CW00661038

To my family, who endured the fieldwork and its aftermath,
and to the memory of Eric Higgs, who started it all.

ποταμοῖσι τοῖσιν αὐτοῖσιν ἐμβαίνουσιν ἕτερα και ἕτερα
ὕδατα έπιρρει

Heraclitus

῞απανθ᾽ ο μακρὸς κἀναρίθμητος χρόνος
φύει τ᾽ ἄδηλα και φανέντα κρὺπτεται

Sophocles, Ajax

A view of the Voïdomatis valley looking westwards from in front of the Klithi rockshelter. The goats in the foreground are on the talus slope below the wall at Klithi, and in the distance are the cliffs of Astraka, guarding the entrance to the Vikos Gorge.

McDONALD INSTITUTE MONOGRAPHS

Klithi: Palaeolithic settlement and Quaternary landscapes in northwest Greece

Vol. 2: Klithi in its local and regional setting

Edited by Geoff Bailey

Publication has been subsidized by grants from the British Academy, the Institute of Aegean Prehistory and the British School of Archaeology at Athens.

Published by:
McDonald Institute for Archaeological Research
University of Cambridge
Downing Street
Cambridge
CB2 3ER
(0)(1223) 339336

Distributed by Oxbow Books
United Kingdom: Oxbow Books, Park End Place, Oxford, OX1 1HN.
Tel: (0)(1865) 241249; Fax: (0)(1865) 794449
USA: The David Brown Book Company, P.O. Box 511, Oakville, CT 06779, USA.
Tel: 860-945-9329; FAX: 860-945-9468

ISBN: 0-9519420-2-6
ISSN: 1363-1349

Edited for the Institute by Chris Scarre (*Series Editor*) and Dora A. Kemp (*Assistant Series Editor*).

Scans produced by Gwil Owen, Photographic Unit, Faculty of Archaeology & Anthropology, University of Cambridge, Downing Street, Cambridge, CB2 3DZ.
Film produced by Gary Reynolds Typesetting, 13 Sturton Street, Cambridge, CB1 2QG.
Printed and bound by Short Run Press, Bittern Rd, Sowton Industrial Estate, Exeter, EX2 7LW.

Cover photo: *View across the Voïdomatis valley from the mouth of Klithi at the end of the 1983 field season.*

Contents

Vol. 2: Klithi in its local and regional setting

Note: Uncalibrated radiocarbon dates are expressed as years BP, calibrated radiocarbon dates as cal BP or cal BC; ka is used as an abbreviation for thousands of years ago.

Contributors

1. Eugenia Adam
   Ephoreia of Prehistoric & Classical Archaeology, Museum of Archaeology, Plateia 25 Martiou, 6, Ioannina 452 21, Greece

2. Geoffrey N. Bailey
   University of Newcastle, Department of Archaeology, Newcastle-upon-Tyne, NE1 7RU

3. Thomas H. Cadbury
   University of Cambridge, Faculty of Archaeology & Anthropology, Downing Street, Cambridge, CB2 3DZ

4. Pat L. Carter
   University of Cambridge, Faculty of Archaeology & Anthropology, Downing Street, Cambridge, CB2 3DZ

5. Nick C. Debenham
   Quaternary TL Surveys, 19 Leonard Avenue, Nottingham, NG5 2LW

6. Nena Galanidou
   University of Cambridge, Clare Hall, Herschel Road, Cambridge, CB3 9AL

7. Clive S. Gamble
   University of Southampton, Department of Archaeology, Southampton, SO17 1BJ

8. John A.J. Gowlett
   University of Liverpool, Department of Archaeology, The Hartley Building, P.O. Box 147, Liverpool, L69 3BX

9. Sarah F. Green
   University of Manchester, Department of Social Anthropology, Roscoe Building, Brunswick Street, Manchester, M13 9PL

10. Robert E.M. Hedges
    Oxford Radiocarbon Accelerator Unit, Research Laboratory for Archaeology & the History of Art, 6 Keble Road, Oxford, OX1 3QJ

11. Helen P. Higgs
    University of Cambridge, Faculty of Archaeology & Anthropology, Downing Street, Cambridge, CB2 3DZ

12. Rupert A. Housley
    University of Glasgow, Department of Archaeology, 10 The Square, Glasgow, G12 8QQ

13. Geoffrey C.P. King
    Institut de Physique du Globe, Laboratoire Tectonique, Tour 24, Boîte 894, Place Jussieu, 75252 Paris, Cedex 05, France

14. Eleni Kotjabopoulou
    Ephoreia of Palaeoanthropology-Speleology, Ardittou 34B, 116 36 Athens, Greece

15. Michel Lenoir
    Université Bordeaux I, UMR 9933 C.N.R.S., Institut de Préhistoire et de Géologie du Quaternaire, avenue des Facultés, 33405 Talence (Cedex), France

16. John Lewin
    University of Wales, Aberystwyth, Institute of Earth Studies, Aberystwyth, SY23 3DB

17. Mark G. Macklin
    University of Leeds, School of Geography, Leeds, LS2 9JT

18. Emily H. Moss
    Harvard University, Department of Anthropology, Peabody Museum, 11 Divinity Avenue, Cambridge, MA 02138, USA

19. Eleni Panagopoulou
    Ephoreia of Palaeoanthropology-Speleology, Ardittou 34B, 116 36 Athens, Greece

20. Vangelis Papaconstantinou
Dyrrou 12, Agrinion, 30100 Greece

21. Colette Roubet
Muséum National d'Histoire Naturelle, Institut de Paléontologie Humaine, 1 rue René Panhard, 75013 Paris (Cedex), France

22. Maria-Fernanda Sanchez-Goñi
Université Bordeaux I, Département de Géologie et Océanographie, URA C.N.R.S. 197, avenue des Facultés, 33405 Talence (Cedex), France, and Instituto de Ciencias de la Tierra Jaume Almera, CSIC. C/Lluis Sole i Sabaris s/n. 08028 Barcelona, Spain

23. F. Wilf Shawcross
Australian National University, Department of Archaeology & Anthropology, The Faculties, Canberra, ACT 0200, Australia

24. Anthony Sinclair
University of Liverpool, Department of Archaeology, The Hartley Building, P.O. Box 147, Liverpool, L69 3BX

25. Derek A. Sturdy
University of Liverpool, Department of Archaeology, The Hartley Building, P.O. Box 147, Liverpool, L69 3BX

26. Gwyn Thomas
Kingswood Villas, Mynydd-y-Garreg, Kidwelly, Dyfed, SA17 4RA

27. Charles Turner
The Open University, Department of Earth Sciences, Milton Keynes, MK7 6AA

28. Dimitra Vassilopoulou
Dyrrou 12, Agrinion, 30100 Greece

29. Derrick P. Webley †
University of Wales, Cardiff, School of History & Archaeology, P.O. Box 909, Cardiff, CF1 3XU

30. Francis F. Wenban-Smith
University College London Boxgrove Project, Institute of Archaeology, 31–34 Gordon Square, London, WC1H 0PY

31. Katherine J. Willis
University of Cambridge, Department of Plant Sciences, Downing Street, Cambridge, CB2 3EA

32. Nick P. Winder
University of Newcastle, Department of Archaeology, Newcastle-upon-Tyne, NE1 7RU

33. Jamie C. Woodward
University of Leeds, School of Geography, Leeds, LS2 9JT

Figures

Part IV

Klithi in its Local Setting

Part IV: Editorial

Geoff Bailey

The chapters in this section deal with two sorts of issues: the relationship between Klithi and its local environmental setting, and the relationship between Klithi and other Palaeolithic sites in the Voïdomatis catchment. The boundary between local and regional issues is to some extent an arbitrary one, and there is some overlap between the studies in Part IV and some of the studies in Parts V & VI. The chapters in Part IV deal for the most part with evidence that is located within the Voïdomatis catchment, and with processes that operate on a local scale. They provide some of the most important local evidence for Late Pleistocene–Holocene environmental changes and their potential impact on the attractions of the rockshelter sites as a base for human activities. Part VI deals with processes that operate on a regional scale, or need a regional perspective for their comprehension, and with the comparison between evidence from sites within the Voïdomatis catchment and sites occurring further afield in the Epirus region.

Chapter 16 sets the scene for the more detailed material of later chapters by giving a general review of the present-day climate, geology, geomorphology and vegetation of the Voïdomatis basin, including some reference to the wider regional picture, and a general description of the Palaeolithic sites in the area. Chapter 17 presents the evidence for Late Pleistocene and Holocene changes in the geomorphology of the valley. A succession of dated river terraces formed over the past 30,000 years or so bears witness to a succession of episodes of aggradation, with intervening periods of incision. These in their turn reflect changes in the pattern of erosion and sedimentation within the wider catchment as a result of climatic and vegetational change. They also provide the more general catchment-wide context for interpretation of the detailed sediment sequences from Klithi (Chapter 18) and Megalakkos (Chapter 19).

Variation in rockshelter sediments is often interpreted in terms of climatic change, and the assumptions on which such interpretations are based have already been critically assessed in Chapter 4 in relation to the analysis of the coarse fraction. Chapters 18 and 19 mainly focus on the physical and chemical composition of the fine sediment fraction and disentangle the varying impact of climatic change, purely local hydrological and geological influences, and human activities. The marked differences in the sediment sequences at Klithi and Megalakkos, even though they were formed over a similar time span in the same valley system, highlights the value of inter-site comparisons and the importance of larger-scale geological studies of the catchments from which the sediments are derived as a control on intra-site interpretation. Chapter 20 completes the sequence of palaeoenvironmental studies by discussing the pollen evidence from the Rezina Marsh and Lake

Gramousti, respectively at higher and lower altitude than Klithi. Unfortunately, the poor preservation of pollen in the Klithi and Megalakkos rockshelter sediments, combined with the high probability of intrusion and contamination, have precluded useful results, and have meant that we have had to rely on the lake record for details of vegetational history even though it is derived from different locations. The Rezina and Gramousti results are further constrained by the fact that they are largely confined to the Holocene and barely overlap with the period of Palaeolithic occupation at Klithi (see Chapter 2 for discussion of the dating issues). On the other hand they provide important detail about local vegetational history and the spatial contrast in vegetational records separated by quite short distances. The value of inter-site comparisons emerges strongly here as in the discussion of rockshelter sedimentology. The lake records also give a detailed insight into full Postglacial conditions immediately following the period when Klithi was abandoned, a period which is virtually unrepresented in the rockshelter sedimentary sequences or the wider river sedimentary sequence of the Voïdomatis basin. Late Glacial pollen records from Tseravinas, Ziros and Ioannina, covering the period of occupation at Klithi, but more geographically distant and probably less sensitive to local variation, are discussed in Chapter 29.

As with the palaeoenvironmental data, inter-site comparisons play an important role in the evaluation and interpretation of the archaeological sequences. Chapter 21 presents the archaeological results from Megalakkos, and Chapter 22 the preliminary results of excavations at Boïla. Both sites cover a time span of occupation similar to Klithi, although the nature of the available archaeological samples is more variable. Much of the deposit at Megalakkos has been removed by natural erosion, and only a very limited sampling operation was possible. Boïla has been the focus of more extensive investigation, and excavation, analysis and interperetation are still ongoing. Notwithstanding these problems of comparability, significant differences are apparent in the faunal and lithic assemblages.

Chapter 16

The Voïdomatis Basin: an Introduction

Geoff Bailey, Charles Turner, Jamie Woodward,
Mark Macklin & John Lewin

The first step in placing the archaeological information from Klithi into a broader framework is the examination of the local setting within which the site occurs. The most obvious geographical unit for such purposes is the catchment of the Voïdomatis, and this area, together with some of the adjacent areas such as the Doliana basin to the west, has been the focus for our most detailed palaeoenvironmental and archaeological analysis. The Voïdomatis flows westwards from the highest part of the central Pindus Mountains, then northwestwards towards Albania, extending over a distance of some 30 km and an altitudinal range of more than 2000 m. This results in a considerable diversity of climatic, physiographic, geological and ecological conditions. During the Late Pleistocene, glaciation in the upland areas of the catchment imposed strong controls on local climate, hydrology, geomorphology and vegetation, causing substantial changes in the potential of the landscape for human occupation. The lower reaches of the catchment are dominated by limestone bedrock, and the effects of limestone weathering, tectonic faulting and fluvial erosion have created a large number of caves and rockshelters. Many of these are suitable for human use, and some contain archaeological deposits, offering the potential for comparative analyses of sedimentation and human activities in different localities. The aim of this chapter is, then, to outline the major features of the physical environment in the vicinity of Klithi and the wider Voïdomatis basin, and to provide general descriptions of geological history, geomorphology, climate, vegetation and archaeological sites as an introduction to the more detailed analyses of the following chapters.

Regional geological and geomorphological setting

Many of the features of the Voïdomatis basin are the result of an interplay between local lithological controls and the regional climatic and tectonic history, and it is to the latter that we turn first (for a more detailed discussion of tectonics see Jones & Robertson 1991; King *et al.*, Chapter 28). Epirus has a complex geological history and changing interpretations have been paralleled by the development of plate tectonic theory and associated concepts over the last four decades. In the early 1960s, following the classic work of Aubouin (1959), the structural arrangement of the Hellenide belt was viewed in terms of the development and subsequent deformation of a major geosyncline. Over the next two decades, however, this initial model was modified significantly as new field data became available and the implications of plate tectonic theory attained general acceptance (see Smith & Moores 1974; Smith *et al.* 1979). As a result of this reappraisal, the Epirus region is now regarded as a distal portion of the intricate tectonic terrain that makes up the Alpine Mountain system (Everett *et al.* 1986). Whilst there is little doubt that the structural evolution of northwest Greece is complex, and that processes of crustal deformation continue to the present, details on uplift rates and seismic activity are still under investigation (King *et al.*, Chapter 28).

As a consequence of its tectonic history, the entire region is characterized by intense folding and overthrusting, the direction of compression being from the northeast toward the Ionian Sea. Traditionally, the solid geology of Greece has been divided into twelve geotectonic units and in Epirus these zones are characterized by a series of overlapping lithofacies belts which trend NNW–SSE at right-angles to the general direction of compression and parallel to the present Ionian coastline. The Voïdomatis basin is easily visible on the Landsat image (Fig. 16.1) located due west of the image centre (H12) close to the thrust line separating the Ionian frontal zone and the highest mountains of the Pindus Range. On a regional scale, it is apparent that a close relationship exists between the nature of the individual structural units and the style and patterning of geomorphological features within them. This terrain variability is expressed through inter-unit contrasts in relief, slope angles and drainage geometry and density. The landforms themselves express the structural configuration and lithological composition of each zone and graphically display the tectonic framework of the entire deformed belt (Everett *et al.* 1986). Regional lithology and structure have exerted a strong influence on the geomorphological evolution of Epirus and each structural zone is characterized by differing soils and vegetation as well as slope forms and drainage patterns.

This highly distinctive crustal alignment evolved throughout the Cretaceous and Tertiary periods as a

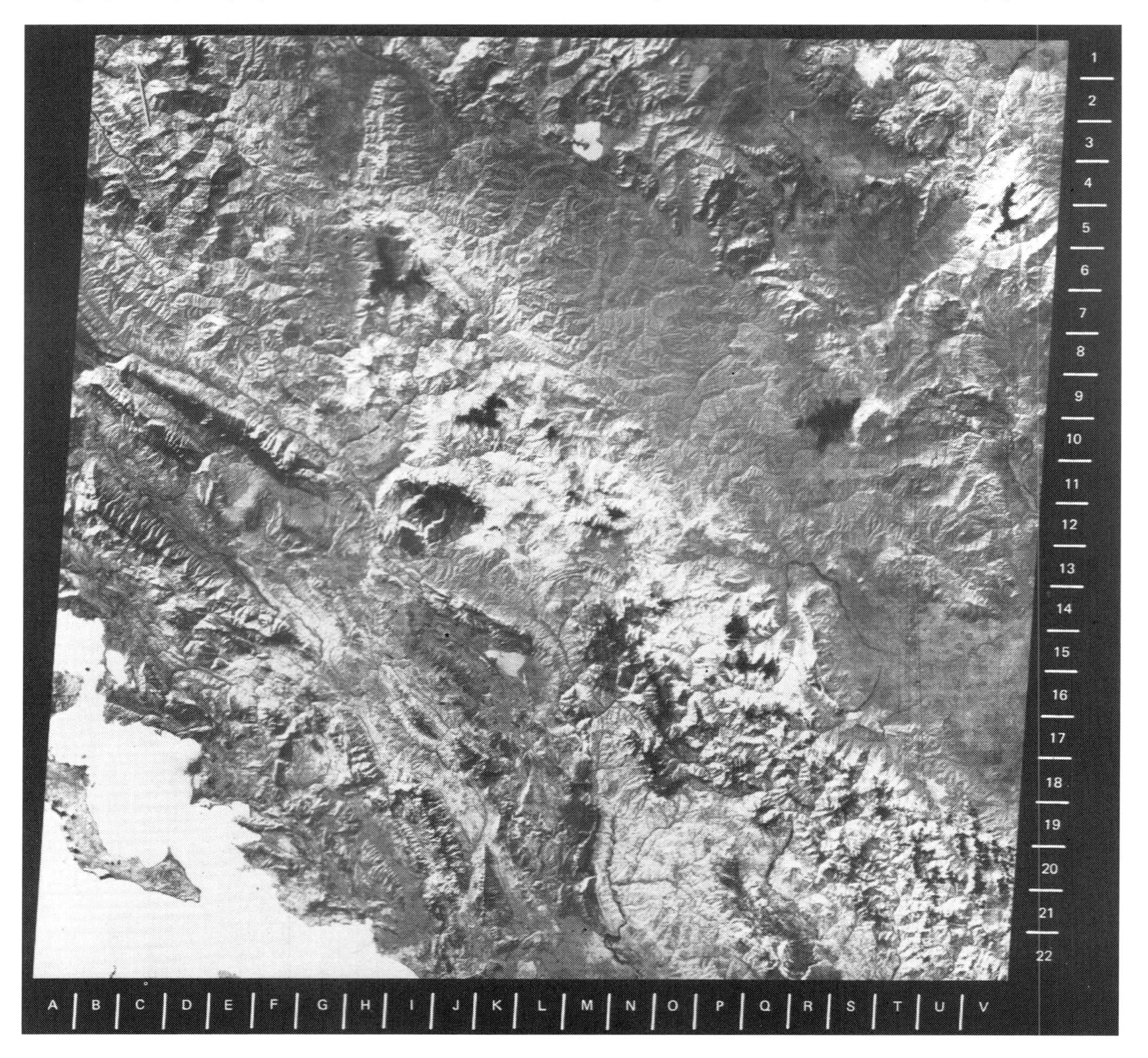

Figure 16.1. *A LANDSAT scene (185 × 185 km) of northwest Greece and southern Albania to illustrate the steepland relief of much of Epirus. The Voïdomatis River basin is located immediately west of the scene centre (H12). Lake Ioannina is situated SSE of the Voïdomatis basin (K15). The highest peaks and karst plateaus of the central montane belt of the Pindus Mountains lie approximately NNW–SSE and bisect this scene from top left to bottom right. The lower part of Kerkyra (Corfu) in the Ionian Sea is also shown.*

succession of compressional features developed (Smith & Moores 1974). In terms of lithology, calcareous, mainly pelagic sediments accumulated across the entire area throughout the Mesozoic era and during the Palaeocene and early Eocene (*cf.* De Mulder 1976). By mid-Eocene times, the Pindus thrust had been initiated and this feature remained active until Oligocene times, leading to the creation of the Pindus Mountains (Clews 1989). During the Oligocene and Miocene epochs, flysch-type sedimentation was dominant and disrupted the extensive carbonate sedimentation which had prevailed since early Mesozoic times. The great thickness of these flysch successions (up to 4000 m in the east of the Ionian zone) indicate the influx of huge volumes of fine-grained, quartz-rich, suspended sediment eroded from the newly uplifted mountain belt. According to Richter *et al.* (1978), flysch deposition ceased in the Aquitanian with the beginning of the main tectogenesis, and Meulenkamp (1985) has described the entire area as a 'mosaic of horsts and grabens'.

The main occurrences of igneous rocks are associated with the Pindus Ophiolite which covers an extensive area in the Aoos River basin to the east of the modern Voïdomatis catchment (IGME 1987; IGRS/IFP 1966). The dominant lithologies here are serpentinite, dunite and tectonized harzburgite and all the available field evidence suggests that only the deepest structural levels of this ophiolite are present. The ophiolite complex is probably continuous at depth below the Meso-Hellenic Trough molasse with the Vourinous and Othris ophiolites together forming a single ophiolite sheet (Smith *et al.* 1979). On exposure to sub-aerial conditions the ophiolite materials can be rapidly broken down by chemical weathering processes. Whilst the modern channel of the Voïdomatis River contains only a very small proportion of ophiolite gravels (see Macklin *et al.*, Chapter 17), the floodplain of the Aoos River to the north and east contains a much greater proportion of ophiolite material.

The drainage basin of the Voïdomatis River (384 km^2) is developed in hard crystalline limestones which are overlain in places by Late Eocene to Miocene flysch rocks — the latter are often tilted and/or deformed. In the southeastern corner of the basin a small portion (*c.* 5 km^2) of the Pindus Ophiolite crops out. In structural terms, the basin is marked by three major NE–SW trending faults which combine to produce the broad 'stepped' relief of the catchment.

The flysch rocks consist of thin bedded (*c.* 10 cm) alternations of fine-grained, clayey siltstones and coarser-grained, siliceous sandstones (Fig. 16.2). The Palaeocene to Upper Eocene limestones which dominate much of the basin are hard, crystalline rocks with occasional bands of chert. In general, these rocks are very pure, with a calcium carbonate content which is typically >99.5 per cent (see Woodward, Chapters 18 & 19). The limestones are dominated by calcium carbonate in the form of calcite and the major non-carbonate minerals are quartz and mica, while the flysch rocks are highly siliceous with significant proportions of plagioclase, calcite, mica and other clay minerals (Woodward *et al.* 1992). The ophiolite material, which occurs as a small, isolated outcrop on the eastern margin of the catchment, delivers coarse gravel-sized clasts of tectonized harzburgite to the main Voïdomatis channel via a small tributary stream. This dark, dense ultramafic lithology has a distinctive mineral assemblage which includes olivine, pyroxene and spinel.

The Epirus landscape is dominated by the uplifted and faulted limestones of the Pindus Mountains, and this uplifted terrain has been deeply incised by a series of steep river systems to form tracts of dramatic steepland topography (see Fig. 16.1). The surface drainage on resistant limestone formations is frequently channelled through ravines and deep gorges whereas the weaker flysch formations are commonly heavily dissected by intermittent headwater streams. This high-relief landscape also encourages sediment transfer by mass movements such as landslips and debris flows, providing large volumes of unconsolidated material for subsequent removal and sorting by fluvial action.

Between these uplifted steepland zones lie fertile low-relief basins of various shapes and sizes such as Ioannina, Doliana and Konitsa. These basins act as sedimentary sinks where lake and alluvial deposits have been preserved. This alternation of terrains gives rise to a 'basin and range' topography across much of the Epirus region (*cf.* Bloom 1991; Macklin *et al.* 1995). It is clear that tectonic or endogenic processes provide the dominant long-term control on drainage network evolution and drainage basin size as well as on the broad pattern of river erosion and sedimentation in the landscape (*cf.* Collier *et al.* 1995; King *et al.* 1994 & Chapter 28; Macklin *et al.* 1995; Mather & Harvey 1995). It is also apparent, however, that climate- and human-induced episodes of river aggradation and incision may be superimposed upon this regional tectonic framework (see Macklin *et al.*, Chapter 17).

Prior to Alpine mountain building during the Tertiary Period, this region — in common with much

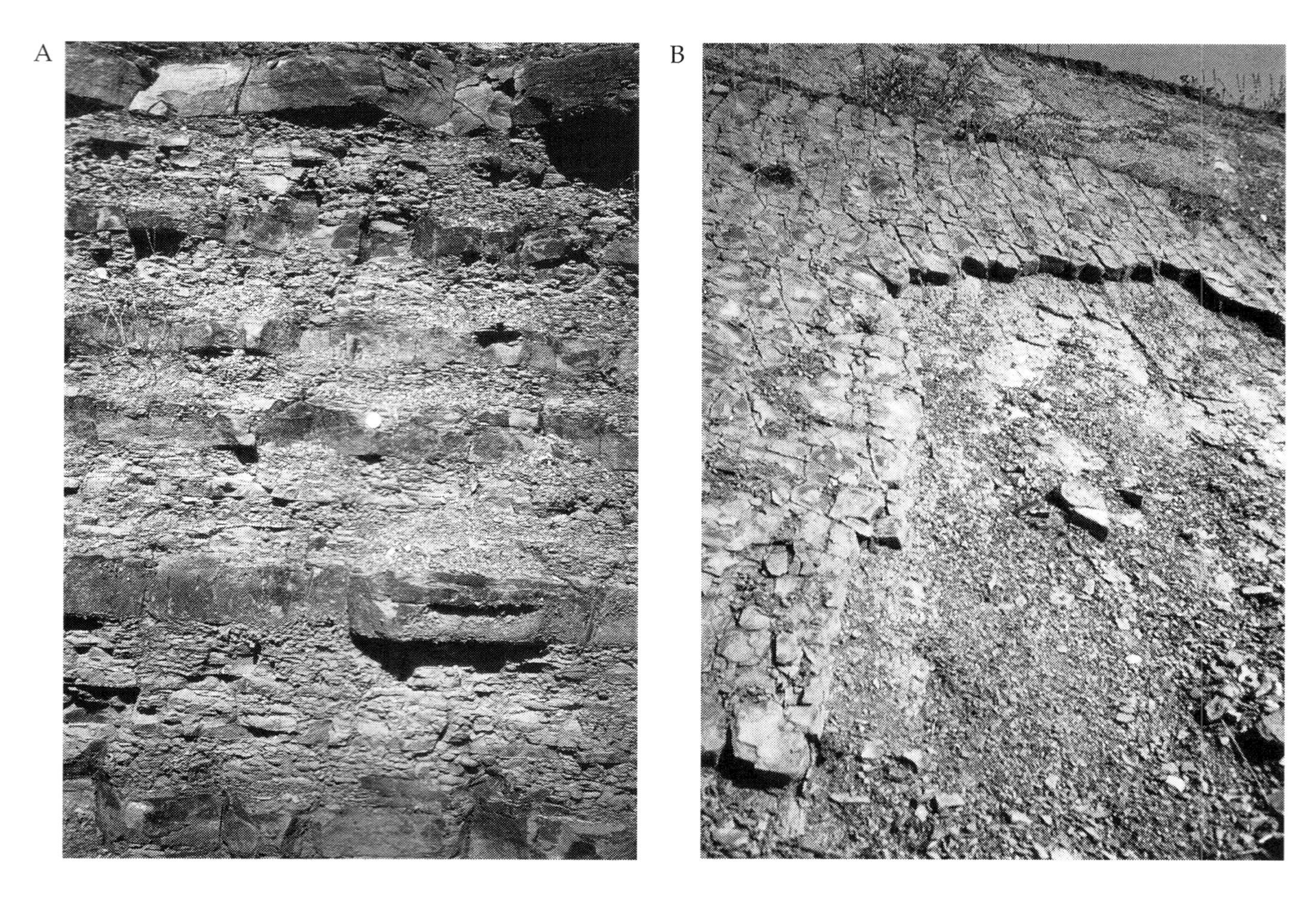

Figure 16.2. *(A) A typical section in flysch bedrock exposed in a road section c. 1 km from Aristi on the Aristi–Papingon road in the Lower Vikos Gorge. In this section the darker resistant sandstone beds are approximately 10 cm in thickness. (B) Following vegetation clearance and the removal of the coarser sandstone beds, the fissile siltstone beds rapidly break down into sand-sized aggregates and primary fine sand and silt particles. When tilted, these bare rock surfaces encourage rapid runoff and yield large volumes of fine sediment to the karst and fluvial systems. The fractured sandstone bed is c. 12 cm thick.*

of the Mediterranean zone — formed part of an extensive marine shelf in which limestones were laid down. The break up and deformation of this carbonate basement has produced limestone mountains and tablelands and, where climate and structure have permitted, karstic features have developed. These hard-rock massifs are commonly juxtaposed with flysch formations, as active Late Cenozoic uplift has elevated such highly erodible materials to create slope instability and high rates of erosion in headwater catchments (Woodward 1995). As in other parts of Greece, such as the Peloponnese, where marked contrasts in rates of denudation between resistant limestones and easily erodible flysch formations result in completely different relief (Gaki-Papanastassiou & Maroukian 1995), lithological contrasts have had an important influence on the evolution of the Epirus landscape.

The development of landscapes on hard limestone on the one hand, and flysch or other relatively easily eroded sediment on the other, is of particular significance in the Voïdomatis basin, and bears witness to the contrasting impact of erosive forces on different terrains. While erosion has been exacerbated by human action in more recent times, there is also an abundance of evidence recording extensive stripping of soil mantles and high river sediment loads during the Pleistocene. The thick 'red beds' of Epirus and the ancient braided river deposits preserved in valley bottoms point to significant episodes of hillslope instability and high sediment availability prior to major human vegetation disturbance in the Holocene. In more recent times, however, extensive grazing by sheep and goats and cutting of wood for fuel has led to the removal of

A

B

Figure 16.3. *Typical slope forms in Epirus on limestone and flysch bedrocks. (A) A steep slope on hard limestone with a discontinuous soil cover in the headwaters of the Louros River. (B) A heavily dissected flysch terrain east of Konitsa in northern Epirus. Note the difference in vegetation cover between the two slope forms.*

shallow soils from resistant limestones, producing bare rock slopes, while readily-erodible bedrock, including flysch and marl deposits may undergo extensive gullying, slope instability and even badland formation (Fig. 16.3). Such processes deliver large quantities of fine-grained sediment to the fluvial system and these materials may become an important part of alluvial sediments accumulating in the lower reaches of river networks and tectonically-controlled basins (Macleod & Vita-Finzi 1982; Woodward *et al.* 1992; Macklin *et al.* 1995; see Chapter 17).

Climate and hydrology

The climate of Epirus is transitional between central Europe and the Mediterranean with considerable local variability due to contrasts in aspect and relief. The climate of the Voïdomatis basin may best be described as a modified Mediterranean regime since the altitude of the basin (which locally exceeds 2400 m) imparts certain distinctive alpine characteristics and has an important effect on the timing and magnitude of precipitation and stream-channel runoff. The summer months are not as dry as the true Mediterranean coastal belt of southern Greece (Fig. 16.4). Periodic thunderstorms interrupt the summer drought and contribute to a total annual rainfall of *c.* 1000 mm near the Ionian coastal fringe and up to 2000 mm in the upland interior, where much of this rainfall is orographic. As in most mountain environments, the weather is capricious and the diurnal temperature range high (Legge 1972; McNeill 1992).

Streamflow records are not yet available for the Voïdomatis River itself, but a twenty-four year record is available for the Aoos River at the Konitsa bridge gauging station, only *c.* 10 km NNE of the mouth of the Lower Vikos Gorge (Fig. 16.5). It is likely that the annual flow regime of the two rivers is very similar

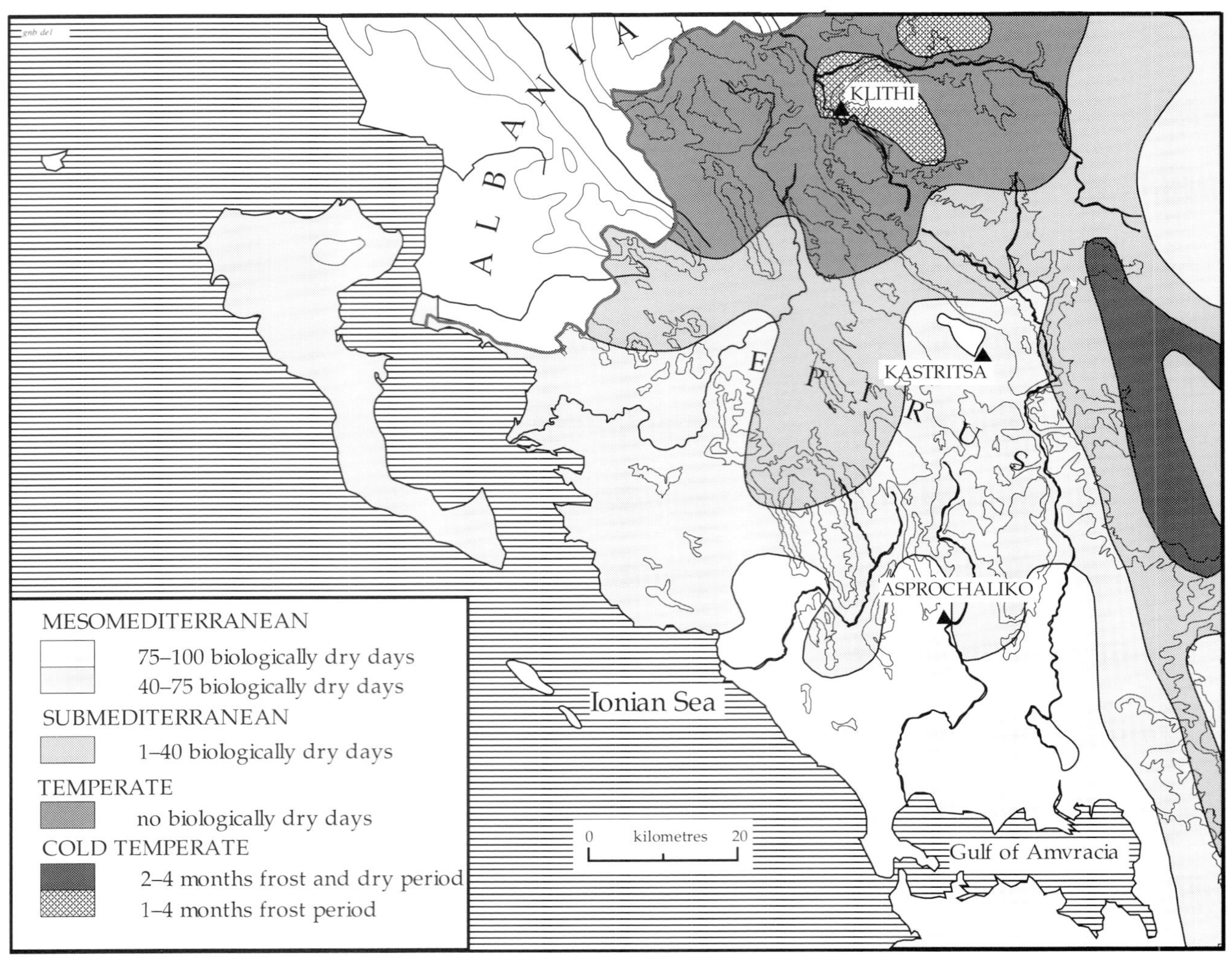

Figure 16.4. *Bioclimatic map of Epirus, showing principal Palaeolithic sites. (After Higgs* et al. *1967.)*

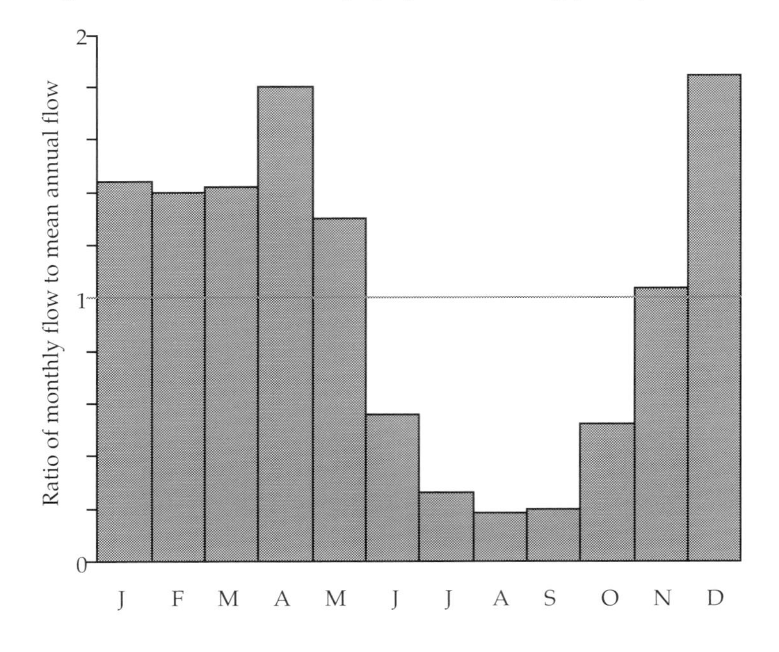

Figure 16.5. *Mean monthly flow of the Aoos River at the Konitsa station, expressed as a proportion of the mean annual flow for the period October 1963 to September 1987 (24.66 $m^3 s^{-1}$). During the five driest months of the year (June to October) the mean monthly flows are well below the mean annual discharge. December is normally the wettest month and the region's river regimes are shaped mainly by the timing and form of precipitation as well as by contributions from snowmelt and karstic storage. (Streamflow data kindly supplied by the Public Power Corporation of Athens.)*

in view of their common watershed and comparable relief and geology. These data highlight the strong contrast between a relatively brief dry summer spell characterized by low discharges and much higher flows during the rest of the year, particularly during March, April and May, when snowmelt forms an important component of the total runoff. Hammond (1967, 16) observes that 'in the winter and spring it is impossible to ford the major Epirus rivers and their tributaries, because the rainfall and snowmelt come down from the limestone massifs in raging torrents' (see also Woodward *et al.* 1995).

Mean July temperatures of 15°C are typical of the highest central montane belt of the Pindus Mountains, although these may rise to 20°C at intermediate altitude. This contrasts with a mean value of 25°C for the western coastal zone and Ionian islands. The highest plateaus and karst ridges of the Pindus Mountains run parallel to the Adriatic and Ionian coasts and lie in close proximity to them. At the coldest time of the year these mountain ranges provide effective shelter for the narrow coastal region against invasions of polar air, and not infrequently, even arctic air (Furlan 1977). Thus, while the nearby city of Ioannina has an average January temperature of *c.* 7.5°C (Lake Ioannina very rarely freezes), it is much colder in the inland montane belt of the Pindus Mountains where freezing winter temperatures are the norm and average January temperatures range from –2.5 to –5°C. Severe winters with prolonged snowcover are typical in the Voïdomatis basin and the highest peaks of the northern Pindus Mountains may have a snow cover until the end of June (Sfikas 1979). Frosts are common from October to May and the freezing temperatures and harsh conditions of the Epirus winter have been well documented. In the winter of 1940–41 the Greek army in northern Epirus had more casualties through frostbite than it had in battle throughout the whole campaign (Hammond 1967, 17).

Physiography of the Voïdomatis basin

The marked regional physiographic diversity in northwestern Greece is mirrored by the juxtaposition, on a more local scale, of equally striking terrain units within the boundaries of the Voïdomatis basin. Five major landscape units, identified on the basis of distinctive geological and topographical associations, have been identified in the catchment (Fig. 16.6).

1. The glaciated Tsepelovon district

The upland (Palaeocene–Eocene) limestone massif in the central part of the basin forms the highest part of the catchment, with elevations locally exceeding 2400 m. In the Tsepelovon district, there is an impressive range of morphological and sedimentological evidence for recent Pleistocene glaciation (Fig. 16.6). Well-developed glacial erosional features such as corries and hanging valleys carved into the limestone bedrock, fringe the stepped, U-shaped valleys of the area. Extensive deposition of glacially modified and transported sediments has produced a distinctive series of morainic lobes with associated glacio-fluvial landforms. These moraines, capped by boulder-strewn surfaces, mantle almost the entire south-facing slopes from above the village of Tsepelovon down into the Voïdomatis valley. Kame terrace features can be identified — these forms have been deeply incised by seasonal, snow-melt fed streams. Natural sections created by small landslips in these limestone dominated moraines appear as distinctive white scars in the landscape.

The glacial history of Greece is not well documented (see Denton & Hughes 1981; Sibrava *et al.* 1986). Although 'moraines des glaciers quaternaires' are marked on the geological sheets for the area, their age and geomorphological significance has only recently been established (Bailey *et al.* 1990; Lewin *et al.* 1991; Woodward *et al.* 1992; 1994; 1995). The original geological survey outlines the broad spatial extent of glacial sediments in the basin (IGRS 1970), but does not attempt to assign these deposits to specific Pleistocene stages (see also Sestini 1933; Pechoux 1970). The Tsepelovon to Skamnelion road provides impressive sections (up to 20 m high) in these glacial deposits (Fig. 16.7). Fresh, largely unweathered sediments form massive diamictons (poorly sorted deposits including a very wide range of particle sizes) of sub-rounded boulder- to gravel-sized material in a distinctive, creamy silty/sand matrix. Close inspection of individual clasts reveals glacially-etched and striated rock surfaces. The brilliant creamy-white colour of these sediments reflects their derivation from the pure local limestone. Isolated pockets of flysch bedrock are also present in this area, accounting for the small flysch gravel and fines component in these sediments.

2. Headwater flysch terrain

Lying below the limits of Pleistocene glacial activity, this distinctive topography is typical of areas underlain by actively eroding flysch strata. Such terrain consists mainly of fairly steep, erosional slopes producing a compact arrangement of short ridge and valley forms (Fig. 16.8). These unstable slopes do not support a continuous vegetation cover and are highly susceptible to rapid runoff during high intensity storms, thus promoting widespread gullying and erosion. In some areas the erodibility of the terrain and the high rainfall totals have combined to produce a badlands topography (see Campbell 1989; Woodward 1995). The flysch rocks consist of fine-grained, quartz-rich sandstones and fissile siltstones (shales) which contain large amounts of easily erodible and transportable fine sediment. This part of the catchment is a major source of fine (suspended) sediment during storm runoff events. The relatively high density, modified dendritic drainage network, may be described as a pinnate drainage pattern (Bloom 1991), since the second order tributaries run parallel and join the main tributary streams at acute angles. This forms a highly effective water and sediment transport system, maximizing sediment delivery during peak flows. This heavily dissected area produces a landform style and texture in stark contrast to the glaciated limestone relief of the Tsepelovon district north of the modern Voïdomatis channel (see Fig. 16.6).

3. The Vikos Gorge

Mount Gamila is arguably the most extensive and most majestic of the Greek mountains (Sfikas 1979). The northern side consists of a range of cliffs which are dissected by deep ravines, whereas the southern flanks slope down gently to an extensive tableland which is cut off abruptly by the great gorge of the Voïdomatis River. This spectacular karst canyon is one of the most impressive topographic features in southeast Europe (Jennings 1985). It

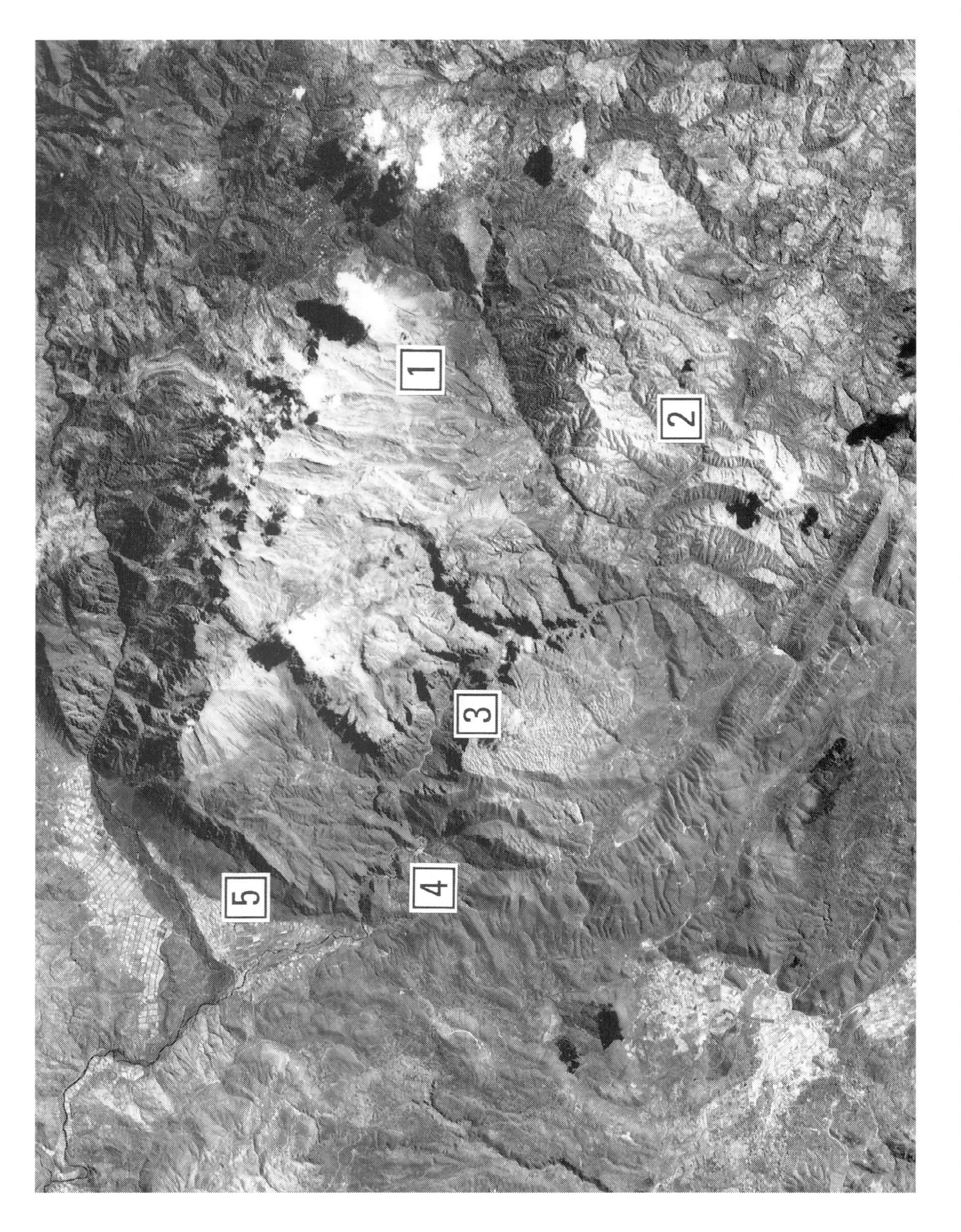

Figure 16.6. *SPOT satellite image of the Voïdomatis River and the Ioannina Lake basin to the southeast. This image provides a useful illustration of the terrain variability in and around the Voïdomatis basin. This scene covers an area of approximately 40 × 28.5 km. Voïdomatis terrain units discussed in the text: (1) Glaciated Tsepelovon district; (2) Headwater flysch terrain; (3) Vikos Gorge; (4) Lower Vikos Gorge; (5) Konitsa basin. Each of these terrains can be identified in the LANDSAT scene of the wider Epirus region (Fig. 16.1).*

is cut into resistant Tertiary and Mesozoic limestones and in places is almost 1000 m deep, yet only about 2.5 km across, with near vertical sides in parts (Fig. 16.9A). The bedrock floor of the gorge, which is locally well exposed in the active channel, is composed of resistant Jurassic carbonates. These rocks form an outcrop up to 700 m thick in the Vikos Gorge, and Palaeocene to Late Eocene limestones (>300 m in thickness) complete the carbonate sequence (Fig. 16.9B).

Large-scale talus cones form an extensive colluvial blanket along the gorge sides. These massive limestone screes are dominated by angular and multifaceted clasts, are locally calcreted and frequently interfinger with the thick veneer of alluvial sediments that mantles the gorge floor (Lewin *et al.* 1991). At the western end of the gorge the presence of a series of talus cones on the right bank indicates that the rockwall is not weathering uniformly over its surface (Fig. 16.6). Preferential erosion of local structural lines of weakness may account for this group of steep debris cones as material is delivered from chutes in the gorge wall. The discontinuity between the talus cone mantles and the floor of the chutes indicates that sediment is delivered to the cones predominantly by rockfall rather than by debris flows. During uplift of the block-faulted terrain, these hard, resistant limestone rocks have restricted slope processes from cutting back the rock walls of the valley sides.

In this part of the basin the active stream flows in a steep boulder-lined channel (Fig. 16.10) where bed material calibre may exceed two metres, indicating the occurrence of very high stream powers, typical of narrow gorge environments during extreme flood discharge events (*cf.* Baker & Pickup 1987).

4. The Lower Vikos Gorge

Intermediate in relief between the Vikos Gorge (upstream) and the Konitsa Plain (downstream), this reach of the Voïdomatis River is characterized by a series of deeply incised meander bends (Figs 16.11 & 16.12). These perhaps reflect slower uplift than in

Figure 16.7. *Glacial sediments exposed in a section along the Tsepelovon–Skamnelion road. These are overwhelmingly dominated by limestone-derived material and incorporate all grades of sediment from clay- to boulder-sized particles. They also contain a large proportion of $CaCO_3$-rich rock flour.*

Figure 16.8. *The degraded flysch landscape south of the modern Voïdomatis stream channel in the catchment headwaters. These steep erosional slopes do not maintain an effective vegetation canopy and constitute an extremely fragile ecosystem. The poor vegetation cover on these highly erodible sediments has encouraged the development of a badlands topography. Goat shelter and telegraph pole in foreground for scale.*

A

B

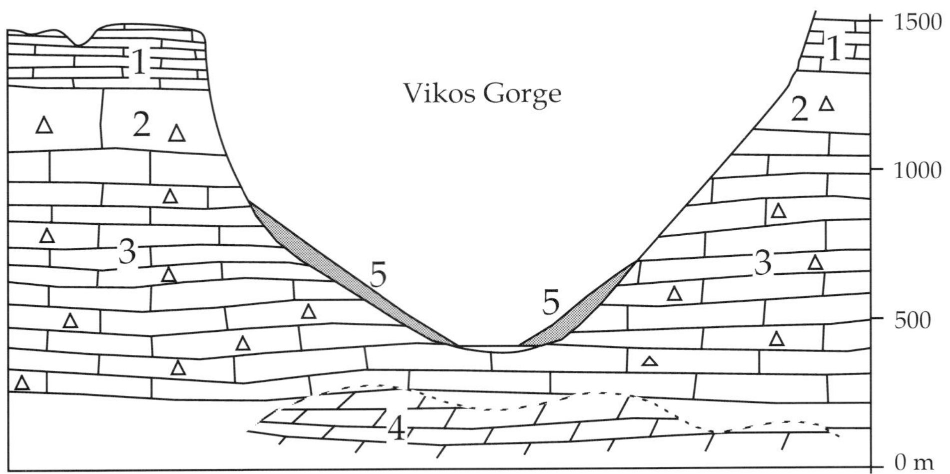

Figure 16.9. *(A) The Vikos Gorge viewed from the western (downstream) end of the canyon near the village of Vikos. The widest parts of the canyon are lined with great thicknesses of coarse-grained colluvial sediments. The basal sections of these talus formations frequently interdigitate with coarse alluvial materials. The course of the modern channel is shaded by a corridor of plane trees. (B) A geological cross section through the main Vikos Gorge (after IGRS 1968): 1. Palaeocene to Eocene limestone; 2. Upper Senonian limestone; 3. Vigla limestone (Lower Senonian); 4. Dolomitic limestone (Lower Senonian); 5. Pleistocene scree sediments.*

Figure 16.10. *The boulder-lined channel of the Voïdomatis River in the main Vikos Gorge. The moss-covered boulders indicate that the coarsest bed materials are moved only during very large flood events.*

Figure 16.11. *View looking westwards into the Lower Vikos Gorge from the Aristi–Vikos road. The Aristi–Papingon road bridge over the Voïdomatis is shown in the bottom left of this photograph. Note the dense vegetation on the flysch slopes either side of the gorge. The sheer limestone cliffs in the vicinity of the Klithi rockshelter can be seen further downstream (compare Fig. 1.1).*

Figure 16.12. *(On left) A SPOT satellite image of the lower basin showing the western end of the Vikos Gorge, the incised meanders of the Lower Vikos Gorge and the Konitsa basin. This scene provides a useful illustration of the topography in the vicinity of the Klithi rockshelter which is located in the centre of this scene. The two major faultlines trending NE–SW mark the upper and downstream ends of the Lower Vikos Gorge and highlight the broad stepped relief of the basin. Both the Voïdomatis and Aoos rivers drain glaciated headwater catchments and both systems exit via fault-bounded limestone gorges onto the Konitsa basin. The Aoos–Voïdomatis confluence in the centre of the Konitsa basin is approximately 5 km from the Konitsa gauging station situated at the downstream end of the Aoos Gorge (see Fig. 16.5). This fluvial system drains into Albania and eventually into the Adriatic Sea.*

Figure 16.13. *View looking NNE across the Konitsa basin showing the active floodplain of the Voïdomatis River. This fertile alluvial basin is fed with irrigation waters abstracted from the Voïdomatis and Aoos Rivers. The eastern side of the basin is draped by a steep colluvial prism which contains evidence of mass movements including debris flows.*

the main gorge upstream, allowing progressive lateral fluvial erosion of the gorge walls as well as vertical incision. These incised or entrenched meanders may result from headward migration of a nickpoint after base-level lowering (see Chorley *et al.* 1984, 312). At a number of locations in this part of the basin the modern river channel is actively eroding the limestone gorge walls and it is highly likely that the Klithi rockshelter itself, which is located on the outside of a large entrenched meander, is the product of fluvial erosion. Further, in contrast to the deeper Vikos canyon, occurrences of bedrock in the channel are quite rare in the Lower Vikos Gorge and would seem to imply that vertical incision is proceeding at a slower rate along this particular reach of the Voïdomatis River.

The Lower Vikos Gorge is significantly lower (the main gorge walls are about 150–200 m high) and narrower (locally <150 m) than the main Vikos canyon (Fig. 16.11). Flysch rocks overlie the gorge-forming limestones on both sides of the valley, and this accounts for the increase in surface drainage density on the adjacent slopes and the increase in flysch-derived sediment delivery to the main valley floor via a series of small, seasonal streams flowing through steep tributary ravines. The Megalakkos rockshelter is located in such a tributary ravine which joins the main Voïdomatis channel approximately 500 m upstream of the Klithi rockshelter. Small-scale alluvial fans less than 10 m across are locally well developed at a number of tributary junctions (Lewin *et al.* 1991). Large floods generated by torrential rainfall and/or rapid snowmelt can transfer large volumes of coarse angular sediment to the main valley floor. Debris flows are also locally important and coarse-grained alluvial fans may build out onto the modern floodplain and this material is reworked by the main Voidomatis River and incorporated into the main channel sediments.

Slope deposits in this part of the basin are of two main types. Firstly, unvegetated scree slopes and talus cones consisting of openwork (clast supported) coarse limestone clasts of all size grades, from gravel to boulder size, are common on each side of the river channel. These wedges of colluvial debris attain considerable thicknesses and often display local size-sorting. Recent scree deposits do not have a significant fine matrix component. However, tributary-cut sections at a number of sites reveal considerable thicknesses of coarse, colluvial debris with a fine brown, probably flysch-derived, silty matrix filling clast voids. In older sections (probably of Pleistocene age) near the Papingon–Aristi road, this fine matrix has been weathered (rubified) to a reddish silty clay. This part of the river basin provides the main focus for detailed investigation of the alluvial sedimentary record and late Quaternary soil development (see Macklin *et al.*, Chapter 17).

5. The Konitsa basin

The Old Klithonia Bridge spans the Voïdomatis River at the downstream limit of the Lower Vikos Gorge and marks the end of lateral controls which have confined the main channel throughout most of its course. Edged with colluvial sediments, which are particularly well developed on the eastern side of the basin, this is a fault-controlled graben of Tertiary age into which the Voïdomatis and Aoos Rivers flow (Fig. 16.11). On either side of the modern river this broad alluvial plain is mantled with coarse alluvial gravel deposits whose surfaces lie between 5 and 10 m above modern river level. In the absence of detailed borehole records, the full depth of the Quaternary river gravels in this part of the basin is not known, but the geomorphic setting suggests that they may attain a considerable thickness. Here the contemporary channel and floodplain of the Voïdomatis are rarely more than 200 m across (Fig. 16.13). The modern Voïdomatis River bisects the triangular plain and flows roughly NNW to its confluence with the Aoos River in the centre of the basin (see Fig. 16.11).

The present valley-floor environment
The contemporary channel and floodplain system is typical of many steepland karst streams in the Mediterranean region (*cf.* Macklin *et al.* 1995, 18). The steep average slope of the river (0.016) reflects the high relative relief and mountainous headwaters exceeding 2400 m asl. This is a major influence on the geomorphology of the valley floor and on river processes. The active channel and floodplain zone are dominated by landforms comprising coarse-grained bedload sediments dominated by cobbles and boulders derived from the limestone and flysch rocks of the basin. In plan form the Voïdomatis forms a single-channel meandering river and flows through a bedrock gorge which has restricted its lateral development. Fluvial erosion has produced notches in the gorge walls at several sites along the present channel and ancient river-cut features can be observed at higher elevations. Elsewhere the Voïdomatis flows in a self-formed alluvial channel and bank materials are commonly composed of coarse-grained Pleistocene river sediments belonging to the Aristi Unit (see Macklin *et al.*, Chapter 17 for detailed descriptions of this and other alluvial units), colluvial materials, or the recent fine-grained alluvium of the Klithi Unit. The latter sediments form an extensive low terrace which is an important feature of the present valley floor. During flood events these materials are reworked and incorporated into the sediment load of the modern stream. Channel morphology is dominated by coarse gravel point- and side-bar forms, and deep pools which alternate with gravel or cobble riffles. Upstream of the Konitsa basin the present channel is rarely more than 15 m wide and is commonly incised a few metres into the valley floor deposits. The occasional presence of channel margin boulder berms and overbank gravel splays, whose surfaces lie up to a few metres above present river bed level, points to the occurrence of extreme flood flows in very recent times.

Modern vegetation

Epirus is both vegetationally and floristically one of the most diverse regions of Greece and of the Balkan peninsula in general. It is also the most forested region of Greece, and indeed one of the few areas of Europe where forest cover seems actually to be increasing. Under the present prevailing temperate 'interglacial' conditions, it is generally agreed that the 'natural' climax vegetation of this part of Greece would consist of a variety of forest types (Turrill 1929), depending on altitude, aspect and distance from the sea, with more open vegetational conditions restricted to the highest mountain areas, steep unstable cliffs, and seral environments such as marshes and coastal dunes. Clearly this is a theoretical reconstruction and, because of the immense impact of human activities, the nature and distribution of modern vegetation types is very different. Even the composition of existing forests has been greatly affected by direct or indirect human interference. Yet, although vegetation types over the whole region have been substantially modified by human activities, nevertheless a broad zonation, particularly of woodland and scrub vegetation, can be clearly recognized. This zonation has been discussed in detail by Turrill (1929) and is also given in outline in Bottema (1974).

The coastal lowlands to the west (up to about 400 m asl), which are virtually frost-free throughout the year, appear formerly to have supported typical Mediterranean evergreen forests, but these have almost everywhere been destroyed by agriculture and, from Roman times onwards, the demands of the Adriatic timber trade for ship- and house-building, or else they have been degraded by incessant sheep and goat-grazing, burning and culling for firewood, leading to the formation of shrubby maquis communities. The residual flora suggests forests with oaks, particularly the evergreen species holm oak *Quercus ilex* and kermès oak *Q. coccifera*, *Phillyrea media*, *Pistacia lentiscus*, the native wild olive *Olea europaea* and *Arbutus* spp., together with shrubs such as *Cotinus coggyria*, *Erica arborea*, *Spartium junceum*, *Phlomis fruticosa* and *Cistus* spp. In Epirus *Pistacia lentiscus*, *Erica arborea* and *Arbutus* spp. are virtually confined to this zone.

Inland, at altitudes between 400–700 m asl, deciduous tree species become important, particularly deciduous or semi-deciduous oaks such as *Quercus pubescens* and Turkey oak *Q. cerris*, likewise oriental hornbeam *Carpinus orientalis*, terebinth *Pistacia terebinthus*, elm *Ulmus* spp. and maple *Acer* spp. In this zone too much of the forest vegetation has been strongly affected in the past — and still to a decreasing extent today — by burning and grazing, producing shrubby communities that range from maquis to pseudomaquis or shiblyak (Turrill 1929). Some of the evergreen Mediterranean elements are still abundant, notably *Quercus coccifera* and *Phillyrea*, as are prickly shrubs such as junipers *Juniperus* spp. and Christ's thorn *Paliurus spina-christi*. Nevertheless, large or small areas of well-grown woodland can be found, for example as woods that are actively managed for forestry or at least preserved as a supply of timber and firewood, or as groves of trees, particularly stands of ancient oaks, which have clearly been protected by local communities and are often associated with shrines. Another residual site for woodland is in relatively inaccessible gorges where the rivers of Epirus have deeply dissected particular geological formations.

As one moves further from the coast and up into the foothills of the Pindus Mountains, although some of the Mediterranean elements become sparser or confined to sheltered or south-facing slopes, the diversity of the tree and shrub flora increases. Not only are southern European tree species such as *Ostrya carpinifolia*, *Quercus frainetto*, *Q. trojana*, *Tilia tomentosa* and *Acer obtusatum* present, but also trees such as *Carpinus betulus* and shrubs like hazel *Corylus avellana* and *Viburnum lantana*, whose native distribution extends up the Balkan peninsula and into central and even northern Europe. A number of rare Balkan endemic species also occur, the most notable being the horse chestnut *Aesculus hippocastaneum*. The sweet chestnut *Castanea sativa* also occurs, particularly in managed woodland, but should probably be regarded as a very ancient introduction in this area.

In the Pindus Mountains themselves, particularly above altitudes of *c.* 1000 m asl, the mixed-deciduous forests, usually dominated by *Quercus pubescens*, give way to more uniform forests of fir *Abies* and pine *Pinus nigra* (sometimes *P. heldreichii*) or, depending on altitude and aspect, of beech *Fagus sylvatica*. Alpine grasslands occur above the treeline, but it is clear that the altitude of the treeline is very often determined by human activity, since the mountain pastures are heavily grazed and the high-level forests have long been exploited for fuel, some being carefully managed, others ravaged by man and beast beyond any possibility of regeneration.

The Western Zagori

The site of Klithi lies within the Western Zagori, the cluster of ancient villages and their territories occupying the foothills of the northern Pindus mountains between the Doliana basin on the lower western side, where the Kalamas River has its source, and the great cliffs of the Gamila and Astraka in the Tymfi massif. Because of the range of altitude and geology, the vegetation must always have been diverse, at least during Postglacial times.

Large tracts of land within the Doliana basin have only been drained in recent times and are now under intensive cultivation. A century ago much of the area was probably covered in reed swamp and willow scrub. Nevertheless such areas must have been economically important; for example, Aristi, an upland village, has as a detached part of its territory called Limni, a small enclosed basin at lower altitude, again now drained, situated to the north of Kalpaki. Such basins may have held stretches of open water during the winter and spring months, as is still the case with Lake Gramousti on the northern margin of the Doliana basin (Willis 1992a; Chapter 20).

Travelling by road from Kalpaki on the edge of the Doliana basin through the villages of Mesovouni and Aristi, then crossing the Voïdomatis river and its gorge to reach the twin villages of Papingon below Astraka, one passes through a dissected, increasingly steep and rugged, but often densely wooded terrain. Meadows and small cultivated plots are found around the villages, more extensively at lower altitudes, and occasionally along the floors of small side valleys. The bedrock throughout this area is either limestone or flysch, and, particularly in limestone areas, there are still poorly vegetated slopes with scattered grazed scrub. Survey of the woodland vegetation has led to two observations. First there are small but significant differences between the vegetation on limestone and flysch bedrock, although these are obscured where soil and rock material has moved downslope, particularly adjacent to the fault scarps that traverse the area. Secondly there have been considerable recent changes in the physiognomy of these woody plant communities.

On limestone substrates the trees and shrubs and the ground flora tend to be slightly more diverse than on flysch (though in either case diversity is much greater than in any woodland communities in northern Europe). In many stands the dominant trees are *Phillyrea media*, *Quercus coccifera* and *Carpinus orientalis*, but in others the deciduous oak *Quercus pubescens* is plentiful. Other trees present include *Pistacia terebinthus*, *Acer campestre* and *A. monspessulanum*, *Ostrya carpinifolia*, *Fraxinus ornus*, *Ulmus* sp. and sometimes *Cercis siliquastrum* and *Celtis australis*. In sheltered gullies less common trees such as *Tilia tomentosa* and *Acer obtusatum* may be present. The associated shrubs, seldom forming a true shrub layer, are also diverse with, amongst others, *Corylus avellana*, *Cornus mas*, *Prunus spinosa*, *Pyrus* spp., *Malus sylvestris*, *Crataegus monogyna* and *Juniperus* spp. What is clear is that most of the dominant trees are multi-stemmed and ring-counts show that their main stems are only between 10–20 years old. Larger older trees do exist within the woods, with thick single trunks (for example, *Acer* spp.), but these usually show signs of once having been repeatedly pollarded at heights of *c.* 2 m above ground level. The conclusion must be that about twenty years ago these woodland areas were heavily browsed scrub, gnawed down to less than a metre in height, in which only resistant species such as *Quercus coccifera*, *Phillyrea* and *Carpinus orientalis* could easily survive. The trees would form a mosaic of clumps separated by almost bare ground. In places where goat browsing is still intense, and this pattern can still be seen (Fig. 16.14), a few other trees and shrubs can just about survive though almost smothered within the densely branched and stunted clumps of the dominants. Virtually none of the woody species are able to flower or set fruit under these conditions. The rapid decline in traditional goatherding, as young people have left the land for city life has allowed the trees to grow up and spread out to form a canopy. Subsidiary species have also been able to grow up, or have been brought in by bird dispersal, enriching the diversity.

To some extent the same process must have taken place on flysch soils, but in many places the woodland dominants are now *Quercus pubescens* and perhaps the Turkey oak *Q. cerris*. *Phillyrea* and *Q. coccifera* are seldom abundant and often confined to woodland margins, along with another browsing-tolerant species *Paliurus spina-christi*. Most of the subsidiary trees and shrubs found in the limestone woodland communities, including *Carpinus orientalis*, are actually present in the flysch woodlands, but in sparser quantity, the exception being *Cornus mas* which may be abundant. Although the older oaks are multi-stemmed and pollarded trees are also present, there is often active regeneration of *Quercus pubescens*. In the absence or sparsity of the evergreen *Phillyrea* and *Quercus coccifera* light can penetrate to the woodland floor and probably encourages germination. Quite well-developed oak woodland is present on flysch in the neighbourhood of Kipi and many other places and also on the Triassic strata outcropping in the Doliana basin, where *Quercus trojana* is also an important species.

The explanation for differences in regeneration cannot simply be the edaphic preferences of *Phillyrea* and *Quercus coccifera*. There are still sites on flysch, particularly close to villages or along well-used tracks, where these species are clearly dominant. A better explanation might be that many flysch areas simply did not suffer such an intensity of grazing activity, perhaps because from a nutritional point of view it was always better to pasture sheep and goats for a longer period on limestone terrain if that was also locally available (Sturdy *et al.*, Chapter 30). This might have enabled deciduous oaks to maintain a competitive advantage on flysch soils over the kermès oak and *Phillyrea*. Another point is that with flysch soils so obviously susceptible to erosion on sloping ground, over-use by stock would clearly damage the extent of the resource, whereas limestone areas do not degrade in the same very visible way.

The Vikos Gorge

Botanically the most important feature of the area is the Vikos Gorge, together with the Aoos Gorge which lies to the north of the Gamila. It should be noted that there are other gorges in the area, notably the Kalamas Gorge actually within the Doliana basin, and the Gormos Gorge that adjoins it to the north-west. Neither of these gorges are on the scale of the Vikos Gorge, but they are nevertheless deep, to a large extent inaccessible and provide a refuge for woodland and cliff-face plant communities, but they are at a much lower altitude and lack the physical connection with the high Pindus that has made both the Vikos and Aoos Gorges so floristically rich.

Although vegetation conditions in the Vikos Gorge are now very different from what they were during the Late Glacial period, it is worth describing the main features of the present-day vegetation and the historical and physical processes that have shaped it, because these have a bearing on the special nature of the gorge as a habitable environment.

Vegetation surveys were carried out in the lower Vikos Gorge primarily between 1984 and 1987, usually during the months of July and August, so that much of the herbaceous plant cover was already becoming desiccated, but the area was also visited in May 1977. The upper Vikos Gorge around Monodendri and Kipi was examined in particular in July 1992, a year when spring and early summer were unusually wet, so that the vegetation was unusually fresh compared with previous years. Additional information has been obtained from what are basically floristic lists (Polunin 1980; Strid 1986; 1991; and P. Authier pers. comm.), since the Vikos Gorge, together with the neighbouring Aoos Gorge and the limestone cliffs of the northern Pindus, form a veritable 'Mecca' for amateur and professional botanists because of their floral richness. Here, however, only the main features of vegetation stands are mentioned rather than exhaustive listing of species present.

The floodplain of the Voïdomatis consists partly of the active channel with its poorly vegetated bars and gravel spreads, usually consisting of coarse- to medium-sized rounded cobbles, partly of abandoned gravel spreads at much the same level, which have been colonized by willows or other trees and shrubs, over which a thin soil begins to develop in favourable areas, and partly by the slightly higher surface of the Klithi Unit, about 3 m above river-bed level, the youngest (late Holocene) unit of the alluvial fill of the gorge (Macklin *et al.*, Chapter 17). In fact all these surfaces are regularly covered by the winter and spring floodwaters of the modern river.

On the bare gravels of the banks and bars of the river sprout young bushes and seedlings of the willows *Salix eleagnus* and *S. alba* and plane *Platanus orientalis*, perhaps regenerating from the severed roots of trees long swept away. Some bars are partly stabilized by clumps of *Petasites hybridus* and *Calamagrostis*, otherwise the vegetation is restricted to scattered plants of ruderal or marsh species. Where the floodplain has been abandoned, thickets of willow or alder *Alnus glutinosa* may grow up into floodplain woodland or a less dense woodland dominated by *Platanus* may emerge and a thin soil develop over the cobbles. The regular flooding carries in a large range of fruits and seeds of both woodland and open-ground species, so that eventually patchy shrub and herb layers develop, but this is subject to frequent grazing and browsing by the flocks of goats that pass daily along the valley-floor from spring to autumn. The trees include very stunted specimens of *Quercus coccifera* and *Carpinus orientalis*, both goat-tolerant, together with seedlings of *Cercis siliquastrum*, *Pistacia terebinthus*, *Sorbus* sp. and bramble *Rubus fruticosus agg*. Stagnant pools of water may persist for much of the summer. The older surface of the Klithi Unit (Macklin *et al.*, Chapter 17) provides more varied habitats with woodlands such as those just described or patches of open grassland, possibly developing on spreads of finer-grained alluvium, and probably encouraging its deposition during floods. These grassland areas, such as those around the camp-site near the Agii Anargyri monastery, partly shaded by large plane trees, are clearly very important to domestic animals. Nearby, isolated trees such as specimens of *Acer monspessulanum* have been pollarded, presumably to provide an occasional but readily available emergency supply of green foliage for goats. These grasslands have a rich and diverse flora of grasses and other herbs, though sometimes invaded by bracken *Pteridium aquilinum*. In spring and early summer they are bright with the flowers of anemones and of many species of bulbous plants and wild orchids.

Figure 16.14. *Bushes of kermès oak (*Quercus coccifera*), close to the village of Doliana. These have been stunted by intensive goat browsing. Note the ring of bare ground which separates each bush.*

In some places on the edges of the floodplain and particularly on the steep lower slopes a rather dense multi-stemmed, thorny scrub has developed, consisting primarily of *Phillyrea media*, *Quercus coccifera* and *Carpinus orientalis*. By 1987 these bushes had grown to be 8–10 m tall, with the appearance of an even-aged stand. Tree-ring counts confirmed that the upright stems were about 10 years old at that time. The interpretation is that until about 1977 these trees were contained by heavy browsing pressure to heights of less than a metre. This suggests that the pattern of vegetation cover, and indeed the whole appearance of much of the Lower Vikos Gorge may have changed dramatically in the last 20 years.

Associated with this regeneration of woodland within the Lower Vikos Gorge has been the appearance within lightly grazed areas of the floodplain of young seedlings of a great variety of trees and shrubs, many of which (for example the horse chestnut *Aesculus hippocastaneum* and the silver fir *Abies alba* (or possibly the hybrid *A. borisii-regis*) are not represented in the present floodplain woodland by mature flowering and fruiting adult specimens, or seldom so. Apart from the extraordinary botanical richness of the gorge, reflected too in the herb flora, this emphasizes two further points: (1) the role of seasonal river floods in distributing fruits and seeds from upstream; and (2) the role of the steep cliffs along the whole gorge and perhaps even more importantly of the densely wooded and almost impenetrable side valleys of the upper Vikos Gorge as refugia for these woody plant species.

The cliffs of the gorge not only support scattered stands of trees, high and impregnable to the efforts of even the most determined goats, but also a rich herb flora, in part of shade-tolerant woodland species, in part of open-ground alpine species. These contain many local rarities and some endemic species, as also do the cliffs of Astraka 1500 m higher. Today these cliff localities act as refugia from the destructive forces of browsing, grazing and human deforestation, both for woodland and open-ground species, a role also reinforced by the climatically sheltered nature of the gorge with its many aspects and the moderating and freshening influence of the river below. It is probable that these same sites were available as potential refuges for woody and herbaceous plants during the glacial stages, when climatic conditions were generally more hostile, and large populations of agile and voracious herbivorous mammals such as ibex and chamois, as shown by the Klithi excavations, were present in the area.

Archaeological sites

Systematic surveys at various stages in the course of the project, particularly in 1987 and 1992, have explored most areas of the catchment, including a search for open-air finds as well as rockshelters (Fig. 16.15). Particular attention was devoted in 1992 to river courses in order to identify rockshelters, and to three other types of locations: (1) the heavily eroded, red, gravelly fan deposits which are found extensively in the middle reaches of the Kalamas, and north of the Doliana basin towards the Albanian border; (2) 'strategic' locations (ridge-tops and routeways) in and around the Pedina basin, which forms a potentially important intermediate grazing basin between the lowlands of the Doliana and Ioannina basins, on the one side, and the high summer grazing territories on the Gamila mountain massif, on the other, which were exploited from known sites such as Klithi (see Sturdy *et al.*, Chapter 30); (3) the edge of the flysch basin east of the village of Kipi, where a series of ridge tops and valley-edge locations were searched, as an exercise in the testing of a 'negative' area of occupation (see also Bailey *et al.*, Chapter 27 for further discussion of site survey in flysch areas and for sites discovered outside the Voïdomatis catchment).

Coverage is by no means exhaustive, however. Even such a definable target as the discovery of rockshelters in the Vikos Gorge is open to considerable uncertainty. Different pathways through the deep central portion of the gorge offer different perspectives, and visibility can be affected by such imponderables as seasonal vegetation cover, light conditions and the time of day, while local information can be invaluable. We were told of several rockshelters in the main Vikos Gorge which were theoretically visible, but which we would not have spotted if they had not been drawn to our attention. Within the deepest sector of the Vikos gorge, the side gorges of Megas Lakkos and Mezaria are of potential interest but have not yet been explored. Steep slopes, thick vegetation, difficulties of access, and the absence of any significant finds in the rockshelters of the main gorge nearby have dissuaded us from giving priority to the search of these side gorges.

Many of the rockshelter sites are empty of deposit, and appear not to have been used except perhaps fleetingly in recent periods. Other sites have signs of prehistoric occupation but no clear indication of age, while some have yielded diagnostic Upper Palaeolithic artefacts. There are also a number of open-air sites, mostly surface finds, the age of which is difficult to establish with confidence (Table 16.1). The most important sites in this category, because they have given radiometric dates, are the flints exposed in the eroded section of the Aristi Unit by the Old Klithonia Bridge, just downstream of the Boïla rockshelter (Macklin *et al.*, Chapter 17).

Rockshelters

Klithi is one of at least 26 rockshelters within the Voïdomatis basin, distributed throughout the limestone areas of the catchment in physiographic zones 3, 4 and 5, from the edge of the Konitsa basin to the edge of the flysch terrain near Kipi. The rockshelter sites with indications of prehistoric occupation fall into two main groups, one in the Lower Vikos Gorge associated with Klithi, and a second group near the village of Kipi in the upper reaches of the Vikos Gorge where it opens out into flysch terrain.

Konitsa basin and Lower Vikos Gorge

Out on the edge of the Konitsa plain is the Agios Menas rockshelter (so called after the village within whose territory it is located). It has an opening 7 m

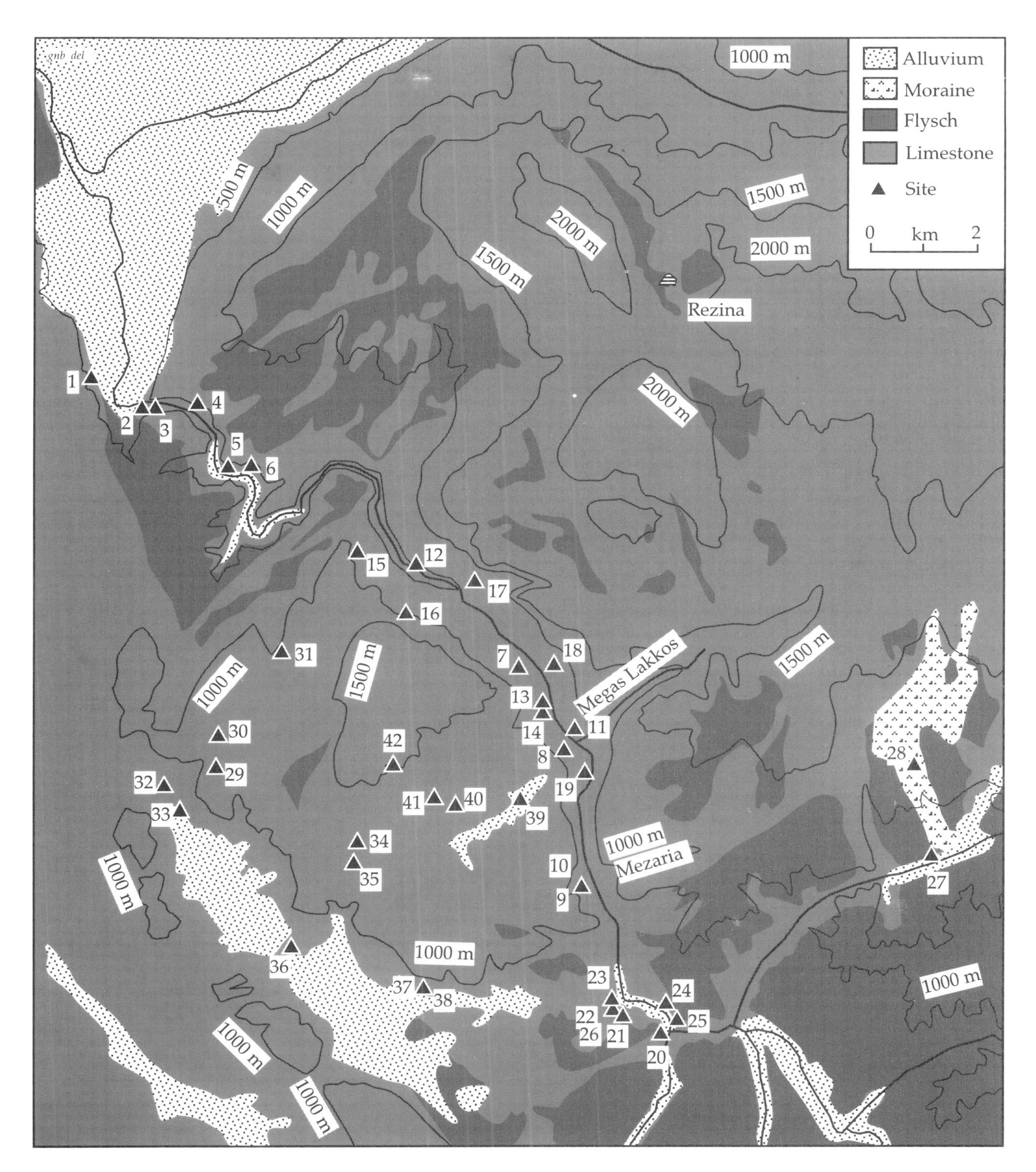

Figure 16.15. *Distribution of archaeological sites in the Voïdomatis basin. Site numbers refer to Table 16.1.*

wide and faces east-northeast, looking out over the plain (Fig. 16.16). The site was visited by Higgs in the 1960s (Higgs & Vita-Finzi 1966). Since that time a new road has been built across the mouth, obscuring any deposits outside the dripline. Inside the shelter large blocks have fallen from the ceiling, but intact

Table 16.1. *List of sites in the Voïdomatis catchment.*

O = Open-air site, R = Rockshelter. Local altitude is the height of the site above the adjacent valley floor. Width, Depth and Height are the gross dimensions of rockshelter openings. Data missing or not recorded are indicated by – . Names in brackets are the local names for rockshelters, where known. Numbers after rockshelters, or numbers in brackets after open-air sites, are the local identifiers used at the time of survey. Map no. refers to Figure 16.15. * = many artefacts resulting from excavation.

		Longitude	Latitude	Map no.	Altitude (m asl)	Local altitude (m)	Width (m)	Depth (m)	Height (m)	No. of artefacts
KONITSA PLAIN										
Agios Menas	R	20°39.50'E	39°58.2'N	1	420	–	7	7	5	3
LOWER VIKOS GORGE										
Old Klithonia Bridge	O	20°40.0'E	39°58.0'N	2	410	10	–	–	–	6
Boïla	R	20°40.0'E	39°58.0'N	3	410	10	20	3	10	*
Klithonia	R	20°40.5'E	39°58.0'N	4	415	20	5	5	5	1
Klithi	R	20°41.0'E	39°57.5'N	5	430	30	30	10	10	*
Megalakkos	R	20°41.5'E	39°57.5'N	6	430	10	5	3	5	*
VIKOS GORGE (CENTRAL)										
Rockshelter 2 (Dragousiani)	R	20°44.7'E	39°55.5'N	7	540	7	60	4	4	4
Klima	O	20°45.4'E	39°54.8'N	8	540	–	–	–	–	1
Rockshelter 6	R	20°45.4'E	39°53.4'N	9	700	30	15	3	9	1
Rockshelter 7	R	20°45.4'E	39°53.5'N	10	710	35	30	8	20	1
Vikos Site 8	O	20°45.5'E	39°54.4'N	11	730	50	–	–	–	3
Supplementary List of Rockshelters										
Rockshelter 1	R	20°43.4'E	39°56.6'N	12	540	40	10	3	4	–
Rockshelter 3	R	20°45.0'E	39°55.1'N	13	600	30	6	4	10	–
Rockshelter 4	R	20°45.0'E	39°55.1'N	14	600	30	3	3	3	–
Rockshelter 8	R	20°42.5'E	39°56.7'N	15	1000	500	10	–	15	–
Rockshelter 9	R	20°43.3'E	39°56.0'N	16	900	400	10	2	2	–
Rockshelter 10 (Cochista)	R	20°44.2'E	39°56.5'N	17	*c.* 950	*c.* 350	–	–	–	–
Rockshelter 11 (Greksta)	R	20°45.2'E	39°55.5'N	18	*c.* 900	*c.* 300	–	–	–	–
Rockshelter 12 (Kapnismeni)	R	20°45.3'E	39°54.7'N	19	620	40	6	3	7	–
VIKOS GORGE (UPPER)										
Kipi 1 (Kokoris)	R	20°46.4'E	39°51.8'N	20	730	10	20	10	12	5
Kipi 2	R	20°45.9'E	39°52.0'N	21	720	12	10	12	10	1
Kipi 4	R	20°45.8'E	39°52.1'N	22	720	7	12	6	4	144
Kipi 5	R	20°45.8'E	39°52.1'N	23	740	25	10	2	2	5
Kipi 3	R	20°46.4'E	39°53.0'N	24	720	–	8	2	3	–
Kipi 6	R	20°46.5'E	39°51.9'N	25	730	–	8	4	8	–
Kipi 7	R	20°45.8'E	39°52.1'N	26	720	7	10	3	–	–
HEADWATER FLYSCH										
Tsepelovon	O	20°49.9'E	39°53.5'N	27	880	–	–	–	–	3
Tsepelovon fan	O	20°50.0'E	39°54.0'N	28	1100	–	–	–	–	1
PEDINA										
Elafotopos	O	20°41.0'E	39°54.5'N	29	1120	–	–	–	–	6
Drabala 1	O	20°41.0'E	39°54.8'N	30	1140	–	–	–	–	4
Drabala 2	O	20°41.9'E	39°55.5'N	31	1040	–	–	–	–	5
Pedina (P0)	O	20°40.0'E	39°54.2'N	32	850	–	–	–	–	2
Pedina (P1)	O	20°40.2'E	39°53.8'N	33	850	–	–	–	–	10
Pedina (P2)	O	20°42.5'E	39°53.5'N	34	1310	–	–	–	–	6
Pedina (P3)	O	20°42.4'E	39°53.4'N	35	1290	–	–	–	–	4
Pedina (P4)	R	20°41.5'E	39°52.5'N	36	850	2	12	15	12	?1
Pedina	R	20°43.4'E	39°52.2'N	37	860	20	4	1	2	1
Pedina	R	20°43.4'E	39°52.2'N	38	860	–	–	–	–	1
Tsouknida 1	O	20°44.6'E	39°54.1'N	39	1290	–	–	–	–	5
Tsouknida 2	O	20°43.6'E	39°53.9'N	40	1360	–	–	–	–	3
Tsouknida 3	O	20°43.5'E	39°54.1'N	41	1380	–	–	–	–	16
Episkopou	O	20°43.0'E	39°54.0'N	42	1520	–	–	–	–	1

scree deposits are present and artefacts of Upper Palaeolithic type have been reported including backed bladelets.

The Boïla shelter is just inside the mouth of the gorge close by the old bridge and faces north-north-east (Fig. 16.17). The opening here is about 20 m wide with quite a shallow overhang and a scree deposit sitting on top of a river terrace comprising the Aristi unit (Macklin *et al.*, Chapter 17). The site was first noted by Derek Sturdy in 1970. In 1992 the Ephoreia of Speleology began a programme of excavation (Kotjabopoulou *et al.*, Chapter 22).

Within the Lower Gorge proper, the key sites are Klithi and Megalakkos. Other shelters are present, but these are small, at low level liable to flooding, or bare of deposit. The first shelter inside the gorge, upstream of Boïla, is small and of little significance: its only claim to mention is the discovery of a worked flint artefact on the surface. Klithi is undoubtedly the largest rockshelter of the group with the largest and most obviously intact deposit. Its use as a winter shelter for goats in recent times also attests to its superior attractions. Notwithstanding its position in a narrow gorge with cliffs rising to 300 m above the site (frontispiece, vol. 1), it would have been easily approachable on foot from a number of directions during the period of prehistoric occupation. There are several routes near Klithi which provide steep but passable access from the valley bottom to the heights above the site and thence to the gentler slopes between Old Klithonia and Papingon. The higher slopes on the opposite side of the river near Agios Menas can be similarly reached without difficulty. It should also be emphasized that when the site was occupied, the river was flowing at a higher level than today, and the valley floor was broader and more easily negotiable (Macklin *et al.*, Chapter 17). All these factors make Klithi an attractive shelter for occupation, and an obvious first choice for investigation, as the results of excavation have amply demonstrated.

Megalakkos is about 400 m east of Klithi in a narrow, steep-sided tributary stream and some 100 m upstream of its junction with the main river. The shelter is about 10 m above the local stream bed, which today is dry in summer, and at about the same height above the main river as Klithi (Fig. 16.18). Otherwise it is very different from Klithi, with a small shelter opening about 5 m wide which faces southwest. The site was discovered by John Lewin and Mark Macklin in 1986 during the couse of survey of the valley-fill sequence (Macklin *et al.*, Chapter 17). The deposit is about the same depth as at Klithi but has been heavily eroded and partially cemented to reveal a standing section readily available for inspection and sampling with minimal excavation. The upper part of the deposits has been undercut by erosion to form an overhang. Megalakkos is of particular interest because the archaeological deposits

Figure 16.16. *General view of the Higgs rockshelter (Agios Menas) on the side of the main Ioannina–Konitsa road, looking west.*

Figure 16.17. *General view of the Old Klithonia Bridge, looking southeast from the right bank of the Voïdomatis at the mouth of the Lower Gorge. The cliffs visible beyond the trees are directly above the Boïla rockshelter opening, which is hidden from view. The dated open-air sites exposed in the section of the Aristi Unit are just beyond the right of the picture.*

Figure 16.18. *General view of the Megalakkos rockshelter from immediately below the shelter opening.*

Figure 16.19. *General view of the Kokoris rockshelter near Kipi. The dry river-bed of the Voïdomatis is in the immediate foreground.*

cover a similar time span to those at Klithi but show significant differences in sedimentology (Woodward, Chapters 18 & 19) and cultural content (Sinclair, Chapter 21).

The Kipi group

Kipi 1 is opposite the old bridge of Kokoris, close to the modern road from Pedina to Tsepelovon (Fig. 16.19). The shelter opening is about 20 m wide by 10 m deep and 12 m high. There are at least 3 types of deposit here: a heavily cemented and eroded deposit, now existing only in small patches cemented to the back wall, but containing worked flint (undiagnostic of period though possibly Upper Palaeolithic) and bone fragments, from which we have attempted to obtain radiocarbon dates but without success; a second cemented and partially eroded deposit on the lower floor of the shelter, which appears to be more extensive but culturally sterile, and a loose brown deposit on the lowest part of the shelter floor which has been partly disturbed and removed by recent use as an animal shelter.

An additional 6 rockshelters are located further downstream, 3 of which have definite indications of prehistoric use. The most promising is Kipi 4 (Fig. 16.20). This is an east-facing shelter with two openings, the larger of which is about 15 m wide and 3 m deep, and some 6 m above the present river bed. There are traces of eroded and cemented deposit on the back wall which appear to be sterile, but in front of the opening there is a talus deposit of loose, brown sediment, which is about 5 m deep and extends some 15 m in front of the overhang. Numerous flint artefacts were found on the surface of the talus and one or two pieces under the overhang.

Kipi 5 is about 50 m downstream of Kipi 4 and some 25 m above the present river bed, close to the old bridge which linked the villages of Vitsa and

Koukouli. The opening is 10 m wide by 2 m deep with a 2 m high ceiling. The bedrock of the shelter and the slope in front of it are steeply angled. There are pockets of sediment on the slope in front of the overhang containing flint artefacts including a patinated backed bladelet, but there appears to be very little remaining *in situ* deposit.

Kipi 2 is a solution cavity with a steep talus

Figure 16.20. *General view of the Kipi 4 rockshelter. The Voïdomatis river-bed is in the foreground.*

Figure 16.21. *Section downstream of Boïla showing a thin lens of soil and charcoal marking exposure of flint artefacts within sandy sediments in the upper section of the Aristi Unit: left-hand picture shows general view looking east (Derek & Carolyn Sturdy); right-hand picture shows close-up of section with slope deposits stratified on top of the fluvial sediments. The artefact-bearing horizon is the dark line about one third of the way down the shepherd's staff and to its right.*

slope of jumbled stones and boulders and little sign of cultural material apart from one struck flint found on the surface.

In all cases the deposits have been subject to a variety of disturbing and destructive processes, including human disturbance at Kipi 1, and are vulnerable to further disturbance. The Kipi sites are of particular interest because they represent a focus of activity at the upstream end of the Vikos Gorge where it opens out to more accessible terrain, and in this sense they are closely analogous to the group of sites centred on Klithi. They differ from the Klithi group in being at higher altitude. Also Kipi 1 and Kipi 4 are too low above the present river level to have been used during the Last Glacial period when the stream bed would have been considerably higher than the present. These are clues to the possible presence of late Upper Palaeolithic or even post-Upper Palaeolithic cultural material in these deposits, but this possibility will only be resolved by future excavation.

Open-air sites

Two open-air sites with a small number of artefacts have been located in river-terrace deposits about 50 m downstream of Boïla, just beyond the old bridge (Gillespie *et al.* 1985; Bailey *et al.* 1990). The first of these comprises a handful of flints in a thin ashy lens within a soil horizon exposed in a section of sandy, slack water river sediments now exposed some 8 m above the present river channel (Fig. 16.21). The site was discovered by Derek Sturdy and Derrick Webley in 1983 (Bailey, Chapter 1) and has yielded two series of radiocarbon dates (Gowlett *et al.*, Chapter 2), respectively of about 11,000 BP (from charcoal) and 15,000 BP (from the humic acid fraction of the charcoal samples). Lower down in the same terrace sequence is a lens of similar sandy sediments sandwiched between typical gravels of the Aristi unit (Fig. 16.22). A flint artefact and a red deer mandible were recovered from the sandy lens by John Lewin and Mark Macklin in 1986 (Bailey, Chapter 1), and the red deer mandible has yielded an ESR date of about 25,000 years (Macklin *et al.*, Chapter 17).

There is also a group of sites in and around the Pedina basin. These sites are of uncertain age and significance but are worth brief comment because the Pedina basin forms a potentially important intermediate grazing basin between the lowlands of the Doliana and Ioannina basins, on the one side, and the high summer grazing territories on the Gamila mountain massif, on the other, which were exploited from known sites such as Klithi and possibly from Kipi.

None of these finds provides unambiguous

Figure 16.22. *Section of Aristi Unit downstream of Boïla showing exposure of sandy lens from which the ESR-dated red deer mandible and artefact were recovered, next to the folded arms of the human figure (John Lewin). This section is immediately below that illustrated in Figure 16.21. The sandy lens is of similar composition to the sandy sediments in the Figure 16.21 section.*

indications of age, and the material could well be post-Palaeolithic. In view of the strategic location and ecological potential of this intermontane valley system, further investigation would be desirable. Perhaps the best prospect for providing further information is the small rockshelter (site 13, Table16.1). This is a small west-facing rockshelter in the middle of the Pedina basin, about 2 m above the valley floor, and by the side of the road from Kato Pedina to Monodendri. The shelter opening is about 12 m wide by 15 m deep, with a hole in the roof, and has been used in modern times as an animal shelter. In front of the opening is a nettle-covered talus at least 1 m thick. The site has been visited on a number of occasions since at least 1983, but has failed to give unambiguous surface indications of archaeological potential.

Comparisons

It should be emphasized that the group of sites as a whole offers interesting opportunities for the analysis of inter-site variation at a local scale within a single valley-catchment. Such comparisons may reveal a wider range of variation than might be apparent from the study of individual sites, and an important control on the interpretation of both archaeological and sedimentological data. This opportunity was recognized at an early stage, but practical and permit constaints have so far limited comparative investigations to Klithi and Megalakkos, while excavation of Boïla has recently got under way, and preliminary findings are reported later (Kotjabopoulou *et al.*, Chapter 22).

In a more general sense the evidence at present available emphasizes another point of importance. There are a considerable number of cave or rockshelter sites within the valley as a whole. Not all are listed here, and some can be ruled out as improbable locations for prehistoric occupation because of difficulties of access, poor shelter, or small size. However, it is clear that the location of sites with prehistoric occupation is not simply a function of the location of caves and/or rockshelters. Nor are the sites that were occupied of equal weighting. Some, such as Klithi, appear to have been preferred sites in the sense of being the focus of repeated or prolonged visits, while others were less so. Clearly the evaluation of the comparative weighting to be placed on each site is problematic in view of the limited number of sites that have been excavated. The point, however, is that the data as a whole provide considerable evidence for variation in the use of particular rockshelter locations — or in the geological conditions that favour survival of evidence — and opportunities for identifying the factors underlying such variability.

Chapter 17

Quaternary River Sedimentary Sequences of the Voïdomatis Basin

Mark Macklin, John Lewin & Jamie Woodward

Quaternary river deposits both in the Old World (e.g. Huntington 1910; Higgs & Vita-Finzi 1966; Vita-Finzi 1969) and the New World (e.g. Bryan 1941; Hack 1942) have long been recognized by archaeologists and geomorphologists alike as being particularly important sources of evidence for elucidating interrelationships between environmental change and prehistoric human activity. They provide data which complement those from lake and rockshelter sediments, with an additional attribute in that river terraces and alluvial fills may be major landscape features which change over time to provide a varying setting for human activity and exploitation. River systems in the Mediterranean region during Quaternary times, in common with many others in central and northern Europe (Starkel 1985), responded in a sensitive manner to variations in sediment delivery rates to valley floors and also changes in hydroclimatological regimes (see Macklin *et al.* 1995 for a recent review). Episodes of alluviation in the Mediterranean have been attributed both to climatic controls (Bintliff 1975; 1977), epitomized by Vita-Finzi's (1969) now classic subdivision of valley sediment sequences in the region into 'Younger' and 'Older' Fills, and also anthropogenic influences (Davidson 1980). Later workers (Gilbertson *et al.* 1983; Gomez 1987; Lewin *et al.* 1991; Pope & Van Andel 1984; Van Andel & Zangger 1990; Wagstaff 1981), however, have questioned the applicability of Vita-Finzi's model to regionally diverse and stratigraphically complex alluvial chronologies, whilst neotectonic activity is now seen as an important factor (King *et al.*, Chapter 28; Harvey & Wells 1987), as Vita-Finzi's own later work has underlined (Vita-Finzi 1986).

The Upper Palaeolithic coincided with the climatic fluctuations of the last major glacial–interglacial cycle, when the development and decay of glaciers, and the effects of cold-climate periglacial processes transformed the erosion/deposition systems of many Mediterranean rivers. Whilst Late Würm glaciation of mountains in the Mediterranean is now quite well established (Lewin *et al.* 1991; Sibrava *et al.* 1986; Woodward *et al.* 1995), with cirque glaciers down to 1500–1900 m in southern Italy for example (Palmentola *et al.* 1990), the exact timing of glacial conditions in relation to human activities is not well understood. The examination of Palaeolithic sites in Epirus by the Klithi project provided an ideal field setting in which to use modern geomorphological, sedimentological and geochronological techniques to examine prehistoric archaeological sequences within the context of changing Quaternary riverine environments in a key area for European Palaeolithic studies. Fieldwork in the Voïdomatis was carried out by the authors between 1986 and 1988. A series of papers have already been published on the relationship between Pleistocene glaciation and human settlement (Bailey *et al.* 1990; Woodward *et al.* 1995), river response to Late Quaternary climate change (Lewin *et al.* 1991), and long-term variations in alluvial sediment sources (Woodward *et al.* 1992) and soil chronosequences on river terraces (Woodward *et al.* 1994). This chapter summarizes this work within the broader context of the Klithi project, presents a new interpretation of the Late Pleistocene river record of the Voïdomatis in the light of recent palaeoclimate reconstructions from the GRIP and GISP2 ice cores drilled through the Greenland ice sheet at Summit (Johnsen *et al.* 1992; Taylor *et al.* 1993), and focuses on the implications of these environmental and climatic changes for human occupation of the Voïdomatis basin.

The Voïdomatis basin

Geomorphological investigations have centred on the Voïdomatis basin (drainage area 384 km^2) and in particular on a 17.8 km reach of the Vikos and Lower

Vikos Gorge (Fig. 17.1). In broad terms, this catchment is developed in hard limestones overlain by folded and deformed flysch strata, the latter being thin-bedded alternations of fine-grained clay/silt and coarser-grained siliceous sandstones (Bailey *et al.*, Chapter 16). Some of the limestones contain bands of chert, but for the most part they are extremely pure calcium carbonates. There are also some limited areas with igneous rock outcrops, the Pindus Ophiolite. This is found more widely further to the east of the Voïdomatis basin itself.

On the basis of geology and topography, five separate physiographic zones can be recognized in the Voïdomatis basin (Table 17.1) (Lewin *et al.* 1991; Bailey *et al.*, Chapter 16). There is, first, a mountainous limestone region in the eastern and northeastern part of the catchment close to the village of Tsepelovon. Here, fresh glacial landforms (cirques,

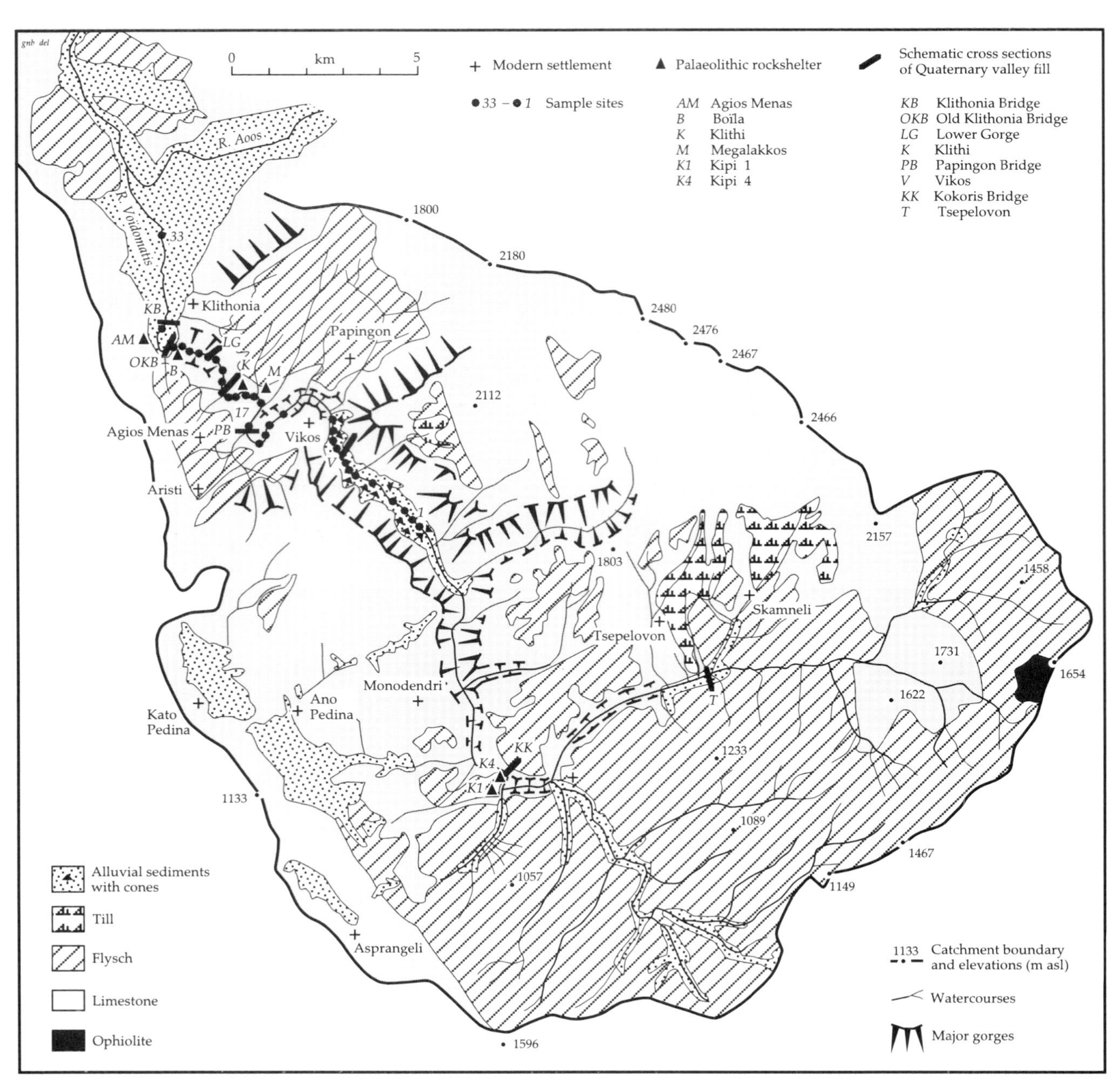

Figure 17.1. *The Voïdomatis River basin, showing its drainage network, solid geology, location of major Palaeolithic rockshelters and location of study and sample sites. (Redrawn from Lewin* et al. *1991.)*

U-shaped valleys, lateral moraines, and kame terraces) are well developed, and extensive glacially-related sediments (tills, glaciofluvial deposits) indicate recent glaciation. Mountain elevations exceed 2400 m along the crests of the Gamila range. Second, a dissected flysch basin (of Late Eocene–Miocene age) is to be found upstream of Kipi; this lay beyond the limits of glaciation and displays many of the classic 'badland' slope forms typical of semi-arid regions elsewhere in Greece and the Mediterranean (Woodward 1995). The third subregion is the Upper Vikos Gorge, between Monodendrion and Vikos, which is judged to be one of the most spectacular in the whole of the Balkans. The gorge is cut in Eocene and Jurassic limestone and has near vertical sides which are in places >800 m high, although the gorge itself is only about 2.5 km across at its widest point. Talus cones (>40 m thick) and aprons mantle the walls of the gorge and locally cover or interdigitate with coarse-grained alluvial sediments (>20 m thick) that infill the gorge floor. The fourth physiographic unit is the Lower Vikos Gorge that contains the majority of the Palaeolithic rockshelter sites. This is separated from the main Vikos Gorge at a point, 2 km southeast of Papingon, where the Voïdomatis leaves the confines of the Gamila Massif. It extends downstream as far as Old Klithonia Bridge where its narrow limestone walls, up to 150 m high, open out onto the Konitsa basin. Alluvial fans are well developed at the mouths of a number of tributary streams in the lower gorge that drain areas of flysch bedrock (e.g. 2 km northeast of Aristi), which outcrop on the upper slopes of a considerable part of the Lower Vikos Gorge. Where the floor of the gorge widens, dissected colluvial sediments (>15 m thick), and terraced alluvial deposits (>25 m thick), are well preserved. The fifth and final physiographic unit is the Konitsa basin. This is a fault-controlled graben of Tertiary age into which the Voïdomatis and Aoos Rivers flow. The active channel and floodplain of the Voïdomatis are rarely more than 200 m wide in the Konitsa basin, but on both sides there are extensive Quaternary alluvial deposits whose surfaces lie 1–5 m above river-bed level.

These five physiographic units have all delivered sediment to the river though each area has operated differentially over time. The upper part of the Voïdomatis catchment has also provided material whose characteristics are diagnostic of source area. These lithologically distinctive headwater sub-basins are underlain either by a single rock type, for example, the flysch basin upstream of Kipi and the Eocene and Jurassic limestone in the Upper Vikos Gorge and Tsepelovon district, incorporate a small area of petrographically distinctive bedrock, e.g. the ophiolite complex in the most eastern corner of the catchment — or contain localized glacigenic deposits. Analysis of the lithological composition of Quaternary alluvial deposits in the middle and lower reaches of the Voïdomatis has allowed these sediment sources to be readily identified (Lewin *et al.* 1991; Woodward *et al.* 1992).

The rockshelters of the Voïdomatis basin are all located in close proximity to areas of Quaternary alluvial sedimentation, even though later dissection has eroded and lowered the valley floor deposits. Alluvial and colluvial units are well exposed on both the sides and floor of the Vikos Gorge, and in conjunction with the archaeological material, they provide a very useful basis for environmental reconstruction. Fluvial sedimentation is inherently episodic in nature, with periods of cut and fill, erosion and deposition episodes following one another, and for that reason they provide a less continuous record than that available from other sorts of deposits, for example lacustrine ones. Locally, however, alluvial units can cover a more extended timespan than is available from either rockshelter or lake deposits (see Chapters 18–20), and this is certainly true of the Voïdomatis. The environmental changes recorded also reflect an intermediate *spatial* scale, integrating environmental effects in the 384 km^2 of the river catchment, which is somewhat larger than that of the main rockshelter sediments (though some

Table 17.1. *Physiographic units in the Voïdomatis basin.*

	Area	Geology	Drainage density	Local relief
Glaciated region	19.2 km^2	Palaeocene to Eocene limestone	0.16 km/km^2	≈500 m
Headwater flysch terrain	153.6 km^2	Late Eocene to Miocene flysch	0.84 km/km^2	≈150 m
Vikos Gorge and adjacent karst plateaus	117.2 km^2	Jurassic to Eocene limestones	0.26 km/km^2	≈1000 m
Lower Vikos Gorge & adjacent flysch exposures	57.6 km^2	Palaeocene to Eocene limestones & Late Eocene to Miocene flysch	0.76 km/km^2	≈200 m
Konitsa plain	38.4 km^2	Quaternary alluvial sediments	0.24 km/km^2	<20 m

fine-grained aeolian material may have blown in from outside the basin: Woodward, Chapter 19), and probably the lake pollen evidence, but less than the regional scale discussed in Chapters 28–30.

Methods of investigation

Morphostratigraphic relationships between Quaternary alluvial and colluvial fills in the Voïdomatis basin were established by extensive field reconnaissance and detailed morphological mapping. In addition, at 33 sites within the Vikos Gorge and the Konitsa basin, from a point 5 km north of Monodendrion, to a point 1 km northeast of Klithonia (Fig. 17.1), an aneroid barometer was used to measure the height of river terraces and fans (to the nearest 0.3 m) above a fixed local datum. The heights of the rockshelters, measured at present floor level, were also determined. At 8 locations along the Voïdomatis (shown and listed in Fig. 17.1) exceptionally good exposures of valley fill sediments, mostly in currently eroding river bank sections, allowed detailed examination of Quaternary alluvial and colluvial deposits in all of the 5 major physiographic units described above. At these sites the sedimentary properties, sequence and architectures of all Quaternary units were recorded. Sediment logs from a further 32 sites, at which sections were rather less extensive laterally or vertically, were used to supplement and in places refine lithostratigraphic relationships (see Lewin *et al.* 1991).

Lithological and mineralogical analyses of both the gravel (8–256 mm) and fine sediment (<63 μm) fractions were carried out on a range of fluvial, colluvial and glacial Quaternary deposits. More than 50 samples of the fine-grained sediment that forms the matrix of the coarse-grained Quaternary deposits were examined for their mineralogical composition with XRD techniques (Woodward *et al.* 1992). The lithologies of 21 gravel-size sediment samples, including present day river bed material and all Quaternary alluvial units hitherto identified in the study area, have also been analyzed (Lewin *et al.* 1991). Field procedure for analyzing gravel lithologies consisted of marking-out a one metre square on the section to be sampled, removing all clasts exposed on the surface, and then establishing their size over the range 8–256 mm using templates graduated at 0.5 Ø intervals (Fig. 17.2). The weight and number of clasts in each size fraction were counted and all were assigned to one of four predetermined lithological classes — limestone, flysch, flint or ophiolite rock types. This entailed hand sieving 4.75 tonnes of gravel and measuring 16,263 clasts.

The degree of soil development on the major terrace surfaces was also investigated, with analysis of $CaCO_3$ and organic content, particle size, magnetic susceptibility and iron content (Woodward *et al.* 1994). Though not the primary means of age sequencing of alluvial units (*cf.* Pope & Van Andel 1984), this analysis has been used to confirm and extend conclusions reached through other dating and lithostratigraphic procedures.

Finally, the alluvial deposits in the basin have been dated by a range of isotopic (radiocarbon) and radiogenic (TL, ESR) dating techniques. Organic materials have been dated at two sites in the Konitsa basin and at one in the Lower Vikos Gorge. Three TL sediment dates, and three ESR dates from a deer tooth incorporated into alluvial sediment at Old Klithonia Bridge, have also been obtained.

Quaternary river deposits in the Voïdomatis basin

Four Quaternary alluvial units that pre-date the contemporary floodplain have been identified in the Voïdomatis basin. Their sedimentary properties, height relationships, depositional environments and estimated ages are summarized in Table 17.2, and Figures 17.3 & 17.4. The names used for all alluvial units are informal and they are described below in order of apparent age.

(i) Kipi Unit

This is the oldest alluvial fill yet identified in the study basin. To date it has been recognized only at one site near Kokoris Bridge, 1.5 km west of Kipi, in a road cutting where 22.9 m of the unit was exposed (Fig. 17.5). A TL date of >150,000 ka (BM ref VOI26, Appendix A) was obtained from silts close to the base of the section, and this gives a minimum age for the deposition of the unit.

The Kipi alluvial fill is highly weathered and comprises flat-bedded, imbricated sandy gravels which grade down valley into cross-stratified sands. The contact between vertically contiguous gravel units is generally non-erosional and frequently marked by thin beds (<0.2 m) of laminated silts. Coarser sediments within the Kipi Unit are interpreted as longitudinal/mid channel bar-forms deposited in an aggrading, low-sinuosity river system, with sands and silts representing bar-tail fines and bar-surface drapes, respectively. The surface of the Kipi terrace lies 56 m above present river-bed level, is underlain by Late Eocene–Miocene flysch, and was clearly deposited before the formation of the limestone gorge in which the Voïdomatis now

Figure 17.2. *Particle size and lithological analyses of Voïdomatis River gravels. Well-rounded limestone gravels above, flatter and rounded flysch gravels below.*

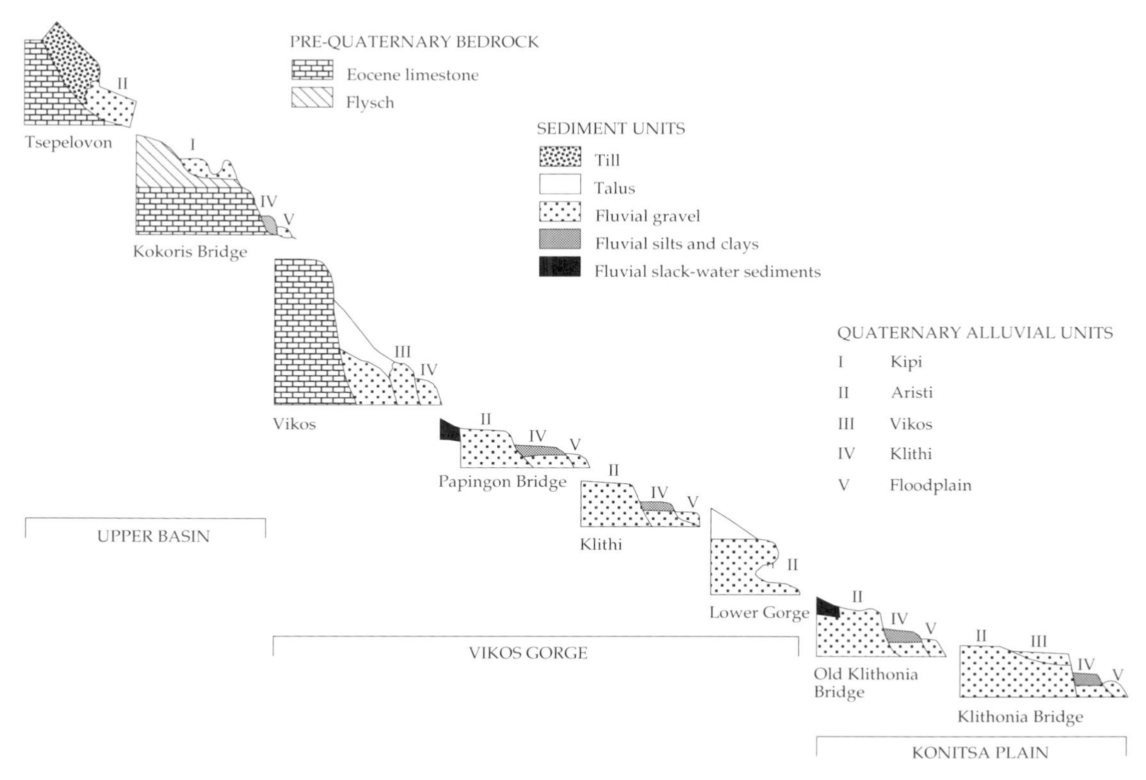

Figure 17.3. *Quaternary valley fill sequence in the Voïdomatis basin. Locations of schematic cross sections are shown in Figure 17.1.*

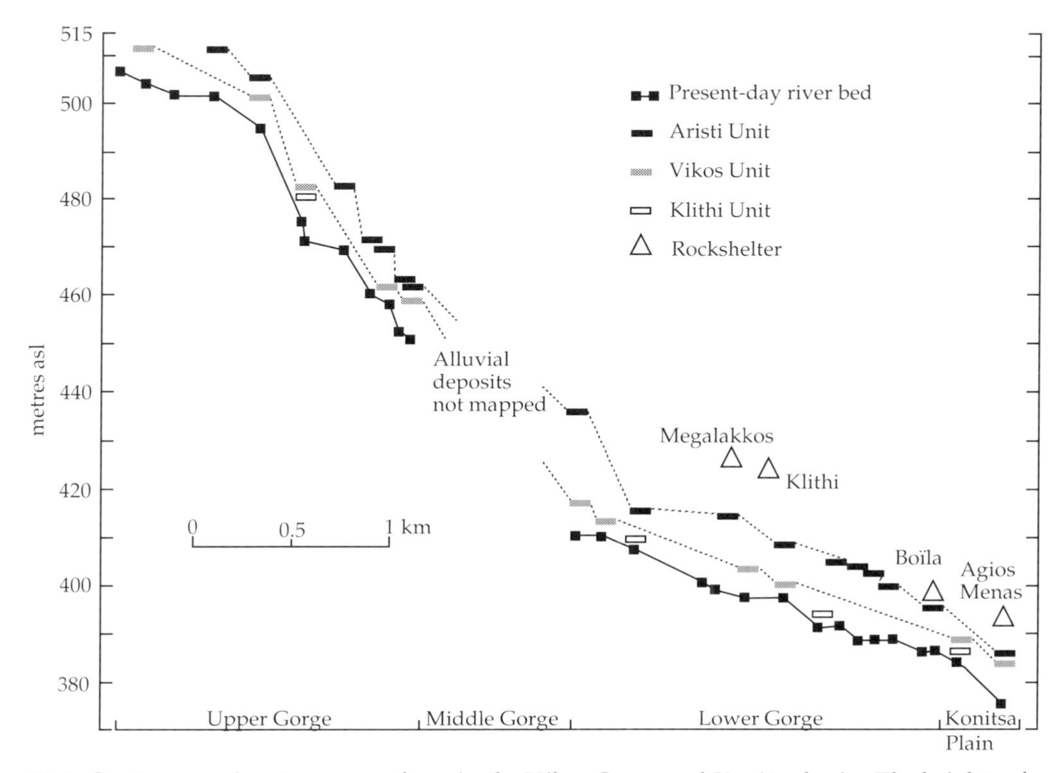

Figure 17.4. *Quaternary river terrace surfaces in the Vikos Gorge and Konitsa basin. The heights of major rockshelters above present river bed level are also shown.*

flows in this part of the basin. High proportions of ophiolite and flysch rock types and low amounts of limestone (Table 17.2 & Fig. 17.6) distinguish the Kipi Unit from other Quaternary alluvial fills in the Voïdomatis basin. This strongly suggests that in Kipi times the Voïdomatis catchment extended further to the east and drained a much larger area of ophiolite terrain than at present. This sub-basin was subsequently captured by the Aoos River.

(ii) Aristi Unit

This is the major alluvial fill in the catchment and it can be traced almost continuously from the Tsepelovon moraine complex (Figs. 17.1 & 17.3), where it interdigitates with glacial till, to the present Aoos–Voïdomatis junction in the Konitsa basin, more than 40 km downstream. It forms a prominent terrace (Fig. 17.4) whose surface lies on average 12 m above river-bed level. In places the Aristi Unit is more than 26 m thick and consists almost entirely of flat-bedded or massive matrix-rich cobble gravels with occasional boulder-sized clasts (Figs. 17.7 & 17.8). Imbrication of clasts is locally well developed where there is a lower proportion of silt-sized matrix. XRD analysis of the <63 µm (silt and clay) size fraction in the Aristi Unit (Fig. 17.9) shows a mineralogical composition very similar to glacial till at Tsepelovon from which, at least in part, it appears to have been derived. The gravel size fraction of the Aristi alluvial fill also has a similar lithological composition to the till, containing up to 95 per cent limestone and significant amounts of flint (Fig. 17.6).

The Aristi Unit is believed to be the terraced remnant of a formerly extensive glaciofluvial outwash system that was deposited by an aggrading, low-sinuosity pro-glacial stream which drained a series of valley glaciers in the Tsepelovon region. In common with many contemporary and Pleistocene glacially-fed river systems, suspended sediment loads of the Voïdomatis were high during full glacials, as shown by the large proportion of silt and sand-size matrix in the Aristi gravels. The combination of high suspended sediment loads during these periods with the backing-up of tributary streams by the Voïdomatis during major floods also resulted in the deposition of several metres of fine-grained slack water sediment (*cf.* Baker *et al.* 1983) at a number of tributary and main valley junctions (e.g. at the Papingon Bridge and Old Klithonia Bridge: Figs. 17.1 & 17.3).

Towards the base of gravels underlying slack-water sediments at Old Klithonia Bridge, part of a red deer jaw bone and a number of Palaeolithic flint flakes were discovered in a small palaeochannel infilled with sandy silts (Fig. 16.19). The fragility of the bone and the unmodified condition of the flints attest to minimal river transport. A tooth from the mandible was submitted for enamel dating by ESR, using the linear, continuous U-uptake model (Grün *et al.* 1987), and yielded ages of 24,300 ± 2600,

Figure 17.5. *Kipi Unit sediments exposed in a road cut section near Kokoris Bridge.*

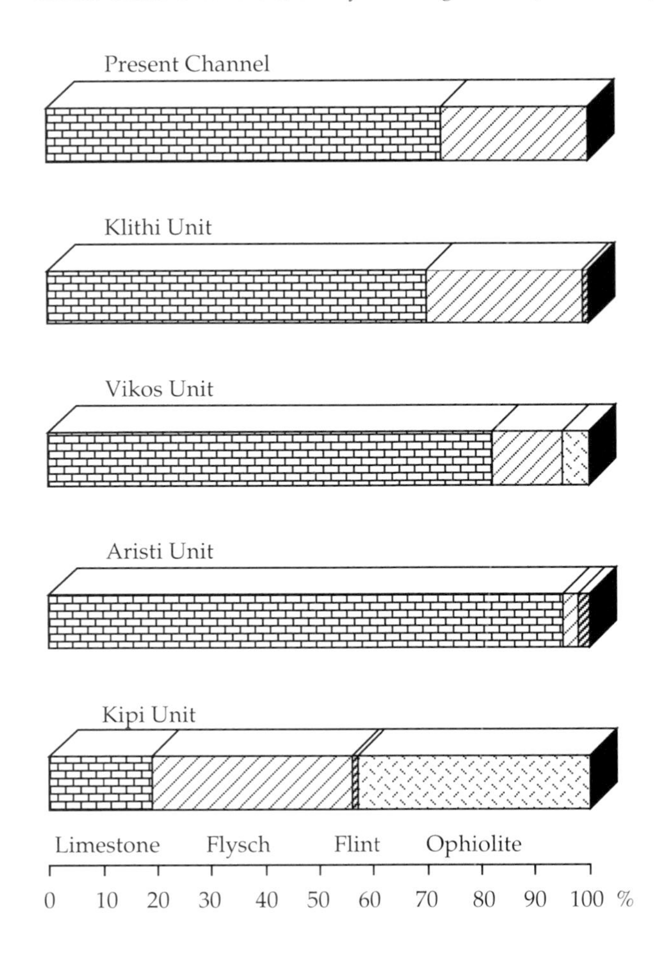

Figure 17.6. *The lithological composition of the coarse-grained sediment (8–256 mm) in each of the Quaternary alluvial units.*

Table 17.2. *Alluvial units in the Voïdomatis basin. See text for the different dating methods used to obtain ages.*

Alluvial Unit	Height of terrace surface above river bed level (m)	Maximum observed thickness of alluvial unit (m)	Lithological composition (8–256 mm) % Limestone	% Flysch	% Flint	% Igneous	Coarse (*C*)/ fine sediment (*F*) member ratio	Fluvial sedimentation style	Age (BP)
Present channel	–	–	*72.7*	*26.6*	*0.5*	*0.2*	C > F	Incising, confined meandering gravel bed river. Low suspended sediment load.	< 30
Klithi	x = 3.2 s = 0.7 Range = 1.8–4.5	4.5	*69.3*	*29.6*	*1.0*	*0.1*	C < F	Aggrading, high sinuosity gravel bed river. High suspended sediment load.	1000 ± 50
Vikos	x = 6.8 s = 1.7 Range = 3.9–9.7	8.3	*82.3*	*12.8*	*0.6*	*4.3*	C > F	Incised wandering gravel bed river. Low suspended sediment load.	24,300 ± 2600–19,600 ± 3000
Aristi	x = 12.4 s = 3.9 Range = 6.7–25.9	25.9	*94.6*	*3.1*	*2.2*	*0.1*	C > F	Aggrading, low sinuosity, coarse sediment river system. High suspended sediment load.	28,200 ± 7000–24,300 ± 2600
Kipi	56	22.9	*18.7*	*36.7*	*0.9*	*44.0*	C > F	Aggrading (?) low sinuosity, coarse sediment river system.	>150,000

25,000 ± 500 and 26,000 ± 1900 from three separate dating assays. These ages, together with a TL date of 28,200 ± 7100 (British Museum ref. VOI23, Appendix A) from fine sediments at Old Klithonia Bridge suggest a Late–Middle Würm date for the Aristi Unit, and for the glaciation to which it relates. The alluvial unit was also at least in part being deposited whilst there was Upper Palaeolithic human activity in the Konitsa basin.

Recent analysis of soil profiles developed on the Aristi Unit (Woodward *et al.* 1994) has revealed significant variations in the degree of pedogenic weathering (Fig. 17.10). This suggests that it comprises at least two alluvial fills which relate to different glacial episodes. The youngest of the alluvial fills with Aristi-type sedimentary characteristics can be assigned, as outlined above, to the Late–Middle Würm substage. The older unit obviously pre-dates this, but at the moment, in the absence of independent dating control, it is unclear whether it is of Early Würm age, or, quite possibly, was deposited during a pre-Last Interglacial glaciation.

Figure 17.7. *Aristi Unit sediments exposed in a road-cut section near the Papingon–Aristi road bridge on the right bank of the Voïdomatis.*

(iii) Vikos Unit

Considered on the basis of the proportion of valley floor that it occupies at any one site, this is a minor unit, but a lithologically and sedimentologically distinctive alluvial fill (Fig. 17.11). Its terrace surface lies 4 m to 10 m above river-bed level and it has a maximum thickness of just over 8 m. It consists of contact-imbricated sandy gravels with a significantly lower matrix content than the Aristi Unit. A fine-grained sediment fill in a channel in the upper part of the Vikos Unit, at sample site 13, 1 km west of Vikos village, has been dated by TL to 19,600 ± 3000 (British Museum ref. VOI24, Appendix A), and gives a minimum age for the unit. Although the fill cannot be traced upstream to the Tsepelovon glacial deposits, the predominance of limestone clasts in its coarse fraction, which is much higher than in more recent alluvial sediments, together with the intermediate mineralogical composition of the fine fraction, suggests input of glacial materials

Figure 17.8. *Close-up of Aristi Unit matrix.*

(Fig. 17.9). The high percentage of ophiolite rock types, and the flysch-derived matrix fines, also indicate significant erosion of the non-limestone areas of the catchment.

(iv) Klithi Unit

The Klithi Unit (Fig. 17.3) represents the only important episode of valley floor alluviation of demonstrable Holocene age in the catchment. It has many of the sedimentary characteristics of alluvial deposits that have been described in many parts of the Mediterranean basin by Vita-Finzi (1975) and subsequent workers (Wagstaff 1981) as 'Younger Fill'.

The Klithi Unit forms a terrace *c.* 3 m above present riverbed level and is composed of two distinct lithofacies: an upper unit of thick (up to 2.5 m) crudely bedded sandy silts which fine upwards, and a lower unit of flat-bedded, contact-imbricated, sandy gravels (Fig. 17.12). This coarse/fine couplet with upward fining is a 'type' example of a sedimentary sequence produced by lateral migration and associated sedimentation in a high sinuosity meandering river (Jackson 1978). The sandy-silts are interpreted as overbank fines and the sandy gravels as within-channel sediments resulting from river bed/bar accretion. The Klithi Unit appears to have been deposited by an aggrading, meandering river system with suspended sediment concentrations in flood waters significantly higher than those of the present day. Comparatively low rates of lateral channel movement during this period allowed the development and subsequent preservation of thick sequences of vertically accreted fine sediment. The fine-grained lithofacies of the Klithi Unit attains its maximum thickness in the Lower Vikos Gorge where mineralogical analyses (XRD) show that it has been derived from erosion of local flysch rocks and soils (Fig. 17.9). Clast lithological analyses also show the Klithi fill to have a high proportion of flysch rock types in its gravel size fraction (Fig. 17.6). Flysch outcrops extensively in this part of the basin and is dissected by

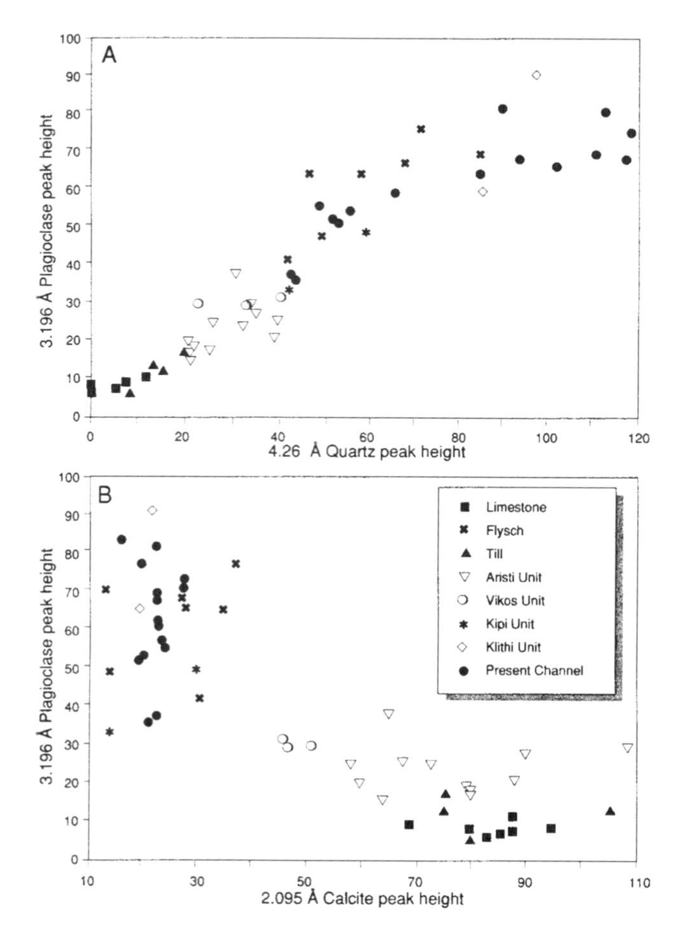

Figure 17.9. *Peak height data from X-ray diffraction traces showing the broad mineralogical composition of the <63 µm component of the Voïdomatis glacial and alluvial sediments. (A) Plot showing the strong positive correlation between quartz and plagioclase in the basin sediments (r^2 = 0.86). B) Plot showing calcite and plagioclase relationships (after Woodward et al. 1992). Aristi Unit sediments contain low amounts of plagioclase and quartz and are rich in calcite reflecting their derivation from limestone-rich glacial sediments. Klithi Unit fine sediments are dominated by flysch-derived materials. The fine fraction of the Vikos Unit sediments is intermediate between these two extremes.*

numerous gully systems that feed directly into the Voïdomatis, many of which are partially stabilised by vegetation (see Bailey *et al.*, Chapter 16).

Sheets of colluvium consisting entirely of flysch lithologies mantle many parts of the Lower Vikos Gorge and slopes surrounding the Konitsa basin. When seen in section at the margins of the valley floor, colluvial sediment frequently interdigitates with the fine member of the Klithi Unit. Charcoal recovered from the upper part of a sequence of colluvial sediments 200 m downstream from the road bridge at Klithonia (Fig. 17.1) has been dated to between 800 ± 100 BP (OxA-192) and 1000 ± 50 BP (OxA-191), and suggests that this major period of hillside erosion and coeval deposition of the Klithi alluvial fill ended at about 1150 cal AD (Gowlett *et al.*, Chapter 2, Table 2.2). Near the Klithi rockshelter, however, organic deposits radiocarbon-dated as modern (OxA-1747) underlie more than 2 m of flysch-derived alluvial and colluvial sediments, and indicate the continued and rapid development, at least locally, of the Klithi Unit until quite recent times.

There is a close similarity between the thick sequences of overbank fines and colluvium that characterize the Klithi Unit and the widespread 'haugh loams' of central and northwest Europe (Butzer 1980; Macklin & Lewin 1986) and 'Post-settlement alluvium' of North America (Knox 1977), which formed in response to anthropogenically related deforestation and the advent of cultivation. It is probable that deposition of the Klithi Unit followed disturbance of the catchment vegetation by human agency, especially the readily erodible soils on the flysch terrains (Woodward 1995).

Quaternary river environments in the Voïdomatis

It is clear from the evidence presented above that the Quaternary fluvial sedimentary sequence of the Voïdomatis is indeed more complex than the Older/Younger subdivision suggested by the Vita-Finzi model (Vita-Finzi 1969). We have also not found evidence in the local alluvial record for major tectonic activity in the last *c.* 30,000 years, such as faulting within Quaternary river deposits or distortion of river terrace profiles. Over a longer timescale as elsewhere in Northern Greece, tectonics has been important in controlling the pattern of fluvial sedimentation (King & Bailey 1985; King *et al.*, Chapter 28), but within the Voïdomatis basin it appears that climatic fluctuations have had by far the strongest effect on Late Pleistocene river development and the alluvial record.

The Voïdomatis Late Pleistocene alluvial sequence can be usefully assessed in relation to two other palaeoenvironmental records. The first is quasi-continuous long pollen sequences from a number of lake basins in northern Greece. These include the

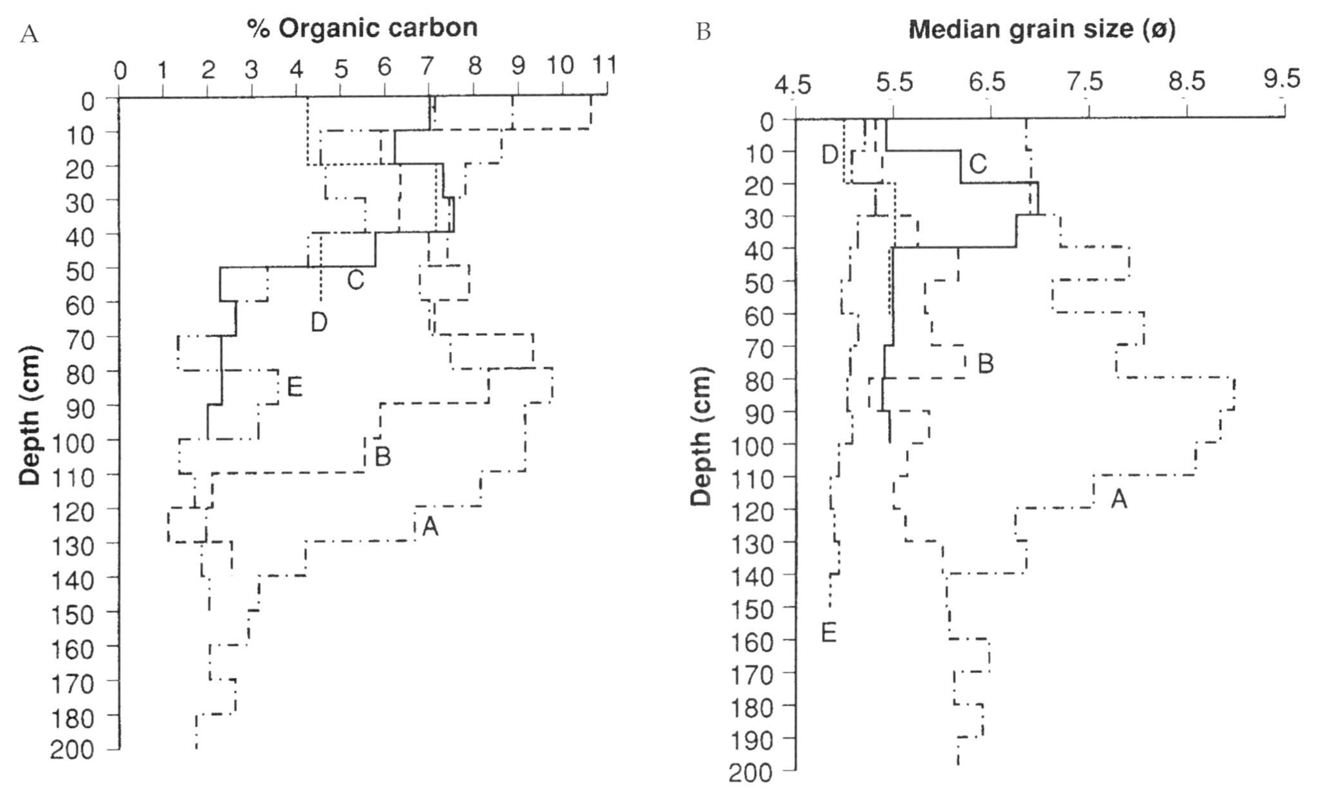

Figure 17.10. *Soil profile data from Quaternary alluvial sediments in the Lower Vikos Gorge and Konitsa basin. These plots show (A) changes with depth in organic carbon content and (B) the mean grain size of the fraction <63 μm. Profile A = Aristi Unit at site 4, profile B = Aristi Unit at site 7, profile C = Vikos Unit at site 3, profile D = Klithi Unit at site 7, profile E = Klithi Unit at site 5. (After Woodward* et al. *1994.)*

relatively well-dated Tenaghi Philippon site in Macedonia which covers the entire Würm stage (Wijmstra 1969), and also the less well-dated but longer sequence from nearby Lake Ioannina (Bottema 1974; Tzedakis 1993). The second record which can be used as a palaeoclimatological framework is the profile of oxygen isotope ratios from the Summit deep Greenland ice-core Project (GRIP, Johnsen *et al.* 1992). This gives a continuous and very high-resolution record (annual for the most part) of changes in climate and atmospheric circulation for the North Atlantic and adjacent land areas including Europe for the entire period of relevance to the Klithi investigations.

Comparable Late Pleistocene river sequences in Greece, which like the Voïdomatis evidence relate to discontinuous phases of alluviation, have been studied in the Larissa Plain, Thessaly (Demitrack 1986) and, more distantly, in the Southern Argolid (Pope & Van Andel 1984). These studies place greater emphasis on soil mapping and on dating via the age-characteristics of soils than do our Voïdomatis studies, but there are also radiocarbon and U-Th dates available. However, correlations between alluvial phases from these studies and those in the Voïdomatis are difficult (Lewin *et al.* 1991).

Figure 17.11. *Vikos Unit sediments exposed in a river cut section in the upstream section of the Lower Vikos Gorge.*

A particular problem with both lake and alluvial data lies in the comparability and reliability of different dating techniques. For example, work by Bard *et al.* (1990) using U-Th dating of corals has shown that the radiocarbon timescale may be significantly compressed between 9000 and 30,000 BP, with a maximum difference of around 3500 years at around 20,000 BP (see also Gowlett *et al.*, Chapter 2). As we are especially concerned with environmental reconstruction in precisely this time period, it is important to appreciate that alternative dating techniques may need some reconciliation. In order to achieve this, we have used the Bard chronology to convert radiocarbon dates to 'calendar' ages, so that we can directly compare the archaeological sequence with both the TL- and ESR-dated Voïdomatis alluvial fills and the GRIP ice core record. Establishing a common and consistent timescale for both palaeoenvironmental and archaeological data sets is of critical importance for the correct interpretation of human interactions with environmental change in the Voïdomatis basin during the latter part of the Late Pleistocene.

As far as the Upper Palaeolithic is concerned, the Aristi and Vikos Units are the most significant. The Aristi Unit has been dated to between 24,300–26,000 and 28,200 BP using ESR and TL methods, respectively. Judging by the GRIP oxygen isotope ice core record (Fig. 17.13), sedimentation in Aristi times, and the period of glaciation in the upper Voïdomatis catchment to which it is linked, falls within the severest climatic phase of the Late Würm. This coincided with a massive iceberg release (Heinrich event 3: Bond *et al.* 1992) into the North Atlantic Ocean, dated to 27,000 BP, associated with cold North Atlantic surface water, and cold air over Greenland. Low temperatures would also have accelerated rates of frost weathering and rock breakdown. Much of the thick limestone scree deposits in the Vikos Gorge, including the archaeologically sterile basal scree units of the Klithi rockshelter (Bailey & Woodward, Chapter 4; Woodward, Chapter 18), probably formed during this period. The Voïdomatis dates for glaciation are somewhat older than the often quoted time of maximum glacial extent in Europe for the Last Glacial Maximum at *c.* 18,000, corresponding to 21,500 cal BP. This most likely reflects the more rapid response, and greater sensitivity, of small Mediterranean mountain glaciers to climate change compared to the much larger continental-scale ice sheets of northern Europe.

The broader regional picture given by palynological evidence and lake-level data from Tenaghi Philippon, Lake Ioannina and from elsewhere in the eastern Mediterraenan, indicates cold winters, intense winter precipitation and summer drought (Harrison & Digerfeldt 1993; Prentice *et al.* 1992). Markedly reduced winter temperatures resulted from strong westerly advection from the cold North Atlantic and the development of a fixed anticyclone over the northern European ice sheet. The drying and cooling effect of these was most likely counteracted in winter by increased storm frequency under a southward-shifted jet stream. This may account for greater runoff and higher lake levels, while at the same time low winter temperatures and a soil moisture deficit during the growing-season would have maintained an open vegetation dominated by *Artemisia* and *Chenopodiaceae* (see also Turner & Sánchez-Gõni, Chapter 29). The river regime of the Voïdomatis under full-glacial conditions would have been different from that of today. At present, from early summer to late autumn stream flow is maintained only in the lower reaches of the river, downstream of a major exurgence in the Vikos Gorge. In central and upper parts of the basin, main channel flows are ephemeral and controlled by late autumn and winter precipitation. During Late Pleistocene and earlier glacials, however, peak river flows would have been associated with spring and early summer glacial meltwater discharges, making access to and movement along the floor of the Vikos Gorge very difficult for animals and humans alike. Indeed, the fact that the only archaeological material of this age so far recovered in the Voïdomatis basin is located downstream of the gorge by the Old Klithonia Bridge, points to a very hostile river environment at this time.

Deposition of the Aristi Unit was followed by a major phase of valley floor entrenchment which, on the basis of the 1σ error ranges of the TL and ESR dates for the Aristi and later Vikos Unit, can be bracketed to some time between 24,500 and 21,000 BP. This places this interval of erosion within Johnsen *et al.*'s (1992) interstadial number 3 (Fig. 17.14). Climatic amelioration would have reduced sediment supply both from glacial sources (with glacier retreat) and also from those parts of the Voïdomatis basin unaffected by glaciation, which would have witnessed lower rates of mechanical rock weathering and stabilization of hillslopes by vegetation.

The TL date on the upper part of the Vikos fill indicates that renewed valley floor aggradation had begun before *c.* 19,000 BP and broadly coincides with a return to full-glacial climatic conditions, dated in the GRIP ice core record to *c.* 21,000 bp (Fig. 17.13). There is, however, a marked change in lithology between the Aristi and Vikos Units: the later fill has a much higher proportion of flysch-derived material but retains a significant glaciogenic element in its fine-grained sediment fraction (Fig. 17.9). This may relate either to higher rates of erosion from flysch terrains than in Aristi times or to reduced glacial erosion of limestone terrains in the catchment. The decline in the limestone-derived sediment component in the Vikos fill, which is particularly evident in the gravel-size fraction, could be attributed to two principal causes:

Figure 17.12. *Klithi Unit sediments exposed in a natural river cut section approximately 300 m downstream of the Klithi rockshelter. Survey staff for scale.*

- A much smaller proportion of the mountain headwaters of the Voïdomatis were occupied by glaciers than during the earlier Late Würm glacial phase at *c.* 27,000 BP. Nevertheless, glacial rock flour still appears to have been the primary source of calcite-rich sediment in the <63 μm size fraction.
- There may have been less active slope processes and mechanical weathering during this period. These, to a large degree, regulate the delivery of coarse rock debris to the Voïdomatis especially in the more confined reaches of the river such as the Vikos Gorge. Erosion of the lower relief flysch terrain, on the other hand, was probably controlled more by vegetation cover which, as discussed above, has been shown to be very sensitive not only to altered temperature and rainfall regimes but also to changes in the seasonality of precipitation. A decline in effective precipitation in the Vikos period, coupled with low temperatures, could have severely affected vegetation growing on flysch bedrock. In some areas this may even have initiated accelerated erosion and the development of extensive badlands that are one of the characteristic features of these areas today.

It appears that the Klithi rockshelter first started to be used in Vikos times at about 20,000–19,000 cal BP. The river, however, was flowing at about 7 m above present levels, though it is likely that the main phase of occupation at Klithi post-dates the Vikos Unit and took place while the river was incising into its alluvial valley floor. Indeed, the formation of a low terrace above the river, which at this time would still have had a prominent spring/early summer nival flood, may have greatly facilitated access along the gorge both for humans and their ibex and chamois prey.[1]

Conclusion

The Late Pleistocene alluvial record of the Voïdomatis river has been used both to reconstruct the local valley floor environment in the Upper Palaeolithic, and, in conjunction with rockshelter and lacustrine evidence, to establish the broader environmental

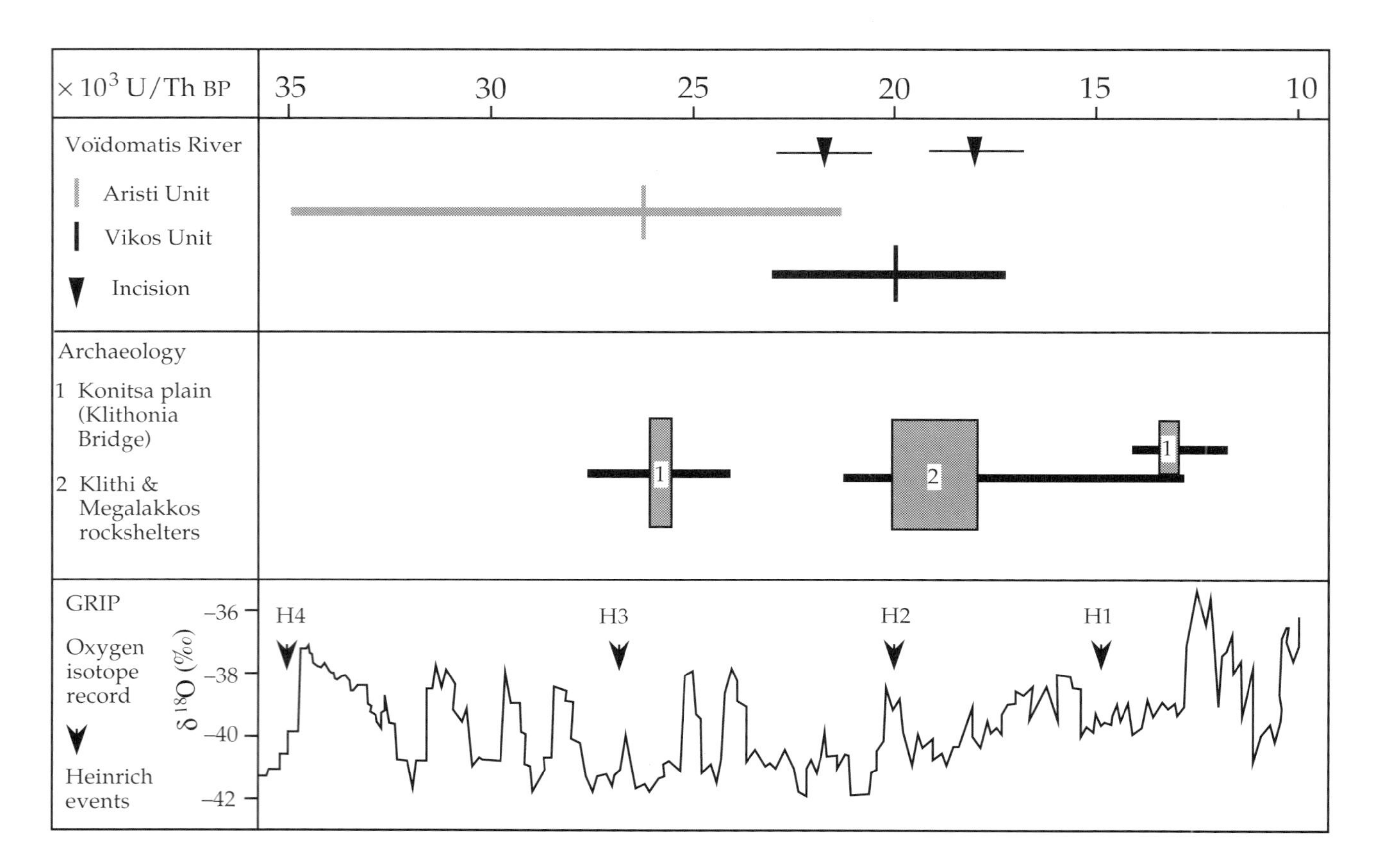

Figure 17.13. *Correlation of environmental changes in the Voïdomatis basin with the GRIP oxygen isotope ice core record.*

context of human occupation in the basin. It is clear that before 20,000 cal BP the Vikos Gorge must have been a very harsh and uninviting environment. In the spring and early summer, with the river swollen by glacial meltwater, movement along the floor of the gorge must have been particularly difficult and hazardous. The absence of evidence of occupation at Klithi and at Boïla and Megalakkos before 20,000 cal BP strongly suggests that the Vikos Gorge was very infrequently visited. By some time after 19,600 cal BP, river incision and an improving climate appear to have facilitated both physical access to and availability of food resources in the gorge. This marks the beginning of the main phase of occupation at Klithi. Though there is little further local geomorphological evidence to go on, the GRIP ice core record (Johnsen *et al.* 1992) shows that the climatic 'window of opportunity' may have been terminated by a return to colder conditions in the Oldest Dryas at *c.* 15,000 cal BP (Heinrich event 1: Bond *et al.* 1992) rather than at the beginning of the Younger Dryas as originally proposed by Bailey *et al.* (1990).

The Late Pleistocene fluvial sequence of the Voïdomatis basin is probably as well dated and as fully documented lithostratigraphically as any available at present in Greece. Nevertheless, the alluvial record is fragmentary, with no information presently available for the many thousands of years between the Vikos and Klithi Units. Since the late 1980s, when geomorphological fieldwork in the Voïdomatis was completed, there have been important developments in a number of new luminescence dating methods which now offer dating precision for Late Pleistocene and Holocene river sedimentation events which could not have been foreseen even ten years ago (e.g. Fuller *et al.* 1996). In conjunction with the high resolution continuous climate records of the GRIP and GISP2 ice cores, the wider application of optically stimulated luminescence dating methods promises to revolutionize our understanding of human interactions with environmental change, especially for the Late Glacial–early Holocene periods which witnessed important changes in the human economy.

Acknowledgements

We would like to extend special thanks to Geoff Bailey for inviting us to join the Klithi project and also to Jane Lewin, the fourth member of the infamous 'rubble-grading' team. We also thank Rainer Grün, formerly of the Godwin Laboratory, Cambridge, and Nick Debenham and the British Museum Department of Scientific Research for arranging ESR and TL dating respectively.

Note

1. The slack-water sediments at the Old Klithonia Bridge have been radiocarbon-dated to about 13,000–11,000 cal BP (Gowlett *et al.*, Chapter 2; Bailey *et al.*, Chapter 16), or 18,000–19,000 cal BP on the humic acids from the charcoal samples (Chapter 2). This deposit appears to form the topmost part of the Aristi Unit. It is also at the same height as the uppermost level of the typical Aristi Unit gravels which underlie the Boïla archaeological sequence where the earliest archaeological deposits immediately above the Aristi Unit are dated by radiocarbon to 16,000–17,000 cal BP (Gowlett *et al.*, Chapter 2; Kotjabopoulou *et al.*, Chapter 22). This suggests that the TL date of 19,600 ± 3000 for the Vikos Unit is too old with respect to the calibrated radiocarbon time scale, although it could be reconciled with the radiocarbon dates by taking the lower end of the 1σ range. It also suggests that the radiocarbon dates from the humic acids of the Old Klithonia Bridge sample are to be preferred to those from the charcoal. The effect of these adjustments would be to make the main period of occupation at Klithi contemporaneous with the period of river incision between the Aristi and Vikos Units, and the occupation at Boïla contemporaneous with the Vikos Unit. Further resolution of these issues must await a more extensive programme of dating including paired luminescence and radiocarbon samples.

Chapter 18

Late Pleistocene Rockshelter Sedimentation at Klithi

Jamie Woodward

From the earliest days of the Klithi project it was apparent that the sedimentary sequence at Klithi would play a central role in any attempt to compare the environmental and archaeological records. The purpose of this section, therefore, is to describe and interpret the sedimentary sequence within the rockshelter depositional environment of Klithi, and to attempt to place these deposits within a broader environmental context. In contrast to the detailed examination of *lateral* variation presented previously (Bailey & Woodward, Chapter 4), this contribution is primarily concerned with a *vertical* or *temporal* sequence and especially the properties and origin of the pre-occupation sediments in comparison with the sediments in the upper part of the sequence associated with human occupation. By focusing on the full stratigraphic succession, and by drawing comparisons with the Quaternary alluvial sediments and soils in the vicinity of the rockshelter site, the aim is to establish the wider stratigraphic and environmental context of the Klithi sequence (*cf.* Woodward 1990; 1996).

To this end, this chapter focuses on the sedimentary sequence recovered from the cores and on the fine sediment fraction of this material. Unlike the excavated trenches, the core sequences actually penetrate the pre-occupation deposits and form a potentially valuable record of Late Pleistocene conditions prior to, and during, human occupation of the site. Palaeoenvironmental interpretation of rockshelter sediments often relies heavily on measured variation in the size and form of the coarse limestone clasts within a sequence (e.g. Goldberg 1972; Laville 1976; Laville *et al.* 1980). Nonetheless, there are good reasons for departing from this traditional approach and for concentrating sedimentological analysis on the fine sediment fraction in the present study. Such an approach is adopted here partly because of evidence presented earlier for considerable lateral variation in the particle size characteristics of the coarse limestone rock fragments at Klithi (Bailey & Woodward, Chapter 4), and also because a coarse sediment based methodology is precluded by the small diameter of the cores, which does not yield large enough samples for coarse sediment analysis to be conducted on the entire sequence.

Numerous investigations have shown that Quaternary sediments can provide both stratigraphic control and environmental context for many kinds of archaeological materials in a range of depositional settings (e.g. Hassan 1978; Rapp & Gifford 1982; Stein & Farrand 1985; Waters 1988). In the case of rockshelter and cave-mouth environments, it has been recognized for well over a century that cultural and faunal remains are often preserved within considerable thicknesses of Quaternary sediment. Yet realization of the potential provided by rockshelter sediments (rather than the artefacts and fossils within them) as a basis for reconstructing past environments and solving archaeological problems represents a comparatively recent innovation (*cf.* Farrand 1975; Gamble 1986). During the last three decades the scientific analysis of rockshelter sediments has become a firmly established line of enquiry in environmental archaeology (Collcutt 1979; Farrand 1975; 1979) and now more commonly forms an important consideration in excavation strategy (Stein & Farrand 1985). Indeed, it is now widely recognized that most Palaeolithic materials are found in situations where sediment-based environmental reconstruction must be an integral part of their study. To date, however, many workers have tended to concentrate their attention almost exclusively on the 'site' sedimentary record, without either considering the position of a particular sediment column within a wider environmental framework, or evaluating the nature and composition of adjacent sedimentary environments and the possibility of material exchanges between them. A major goal of this contribution is to show how careful integration of both the 'on-site' *and* 'off-site' sedimentary records with the archaeological sequence is essential if we are to advance our understanding of human activity in Pleistocene environments.

Throughout this and the following chapter on Megalakkos, the rockshelter or 'on-site' sediments are treated as a component within a larger and dynamic catchment-wide sedimentary system which has responded in a sensitive way to Quaternary environmental change. For example, Chapter 17 gives details of the striking changes that have taken place in the adjacent river environment as both depositional style and sediment lithology shifted in response to the waxing and waning of headwater glacial activity during the Late Pleistocene. It is to be expected that the nature of the sediments deposited at Klithi was strongly influenced by the immediate geomorphological surroundings and that any changes in the dominant processes operating there can be expected to influence the sedimentary record within the rockshelter. For these reasons it is clearly important to avoid viewing 'on-site' processes and sediments in isolation, and to construct a catchment-wide lithostratigraphic and chronological framework which allows the rockshelter sediments to be placed within an appropriate local and regional environmental setting. The drainage basin of the Voïdomatis forms a convenient unit of study for such an approach (Woodward 1990; Woodward *et al.* 1995; Bailey *et al.*, Chapter 16).

The rockshelter depositional environment

Almost by definition, rockshelters tend to favour sediment preservation rather than erosion, and in most cases they provide highly favourable sites for sediment accumulation. In most instances this is because rockshelter and cave-mouth locations are largely protected from sub-aerial weathering and form comparatively low-energy geomorphological environments. Thus even though rates of sediment delivery are usually quite modest in most mid-latitude settings, sediment removal capacities are also low, and these locations are able to function as effective repositories for the accumulation and protection of a variety of sediments for extended periods of time. In favourable locations, as for example at Asprochaliko in the Louros valley (Gowlett & Carter, Chapter 23), rockshelter and cave stratigraphies can often represent a considerable portion of late Quaternary time (see Butzer 1981; Huxtable *et al.* 1992; Laville *et al.* 1980).

The lithological and textural characteristics of the sediment accumulating on a rockshelter floor are governed by the influence of a number of environmental controls (Farrand 1985; Woodward 1990). These include external macro-scale climatic and tectonic factors such as thermal and precipitation regimes and seismicity, and more local site-specific controls such as host bedrock properties, geomorphological setting (including site geometry, aspect and local karst hydrology), and biological activity. Superimposed on these 'natural' factors may be the influence of human occupation. The principal influence on sedimentation style at any point in the history of a site may be a single dominant control, or more often the product of two or more of these variables. Many of these controls are strongly interrelated and each can influence sediment source, sediment transport mechanisms, and the nature and degree of post-depositional alteration.

In considering the rockshelter depositional environment, it is first useful to make the simple distinction between two principal routes for sediment transfer. Sediment may reach the rockshelter floor either *vertically*, by the action of gravity from the shelter walls and ceiling, or by means of percolating water from the land surface above, or *laterally*, mainly by the action of water, wind and human or animal activity. Each of these routes can deliver sediment particles of various sizes and lithologies from sources which are either *autogenic* (internal) or *allogenic* (external) to the particular rockshelter niche under consideration. It is also helpful, where appropriate, to further differentiate the allogenic contribution into its *proximal* and *distal* components. In reality, all rockshelter sedimentary sequences are composed of a mixture of autogenic and allogenic material although one or the other may dominate as environmental conditions change (between sites and over time). A hypothetical, yet commonly encountered combination, for example, could involve a sediment body composed of coarse limestone debris derived from frost weathering of the rockshelter walls (*vertical, autogenic)* with the inter-clast voids filled with a fine-grained silty matrix of far-travelled loess (*lateral, allogenic, distal).* An example of the latter association is provided by the middle sedimentary units (12–14) at the Cueva Morín cave in Santander, where 'loessic components' are found within coarse deposits described as limestone 'roof rubble accumulation' (Butzer 1981, 148, 175).

This simple classification based on sediment provenance provides a useful framework for the interpretation of rockshelter sediment records. It serves to highlight their position within a wider sedimentary system and underscores the fact that such sites can provide sinks for a wide variety of sediment imports. In attempting to make linkages between the rockshelter sediment record and the climatically-driven changes in the wider Pleistocene environment, it is suggested that a thorough consideration of sediment *source* is essential to achieve a proper appreciation of the wider stratigraphic and environmental significance of rockshelter sediments.

General features of the sediments

In very general terms the Klithi rockshelter deposits are composed largely of unconsolidated angular limestone clasts of various sizes within a predominantly silt-grade calcareous fine matrix (see Bailey & Woodward, Chapter 4). These coarse sediments are typically roughly stratified and very poorly sorted. The following discussion is largely based on information derived from detailed analyses of the two longest sediment cores collected during the site drilling programmes in 1986 and 1988 (Bailey *et al.*, Chapter 3), and on the fine sediment fraction (<63 μm). Most attention has been concentrated on core Y25, which was collected in 1986, and which provides the most complete record of the pre-occupation deposits. The sedimentological characteristics of this core were first reported in Woodward (1990), and the second sediment core (CC27) was analyzed in 1992 to provide an independent test of the results from core Y25. From the results of the coring programme we know that the sedimentary fill is at least 7 m in thickness. It is likely, though not certain, that the Y25 core reached bedrock, and the total depth of the Pleistocene deposits may therefore be greater than 7 m, although the external geometry of the site suggests that the sediment fill is unlikely to be much deeper than this.

Silt-sized and clay-sized particles account for a significant part of the sediment matrix across the entire site and throughout both cores. They are of particular interest because they can provide a detailed record of changing environmental conditions and post-depositional alterations (Farrand 1975; Birkeland 1984; Woodward *et al.* 1994). In most rockshelter settings the fine sediments are derived from a wider range of sources than the coarse sediment fraction (e.g. Butzer 1981; Farrand 1975) and even where a significant proportion of the fine fraction has been derived from an allogenic or 'off-site' source, such materials can be expected to display considerable textural and lithological homogeneity within coeval sedimentary units. This is often the result of sorting prior to, and during, deposition within the site. As the transport processes commonly involve wind or water, this will often effect a fairly even distribution of such material across the site. Human occupation can also contribute to this process, although it is recognized that site activities can result in marked lateral changes in some primary and secondary fine sediment properties (Butzer 1981). In comparison to the coarse limestone rock fragments, whose particle size characteristics can vary substantially across the site within coeval sedimentary units due to the influence of various factors (see Bailey & Woodward, Chapter 4; Farrand 1975, fig. 3), the primary attributes of the fine matrix are likely to be much more uniform across the site and less susceptible to local variation. The fine sediments forming the matrix within a coarse limestone gravel unit may be very similar in composition and texture to the fine sediments within a stratigraphically-equivalent, but much coarser-grained, limestone gravel unit a few tens of centimetres away. This is also the case in many 'off-site' colluvial deposits, particularly 'stratified screes' (see DeWolf 1988). Such observations place a question mark against the usefulness of approaches which rely heavily on variations in the calibre of limestone rock fragments as a basis for palaeoenvironmental reconstruction (*cf.* Laville 1976). This is not to say that fine sediments will not display some degree of primary spatial variability, only that fine sediments often display less lateral variation than coarse sediments in rockshelter environments. Ideally, of course, and wherever possible, the information derived from both coarse and fine sediments should be used together for the purpose of section description and site interpretation (Woodward, Chapter 19). At least at Klithi, however, it is the argument of this section that the fine sediments provide both a more reliable indicator of temporal changes in the local Late Pleistocene palaeoenvironment, and a valuable means of establishing correlations with 'off-site' sedimentary environments.

Field and laboratory methods

Coring the Klithi sequence

The particular logistical and engineering considerations posed by the Klithi rockshelter deposits in this exercise are reported in detail elsewhere (Bailey & Thomas 1987; Bailey *et al.*, Chapter 3). During the 1986 field season three boreholes were drilled into the Klithi fill — the longest and most successful (Y25) reaching a depth of 6.93 m below the surface. The sediments were retrieved using 1 m coring tubes of 75 mm and 60 mm diameter. Following extraction and sediment description, the cores were photographed, drawn and sampled on-site at 5 cm intervals in the upper, archaeologically-rich, sediments, and then mostly at 10 cm intervals to the base of the sequence. Although the 7 m core contained 8 voids, the sequence forms an internally consistent, stratigraphic succession of great significance as it provided the first detailed insight into the nature of the pre-occupation horizons. Core CC27 was recovered during the 1988 drilling programme.

Laboratory procedures
Core Y25 was sub-divided into 56 sediment samples which were air-dried in the laboratory at room temperature for 48 hours prior to screening through a 1 mm mesh sieve. Magnetic susceptibility measurements were conducted on the <1 mm component of all sediment samples using a standard Bartington Instruments meter and sensor (Thompson & Oldfield 1986). The analytical procedure involved placing approximately 10 g of sediment into pre-weighed cylindrical plastic sample pots of 10 cm^3 volume. These samples were firmly packed using cling film to prevent particle movement. Magnetic susceptibility is a *non-directional* magnetic parameter which provides a measure of the 'magnetizability' of sediment. This in turn is largely determined by the concentration of magnetic minerals within a sediment sample. The minerals of major interest in magnetic studies are the iron oxides including haematite, goethite, maghemite and magnetite (see Maher 1986). Magnetic susceptibility represents the ratio of the magnetization produced in a sediment sample to the intensity of the magnetic field to which it is subject and is measured within a small magnetic field of about 0.1 mT (millitesla). This parameter can be measured at low or high frequency using a dual frequency susceptibility sensor (measured at 1 and 10 kHz), and the difference between the two readings can be expressed as a percentage of the low frequency reading and is referred to as *frequency dependent susceptibility* (Maher 1986). Measurements were taken on all the samples in core Y25. Magnetic susceptibility results are expressed on a mass specific basis ($m^3\ kg^{-1}$) and frequency dependent values are expressed here as a percentage of low frequency susceptibility.

The proportion of insoluble residue (i.e. non-carbonate material) present within seven limestone rock samples from Klithi was determined by weighing following dissolution in dilute hydrochloric acid (*cf.* Macleod 1980). All the core sediment samples were also screened through a 63 µm mesh sieve to obtain the silt and clay component. This fraction was then analyzed for total calcium carbonate ($CaCO_3$) content and detailed particle size analyses were also undertaken. $CaCO_3$ determinations were carried out following dissolution in dilute hydrochloric acid (Gross 1971). Prior to particle size analysis all samples were treated with hydrogen peroxide to remove the organic component and then chemically dispersed using sodium hexametaphosphate (McManus 1988). The particle size characteristics of the fine sediment fraction (<63 µm) of core Y25 and of the bedrock insoluble residues were measured in the Department of Earth Sciences at the University of Cambridge using the computer-interfaced SediGraph 5000ET system reported by Jones *et al.* (1988). This apparatus provides detailed particle size information within the silt fraction (i.e. in the 63 µm to 2 µm range) as well as total clay content (i.e. the proportion <2 µm). Within the silt fraction the proportion of coarse silt, 63 µm to 16 µm, medium silt, 16 µm to 8 µm, and fine silt, 8 µm to 2 µm can also be determined (Table 18.1). For Core CC27 the particle size characteristics of the sediment fraction <63 µm were measured in 1992 at the University of Exeter using a Malvern Mastersizer laser diffraction particle size analyzer (Agrawal *et al.* 1991). Previous studies of the particle size characteristics of rockshelter fine sediments have used traditional and time-consuming sizing methods based on particle settling velocities, such as the hydrometer and pipette methods (e.g. Butzer 1981). The methods employed in this study are less prone to operator error and allow rapid and precise particle size determination on a large number of samples. This has facilitated perhaps the first detailed investigation of changing fine sediment size modes in a rockshelter environment.

Local bedrock properties

In order to determine the source of the rockshelter fine sediments it is necessary to consider the lithological composition of likely source materials and the form and size of their erosional products. In the cave-mouth or rockshelter environment this must begin with an evaluation of local bedrock structure and composition.

General features of the Klithi limestone
The limestone bedrock at Klithi (and throughout the Lower Vikos Gorge) is Palaeocene to Upper Eocene in age. These limestones are massive resistant rocks and the upper members have been described as *sublithographic* (IGME 1968), indicating a hard and resistant lithology. These dense crystalline limestones contain occasional chert bands, are of low primary porosity, and solutional weathering processes predominate, mainly concentrating along bedding planes. These rocks form near-vertical cliffs, deep gorges and steep-sided tributary ravines (Bailey *et al.*, Chapter 16). In places these rocks are tectonically deformed and fractured, providing a major source of coarse alluvial and colluvial material in a wide range of particle sizes. It is apparent that limestone bedding and joint frequency exerts an important control on the size of rock fragments detached from a rock wall, and bedding frequencies in the Lower Vikos Gorge may vary from a few centimetres to several metres. In lithological terms the limestone bedrock at Klithi is very pure, yielding only tiny amounts of residual material following solution (Woodward 1990). The acid insoluble residue (non-carbonate fraction) of seven rock samples collected

Table 18.1. *Units of measurement used in the classification of sediment particle size in this study. (After Friedman & Sanders 1978.)*

phi (φ)	mm		
		V. large	Boulder
−11	2048		
		Large	
−10	1024		
		Medium	
−9	512		
		Small	
−8	256		
		Large	Cobbles
−7	128		
		Small	
−6	64		
		V. coarse	Pebbles
−5	32		
		Coarse	
−4	16		
		Medium	
−3	8		
		Fine	
−2	4		
		V. fine	
−1	2		
		V. coarse	Sand
0	1		
	microns	Coarse	
1	500		
		Medium	
2	250		
		Fine	
3	125		
		V. fine	
4	63		
		V. coarse	Silt
5	31		
		Coarse	
6	16		
		Medium	
7	8		
		Fine	
8	4		
		V. fine	
9	2		
			Clay

from various levels within the Klithi sequence and from the rockshelter wall range from 0.32 per cent to 1.04 per cent with a mean value of 0.57 per cent. The host strata is thus extremely pure and dominated by $CaCO_3$ (>99.4 per cent) in the form of calcite, with quartz and mica grains accounting for most of the limestone impurities. A typical particle size distribution of this insoluble residue fraction is shown in Figure 18.1. This material is composed almost exclusively (>75 per cent) of clay particles (<2 μm) and fine silt particles, with a silt/clay ratio of 0.32. It is worth noting that the residual portion of the bedrock is effectively free of coarse silt-sized and sand-sized particles (see Table 18.1).

Flysch mineralogy and texture

On either side of the Lower Vikos Gorge the limestone rocks are overlain by flysch rocks of Late Eocene to Miocene age (see Bailey *et al.*, Chapter 16). These rocks consist of thin beds (10–20 cm in thickness) of hard, graded sandstones interbedded with softer, brown to buff-coloured, fissile siltstones. Microscopic examination of thin sections and X-ray diffraction analysis of powdered bedrock samples has shown that the flysch rocks are rich in quartz, plagioclase, mica and other phyllosilicates, with a calcite content of between 10 and 15 per cent. The flysch beds are readily erodible and the siltstones break down relatively easily into their primary particles, and thus represent an important source of fine sediment for the modern river system (Woodward *et al.* 1992) and frequently form the matrix material in colluvial sediments. Many of the flysch-derived fine sediments in the Voïdomatis basin show a distinctive size mode in the coarse silt range (63 μm–16 μm).

Lithology and texture of the core sediments

In the following descriptions of the core sediments, particular attention is focused on downcore changes in the lithology and particle size characteristics of the sediment and on contrasts between the pre-occupation and occupation horizons.

Calcium carbonate and organic matter content

The fine sediment fraction is rich in $CaCO_3$ throughout the entire core sequence, with all values >50 per cent and a mean value of 64 per cent (Fig. 18.2). The $CaCO_3$ profile may be divided into two main parts: above 2.5 m the $CaCO_3$ values range from 54 per cent to 64 per cent with a mean value of 58.5 per cent, while the lower section of the profile has a range of 61.4 per cent to 80.6 per cent with a mean of 71.7 per cent (Table 18.2). In the upper section the fine sediments show a variety of reddish brown to brown and grey colours, reflecting the increase in non-carbonate minerals and the variable presence of human habitation debris including sediments rich in ash and organic detritus. In marked contrast, the fine sediments in the lower section of the core sequence contain only very small amounts of organic material and display a distinctive creamy-white colouration reflecting the dominance of silt-grade $CaCO_3$.

Clay content

The insoluble residue of the fraction <63 μm is composed of clay particles and non-carbonate silt material. The $CaCO_3$ boundary identified at 2.5 m is also equivalent to the lowest clay content in the sequence, where two successive samples, representing 15 cm of the deposit, record the highest silt/clay ratios in core Y25. The lower portion of the core sequence (4.2–7 m) is quite rich in clay grade (<2 μm) material with values up to 28 per cent. The largely clay-free band at the base of the archaeological horizons is a distinctive feature of the sequence since this horizon marks the end of a gradual decline in the profile clay component in the central part of the sequence which begins at 4.2 m (Fig. 18.2). It is of particular interest to note that the rather abrupt transition between the $CaCO_3$ zones and the profile clay minima coincides with the base of the cultural horizons. Low clay values are a distinctive feature of the lower part of the occupation horizons.

Non-carbonate silt content

The proportion of non-carbonate silt at each point in the sequence may be estimated by subtracting the clay component from the total insoluble residue content of all samples (assuming little or no $CaCO_3$ in the clay fraction). At each level in core Y25 the proportion of non-carbonate fine sediment (i.e. the acid insoluble residue of the <63 μm fraction) is always greater than the clay component, indicating the variable presence of non-carbonate (quartz-rich) silt throughout the sequence (Fig. 18.2). This non-carbonate silt fraction is a minor component in the lower core (below 4.2 m) ranging from 0.9 per cent to 14.8 per cent (mean = 4.9 per cent). However, in the central section of the core (2.5–4.2 m), $CaCO_3$ content declines slightly (but still averages 69 per cent), while total silt content increases markedly to almost 90 per cent (Fig. 18.2). As these data refer to the fraction < 63 μm, the clear divergence of these curves at 4.2 m records a significant influx of non-carbonate silt material, signalling a major transition in the nature of the Klithi fine sediments. The non-carbonate silt component increases steadily in the central part of the sequence to a maximum of 43.9 per cent at the base of the archaeological horizons. In the upper section of the core (above 2.5 m) the non-carbonate silt component is always greater than 21.1 per

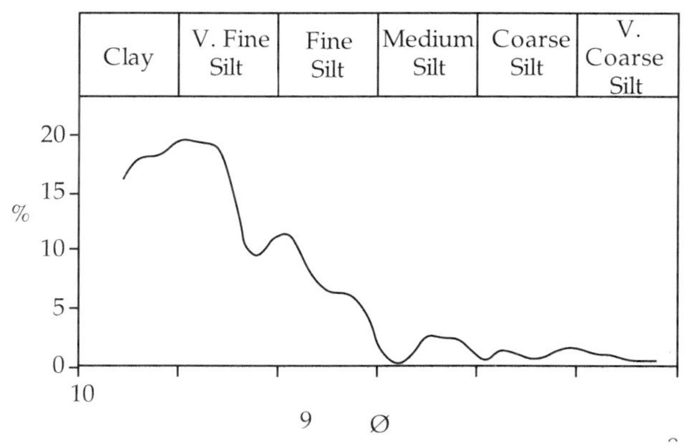

Figure 18.1. *Typical particle size distribution curve for the insoluble residue fraction of the host limestone bedrock at Klithi. Note the fine-grained nature of this material and the virtual absence of coarse silt. 4 ϕ (63 μm) is the sand/silt boundary and 9 ϕ (2 μm) is the silt/clay boundary (see Table 18.1).*

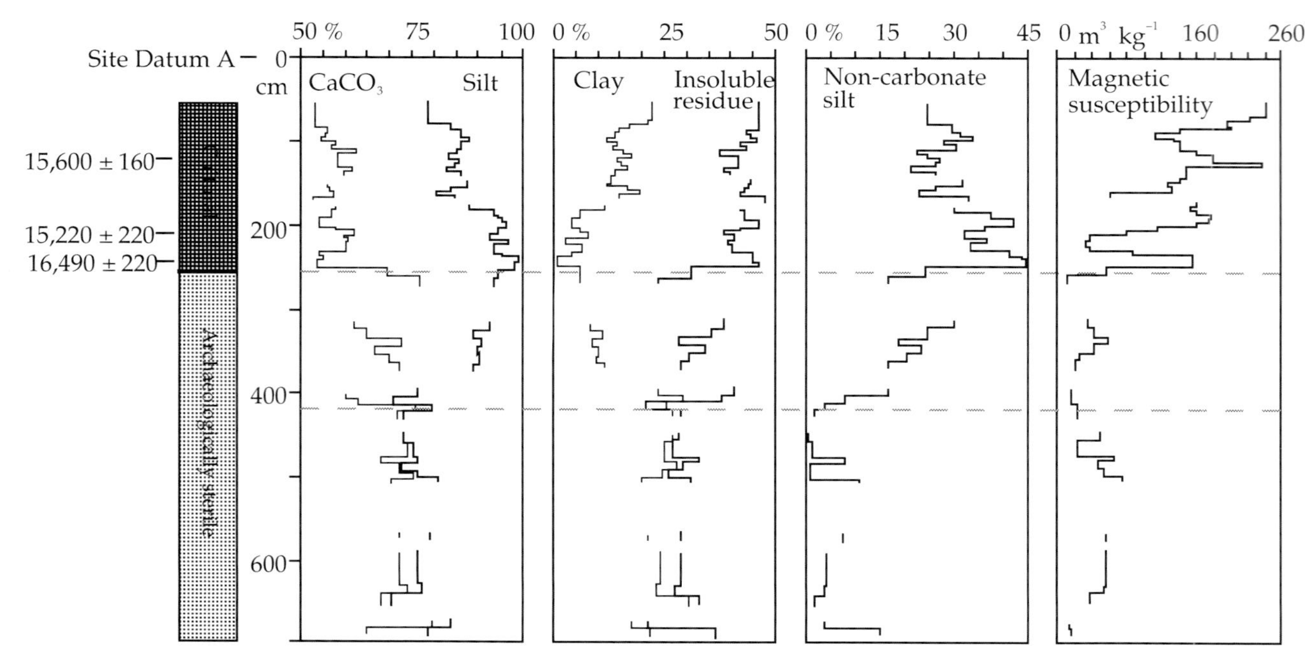

Figure 18.2. *Downcore changes in various sedimentological parameters and magnetic susceptibility for the Y25 core sediments. Laboratory numbers for radiocarbon dates from top to bottom: OxA-1155, OxA-1091, OxA-1092. The horizontal dashed lines mark the probable boundary between full glacial conditions (lower), transitional climatic conditions (middle), and milder climatic conditions (upper).*

Table 18.2. *Selected sediment properties from core Y25, showing ranges and mean values for the sediment fraction < 63 μm from each core section (Fig. 18.2). The proportion of non-carbonate silt has been estimated as the difference between the total insoluble residue fraction and the clay content of each sample. Bulk magnetic susceptibility measurements (low frequency) were carried out on a mass specific basis on the <1 mm sediment fraction using a standard Bartington system.*

Sediment property	Upper section (0–2.5 m)	Central section (2.5–4.2 m)	Lower section (4.2–7 m)	Whole core (0–7 m)
$CaCO_3$ (%)	54.0–64.0 58.5	61.4–78.1 69.0	65.2–80.6 72.9	54.0–80.6 64.0
Clay (%)	0.28–20.5 10.4	5.2–27.8 11.4	15.7–28.7 22.2	0.28–28.7 13.5
Non-carbonate silt (%)	21.1–43.9 31.1	8.2–29.4 19.7	0.9–14.8 4.9	0.9–43.9 22.5
16–32 μm (%)	26.3–37.9 31.3	23.8–30.7 27.3	13.3–25.9 20.7	13.3–37.9 27.9
Magnetic susceptibility (m^3 kg^{-1})	28.1–239.6 143.3	8.7–54.5 27.3	5.5–68.7 39.0	5.5–239.6 95.7

cent and averages 31.1 per cent.

Summarizing the Y25 sedimentological data, the Klithi sequence can be divided broadly into three lithologically and texturally distinctive sections (Fig. 18.2; Table 18.2): a lower section between 7 m and 4.2 m with high values of $CaCO_3$, a high clay content, and low values of non-carbonate silt; a middle section, from 4.2 m to 2.5 m, characterized by declining values of $CaCO_3$ and clay content — the latter reaching a minimum at the top of this middle section — and a marked increase in non-carbonate silt; and an upper section, from 2.5 m to the top of the sequence, coinciding with the archaeological deposits, and characterized by lower values of $CaCO_3$, increased clay content and high values of non-carbonate silt (Fig. 18.2).

Core CC27

To provide an independent test of the wider significance of the sequence derived from Y25, a limited analysis of the second long core, CC27, was undertaken. The downcore changes in the coarse silt fraction (63 μm–16 μm) are shown in Figure 18.3. While some differences between the two cores are to be expected, there is a good general agreement between the two cores in terms of the overall sequence, with CC27 also clearly showing the three main sections identified in Core Y25. Coarse silt varies from 26 per cent at the base of the sequence in the pre-occupation sediments to a maximum value of 44 per cent in the sediments associated with human occupation. In common with the non-carbonate silt trend in core Y25, the smoothed curve in Figure 18.3 also indicates that the influx of coarse silt particles decreased towards the end of the period of human occupation in the upper 1 m of the core.

Sediment sources and sediment transfer processes

In the following discussion, the dominant lithological character of specific sediment size fractions within the Y25 sequence is used to provide a basis for determining the major sediment sources and modes of sediment transfer.

Relationships between sediment texture and composition
Relationships between the textural and lithological parameters described in the above section are shown in Figure 18.4. The source of the non-carbonate silt fraction, which represents an important component of the core sediments (up to 43.9 per cent), is of particular interest. This material correlates strongly with the coarse silt fraction, 63 μm–16 μm (Fig. 18.4, r = 0.79), and this coarse silt component reaches a maximum of 59.6 per cent of the total fine sediment fraction (< 63 μm) at a depth of 95 cm. The strong positive relationship between the coarse silt and non-carbonate silt fractions, and the abundance of this coarse silt material throughout the sequence (mean = 44.9 per cent), shows that a considerable proportion of the fine sediments at Klithi are *allogenic* and cannot be a breakdown product of *in situ* limestone weathering. The strong negative relationship between coarse silt and fine silt (Fig. 18.4, r = –0.75) suggests that these materials derive from different sources.

The role of limestone solution in fine sediment production
As the non-carbonate portion of the limestone bedrock accounts for <0.5 per cent of its mass, the significant proportion of non-carbonate material within the rockshelter fine sediments would seem to argue against a limestone source for this material. The insoluble residue component of the Y25 core sediments ranges from 19.4 per cent to 46 per cent with a mean value of 36 per cent. Most significantly, however, the *texture* of the Klithi fine sediments argues against a limestone source as the bedrock is effectively free of non-carbonate coarse silt material (Fig. 18.1) and this is a major component of the core sequence (Fig. 18.2; Table 18.2). The absence of non-carbonate coarse silt in the local bedrock rules out limestone solution as a major fine sediment (<63 μm) source in this context and also removes the need to invoke perhaps geologically unreasonable amounts of limestone solution to account for the rockshelter fine sediments.

In an attempt to identify the dominant size class of the non-carbonate silt fraction, this component was compared with all the size classes at 0.5ϕ and 1ϕ intervals within the silt range (4ϕ to 9ϕ). The relationships shown in Figure 18.4 suggest that the non-carbonate silt fraction is dominated by coarse silt material and is largely concentrated in the 4ϕ to 5.5ϕ range (Table 18.1).

Coarse silt and non-carbonate silt fractions
Parts of the limestone bedrock wall at the back of the rockshelter show evidence of a thin coating of

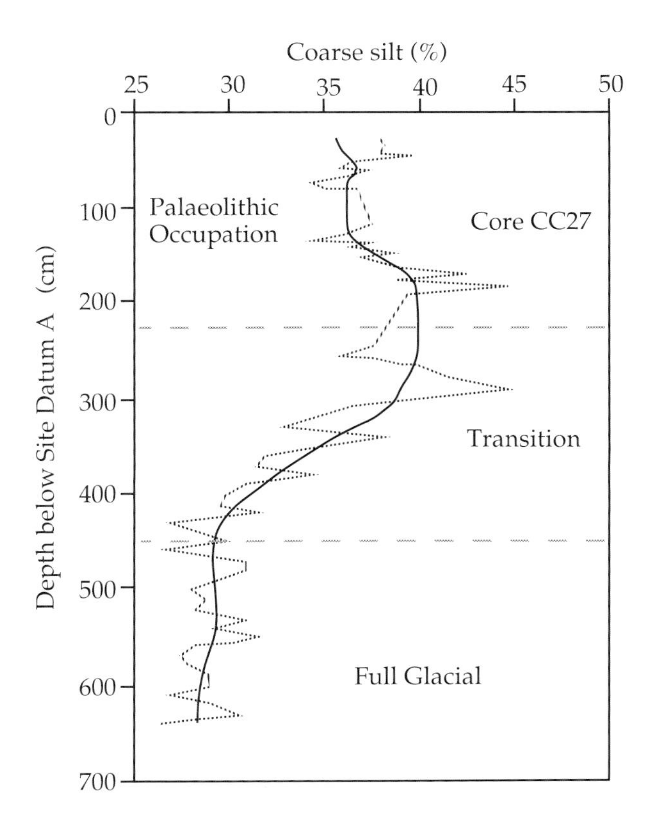

Figure 18.3. *Downcore changes in coarse silt in the sediments of core CC27. The solid line represents a five point moving average. Compare the non-carbonate silt curve of core Y25 in Figure 18.2. It is important to note that the CC27 sediments were analyzed in 1992 using a Malvern Mastersizer Laser diffraction particle size analyzer. All particle size methods are operationally defined; the size data derived from this apparatus are not based on Stokes' Law of settling, in contrast to the Y25 sediments analyzed with a SediGraph (Fig. 18.2). The absolute size values of the two cores are therefore not directly comparable, although the* form *of the two curves can usefully be compared.*

brown- to buff-coloured fine-grained sediment. This silty material is also present in cracks behind fractured limestone slabs at the nearby site of Megalakkos, where XRD analysis has demonstrated that this is flysch-derived sediment (Woodward, Chapter 19). Elsewhere in the Lower Vikos Gorge there is a large body of evidence to suggest that the movement of silts and clays within the interior drainage system of the limestone bedrock is a significant geomorphological process and that this material is dominated by fine sediments eroded from the overlying flysch deposits (Woodward 1990).

Sediment-laden groundwater has been identified

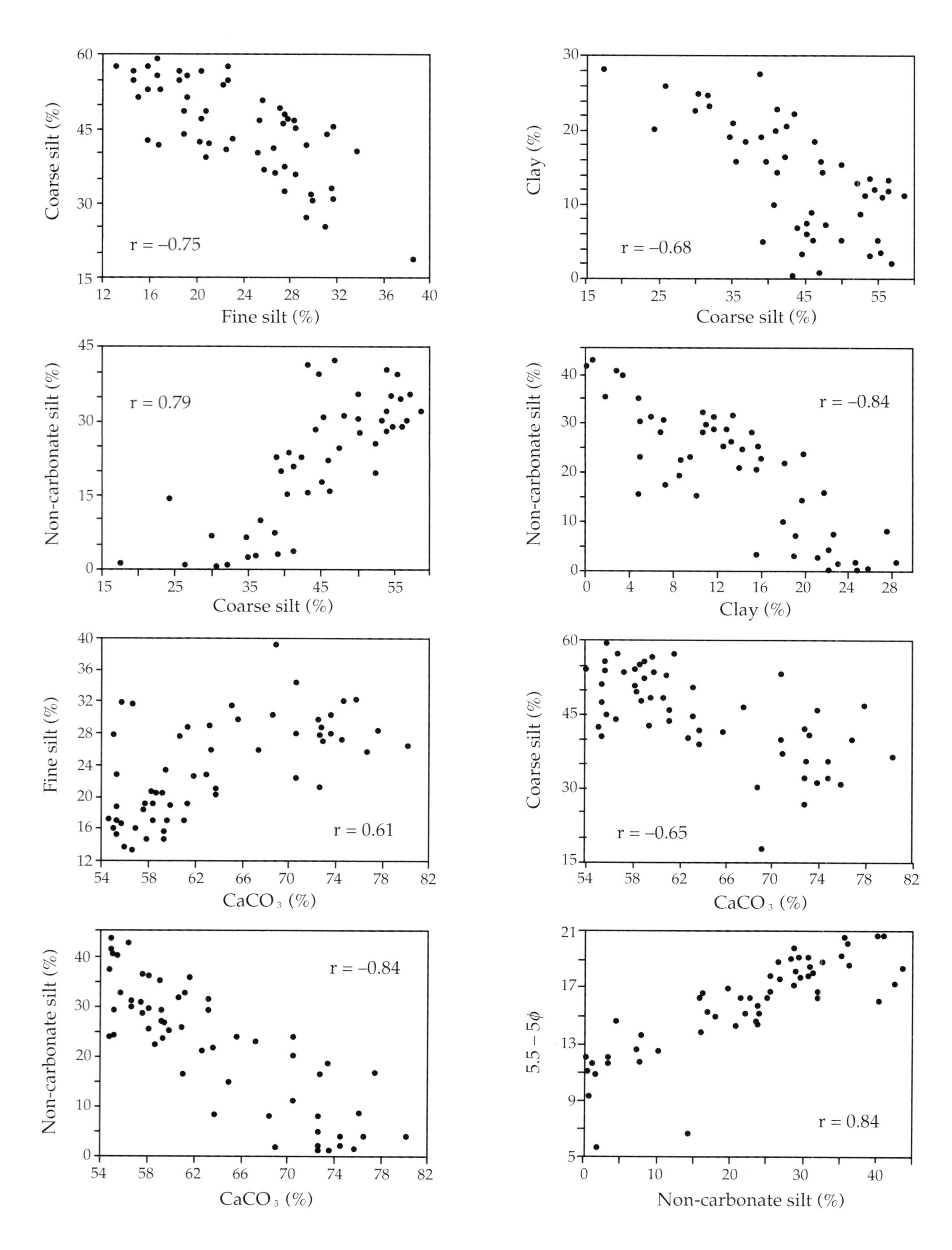
Coarse silt (%)
Fine silt (%)
r = –0.75
Clay (%)
Coarse silt (%)
r = –0.68
Non-carbonate silt (%)
Coarse silt (%)
r = 0.79
Non-carbonate silt (%)
Clay (%)
r = –0.84
Fine silt (%)
CaCO3 (%)
r = 0.61
Coarse silt (%)
CaCO3 (%)
r = –0.65
Non-carbonate silt (%)
CaCO3 (%)
r = –0.84
5.5 – 5ϕ
Non-carbonate silt (%)
r = 0.84

as a major agency in fine sediment transfer in karst regions across the world (Bull 1981; White 1988; Ford & Williams 1989) and these sediments have been called *infiltrates* (see Jancin & Clark 1993; White 1988). Infiltrates can often represent an important and even the dominant mechanism of fine sediment delivery to rockshelter and cave-mouth environments, especially in humid, high-relief environments (Butzer 1981; Woodward 1990). The Voïdomatis basin currently receives up to 2000 mm of precipitation annually (*cf.* Furlan 1977) and high intensity rainfall events are not uncommon during the summer months.

Infiltrates are fine-grained clastic sediments transported in suspension by percolating groundwater through the interior drainage system and may be deposited in cave and rockshelter locations under the action of gravity. The chief sources of infiltrates are surface soils which have been washed or slumped into open rock crevices or sinkholes in the limestone surface (White 1988). Infiltrates can be stored within the karst drainage system for extended periods, and later can be remobilized and eventually discharged into interior cavern systems or rockshelter environments with little chemical alteration. While there is little dispute regarding the efficacy of this transport mechanism in karst environments, the original *source* of the fine sediments in transit has generated considerable debate (see Jennings 1985; White 1988).

The relationships shown in Figure 18.4 suggest that the non-carbonate silt component is composed primarily of coarse silt (63 µm–16 µm) material and that the 5ϕ–6ϕ, 32 µm–16 µm, size range is especially rich in flysch-derived silt. It has already been noted that many of the flysch-derived fine sediments in the Voïdomatis basin show evidence of a distinctive size mode in the coarse silt range (63 µm–16 µm). The unstable flysch slopes on both sides of the Lower Vikos Gorge provide an obvious local source of quartz-rich silty material. The colour, mineralogy and particle size characteristics of the fine matrix fraction of many recent slope and river sediments, as well as cave and rockshelter materials, indicate a flysch origin (Woodward 1990; Woodward *et al.* 1997).

Medium silt fraction

The medium silt component (16 µm–8 µm) displays only a comparatively small degree of downcore variation with mean values of 18.3, 17.5 and 16.2 per cent in the upper, central and lower core sections respectively. This size fraction does not show a strong positive or negative relationship with any of the other parameters mentioned above. This has precluded an accurate assessment of its lithological characteristics and source, and this parameter is therefore of limited value for purposes of environmental reconstruction.

Figure 18.4. *Bivariate plots to illustrate the relationship between various sedimentological parameters in the Y25 core sequence. All the product moment correlation coefficients (r) are significant at the 0.001 confidence level (n = 56).*

Fine silt fraction

The positive correlation between $CaCO_3$ content and fine silt (8 µm–2 µm) and the negative relationship between $CaCO_3$ and coarse silt suggests that a significant proportion of the fine silt fraction is composed of $CaCO_3$ (Fig. 18.4). Thus, while the coarse silt material is composed largely of non-carbonate or flysch-derived mineral grains, a significant proportion of the fine silt fraction appears to be dominated primarily by $CaCO_3$ or limestone-derived material.

At the nearby rockshelter site of Megalakkos, the $CaCO_3$ content of the fine sediment matrix is generally significantly less than the Klithi sediments and always less than the lower sections of core Y25 (Fig. 18.5). Thus, fine sediments with a $CaCO_3$ content greater than *c.* 60 per cent are not present at Megalakkos, even though micromorphological evidence suggests that some *secondary* deposition of carbonate has taken place within the Megalakkos fine sediments (Woodward, Chapter 19). If we assume that the chemistry of the groundwater at Megalakkos does not differ substantially from that at Klithi, then we need to invoke an additional source of fine-grained limestone-derived sediment to account for the Klithi material in the lower section of core Y25.

Between *c.* 28 ka and 24 ka the Voïdomatis River was a glacially-fed outwash stream, transporting coarse and fine sediments dominated by limestone-derived material (Lewin *et al.* 1991; Macklin *et al.*, Chapter 17). The high suspended sediment load of this glacio-fluvial system resulted from the influx of huge amounts of finely comminuted limestone detritus (rock flour) in the Tsepelovon district of the basin (see Woodward *et al.* 1992; Macklin *et al.*, Chapter 17). During periods of seasonally-reduced discharge, reworking of loosely consolidated fine alluvial sediment by wind action would have been a significant agent of sediment redistribution within the gorge environment. In addition, the absence of an effective vegetation cover on the braided floodplain beneath the site would have fostered an effective deflation surface where aeolian entrainment and redistribution of fine sediment could have occurred throughout the glacial period. The transfer of fine sediments by wind action from local floodplain sources to rockshelter environments has been reported elsewhere in Europe during the Last Glacial Maximum. At the Abri Pataud in the Dordogne, for example, heavy mineral analysis has indicated the presence within certain sedimentary units of fine sands and silts blown by wind action into the rockshelter site from the floodplain of the nearby Vézère River at around 27 ka (Farrand 1975, 17).

It is also important to emphasize that the level of the full glacial 'Aristi' floodplain would have been significantly higher than at present, bringing the valley floor closer to the rockshelter mouth, and so increasing the exposure of the rockshelter to input of such allogenic materials. The modern shelter floor (the top of the Palaeolithic surface) is 29 m above the present-day river level. The Aristi Unit (Macklin *et al.*, Chapter 17) is a striking alluvial terrace reaching maximum elevations of 25.9 m above the level of the modern river bed, with an elevation estimated at about 19 m above the modern level in the immediate vicinity of Klithi. The full glacial river thus flowed at a level some 10 m below the shelter floor (Fig. 18.6).

Further support for an additional allogenic contribution to the rockshelter sequence comes from experimental work on patterns of limestone breakdown. Experimental studies of rock disintegration suggest that the minimum size limit to which

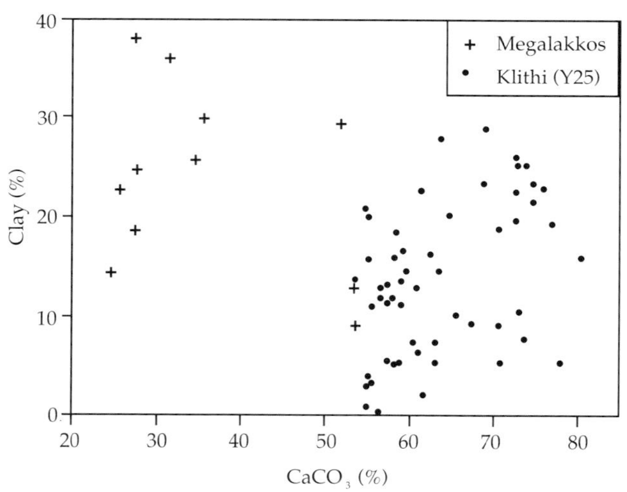

Figure 18.5. *Bivariate plot to highlight the contrasting particle size characteristics and lithology of the Megalakkos fine sediments (see Chapter 19) and the Klithi core (Y25) fine sediments. The mean $CaCO_3$ content of the Klithi core Y25 fine sediments is 64.0 per cent with a range of 54.0 to 80.6 per cent. In contrast, the mean $CaCO_3$ content of the Megalakkos fine sediments is 36.2 per cent with a range of 25.0 to 54.0 per cent.*

lithographic limestone rock particles can be broken down by frost action is approximately 1.0 mm (*cf.* Lautridou 1988). Most of the $CaCO_3$-rich material in the rockshelter record at Klithi is much finer (< 63 μm) and a proportion of this is concentrated in the fine silt (8 μm–2 μm) range. Furthermore, it is likely that, except under direct glacial action in the Tsepelovon district — where processes of physical grinding and crushing of bedrock by glacier ice were important — the pure, hard limestones of the Voïdomatis basin do not liberate significant amounts of sediment in the <63 μm grade (Woodward *et al.* 1992). It is probable that a proportion of the fine-grained material within the Klithi sediments *is* a byproduct of on-site rock reduction processes such as frost action. This mechanism of $CaCO_3$-rich fine sediment production, however, is thought to be minor in comparison with allogenic aeolian inputs. Another process that may be important is the deposition of secondary carbonate material by solute-laden percolating waters. It is also important to remember that flysch-derived sediments contain a significant calcite component (Woodward, Chapter 19), and both flysch-derived infiltrates and aeolian sediments contain $CaCO_3$, thus representing an additional allogenic contribution of fine-grained carbonate material.

In view of these arguments it seems highly likely that a significant proportion of the $CaCO_3$-rich fine sediments in the Klithi sequence (particularly the fine silt fraction) is also of external origin. The lithology of the fine fraction in the lower part of the sequence (between 4.2 m and 7.0 m) is similar to the fine fraction of unweathered Aristi Unit sediments (Woodward *et al.* 1994). Both contain up to 80 per cent $CaCO_3$. Both also clearly pre-date the Palaeolithic occupation at Klithi, and while the lower part of the Klithi sequence is not dated by radiometric means, it is highly likely that it overlaps in time the period of deposition of the Late Würm Aristi alluvial Unit.

The clay fraction

The origin of the non-carbonate silt material discussed above appears to be largely unrelated to the source of most of the clay fraction, which forms the remainder of the insoluble residue component. These two size fractions show a negative correlation (Fig. 18.4, r = –0.68), perhaps indicating contrasting sediment sources or the operation of different transfer pathways and depositional processes. The total insoluble residue component in the lower core sediments (below 4.2 m) is dominated by clay grade material (Fig. 18.2). As the flysch rocks contain a significant clay component, it was first considered that a proportion of this clay grade material could be locally derived. This is unlikely, however, because during the full-glacial period the flysch rocks of the catchment made only a comparatively minor contribution to the suspended sediment load of the Voïdomatis River. Also, Aristi Unit fine sediments sampled at the unweathered base of soil profiles are largely free of clay particles (Woodward *et al.* 1994) and this argues against a local riverine source for this fine material. It is also rather improbable that this clay material is infiltrated sediment, as the pronounced coarse silt mode which characterizes all local flysch-derived sediments is absent in most samples. On balance, then, it is likely that a considerable proportion of the clay within the site sediments is derived from off-site sources and represents the deposition of aeolian dust (see Pye 1992).

There is some evidence to suggest that iron-rich windblown silts and clays were incorporated into alluvial soil profiles in the Lower Vikos Gorge during the Last Glacial (Woodward *et al.* 1994). From the evidence available, it is not yet possible to pinpoint specific sources for this clay material, but it does seem likely that windblown dust from outside the adjacent river environment provided an important contribution to the fine matrix of the rockshelter sediments — particularly during the full-glacial period (Pye 1987; 1992). A minor *autogenic* supply of clay from the host limestone bedrock is also to be expected (Fig. 18.1).

In view of the above, the absence of clay particles at the base of the cultural horizons, and the very low values around 2 m depth in core Y25 (Fig. 18.2), would seem to represent a significant change in the wider environment, when the aeolian transfer of very fine particles from both the catchment slopes and from outside the basin was restricted — perhaps by an increase in humidity and vegetation cover at around 16 ka. This scenario receives some support from the pollen record at Tenaghi Philippon (Wijmstra 1969; Turner & Sánchez-Goñi, Chapter 29).

The above discussion impinges directly on the well-worn debate concerning the importance of far-travelled aeolian dust as a soil-forming factor in the soils of Epirus and the wider Mediterranean region (Macleod 1980; Pye 1992). This controversy is ongoing and worth comment here because, if dusts rich in iron oxide were deposited at Klithi during the full-glacial period, then their presence within the sequence would provide an extremely plausible explanation for the magnetic susceptibility values greater than *c.* 20 $m^3\ kg^{-1}$ recorded in the lower core (Fig. 18.2), which are clearly not the result of human occupation. Finally, it is important to appreciate that it is not necessary to invoke a Saharan source for this type of windblown material at Klithi, as outcrops of iron-rich rocks, sediments and soils are widespread in Epirus itself (Woodward 1990; Woodward *et al.* 1994).

Post-depositional alterations

A number of secondary or post-depositional features are apparent in the Klithi rockshelter sediments. These include marked increases in the magnetic susceptibility of the fine sediments in the archaeologically-rich deposits, changes in fine sediment colour, the incorporation of human habitation debris such as organic detritus, charcoal fragments, ashy materials, and lithic and faunal remains. It can be argued that all of the cultural materials within the site should be regarded as primary depositional features. Much of the human activity within the site, however, would have resulted in a degree of sediment reworking and modification. The nature and extent of some of these

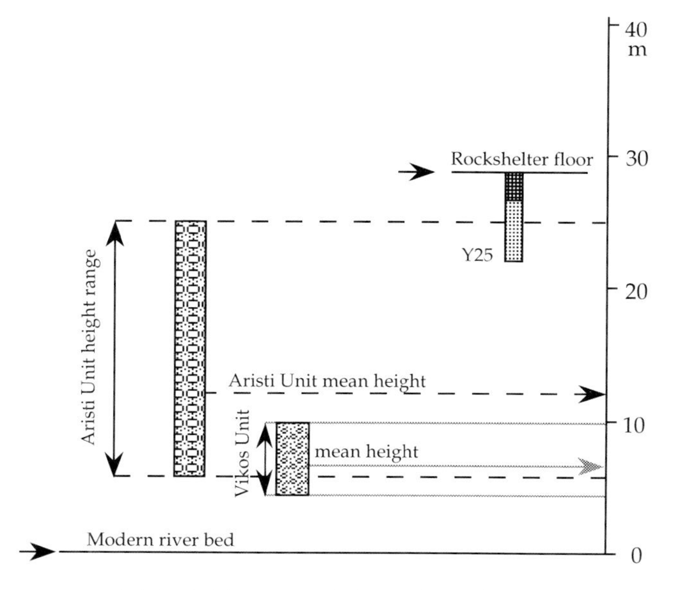

Figure 18.6. *Altitudinal relationships between the sedimentary sequence at Klithi (core Y25) and the Aristi and Vikos alluvial units. The mean height of the Aristi terrace is 12.4 m and the mean height of the Vikos terrace is 6.8 m (see Chapter 17). The modern river bed is approximately 28 m below the base of the Palaeolithic strata in the Klithi fill. The geomorphological setting of Klithi and the high fine sediment load of the cold stage, braided, glacio-fluvial river would have made the site a favourable location for the accumulation and storage of aeolian fine sediment from the adjacent floodplain environment.*

alterations can be tested by comparing the occupation sediments with both the pre-occupation deposits and the alluvial sediments and soils in the adjacent floodplain environment. The Pleistocene alluvial units of the Lower Vikos Gorge contain sediments of similar age to those at Klithi, and of similar lithological composition, composed principally of coarse limestone clasts in a silty $CaCO_3$-rich matrix. This allows comparisons to be drawn between the processes operating within the local pedogenic weathering regime (sub-aerial diagenesis) and the processes operating in the rockshelter environment.

Soil development in the Voïdomatis basin

The nature of soil profile development in the Voïdomatis valley has been described in detail in Woodward *et al.* (1994). The two alluvial units which broadly correspond to the time interval of the Klithi core sequence are the Vikos and Aristi Units (see Macklin *et al.*, Chapter 17). Both are characterized by the development of mature reddish-brown soils with decalcified *A* horizons and clay-rich *B* horizons enriched in ferric iron (Fig. 18.7). These profile features are the result of pedogenic alteration in a strong leaching environment over many millennia. Total decalcification of these soils to a depth of 50 cm or more is common, and is a necessary prerequisite for the accumulation of pedogenic iron and pedogenic clay and for the development of the distinctive 'Mediterranean' red-brown colouration. Whilst total decalcification of surface soil horizons can occur in as little as 1000 years in the soil profile environment (Woodward 1990), the rockshelter environment at Klithi is not exposed to such leaching processes. In contrast to the high solvent capacity of the soil moisture derived from direct rainfall input, the solvent capacity of the water percolating through the limestone bedrock at Klithi is negligible. Any groundwater that percolates into the Klithi sediments must be too alkaline to remove any $CaCO_3$. The rockshelter sediments are thus rich in $CaCO_3$ material in all size fractions throughout the sequence. All the sediment samples from core Y25 contain >50 per cent $CaCO_3$ in the <63 µm grade. This is in marked contrast to the observed pattern of upper profile decalcification which is so pronounced in the soil environment on the local river terrace surfaces (Fig. 18.8). Even though the site has been used in recent years to shelter a herd of goats, which must have produced considerable amounts of uric acid, the rockshelter sediments show no evidence of carbonate removal by solution.

Mineral magnetic properties

Magnetic susceptibility is roughly proportional to the concentration of magnetic minerals within a sediment sample and can be an especially sensitive indicator of weathering and oxidation (Dearing *et al.* 1985; Thompson & Oldfield 1986). In common with the soil profile environment, a negative relationship exists between magnetic susceptibility and $CaCO_3$ content in the core sediments (Figs. 18.2 & 18.8). Unlike the soil profile environment, where magnetic susceptibility maxima are always associated with strongly leached and decalcified horizons (Fig. 18.8), in the rockshelter sequence, high magnetic susceptibility values are found in carbonate-rich deposits. The highest values for low frequency magnetic susceptibility clearly coincide with the onset and duration of human occupation. Magnetic susceptibility enhancement of sediments through burning is typical at sites with extensive hearth areas subjected to intensive human occupation (Thompson & Oldfield 1986). Thus it is likely that the highest susceptibility values in the rockshelter sediments are a product of *sediment firing* as a direct consequence of human occupation.

The magnetic susceptibility values of the pre-occupation sediments range from 8.8 to 68.7 $m^3\ kg^{-1}$. The maximum values in the lower core are too high for unweathered, carbonate-rich materials (mean = 35.8 $m^3\ kg^{-1}$), especially since similar sediments at the base of the Pleistocene soil profiles have values of <40. Nor can the high values in this part of the core be attributed to burning. The deposition of aeolian dust, however, derived from previously weathered or burnt surfaces (i.e. surfaces with enhanced susceptibilities) or sediments rich in iron oxides could produce such high values. This explanation would also account for the significant proportion of clay in the lower part of the sequence, as discussed above.

The downcore pattern of *frequency dependent susceptibility*, which is a function of the contribution to total low frequency susceptibility by fine viscous ferrimagnetic grains (*cf.* Dearing *et al.* 1985; Maher 1986), has also been determined. These fine grains are significant contributors to total susceptibility in weathered horizons and in sediments affected by high temperatures. In core Y25, the values range from 2.4 per cent to 7.8 per cent , with a mean value of 6.4 per cent. In the upper part of the core, values range from 3.2 per cent to 7.8 per cent with a mean value of 7.1 per cent, whereas in the pre-occupation deposits the values are much lower. Since the rockshelter sediments have not been fully exposed to sub-aerial weathering processes, the high values in the archaeologically-rich sediments must reflect the impact of sediment firing. The highest value, 7.8 per cent, was recorded for the sample at the top of the core. This surface enhancement, and the reddening of the fine matrix in the uppermost levels of the Klithi fill, could represent the formation of magnetic minerals through the burning of the goat dung surface in recent decades. The formation of maghemite (a fine-grained magnetic mineral) due to burning was first demonstrated by Le Borgne (1955). More recently, Mullins (1977) has proposed a mechanism whereby the combustion of organic detritus produces reducing gases such as carbon monoxide, which reduce finely divided oxides and hydroxides of iron to magnetite. When the sediment cools, air enters and oxidizes the magnetite to maghemite.

It can often prove difficult to differentiate between the *primary* or natural environmental signal in rockshelter sediments and the *secondary* or cultural imprint in such archaeologically-rich sequences (see Butzer 1981; 1982; Gillieson *et al.* 1986). Nevertheless, by analyzing the sedimentary record spanning the pre-occupation history of the site with an appropriate range of techniques, and by comparing sediments of similar composition and age from contrasting local depositional and weathering environments, it has proved possible to begin to decouple the relative importance of cultural and environmental components in the rockshelter sediments. The fine sediments have been strongly influenced by the geomorphological setting of the site, and in particular by the nature of the fine sediment load of the adjacent river, which has changed over time in response to environmental changes, resulting in

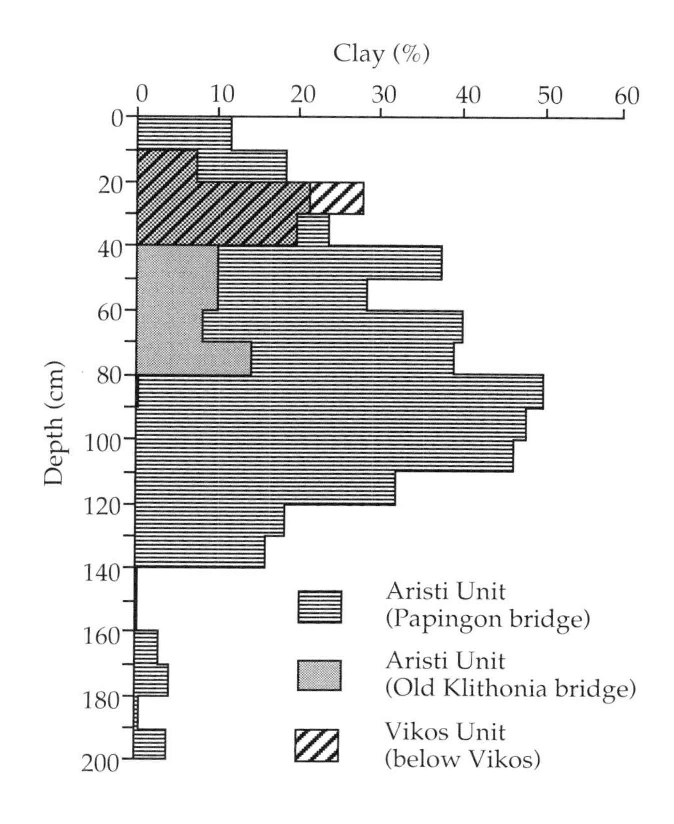

Figure 18.7. *Clay-rich B horizons developed in alluvial soils on Pleistocene terrace surfaces in the Lower Vikos Gorge and Konitsa basin (Chapter 17). These soils have formed under long periods of seasonal leaching (Woodward* et al. *1994).*

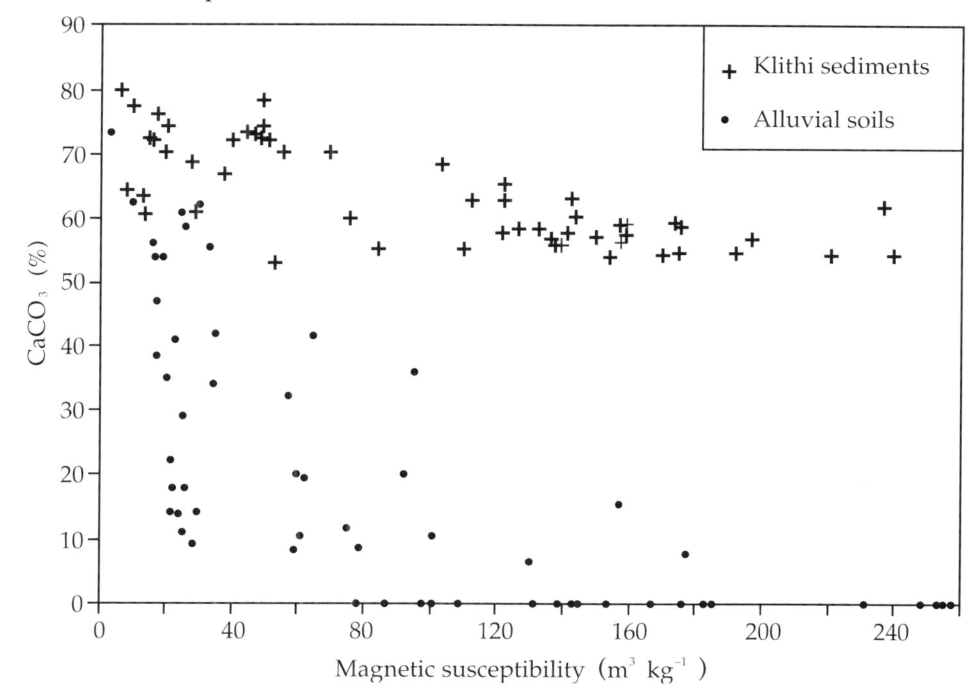

Figure 18.8. *The relationship between the $CaCO_3$ content and magnetic susceptibility of the Klithi core sediments and the alluvial soils from the local valley-floor environment. The high magnetic susceptibility values in the alluvial soils are the result of pedogenic weathering, whereas the high values in the rockshelter environment are the result of sediment firing.*

gradual changes in such lithological and textural parameters as $CaCO_3$ and non-carbonate silt. Superimposed on this environmental signal are cultural changes characterized by abrupt changes in colour and magnetic susceptibility.

Environmental change and sediment sources

The sedimentary sequence at Klithi records the changing importance of three principal fine sediment sources — namely materials ultimately derived from the limestone and flysch rocks of the catchment and aeolian dust of uncertain provenance. The transfer pathways involved in the delivery of fine sediment to the rockshelter floor are, however, complex, with evidence for the storage, weathering and reworking of materials prior to deposition in the rockshelter. The examples discussed above emphasize the importance of carefully evaluating the local geomorphological setting and the value of drawing comparisons with other local sedimentary environments (including other rockshelters) to provide a more rigorous basis for palaeoenvironmental interpretation. Through careful consideration of the particle size characteristics and lithological composition of the fine sediment fraction it has been possible to establish correlations with other Quaternary sediments in the Voïdomatis basin on *lithostratigraphic* grounds. This approach has been adopted in preference to establishing correlations on the basis of inferred climatic characteristics for particular sedimentary associations, or *climatostratigraphy*, the use of which has characterized many of the correlation schemes devised from rockshelter sedimentology (*cf.* Laville *et al.* 1980).

While it is difficult to estimate the absolute contribution to the fine sediment fraction from *in situ* limestone weathering, this fine sediment source is thought to be minor in comparison with external sources (see also Jennings 1985; Macleod 1980; White 1988). Sedimentological and geomorphological evidence suggests that the lower portion of the core sequence correlates with the Late Würm Aristi Unit of the Voïdomatis alluvial sequence and represents full-glacial conditions in the Voïdomatis basin before approximately 24 ka (Lewin *et al.* 1991; Macklin *et al.*, Chapter 17). During this period two main kinds of aeolian sediment were blown into the rockshelter: $CaCO_3$-rich silts from the braided floodplain of the Voïdomatis River; and significant amounts of clay-rich dust derived from further afield.

The central and upper sections of the core sequence correlate with the Vikos alluvial Unit (Macklin *et al.*, Chapter 17). This unit was deposited following incision and terracing of the Aristi Unit sediments and the associated reduction in suspended sediment load and narrowing and deepening of the channel system would have considerably restricted aeolian activity, especially if the higher parts of the former floodplain were colonized by vegetation. The corresponding parts of the rockshelter sediments record a considerable change in sediment character as the supply of limestone-derived fine sediment from the suspended load of the Voïdomatis River eventually waned and the delivery of flysch-derived (quartz-rich) silts increased in importance (Fig. 18.9). This non-carbonate silt component of the fine sediment matrix was transported *vertically* by karst infiltration processes, and also *laterally* by local riverine/aeolian processes.

The upper part of the sequence shows evidence of alteration as a result of human occupation. In the upper metre or so of the core sequence, inputs of aeolian dust begin to increase, but do not attain pre-occupation (full-glacial) levels. At the same time the non-carbonate silt component declines towards the upper part of the rockshelter fill, perhaps reflecting a return to cooler and drier conditions and reduced fine sediment infiltration and/or further incision of the Voïdomatis River which would have reduced any aeolian inputs by increasing the height difference between the active floodplain and the rockshelter floor.

In summary, the lithological and environmental changes recorded in the Late Pleistocene rockshelter sequence broadly mirror the major changes in the alluvial sedimentary record of the adjacent river environment. Following the Last Glacial Maximum, run-off and sediment delivery from the flysch terrains of the catchment made an increasingly important contribution to the suspended sediment load of the Voïdomatis River. During this period, after about 16 ka, a marked increase in the importance of flysch-derived materials as a fine sediment source is clearly recorded throughout the basin in both the rockshelter and alluvial records (Fig. 18.9).

Conclusions

A central concern of this contribution has been to demonstrate how careful integration of both the 'on-site' and 'off-site' sedimentary records with the archaeological sequence can provide a major contribution to an understanding of the interactions between large-scale changes in the Pleistocene environment and human activity. The sedimentary sequence at Klithi has provided an important bridge between the archaeological and environmental records. By focusing on the full stratigraphic succession and by making comparisons with the river sediments and soils in the vicinity of the site, it has been possible to establish the wider stratigraphic and environmental context of the Klithi sequence. In order to fully evaluate the environmental significance of rockshelter sediments, it is important to establish linkages with other sedimentary environments such as well-dated glacial, alluvial and lacustrine successions where the evidence for climatic change is much less equivocal and often incontrovertible. Without a detailed appreciation of the catchment-wide geomorphological changes which took place during the Late Pleistocene, aspects of the rockshelter sequence at Klithi would have appeared puzzling, posing fundamental problems of interpretation. For example, it is difficult to reconcile the general rule that 'sound rocks produce few fines' (DeWolf 1988) with the presence of hard limestone bedrock at Klithi and the abundance of limestone-derived fine silt in the pre-occupation sediments. Furthermore, a major conclusion from experimental research on frost weathering of resistant limestone is that the fine fraction within coarse sediments cannot result solely from the breakdown of the host bedrock (Lautridou 1988).

As far as the rockshelter sediments are concerned, the main conclusions to emerge are as follows:

1. There is a marked contrast between the pre-16 ka deposits and those associated with the human occupation of the site.
2. Allogenic materials dominate the fine sediment component *throughout* the sequence.
3. The production of fine sediments through *in situ* limestone breakdown is a comparatively minor process.

It has only been possible to account for the origin of the allogenic fine material through detailed investigation of local bedrock composition and a range of late Quaternary sedimentary environments throughout the Voïdomatis basin. It is clear that a substantial shift in the dominant sediment sources and depositional processes took place between *c.* 20 ka and 16 ka (middle core section), which can be related to major climatic and basin-wide geomorphological changes. The pre-occupation levels are dominated by limestone erosion products associated with headwater glaciation, fluvial transport and local aeolian reworking. The occupation deposits mark a period of reduced glacial influence, which corresponds to a change in the composition of the Voïdomatis suspended sediments, and an increase in fluvial transport and infiltration of flysch-derived sediments. This switch in sediment provenance in the middle part of Y25, prior to human occupation of Klithi, is indicated by a considerable change in the character of the fine sediment as coarse insoluble silt material assumes increasing importance. These sedimentological changes were under way *prior to* the occupation of the site.

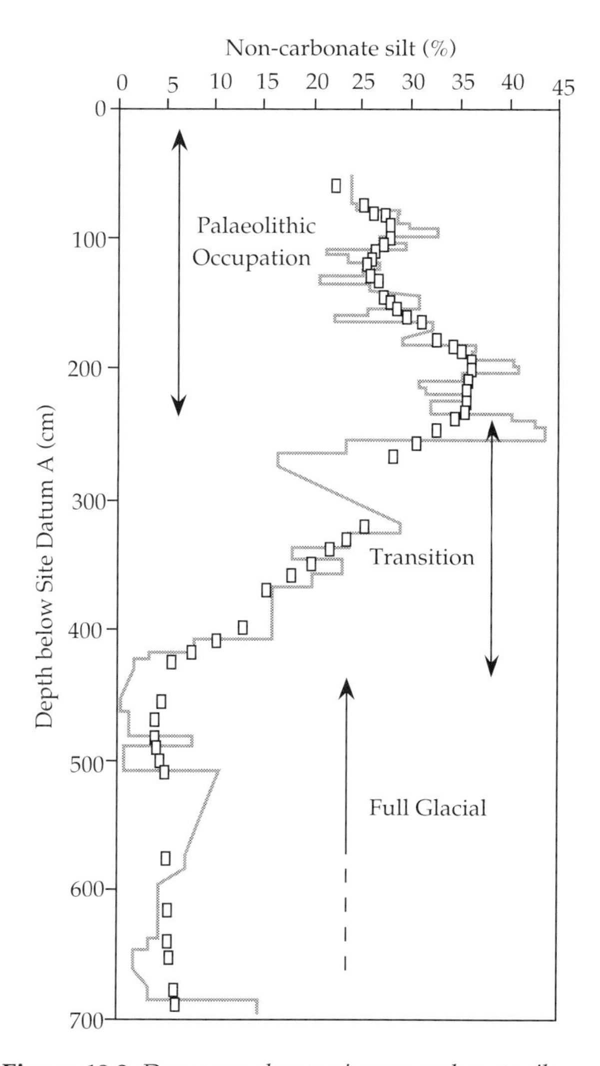

Figure 18.9. *Downcore changes in non-carbonate silt content in the Y25 sediments. The open squares represent a five point moving average and provide a useful proxy for the major environmental changes which took place during the Last Glacial–Interglacial Transition. The transitional phase (climatic warming) after the full-glacial period which preceded the earliest Palaeolithic occupation of the site is also shown. The progressive decline in non-carbonate silt material in the upper part of the core may indicate a return to cooler conditions.*

From the available sedimentary data at Klithi,

it is not possible to resolve in detail the nature of environmental fluctuations which may have taken place during the occupation of the site between *c.* 16 ka and 10 ka. It is of considerable interest, however, to note that the proportions of non-carbonate silt and coarse silt material, which markedly increase immediately preceding the period of human occupation, show a systematic decrease in the upper 1 m of the deposit. As the increase signals a reduced glacial influence and possibly also a significant climatic amelioration between *c.* 20 ka and 16 ka, then it is tempting to relate the later decrease to renewed cooling. Some support for this interpretation is the coeval increase in clay content, which reaches levels comparable to those in the full-glacial pre-occupation sediments. This suggests a wider, perhaps regional, increase in aridity which promoted the entrainment and transport of aeolian dust. This deterioration may not have been sufficiently prolonged or intense for renewed glacier expansion, and is thus not recorded in the Voïdomatis alluvial sequence, nor do the $CaCO_3$ values in the Klithi sediments show any significant change throughout this period. It is tempting to relate these trends to the Younger Dryas cooling which took place between *c.* 11 ka and 10 ka, but poor dating resolution at the top of the Klithi sequence does not allow this point to be pursued.

A more detailed insight into local environmental changes during this crucial episode between 16 ka and 10 ka is offered by the more finely resolved and accessible sedimentary sequence at the neighbouring site of Megalakkos, where there are sharp alterations in sediment style over this period and a relatively small human impact on the sedimentary record (Woodward, Chapter 19).

Acknowledgements

Much of the work reported here was carried out during the tenure of an SERC Ph.D. studentship at Darwin College, the Sub-Department of Quaternary Research (Godwin Laboratory) and the Department of Archaeology at the University of Cambridge. I would especially like to thank Geoff Bailey and all the members of the Klithi Project for their support and also IGME for permission to undertake 'off-site' field research in Epirus. In the Godwin Laboratory Simon Crowhust provided software advice and Simon Robinson provided assistance with the magnetic susceptibility measurements. I also thank Professor I.N. McCave of the Department of Earth Sciences in Cambridge for generously allowing access to the SediGraph and XRD facilities. This manuscript has benefited considerably from valuable comments by Geoff Bailey, and at various stages of this work John Lewin, Mark Macklin and Phil Gibbard have provided helpful discussions.

Chapter 19

Late Pleistocene Rockshelter Sedimentation at Megalakkos

Jamie Woodward

Megalakkos is a small rockshelter which was discovered in 1986 during the geomorphological survey of the tributary stream network in the Lower Vikos Gorge (Bailey, Chapter 1). The site is located in a narrow and steep-sided right-bank tributary ravine about 100 m from the point where it joins the main Voïdomatis River approximately 500 m upstream of the Klithi rockshelter. Megalakkos has an opening 4.5 m wide which faces to the southwest and is perched about 10 m above the seasonal stream bed (Fig. 19.1). Today it can only be reached with some difficulty by scrambling up a steep slope. The stream channel drains a fairly narrow and steep catchment whose headwaters lie in the flysch terrain to the west and northwest of the village of Papingon. Stream bed materials include a wide range of particle sizes ranging from coarse (>2 m) limestone boulders derived from rockfalls, angular to sub-angular limestone gravel clasts derived from channel bed and rock bank erosion and rounded flysch gravel and flysch-derived sands and coarse silt. River terraces are not present along the Megalakkos tributary and colluvial material is delivered directly into the channel system from the steep valley sides.

Within the rockshelter a Late Pleistocene and Holocene sedimentary fill attains a thickness of at least 5.3 m and these sediments have been investigated through a combined programme of field-based and laboratory-based analysis. In contrast to the sedimentary sequence at Klithi, natural erosion at the site opening has allowed direct observation of the Megalakkos sequence (Fig. 19.1). This has facilitated detailed subdivision of the sequence and twelve lithostratigraphical units have been identified with only minimal excavation. Four of these sedimentary units contain cultural and faunal remains which indicate a Late Upper Palaeolithic age for part of the sequence, covering a similar time span to the cultural deposits at Klithi.

The presence of ready-made vertical exposures in the Megalakkos fill removed the need to excavate deep trenches or to conduct site drilling to uncover the nature of the stratigraphic record. Good exposure of sections also permitted the use of a more detailed sediment sampling strategy and methodology than that employed at Klithi, incorporating textural analysis of the coarse sediment fraction and micromorphological analysis of fine-grained sediments (*cf.* Butzer 1982, 87). As in the previous chapter, emphasis is placed on the *temporal* sequence and on establishing the *source* of the fine sediments. The latter aim is again regarded as an important element in the reconstruction of the transport mechanisms and depositional processes responsible for sediment accumulation and the reconstruction of the wider environmental context.

The sedimentary sequence at Megalakkos provides a valuable local source of comparison with the Klithi rockshelter deposits described earlier (Woodward, Chapter 18). Like Klithi, Megalakkos also presents an opportunity to integrate the study of 'on-site' archaeological materials and sediments with the 'off-site' Late Pleistocene sediments in the immediate and basin-wide geomorphological environment. The Megalakkos sequence is particularly noteworthy because archaeologically rich sediments, characterized by coarse and angular limestone clasts, are interbedded with highly distinctive fine-grained, archaeologically-sterile deposits. The repeated alternation of markedly contrasting coarse and fine sediment facies at Megalakkos provides an additional contrast to the Klithi sedimentary record. The clear differences in sedimentation style between the Klithi and Megalakkos sites present an unusual opportunity to evaluate the importance of local or site specific environmental factors in controlling the nature of rockshelter sedimentation (*cf.* Farrand 1985; Woodward 1990).

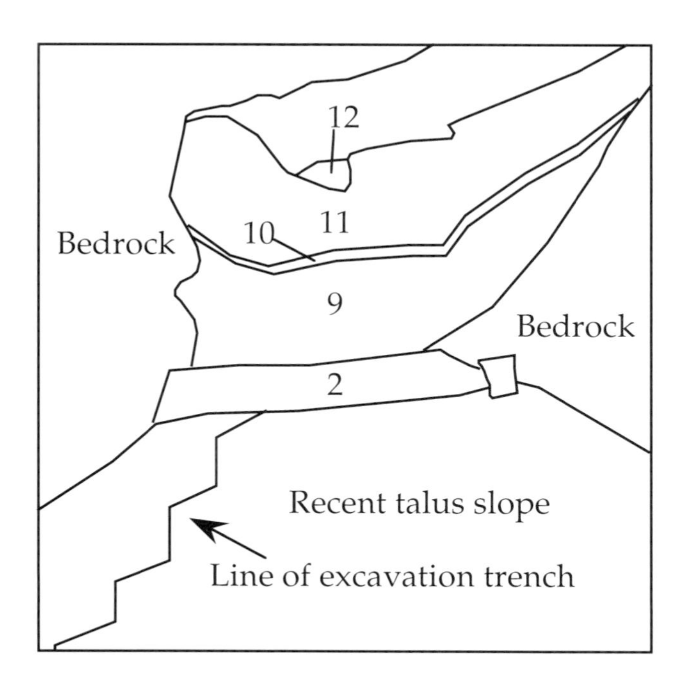

Field and laboratory methods

The erosive action of natural slope processes has created a useful section in the upper deposits and much of the sedimentary fill is exposed at the cave-mouth (Fig. 19.1; see also Fig. 21.1). The stratigraphical relationships within the site were further explored by means of a narrow (*c.* 25 cm) trench cut into the central and lower parts of the sequence. This trench was extended laterally in the central part of the sequence to a maximum width of *c.* 75 cm (see Sinclair, Chapter 21). The stratigraphical relationships within the sedimentary fill were logged, sketched and photographed. The 5.3 m thickness of Quaternary sediments was subdivided into twelve lithostratigraphic units and their sedimentological characteristics were described and logged in the field. Host limestone rock samples were collected from within the sequence and from the shelter walls for lithological and textural analysis. Sediment samples were taken from both the excavated units and the exposed upper section, and where possible sediment samples were taken in vertical columns (*cf.* Colcutt 1979). Because of the presence of a deep natural section, bulk samples of coarse (>11.2 mm) material were also taken for particle size analysis. This was not possible at Klithi because of the relatively small samples recovered from the cores (see Chapter 18). Fine fraction sediment samples were also collected for laboratory analysis and samples of charred material were taken for radiocarbon dating. As the fine sediments of interest were

Figure 19.1. *An oblique view of the Megalakkos rockshelter looking up from the recent talus slope. The site opening is approximately 4.5 m across. The evolution of the site appears to be related to the erosion of a local structural weakness in the limestone bedrock — enlarged initially by solutional weathering — and later also by physical weathering processes and bedding stress release. Part of the uncemented central portion of the fill has been eroded away leaving a precarious overhang of mildly cemented limestone clasts. Calcite deposition is evident on the sediments and bedrock wall in the upper left of this photograph. The high bedding frequency and brittle nature of parts of the limestone bedrock walls is also apparent. The shallow trench excavated during the 1986 field season is located in the central part of the fill. Sedimentary units are shown on the attached legend.*

frequently too compacted for the insertion of Kubiena tins, small blocks of fine-grained sediment were collected for impregnation and subsequent micromorphological analysis. Thin sections were studied under a petrological microscope.

As at Klithi, the lithological composition of the host limestone strata at Megalakkos was examined in a number of ways (see Woodward, Chapter 18 for details). Initial observations on bedrock hand specimens were supplemented by qualitative assessment of rock thin sections viewed under a petrological microscope. Semi-quantitative evaluation of mineralogy was achieved by XRD analysis of both powdered rock samples and their acid-insoluble residues. The proportion of non-carbonate minerals present — a measure of limestone purity — was also determined following dissolution in dilute hydrochloric acid. The particle size characteristics of the acid-insoluble residue of the Megalakkos host rock were also examined in detail using a SediGraph. In addition, the organic content of the fine sediments was estimated by loss on ignition using the procedure described by Gross (1971). For mineralogical analysis by XRD, all bedrock samples were crushed and ground with a mortar and pestle to powders which would pass through a 63 μm sieve. Rockshelter fine sediment samples were also screened through a 63 μm sieve. The bedrock and fine sediment sample powders were mounted as slurries in an acetone solution on circular glass slips (20 mm diameter) and air dried at room temperature (see Woodward *et al.* 1992). All samples were analyzed under the same instrument conditions using a Philips PW 1730 X-ray generator and PW 1050/25 vertical goniometer. Peak height measurements were recorded for quartz 4.26 Å (100 hkl), plagioclase 3.196 Å (002 hkl), and calcite 2.095 Å (202 hkl), on all diffractogram traces for comparative analysis. While estimates of mineral abundance obtained by this technique are no more than relative and semi-quantitative, they provide an extremely useful means for comparing intersample composition (see Griffin 1971; Wood 1978; Woodward *et al.* 1992).

Lithostratigraphy and facies types

Twelve sedimentary units are recognized at Megalakkos (Figs. 19.2–19.4) and are described below in terms of overall texture, matrix colour, nature of unit boundaries and other salient features. Units are described in order of age, beginning with the lowest (Unit 1), and mean unit thicknesses are given in brackets.

Unit 1 (150 cm)
Coarse-grained and crudely stratified, angular limestone clasts, with some cobble-sized material. Poorly sorted with red/brown coloured fine matrix but generally matrix poor. Archaeologically sterile. The upper part of this unit was observed in the narrow section in the scree slope in front of the rockshelter opening.

Unit 2 (70 cm)
Compacted, stratified, angular limestone clasts. Finer-grained and better sorted than Unit 1. The lower 45 cm of the unit displays a yellow/brown (10 Y/R 5/6) colour. In the lower part of the unit the limestone clasts are less compacted and are contained within the silt-dominated fine matrix. The upper part of the unit is well bedded and clast supported. Very sharp contact with Unit 3. The upper 25 cm includes a dark grey ashy lens and contains archaeological material.

Unit 3 (35 cm)
Fine-grained sediment dominated by clayey silt. Occasional, isolated, large angular limestone clasts. Silt (63–2 μm) is the dominant particle size, with some clay grade material. Finely laminated and compacted. Very distinctive unit. Yellow/brown colour (10 Y/R 6/6). Archaeologically sterile.

Unit 4 (12 cm)
Poorly sorted angular limestone clasts supported in a clayey silt

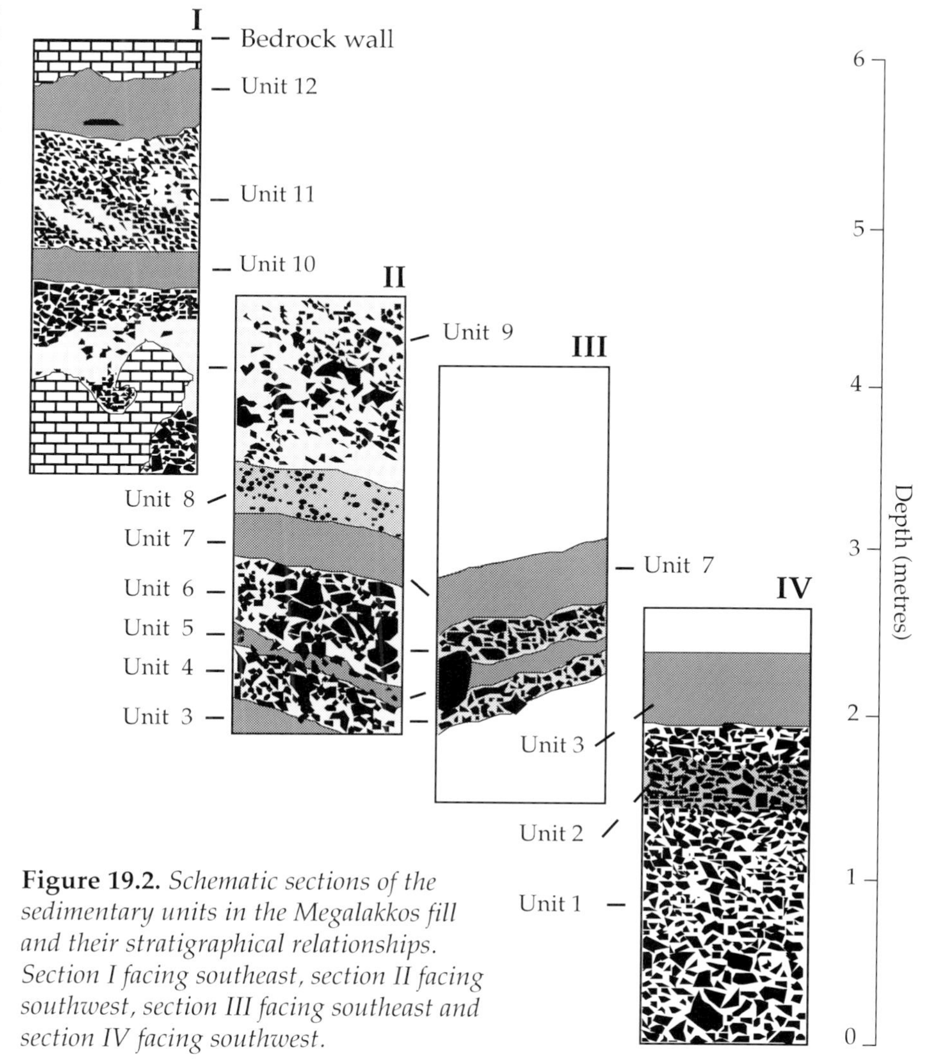

Figure 19.2. *Schematic sections of the sedimentary units in the Megalakkos fill and their stratigraphical relationships. Section I facing southeast, section II facing southwest, section III facing southeast and section IV facing southwest.*

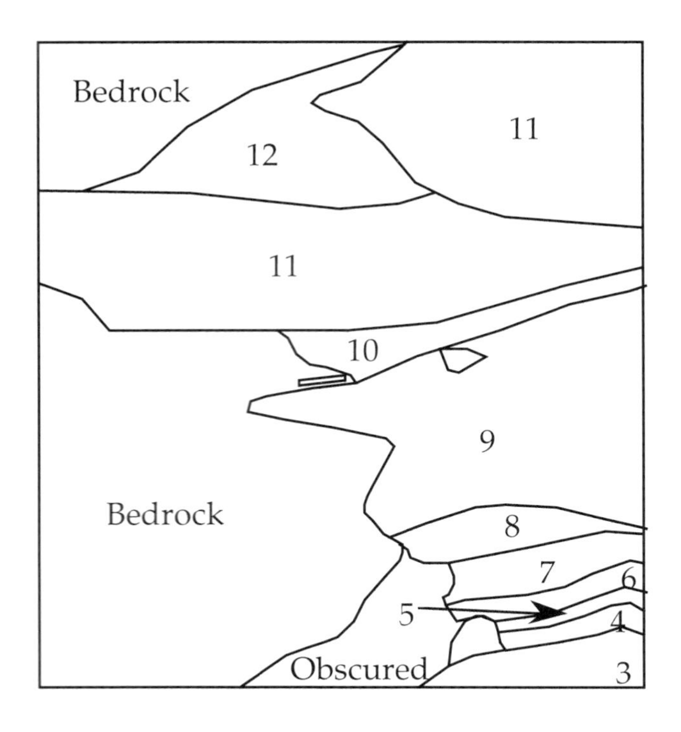

matrix with a significant ashy component. Matrix colour 7.5 Y/R 5/8. Maximum clast size is 128 mm. Rich in archaeological material.

Unit 5 (10 cm)
Fine-grained, clayey silt. Laterally discontinuous unit which is well developed in the southeast facing section. Sharp contact with Unit 4. 10 Y/R 6/6. Archaeologically sterile.

Unit 6 (15 cm)
Coarse, angular limestone clasts, similar grade to Unit 4 and poorly sorted. Matrix supported with a clayey silt matrix. Matrix colour is 7.5 YR 5/8. Ashy component with fine charcoal debris. Cultural and faunal remains.

Unit 7 (20 cm)
Homogeneous olive yellow 2.5 Y 6/6 clayey silt. Limestone clasts absent. Fine laminations. Very sharp contact with Unit 6 and Unit 8. Generally a very distinctive unit. This unit was sampled for micromorphological analysis. Archaeologically sterile.

Unit 8 (15 cm)
Well-rounded alluvial gravel with slight fining upwards. Some traces of imbrication (i.e. a bedding structure where individual clasts have their long axes oriented in the same direction, indicating deposition by flowing water). Brown silty matrix. Maximum clast size 25 mm (intermediate (b) axis). Flysch-derived fine, flat gravel. Sharp contact with Unit 7. Archaeologically sterile.

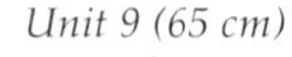

Unit 9 (65 cm)
Fine, brown silty matrix-supported deposit with stratified, angular limestone clasts throughout. Slight fining upwards grading into upper Unit. Recent carbonate deposition on the southwest face of this Unit and cementation of limestone fragments. Gradational contact with Unit 8. Archaeological material with lithics and some faunal remains and a large (cobble-sized) rounded flysch pebble probably carried in by hand from the main Voïdomatis floodplain.

Unit 10 (15 cm)
Laterally continuous fine-grained, stoneless, clayey silt. Sharp contact with Unit 11. Carbonate

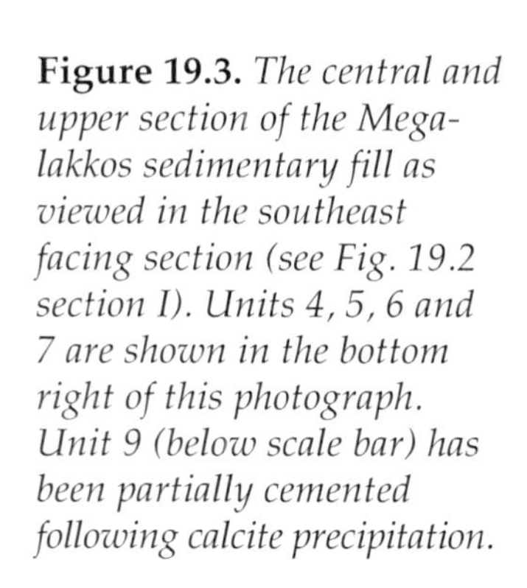

Figure 19.3. *The central and upper section of the Megalakkos sedimentary fill as viewed in the southeast facing section (see Fig. 19.2 section I). Units 4, 5, 6 and 7 are shown in the bottom right of this photograph. Unit 9 (below scale bar) has been partially cemented following calcite precipitation.*

deposition on southeast facing section. Evidence for development of a vertical blocky ped structure. Archaeologically sterile.

Unit 11 (50 cm)
Angular limestone fragments. Clast supported and lightly cemented. A finer grade, with a paucity of fine matrix and an increase in sorting, distinguishes this unit from the other coarse units in the sequence apart from Unit 2. The upper part of this unit is weathered and displays three discrete horizons. These indicate partial decalcification of the top few centimetres of matrix and the development of a reddish/brown secondary layer. Sharp contact with Unit 12. Archaeologically sterile.

Unit 12 (75 cm)
Fine-grained clay/silt dominated unit. Laminated and stoneless. Archaeologically sterile.

From the field sedimentary logs summarized above and the section drawings shown in Figure 19.2, four main lithofacies types may be recognized within the Megalakkos sedimentary fill:

1. Facies A. A finely laminated clayey-silt facies. This facies is very distinctive, typically yellow/brown in colour, devoid of coarse material, forming sharp contacts with adjoining units. Units 3, 5, 7, 10 and 12.
2. Facies B. A poorly stratified, matrix supported, angular limestone debris facies characterized by coarse, poorly sorted, angular limestone clasts with a significant proportion of fine 'earthy' clayey/silt matrix. Units 1, 4, 6 and 9.
3. Facies C. A well sorted, stratified, deposit of fine, angular limestone clasts, partly clast supported with a predominantly yellow brown or creamy/brown silty matrix. Units 2 and 11.
4. Facies D. A fine fluvial

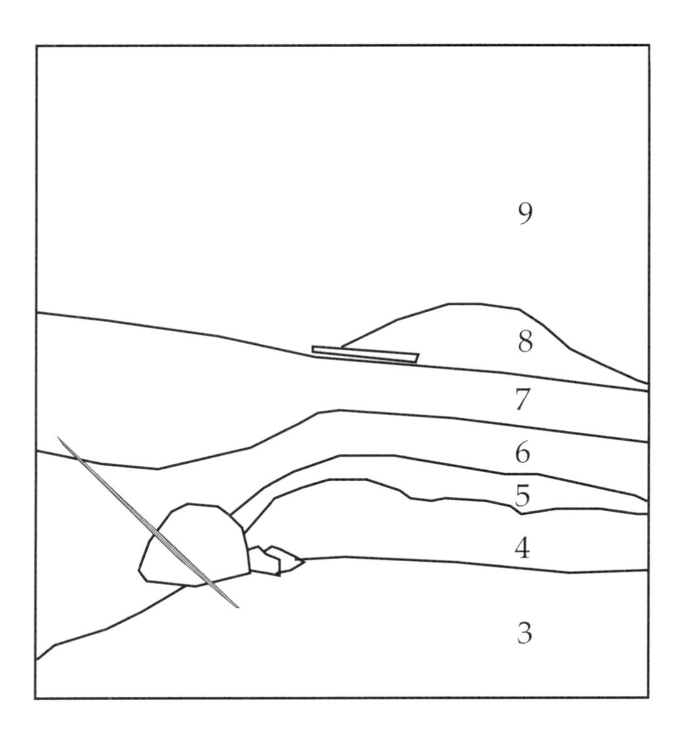

Figure 19.4. *The southwest facing section of the excavated trench in the central part of the fill (see Fig. 19.2 section II). Unit 5 is laterally discontinuous and is recognizable, but not so clearly defined at the back of the trench.*

gravel facies containing well-rounded flysch gravel up to 2.5 cm (b axis), largely matrix supported with some evidence of imbrication. Unit 8.

General bedrock features and site formation

The limestone bedrock at Megalakkos, as at Klithi, is Palaeocene to Upper Eocene in age. In many places these rocks are tectonically deformed and fractured and often display high bedding and joint frequencies. A typical section in fractured Eocene limestone is shown in Figure 19.5. In contrast to Klithi, where it seems likely that fluvial erosion of the gorge wall was a major factor in site formation, the evolution of the small rockshelter opening at Megalakkos appears to be related to the presence of a local structural weakness which was probably exploited initially by solutional activity and later by chemical and physical weathering processes (*cf.* Woodward 1990). In general, solutional weathering processes are concentrated along the bedding planes of these hard and low porosity limestones.

Figure 19.5. *A section in the Palaeocene to Eocene limestone of the Lower Vikos Gorge exposed along the Aristi to Papingon road. Note the often brittle and fractured nature of the limestone bedrock, the local variation in bedding thickness, and the importance of the karst system as a conduit for fine sediment transfer (see also Fig. 19.11).*

Lithological composition

A typical XRD pattern for a bulk powdered bedrock sample is shown in Figure 19.6. This indicates that the limestone bedrock is dominated by $CaCO_3$ in the form of calcite with tiny amounts of detrital quartz. The acid-insoluble residue content of 7 rock samples ranged from 0.34 to 0.89 per cent with a mean content of 0.54 per cent. These limestones are thus >99.4 per cent $CaCO_3$ and may be classified as *extremely pure* (*cf.* Bögli 1980). Three of the insoluble residues from the Megalakkos rock samples were also analyzed by XRD. The insoluble residues are clay-rich (Fig. 19.7) with a mineralogy dominated by quartz and mica. In view of the known tendency of limestones to display lithological uniformity over wide areas, it is not surprising that the host limestone bedrock at Megalakkos and Klithi is very similar in both texture and composition (Fig. 19.7). The lithological character of the flysch rocks of the Lower Vikos Gorge has been described in Chapter 18.

Lithological properties and sources of sediments

Fine sediment sources

A large proportion of the Megalakkos sequence is made up of fine-grained material in the silt and clay (<63 μm) size range. This material is present in varying proportions in all the sedimentary units and various properties are summarized in Table 19.1. Non-carbonate silt forms an important component of the fine element of all the units, reaching a maximum of 60.8 per cent in Unit 8. The $CaCO_3$ content ranges from 25 per cent to 54 per cent with a mean value of 36 per cent. Silts and clays form the interclast matrix within the coarser units where limestone rock fragments form a major component, and they dominate the exclusively fine-grained units.

The provenance of silts and clays in cave and rockshelter environments has generated much debate (*cf.* Jennings 1985) and this controversy may be usefully compared with the debate surrounding the origin of the Epirus *terra rossa* soils since it involves an assessment of limestone purity and the geological significance of limestone dissolution products (*cf.* Macleod 1980; Woodward 1990; Pye 1992).

Both the XRD results and the insoluble residue proportions indicate that, in common with the Klithi sediments, most of the Megalakkos fine sediments are not derived from the limestone bedrock. The bedrock is extremely pure — composed almost exclusively of $CaCO_3$ (>99.4 per cent) in the form of calcite, with tiny amounts of predominantly clay-grade, quartz and mica (Fig. 19.7). The XRD traces shown in Figure 19.6 demonstrate the relatively simple bulk mineralogical composition of the Megalakkos

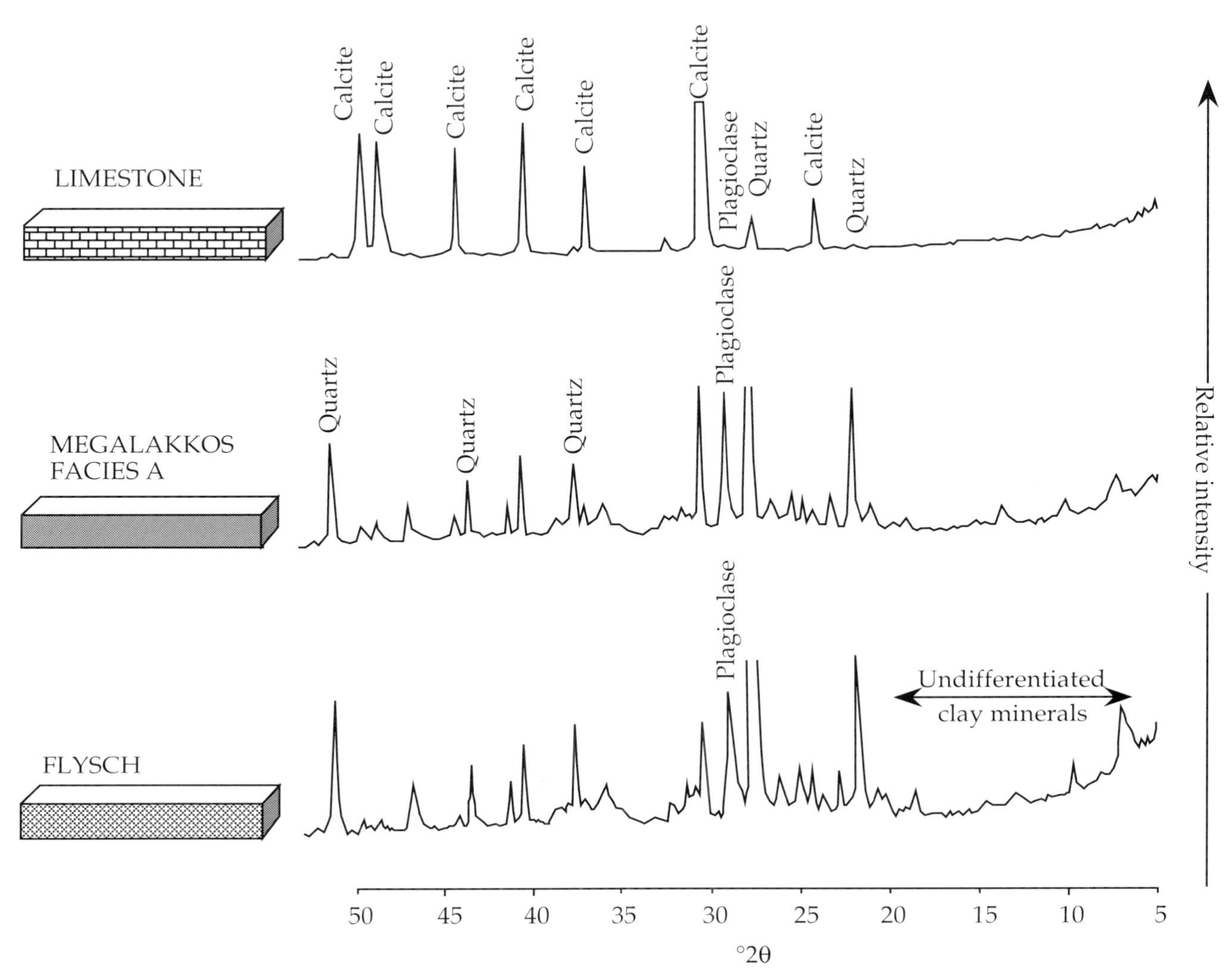

Figure 19.6. *Typical X-ray diffraction (XRD) traces for powdered (<63 μm) limestone and flysch bedrock samples and the facies A fine sediments (Unit 7) at Megalakkos.*

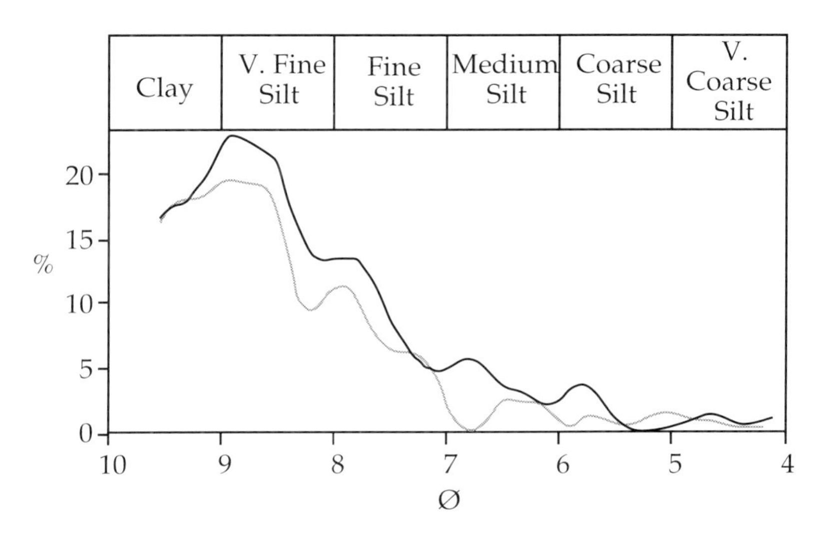

Figure 19.7. *Typical particle size distribution curves for the insoluble residue fraction of the host limestone bedrock at Megalakkos (grey line) and Klithi (black line). Note the fine-grained nature of this non-carbonate material and the virtual absence of coarse silt. 4 ϕ (63 μm) is the sand/silt boundary and 9 ϕ (2 μm) is the silt/clay boundary (see Table 18.1).*

limestone in contrast to the more complex mineral suite found in the overlying flysch strata and the rockshelter fine sediment. The composition of the local flysch strata is identical to that of the Megalakkos fines (Figs. 19.6 & 19.8). The mean insoluble residue content of the Megalakkos limestone is 0.54 per cent. In common with the Klithi host rocks the paucity of non-carbonate minerals within the Megalakkos limestone and their very fine *texture* rules out a simple residual origin for the Megalakkos fine sediments. All the sedimentological evidence indicates that these sediments are *allogenic* — derived ultimately from sources *exterior* to the limestone system. The overlying flysch rocks and soils provided the main source of this material (Woodward 1990). This conclusion is supported by the colour of the fine units — their light-brown or 'buff' colour is similar to that of the alluvial fine sediments of the Klithi alluvial unit which are largely a byproduct of local flysch erosion (Lewin *et al.* 1991; Woodward *et al.* 1992; Macklin *et al.*, Chapter 17). The insoluble products of limestone weathering make only a very minor contribution to these sediments.

The central and upper sections of the sediments described from core Y25 at Klithi display some lithological and textural similarities to the fine sediments at Megalakkos (see Chapter 18, Table 18.2). In contrast, however, the fine sediment fraction within the basal sections of core Y25 contains a significantly greater proportion of $CaCO_3$ than the Megalakkos sediments.

Bearing in mind the apparent significance of aeolian processes at Klithi, it could be argued from a cursory inspection of the fine-grained units (Facies A) that wind action was largely responsible for their transport and deposition. Indeed, Butzer (1971) has argued that aeolian activity is a major agent of fine-sediment deposition in rockshelter and cave-mouth environments. In this respect, it is interesting to note that loess-like sediments which share a number of similarities with the Megalakkos Facies A deposits have been reported in the Doliana basin west of the Voïdomatis catchment (Sturdy *et al.*, Chapter 30). In very general terms the silty texture, yellow/brown colouration and absence of coarse material in these fine units are features which characterize many aeolian deposits (*cf.* Brunnacker 1980; Pye 1987; Wintle *et al.* 1984).

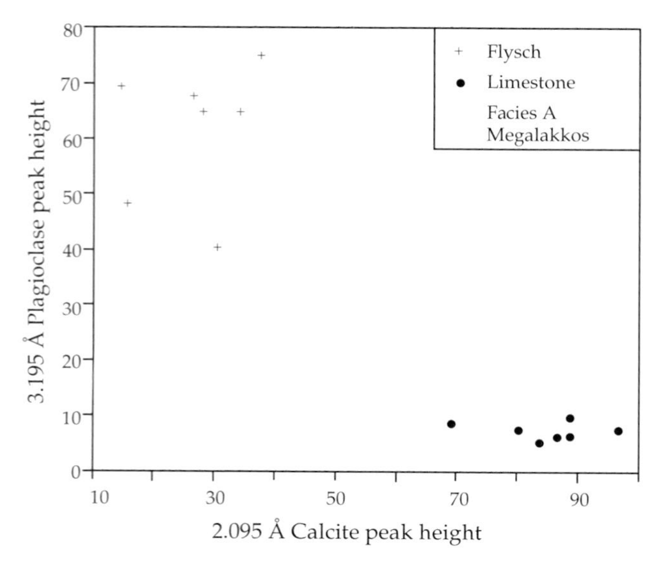

Figure 19.8. *A plagioclase and calcite XRD peak-height plot for 14 bedrock samples (7 limestone and 7 flysch) and the 5 Facies A units in the Megalakkos sequence.*

The Doliana basin loess. Loess has been defined as a terrestrial windblown silt consisting chiefly of quartz, feldspar, mica, clay minerals and carbonate grains in varying proportions (Pye 1984; 1987). The mineralogical and particle size characteristics of the Megalakkos fine units are undoubtedly loess-like in a number of respects. The particle size distribution of 'typical' loess shows a pronounced mode in the range 20–40 μm and is positively skewed (Pye 1987).

A number of sedimentological comparisons were made between the Megalakkos sediments and loess samples from an exposure in the Doliana basin approximately 15 km west of the Voïdomatis basin. Figure 19.9 illustrates the relationship between silt content and $CaCO_3$ content, and these parameters show a clear separation between the two sample groups. The Megalakkos deposits are generally finer-grained (richer in clay) and contain more $CaCO_3$ than the Doliana loess sediments. It is unlikely that these contrasts are primarily a function of post-depositional modifications (*cf.* Woodward 1990). In addition, the distinctive vertical (prismatic) ped structure frequently present in loess sediments is largely absent in the Megalakkos sequence.

As well as these textural and lithological differences between the Megalakkos fine sediments and the Doliana loess, the geometry of the site and its local topographic setting combine to create an unfavourable location for aeolian deposition. In contrast to the local setting and aspect of the much larger Klithi rockshelter, where proximity to a well developed floodplain system afforded a ready supply of local windblown material, Megalakkos is situated in a narrow and steep-sided tributary ravine and this sheltered setting is not a favourable location for prolonged and repeated episodes of aeolian deposition. Furthermore, the youngest fine unit in the sequence, Unit 12, which is *c.* 75 cm thick, is unweathered and the top of this unit lies *above* the upper level of the shelter opening. This unit was probably deposited in Holocene times and may still be accumulating today.

Table 19.1. *Lithological and textural properties and organic content of the <63 μm fraction of the Megalakkos sediments. The facies groups are also shown. Asterisks indicate the presence of Palaeolithic material.*

Unit	Facies type	$CaCO_3$ %	Insoluble residue %	Clay %	Silt %	Non-carbonate silt %	Median size (φ)	Organic carbon %
12	A	36	64	29.8	70.2	34.2	6.86	0.08
11	C	54	46	8.8	91.2	37.2	5.82	0.11
10	A	35	65	25.6	74.4	39.4	6.34	0.08
9	B*	28	72	18.4	81.6	53.6	5.96	0.10
8	D	25	75	14.2	85.8	60.8	5.37	0.06
7	A	28	72	24.6	75.4	47.4	5.98	0.08
6	B*	26	74	22.6	77.4	51.4	5.89	0.10
5	A	28	72	38.0	62.0	34.0	7.43	0.05
4	B*	52	48	29.3	70.7	18.7	6.78	0.10
3	A	32	68	35.9	64.1	32.1	7.71	0.06
2	C*	54	46	13.4	86.6	32.6	5.82	0.12

Micromorphology and fine sediment laminations. Close examination of the Megalakkos fine units shows the presence of fine laminations. These laminae can be several millimetres in thickness, which suggests that these sediments were laid down in ponded water under low energy conditions (see Gillieson 1986). Intact sediment blocks were collected from Unit 7 for micromorphological analy-

suggests that they may be terminal Pleistocene cold climate sediments, and a modern date is thus highly unlikely. The seed from which this date was obtained may have been introduced by recent geomorphological or biological processes. It is clear that more dates are needed from the Megalakkos sequence to clarify its chronological relationship with the sediments at Klithi and with Late-Glacial events in the catchment. Additional samples submitted for dating, however, have failed to yield sufficient carbon even for AMS dating.

On the basis of radiocarbon dating, archaeological equivalence, and lithological similarities, the bulk of the Megalakkos sequence (Units 2 to 9) can be correlated with the central and upper sections of core Y25 at Klithi. It is notable that both sites contain a significant component of flysch-derived fine sediment. With the commencement of Palaeolithic occupation of Klithi and Megalakkos after *c.* 16 ka, the erosion and transfer of flysch-derived silts and clays through the karst system assumed greater importance, and this process had a profound impact upon the nature of rockshelter sedimentation in the Lower Vikos Gorge. It is notable that the cultural horizons at both sites contain a significant component of allogenic fine sediment although the ratio of aeolian to infiltrated sediment contrasts markedly between the two rockshelters.

Post-depositional alterations

Natural alteration

The bulk of the Megalakkos sediments has not been significantly altered by post-depositional processes. An important secondary feature in the sequence is the result of cementation processes which have selectively brecciated a section of the fill (*cf.* Bull 1983), particularly part of Unit 9. This calcite deposition has preferentially affected the northwest face of the site (Fig. 19.3) and seems to be taking place under modern conditions. Its selective operation along the west side of the bedrock wall and sediments is probably related to very local hydrological pathways. As mentioned previously, there is also some micromorphological evidence to suggest that secondary carbonate deposition has taken place within some of the Facies A Units (Fig. 19.10). In view of the importance of water-laid sedimentation at Megalakkos and the clear evidence of carbonate deposition within many of the units, it seems reasonable to conclude that the emergence of karst waters at Megalakkos has had a much more important influence on site sedimentation than at Klithi. It is evident that the local hydrogeology and related water quality parameters (such as suspended sediment and solute concentrations) have had a profound impact upon both primary and secondary sedimentation processes at Megalakkos. Indeed, it seems likely that the hydrogeological features of the host bedrock were also a major factor in site formation. By contrast, at Klithi, it appears that the behaviour of the Voïdomatis River and the lithology of its suspended sediment load were major determinants of rockshelter sediment properties.

The top of Unit 10 contrasts with the earlier fine beds in terms of its structure. This unit is characterized by a blocky ped structure which can be indicative of moisture deficiency (Birkeland 1984). The significant clay content of these sediments aids in the development of such ped structures, as clay mineral shrinkage accompanies dehydration. Unit 10 forms a very sharp contact with the overlying scree deposit and its distinctive structure may reflect desiccation and the onset of more arid conditions. The break in water-laid fine sediment deposition at the Unit 10/Unit 11 contact provides further support for this interpretation (Fig. 19.14).

The development of horizontal zonation at the top of Unit 11 provides the only indication of post-depositional chemical weathering in the sedimentary column. The unweathered matrix of Unit 11 is generally a creamy/light brown colour. This has been pedogenically altered, through partial decalcification, to a slightly reddened surface layer overlying a grey/brown horizon. This feature is not observed elsewhere in the sequence and could be the product of an increase in the solvent capacity of the moisture percolating into the sediments. This change in chemistry may reflect the influence of atmospheric precipitation locally seeping into the site possibly via the hole in the site ceiling.

Apart from these modifications, the most striking post-depositional change is the extensive erosion of the fill itself. The central part of the sequence has been eroded away leaving the precarious overhang formed by the mildly cemented Unit 11 (Fig. 19.3).

Human impact

The sedimentary units containing archaeological material are all dominated by coarse, angular limestone clasts. The matrix within these units is primarily flysch-derived fine sediment containing an abundance of fine charcoal fragments and some lithic and faunal debris. In general, there has not been any significant human impact upon the sedimentation style or physical properties of the deposits at

Megalakkos. Accordingly, the organic content of the Megalakkos sediments is quite low (Table 19.1) averaging 0.07 per cent for the Facies A sediments and 0.1 per cent for the Facies B sediments associated with human occupation. Organic material is similarly present in greater quantities in the cultural horizons within the Klithi rockshelter sediments. In contrast to Klithi, the sedimentological evidence at Megalakkos, e.g. distinctive and undisturbed sedimentary units, and presence of archaeologically-sterile units, suggests that the site was not a focus of intensive and prolonged occupation, and this is consistent with the archaeological evidence (Sinclair, Chapter 21).

Controls on sedimentation style and palaeoenvironmental implications

In palaeoclimatic terms, the observed variations in sedimentation style can be interpreted in at least two ways. Firstly, it is possible that the main influence on sedimentation style was local and regional climatic variability. Therefore, the sequence records episodes of freeze–thaw activity when sedimentary units consisting of coarse and angular limestone rock fragments derived from weathering of the site walls and ceiling were deposited. These deposits are present in two main types. They occur as crudely stratified and poorly sorted sediments in an abundant clay-rich matrix (Facies B). These sediments could indicate cold and humid conditions. Limestone clasts are also found in fairly well-sorted and finer-grained coarse units — characterized by a less extensive, predominantly silt-grade fine matrix (Facies C). These sediments may indicate the presence of cold and dry conditions. The archaeological material in the site is concentrated in the Facies B deposits and the upper 25 cm of Unit 2 (Table 19.1).

A particularly distinctive feature of the sedimentary fill is the recurrence of discrete, stoneless beds of clayey-silt (Facies A). These clay-rich units are normally interbedded within the coarser facies and record intervals of ponding in the site, when large amounts of clay-grade, allogenic material were able to accumulate, and freeze–thaw weathering was retarded. These sediments may indicate the presence of milder and more humid conditions than those of Facies

Figure 19.14. *Part of the northwest facing section in the Megalakkos fill (scale bar in cm). This part of the sequence is comparatively free from calcite cementation. This section shows the clay-rich facies A sediments of Unit 10 and its sharp upper contact with Unit 11 (Facies C). The contact between these units marks a significant change in sedimentation style. The deposition of water-lain clays and silts ends, and is followed by the accumulation of a considerable thickness (c. 0.75 m) of frost-riven, angular limestone clasts. These units are both archaeologically sterile.*

B and more humid conditions than those of Facies C. Because of their small size and irregular shape, discrete clay particles have very low fall velocities and will remain in suspension even in very slow-flowing waters. Thus, the deposition of Facies A sediments requires the presence of standing water in the rockshelter to facilitate sedimentation of the large clay fraction in these units and to permit the development of laminations and fining-upward features. The absence of coarse limestone clasts in these units suggests either that freeze–thaw processes were not important at this time or that these sediments accreted very rapidly. The considerable thickness of Units 3 and 12 in particular, and Unit 7 do not favour the latter interpretation. In addition, the very low energy conditions under which these sediments developed and the delicate sedimentary features highlighted by the micromorphological observations are probably not indicative of a rapid sedimentation rate within a rockshelter environment. In summary, these sediments suggest the presence of humid conditions in the site with the presence of pools of standing water and with freeze–thaw activity much reduced or absent. Unit 12 is at least 75 cm in thickness and forms the uppermost unit in the Megalakkos fill. This unweathered and uncompacted unit is probably of Holocene age (Woodward 1990) and supports the hypothesis that the fine units in the sequence accumulated under fairly moist and temperate conditions not dissimilar to those of the present day.

Alternatively, rather than invoking changes in Late Glacial climate, we might argue that part of the variability within the sequence represents fluctuations in the supply of flysch-derived fine sediment in response to local karst hydrological dynamics. The opening and closing of sediment-caked karst fissures — the influence of which could have been sufficient to *overprint* local and regional climatic influences — is one possibility. Such a theory implies that the observed inter-unit variations in the ratio of fine and coarse sediment components would simply be a consequence of changes in the rate of fine sediment *supply*. However, such an explanation is unlikely in view of the repeated alternation of sedimentation styles producing sedimentary units of comparable thickness implying a fluctuating *climatic* control rather than internal karst dynamics. The temporary plugging and clearing of underground limestone conduits is unlikely to be evenly spaced in time. Furthermore, the supply and movement of sediment and water to and through the karst system is often intimately linked to climate as this largely controls surface hydrology and vegetation cover (*cf.* Ford & Williams 1989; Gillieson 1986; White 1988).

The sharp contacts between the fine units and those units dominated by limestone debris indicate a relatively rapid shift in sedimentation style. The regular occurrence of these distinctive units requires the repeated operation of a particular assemblage of environmental conditions, i.e. humid conditions to produce sediment-laden karst drainage waters and standing water in the site, as well as a milder climate to repress freeze–thaw activity. On balance, the orderly and repeated fluctuation in sedimentation style is more likely to be a response to changing climatic factors rather than solely a product of local karst dynamics. If it is assumed that, as at Klithi, the end of Palaeolithic occupation at Megalakkos was between about 13 ka and 10 ka, then Unit 11, which effectively seals the archaeological horizons and implies a return to colder conditions, may be time-equivalent to the Younger Dryas Event (see Bailey *et al.* 1990; Woodward 1990). Overall, then, the sediment variations at Megalakkos suggests a climatic sequence which began with cold and dry conditions (Unit 2). The date at the top of this unit of 15.4 ka suggests that this climatic episode might represent the tail end of maximum glacial conditions, with archaeological evidence of occupation coming in at the very end of this period, while the radiocarbon date from Unit 4 suggests slightly earlier occupation at *c.* 16.1 ka. The initial occupation of the site was followed by a period of perhaps 5000 radiocarbon years of generally milder climate which fluctuated between colder conditions (Facies B sediments) and warmer and wetter conditions (Facies A sediments). This was terminated by a return to colder and drier conditions (Unit 11), tentatively associated with the Younger Dryas. It is important to note that the Last Glacial Maximum in the Pindus Mountains could not have been characterized by arid conditions as ice build up and glacier expansion at this latitude requires a plentiful supply of effective precipitation (*cf.* Sugden & John 1976; Woodward *et al.* 1994; 1995). In the absence of other sources of evidence, it is not possible to attach absolute values for ambient temperature and precipitation conditions for the Late Pleistocene from the rockshelter sedimentological data, which can give, at best, only indications of relative climatic changes.

Conclusions

The deposition of sediments eroded from flysch bedrock and soils and washed down into the karst drainage system is a distinctive feature of the sedimentary fill at Megalakkos. The accumulation of these flysch-derived clay-rich sediments in shallow pools of standing water after *c.* 16 ka may have been linked to a warmer climate and an increase in precipitation during the deglaciation of the catchment. This interpretation receives support from the core sequence at Klithi where a cessation in aeolian dust deposition in core Y25 is coeval with the initial occupation of the site at around 16 ka to 15 ka. Unfortunately, this interpretation cannot be corroborated by pollen data from Megalakkos itself, because preliminary studies showed that pollen had been introduced post-depositionally into these fine-grained sediments by biological activity (Willis, Chapter 20). At the same time, it is now well established that cave sediments are not an ideal medium for pollen studies (see Turner 1985) because of problems of differential preservation and the unknown residence times for pollen grains derived from within the karst system. Mineralogical analyses have demonstrated that these fine sediments, in common with a significant proportion of the sediments at Klithi, are derived from local flysch rocks and soils and are *not* the products of limestone dissolution. Micromorphological investigations have corroborated earlier field observations and confirmed that these sediments are infiltrates which were laid down in standing water and *not* windblown sediments.

The alternation of fine and coarse sedimentary units in the Megalakkos sequence records a period of fluctuating environmental conditions after *c.* 16 ka during the Late Glacial period. The archaeologically sterile sediments of Unit 11 may record a return to cold conditions at the end of the Late Glacial period. This event may be equivalent to the Youger Dryas cold phase, although this will only be confirmed by more detailed dating evidence.

In relation to the alluvial sedimentary record discussed in Chapter 17, the greater part of the sedimentary fill at Megalakkos probably accumulated during the deposition and subsequent incision of the sediments of the Vikos alluvial unit. The composition of Unit 8 demonstrates that flysch-derived alluvial sediments were being delivered to the Voïdomatis River between *c.* 15 ka and 12 ka via the tributary systems of the Lower Vikos Gorge. This is in accord with the composition of the fine sediments of the Vikos Unit (which contain a significant flysch component) and the inferred riverine/aeolian origin for part of the fine sediment within the middle and upper sections of core Y25 at Klithi (Woodward, Chapter 18).

The Klithi core record described in the previous chapter shows that the texture and lithology of the rockshelter sediments at Klithi have changed markedly during the Late Pleistocene. At Megalakkos, limited human use of the site has allowed preservation of a detailed (perhaps intact) primary sedimentary record that suggests the local environment was not constant during the period of Palaeolithic occupation, alternating between episodes of relatively warm and wetter climate and cold and humid conditions. An interesting feature of the Megalakkos fill is that the archaeological material begins in the upper 25 cm of Unit 2 and ends in Unit 9, and this represents almost 2 m of deposition. The sediments associated with human occupation at Klithi are also approximately 2 m in thickness. In contrast to Megalakkos, however, post-occupation and Holocene sediments at Klithi are not well developed and it is not clear whether this represents a real hiatus in deposition or levelling of the site in recent times (see Bailey & Woodward, Chapter 4).

In addition to broadly similar lithic and faunal assemblages, the limited number of radiocarbon dates from the archaeologically-rich sedimentary units suggests that the timing of human occupation at Megalakkos was broadly equivalent to the neighbouring rockshelter site of Klithi. The date of 8.8 ka in Unit 6 seems too young for the stratigraphic context, but since it is on a piece of burnt caprid bone, it indicates some human activity at this time. Unfortunately it has proved impossible to obtain additional dateable material from Unit 6, or from the stratigraphically younger Unit 9, which also contains archaeological material, to establish the upper chronological limit on human occupation at Megalakkos. Thus it remains unclear how much later than *c.* 15 ka human use of the site persisted into the Late Glacial.

Given the palaeoclimatic interpretation of the Megalakkos sediments, it would appear that the most favourable window of opportunity for Palaeolithic occupation in the lower Voïdomatis valley occurred in conditions intermediate between the cold and drier climate of the Last Glacial Maximum and of the Younger Dryas, on the one hand, and the warm and wet conditions of the Holocene (and perhaps of the milder episodes of the Late Glacial indicated by the Facies A sediments at Megalakkos), on the other hand. It is difficult to resolve further the relationship between human occupation and climatic fluctuations. The absence of archaeological remains in the Facies A fine-sediment units may reflect a temporary reduction in human presence in the wider Voïdomatis basin because of vegetational changes associated with milder climatic conditions that inhibited ibex-hunting, or quite simply the fact that the Megalakkos rockshelter itself became unsuitable for occupation because of damp conditions and standing pools of water. Progressive incision of the local tributary stream in the Late Glacial may also have made the site increasingly difficult of access. The absence of archaeological materials during the renewal of coarse sediment deposition in Unit 11 may simply reflect the unsuitability of the site for human use at this time because of reduced headroom within the shelter itself and a steep slope in front of the site, rather than the onset of colder climatic conditions. Here, as at Klithi, the evidence for assessing the impact of environmental and climatic changes on human occupation in the closing few millennia of the Last Glacial period and the period of transition to Holocene conditions is tantalizingly incomplete.

Acknowledgements

Most of the field and laboratory work reported here was carried out during the tenure of a SERC postgraduate research studentship at Darwin College, the Sub-Department of Quaternary Research (Godwin Laboratory) and the Department of Archaeology at the University of Cambridge. I am grateful to the SERC, Darwin College and the Henry Giles Fund for financial support. I thank IGME for providing geological fieldwork permits and the Department of Earth Sciences in Cambridge for allowing access to their analytical facilities and excellent technical support. Ken Pye provided helpful discussions on XRD analysis and John Lewin kindly arranged for the impregnation of sediment samples and for the production of thin sections for micromorphological analysis at the Institute of Earth Studies, University College Wales Aberystwyth. I am particularly grateful to John Lewin and Mark Macklin who discovered Megalakkos in July 1986 and carried out the initial survey and interpretation of the site with the author. Geoff Bailey provided many valuable comments during the preparation of this chapter.

Chapter 20

Vegetational History of the Klithi Environment: a Palaeoecological Viewpoint

Katherine Willis

Within a multidisciplinary study such as the Klithi project, the role of the palaeoecologist is to provide information on the environmental situation surrounding the sites from an ecological perspective, in particular, to focus on the type and scale of change in the plant community with changing environmental variables over time, and to identify the interrelationships between such changes and human activity. The following study concentrates on the analysis of lake sediments within the general vicinity of Klithi and Megalakkos rather than on the sediments from the rockshelter sites themselves. This reflects the poor preservation of pollen in the rockshelter deposits and the high risks of contamination, and the availability of sediments in small nearby lake basins within a *c.* 10 km radius, which may be expected to give a more reliable picture of local vegetational history on a spatial scale relevant to the behavioural catchment of the archaeological sites.

Three techniques have been employed: pollen and plant-macrofossil analysis for the reconstruction of the vegetational history; mineral magnetics and sediment chemistry for the reconstruction of the sedimentary environment in which the pollen and plant macrofossils were deposited; and AMS radiocarbon dating to provide a timescale. Pollen analysis is the primary study and will be the main focus. Results from the other techniques are briefly presented to corroborate interpretations, but are discussed more fully elsewhere (Willis 1992a,b,c).

Site selection

The primary archaeological evidence comes from the rockshelters of Klithi and Megalakkos, and thus the first and most obvious step in palaeoecological interpretation might seem to be the analysis of pollen from the rockshelter sediments themselves as a control on the sedimentological interpretations discussed earlier (Woodward, Chapters 18 & 19). Studies of cave pollen represent a well-established tradition, particularly in conjunction with sedimentological and archaeological analysis of rockshelter deposits, where the emphasis has typically been on the refinement of palaeoclimatological and chronological sequences (e.g. Laville *et al.* 1980). Poor preservation of pollen in such deposits, small sample size, risks of contamination, and uncertainties about sources of pollen and agents of transportation, pose formidable obstacles to interpretation (Sanchez-Goñi 1991; Turner 1985; Turner & Hannon 1988), although taphonomic biases may, in themselves, provide a potentially interesting additional source of information about the formation of a rockshelter deposit and the activities — human and otherwise — associated with it. Pilot studies of pollen were carried out on samples from Klithi and Megalakkos, and in both cases showed very poor preservation. In addition, at Klithi, the likelihood that modern pollen contaminants had been washed from the surface layers of goat dung into the loose and unconsolidated scree sediments that characterize the immediately underlying Palaeolithic levels was considered unacceptably high. At Megalakkos, the clay sediments that alternate with layers of scree (Woodward, Chapter 19) offer a potentially more favourable sedimentary matrix for recovery of pollen, but, apart from poor preservation, there is the additional problem that bees have bored nesting holes into the exposed sections.

On the other hand, the analysis of fossilized pollen within lake sediments has long been recognized as a highly versatile technique which can provide ecological information on a variety of scales about the composition of the surrounding vegetation, its density, and in certain instances total plant biomass. Work on the size of the basin in which pollen is deposited by atmospheric transport has indicated that the larger the basin, the greater the input of 'long distance pollen' (Bradshaw & Webb 1985; Jacobson & Bradshaw 1981; Tauber 1965; 1977). Conversely, the smaller the basin, the greater the percentage of pollen from local sources (Fig. 20.1). Basin size can therefore be used as a crude measure of the extent of the landscape represented in the pollen record.

The availability of small lake basins in the study area has obvious advantages, not only from the archaeological point of view, but also from the point of view of environmental interpretation. The Vikos Gorge contains one of the most diverse mixtures of central European and Balkan woody species in the Balkans (Polunin 1980). The wider region also offers large altitudinal differences over a small latitudinal range, which has resulted in a variety of micro-environments. The geology of the region is diverse, with alternating zones of flysch and limestone, each creating its own distinctive soil type, as well as intermediate soil conditions where flysch fans spread out over a limestone substrate (Bailey *et al.*, Chapter 16). Because of the great variation in environment over small distances, a large lake basin, such as the Ioannina Lake some 40 km distant from Klithi, which incorporates a regional pollen rain derived from many different landscape units over a large area, is clearly less suitable for identifying small-scale spatial variability in vegetation patterns, although it offers a long sequence of vegetational history extending through a substantial part of the Pleistocene (Bottema 1974; Tzedakis 1993; Turner & Sánchez-Goñi, Chapter 29).

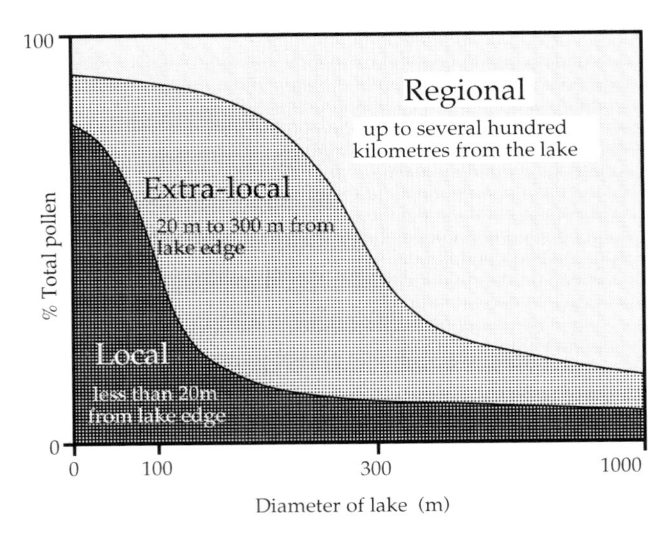

Figure 20.1. *Theoretical relationship between pollen source area and lake basin size. (After Jacobson & Bradshaw 1981.)*

The two sites selected for palaeoecological analysis, Gramousti Lake and Rezina Marsh, are each approximately 10 km from the Klithi rockshelter and at contrasting heights of 400 m asl (not 285 m as previously published) and 1800 m asl respectively. The distance between the two sites is approximately 20 km with the Klithi rockshelter located approximately mid-way (Fig. 20.2). Both basins are less than 500 m in diameter and thus each should contain a pollen record representative of a relatively local vegetation.

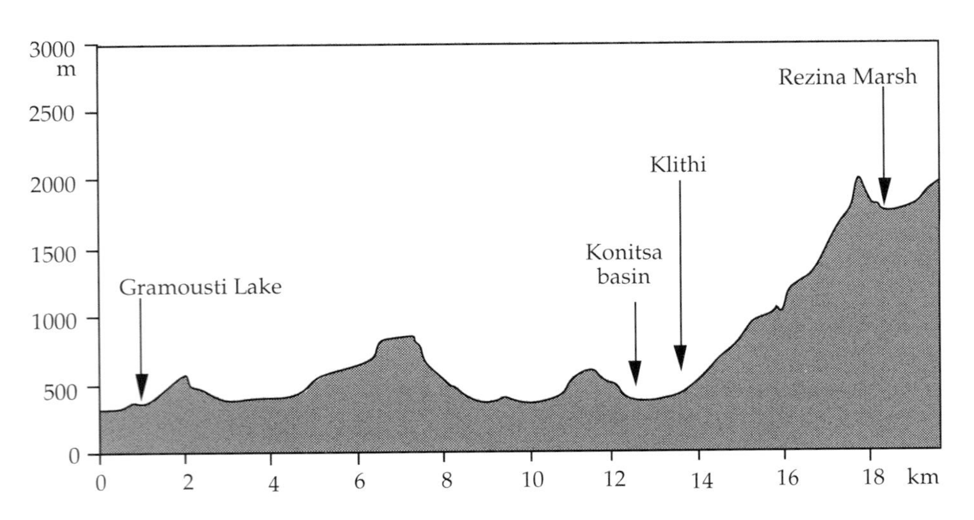

Figure 20.2. *Profile of topographical relief between the two palaeoecological sites of Gramousti Lake and Rezina Marsh. Also indicated are approximate positions of the Konitsa basin and the Klithi rockshelter.*

Gramousti Lake at 400 m asl is a drained lake basin within the wider environs of the Doliana basin (Fig. 20.3) and is situated on alluvial sands and gravels overlying Trias sediments which are composed of brecciated sandstone, siltstone, thick beds of anhydrite (calcium-magnesium sulphate) and dedolomotized limestone (IGRS/IFP 1966; Willis 1992a). The basin forms an irregular rectangle, with its long axis running approximately 500 m in an east–west direction. To the north it is bounded by steep limestone terrain, to the east and west by slopes of alluvial

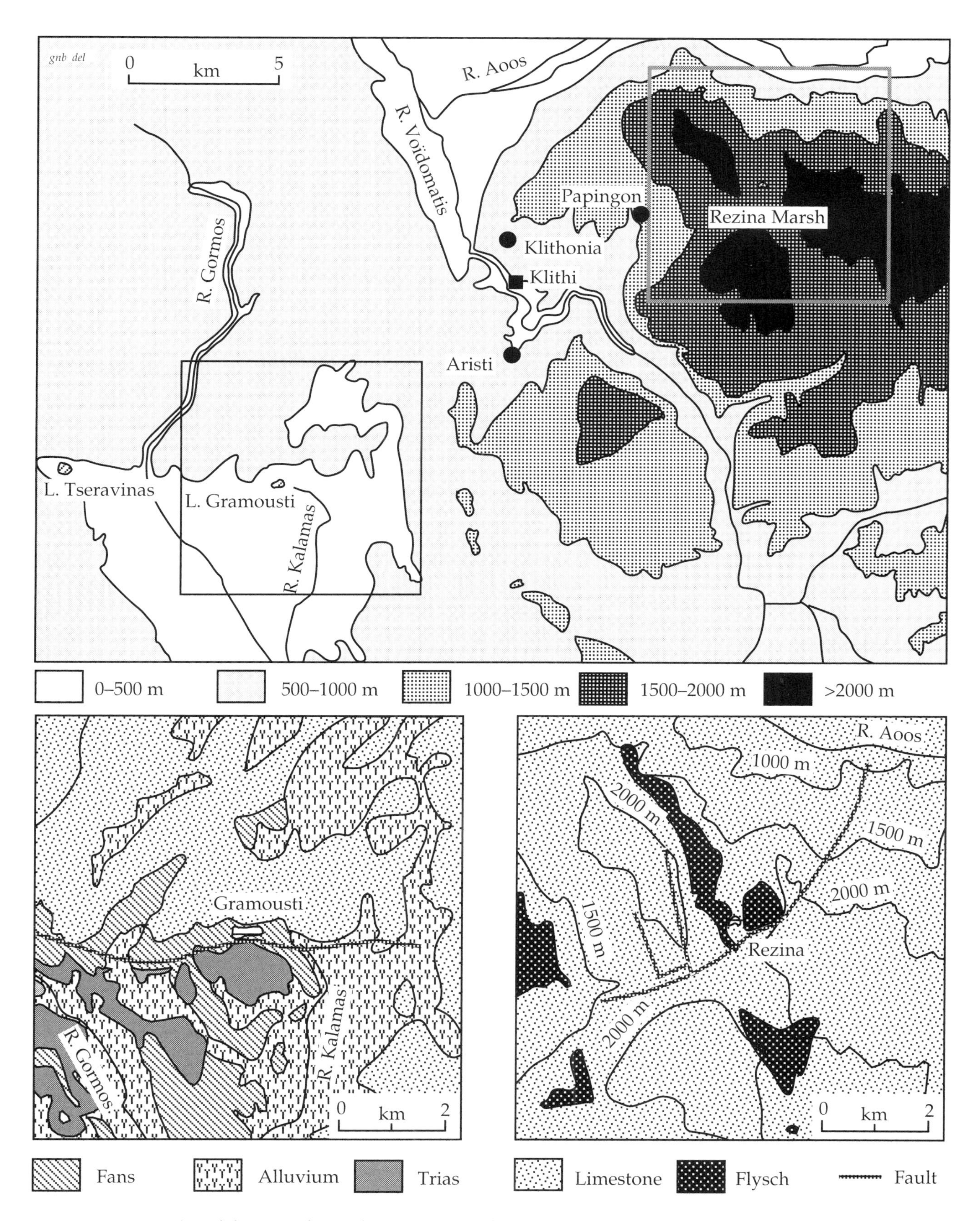

Figure 20.3. *Location of the two palaeoecological sites in relation to topography (upper), and the local geology around Gramousti (lower left) and Rezina (lower right).*

sands and gravels, and to the south by Triassic outcrops. There are no visible inlets and the basin is probably a hydrological feature of the limestone such as a doline. The present-day vegetation surrounding the basin is strongly influenced by anthropogenic activity, in particular grazing and agriculture. The slopes surrounding the basin are composed of 'chew-resistant' crops such as Christ's thorn (*Paliurius spina-christi*), Kermès oak (*Quercus coccifera*), cornelian cherry (*Cornus mas*) and hawthorn (*Crataegus monogyna*).

Rezina Marsh at 1800 m asl is the highest palaeoecological site to be studied in Greece and also the smallest (Willis 1992b). The marsh approximates the shape of an equilateral triangle, with sides 250 m in length, and is surrounded by alternating slopes of flysch and limestone. The topsoil on the flysch is heavily eroded and coarse limestone scree overlies much of the lower flysch slopes. The scree slopes are possibly a relict feature of the frost shattering that occurred during the last glacial period. The basin itself lies within an area of glacial till (Bizon 1970), and localized glaciation is known to have occurred in the region (Lewin *et al.* 1991; Macklin *et al.*, Chapter 17). The origin of the basin is uncertain but it is thought to be either a relict feature of glaciation such as a kettle-hole, or a tectonic basin. The region is tectonically active and a fault margin between the limestone and flysch runs in an east–west direction to the south of the basin (Fig. 20.3). As at Gramousti, the surrounding vegetation is heavily influenced by anthropogenic activity, although in this environment the effect is more dramatic. The vegetation is almost totally devoid of trees and is dominated by grasses and herbs. Areas of flysch that have been heavily grazed show signs of significant soil erosion, whereas heavily grazed areas on the limestone indicate little evidence of erosion (see King *et al.*, Chapter 28 for further discussion of erosion on flysch).

It should be noted that the advantages of spatial scale and resolution offered by Gramousti and Rezina are offset by certain disadvantages in the temporal dimension. The Gramousti sequence extends back to an estimated date of 13 ka, and thus overlaps with the latter part of the archaeological sequence in the Voïdomatis, while the Rezina sequence offers virtually no overlap at all, since it does not extend back beyond *c.* 10 ka. This is almost the exact converse of the Ioannina lake sequence, noted above, which offers excellent time-depth, but relatively poor chronological resolution, and very poor resolution in the spatial dimension. Lake Tseravinas, some 10 km to the west of Gramousti (Fig. 20.3), offers perhaps the best compromise between spatial and chronological resolution, since it is a relatively small basin but appears to have a long sequence. Cores have also been extracted from the upper part of the Tseravinas sediments (Turner & Sánchez-Goñi, Chapter 29). Notwithstanding these limitations, both the Gramousti and the Rezina sequence give important insights into the nature of the Late Glacial vegetation cover, as well as a detailed picture of the vegetational changes associated with the transition to Postglacial climatic conditions and subsequent developments.

Analytical techniques and methodology

The two basins were cored using a modified Livingstone piston corer (Wright 1967). Sediment to a depth of 18.45 m was collected from Gramousti Lake basin and to a depth of 12.42 m from Rezina Marsh. Samples were extracted from both cores for the analysis of mineral magnetics, sediment chemistry, pollen and plant macrofossils (Willis 1992a,b). From the Rezina core 105 levels were sampled for pollen, and from Gramousti 90 levels.

The usual method for reconstructing the vegetational history of a region is the construction of pollen percentage diagrams. However these are often of limited use in a more detailed assessment of the vegetation around a site because they do not take into account changes in plant biomass (Magri 1994). A region with a low plant biomass but with vegetation dominated by pine trees, for example, will produce a pollen percentage record that is similar to a pine-dominated vegetation high in plant biomass. In recent studies it has been shown that a more realistic estimate of plant biomass can be obtained from measurements of pollen concentration or pollen influx values (Magri 1994). Therefore, both pollen percentage diagrams and influx diagrams have been calculated in this study.

Pollen percentage data are based on a pollen sum of total land pollen excluding indeterminates. In the Rezina sum, Cyperaceae were also excluded and in the Gramousti sum, Umbelliferae and *Polygonum*, since macrofossil analysis revealed that these types were aquatic taxa growing in the lake and therefore not representative of the surrounding terrestrial vegetation (Willis 1992a,b). Selected percentage data of the two sites are plotted against age (Figs. 20.4–20.7). Also for descriptive purposes, zonation of the pollen diagrams into local pollen assemblage zones has been carried out using the BBCBASIC program SPLITINF and SPLITLSQ written by L.J. Maher Jr from an original FORTRAN program by Gordon & Birks (1972).

Pollen catchment areas

Analysis of local vegetational history requires comment on the inferred pollen catchment area of these two basins. Both basins are less than 500 m in diameter and therefore fit into that category of lake that receives most of its pollen from plants growing in the nearer vicinity rather than from the regional pollen rain (Jacobson & Bradshaw 1981). However, these terms need further definition in a study such as this, where the emphasis is on the relationship between archaeological sites and human land-use activities, and where the degree of spatial resolution is therefore of primary concern.

The term 'local' was first given an explicit definition by Tauber (1965; 1977) to refer to the vegetation up to 20 m from the depositional basin, while the term 'extra-local' was used to refer to pollen derived from distances of between 20 m and 300 m.

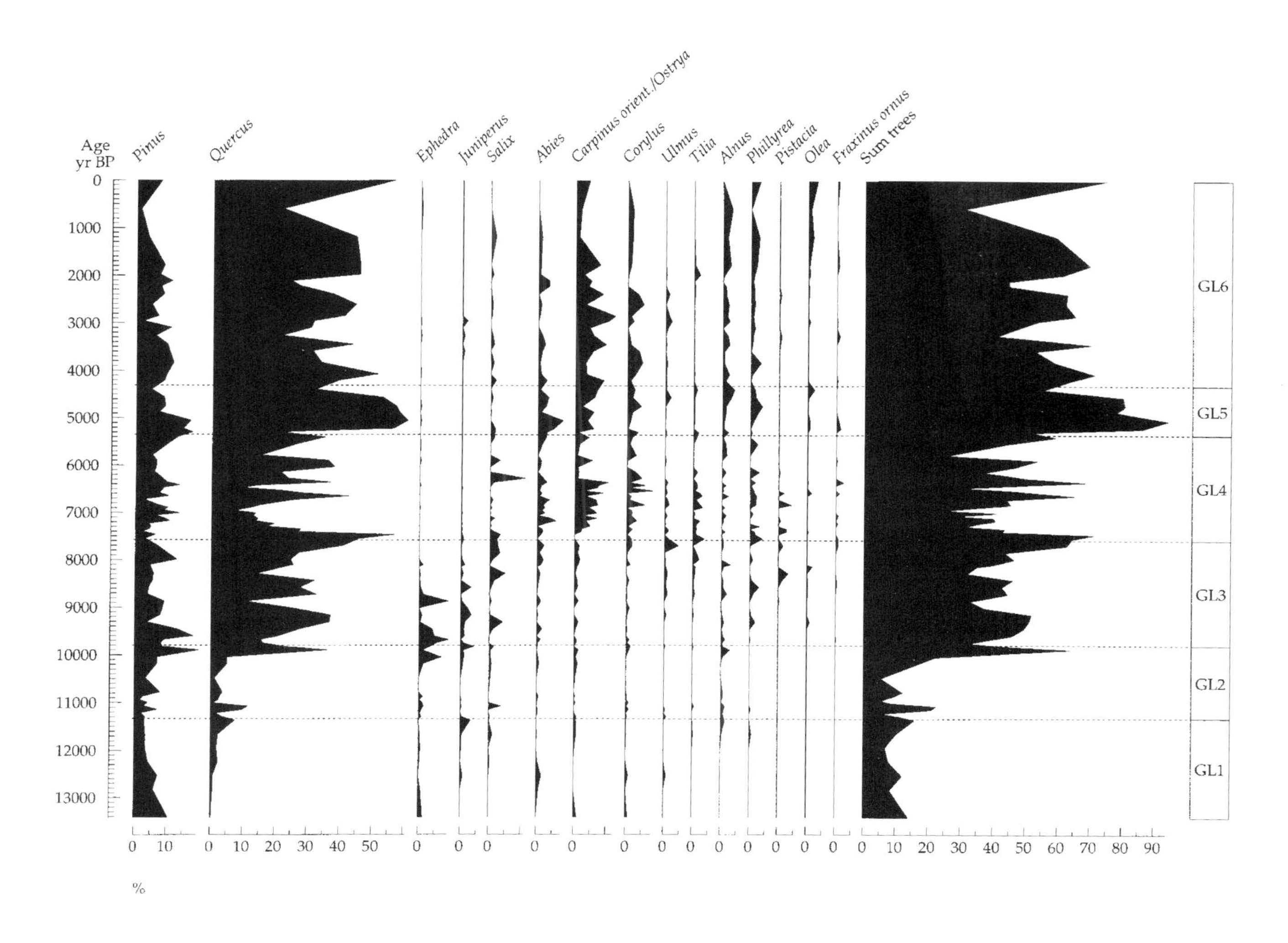

Figure 20.4. *Pollen percentage diagram of selected tree taxa from Gramousti Lake. The percentage of each taxon is plotted against a radiocarbon timescale.*

Local and extra-local pollen together refer to vegetation in the immediate surroundings of the basin. These figures should not, of course, be applied literally to all circumstances and need to be adjusted to allow for local topography, circulatory effects and so on, but they do highlight a useful contrast between pollen that records vegetation growing in relative proximity and pollen likely to have been brought in from much greater distances by the 'regional' pollen rain. Regional pollen rain is pollen brought in from greater distances by the action of wind in the upper atmosphere, and may come from distances of up to several hundred kilometres, depending on the size and dispersal characteristics of the pollen grains. The relationship between the proportion of pollen from these various sources and the size of the collecting basin is based on the principle that the larger the basin, the smaller the contribution of pollen from local and extralocal sources in comparison to pollen transported over long distances in the atmosphere (Fig. 20.1). The analysis of the pollen catchment area must also include information on the differential pollen productivities of the plants in the landscape. Copious pollen producers such as *Pinus* (pine) and *Quercus* (oak) are far more likely to be represented in the regional pollen rain than poor pollen producers or trees with low pollen dispersal characteristics such as *Tilia* (lime), *Ulmus* (elm) and *Abies* (fir) (Bradshaw & Webb 1985; Jackson 1990). Various studies have shown that presence within a pollen diagram of poor pollen producers such as elm, fir and lime usually represents a local stand rather than a regional presence (Gaudreau *et al.* 1989; Janssen 1966; Reille 1990). In a hydrologically closed basin such as Gramousti, therefore, it is expected that the majority of the pollen contained within the sediment will have come from local and extralocal sources, with only a small amount of regional pollen, most of which is likely to be from the more copious pollen producers. The term 'hydrologically closed', however, must also be qualified. The Gramousti basin is located within the much wider Doliana basin, at least 5 km in diameter, and at certain times of year pollen may be washed in from the slopes of this wider catchment, particularly pollen emitted during periods of snow cover in spring. Unlike the pollen that falls at other times of year, winter pollen falling on snow-covered slopes remains well preserved and could easily be washed into the lake by the spring meltwater. Thus, during spring the Gramousti basin must be considered as having a more extensive pollen catchment, probably including vegetation present within the wider Doliana basin.

Similar comments apply to the Rezina basin, although

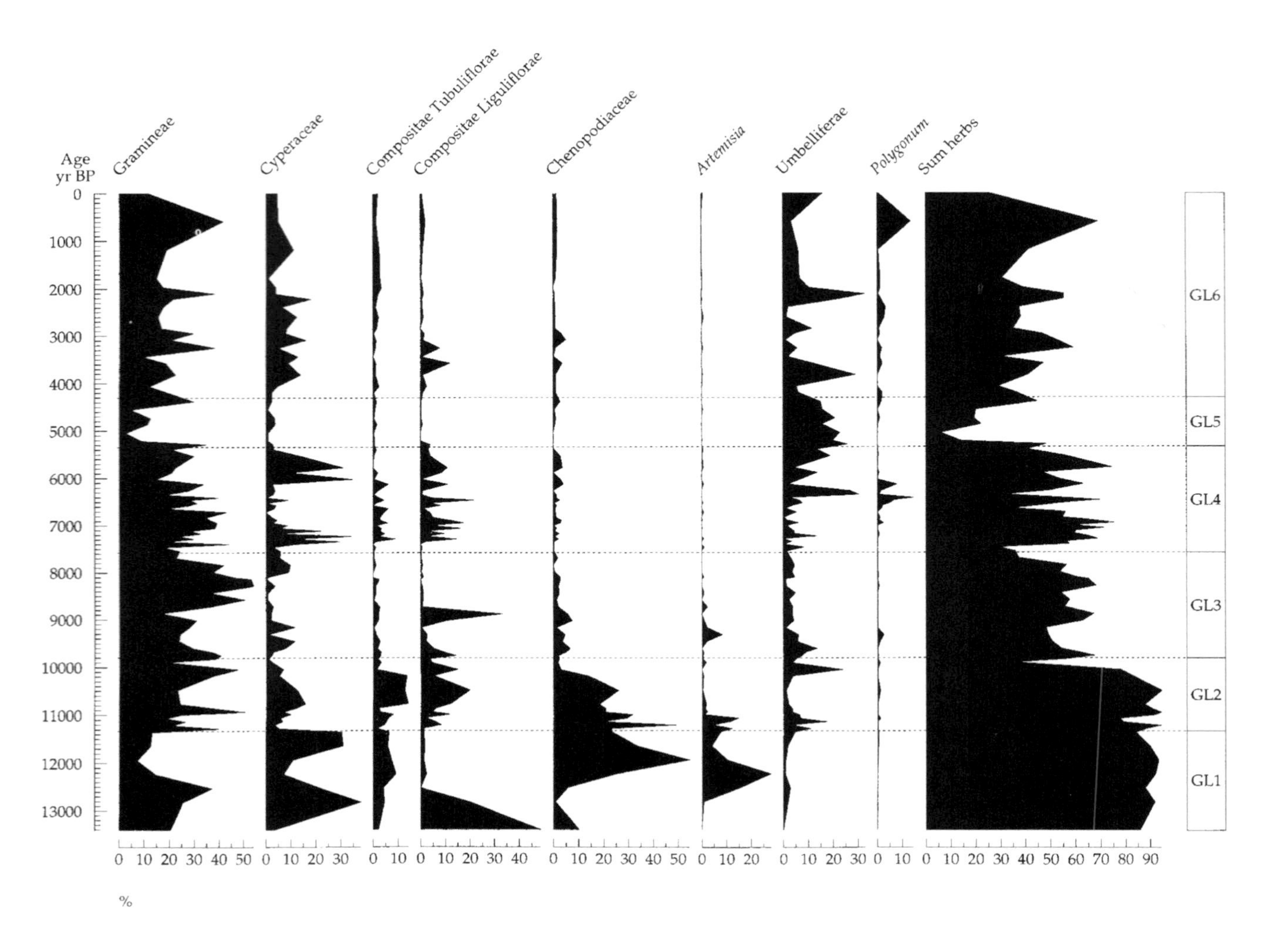

Figure 20.5. *Pollen percentage diagram of selected herbaceous taxa from Gramousti Lake. The percentage of each taxon is plotted against a radiocarbon timescale.*

circulatory effects have to be taken into account as well for this montane site. At a height of 1800 m asl, pollen transportation to Rezina Marsh will be strongly influenced by topography and associated climatic conditions (Willis 1992b; 1994). Work on the circulatory effects caused by anabatic, katabatic and convection winds in mountain regions has indicated varying degrees of effect upon pollen deposition (Davis *et al.* 1980; Gaudreau *et al.* 1989; Markgraf 1980; Solomon & Silkworth 1986). Markgraf (1980), for example, has shown that with increasing elevation, regardless of the density of the woodland, the proportion of long-distance pollen increases in the sample and finally surpasses local pollen production. Solomon & Silkworth (1986), however, demonstrate that in mountain regions constant values of deposition occur, irrespective of distance from the source, and that abundant pollen originates locally.

Studies by Davis *et al.* (1980) and by Gaudreau *et al.* (1989) indicate that dispersal from one elevation to another tends to be taxon specific. Markgraf (1980) also examined dispersal characteristics with elevation and found that of thirteen tree taxa, only four — *Pinus, Quercus, Alnus* (alder), *Corylus* (hazel) — were well dispersed. Of the remaining nine — *Fagus* (beech), *Ilex* (holly), *Hedera* (ivy), *Acer* (maple), *Ulmus, Picea* (spruce), *Abies, Tilia* and *Juglans* (walnut) — poor dispersal characteristics or low pollen production resulted in pollen deposition in close proximity. Thus the hypothesis that increasing elevation results in an increase in regional deposition can only be the case for certain taxa, and the presence of poor pollen producers in a montane pollen diagram cannot be dismissed as being the result of long-distance transport.

A brief study carried out on the present day pollen deposition at Rezina Marsh (Willis 1992b; 1994) shows that pollen from eight tree types — *Pinus, Alnus, Carpinus orientalis/Ostrya* (hornbeam), *Quercus, Juglans, Corylus* and *Juniperus* (juniper) — which are known to be growing on the lower western flank of the mountain in the vicinity of Papingon up to an elevation of approximately 1200 m asl (Polunin 1980), were present in the pollen rain and must have been carried 600 m up the mountain as a result of circulatory currents (Table 20.1). The absence, however, of pollen from other trees also growing on the western flanks, such as *Tilia, Ulmus, Acer, Abies, Fraxinus* (ash) and *Phillyrea*, is equably notable. This suggests that if pollen from these latter taxa are present in the sediments at Rezina Marsh, the trees must in all probability have grown nearer to the site than they do at the present day. Thus tree pollen in the Rezina sediments may represent trees growing in the near vicinity of the basin, or trees growing further away on the lower mountain slopes, depending on the taxon.

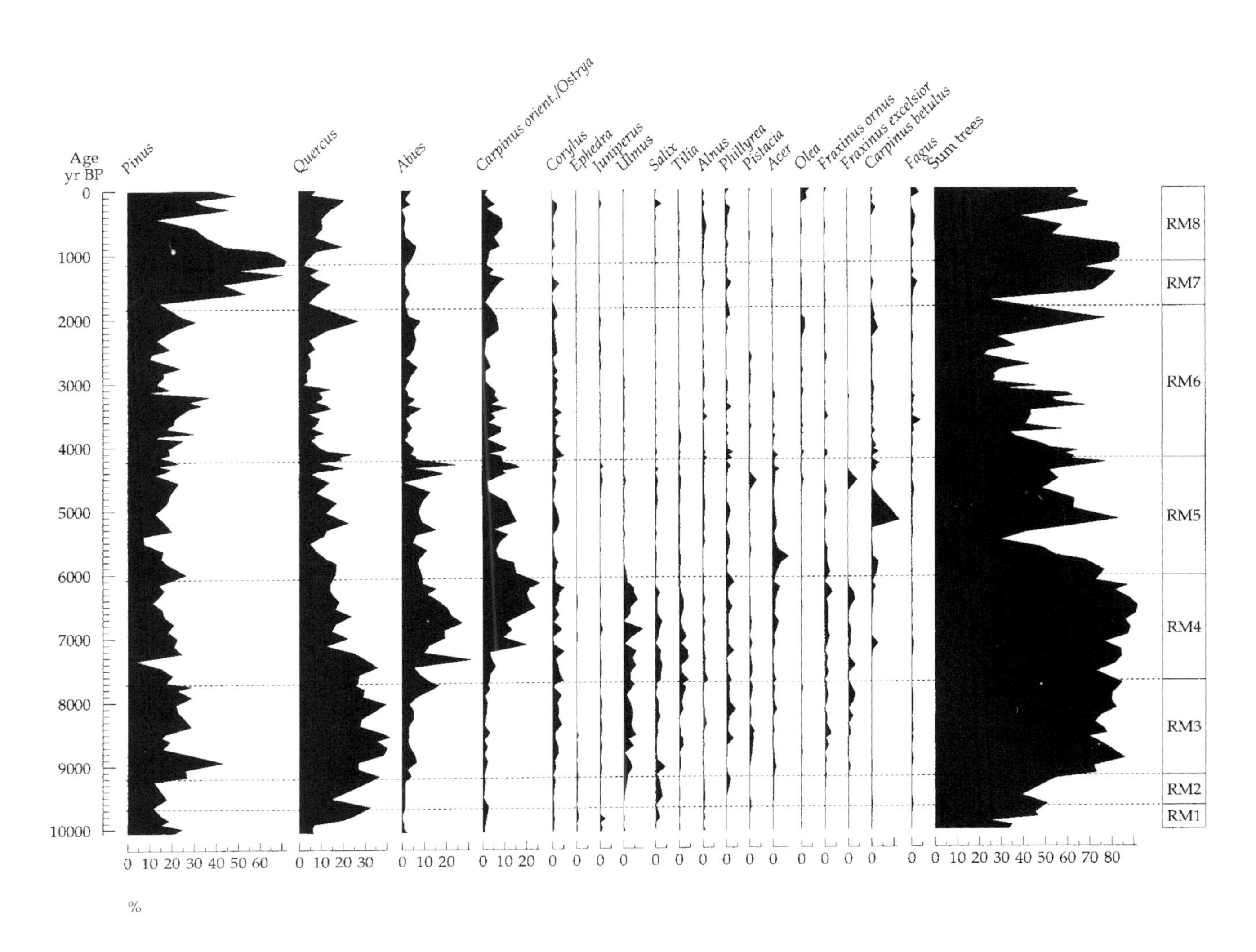

Figure 20.6. *Pollen percentage diagram of selected tree taxa from Rezina Marsh. The percentage of each taxon is plotted against a radiocarbon timescale.*

The question of the enlargement of the pollen collecting source at Rezina Marsh through seasonal snow must also be addressed. In the mountains this effect is probably more pronounced because of the increased length of time that the ground is covered by snow (up to six months). As at Gramousti, therefore, the potential size of the pollen catchment must be viewed as varying with season.

Pollen influx and plant biomass

An important consideration when analyzing pollen data is that different plants produce different amounts of pollen. This leads on to the further consideration that the pollen output of different vegetation types may vary, such as tundra, boreal forest, and temperate forest. In a study of surface samples, for example, Ritchie & Litchi-Federovich (1967) demonstrated that modern values of pollen influx (grains cm^{-2} $year^{-1}$) are highest for northern coniferous forest and decrease in value for tundra (dwarf-shrub), tundra (moss-sedge) and rock-desert respectively. Davis *et al.* (1973; 1975) found similar variations in influx values, but showed that the highest values are from mixed coniferous-deciduous forest and deciduous forest, and that influx values of similar vegetation units vary considerably from area to area. From these studies, two interesting relationships emerge: (1) there is a marked decline in pollen influx in areas beyond the tree limit; (2) the modern pollen influx from forest communities shows a much broader range of values than from herbaceous formations (Magri 1994).

Magri's (1994) interpretations provide the basis for an alternative approach to the analysis of pollen influx data. Variations in pollen influx between different vegetation types represent variations in biomass. Changes in influx at a site, therefore, can be interpreted as being representative of changing plant biomass over time. For example, a change from tundra vegetation to coniferous forest would be represented by an increase in total pollen influx in the sediment.

In order to examine the changes in total pollen influx at Gramousti and Rezina, frequencies of total tree pollen and total herbaceous pollen are presented as influx values (cm^{-2} $year^{-1}$) (Figs. 20.8 & 20.9). Figures 20.8 and 20.9 also show the ratio of tree pollen to herbaceous pollen in terms of influx values. Magri (1994) applied this ratio to the 250,000 year sequence from Valle di Castiglione (Follieri *et al.* 1988), and found that through time the concentration of herbaceous pollen hardly altered, whereas the concentration of tree pollen increased significantly at the

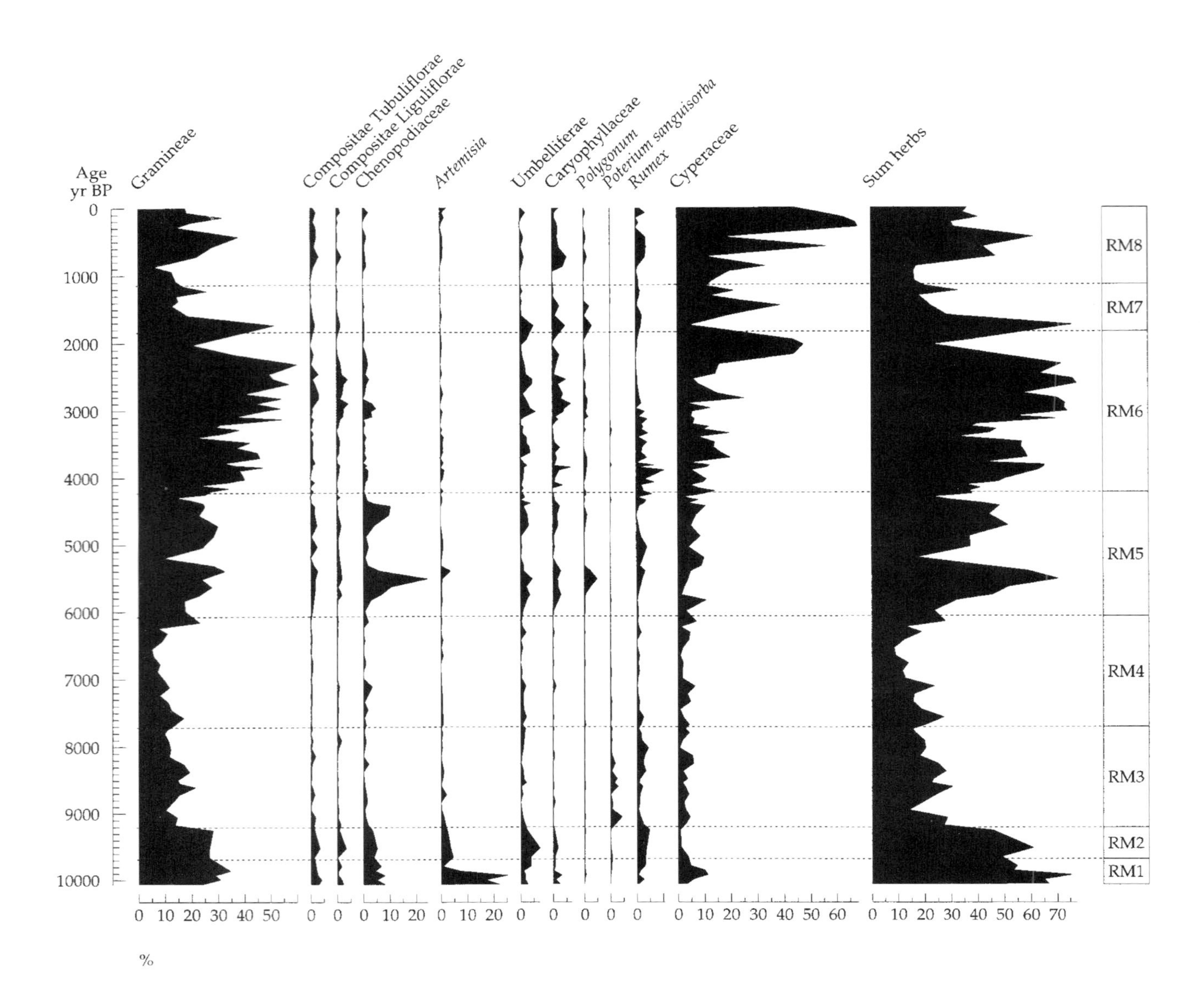

Figure 20.7. *Pollen percentage diagram of selected herbaceous taxa from Rezina Marsh. The percentage of each taxon is plotted against a radiocarbon timescale.*

beginning of each interglacial and then decreased at the end.

The ratio of tree pollen to herbaceous pollen influx-values also provides a means of assessing the sediment accumulation rate. Normally a linear relationship is assumed, and the radiocarbon dates are used to determine the average sedimentation rate. However, this is far from ideal, because the relatively poor chronological resolution of radiocarbon dating may obscure short-term fluctuations in rates of sediment accumulation. Correlated sharp peaks in the influx of tree taxa and herbaceous taxa can be seen in both the Rezina and Gramousti influx diagrams. It is difficult to imagine an environment where tree biomass and herbaceous biomass both show a simultaneous and rapid increase, and the most obvious explanation for these peaks is short-term fluctuations in sediment accumulation. The ratio of tree to herbaceous pollen influx-values thus makes it possible to control for the 'noise' of varying sedimentation rates and to achieve more realistic interpretations.

The combination of pollen percentages and pollen influx-values, thus, gives information not only on the diversity and composition of the vegetation but also on its biomass. One note of caution, however, must be added. As mentioned at the beginning of this section, the quantity of pollen produced by various plants must also be taken into account when considering plant biomass. A woodland dominated by poor pollen producers such as lime, elm and fir, for example would give much lower influx values than a woodland dominated by pine and oak, and this is an added factor that needs to be taken into account in interpretation.

Plant macrofossil analysis

Plant macrofossils are well preserved in both sequences, represent plant taxa growing in the immediate vicinity of the lake, and are often easier to identify to species level than the corresponding

Table 20.1. *Results from the measurement of present day arboreal pollen rain at Rezina Marsh (taken from four sample sites on surface of marsh), compared to trees and shrubs growing up to 1600 m in the northern Pindus Mountains (Polunin 1980). (From Willis 1994.)*

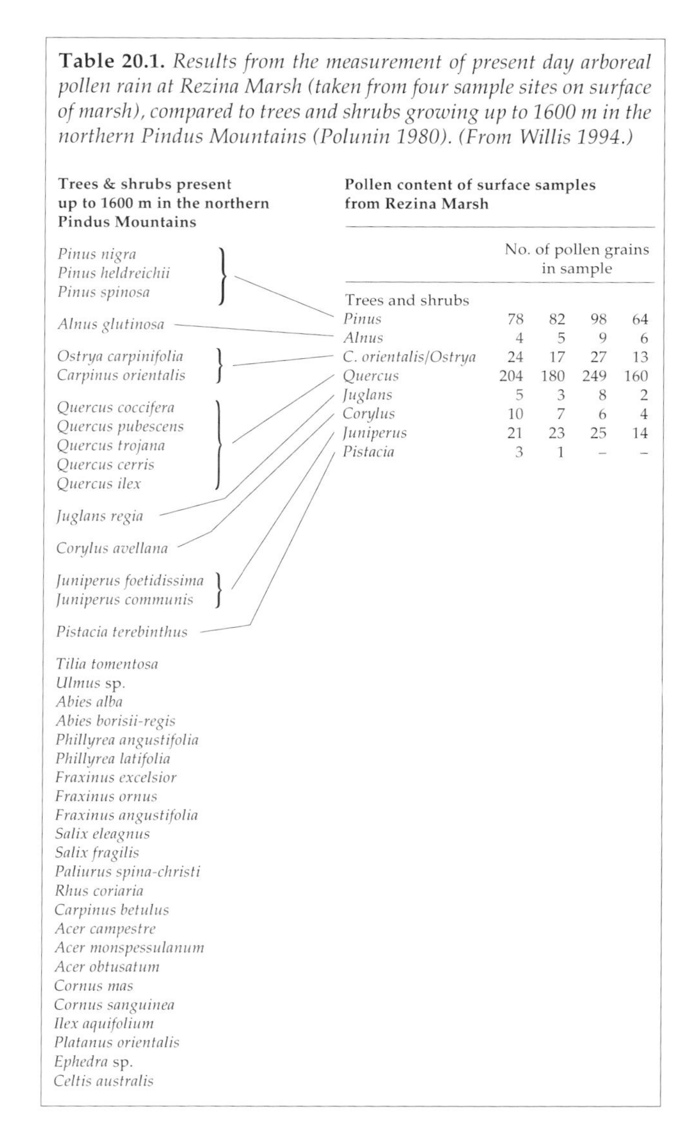

Trees & shrubs present up to 1600 m in the northern Pindus Mountains

Pinus nigra
Pinus heldreichii
Pinus spinosa
Alnus glutinosa
Ostrya carpinifolia
Carpinus orientalis
Quercus coccifera
Quercus pubescens
Quercus trojana
Quercus cerris
Quercus ilex
Juglans regia
Corylus avellana
Juniperus foetidissima
Juniperus communis
Pistacia terebinthus
Tilia tomentosa
Ulmus sp.
Abies alba
Abies borisii-regis
Phillyrea angustifolia
Phillyrea latifolia
Fraxinus excelsior
Fraxinus ornus
Fraxinus angustifolia
Salix eleagnus
Salix fragilis
Paliurus spina-christi
Rhus coriaria
Carpinus betulus
Acer campestre
Acer monspessulanum
Acer obtusatum
Cornus mas
Cornus sanguinea
Ilex aquifolium
Platanus orientalis
Ephedra sp.
Celtis australis

Pollen content of surface samples from Rezina Marsh

Trees and shrubs	No. of pollen grains in sample			
Pinus	78	82	98	64
Alnus	4	5	9	6
C. orientalis/Ostrya	24	17	27	13
Quercus	204	180	249	160
Juglans	5	3	8	2
Corylus	10	7	6	4
Juniperus	21	23	25	14
Pistacia	3	1	-	-

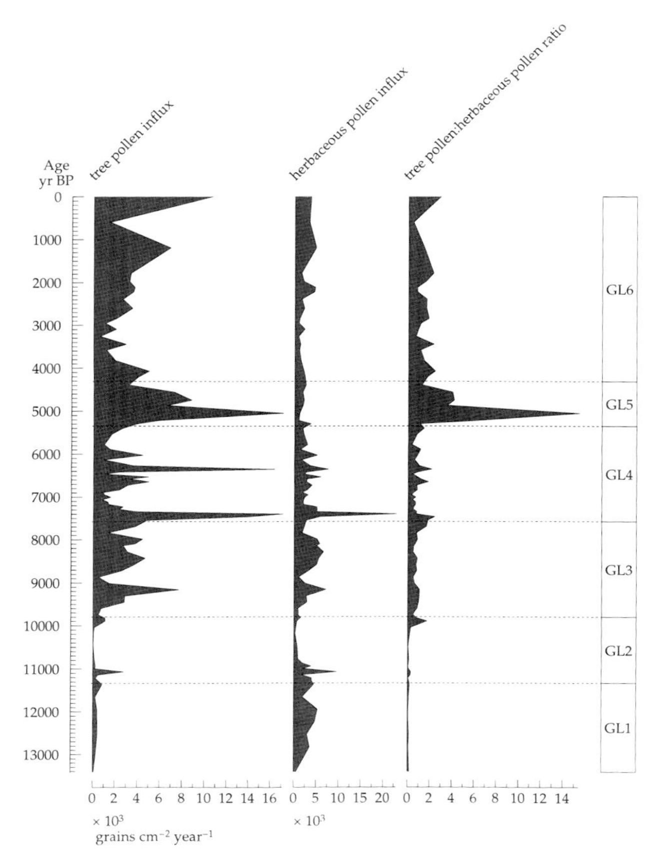

Figure 20.8. *Pollen influx diagram of total tree and total herbaceous pollen influx (grains cm^{-2} year^{-1}) from Gramousti Lake. Also plotted is the ratio of tree pollen influx to herbaceous pollen influx.*

pollen. In this study plant macrofossil analysis has concentrated on those taxa which are well represented in the pollen record but whose pollen is not identifiable to the species level (Figs. 20.10 & 20.11).

Mineral magnetics and sediment chemistry

Two types of magnetic measurement have been made on the sediments — magnetic susceptibility and magnetic quadrature (Figs. 20.12 & 20.13). Magnetic susceptibility can be described as a measure of the ease with which material can be magnetized, and gives an indication of the fraction of magnetic grains contained within a sample (Thompson & Oldfield 1986). Magnetic quadrature measures the percentage difference between grains with high magnetic frequencies and those with low magnetic frequencies. Materials with high magnetic frequencies tend to be fine-grained and magnetically enhanced, and include materials such as topsoil and aeolian dust (Mullins 1977). Gramousti and Rezina are in predominantly limestone catchments, so that sediments derived from the local bedrock are likely to have low concentrations of magnetic material (Thompson & Oldfield 1986). It is thus reasonable to assume that the presence of high frequency magnetic material represents inwashed material derived from sources other than the local bedrock such as surface erosion. Sediment samples have also been analyzed for the presence of sodium, magnesium, iron, calcium and manganese. Downcore variations in these elements can indicate changes occurring within the basin and on the surrounding slopes, and provide a useful complement to variations in pollen frequencies (Figs. 20.12 & 20.13). Broad trends are presented here to aid in the interpretation of the pollen data, while fuller details are presented elsewhere (Willis 1992a,b).

Radiocarbon dating

Given the calcareous nature of the lake environments, accelerator dating has been used to obtain radiocarbon dates, because of the facility for dating small samples and thus for avoiding the problem of hard-water contamination commonly encountered when dating larger samples by conventional techniques. Dates have been obtained for six samples of organic material spaced evenly throughout the Gramousti core and seven samples evenly spaced in the Rezina core (Hedges *et al.* 1990) (Table 20.2; Gowlett *et al.*, Chapter 2).

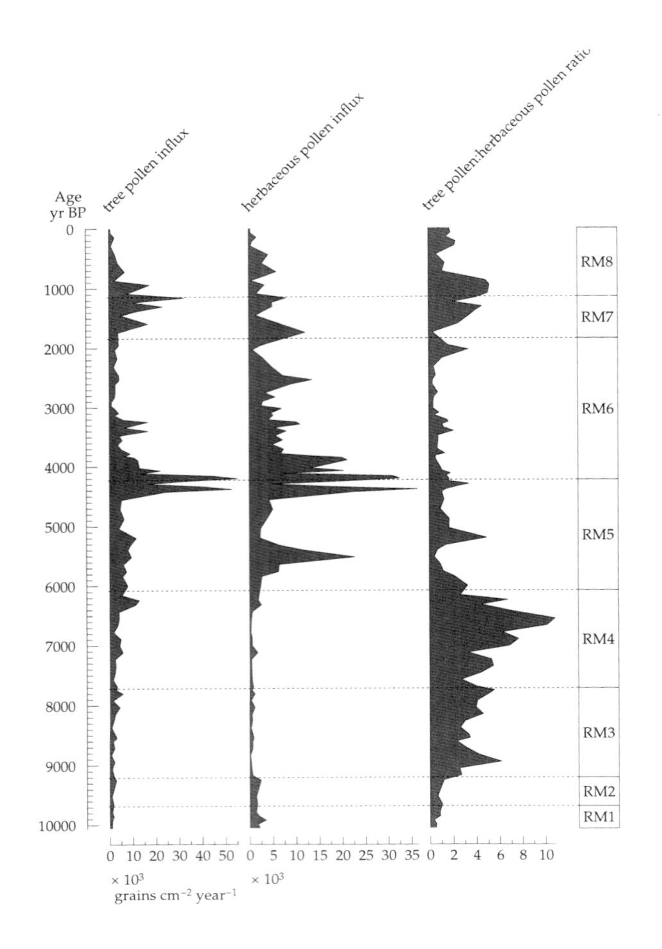

Figure 20.9. *Pollen influx diagram of total tree and total herbaceous pollen influx (grains cm^{-2} year^{-1}) from Rezina Marsh. Also plotted is the ratio of tree pollen influx to herbaceous pollen influx.*

Environmental reconstruction

Discussion of the environmental reconstruction is divided below into four sections: Late Glacial; Late Glacial/Postglacial transition; early Postglacial; and the later Postglacial, which is a period of widespread anthropogenic disturbance.

Late Glacial of the Klithi region (13,000–9800 BP)

In this discussion the Late Glacial is taken to represent the time period represented in the Gramousti diagram by zones GL1 and GL2, estimated to be between 13,000–9800 BP (see Gowlett *et al.*, Chapter 2 and Turner & Sánchez-Goñi, Chapter 29 for discussion of dating problems). Because of the uncertain representation of the Late Glacial in the Rezina diagram, most of the discussion in this section will be confined to the results from the Gramousti profile. From evidence in the pollen percentage diagram (Figs. 20.4 & 20.5), the temptation would be to classify the vegetation around the Gramousti basin during the Late Glacial as sparse tundra made up of open-ground herbaceous types such as grasses, *Artemisia*, Chenopodiacae, and Compositeae with large areas of open uncovered ground. However, an

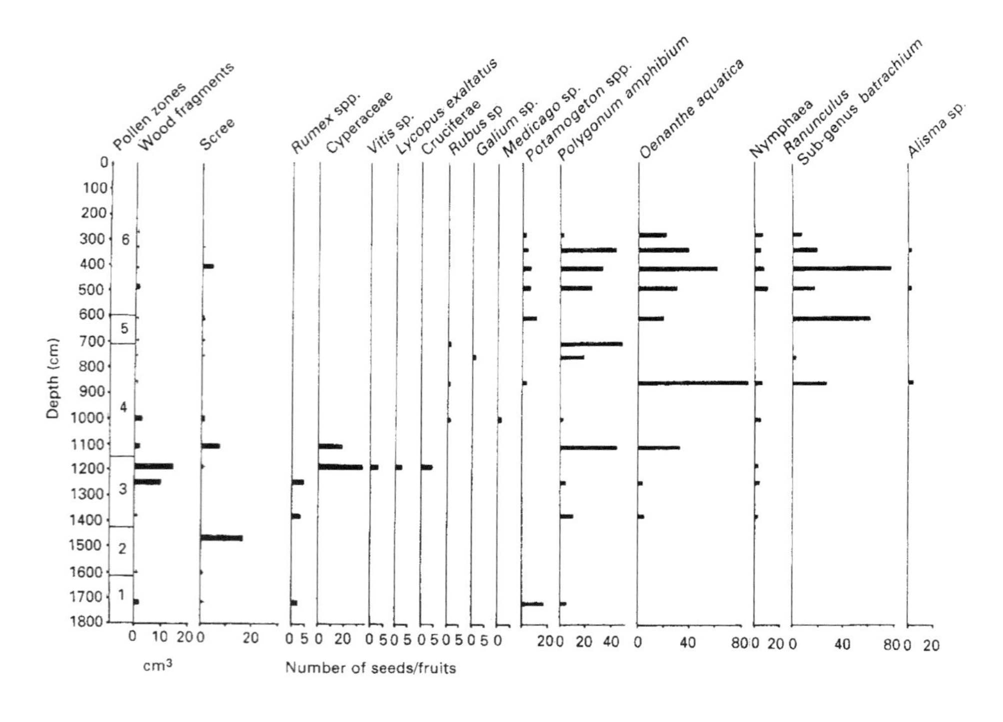

Figure 20.10. *Plant macrofossil diagram from Gramousti Lake. (Redrawn from Willis 1992a.) The number of macrofossils contained within each sample (160 cm³ of sediment) are plotted against depth.*

examination of the pollen influx and inferred plant biomass would suggest otherwise. Between 13,000 BP and 10,600 BP herbaceous pollen influx averaged 4500–5000 grains cm^{-2} yr^{-1}. Influx values from present-day tundra ecosystems (e.g Ritchie & Litchi-Federovich 1967) may be around 53–763 grains cm^{-2} yr^{-1}, and Davis *et al.* (1973) measured an influx of 1120–2000 grains cm^{-2} yr^{-1} for tundra (dwarf-shrub). The higher values at Gramousti thus suggest that the vegetation from around the Doliana basin was far from sparse, and thus the term 'steppe' is preferred to 'tundra'. Admittedly, there are problems in comparing ecosystems from different time periods and geographical regions, but some further support for the interpetation offered here is provided by a comparison of Postglacial herbaceous-pollen influx-values with Late Glacial values. This suggests that the density of herbaceous vegetation was no less in the Late Glacial than in the Postglacial.

The few trees present in this Late Glacial vegetation included oak and pine, although the low percentage of these two types, accounting for only 15 per cent of the total pollen sum, suggests that the pollen was brought in from at least as far as the wider Doliana basin, rather than from local or extralocal sources. Other trees and shrubs present are *Ephedra* (joint pine) hornbeam, willow (*Salix*) and fir. Again, it is probable that these were growing within the wider catchment of the Doliana basin. Sediment influx during this time contains a high input of magnesium, probably allogenic in origin, eroded from the surrounding slopes.

The Late Glacial environment around Rezina Marsh can only be inferred by extrapolation from the very base of the pollen profile (RM1), which probably spans the boundary between the latest part

Table 20.2. *Radiocarbon age determinations from Gramousti Lake and Rezina Marsh. Three dates (OxA-1748, OxA-1600, OxA-1652) were excluded from calculation of the age-depth curve (Willis 1992a,b; see also Chapter 2).*

Depth (cm)	Material	Age (yr bp*)	Laboratory no.
Gramousti Lake			
278	leaf litter	1930 ± 180	OxA-1502
482	wood	7880 ± 140	OxA-1748
854	wood	6330 ± 180	OxA-1749
1182	wood	7490 ± 110	OxA-1446
1375	wood	9260 ± 170	OxA-1447
1600	wood	8790 ± 150	OxA-1095
Rezina Marsh			
510	leaf litter	2990 ± 80	OxA-1650
686	wood	3830 ± 60	OxA-1652
904	*Abies* needle	4440 ± 150	OxA-1379
1092	wood	6320 ± 130	OxA-1380
1193	wood	9200 ± 130	OxA-1381
1234	wood	9890 ± 120	OxA-1094

* uncalibrated dates in radiocarbon years before present using the Libby half life of 5570 years.

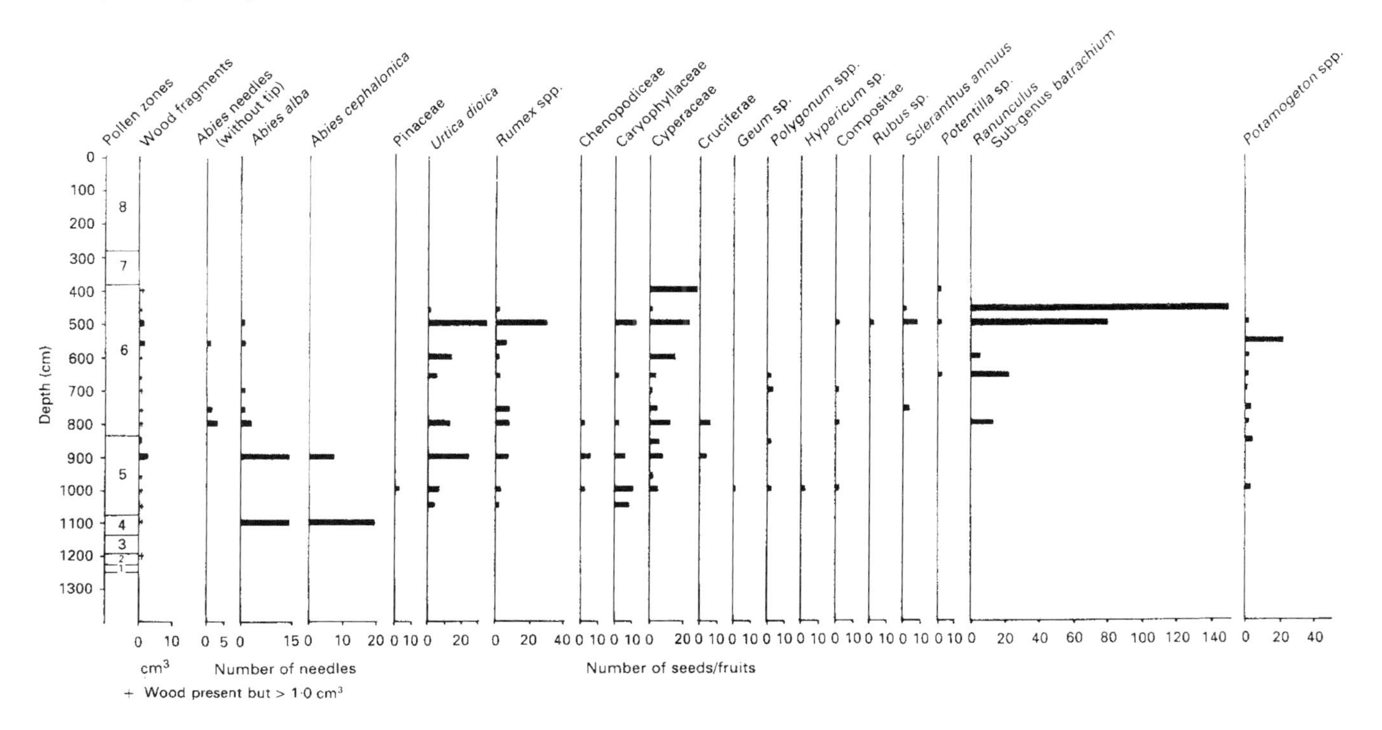

Figure 20.11. *Plant macrofossil diagram from Rezina Marsh. (Redrawn from Willis 1992b.) The number of macrofossils contained within each sample (160 cm³ of sediment) are plotted against depth.*

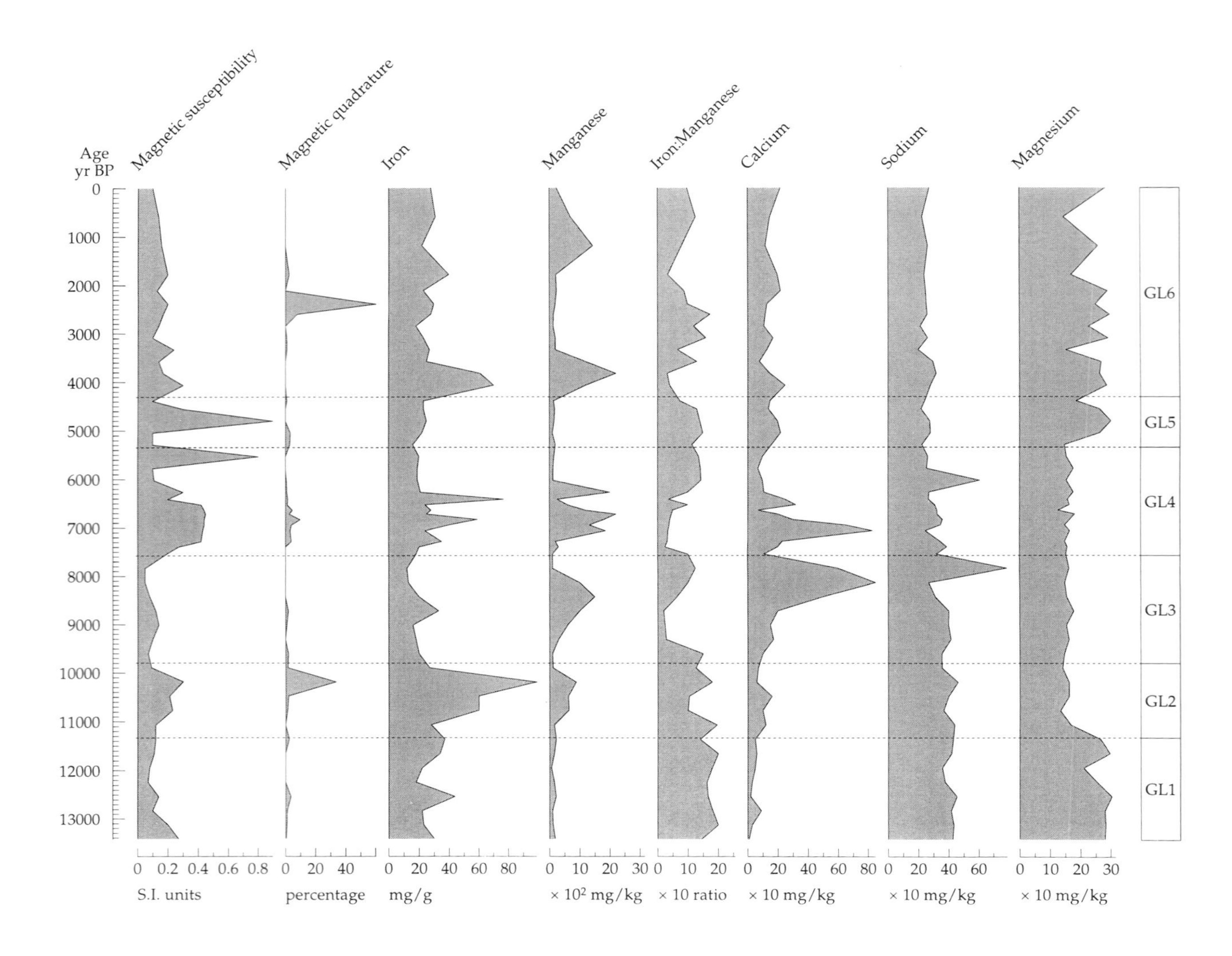

Figure 20.12. *Magnetic characteristics (SI units) and elemental concentrations of the Gramousti core plotted against an estimated timescale. Pollen zone boundaries are shown for comparison.*

of the Late Glacial and the earliest Postglacial. Allowing for that uncertainty, the Rezina data suggest a comparable Late Glacial environment to the Gramousti basin in that vegetation representative of a steppe community covered the slopes around the basin (Figs. 20.6 & 20.7) However, there are also significant differences. Although dominated by grasses, sedges, Chenopodiaceae and *Artemisia,* the pollen diagram also indicates the presence of a variety of trees including pine, oak, fir, hornbeam, hazel, *Ephedra,* elm, willow, lime and alder. As at Gramousti, pine and oak pollen may be the product of long-distance transport, but the presence of elm, lime and fir, even at low percentages, suggests that these were growing quite close to the site, at least by about 10,000 years ago.

It is also interesting to compare the pollen influx values (Figs. 20.8 & 20.9). In the Gramousti basin at the end of the Late Glacial the ratio of tree pollen to herbaceous pollen is approximately 0.2:1. In comparison the tree pollen to herbaceous pollen influx-ratio at the base of the Rezina diagram is on average 1:1, suggesting a denser tree cover. The tree taxa contributing to these influx values also differ between the two sites. At Gramousti the tree pollen comprises the high pollen producers oak and pine. At Rezina oak and pine also contribute to the pollen influx, but the presence of low pollen producers such as fir, elm and lime suggests that trees of these taxa were growing closer to Rezina at an earlier date than at Gramousti. It is, therefore, inferred that small pockets of Late Glacial refugia for temperate tree taxa

vegetation around Gramousti and Rezina between 5000 and 4300 BP, further signs of anthropogenic activity can be detected from approximately 4000 BP onwards. The impact of anthropogenic influence, however, had differing effects at the two sites, and the present-day contrast was probably established at this time. In the lowlands around Lake Gramousti, an oak and hornbeam woodland became established, and, as mentioned above, probably consisted of the more chew-resistant species. Input of allogenic material from the slopes surrounding the basin increased (Fig. 20.12) and in particular, magnesium shows an increase from 4000 BP to the top of the core (Willis 1992a); this is taken to be indicative of a variable vegetation cover resulting in the leaching of magnesium from exposed topsoil.

In the mountains, the initial removal of the wooded vegetation and the subsequent grazing activity resulted in irreversible damage. From approximately 4300 BP onwards, the sedimentary evidence suggests that large-scale topsoil erosion occurred (Fig. 20.13) and herbaceous taxa such as Chenopodiaceae, Umbelliferae and Rumex became established on the disturbed soils (Willis 1992b). The soils were no longer able to support a diverse woodland, and probably an environment similar to the present day became established around the basin. The pollen influx-ratios also record this trend. A large increase in the sedimentation rate at around 4000 BP is also reflected in the rapid increase in influx of both tree and herbaceous pollen (Fig. 20.9). The ratio of tree pollen to herbaceous pollen falls to around 1:1, its lowest level since the Late Glacial period, and the tree pollen is probably from the regional pollen rain rather than from trees growing directly around the basin. Intermittent visits to Klithi seem to have resumed at about this time, judging from the date of 3560 ± 100 (OxA-747) on a piece of charred bone (Gowlett *et al.*, Chapter 2; Bailey & Woodward, Chapter 4). The large-scale erosion from the flysch terrain that resulted in the formation of the Kipi Unit of the Voïdomatis alluvial sequence seems to correspond mainly to the latter part of this period after about 1000 years ago (Macklin *et al.*, Chapter 17).

At both sites these vegetational conditions persisted until the present day, apart from a period between approximately 1990 and 1200 BP when a pine forest became established on the slopes around Rezina marsh. This reafforestation was due either to a climatic event, such as increased precipitation, or to local depopulation and/or abandonment of grazing on the mountain slopes. This event would suggest that, although the environment around Rezina no longer supports a dense woodland, it is capable of doing so — although perhaps not with the same diversity of taxa as in early Postglacial times — and that the most likely cause for the lack of trees at this altitude today is grazing pressure. Following this brief interlude of woodland development, the environment around Rezina Marsh returned to an open grassland devoid of trees, and has remained this way up to the present.

Conclusions

From this palaeoecological study a number of conclusions can be made about the environmental conditions that existed in the Klithi region. In the Late Glacial period, both upland and lowland areas were dominated by open conditions with few trees, a picture that is entirely consistent with the dominance of ibex and chamois in the archaeological deposits of Klithi.

Scattered stands of trees were also present in both environments. At lower altitude, oak and pine were probably widely distributed, with pockets of hornbeam, fir and willow available locally at Gramousti. Such conditions would have provided additional attractions in summer for red deer, which are known to have been present in the area during the Last Glacial (Sturdy *et al.*, Chapter 30), as well as winter shelter and browse for caprids descending from higher altitude summer pastures. It is probable that, at higher altitudes, there was a similar suite of tree species, but with the addition of hazel, elm, lime and alder. Some of the tree pollen present at this time, notably oak and pine, could have been brought in from distant sources at lower altitude, but the presence of elm and lime at the base of the Rezina sequence is of particular significance. Both species are poor pollen producers and must have been growing nearby, suggesting the presence of high altitude micro-environmental refugia on protected cliffs and slopes that allowed deciduous tree species such as these to persist locally in an otherwise unfavourable climatic region. The presence of these tree species probably had little impact on the human subsistence economy at this time, because they were present in too low densities or in too inaccessible locations to have much effect on grazing conditions for animals. The significance of their local presence is, rather, that they were able to fuel a rapid expansion of woodland at the first onset of climatic amelioration, and this is exactly what appears to have happened between 9700 and 9300 BP, when the slopes around the Rezina Marsh saw the rapid establishment of a dense and diverse woodland cover. At the lowland site of Gramousti, however, an open parkland prevailed, which was little different from the preceding period except for a slight increase in oak. Thus two totally different environments became established within 20 km of each other during this period, and this difference persisted throughout the early part of the Postglacial for some 3000 years, until approximately 7000–6000 BP, when a combination of climatic change and anthropogenic disturbance resulted in a depletion in both density and diversity of the unique early Postglacial montane woodland.

The mountains of northwest Greece have often been cited as an area that could have provided refugia for temperate tree taxa during the Late Glacial (Bennett *et al.* 1991; Bottema 1974; Huntley & Birks 1983; Lang 1970; Van der Hammen *et al.* 1971; West 1980; Willis 1994a). The evidence from Rezina Marsh suggests that a variety of tree taxa were probably present in low frequencies in the last part of the Late Glacial, with a rapid expansion of at least ten different tree types and the establishment of a diverse and dense woodland at the Late Glacial/Postglacial boundary. The establishment of refugia in the mountains rather than the lowlands is thought to be related to the availability of moisture during the Late Glacial (Bottema 1974). It has often been suggested that the limiting factor for woodland development in the Balkans during the Last Glacial was moisture rather than temperature and that the typical steppe plants (grasses, *Artemisia*, and Chenopodiaceae) that dominated Last Glacial plant communities throughout the lowland regions of the Balkans did so because of low precipitation rather than low temperatures. The mountains would have provided an area of higher moisture content and thus a location for the persistence of temperate trees. It is notable that open parkland conditions persisted at Gramousti throughout the early Postglacial, and this suggests that conditions remained too dry during this period to encourage the migration of climatically sensitive tree taxa to lower altitude.

The potential impact of these changes on human activities offers some interesting insights into the archaeological and sedimentological sequences discussed elsewhere (Bailey & Woodward, Chapter 4; Woodward, Chapter 18; Sinclair, Chapter 21). The rapid reafforestation documented by the Rezina pollen diagram after 9700 BP would almost certainly have destroyed the ibex/chamois habitat that had previously existed on the slopes above Klithi, and would presumably have extended into the valley in front of the site, reducing conditions of visibility and access for the human population. Thus it is no surprise that the lower Voïdomatis valley ceased to be a suitable base for ibex hunting, and any continuation of such activities would presumably have shifted to locations at higher altitude near the tree line. The economic potential of the Doliana basin, however, changed very little, and one might surmise that patterns of land use there could have persisted well into the Postglacial with little need for change.

This raises the further question of what vegetational changes might have occurred during short-lived episodes of climatic amelioration in the Late Glacial period. The sedimentological evidence discussed by Woodward in Chapter 19 suggests that this area may have experienced Late Glacial climatic cycles similar to those documented in northwest Europe, notably the Allerod/Younger Dryas cycle. Unfortunately, the Gramousti diagram, because of its geographical position, is rather insensitive to any changes of tree cover that might be associated with such climatic fluctuations. The slight peak in oak pollen between about 11,000 and 10,600 BP gives a possible hint of climatic change, but could equally well reflect nothing more than a short-lived fluctuation in lake sedimentation rate. The Rezina diagram, of course, does not extend back far enough to give any direct evidence for this period. Given the local presence of temperate-tree refugia, however, and the rapidity of woodland development at the Postglacial transition, it seems possible that partial afforestation, if not fully wooded conditions, would have affected the area around Klithi during Late Glacial episodes of climatic warming, with consequent effects on human activity at the site.

Between 7500 and 5000 BP, change occurred in both environments and similarities began to emerge. At first there was an expansion of hornbeam and fir at both sites, suggesting a possible change to a slightly wetter climate. The earliest date, and at present the only radiocarbon date, for Neolithic activity comes from the Asfaka site in the Ioannina lake basin at the very beginning of this period (Higgs *et al.* 1967; Bailey, Chapter 1), and hints at a possible link between climatic change and the expansion of Neolithic activity in the region. There is no unequivocally dated archaeological evidence of occupation in the Doliana or Voïdomatis areas at this time, but soon after there is evidence in both the Gramousti and Rezina pollen diagrams of a reduction in all tree types, indicating local clearance by human activity by about 6000 BP. This is some of the earliest pollen evidence presently available in the Balkans for human impact on vegetation, and indicates, in addition, that clearance was associated with seasonal use of mountain pastures. After 5000 BP there was a recovery of the woodland vegetation, but renewed and intensified clearance from about 4000 BP onwards, and the establishment of vegetational conditions essentially like those of the present, apart from a brief interlude of pine-woodland recovery between about 2000 and 1200 BP. Ironically, as the montane site became devoid of trees, expansion of oak woodland occurred in the lowlands, although it seems likely that this was an expansion of evergreen oaks as a result of intensive grazing leading to the growth of chew-resistant shrubs, an hypothesis further supported by archaeological evidence of a settlement on the shore of Lake Gramousti at about 4500 BP (Bailey, Chapter 1).

Acknowledgements

I would like to thank Geoff Bailey, Keith Bennett and Janice Fuller for helpful comments and discussion, Charles Turner and many participants of the Klithi project for invaluable aid in the field, IGME for permission to core the two sites, Rupert Housley and the Oxford Radiocarbon Accelerator Unit for accelerator dates, and Mark Macklin for advice and technical assistance with the mineral magnetics and sediment chemistry. Fieldwork was undertaken during tenure of an SERC research studentship at the Department of Archaeology and the Department of Plant Sciences, University of Cambridge. I would also like to thank Corpus Christi College, Cambridge, the Tansley Fund and the Quaternary Research Association for assistance with fieldwork expenses.

Chapter 21

Lithic and Faunal Assemblages from Megalakkos: Some Problems in the Interpretation of Small Sites

Anthony Sinclair

Megalakkos is a small cave situated about two hundred metres up a steep-sided tributary flowing into the Voïdomatis River. The cave is almost completely filled with sediments, leaving just a small gap between the top of the sediments and the roof of the cave; a talus of sediments lies in front of the cave mouth. The Megalakkos section provides a long sedimentary history that has been shown to overlap in time with the deposits at Klithi (Woodward, Chapter 19). Excavation of the sediments has also yielded a series of small archaeological assemblages with both lithic and faunal remains: these can be compared to the larger assemblages excavated at Klithi itself (Roubet, Chapters 8 & 9.1), and to the recently excavated assemblages from Boïla (Kotjabopoulou *et al.*, Chapter 22). The Megalakkos assemblages are broadly similar to those from Klithi in terms of lithic typology and technology, and of bone fragmentation and species representation. The lithic assemblages are bladelet-dominated using both local and exotic raw materials, and ibex and chamois are the major taxa represented. Two sedimentary units (Units 4 & 6) provide assemblages large enough for statistical analysis. The lithic assemblages from these two units differ from each other in terms of the frequencies of comparable tool types and their technological characteristics (raw material procurement and reduction). The younger of these two assemblages is similar to a comparative sample from Klithi, but the earlier assemblage appears to be different. These similarities and differences might reflect a time trend, spatial differentiation of activities within the cave or site-specific activity differences in the use of Megalakkos and Klithi.

The Megalakkos assemblages, however, also provide an interpretative challenge: how do we interpret the archaeological record from small sites? Do models derived from intuitive reasoning or ethnoarchaeological fieldwork help? At first sight, Klithi has the appearance of a specialized site, a site in which a limited range of activities took place. Whilst the marked predominance of ibex and chamois bones in the faunal assemblage seems to support this assumption, the actual size of the site, and the great density of lithic and faunal remains indicates considerable use of the site on a scale which is quite different from Megalakkos. In the latter case, the small size of the cave and the much reduced density of archaeological materials suggests that the site was not a major place of habitation. It, too, may be classed within the category of logistic site, in Binford's (1980) sense, that is a site used for a limited range of activities. Given these similarities and differences between Megalakkos and Klithi, how might the use of Megalakkos differ from Klithi, and what does this tell us about Late Glacial land use in this area of northwestern Greece? This interpretative problem forms the heart of the critical analysis of the lithic and faunal assemblages from this site.

Excavation of the site

Originally the site was examined for its sedimentary record. As a result, the sampling strategy and excavation of the site was determined primarily by non-archaeological requirements. Initial excavation of the sediments took the form of a step trench cutting through the sediments of all the units both in the cave and in the talus slope (Fig. 21.1). It was during the excavation of this step trench that archaeological materials were found: the richest being in Unit 4 and Unit 6. At this stage the excavation was opened horizontally to the width of the cave mouth to improve the archaeological sample for analysis. The excavated area for these units approximated one square metre, and approximately twenty centimetres depth of deposit in both cases. The great height of sediments within the cave restricted access to the top of the

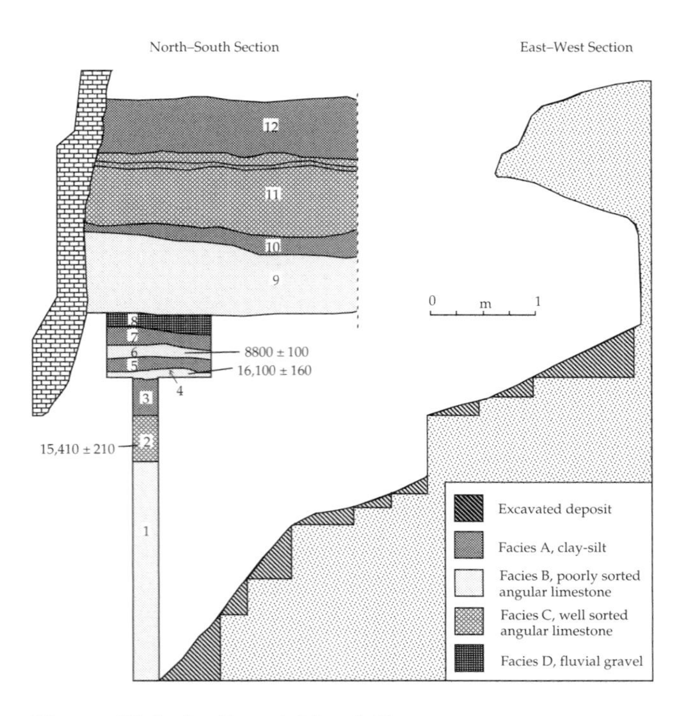

Figure 21.1. *Section at Megalakkos.*

sedimentary column. This and the time constraints of the excavation season restricted sampling of the upper units to the removal of specimens and sediment samples from the exposed outward face of the partly eroded sediments.

The excavation of the archaeological material was carried out using similar methods as at Klithi itself (Bailey, Chapter 3); individual specimens were collected in the trench and bagged separately, and sediment residues were wet sieved. Assemblages are defined according to the sedimentary unit from which they derive. Many are very small, reflecting the limited extent of the excavation. Analysis below concentrates on Units 4 and 6. It should be noted that these two assemblages come from units defined by changes in natural sedimentological processes, rather than by cultural features of the deposit, and thus represent environmentally determined units of time rather than cultural ones.

The artefacts were described according to the detailed system of recording used at Klithi (see Roubet, Chapter 8 for full details). Artefacts were divided into retouched and unretouched pieces ('tools' and 'debitage'). All artefacts were described according to the general lithic type (chert [1] or quartz) and within these general categories according to specific types, defined primarily on the basis of colour (see Appendix 21.1), as well as the presence or absence of cortex (flakes being classified as either fully cortical, semi-cortical or non-cortical). Unretouched pieces were classified according to technological categories based on the scheme devised by Chadelle (1983). Retouched pieces were further classified according to the typological scheme of Tixier (1963). It should be noted that the compacted nature of some of the sediments meant that many of the artefacts had to be cleaned in a solution of hydrochloric acid to remove concretions of calcium carbonate before identification.

Table 21.1. *The density of lithic materials in the Megalakkos assemblages.*

Stratigraphic units	2	3	4	5	6	7	9
Area excavated m^2	0.125	0.25	1.00	1.00	1.00	1.00	3.00
Depth of layer cm	50.0	30.0	7.0	18.0	18.0	20.0	N/A
Number of tools	0	0	25	0	49	0	10
Number of debitage	3	2	322	11	1009	3	17
Number of pieces per m^3	50	29	4609	63	5618	15	2000

Table 21.2. *The frequency of particular debitage types for the layers at Megalakkos.*

Unit	2	3	5	7	9
Debitage type					
Cores - whole	0	0	3	0	0
Cores - broken	0	0	0	0	0
Flakes - whole	0	1	6	0	4
Flakes - broken	1	1	2	0	10
Blades - whole	0	0	0	0	0
Blades - broken	1	0	0	0	0
Bladelets - whole	0	0	0	0	0
Bladelets - broken	1	0	0	0	0
Microbladelets - whole	0	0	0	0	0
Microbladelets - broken	0	0	0	0	0
Microburins	0	0	0	0	0
Krukowski type	0	0	0	0	0
Burinspalls	0	0	0	0	0
Small fragments	0	0	356	0	0
Galets	1	0	0	3	3
Total no. of pieces (excludes small fragments)	**3**	**2**	**11**	**3**	**17**

Table 21.3. *Real and expected frequencies for artefacts from Megalakkos Units 4 and 6. Expected frequencies in italics.*

	Unit 4		Unit 6		Unit 9	
Artefact types						
Burin	1	*1*	0	*1*	0	*0*
Notch	1	*3*	7	*5*	1	*0*
Denticulate	1	*1*	1	*1*	0	*0*
Endscraper	11	*5*	2	*8*	0	*0*
Backed bladelet	2	*12*	31	*21*	5	*2*
Geometric	0	*0*	1	*1*	0	*0*
Borer	3	*2*	1	*3*	0	*0*
Scraper	1	*0*	0	*1*	0	*0*
Composite	0	*0*	1	*1*	2	*0*
Utilized piece	1	*2*	3	*3*	1	*0*
Diverse	5	*4*	5	*6*	1	*0*
Blank	57	*55*	93	*95*	0	*6*
TOTAL	**83**		**145**		**10**	

Table 21.4. *Chi-square results for tool classes from Units 4 and 6.*

Units compared	Score	Degrees of freedom	Significance
Unit 4 & Unit 6	39.410	12	0.0001
Modified tool classes			
Unit 4 & Unit 6	35.251	4	0.0001

Only two of the assemblages, from Units 4 and 6, have sufficient numbers of retouched and unretouched pieces for detailed analysis. The other assemblages, from Units 2, 3, 5, 7 and 9, are significantly smaller in both respects. It should be noted that the artefacts from Unit 9 were obtained by section cleaning. Had it been possible to excavate this Unit in the same way as the others, it is possible that it would have yielded as rich an assemblage as those from Units 4 and 6 (Table 21.1).

General characteristics of the assemblages

The general character of the Megalakkos assemblages is very similar to that from Klithi. They are essentially industries with tools made on flakes, small blades (*c.* 5 cm long) and bladelets. The retouched tools include endscrapers, burins, unretouched but utilized blades (perhaps used as knives), and microliths — primarily backed bladelets (Fig. 21.2). The density of material, however, is an order of magnitude less than at Klithi, where the average density of artefacts per m^3 is 16,000 pieces and the maximum density approaches 80,000 pieces, compared with an average of 1770 at Megalakkos and a maximum of 5618 (Table 21.1).

The backed bladelets, when hafted either individually or in a group, may have formed the cutting/piercing elements of composite tools. Industries of this character have been found in the neighbouring Balkans area, whilst the use of microlithic backed bladelets is a common element in many Late Upper Palaeolithic assemblages from Europe, southwest Asia and farther afield (Adam 1989).

Units 2, 3 and 7 at Megalakkos contain just broken flakes, blades and a single bladelet (Table 21.2). The assemblage from Unit 5 is slightly larger, with 3 cores, all whole. Little can be concluded from this material, except that the cave was used during the periods in question.

The assemblages from Units 4 and 6, and to some extent Unit 9, are quite different from the other Units. These assemblages include a range of retouched tool types comprising burins, notches, denticulates, endscrapers and backed bladelets amongst other items. They are also very much richer in debitage pieces. Both Units 4 and 6 contain specimens from all stages of the reduction sequence, including acquisition of raw materials, preparation and exploitation of cores, and transformation of blanks into retouched tools.

There are also differences between Units 4 and 6. Initial impressions suggest that backed bladelets are more common in Unit 6, followed by notches, whilst endscrapers are the most common tools in Unit 4 (Table 21.3).

The chi-square test shows a highly significant difference, and this significance increases when comparison is restricted to those tool categories which showed the greatest discrepancy between observed and expected frequencies in the first analysis (Table 21.4). There are also more cores in Unit 4 despite the fact that the assemblage is half the size of the Unit 6 assemblage. There would also appear to be differences in the proportion of exotic raw materials (i.e. those not available in the immediate vicinity).

If assemblages are thought of as the byproducts of a mobile hunter-gatherer lifestyle, where tools are manufactured for immediate needs or in anticipation of future ones, and raw materials are collected either incidentally while moving across the landscape for other purposes, as the result of special trips or through exchange, then the differences between the Unit 4 and

Table 21.5. *Debitage types according to raw materials for Units 4 and 6.*

Raw material type	17	1	9	18	19	10	20	14	21	16	Diverse	Indet.	TOTAL
UNIT 4													
Technological type													
Raw block	–	2	–	–	1	–	–	–	–	–	–	–	3
Cortical flake	3	–	–	1	–	–	–	–	–	–	–	–	4
Cortical flake rolled	–	9	–	1	–	–	–	–	–	–	–	–	10
Semi-cortical flake	–	–	–	–	–	–	2	–	–	–	–	–	2
Semi-cortical flake rolled	–	3	2	1	–	–	2	–	–	–	–	–	8
Flake	102	18	3	11	3	4	–	–	–	–	3	3	147
Crested blade	–	–	–	–	–	–	–	–	–	–	–	–	0
Cortical blade	–	1	–	–	–	–	–	–	–	–	–	–	1
Cortical bladelet	–	–	–	–	–	–	–	–	–	–	–	–	0
Blade	22	13	2	7	1	–	–	1	–	–	1	6	53
Bladelet	2	3	1	1	2	–	–	–	–	–	1	1	10
Broken bladelet	6	3	1	2	–	1	–	–	–	–	–	4	17
Crested piece[1]	1	–	–	–	–	–	–	–	–	–	–	–	1
Core tablet	1	–	1	–	1	–	–	–	–	–	–	–	3
Rejuvenation piece[2]	2	1	1	–		1	–	–	–	–	–	–	5
Single platform core	2	2	–	1	1	1	–	1	–	–	1	1	10
Double platfrom core	–	–	1	–	–	–	–	–	–	–	1	–	2
Other core	1	1	–	–	–	–	–	–	–	–	–	–	2
Burinspall	–	–	–	–	–	–	–	–	–	–	–	–	0
Retouch flake[3]	8	2	4	4	–	–	–	–	–	–	3	2	23
Microburin	–	–	–	–	–	–	–	–	–	–	–	–	0
Shatter fragment[4]	107	70	10	9	4	3	–	–	–	–	3	25	212
Tool	–	6	4	4	4	2	–	–	–	–	1	–	21
TOTAL	**257**	**134**	**30**	**41**	**17**	**12**	**4**	**2**	**0**	**0**	**14**	**43**	**554**
UNIT 6													
Raw block	2	4	–	–	1	1	1	–	–	–	–	4	13
Cortical flake	1	–	–	–	–	–	–	–	–	–	–	–	1
Cortical flake rolled	–	15	–	3	–	1	–	–	–	–	–	–	19
Semi-cortical flake	–	–	3	–	2	–	–	–	–	–	–	–	5
Semi-cortical flake rolled	–	9	–	1	–	–	–	–	–	–	–	–	10
Flake	5	30	3	26	1	1	1	–	7	–	5	18	97
Crested blade	–	–	–	–	1	–	–	–	–	–	–	–	1
Cortical blade	–	3	–	–	–	–	–	–	1	–	1	–	5
Cortical bladelet	–	–	–	–	–	–	–	–	–	–	–	–	0
Blade	1	4	6	4	2	1	–	–	1	–	2	–	21
Bladelet	1	7	4	10	1	–	–	–	1	–	12	–	36
Broken bladelet	–	6	4	10	1	2	1	–	2	1	12	8	47
Crested piece[1]	–	1	–	–	–	–	–	–	–	–	–	–	1
Core tablet	–	1	–	–	–	–	–	–	–	–	–	–	1
Rejuvenation piece[2]	–	1	–	–	–	–	–	–	–	–	–	–	1
Single platform core	–	1	–	–	1	–	1	–	–	–	–	–	3
Double platform core	–	1	–	–	–	1	–	–	–	–	–	–	2
Other core	–	2	–	–	–	–	–	–	–	–	–	–	2
Burinspall	–	–	–	–	–	–	–	–	1	–	–	–	1
Retouch flake[3]	13	45	8	30	9	6	2	–	5	2	20	60	200
Microburin	2	3	–	–	1	–	–	–	–	–	5	9	19
Shatter fragment[4]	30	110	25	50	10	7	3	–	10	–	40	190	475
Tool	2	10	6	11	3	1	–	–	1	–	11	7	52
TOTAL	**57**	**253**	**59**	**145**	**33**	**20**	**89**	**0**	**28**	**4**	**108**	**296**	**1010**

[1] Broken blade or bladelet with evidence of cresting
[2] Flake which removes unwanted step fractures from flaking surface
[3] Flake byproduct of retouching
[4] Amorphous debitage fragment

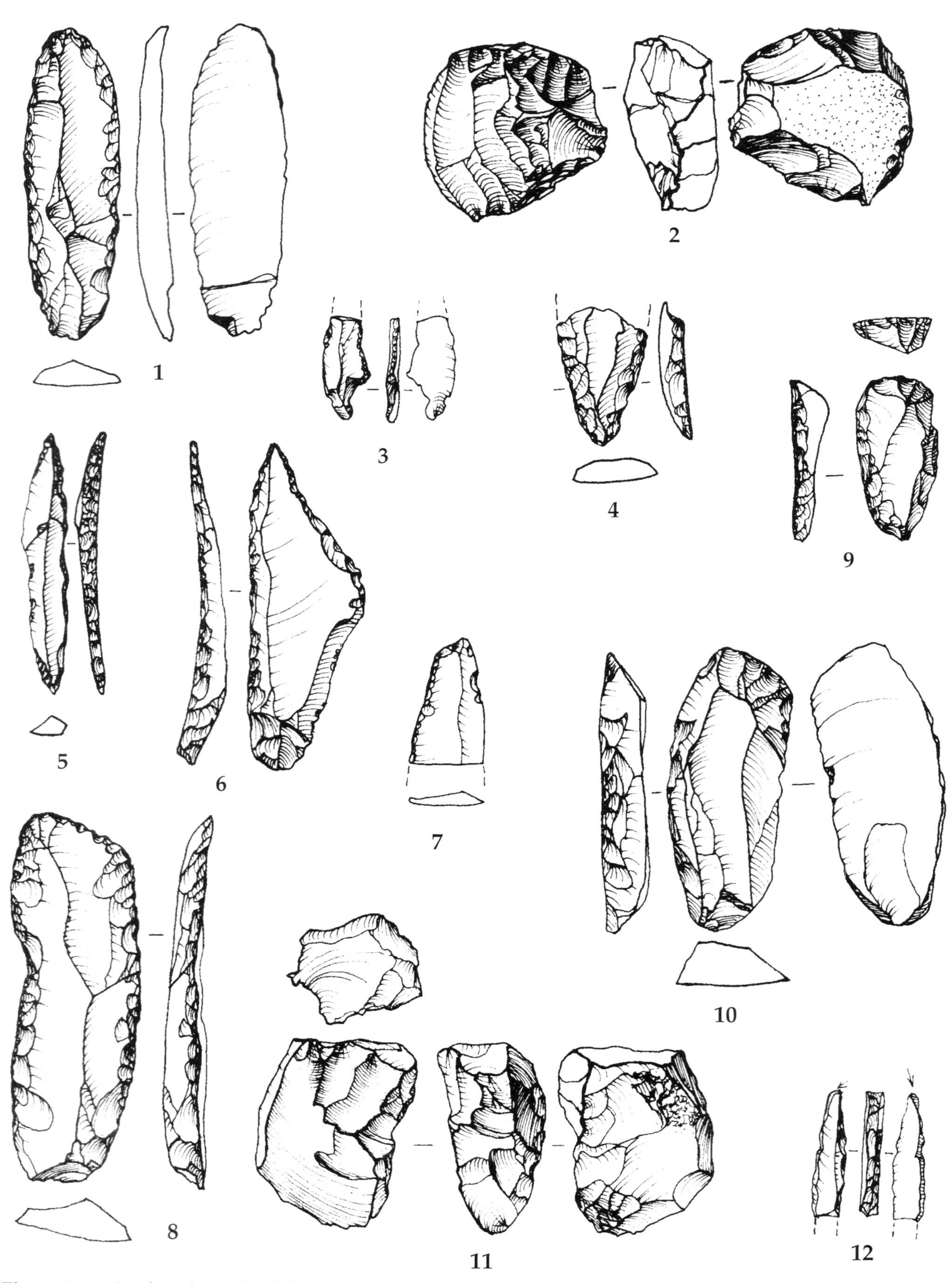

Figure 21.2. *Artefacts from Megalakkos: 1–6. Unit 9; 7–8. Unit 2; 9–10. Unit 4; 11–12. Unit 6. Full size.*

Unit 6 assemblages suggest very different patterns of use of the Megalakkos shelter.

The use of raw materials

The use of different raw materials gives some idea of the catchment area covered by the occupants of the site. Local raw materials are defined here as those procured within approximately a 5 km radius of the site. In the case of Klithi and Megalakkos it includes those cherts which are available within the Voïdomatis basin. The presence of exotic raw materials, obtained from beyond the Voïdomatis, indicates either the exploitation of a greater catchment area by the occupants of Megalakkos, or the arrival of people from a distant site bringing with them raw materials obtained from the vicinity of that site or from even farther afield. In this sense, the implications of this distinction between locally exploited cherts and exotic cherts parallels to some degree the distinction made between the exploitation area and the catchment area of a site (Bailey & Davidson 1983). The likely provenance, local or exotic, is noted in Appendix 21.1.

Raw materials and artefact types

The difference between local and exotic raw materials is also mirrored in the technological debitage types when separated according to raw material type. Local raw materials are generally present in all stages of tool production (raw material acquisition, core production and exploitation, tool production, tool maintenance and discard) as can be inferred by the different technological types (Table 21.5), whereas the exotic materials are generally absent in the earlier stages of tool making (raw material acquisition and core production).

Analysis of raw materials shows that there is a greater frequency of exotic raw materials in the assemblage from Unit 4 than from 6 (Table 21.6). This raises the question of whether the retouched tools which differentiate Unit 4 from the other units, principally endscrapers, are those which were made on exotic raw materials. However, this is not the case. The frequency of raw material types on which endscrapers are made shows no significant differences between observed and expected values. Rather it is the blanks — large enough to be measured but lacking retouch or utilization — that show a significant emphasis on exotic raw materials.

There are also striking differences between Units 4 and 6 in the number of cores, and in the nature of the raw materials of which they were made, which support the conclusions drawn above. Unit 4 has proportionately more cores than Unit 6, and a significant emphasis on exotic raw materials. In addition, the cores in Unit 4 include bladelet cores and cores big enough for the production of blades (i.e. blanks ≥50 mm in length). However, there are no blades present in Unit 4, a significant point that will be considered later. In Unit 6, the cores, all of which are made on local raw materials, include good quality cores for the production of bladelets (up to 25 mm in length), and this is consistent with the dominance of backed bladelets in the tool assemblage.

Summarizing thus far, there are broadly two types of assemblage present at Megalakkos, a chronologically later one (Unit 6), in which retouched tools are dominated by backed bladelets, and the debitage is mostly made on local raw materials, and a typologically more generalized assemblage (Unit 4) with a significant representation of exotic raw materials in both the core and tool categories.

It is possible at this stage to offer a description, as opposed to an explanation, of the events that led to the formation of the lithic assemblages from Units 4 and 6. For the assemblage from Unit 6, the predominance of local raw materials suggests that a group from the local area occupied the cave during this period. On the basis of the typological composition of the assemblage it is possible to say that they either brought a pre-fabricated, specialized toolkit with them when they came to the site and/or they made it at the site. The number of flakes and shatter pieces attests to the fact that knapping occurred at the site at this time. After discarding some of the tools which they had brought or made, people left carrying the remainder of the toolkit and any new tools which they had made as well as many of the cores which they had knapped on site. This is based on the relative absence of cores in the resulting discarded assemblage.

In the case of the assemblage from Unit 4, the predominance of non-local materials suggests the occupation of the site by a group of people who had just arrived in the area from outside of the local exploitation area. The cores and debitage indicate some knapping took place at the site, but the absence of blanks which correspond to the final, negative flake scars observable on the discarded cores suggests that the group moved on having made new tools at the site or simply carrying new blanks that could be retouched into tools at a later date.

The small size of both assemblages suggests the occupation of the site by a small group of people and/or for a brief period of time.

Comparison with Klithi

Initial comparisons with the lithic assemblages from Klithi were made using a sample drawn from Q26. Both the typological and technological characteristics of this assemblage are very similar to Unit 6 at Megalakkos, that is with a predominance of backed bladelets and notches, relatively few (bladelet) cores and a predominance of local raw materials (Tables 21.7 & 21.8). Conversely, there are significant differences with the Unit 4 assemblage.

Interpretation of this pattern is complicated by the question of variability within the lithic assemblages from different levels and areas at Klithi. The task of comparison is further complicated by the fact that the assemblages at Megalakkos are defined in

Table 21.6. *Observed and expected frequencies for local and exotic raw materials from Units 4 and 6. Expected frequencies in italics.*

Raw material type	Unit 4		Unit 6		TOTAL
Local	46	*35*	51	*62*	97
Exotic	37	*48*	94	*83*	131
TOTAL	83		145		228

Table 21.8. *Chi-square results for tool classes from Megalakkos and Klithi (Q26).*

Units compared	Score	Degrees of freedom	Significance
Unit 4 & Klithi	37.014	13	0.0004
Unit 6 & Klithi	19.980	15	0.1727
Modified			
Unit 4 & Klithi	24.443	4	0.0001
Unit 6 & Klithi	4.662	4	0.3237

Table 21.7. *Tool frequencies from Klithi comparative assemblage (Q26).*

Tool types	
Burin	1
Notch	10
Denticulate	5
Endscraper	5
Backed bladelet	28
Geometric	0
Borer	1
Scraper	1
Composite	0
Utilized piece	5
Diverse	6
Blank	198
Indeterminate	7
TOTAL	267

terms of geological layers, whereas the material at Klithi can be grouped according to cultural activities and their associated areas. To cope with this problem, assemblages have been selected from a variety of areas within the Klithi deposit: within the hearth (R21); around the hearth (Q20, Q22); and from the front of the site where predominantly geological conditions of sedimentation prevail (Q24, P26, R27). The material from each square has been treated as a single assemblage without further stratigraphic or contextual differentiation, and described according to the same conventions as the Megalakkos material.

With respect to the tool types, the assemblages from Q22 and R21 have a higher than expected frequency of backed bladelets, notches, denticulates and utilized pieces, while those from Q20, Q24 and P26 show little difference between observed and expected frequencies. The assemblage from R27, however, has relatively few backed bladelets and utilized pieces, while endscrapers are slightly more common (Table 21.9).

With respect to raw materials, assemblages from Q22, Q24 and R21 have observed frequencies close to the expected, those from P26 and Q20 have relatively few exotics and relatively many pieces made on local material, while the assemblage from R27 shows a significant emphasis on exotic raw materials (Table 21.10).

From the point of view of comparison with Megalakkos, the most interesting conclusion to note is that while there are assemblages closely similar to the Unit 6 assemblage at Megalakkos, there are also assemblages at Klithi, notably the R27 assemblage, which correspond more closely to the pattern of material found in Unit 4 at Megalakkos. It would thus appear that the assemblages at Klithi cover the same range of variability as the assemblages at Megalakkos, and that there is significant interassemblage variability at *both* sites. If this is so, then site-specific differences would seem to be ruled out as a basis for interpreting assemblage variability. The alternatives must lie among the following possibilities: (1) variation is due to particular sorts of activities that result in different sorts of lithic assemblages; (2) there is a time trend from one type of activity to another at *both* sites; (3) the activities, or the discard of the materials associated with them, are spatially differentiated at both sites, and the apparent time trend is illusory, due to the fact that, because of limited sampling, particularly at Megalakkos, different layers have sampled different activities. In order to probe these possibilities further, it is necessary to examine more carefully the relationship between activities and the discard of lithic material.

Lithic strategies and archaeological signatures at Megalakkos

The combination of typological and technological characteristics described above can be interpreted from both an intuitive, empirical point of view, in which interpretations are built up from the associations of evidence within the archaeological context, or from an ethnoarchaeological, theoretical point of view, in which the evidence is compared to expectations derived from *a priori* modelling. I shall begin with an empirical approach, and then examine the evidence from the point of view of ethnoarchaeological models taken from Binford's research amongst the Nunamiut.

Empirical considerations

As is discussed in greater detail elsewhere (Roubet, Chapter 8), the specific characteristics of the Klithi stone artefact assemblages, notably an overwhelming abundance of backed bladelets, can be related to a specialized activity, namely the seasonal hunting of ibex and chamois in the local vicinity. In line with this interpretation, one might expect people to arrive at -the site with toolkits already prepared for their first hunting forays. As the various components of the toolkit became broken in the course of use, they would have been discarded and replaced with locally made replacements. The abundance of backed bladelets would therefore represent the major activity undertaken at the site. We would also expect that the discarded items would be biased towards non-local raw materials. Similar arguments can be advanced with respect to the Unit 6 assemblage.

In assessing this interpretation, however, the evidence of tools and raw materials at Megalakkos is somewhat contradictory. The dominance of backed bladelets in Unit 6 gives the impression of a small hunting party moving rapidly over the landscape with their tools made and at the ready,

Table 21.9. *Observed and expected tool frequencies for basic tool types from comparative sample at Klithi. Expected frequencies in italics.*

Tool types	P26		Q20		Q22		Q24		R21		R27	
Burin	0	*1*	4	*4*	1	*3*	0	*0*	3	*3*	8	*6*
Notch	6	*4*	15	*16*	7	*15*	1	*1.2*	14	*11*	30	*26*
Denticulate	1	*3*	8	*11*	0	*10*	3	*1*	6	*8*	31	*17*
Backed blade	3	*1*	5	3	2	*3*	0	*0*	3	*2*	0	*5*
Endscraper	4	*5*	21	*22*	14	*20*	0	*2*	16	*15*	41	*34*
Backed bladelet	26	*26*	105	*106*	61	*95*	7	*8*	128	*73*	149	*168*
Novelty	0	*0*	1	*0*	0	*0*	0	*0*	0	*0*	0	*0*
Borer	1	*2*	5	*7*	2	*6*	0	*1*	2	*5*	19	*10*
Scraper	2	*1*	2	*4*	1	*4*	0	*0*	0	*3*	13	*6*
Composite	2	*1*	5	*4*	0	*4*	0	*0*	4	*3*	8	*7*
Truncated	1	*2*	3	*6*	1	*5*	0	*0*	1	*4*	21	*10*
Utilized	47	*13*	96	*54*	40	*48*	7	*4*	12	*37*	39	*85*
Diverse	2	*2*	10	*7*	2	*6*	2	*1*	3	*5*	12	*11*
Blank	69	*104*	380	*417*	455	*370*	29	*31*	262	*287*	669	*657*
TOTAL	**164**		**660**		**586**		**49**		**454**		**1040**	

Table 21.10. *Observed and expected frequencies for local and exotic raw materials from Klithi. Expected frequencies in italics.*

Raw material	P26		Q20		Q22		Q24		R21		R27		TOTAL
Local	88	*74*	*349*	*307*	*359*	*366*	*34*	*31*	290	*285*	610	*666*	**1730**
Exotic	28	*42*	130	*172*	212	*205*	14	*17*	154	*159*	428	*372*	**966**
TOTAL	**116**		**479**		**571**		**48**		**444**		**1038**		**2696**

stopping briefly here and there to kill an animal or two. However, the fact that the majority of the pieces in this assemblage are made of local raw materials suggests that Megalakkos was used for making and repairing tools and not simply for discarding them. Also the area exploited by this group would appear to have been smaller than we might have expected, since the raw materials suggest a primary exploitation area confined to the Voïdomatis basin, unless we argue the unlikely case that the exotic materials brought into the site were taken away again without leaving any trace.

Conversely, the typological evidence from Unit 4 suggests a diverse assemblage used for a wider range of activities, perhaps reflecting the day-to-day maintenance activities of people living in the cave, whereas the lithic procurement evidence suggests that people travelled into the site from some distance away, and moved on again soon after. The raw materials of which the cores are made, and some of the tools, such as the endscrapers and the blanks, suggest that people visited Megalakkos from some distance away. The fact that the blade products of some of the cores are not present in the assemblage suggests either that the cores were brought into the site ready-knapped and not further used — which seems unlikely — or that the cores were used to produce blanks for tools which were then carried away for use elsewhere. This has also been observed at Klithi (Roubet, Chapter 9; Shawcross & Winder, Chapter 10).

Ethnoarchaeological expectations

The clearest description of the effects of a migratory lifestyle on the manufacture and use of technology has been set out by Binford (1979, 261; see also Binford 1977; 1978; Shott 1986; Torrence 1983; 1989). The key to Binford's analysis is the distinction between curated and expedient tools. Curated tools are made in anticipation of future needs. They are made beforehand with the greatest care and the best materials available, and then kept and carried around until needed. Since they are well made, they are unlikely to break and may well be brought back from the place where they were used, eventually being discarded in a location which may be quite different from the location of use. Expedient tools are made on the spot for a task that has not been anticipated. They are not necessarily made from the most suitable raw materials, nor are they likely to be the best made tools, and they are likely to be discarded at the place of use. If there are no readily available raw materials at the point of use, a previously prepared tool may have to be modified for the immediate purpose. Finally there are tasks requiring tools which are too big or too heavy to carry about ('facilities' in Binford's terminology), and these are used at the point of manufacture and left there for future use. In consequence there are two types of manufacture: 'gearing up' (Binford 1979, 284), which takes place at habitation sites and involves the careful production of tools for future use at another location; and manufacture of tools for immediate needs, which tends to occur at special purpose sites.

In the light of these principles, it is possible to specify a number of expectations — archaeological signatures — for the likely composition of stone tool assemblages that might be recovered from the location of specialized activities as opposed to habitation sites. Evidence of primary manufacturing should be found at habitation sites, whereas any manufacturing debris at specialized sites should correspond to the later stages of the manufacturing process, such as maintenance or retooling. There should also be differences in the types and quality of tools recovered from the two sorts of locations. Although good quality tools (personal gear) are taken to specialized sites, they are unlikely to be discarded there. Rather we would expect to find expedient tools (situational gear) discarded there, and these may include tools made on good quality raw material blanks (personal gear) which have been modified for an important immediate need. Overall, the types of tools discarded at specialized sites are unlikely to reflect exactly the nature of the activities carried out there.

Reinterpretation of the Megalakkos assemblages

The principles outlined above provide a context for the interpretation of the differences between Unit 4 and Unit 6 in terms of the activities of the people who occupied the site in these two periods and the function of the site when occupied.

On the basis of these considerations, we might argue that the Unit 6 assemblage at Megalakkos, with its predominance of backed bladelets and local raw materials, is not indicative of a specialized hunting site at all, but of a habitation site. The evidence for the primary stages in the manufacture of backed bladelets and the discarded endproducts is consistent with the preparation of personal gear in anticipation of future hunting trips, and with subsequent discard of hunting gear that has reached the end of its useful life and needs replacing. Conversely, the range of tool types and exotic raw materials in Unit 4 might be interpreted as evidence of a specialized site: the tools made on exotic raw materials such as endscrapers being evidence for personal gear that has been transformed into expedient tools.

However, such an interpretation raises further difficulties. The notion that Megalakkos might have served as a habitation site at any stage in its history seems hardly credible in view of its small size and unfavourable aspect, not to mention the small size of the stone and bone assemblages present. Hence the reinterpretation of the Unit 6 assemblage as evidence of a habitation site seems implausible. Conversely, the interpretation of all the retouched tools in Unit 4 as abandoned situational gear transformed from personal gear does not work well. Although many of the retouched tools are broken or have clearly reached the end of their useful life, these tools do not show signs of having been transformed from other tools as would be the case if they had been personal gear transformed into situational gear. Moreover, some of the endscrapers made on exotic raw materials have been discarded even though they could still have been used or rejuvenated for further use. Had these items been carefully prepared personal gear, whose use life was determined by their possibilities for future use, in the sense used by Binford, they would not have been discarded at a special purpose site.

Faunal remains

The faunal remains have many of the same characteristics as those from Klithi (Gamble, Chapter 11). They are highly fragmented yet in good condition, and are dominated by the remains of caprids (*Capra ibex, Rupicapra rupicapra*) with relatively few remains of other species (Table 21.11). Carnivores are absent. The fewer number of species relative to Klithi perhaps indicates the short period of time during which Megalakkos was occupied, or it may be due to small sample size.

Analysis of patterns of carcass dismemberment relies on distinctions between high and low utility body parts and the effects that these differences might have on bone transportation to sites (Binford 1978; Stiner 1991; Gamble, Chapter 11). High utility body parts comprise primarily the upper limbs, the low utility body parts comprise the head, the lower limbs and the extremities. A preference for the use of high utility parts has been called 'gourmet' selection, whilst that for both high and low utility body parts has been called 'bulk' selection (Binford 1978, 81). As a prior expectation, we might anticipate that a group which occupied the site for a short period of time with the intention of moving on (as is the case in the logistical use of specialized sites) might use just the choice parts of an animal carcass, such as the upper limbs (the meat carried on the humerus and the femur). Longer-term occupation by a group of individuals, including less mobile individuals (the elderly or children) for whom food would need to be brought back, might lead to the discard of all body parts at a site. The first pattern is what we might predict for Unit 4, the second for Unit 6.

The comparison depends on which parts are classified as high utility and which as low utility, particularly with reference to the limb bones below the 'elbow' and the 'knee' joints (the radius and ulna, and the tibia and fibula respectively). Gamble (Chapter 11) has included these lower limb bones as part of the high utility group, in contrast to Stiner (1991), and I have followed Gamble in the following analysis.

Contrary to prior expectations, the number of individual specimens of bones for the different body parts for the caprids indicates that in both units upper limb and lower limb body parts were brought back to the site (Table 21.12). If these are corrected to account for the differential survival of the different bone types it is clear that the faunal assemblages from both units produce bulk curves. It is, however, worth noting that if the radius, ulna and tibia are classified as members of the low utility group of body parts (following Stiner 1991), then Unit 4 produces a gourmet curve, whilst Unit 6 still indicates a bulk curve.

In his analysis of the faunal remains from Klithi, Gamble has noted a consistent pattern of hunting selection and carcass treatment for the caprids. He has argued that humans hunted randomly, intercepting individual animals either above the site or in the Voïdomatis Gorge below. These animals were then processed and brought back to the site for consumption. In cases where the intercepted animals were prime adults it was possible to bring back predominantly high utility parts, resulting in a 'gourmet' curve. In cases where juvenile and old animals were killed, the complete carcass was brought back to the site for intensive processing particularly for fat, resulting in a 'bulk' curve.

There is another interesting pattern at Klithi. Left-handed elements are better represented than right-handed elements, suggesting prior sharing out of caprid carcasses at kill/primary butchery sites between different social units who camped in separate locations. Such patterns of carcass sharing have been noted amongst many hunter-gatherer groups (Whitelaw 1991). If Megalakkos were part of such a wider system of sharing, we might expect to find a disproportionate representation of right-handed elements. In fact, both sides are equally represented in Unit 4 (10 left-hand and 10 right-hand specimens), whilst right-handed body parts slightly outnumber left-handed body parts in Unit 6 (15 left-hand and 21 right-hand specimens).

One final aspect of the faunal remains at Megalakkos that requires some consideration is the presence of red deer bones in both Units 4 and 6. In both cases the bones are low utility body parts (metatarsals). Red deer bones have also been identified among the faunal remains from Klithi, although in comparison to the vast number of caprid bones they are exceptionally rare. Given the smaller size of faunal sample at Megalakkos, red deer bones appear to be more common. A chi-square test demonstrates

Table 21.11. *Representation by NISP of major taxa at Megalakkos.*

Taxa	Unit 4	Unit 6	TOTAL
Caprid	78	128	206
Cervid	1	1	2
Rodents	3	3	6
Birds	2	1	3
Microfauna	0	2	2
TOTAL	**84**	**135**	**219**

Table 21.12. *Counts and corrected counts for major body-part groupings of all caprid remains from Units 4 and 6 at Megalakkos.*

	Unit 4		Unit 6	
	counts	*corrected*	counts	*corrected*
Teeth	12	*5*	18	*8*
Upper limb parts	30	*30*	27	*27*
Lower limb parts	18	*4*	8	*36*

Correction factors for differential preservation: teeth divide by 2.25, lower limbs divide by 4.5, upper limbs divide by 1.

that when the remains from Klithi are included as part of the total sample population, the number of red deer bones at Megalakkos is significantly greater than expected. Despite this, however, the vary small size of the Megalakkos faunal collection, and the fact that red deer are only represented by a single bone in each unit, suggests that the significance of this result should not be made too much of at this stage.

On the basis of the faunal remains, the processing of the animal carcasses discarded at Megalakkos and Klithi seems to have been similar, despite the differences in the patterning of the respective lithic remains. This seems to suggest a similar approach to carcass processing regardless of the differences in the treatment of lithic artefacts. We might also infer a similar approach to the hunting of caprids as well, with the ambushing of individual animals within the local catchment of the site. In Unit 4 the sidedness of the body parts is even, but in Unit 6 there is a slight bias towards the right-hand side. It is just possible, therefore, that this is the evidence to indicate that occupation of Megalakkos during the formation of Unit 6 was indeed related to the occupation of Klithi.

Problems in current archaeological signatures

Although it has been possible to offer descriptions for the behaviour that may have given rise to the two lithic assemblages from Units 4 and 6, the conflict between an intuitive interpretation of the relationship between assemblage composition and site function, and the ethnoarchaeologically based interpretation, suggests that it may be important to reconsider. In the former interpretation assemblage composition is assumed to be a direct reflection of site use, in the latter there is no such direct reflection, only an indirect reflection through the processes of gearing-up and discard. According to one interpretation, the assemblage from Unit 4 resembles the generalized assemblage to be expected from a habitation site, even though the site is so small, whilst that from Unit 6 is the result of a small hunting party. The alternative interpretation is that the Unit 4 assemblage represents tools that are not directly associated with the primary use of the site, which has a specialist role in planning and tool production, whilst the Unit 6 assemblage is associated with a process of 'gearing-up' which might be expected to occur at a habitation site.

In both cases we assume that the most appropriate typology of sites comprises the habitation and specialized sites that have been noted for logistic collectors such as the Nunamiut, whilst the interpretation of lithic assemblages assumes that hunter-gatherers in Late Glacial Greece managed their technology in a highly planned manner, as implied by Binford's notion of gearing-up and technological optimization.

Two questions emerge from this: (1) what is an appropriate site typology for Late Glacial ibex hunters living in the circumscribed topography of present day northwestern Greece; and (2) where should we look for appropriate archaeological signatures that will allow us to understand the formation of lithic assemblages for the interpretation of site use?

It has been noted by Wobst (1979) that modern studies of hunter-gatherers often provide an overly persuasive analogy for the interpretation of prehistoric remains. This is especially the case with Binford's recent studies of the Nunamiut. It is questionable, however, whether the Nunamiut do provide an appropriate analogy, either for site typologies or technological signatures.

The Nunamiut lead a highly logistic existence, imposed both by their local environmental extremes and also by their main prey species, the caribou. As a fast moving, migratory animal covering long distances, caribou presents particular problems for the hunter (Burch 1972) which are unlikely to match those posed by ibex, especially in the topographically circumscribed area of the Voïdomatis basin. The sharp distinction between residential and specialized hunting sites might need re-thinking as a model for the exploitation of the Voïdomatis basin. There is perhaps no appropriate modern analogy for these prehistoric hunter-gatherers against which we can match site types, and this puts increased pressure on our ability to interpret what went on at individual sites on the basis of the surviving archaeological evidence.

Leaving aside for the moment whether recent cost-benefit approaches to the study of technology are appropriate (Sinclair 1990; 1991), there are other problems associated with the use of modern hunter-gatherer studies as the basis for archaeological analogies. It has already been noted that the transport technology at the disposal of the Nunamiut affects the degree to which they can be logistic and, therefore, the way they can prepare for and organize land use (Weniger 1989). A similar argument might be made for the way in which the nature of the subsistence technology at their disposal affects the structure of their technology and in so doing renders archaeological signatures based on Nunamiut tool use inappropriate for prehistoric hunter-gatherers. This problem revolves around the difference between reliability and maintainability in technology.

Bleed (1986) in his discussion of technology makes a distinction between reliable technology and maintainable technology. Reliable technology comprises items which are over-constructed to the extent that they can be relied upon to perform when needed. This reliability can be engineered through better materials and also back-up systems. Maintainable technology comprises items that can be put back into use quickly when they fail. They are often made of easily replaced component parts. If we return to Binford's distinction between personal and situational gear and the process of gearing up, it is clear that the distinction between these categories is related to reliability and maintainability. When the Nunamiut gear-up their personal equipment, replacing worn out tools and making sure that nothing is likely to break when needed, they are effectively ensuring the reliability of their toolkit. The creation of situational gear in the field is not only evidence of the need to do something unforeseen, but can also be taken as evidence of maintainability, of the ability to repair tools which have broken. However, the tools which the Nunamiut now use (rifles, snowmobiles and so on) are not easily maintained in the field except with large supplies of pre-manufactured, spare parts to allow for all possibilities. Catering for the reliability of these items is, therefore, an essential part of the Nunamiut technological system.

On the other hand, stone tool technology is by its very nature maintainable. The most complex stone tools are necessarily component tools. To employ archaeological signatures derived from the Nunamiut's essentially reliable technological system for the interpretation of prehistoric lithic assemblages is probably highly inappropriate. Whilst recognizing the value of Binford's observation that hunter-gatherers give thought to their technological needs beforehand and prepare accordingly, we also need to recognize that the nature of the technology which they use must come into their calculations. We are left with no direct analogies from modern hunter-gatherer groups for the interpretation of prehistoric lithic technologies, but a series of guiding concepts which we can only apply from first principles. We must take account of the planning of future requirements that goes into stone tool use but also recognise that the inherent maintainability of stone tool technology must mean that the discarded tool components within lithic assemblages reflect the activities which were carried out at the place of discard.

Final interpretations

If we return once again to the lithic assemblages from Megalakkos it is possible to offer some final interpretations for the activities that produced the assemblages within Units 4 and 6.

The raw materials from Unit 4 suggest that the occupants of Megalakkos at this time had come from some area outside of the local exploitation territory. They brought with them good quality cores as well as some backed bladelets, presumably hafted in hunting tools, as well as endscrapers. They made either blanks for tools, or the tools themselves, and then departed. The low proportion of backed bladelets in contrast to endscrapers suggests that the site was not a butchery/hunting location but may have been a small residential camp for a few nights.

The raw materials from Unit 6 indicate that the occupants of the site were local residents, and therefore they were perhaps related in some way to the inhabitants at Klithi. The composition of the discarded assemblage and the abundance of backed bladelets and manufacturing debris in particular suggests that when at the site the occupants took time to gear up their hunting equipment. The quantity of debris is small, however, especially in comparison with Klithi, and so I would suggest that it was not a residential site at this time, and therefore fulfilled some other purpose. The determination of that purpose will require new models for the relationships between subsistence economies, technological systems and the geography of lithic discard processes.

Conclusions

The excavations at Megalakkos have revealed a number of lithic assemblages of which two (from Units 4 and 6) are large enough to make analysis possible. The provenances of the raw materials used and the typology of the tool components discarded differ to such an extent that the assemblages would appear to result from groups engaged in different activities at the site. The characteristics of the earlier assemblage (Unit 4) suggest that the site was perhaps used as a night camp for a small group of hunters who came into the Voïdomatis basin from outside the local area. The characteristics of the later assemblage (Unit 6) suggest that the site was used by a small group of people who were living in the local area. It is clear that some form of tool preparation took place when the site was occupied, some form of gearing up, as well as possibly some small-scale hunting, but the true function of the site is difficult to determine.

One final question remains. When the dimension of time is added to the differences between the Megalakkos assemblages, the evidence can be interpreted in two ways. Either the change at Megalakkos is representative of a change in the use of the wider Voïdomatis basin as a whole, or the nature of the exploitation of the Voïdomatis area remained unchanged throughout the period in question, and what we are seeing at Megalakkos is a change in the pattern of activities at this one particular site. This distinction is central to what Binford (1982) has described as the 'archaeology of place'; which interpretation applies to Megalakkos can only been resolved through a comparison of the lithic assemblages from a number of well-dated contexts from the Voïdomatis area and beyond.

Acknowledgements

Much of the work contained in this piece would have been impossible without the help of Shân Smith who did much of the original recording of tool typology for the materials from Megalakkos and the initial comparative sample from Klithi.

Note

1. In this paper, the term 'chert' is used to refer to all cryptocrystalline, silica-based materials which have been knapped to make stone tools. Following Larrick (1983, 32) the term 'flint' refers to a sub-group of cherts which derive from deposits of Cretaceous age, which in Europe often take the form of flint nodules from chalk deposits.

Appendix 21.1. *Megalakkos and Klithi raw materials and their likely provenances.*

The following list of cherts represents those varieties identified and used as chert types in the Klithi Lithic Catalogue stytem. The cherts were originally separated on the basis of colour and then described in relation to other factors. The provenances of the cherts have been determined by two means. Prospection of the Voïdomatis basin and other local areas for available cherts. In these prospections the locally available cherts were found to be black, semi-translucent, sometimes laminar cherts (Types 1, 3 & 14). It is also possible to estimate whether a material is exotic or local on the basis of the debitage excavated from the sites. A raw material type with a high frequency in the debitage assemblage and which is found in the form of all debitage types from the beginning to the end of the knapping sequence is more than likely to be a local chert. Cherts which are infrequently found and which only appear in debitage forms from the later part of the knapping process are likely to be exotic cherts.

Types 1–16 are those of the Klithi Lithic Catalogue, whilst Types 17–21 have been determined on the basis of the debitage assemblages at Megalakkos. 'Indeterminate' in the raw-material tables refers to materials where the characteristics of the material cannot properly be observed and the raw material types cannot be determined. 'Diverse' refers to raw materials whose characteristics can be observed but which appear in such small numbers, often just one piece, that a proper raw material description cannot be offered. On the basis of their rarity they are likely to be exotic.

Type 1: Black, semi-translucent chert with a fine texture. In many cases there are small black inclusions in the body of the chert. This chert appears to be the same as modern chert in the Voïdomatis basin. It is likely to be of Eocene age.

Type 2: Light-grey, fine-textured chert. It appears to be heavily patinated. Provenance is uncertain.

Type 3: Grey translucent chert with fine texture. It is probably a local chert from the Voïdomatis basin.

Type 4: Brown, fine-grained chert. It is not translucent. This may be a variety of cherts 13 or 15, as the reference example reveals fine cracking in the body of the chert (possible indications of exposure to fire). This is probably an exotic chert.

Type 5: Brown-beige chert, translucent at the edges. There is no obvious patination, colour spots or inclusions in the body of the piece. Probably an exotic chert.

Type 6: Crimson/red and fine textured. The examples reveal evidence of cracking throughout the body of the piece indicating exposure to heat/fire. This was clearly not a red chert until 'fired', but was probably one of the other categories.

Type 7: Milk-chocolate brown, opaque and of fine quality. There are no obvious inclusions, colour spots or signs of patination. An exotic chert.

Type 8: Slate grey, opaque with slightly speckled patination. It is fine textured and the examples indicate that it knaps well. There are no obvious inclusions or colour spots. Probably exotic.

Type 9: Cream-white, slightly opaque but translucent at the edges. It appears to be basically a chalcedoneous chert, with the opaqueness resulting from a slightly milky form of patination. There are no obvious colour spots or inclusions. Probably exotic.

Type 10: Blue-grey, rough textured, opaque with evidence of a milky, spotted patination. No obvious inclusions. The texture seems to have an adverse effect on the knapping quality.

Type 11: Blonde, translucent chert. Very fine textured. Patination takes the form of an opaque, cream coloured covering, beginning at the edges of the pieces. No obvious inclusions or colour spots. The material knaps well. Probably an exotic chert.

Type 12: Black, opaque, rough textured chert. No obvious colour spots or inclusions. Probably a Voïdomatis chert.

Type 13: Lilac coloured, translucent at the edges and rough grained in texture. No obvious inclusions or colour spots. Exotic.

Type 14: Black and white striped, opaque chert. The white stripes may be due to 'preferential' patination of thin chert layers within a laminated chert. This may be a local Voïdomatis chert.

Type 15: Beige, opaque and rough-textured chert. No obvious inclusions of colour spots. Probably exotic.

Type 16: Dark-chocolate brown. Fully opaque, with no outward signs of patination. There are no obvious colour spots, but there seem to be a few cream coloured inclusions, possibly microfossils, throughout the body of the material. Probably a radiolarite chert. Exotic.

Type 17: Cream-grey, opaque chert. Black and white colour spots visible to the eye. No obvious inclusions. No signs of patination. Knaps well, but does not fracture as clearly as the local chert (Type 1). Provenance uncertain.

Type 18: Light, grey-black chert. Semi-translucent with a fine texture. Small black inclusions in the body of the chert. Local. Probably a variant of Type 1.

Type 19: Fine textured, grey chert. No obvious colour spots or inclusions. No evidence of patination. Exotic.

Type 20: Grey-black, rough textured chert. Numerous black colour spots, becoming clearer with patination. No inclusions. Some evidence of desilicification and patination. Possibly a variant of Type 10. Exotic.

Type 21: Fine grey chert. No obvious colour spots or inclusions. No evidence of patination. Exotic.

Chapter 22

The Boïla Rockshelter: a Preliminary Report

Eleni Kotjabopoulou, Eleni Panagopoulou & Eugenia Adam

The Boïla rockshelter is located at an elevation of *c.* 420 m on the left bank of the Voïdomatis River, at the very mouth of the Lower Vikos Gorge, facing northeast onto the Konitsa plain, and has long been recognized from surface indications as having archaeological deposits of probably Late Upper Palaeolithic date (Bailey *et al.*, Chapter 16).

The site is of particular interest within the context of the Klithi investigations for the following reasons:

- Although it is about 2 km from Klithi (Fig. 1.2), its location, orientation and micro-environment are very different from those of Klithi and Megalakkos, and it should therefore give an insight into other aspects of human behaviour, including complementary activities within the gorge environment as well as exploitation oriented to more open terrain to the north and west.
- The archaeological deposits are relatively shallow (*c.* 1 m deep), in comparison with the other excavated Palaeolithic sites in Epirus (Bailey *et al.* 1983), and clearly lie directly on top of the Late Pleistocene terrace termed the Aristi Unit (Macklin *et al.*, Chapter 17), which is exposed on the talus of the site. This offers an opportunity to examine in greater detail the chronological and stratigraphic relationships between the archaeological sequence and the fluvial history of the Voïdomatis valley.
- In terms of chronology, Boïla, due to its location at the very mouth of the gorge, is expected to give indications of earlier and/or later occupation than at Klithi and Megalakkos.

These factors have provided the initial stimulus for the Voïdomatis Palaeolithic Project of the Ephoreia of Palaeoanthropology-Speleology of the Greek Archaeological Service. The general aims of this project are to promote the cause of rigorous Palaeolithic research within the Greek archaeological community and to maintain the momentum of work in the Epirus region, where three decades of research provide a foundation for a new phase of investigations. The specific objectives are to develop new ways of tackling issues raised by the Klithi Project through excavation and survey of new sites and areas. The Project began in 1993, as part of the excavation programme of the Ephoreia of Palaeoanthropology-Speleology, with a preliminary excavation at Boïla, continued in 1994, and is conducted by a team of Greek specialists in a number of fields of Palaeolithic archaeology. To date, the Boïla excavation is the first systematic Greek Palaeolithic project. The purpose of this chapter is to present preliminary results of the 1993 and 1994 excavation seasons on stratigraphy, lithic industries and faunal assemblages.

Site topography

The rockshelter is formed on a fault in the Eocene limestone, and has been subject to further erosion and roof collapse. The overhang today is very shallow and offers little protection from the wind and rain (Fig. 22.1). Because of its north facing aspect and the steep ridges enclosing the gorge at this point, sun only enters the shelter for about one hour in the morning. The presence of large boulders on the talus and within the underlying Aristi Unit indicates that the overhang must have extended further outwards in the past and that it has been subject to more than one episode of collapse. The shape and disposition of the boulders suggest a tectonic origin for these episodes (Mariolakos pers. comm.).

The shelter opening is 17 m wide, the present floor area is *c.* 80 m^2 and the surface of the deposit lies *c.* 11 m above the present river channel (Fig. 22.2).

Excavations

Aims and methods

The aim of the 1993 excavation was to establish the depth and the spatial extent of the cultural deposits. A grid was laid out with a three-dimensional numeric co-ordinate system based on 50 cm intervals (Fig. 22.3). Deposits were removed in 5 cm spits measured with a Sokkisha C3-A level, subdivided where appropriate to follow changes in microstratigraphy. The maximum unit of provenance is, therefore, a 50 cm × 50 cm × 5 cm block of deposit, following experience at Klithi (Bailey, Chapter 3) and thus creating comparable units of analysis. Deposits were loosened with dental tools, finds were removed and bagged directly from the trench, and sediment residues were collected with scoops and brushes, placed in large plastic bags and removed to the adjacent river for wet sieving through a 1 mm nylon mesh. Provenance units were labelled according to a Bagno system as at Klithi (Bailey, Chapter 3). Individual excavators used specially prepared data sheets to record information on sediment lithology, texture, Munsell colour, lithic and bone content and to map features (such as large stones, pebbles and cultural finds) according to a standard descriptive terminology. Samples for geological analysis, dating and wood-charcoal identification

Figure 22.1. *Aspect of Boïla and the mouth of the gorge, looking west. (Photo: T. Cadbury.)*

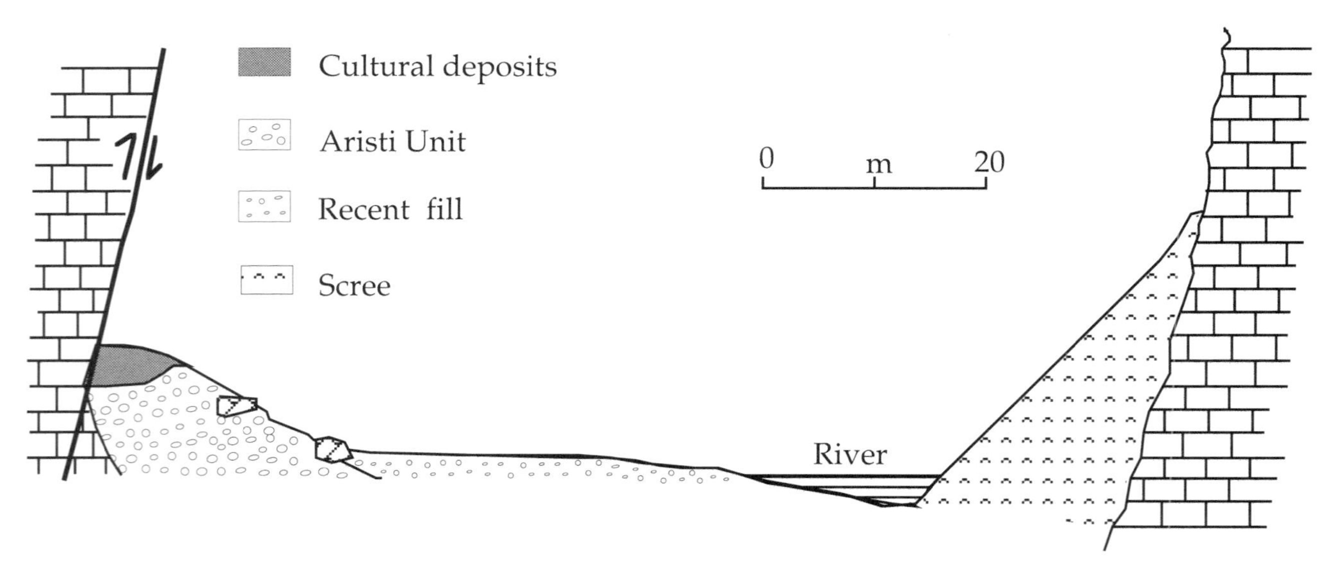

Figure 22.2. *Cross–section of the mouth of the Voïdomatis Gorge showing the relationship between the cultural sequence of Boïla and the river terraces. (Plan: Th. Hatzitheodorou.)*

were collected regularly. This excavation procedure proved to be suited to the nature of deposits and cultural remains at Boïla and was followed unaltered in the 1994 season.

An important goal throughout has been to complete sorting of the wet sieve residues during the digging seasons, a tedious and time consuming procedure, allowing little time for cataloguing and analyzing the cultural assemblages. After each season all excavated areas were filled with sacks containing pebbles from the nearby river terrace in order to protect the deposits from natural and/or anthropogenic destruction. Access to the site is restricted by a temporary fence.

Stratigraphy and chronology

Excavations have been conducted so far along the present dripline, near the talus and in two areas of the more protected part of the site (Fig. 22.3). A total of *c.* 8 m² has been excavated to varying depths, resulting in 31 excavated squares (50 cm × 50 cm). As evidence stands at present, four main stratigraphic units, I–IV from the bottom up, have been identified. Unit IV has only been identified in the area towards the talus, whereas Units III–I are more extensive and give the most informative profile along the present dripline.

Present dripline. The cultural deposits (Figs. 22.4 & 22.5) lie directly on top of the Aristi Unit, dated to between 28–24 ka (Macklin *et al.*, Chapter 17). This juxtaposition is expected to provide more accurate dating at least for the upper limit of the fluvial deposits represented by the Aristi Unit, as the existing dates are thought to be somewhat ambiguous and need further resolution (Gowlett *et al.*, Chapter 2 & Macklin *et al.*, Chapter 17). The deepest excavated profile does not exceed 1.5 m in depth within which the cultural sequence occupies an average depth of 80 cm.

The stratigraphic units are distinguished on the basis of macroscopic observations on lithology, and the relative frequency of cultural remains and other anthropogenic features such as ashy deposits. In addition seven radiocarbon dates are now available from deposits along the present dripline and confirm this initial stratigraphic subdivision. Because of small sample sizes only one was dated at the Demokritos laboratory, Athens, and the other six were processed at the Oxford AMS laboratory (Table 22.1, see also Gowlett *et al.*, Chapter 2). Clearly six dates fall within the expected time range of occupation. OxA-5244 is obviously aberrant, while OxA-5242 has a suspect ∂^{13} value. The remaining four dates, however, offer a stratigraphically consistent chronological framework for occupation of the site.

Unit I. This is a natural deposit, an alluvial gravel fill, devoid of any archaeological remains, which is also exposed on the talus in front of the rockshelter. We have not yet established how far it extends towards the back of the shelter. It was evidently formed at a time when the Voïdomatis River was flowing at a level at least 10 m higher than today and into at least part of the area now

Table 22.1. *List of radiocarbon dates from Boïla.*

Lab. no.	Material	Provenance	∂^{13}C	Date (BP)
OxA-5241	Charred bone	Unit IIIa	-21.2	12,480 ± 120
OxA-5242	Charred bone		-26.7	13,240 ± 110
OxA-5243	Charred bone	Unit IIIb	-21.2	10,190 ± 90
OxA-5244	Charred bone		-26.3	70 ± 55
OxA-5245	Charred bone		-21.2	10,560 ± 110
OxA-5246	Charred bone	Unit II	-20.6	13,810 ± 130
DEM 415-371	Carbon	Unit IIIb	-25.0	11,173 ± 453

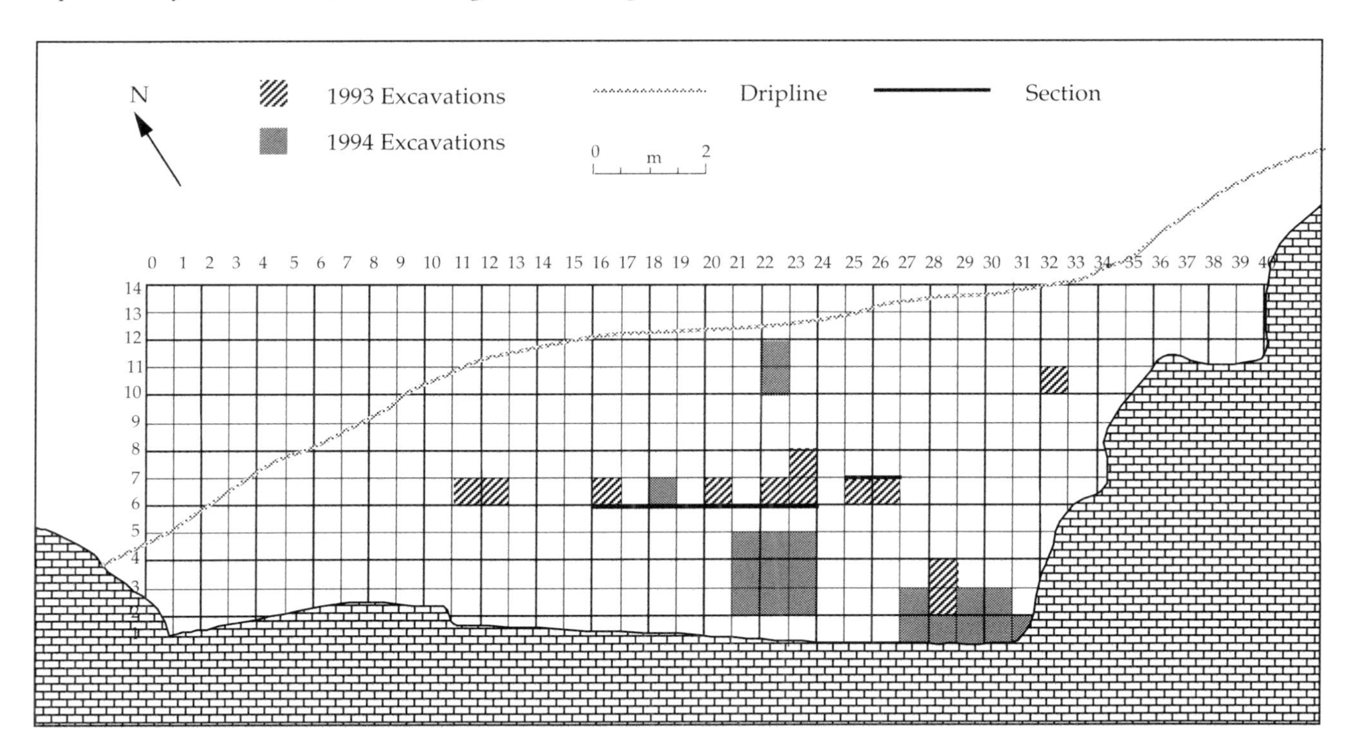

Figure 22.3. *Ground plan and grid of Boïla.*

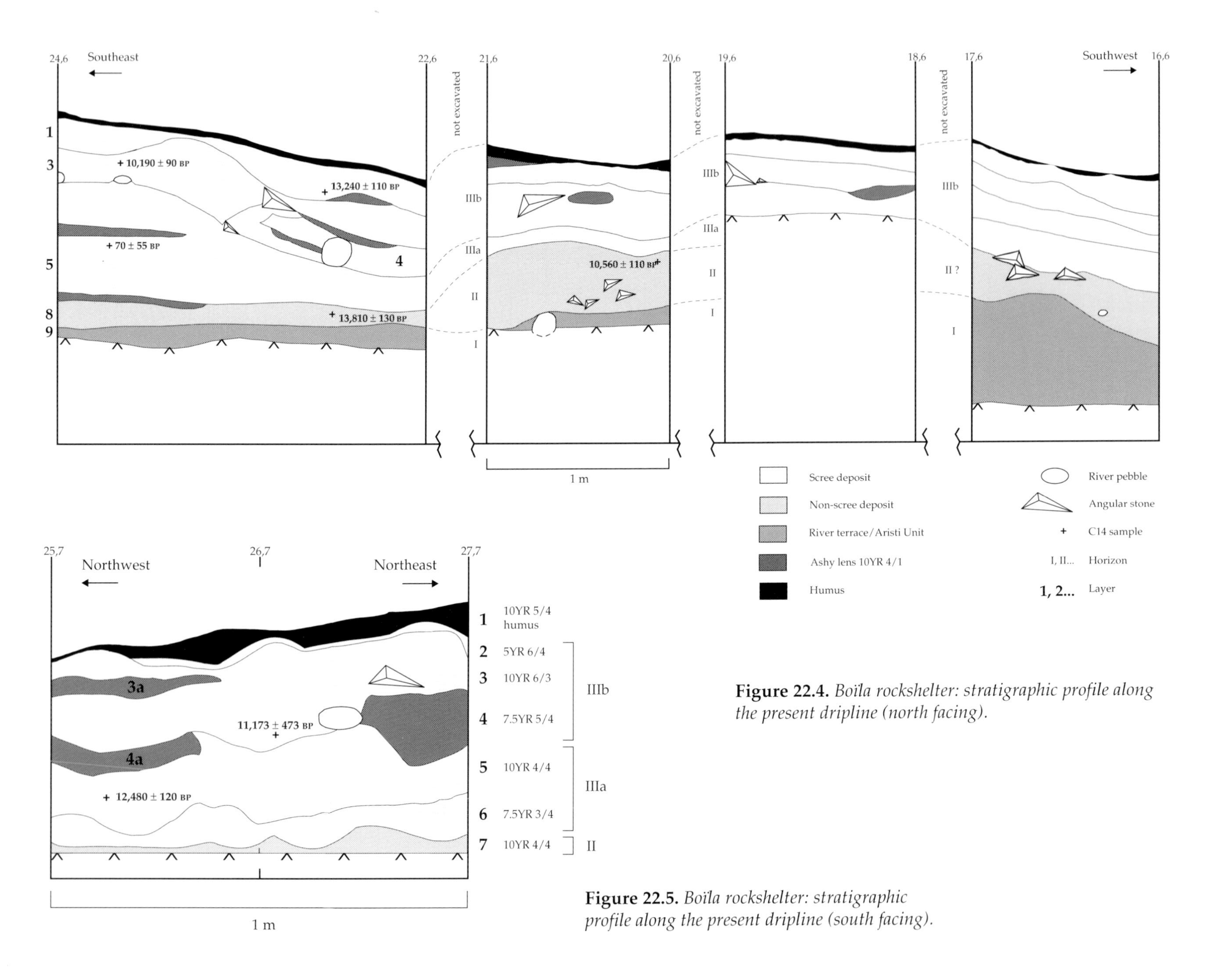

Figure 22.4. *Boïla rockshelter: stratigraphic profile along the present dripline (north facing).*

Figure 22.5. *Boïla rockshelter: stratigraphic profile along the present dripline (south facing).*

forming the rockshelter, making it unavailable for occupation. This remnant of a river terrace formed the natural surface on which the first human occupation took place after the drop in river level.

Unit II. This is a very distinctive fine-grained depositional unit lying directly on fluvial deposits and containing the oldest archaeological material. It is virtually devoid of any scree component. The date of 13,810 ± 130 (OxA-5246) comes from the base, nearly in contact with the underlying unit, and gives the earliest date for occupation at Boïla so far.

Units IIIa & IIIb. The rest of the cultural sequence comprises a complex set of layers characterized by a very pronounced angular limestone scree component. The lower part (Unit IIIa) is relatively poor in archaeological material, whereas Unit IIIb is rich in cultural remains and in features such as hearth deposits and scattered ashy lenses. The date of 12,480 ± 120 (OxA-5241) comes from the middle of Unit IIIa, while Unit IIIb ranges between 11,173 ± 453 (DEM 415-371) and 10,190 ± 90 (OxA-5243). The very top of the sequence is not yet dated.

In general terms the chronological range of occupation at Boïla coincides with that from Klithi and Megalakkos and strengthens the evidence that the Late Glacial was a period of intensive exploitation in the Voïdomatis valley. So far we have failed to find evidence of significantly earlier occupation, and our initial expectations on this point have to be abandoned for the time being. The date of 14 ka which marks the beginning of human occupation is considerably later than the proposed date of the formation of the underlying Aristi Unit, set at about 24 ka based on ESR and TL dates (Macklin *et al.* Chapter 17). Even if we allow for some time lag between the lowering of the river and the first use of the site, we would expect a span of 10,000 years to have left some sort of sedimentary record on the site. The contact between Units I and Unit II, however, is sharp, and there is no evidence for an erosional surface. It is of course possible that additional radiocarbon samples from Unit II at Boïla may give earlier dates, but as the evidence stands we suggest that the apparent discrepancy in the dates can best be resolved by supposing that the earlier set of dates refer to an earlier period in the formation of the Aristi Unit. The ESR date in particular comes from an exposed vertical section of the Aristi Unit just some 20 m away from Boïla, and some 5 m below the top of this unit, and therefore probably does not date the end of its formation. As Woodward (1990, 45) notes, the lens of slack-water silts from which the red deer mandible dated by ESR was recovered, is stratified beneath several metres of gravel accumulation, and this in its turn is overlaid by a further deposit of slack-water silts at the top of the sequence. This upper deposit contains the ashy lens with artefacts dated by radiocarbon to about 11 ka (Gowlett *et al.*, Chapter 2). The fact that this latter date is significantly later than the earliest dates of occupation at Boïla suggests either that the river was still flowing at quite a high level during the early period of occupation at Boïla and occasionally overflowed its banks, or that the radiocarbon dates on the humic acids from the charcoal from the open-air hearth, dated to about 15 ka, are to be preferred to the dates on the charcoal (Gowlett *et al.*, Chapter 2).

Finally, we should comment on the likely date at which prehistoric occupation ceased. Because of disturbances in the uppermost part of the sequence along the present dripline, and growing evidence from other parts of the deposit (discussed below), we suspect that occupation may quite plausibly have persisted into the early Holocene.

Inner part of the rockshelter. After establishing the basic stratigraphic sequence, investigation of the most protected part of the site began, with the aim of detecting the lateral extent and patterning of the cultural assemblages. It soon became apparent that the deposits were indeed rich in lithic artefacts but some sort of disturbance had taken place. With the completion of the 1994 season it became clear that we were faced with a major truncation of the Palaeolithic deposits; a pit approximately 0.5 m deep covering an area of 2 m^2 and with an east–west orientation had been dug right against the backwall of the rockshelter in order to receive a Byzantine burial, itself undisturbed (Fig. 22.6). The skeleton was found complete, in good condition and belongs to a female individual (Stravopodi pers. comm.). It was placed in an extended position, and the upper part — from the skull to the pelvis — rested on a ceramic tile of very good quality (Papadopoulou pers. comm.). The western and part of the northern boundaries were marked by a series of worked limestone blocks. No grave offerings were associated with the skeleton, but within the infill some sherds and two copper coins were found. The presence of this burial, although not out of context in an area where medieval monuments are abundant (Petsas & Saralis 1982), is not easily explicable within the confines of a rockshelter and awaits further investigation. From the stratigraphic point of view, the Palaeolithic deposits continue undisturbed below the burial

Figure 22.6. *Boïla rockshelter: the Byzantine burial. (Photo: E. Kotjabopoulou.)*

and to a greater depth than along the present dripline. Bedrock has not yet been reached in any of the excavated units of this part of the site.

To the west of the Byzantine grave and along the same axis an area of 1.5 m × 1.5 m was opened up during the 1994 season (Fig. 22.3) in order to further investigate the spatial distribution of cultural remains. The slow pace of excavation did not permit the identification of a deep vertical stratigraphy, but two main phases have been recognized: a series of loose, mainly ashy, deposits with a relatively low frequency of cultural remains, probably representing a generalized hearth area; and beneath these a rather compact scree layer rich in lithic and bone remains.

The talus deposits. During the second digging season we investigated the talus deposits (Fig. 22.3) in order to link the cultural sequence with the alluvial terrace exposed in that area. Excavation revealed only the uppermost part of the sequence (Unit IV) as we came across a very fine-grained deposit of a type not previously encountered. This deposit was virtually devoid of limestone scree and remarkably rich in lithic artefacts, but poor in animal bone remains. The technomorphological characteristics of the lithic artefacts suggest either a specialized activity area or a later phase altogether (see below).

The cultural assemblages

Only preliminary results from the ongoing analysis of the lithic and faunal assemblages will be presented here due to the early stage of excavations, the tentative stratigraphic correlations and the limited number of available radiometric dates. We also confine our remarks to the general character of the material and do not attempt a quantitative analysis, which we consider to be premature at this stage if not misleading due to the differential horizontal distribution of the material already noted. On the whole the assemblages are comparable to those recovered from Klithi, but there are indications of important differences in the way the cultural remains were accumulated, modified and re-arranged spatially and this offers ample scope for unravelling the variability in the human use of the Voïdomatis catchment at the end of the Pleistocene.

The lithic industries

A sample of *c.* 2500 artefacts from 10 excavated squares was examined for the following information:

- inventory of the raw materials;
- reconstruction of the reduction sequence(s) (core exploitation, manufacture and maintenance of tools);
- morphological tool classification according to widely accepted and applied schemes (Sonneville-Bordes & Perrot 1954; 1955; 1956a,b; Tixier 1963), supplemented by a system devised specifically for the Epirotic assemblages (Adam 1989).

Briefly, the industries can be assigned to late Upper Palaeolithic industrial phases, i.e. Epigravettian (Gamble 1986; Kozlowski 1992); the presence of even later phases (Epipalaeolithic/Mesolithic) (Bar-Yosef 1970; Perlès 1987; Tixier 1963) is under investigation and can neither be confirmed nor excluded at the present stage of analysis.

The commonest raw material consists of small pebbles collected from the nearby Voïdomatis River. This grey to black flint is usually fine-grained and shatter-prone during knapping, a tendency already recorded in the Klithi industries (Roubet, Chapter 8), and is represented at Boïla in the form of cores, debitage products and tools alike.

The inventory of raw materials includes a range of other, good quality, flint varieties of various colours and textures (dusky red, white, yellow-red etc.) in smaller quantities than the local flint. These varieties are rarely encountered in the local river gravels and could be considered as non-local to the site (exotic flint types have already been recorded at Klithi, but their exact correspondence to those present at Boïla remains to be established). Examination of the outer surfaces indicates that the nodules of non-local flint were not collected from river gravels, in contrast to the local flint where river-rolled surfaces are abundant. Moreover, at least some of them seem to have been processed at the site judging from the presence of cores, technical pieces and primary debitage products along with tools. The Boïla occupants at the end of the Pleistocene obviously had access to other flint sources besides the Voïdomatis; the exact provenance and methods of procurement of these materials are a matter of further research and this applies to the lithic industries of Epirus as a whole.

Most of the cores examined (Fig. 22.7) are exhausted regardless of raw material. A number of them seem to have been exploited intensively, judging from the change of the direction of flaking, their small final size and the crushing of the striking platforms. It is evident that the desired endproducts were bladelets, an observation reinforced by the presence of core tablets (Fig. 22.7:6), platform rejuvenation flakes and crested pieces.

The most frequent tool types are tools made on bladelets (Fig. 22.8:1–6). More specifically these are unilaterally and bilaterally backed bladelets with plain or retouched proximal and/or distal ends, and microgravettes. A remarkable characteristic of the industries is the presence in large numbers of microburins (Fig. 22.8:7–9) which indicates *in situ* manufacture of backed bladelets and other bladelet tools ('armatures'). The use of the microburin technique could eventually prove to be connected to blank segmentation oriented towards the production of geometric microliths.

Other tool types (present in smaller quantities) are simple (Fig. 22.9:1–2) and double (Fig. 22.9:3) endscrapers, mostly on exotic raw materials, burins (Fig. 22.9:4) and notches (Fig. 22.9:5).

Considerable variation in the horizontal distribution of lithic artefacts was observed during the 1994 season:

- differential representation of debitage products in different areas, attested by the presence of such artefacts mostly in the central part of the site (west of the Byzantine burial);
- different tool types inside and outside the present dripline. Endscrapers and burins come from the southeastern part of the rockshelter, that is the most protected area of the site which preserves signs of repeated use. Unfortunately, the major disturbance caused by the Byzantine grave renders stratigraphic correlations with the other units impossible. On the other hand the excavated units nearest to the talus yielded a remarkable number of a specific subtype of bladelet tool that falls within the microgravette category (Fig. 22.8:5–6) in direct stratigraphic correlation to a substantial number of microburins (Fig. 22.8:7–9), a combination unique to the site so far.

In summary, the Boïla lithic industries are comparable to other known Upper Palaeolithic assemblages from Epirus. The tool inventory seems restricted compared both to Klithi (Roubet, Chapter 8) and to Kastritsa Stratum 1 (Adam 1989; Chapter 25), which

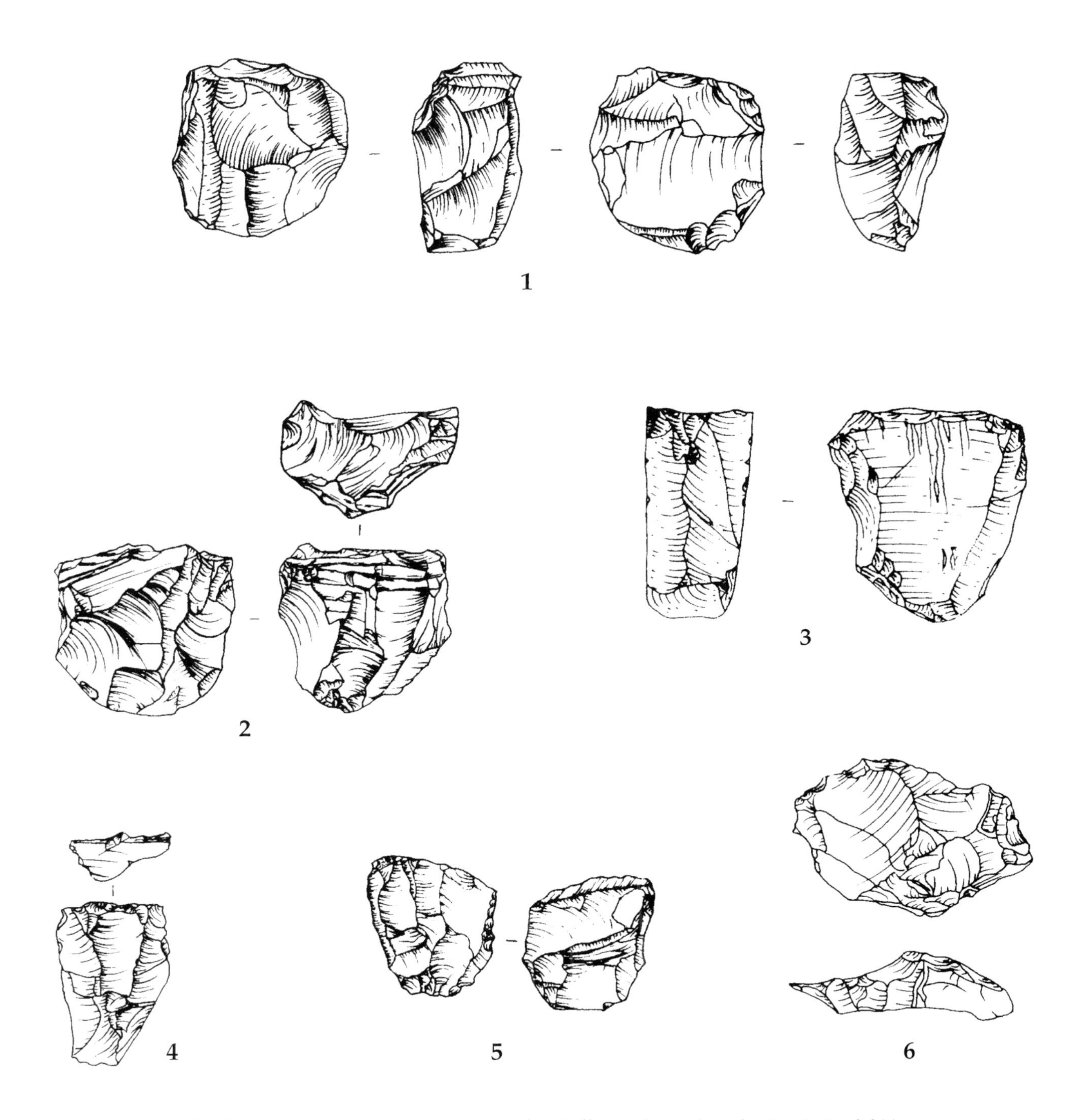

Figure 22.7. *Boïla lithic industries: 1–5. cores; .6 core tablet. Full size. (Drawings by Maria Deïlaki.)*

appears to be the stratigraphic horizon directly comparable to Boïla, as it is dated to 13,400 ± 210 BP (I-1960). This differentiation, if not merely a result of the limited sample size, could be attributed to different circumstances of use and discard of stone tools, i.e. to different site function.

Another important point to make is the different representation of bladelet tool types between the various sites: whereas backed bladelets (unilaterally backed plain) are strongly represented in Kastritsa Stratum 1 and in the Q26 sample from Klithi (Adam 1989, fig. 28:11, fig. 36:2), they appear to be less numerous at Boïla, while at the same time 'armatures' (Fig. 22.8:5–6) make an impressive appearance in the Boïla bladelet tool spectrum and are poorly represented in the former assemblages. This morphological variability has obvious functional connotations; whether it is merely a result of specific site function or indicative of inter-site chronological differentiation remains to be established.

The analysis of the lithic industries supports the stratigraphic

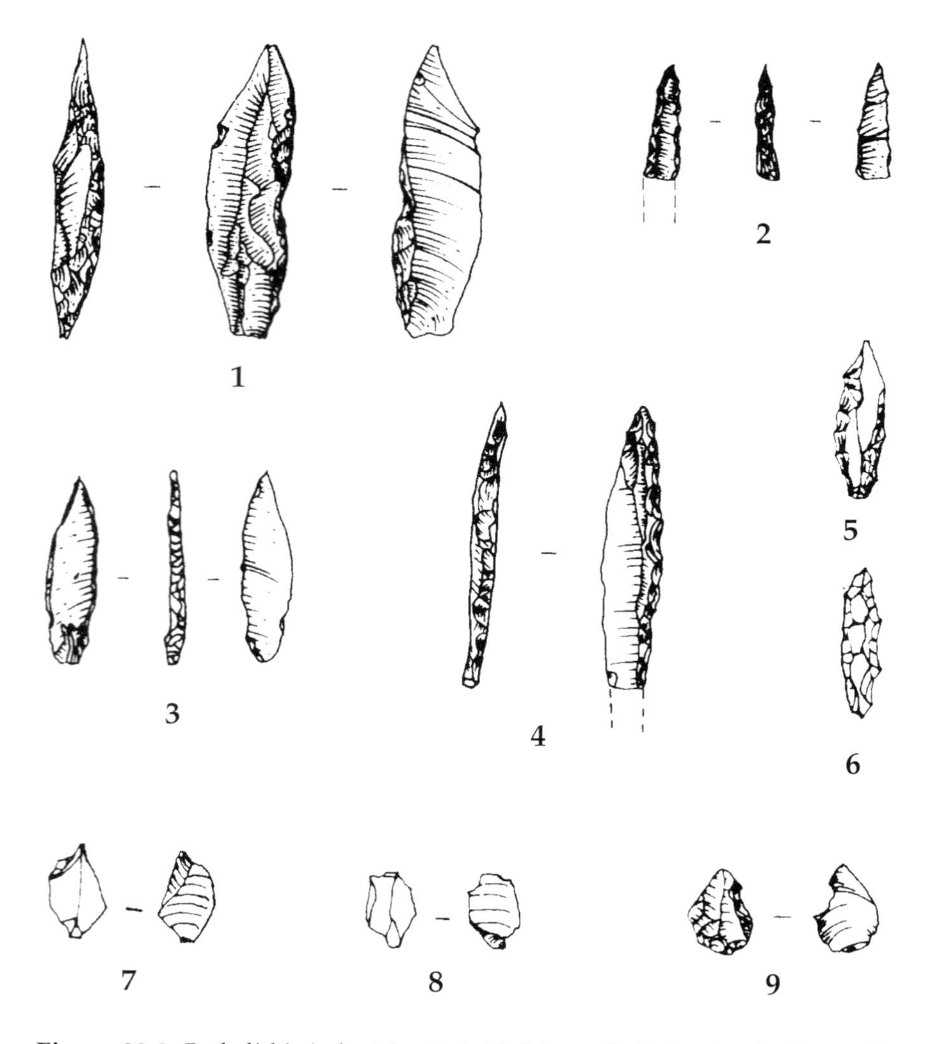

Figure 22.8. *Boïla lithic industries: 1–6. bladelet tools; 7–9. microburins. Full size. (Drawings by Maria Deïlaki.)*

evidence for the existence of discrete cultural horizons at Boïla and seems to indicate the presence of potentially identifiable activity areas as well. If these preliminary observations are confirmed, then a major difference will be established from the Klithi deposits, for which a midden-like taphonomic history is suggested (Bailey & Woodward, Chapter 4; Galanidou, Chapter 15).

The faunal assemblages

The most striking feature of the Boïla faunal assemblage is its poor preservation. This is expressed not only by the extremely fragmentary nature of the bones but also by their badly weathered surfaces in most cases. As a result the bulk of the recovered assemblage consists of long-bone fragments and splinters (not exceeding 6 cm in length) that are difficult to identify to the level of specific anatomical element and/or taxon. This property along with the limited sample size makes it premature to present any meaningful quantitative data.

In terms of species, Boïla, in contrast to Klithi, does not seem to represent an exclusively one-species site. In the identifiable sample caprines predominate, but deer are also well represented. Suids, lagomorphs, some microfauna and remains of fish are also present. Carnivore bones have not as yet been encountered. Chamois is probably the most common caprid (Fig. 22.10), judging from the small size of jaws, loose teeth, bones of the extremities and the characteristic shape of horn cores. Among the deer bones, fragments of antler tines, metapodials and phalanges confirm the presence of red deer. Still, it is possible that *Capra cf. ibex* as well as fallow deer and the more woodland adapted roe may also be present. Tentative as this picture may be, it suggests that the site of Boïla, despite its small size but precisely because of its location, offers a window into patterns of resource exploitation outside the confines of the gorge environment. A precondition, however, for clarifying the role of Boïla in the wider settlement distribution is to disentangle the taphonomic history of the faunal assemblages.

The poor preservation of the bones, frustrating as it may be, requires an explanation. With no evidence so far to the contrary, humans must be held responsible for the accumulation and attrition of the faunal remains; no carnivore- or rodent-inflicted damage has been observed. Within the entire sequence along the present dripline and towards the talus, bone fragments are severely weathered showing signs of moderate to deep exfoliation and are thus extremely brittle. Even teeth, the most resistant parts of the skeleton, are affected. In some cases larger fragments survive, both in terms of length and circumference, but as soon as they are exposed they break into smaller pieces. Thus, great effort has been devoted to consolidating them before removal. The survivability of bone appears to be somewhat better in the inner, more protected, part of the rockshelter.

The very location of the site at the mouth of the gorge, its north facing aspect and the shallow overhang, are all factors which expose the cultural deposits to physical agents of attrition (e.g. wind, water percolation), and hence contribute to the poor preservation. Moreover, the way the deposits have been formed and accumulated via a combination of physical and anthropogenic processes is of crucial importance to the interpretation of site function within the wider settlement pattern. The relatively small quantity and low density of material recovered at Boïla, compared for instance to Klithi, suggests a less intensive pattern of occupation. Given this observation two hypotheses can be advanced. If visits to the site were widely spaced in time and/or of limited duration, and assuming a relatively low rate of sediment accumulation, the bones would have been lying on the surface for a considerable time, thus becoming vulnerable to destruction even before their incorporation in the deposits. Alternatively, if sedimentation rates prove to be high, then post-depositional taphonomic processes must be invoked to explain the poor condition of the bones.

All things being equal, the breakage pattern of the animal bones suggests that some stages of butchering and certainly marrow extraction were taking place at the site. High utility

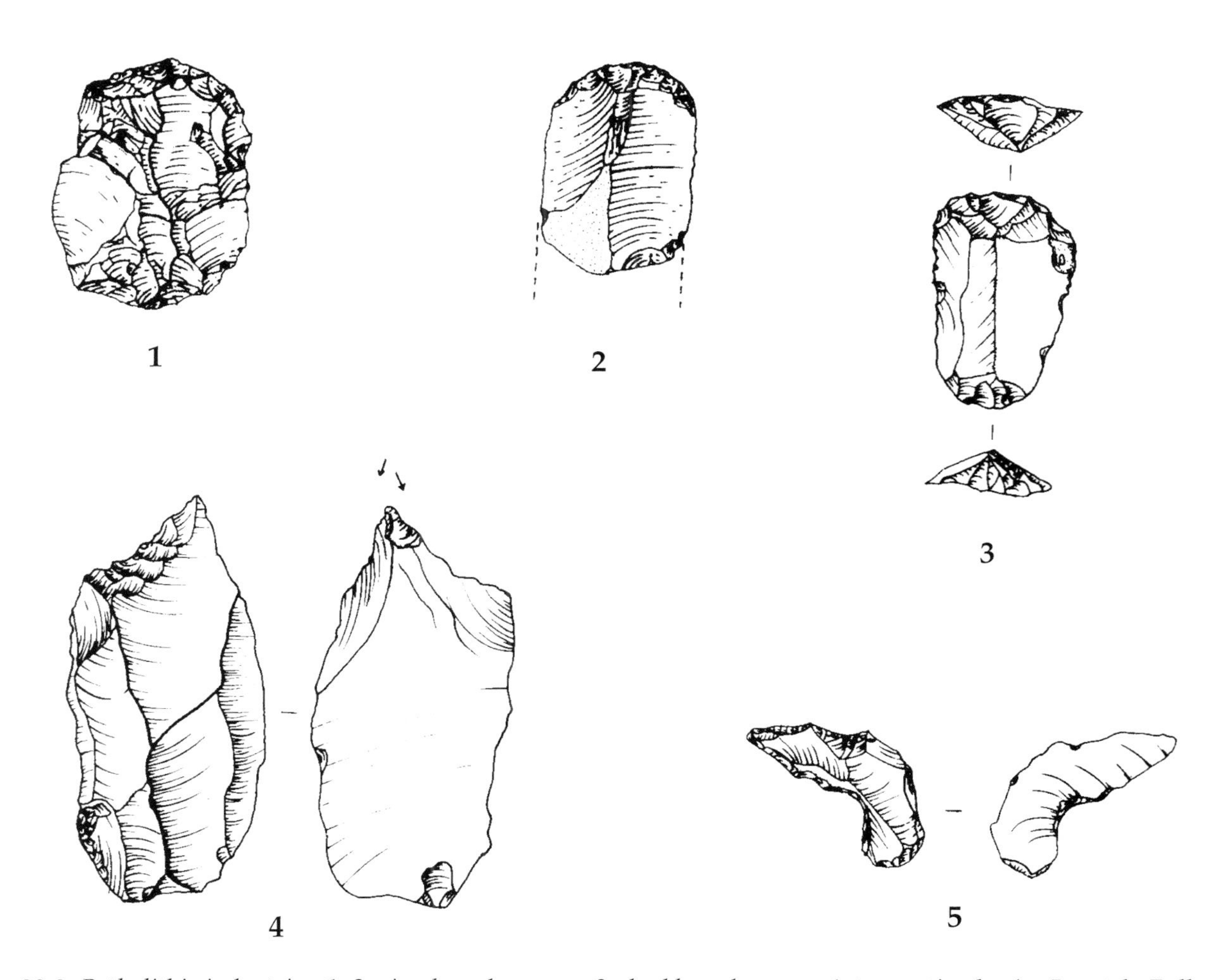

Figure 22.9. *Boïla lithic industries: 1–2. simple endscrapers; 3. double endscraper; 4. truncation burin; 5. notch. Full size. (Drawings by Maria Deïlaki.)*

anatomical parts but also small bones such as phalanges (Fig. 22.11) are clearly chopped and split, in a manner very similar to that recorded at Klithi (Gamble, Chapter 12). The presence of bone tools, such as the awl of Figure 22.12, suggests that at least some bones were further processed in order to complement the lithic tool kit (see also Adam & Kotjabopoulou, Chapter 13). The extent to which this practice contributes to the fragmented state of the material remains to be examined.

Despite the problems related to the taphonomic history of the faunal assemblages, the site of Boïla should provide decisive information on how the specialized hunting of caprines at Klithi was linked to other Late Upper Palaeolithic subsistence strategies of the region. These obviously included a comprehensive system of culling a variety of herbivore taxa across the segmented Epirotic landscape.

Conclusions

Within the Palaeolithic record of Greece a unique case is provided by the Epirus data, and in particular by the combination of on-site and off-site data within the Voïdomatis valley, which open up the possibility of tackling issues related to the contemporaneous use of different parts of the landscape.

Although research at the rockshelter site of Boïla is at an early stage, the existing stratigraphic and artefactual evidence suggests that we should, from now on, view the distribution of sites within the catchment as integral parts of a common settlement-procurement system. While Klithi can be considered as the 'type-site' of the high altitude Voïdomatis environmental niche, it is inadequate by itself to explain, from a regional perspective, the complex web of subsistence decision-making by Late Pleistocene hunter-gatherers. In this context the importance of a site such as Boïla does not lie in its size or depth of stratigraphy, but rather in its very location. Placed at the mouth of the Lower Vikos Gorge, it is a 'bridge' between the gorge environment and the more open terrain to the west.

By and large the chronological range of the cultural sequence at Boïla is analogous to that of

Figure 22.10. *Boïla fauna: Chamois mandibles. (Photo: A. Iliakopoulos.)*

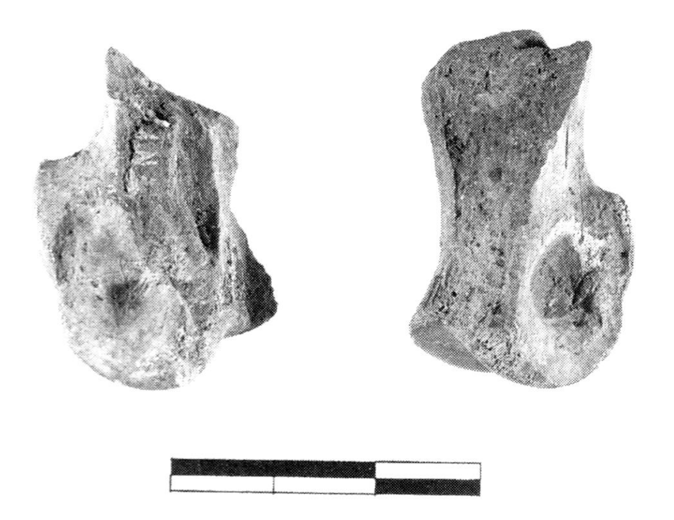

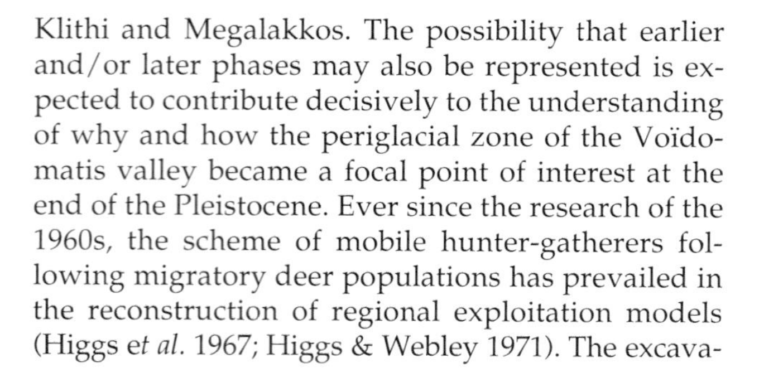

Figure 22.11. *Boïla fauna: Caprine second phalanges, split for marrow extraction. (Photo: A. Iliakopoulos.)*

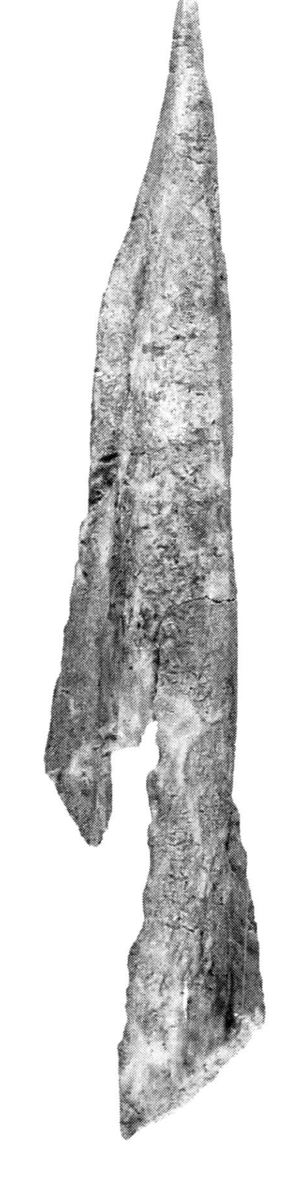

Figure 22.12. *Boïla bone industry: awl fragment, tip damaged. (Photo: A. Iliakopoulos.)*

Klithi and Megalakkos. The possibility that earlier and/or later phases may also be represented is expected to contribute decisively to the understanding of why and how the periglacial zone of the Voïdomatis valley became a focal point of interest at the end of the Pleistocene. Ever since the research of the 1960s, the scheme of mobile hunter-gatherers following migratory deer populations has prevailed in the reconstruction of regional exploitation models (Higgs *et al.* 1967; Higgs & Webley 1971). The excavations at Klithi during the 1980s have stimulated the consideration that alternative resource exploitation strategies co-existed at times of uncertain environmental conditions and biomass availability (Gamble, Chapter 12). Independent palaeogeographical research has re-emphasized the importance of regional long-distance mobility as a dominant theme, while stressing the importance of more localised niches in the overall pattern of subsistence dynamics (Sturdy *et al.*, Chapter 30). The Boïla results clearly offer the prospect of expanding our understanding of inter-site variation on the local scale.

Acknowledgements

Thanks are especially due to Yannis Tzedakis, Geoff Bailey and Alex Kotzambopoulos, without whose support the Boïla Project would never have got off the ground. We also extend our deep gratitude to Thomas Cadbury for his generous help and tolerance of the Greek temperament throughout the digging seasons. Our thanks are also due to Yannis Maniatis and Giorgos Fakorellis of the 'Demokritos' Laboratory and to Rupert Housley of the Oxford AMS Laboratory for the radiometric dating. Panagiotis Karkanas is undertaking the sedimentological analysis, and we extend our thanks for his contribution and insights. Maria Dinou is pursuing anthracological analysis and her contribution to the excavation process is hereby acknowledged. Theodoros Hatzitheodorou and Maria Driva carried out the topographic mapping, and Maria Deïlaki drew the artefacts in Figures 22.7, 22.8 and 22.9. We are grateful to Kostas Kousiandas, Georgia Tsartsidou, Melina Massika, Aristotelis Koskinas and Vangelis Tsakirakis of the University of Ioannina for enduring with remarkable patience the long hours of meticulous digging and sorting of wet-sieve residues. Lakis Kondrolozos has been of valuable help with practical matters. We are also grateful to Chronis Kaltsounis, the Headman of the village of Klithonia, for assistance with field logistics. This chapter is dedicated to the future students of the Palaeolithic of Greece.

Part V

Klithi in its Regional Setting: Archaeology

Part V: Editorial

Geoff Bailey

An important objective of the chapters in Part V is to provide fuller information on the material excavated during the Higgs era, including the presentation of previously unpublished data from the Higgs surveys and the excavations at Asprochaliko, Kokkinopilos and Kastritsa, as well as new data collected during the course of the present project, notably the new dates from Asprochaliko and new site surveys. The subject matter is organized in chronological order, beginning with the Mousterian industries at Asprochaliko in their broader inter-regional context (Chapter 23). Chapter 24 moves on to consider the Asprochaliko and Kokkinopilos Mousterian industries in a regional geographical perspective, including a discussion of the many open-air sites that have been recorded. Succeeding chapters deal, respectively, with the Upper Palaeolithic industries of Asprochaliko and Kastritsa in relation to Klithi (Chapter 25), a comparative analysis of site structure at Kastritsa and Klithi (Chapter 26), and an analysis of site distributions at the regional scale (Chapter 27).

These chapters provide the archaeological context for the Epirus-wide studies of landscape evolution, environmental change and land-use presented in Part VI. The chapters in Part V also complement those in Part VI in another sense, and that is that they bring to the fore the problem of changes in resolution *of the data as one expands the chronological and geographical perspective. Some of this is due to different research strategies: Asprochaliko and Kastritsa were dug differently from Klithi, and inter-site comparison thus raises anew the confounding problem discussed earlier in relation to the differing excavation strategies practised at Klithi (Chapter 6). Much of this loss of resolution, however, is inherent in the data, and no amount of technical virtuosity or judicious research design can recover what has been lost: chronological resolution is inevitably poorer in the Mousterian beyond the range of radiocarbon dating, while open air sites show the poorest chronological resolution of all. Even in stratified sites, the palimpsest effect makes it impossible to talk in any meaningful sense about 'living floors' as these might be observed in an ethnographic context. It is tempting to be defeatist on this issue, to see loss of resolution as a problem and to put it down to inadequate data or inadequate methods of data recovery. But, as the discussions that follow amply demonstrate, this is a misleading way of viewing the situation. Rather than loss of resolution, which implies a value judgement about the superiority of one scale of measurement over others, it would be preferable to refer to differences of resolution, and to welcome these, because they force us to think differently about the data, to frame questions appropriate at different scales of resolution, and to question concepts of accuracy and contemporaneity. In effect, expanding the geographical and temporal perspective opens up different scales of observation, and this is taken up in Part VI, which focuses on the different scales of processes and behaviour revealed by different temporal and geographical perspectives. These twin themes of* resolution *and* scale *are fundamental to what follows, and indeed to much of what has already been presented in earlier chapters, permeating the whole range of studies carried out during the course of the project.*

Chapter 23

The Basal Mousterian of Asprochaliko Rockshelter, Louros Valley

John Gowlett & Pat Carter

In this chapter we seek to evaluate some of the archaeology of Epirus on a longer timescale than can be provided by the important late Pleistocene and late Palaeolithic record of human occupation at Klithi. We describe the basal Mousterian of Asprochaliko rockshelter as part of a study of the wider Palaeolithic context. The work is based on new studies of the shaped tools and of the debitage made during the course of the Klithi project. We examine the nature and size-ranges of the cores and debitage, and consider the shaped-tools as a subset of the whole. Comparisons are made with the overlying assemblages at Asprochaliko and Mousterian material from other sites in Greece. A brief review is given of other Mousterian assemblages of similar age in Europe and around the Mediterranean which have features reminiscent of the Asprochaliko assemblage, such as a prominent blade component.

The Middle Palaeolithic background

There is no means of establishing the full duration of the Palaeolithic in northern Greece, where only one or two isolated finds date back to the Acheulean. Sites dating to the Middle Palaeolithic (*c.* 150,000 BP onwards) are, however, known, especially from the work of the Cambridge projects of the 1960s (Bailey *et al.* 1983; Dakaris *et al.* 1964; Higgs & Vita Finzi 1966) and recent surveys (Runnels & Van Andel 1993a,b).

The rockshelter at Asprochaliko in the Louros valley was central to this work, and remains so now in providing a dated framework (Huxtable *et al.* 1992). The site, however, is not easy to evaluate: there have been major changes in methodologies and research goals since the time of the original excavations, and it also stands almost alone in Greece as a major site of its period. Asprochaliko was excavated in the 1960s; the shaped tools were then re-examined and drawn in 1980, as a preliminary to renewed Palaeolithic investigations in Epirus (see Bailey, Chapter 1). Artefacts from the upper levels of the site were then restudied in new projects (Papaconstantinou 1988, Papaconstantinou & Vassilopoulou, Chapter 24; Adam, Chapter 25). The debitage of the earliest or basal Mousterian — an important component of the assemblage — was first studied in detail in 1989.

Asprochaliko fits into a Mousterian world which has been described much more comprehensively in western Europe and in the Near East. Dated sequences remain rare in southeast Europe, but we have recently presented thermoluminescence (TL) dates, which show that the Asprochaliko archaeological sequence extends to *c.* 100 ka (Huxtable *et al.* 1992). This age applies specifically to the distinctive basal Mousterian industry, which is characterized by numbers of long blade-like flakes (see below). A similar age of sequence has recently been demonstrated for the site of Karaïn in western Turkey (Otte *et al.* 1995).

Middle Palaeolithic archaeology in general passed through a highly typological phase in the 1950s and 1960s, but the Epirus work was largely insulated from this because of the strongly economic approach of the Higgs school (*cf.* Chapter 1). Although the 1980s work caught up with typological norms of the Bordes era, the world of Middle Palaeolithic studies has moved on again, and new questions are in archaeologists' minds. This poses for us a particular question: can old collections, excavated with a previous generation's research goals in view, now serve to address the questions which would be the central focus in new research?

As benchmarks we can take the reports of other Middle Palaeolithic sites recently re-excavated and reanalyzed — for example Tabun Cave (Jelinek 1990) and Kebara Cave in Israel (Bar-Yosef *et al.* 1992). In these the work has been carried out over an even longer period, but it seems conclusively established that it is rewarding to continue analyzing the older material in new terms.

The work at Kebara follows more new directions than can be taken up on a site without re-excavation. But in newer archaeology of this kind, we can trace a general move from typology to technology; from statics to dynamics; from the artefact for its own sake to a seeking of social tradition. This approach need not be accepted uncritically. It is questionable whether the search for social tradition in technology is fundamentally different from the older search for social tradition through typology. The difficulty of separating economic and functional constraints from social patterning seems no less under the new order. Perhaps in truth the new developments represent mainly a humanizing of older research goals.

At Asprochaliko we have attempted to follow this path, even though the analyses did not extend to refitting or microwear studies. They were largely based on metrical studies, which provide some continuity with Lower Palaeolithic research (e.g. Isaac 1977), and can serve to provide some technological insights.

Apart from addressing these general problems of Middle Palaeolithic studies, a principal aim of this paper is to draw any relevant comparisons between Asprochaliko as a rockshelter site of 100,000 years ago, and Klithi as one of 15,000 years ago in a somewhat similar immediate setting. Most of these considerations can be addressed in a series of questions:

- What artefacts were early humans seeking to produce at Asprochaliko?
- What were their technological goals?
- How consistent was their pattern of production?
- How similar or different was it from that on other Mousterian sites?
- What genuine idiosyncracies can we see in the early Mousterian levels? (i.e. distinct from sampling factors).
- Is there information that is relevant to recent research on other sites?
- Is there convincing evidence about when (in the year) and why people used the site?
- How clearly different is the Mousterian adaptation from that visible in Upper Palaeolithic rockshelters?

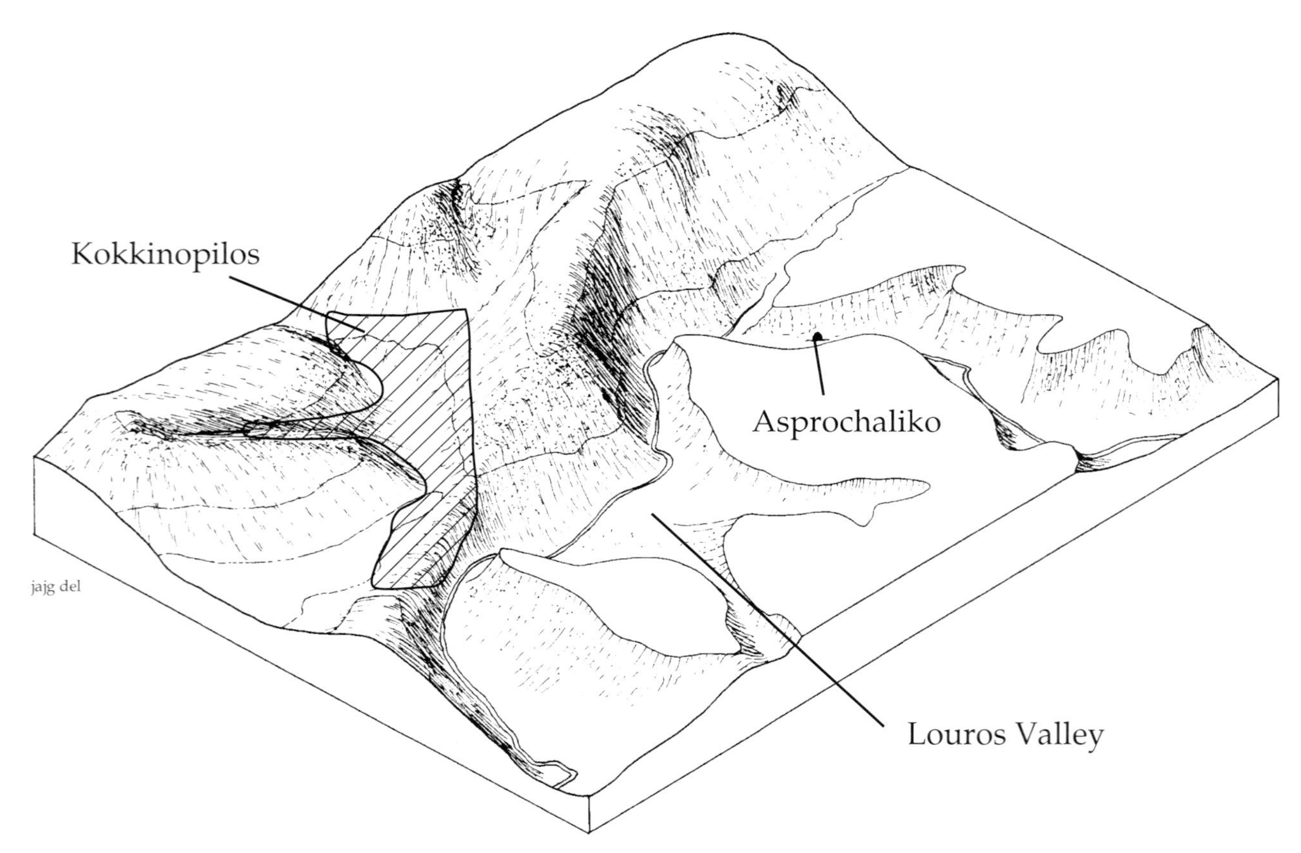

Figure 23.1. *Setting of Asprochaliko and Kokkinopilos in relation to the Louros Valley. The hatched area shows the extent of the Kokkinopilos red beds. North to top right.*

The site and its stratigraphy

Full descriptions of Asprochaliko and its environment are given in earlier papers (Bailey *et al.* 1983; Higgs & Vita-Finzi 1966). Here we summarize only the main features. Asprochaliko is a limestone rockshelter 20 m above the Louros River on the right bank of its gorge between the modern towns of Ioannina and Arta (Fig. 23.1). It was excavated in the 1960s under the general direction of E.S. Higgs, yielding a succession of Mousterian and Upper Palaeolithic stone industries (Bailey et *al.* 1983; Higgs & Vita-Finzi 1966). More recently further studies have been undertaken of the stratigraphy, the radiocarbon sequence and the artefacts, in the context of the renewed research in Epirus mentioned above (Bailey *et al.* 1992; Huxtable *et al.* 1992).

The rockshelter has a relatively shallow overhang. It is about 18 m wide, by 7–10 m deep. The deepest excavation extends about 8 m from front to back of the shelter. We can thus calculate the total area as roughly 150 m^2. The talus slopes fairly steeply, but at the sides, especially to the west, additional areas may have been useful for prehistoric activities.

The deposits were originally excavated to a depth of *c.* 5 m. The upper part of the sequence is dated in outline by two radiocarbon dates from samples taken in the original excavations (Higgs & Vita-Finzi 1966). A date of 26,100 ± 900 BP (I-1965) occurs near the base of a series of deposits within the overhang of the rockshelter (Layers 4, 7 & 10) extending through the top 2 m of the section and containing backed blade assemblages. It is possible that some of these assemblages are late glacial in date (*c.* 14 ka to 10 ka) but at present there is no evidence to indicate how continuous occupation was from *c.* 26 ka to 10 ka (see also Adam, Chapter 25). Attempts were made to obtain further radiocarbon dates, but the bones sampled in 1981 all proved to be depleted in collagen.

This Upper Palaeolithic sequence is underlain

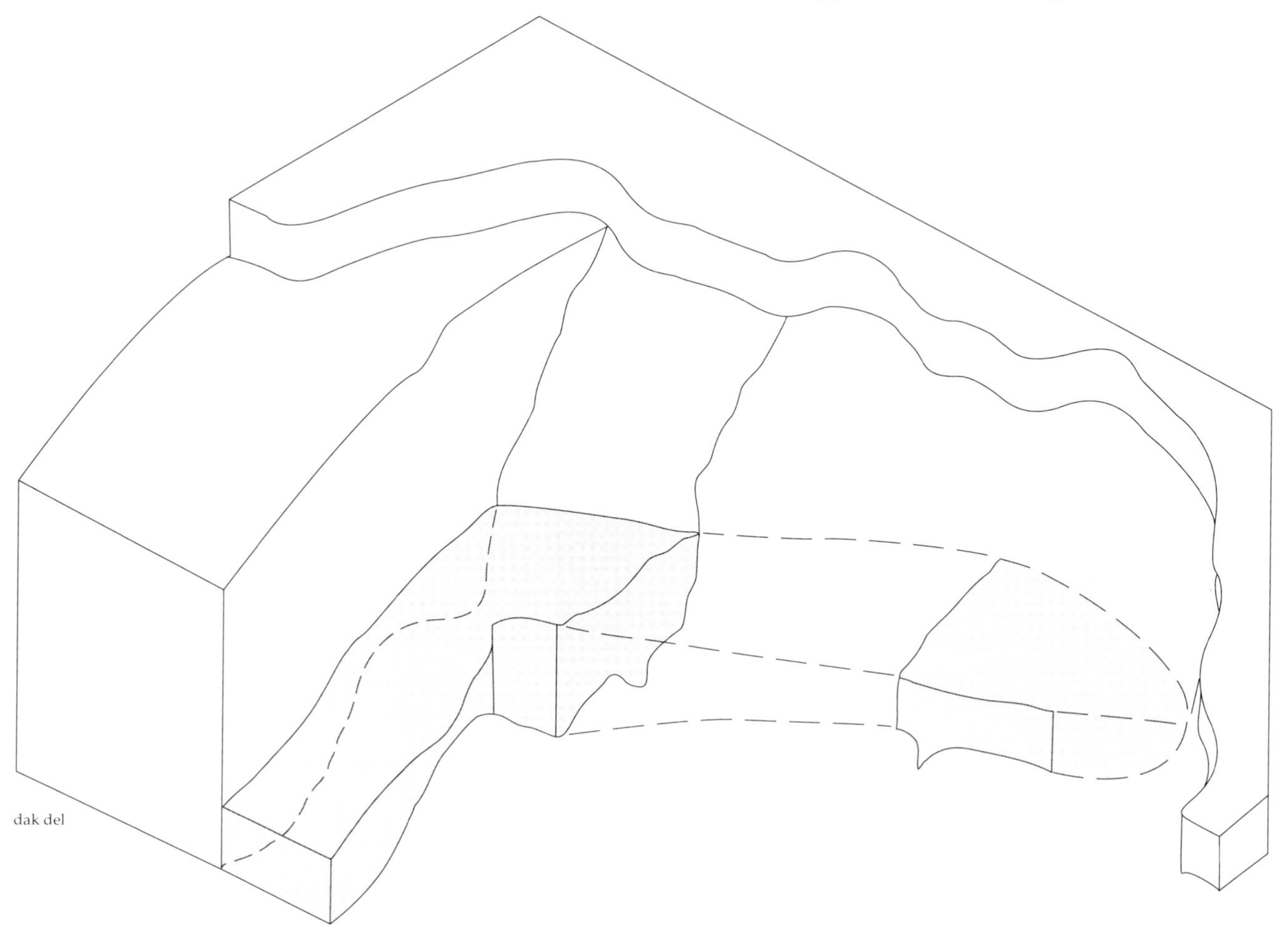

Figure 23.2. *Oblique view of Asprochaliko rockshelter, showing the postulated extent of the basal Mousterian layers, as inferred from the sections of the eastern and western trenches. North to top right.*

by a series of Mousterian assemblages extending from a depth of *c.* 2 m to about 5 m in the sections (Figs. 23.2 & 23.3). The upper levels of Mousterian are characterized by small tools, usually 30–40 mm long, which were described as Micro-Mousterian in the original report, and have subsequently been re-described (Papaconstantinou 1988; Papaconstantinou & Vassilopoulou, Chapter 24; *cf.* Huxtable *et al.* 1992). We refer here to the industry from these upper levels as the upper Mousterian.

In the lower part of the sequence, at a depth of 4 m or more, are the deposits which form the subject of this chapter. Layer 18 extends outside the present rock overhang and contains a different type of Mousterian industry, together with teeth of the extinct Merck's rhinoceros *Stephanorhinus* (formerly *Dicerorhinus*) *kirchbergensis*. The basal Mousterian industry contained within it differs from the overlying material in a number of respects (see below).

Provenance of the material

The extent of the basal Mousterian has not been rigorously defined (see Papaconstantinou & Vassilopoulou, Chapter 24, for concerns about provenance). In the western trench, it is taken to be coincident with Layer 18. This, however, drops some 2 m as one moves out of the rockshelter. At the outer margin it is overlain by Layer 8, itself at a deeper level than the inner part of Layer 18, and it is not plain whether the contents of 8 are exclusively 'basal' Mousterian. Further east in the shelter, Layers 11, 12, 15 and 17 are also regarded as basal Mousterian. The exposure of these layers is limited, however: the greater part of them is unexcavated, and lies between the two Higgs trenches under a very large boulder which subsequently fell from the roof. A thickness of nearly one metre of these sediments extends into the eastern trench (Fig. 23.2).

The sections show that a higher bench of stone existed towards the northeast corner of the cave. Occupation may have been concentrated in this area, and the slope of the sediments suggests that material spilled down from it. Most excavated material of the basal Mousterian comes from the western trench, in its lower area.

Our analysis is based mainly on material from the western trench. The western trench occupies roughly 20 m^2: the specimens examined thus may represent about 10–15 per cent of the total which was deposited in the shelter. The original report (Higgs & Vita-Finzi 1966) mentioned the Mousterian with large blades as coming from Spit 24 and below. This designation would be valid for specimens coming from Spits 28–32 in the inner squares TRBa and TRBb. We are surer of sampling the basal material if we restrict the analysis to material which comes from below Spit 33/34. These spits were encountered only in rectangles TRBc and TRBd. There is still some risk of sampling from Layer 8, but this is minimized by isolating material from Spits 35 and 36 for comparison with the rest of the sample. Layer 8 hardly reached these levels at any point, so they are the most certainly 'uncontaminated'.

Thus finds recorded as from below Spit 35 give the highest probability of belonging exclusively to the basal Mousterian, without likelihood of intermixture with the overlying Mousterian.

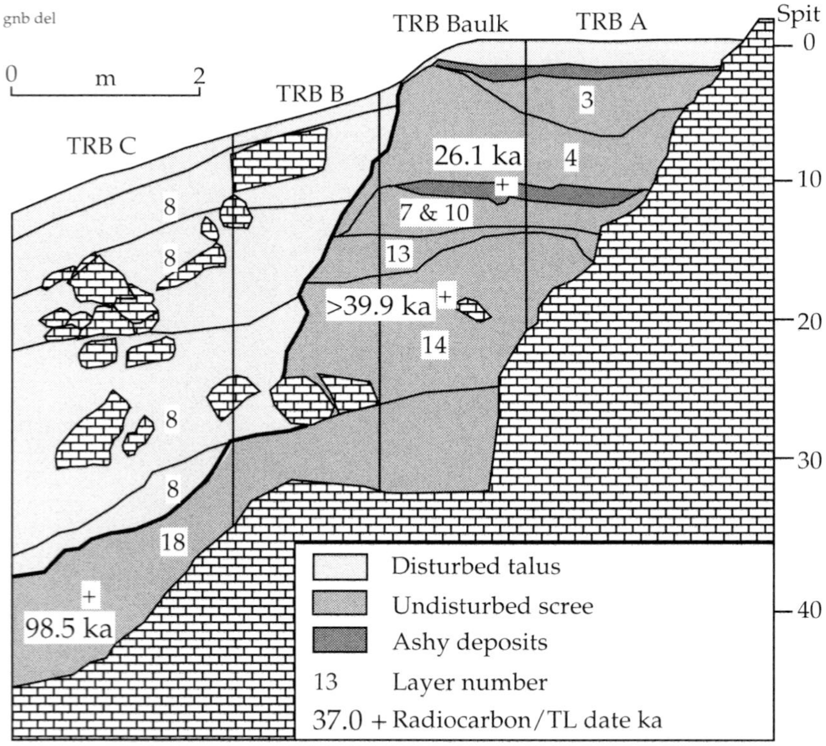

Figure 23.3. *The west section of the TRB trench showing the fit of spits and natural stratigraphy. (After Bailey* et al. *1983; 1992.) According to Higgs & Vita-Finzi (1966) the basal Mousterian began from Spit 24. The status of material from Spits 33/34 and 35/36 is discussed in the text.*

Until the study of the debitage in 1989, no basal Mousterian had been processed from the eastern trench. We examined a series of debitage from Rectangle 52, and take the opportunity to introduce this into the comparisons.

Refinement of the chronology

Apart from the Upper Palaeolithic horizons, most of the sequence is beyond the forseeable range of radiocarbon. A series of bone samples was collected throughout the section in 1981 for AMS radiocarbon dating, but no detectable collagen was preserved. Amino acids extracted from bones produced unsatisfactory results, demonstrating that not all contamination could be removed (Gowlett *et al.* 1987). Burnt flint, however, allowed the thermoluminescence (TL) dating of the lowest levels of the site (Bailey *et al.* 1993; Huxtable *et al.* 1992; Gowlett *et al.*, Chapter 2).

Although section cleaning was undertaken at Asprochaliko in the hope of finding further burnt flints, none was recovered. The flints A9/114 and 115 from the original excavation were found to be satisfactory for dating. The ages of these two flints calculated using the capsule data were 102 ± 1 ka and 96 ± 11 ka respectively. The average age for this level of the site (Layer 18) is 98.5 ± 12 ka (OxTL 229).

This suggests that the basal Mousterian occupation coincides with one of the later phases of the Last Interglacial, an interpretation supported by the spectrum of temperate fauna, including the rhinoceros *Stephanorhinus* (formerly *Dicerorhinus*) *kirchbergensis*. If this date is correct, it also indicates that only about two metres of sediment accumulated between this interglacial occupation and the beginning of the Upper Palaeolithic material about 40,000 years ago.

The dating of the basal Layer at Asprochaliko was regarded as of particular interest, since it establishes the presence in Greece of an unusual lithic industry characterized by many blade-like specimens at some point within the Last Interglacial (isotope stage 5), over 50,000 years before Upper Palaeolithic blade industries appeared in Europe.

Recent work suggests that Middle Palaeolithic with blade elements occurred far earlier than has been supposed, and appeared perhaps on a number of occasions (Mercier *et al.* 1995). Middle Palaeolithic industries which are blade-dominated are known from as early as 200,000 ka in Europe, the Middle East and Africa (Barham & Smart 1996; Mercier *et al.* 1995; Tallon 1978; Wendorf & Schild 1974). It is obviously desirable to make comparisons with other industries of similar appearance, but the blade phenomenon is far from unique, and cannot now justifiably be interpreted as indicating a precursor of the Upper Palaeolithic.

The basal Mousterian stone industry

The lower industry excavated at Asprochaliko consists of at least several thousand pieces including debitage. These come chiefly from *c.* 20 m^2 of the site, in which finds of this nature extend through roughly 1 m in depth. On the basis of calculation of the area of the whole rockshelter, total numbers of shaped tools may amount to about 2000, of cores to about 1500, and of debitage to many thousands. Even with further excavation no close estimate could be made, since other material may have spilled out of the rockshelter and down the talus.

The basal Mousterian assemblage was initially distinguished from the overlying 'Micro-Mousterian' through having larger tools, a more refined retouch, and far larger numbers of racloirs (Higgs & Vita-Finzi 1966, 21). It was regarded as somewhat similar to the material from Kokkinopilos, but had far fewer flakes with facetted butts, and lacked the element of bifacial pieces found there.

Some 284 shaped tools were described in the Bordes analysis which was undertaken in 1980. This shows the industry as a 'typical' Mousterian, in which a rather restricted range of Bordes types is present. Sidescrapers and notches are by far the most common retouched tools (Table 23.1). Although previous analyses have commented on the large size of the tools relative to the overlying layers, some classes such as the notches are fairly small.

We aim now to set this material in a context of production, and to test the questions and assumptions made above.

Raw material procurement

Plainly the industry is produced on river cobbles, as demonstrated by the frequent occurrence of cobble cortex. The variety of rocks, including quartz and quartzite of varied colours, indicates that river cobbles from the Louros were used as the raw material. A size spectrum of the material (Fig. 23.4) shows that very few of the pieces are longer than 80 mm, probably implying that the cobbles selected for use as cores were a maximum of 100 mm in diameter. The curves of the cobble cortex support this idea. Larger cobbles would have been available, so it can be assumed that the size range was a matter of choice, and likewise that any differences in size between the basal industry and later industries reflect choice

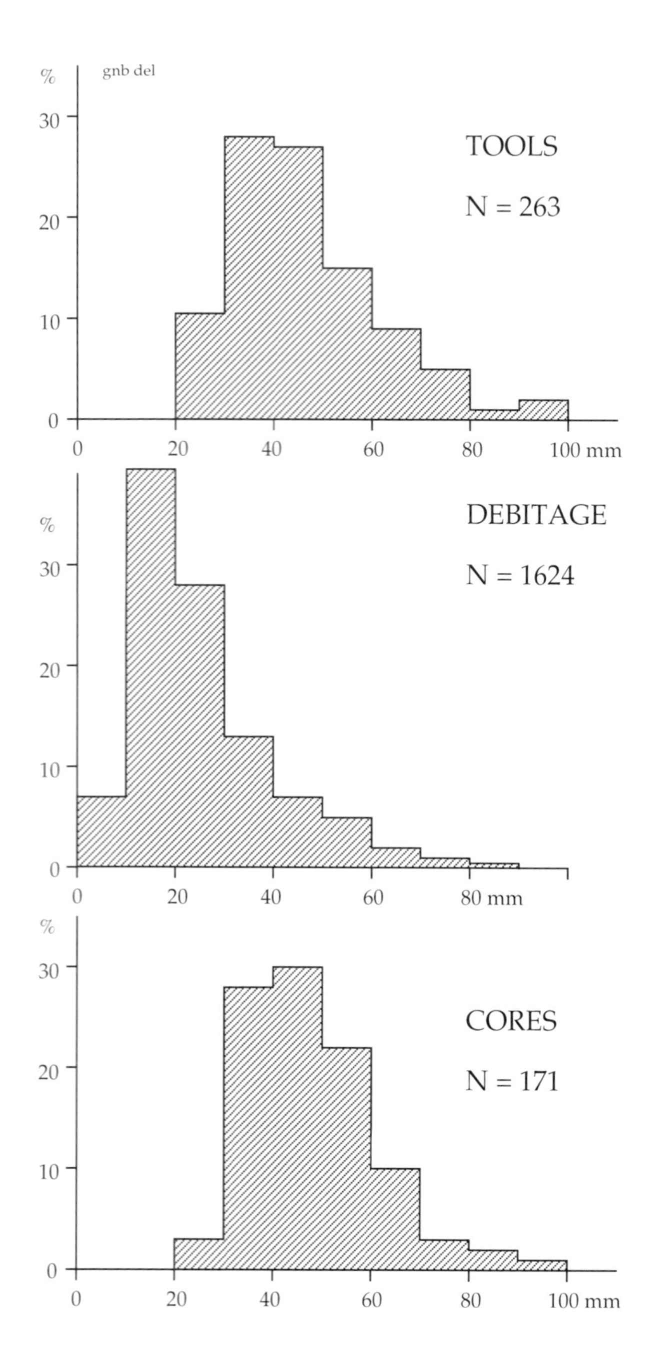

Figure 23.4. *Size spectra of the main elements of the basal Mousterian assemblage (cores, flaking debitage and shaped tools).*

rather than direct environmental constraints.

The knapped material can be treated under a few major categories: cores, which are often discoid, but occur in other forms; the debitage, amongst which some of the larger flakes are notably elongated; and the retouched tools, which it will be seen are often made on blanks far larger than most of the debitage.

Table 23.1. *Bordes analysis of artefact categories.*

No.	Type	N
3	Levallois points	19
4	Retouched Levallois points	5
5	Pseudo-Levallois points	25
6	Mousterian points	2
8	Limaces	8
9	Single straight sidescrapers	7
10	Single convex sidescrapers	46
11	Single concave sidescrapers	11
12	Double straight sidescrapers	2
13	Double straight-convex sidescrapers	3
15	Double convex sidescrapers	4
17	Double concave-convex sidescrapers	1
19	Convergent convex scrapers	1
21	Dejete (offset) scrapers	5
22	Straight transverse scrapers	3
24	Concave transverse scrapers	3
25	Sidescraper on ventral face	1
30	Typical endscrapers	2
31	Atypical endscrapers	2
34	Typical borers	1
38	Naturally backed knives	8
42	Notches	40
43	Denticulates	22
45	Retouches on ventral face	1
46	Abrupt and alternate retouch (thick)	1
54	End-notched pieces	3
62	Miscellaneous	37

The cores

We were able to study 171 cores from the basal Mousterian. Many of these had previously been classified idiosyncratically as 'Sturdy pieces', but most of these did not have definite features of 'tools' and this analysis relies on grouping them and looking at general and metrical characteristics. The cores range in size from around 100 mm maximum dimension down to less than 30 mm. These cores and their flake scars give an indication of both the size range and shapes of flakes desired by the makers.

The larger cores are generally single-platform (e.g. Fig. 23.5:e), and allowed long elongated flakes to be detached, usually along the longest axis of the core. Some of these are classic Levallois cores (Fig. 23.5:d), but on the whole few of the cores or flakes show signs of deliberate platform facetting.

The smaller cores are often discoid (Fig. 23.5: a,c&f), but sometimes irregular, and allowed series of flakes to be detached from each of two opposed faces. More than half of all cores were less than 50 mm in greatest dimension when abandoned.

As surviving cores reflect the endpoint at which they were no longer regarded as useful, it can be assumed that the smallest flake scars indicate directly the smallest sizes of useful flakes. One hypothesis to consider is that in general the knappers started with large cores, and worked them down in a systematic pattern, except when things went wrong. In favour of this is a systematic shape shift which can be documented from large to small cores (Figs. 23.6:a&b). This is remarkably consistent in its trend.

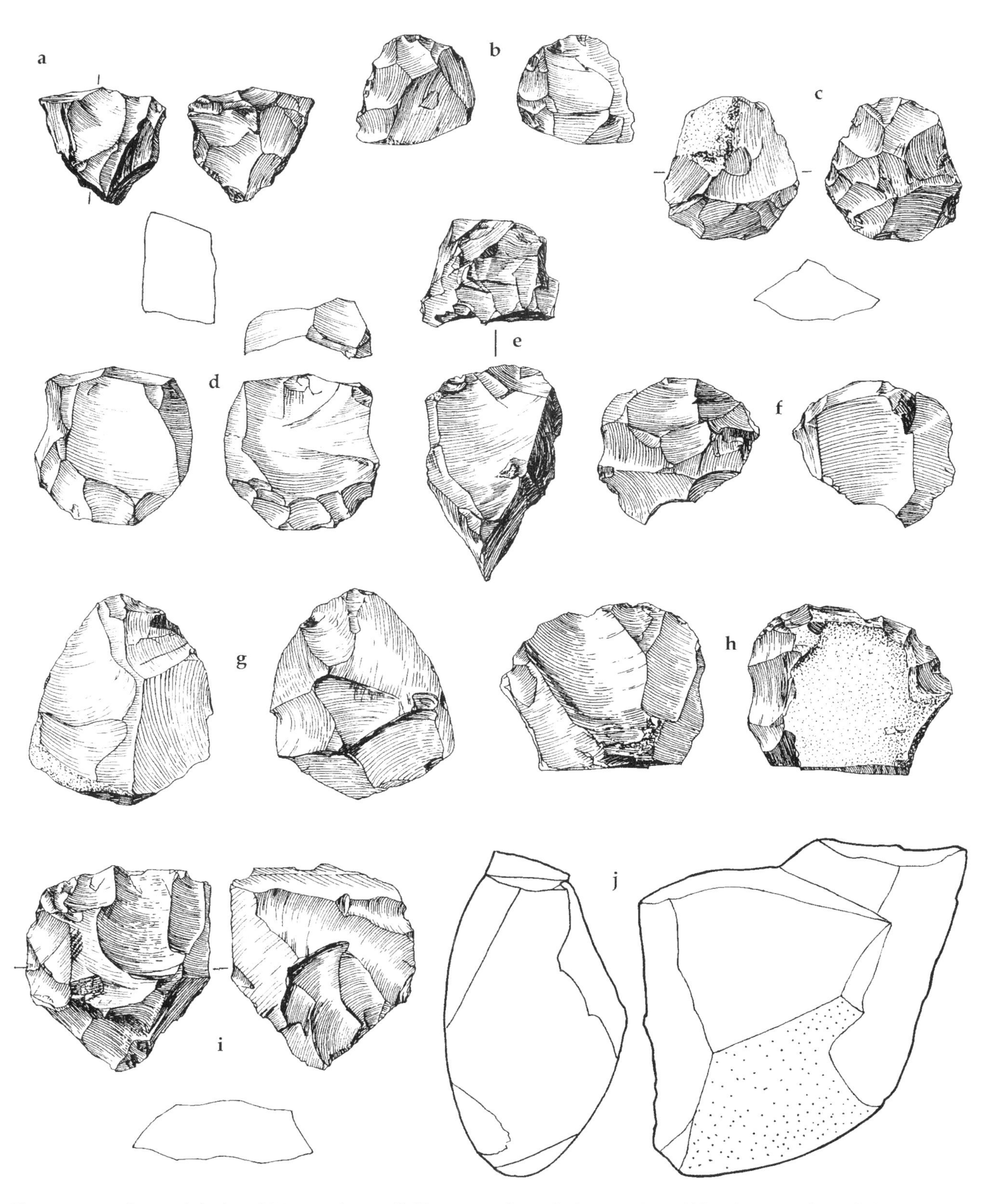

Figure 23.5. *Cores of the basal Mousterian: a–i) flint cores; j) worked quartzite cobble; c) a typical small discoid core, retaining some cortex; d) a small Levallois core, from which flakes* c. *4 cm in length have been released from the opposed faces; i) an unusually thin example, illustrating removals of small flakes from both faces. Scale 2/3 normal size.*

It may suggest that some of the large single platform cores were made discoidal as they were reduced.

There are however contrary indications that large cores were worked principally for large flakes; and that small ones often started small, showing that they were actively selected for the production of small flakes. The principal evidence is as follows:

- There is a very low frequency of large flakes in the debitage. This suggests either that very few cores started large, or alternatively that many large flakes have been removed from the site.
- There is a high proportion of small cores which retain cortex (Fig. 23.6:c). Nearly half (46 per cent) of cores smaller than 50 mm retain at least 20 per cent cortex on one face. This would not be so if several generations of flakes had previously been removed.

The debitage

The flake material *en masse* should in a sense provide a mirror image of the cores, unless substantial quantities of cores or flakes had been transported in or out of the site. Figure 23.4 shows a relationship of fairly close correspondence.

In our work, debitage was studied from a number of spits at different levels of the western trench, and also from Rectangle 52 of the eastern trench. It was felt that this would assist in picking out variations in activities on the site, and also help in assessing any contamination between the upper Mousterian and the basal Mousterian.

Overall the length spectra are fairly consistent in showing that 90–95 per cent of the material is under 60 mm in length, from 9 different contexts (Fig. 23.7). The percentage of material less than 10 mm in length is highly variable. This might well be a result of variations in recovery or storage. Nevertheless, the retention of small flakes in the original excavations was highly useful: the length spectra show that the great majority of knapping happened *in situ*, and that no factors of disturbance have winnowed out the smaller material. There is a growing body of material for comparison from other sites (e.g. Andresen *et al.* 1996; McBrearty 1988; Schick 1991).

Perhaps more surprising is the fact that from all studied samples combined (Fig. 23.7) more than 70 per cent of the debitage is less than 30 mm long. On its own this figure might be interpreted simply to suggest that the knapping produced a great many waste flakes. Taken with the core-size data, it can only be interpreted as showing that the major aim on the site in the basal Mousterian was to produce small flakes in the range 20–40 mm.

This emphasis on artefacts virtually as small as those of Klithi had not emerged from previous analyses which had concentrated on the shaped tools.

The large blades

This finding does not mean that long flakes were not required. The outstanding feature of the basal Mousterian as we and others have described it previously is the presence of numbers of flake-blades (Fig. 23.8:f,i,l&m), skilfully produced. It was argued that these are not a byproduct but a deliberate end. These include numbers of shaped tools which are larger than any tools in the overlying Mousterian (Fig. 23.9:i&p).

Inspection of the larger cores shows that long narrow flakes were regularly produced by intention, making intelligent use of previous flake facets on the cores. Such elongated flakes amount to *c.* 20 per cent of all debitage, a proportion similar to that in the 'Pre-Aurignacian' of the Haua Fteah in Cyrenaica (Fig. 23.11). The large blades were noticed originally as offering a distinction from the 'Micro-Mousterian'. Their size-range would not, however, be unusual in the Mousterian of either western Europe or the Near East.

The flake-blades stand out in the assemblage, however, for both their size, and also for their technique. Until recently, following Bordes (1979), the normally accepted definition of 'Levallois' included any flake whose 'form was predetermined by special preparation of the core before the removal of the flake' (1979, 26). Newer work has tended to emphasize the variety of approaches possible within the Levallois (e.g. Boëda 1993; Dibble & Bar-Yosef 1995). Technically these may be regarded as Levallois flakes, but the principal emphasis is on elongation (Fig. 23.8).

The section below will show that such long flakes were used as blanks for most scrapers. The analysis shows clearly, however, that only 2.5 per cent of flakes struck on the site were greater than 60 mm in length. This may imply that suitable large flakes were struck elsewhere and imported as blanks, a practice known on other sites (Toth 1987; Wilson 1988). On present evidence we cannot prove this,

Table 23.2. *List of bags examined.*

A9-33	A9-77	A9-97	A9-131	A9-376
A9-34	A9-83	A9-99	A9-139	A9-385
A9-35	A9-85	A9-102	A9-142	A9-386
A9-47	A9-86	A9-106	A9-143	A9-392
A9-50	A9-88	A9-110	A9-147	A9-393
A9-66	A9-90	A9-114	A9-318	A9-411
A9-67	A9-92	A9-115	A9-342	A9-412
A9-68	A9-93	A9-124	A9-358	A9-415
A9-70	A9-94	A9-125	A9-359	A9-489
A9-73	A9-95	A9-129	A9-364	R52-2890

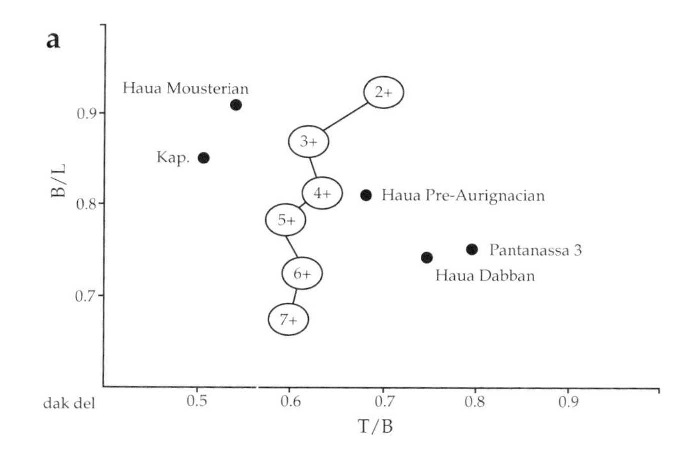

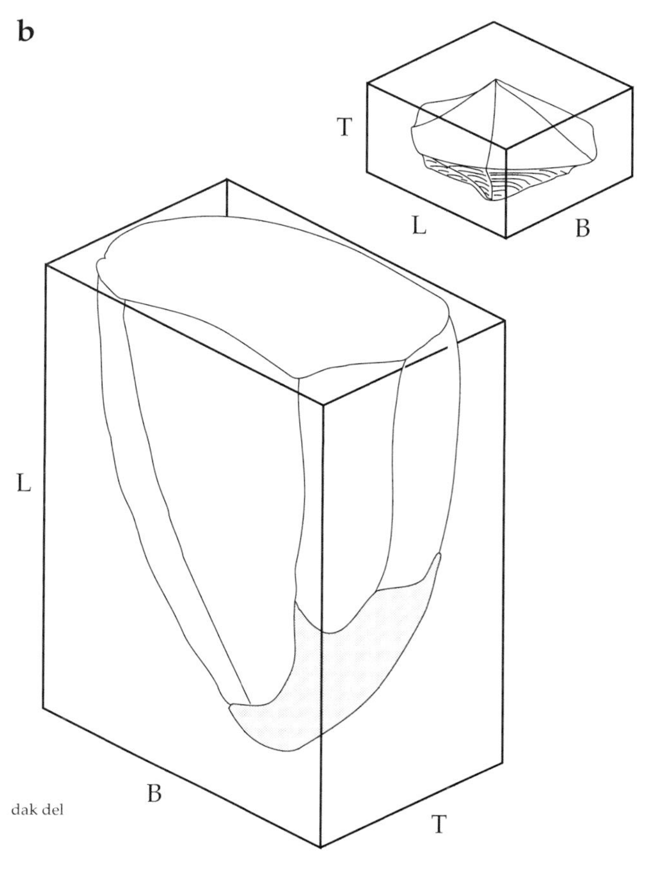

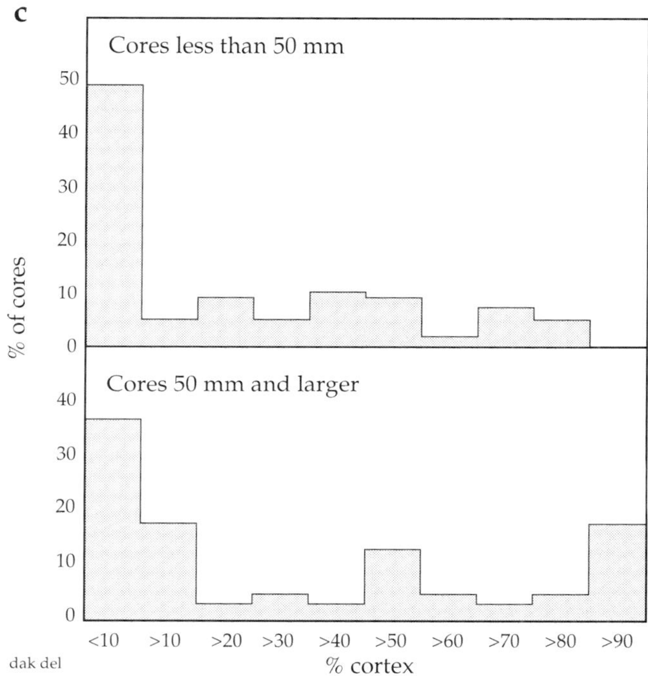

Figure 23.6. *a) Graph of the shape shift (allometry) in cores of the basal Mousterian from largest to smallest. Cores are grouped by length in centimetre classes (2+ cm = cores from 2–3 cm in length, etc.). b) Outline boxes indicating the typical shape of largest cores (6–7 cm) and smallest cores (2–3 cm). c) Proportion of cortex (on at least one face) remaining on smaller and larger cores.*

because the number of large (non-retouched) flakes among the debitage, and the number of large cores, is just high enough that knapping on-site could have generated all the blanks.

The 'big blade' element is clearly real, and it was originally highly noticeable in comparison with the overlying 'Micro-Mousterian' (as it was known). We can also observe an allometry, in which longer flakes tend to be relatively narrow. Nevertheless the new analysis emphasizes not just that such flakes are a very low proportion of the total, but also that these long flakes may have been concentrated in certain spits towards the top of the basal Mousterian (especially Spits 28/29 and possibly 35/36).

The shaped tools

These are predominantly retouched tools, although following Bordes and others they formally include some Levallois flakes. The great majority of pieces are racloirs and notches (Table 23.1; Fig. 23.9). The analysis shows that scrapers in particular were made on selected flake blanks much larger than the average in the debitage. Fine retouch is notable on some of the scrapers. Most are single-sided; they were not however highly standardized in size, ranging from about 30 mm to 100 mm. Notches tend to be smaller, with a higher proportion falling in the 30–50 mm range.

The list for the basal Mousterian includes some

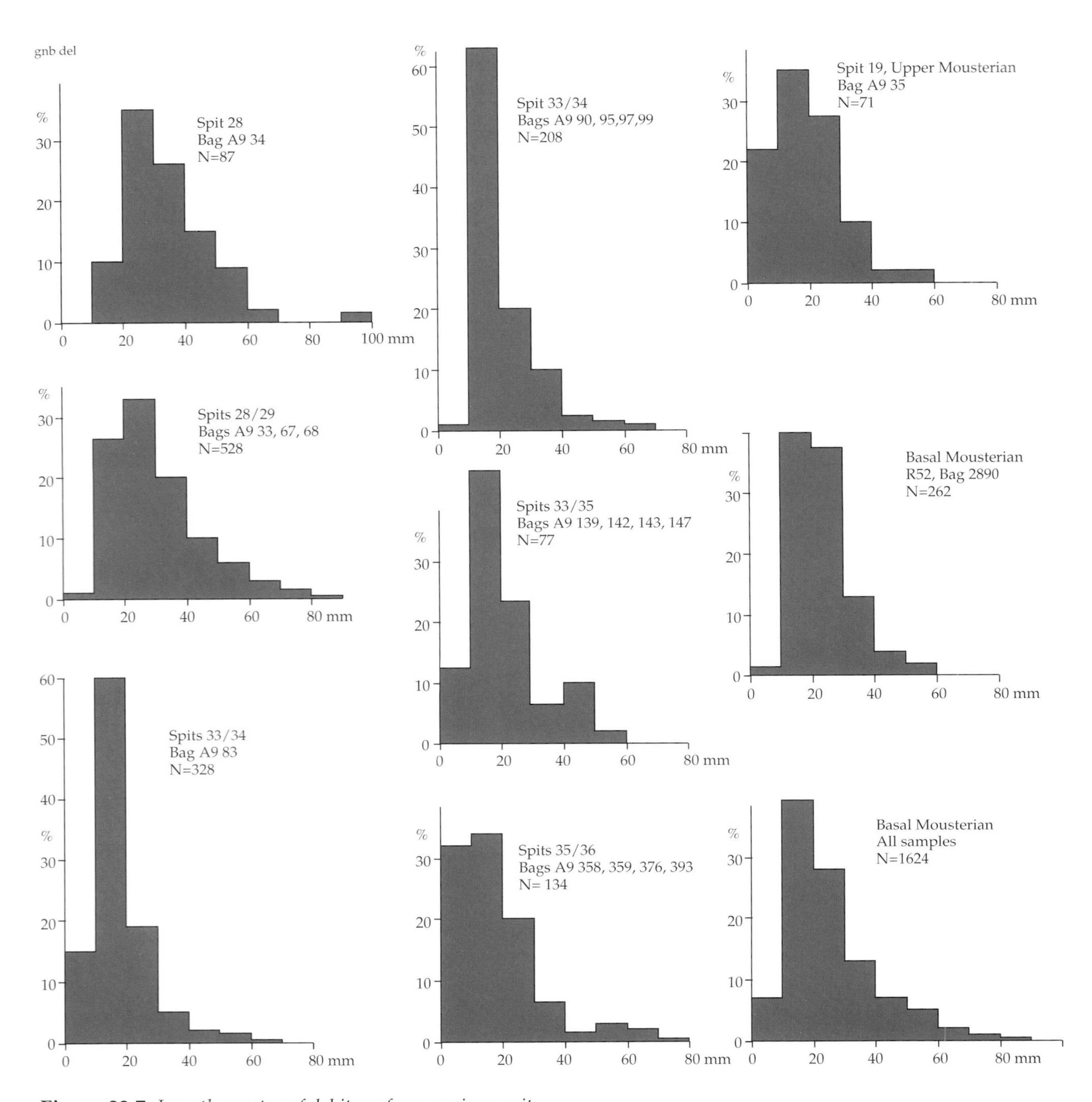

Figure 23.7. *Length spectra of debitage from various spits.*

25 of the Pseudo-Levallois points which are characteristic of the upper Mousterian. It cannot be guaranteed that these are not intrusive. On the other hand, many flakes were produced from discoid cores in the basal Mousterian, and at least some of these might potentially be described as Pseudo-Levallois points. Thus even now further work is required to determine whether these are a continually present feature of the Asprochaliko Mousterian.

Recent work has indicated that hafting was used in the Mousterian, at least in the Middle East (Anderson-Gerfaud 1990; Friedman *et al.* 1995; Shea 1989a,b). At present, the Asprochaliko collections give no direct information on this, but if once a concentration on making very small pieces has been demonstrated, it is difficult to see how they would

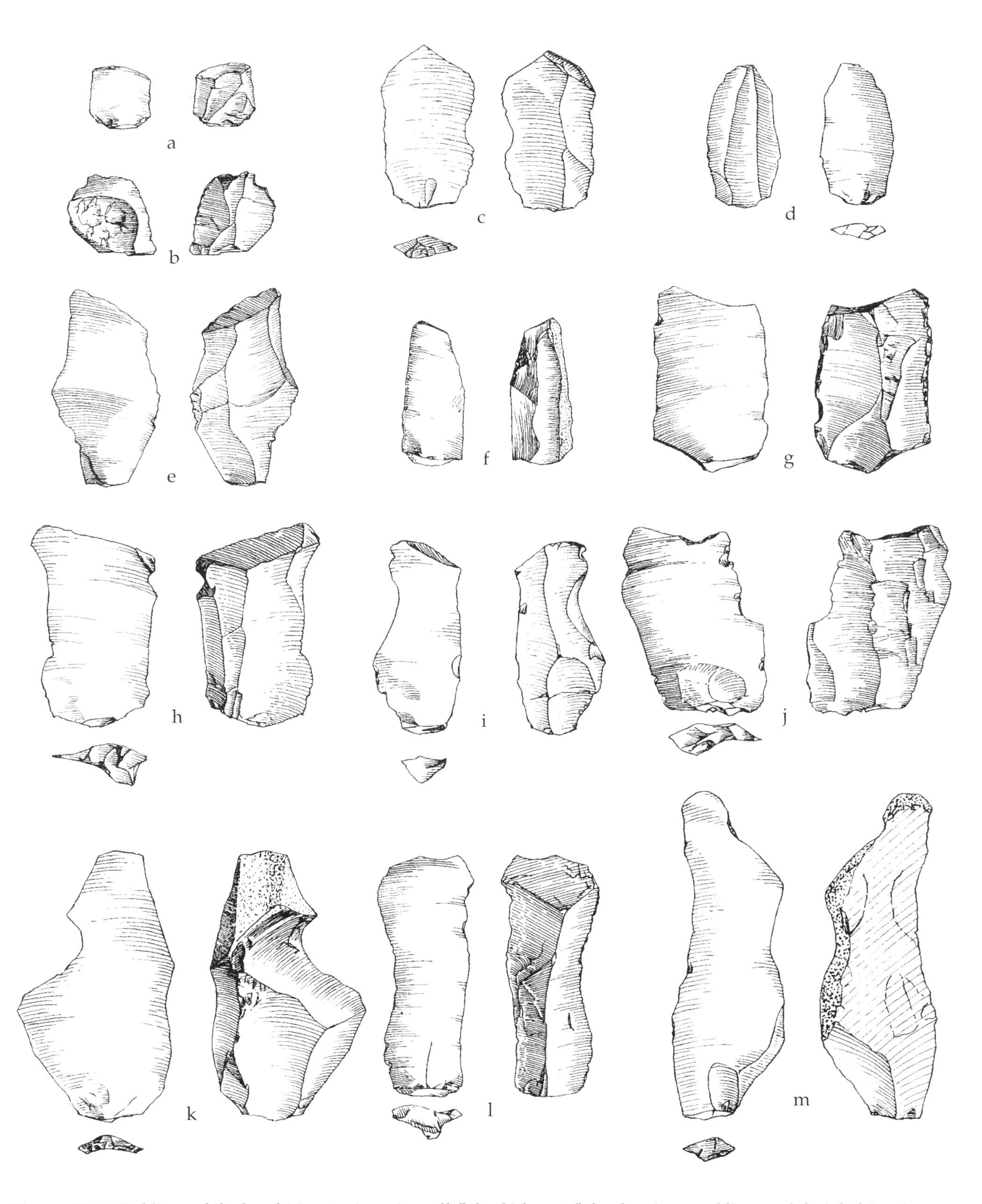

Figure 23.8. *Debitage of the basal Mousterian: a) small flake; b) burnt flake showing crackling; c, d, h, j, k, l & m) flakes with facetted butts; e & i) flakes; f) flake from Layer 14; g) flake with utilization traces. Scale ²/₃ normal size.*

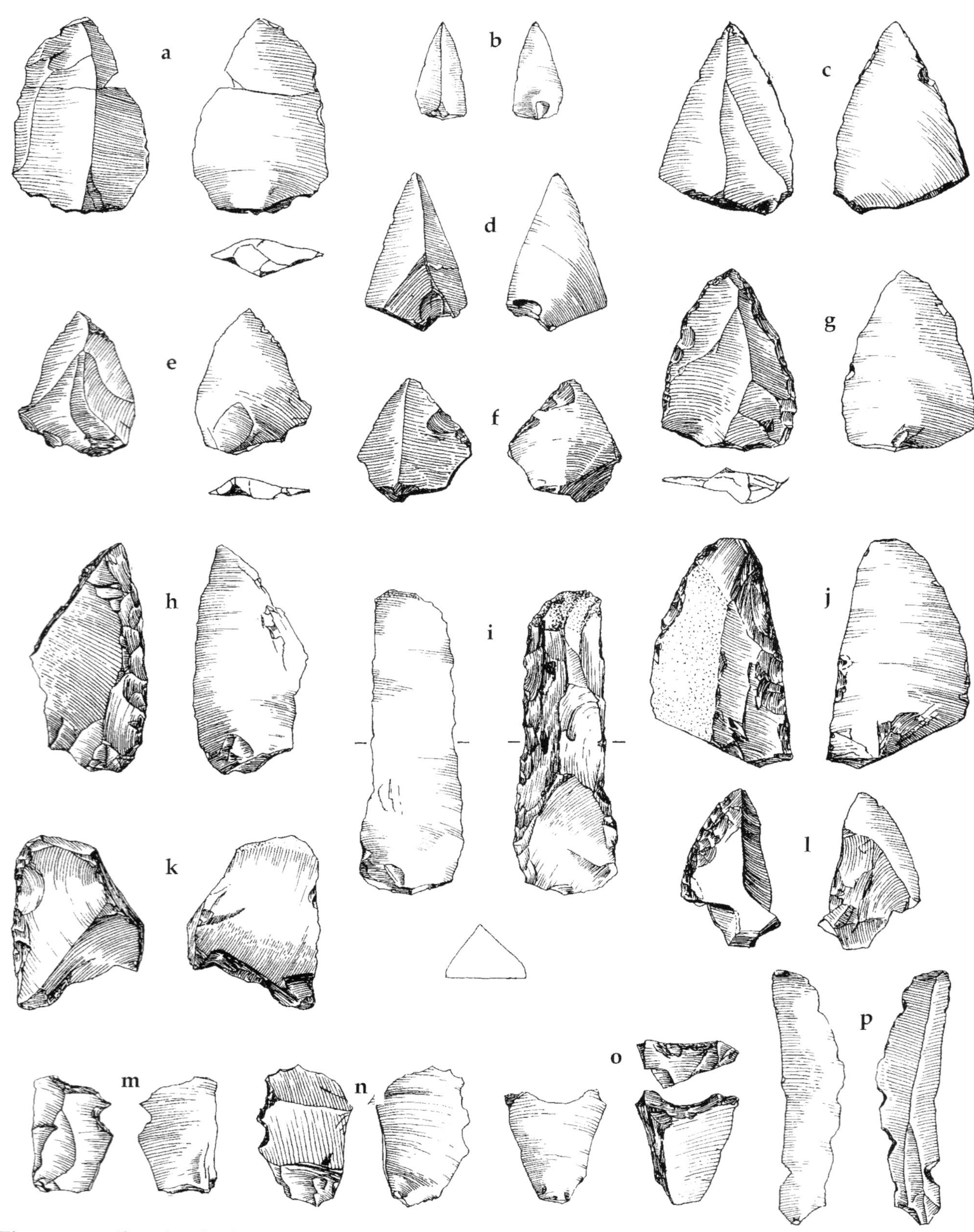

Figure 23.9. *Shaped tools of the basal Mousterian: a, b & d) Levallois points; c & e) retouched Levallois points; f) pseudo-Levallois point; g) Mousterian point on flake with facetted butt; h) single convex sidescraper; i) double sidescraper; j) convergent convex scraper; k) transverse; l) small scraper; m & p) notched pieces; n) denticulate piece; o) end notch. Scale $^2/_3$ normal size.*

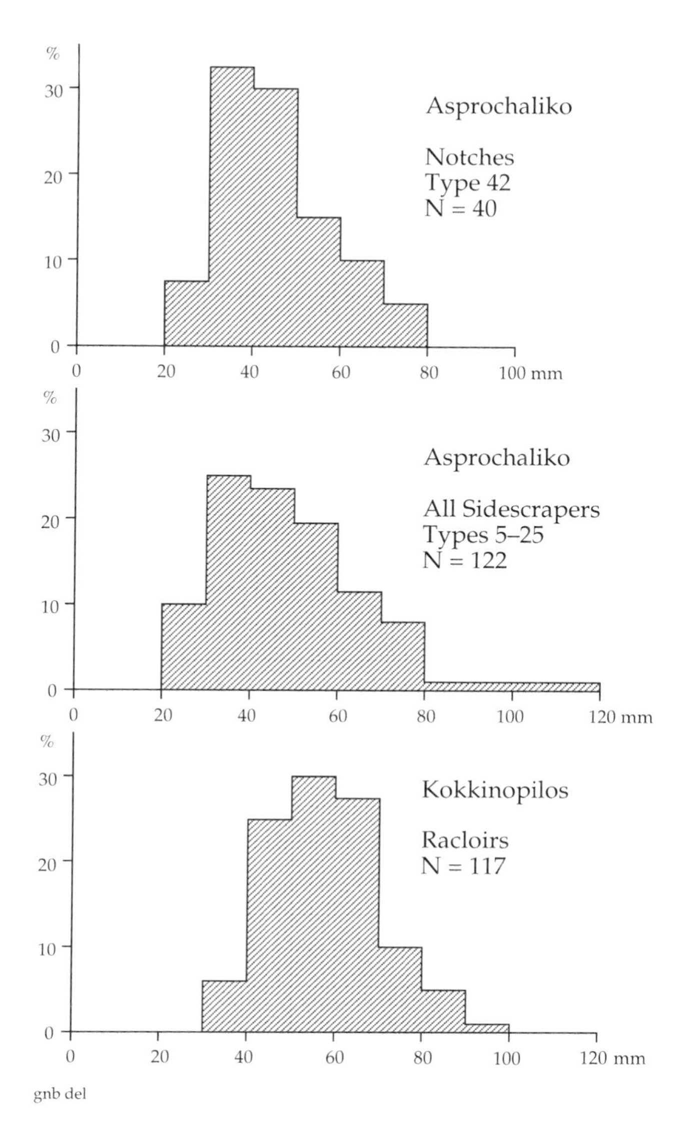

Figure 23.10. *Length spectra of tools from Asprochaliko and Kokkinopilos. (Data from Kokkinopolis are from Dakaris* et al. *1964.)*

have been used without hafting. The notches common on the site may indicate bone-working (Shea 1989a), but otherwise could suggest work on handles or shafts of wood.

Comparisons with the upper Mousterian

The upper Mousterian industry of Layer 14 can now be linked with the earlier part of the Last Glaciation (Huxtable *et al.* 1992; Papaconstantinou & Vassilopoulou, Chapter 24). The industry emphasizes small tools on flakes. Many small discoid cores are preserved from these levels. The characteristic feature is the production from them of 'pseudo-Levallois' points, 25–35 mm long, often retouched to form various kinds of scrapers. Some larger scrapers made on primary flakes are also present, whereas blades are completely absent.

Although the analyses of the 1980s and these descriptions might suggest a fundamental difference between the two Mousterian industries, our recent analysis of the basal Mousterian provides a different impression. The larger flake blades and cores of the basal Mousterian appear as one element within an industry which is also characterized by many small disc cores and associated flakes (Figs 23.5, 23.7 & 23.8). Moreover, the larger flakes may be concentrated at certain levels. The 'pseudo-Levallois' points of the upper levels are smaller than the Levallois flakes of the basal industry, but otherwise the mean size of the other flakes and retouched tools is almost identical in the two industries, which were also made on identical raw materials (Huxtable *et al.* 1992; Papaconstantinou & Vassilopoulou, Chapter 24).

Comparisons within Greece

The nearest Mousterian sites to Asprochaliko are the open sites of Pantanassa 3 and Kokkinopilos (Fig. 23.1). Our analysis of the surface collection from Pantanassa suggests some close similarities with Asprochaliko, especially in the small size of cores, and the size range of debitage (Fig. 23.7). Few shaped tools remain at Pantanassa. In spite of these similarities, the shape of the Pantanassa cores is notably different from those of Asprochaliko (Fig. 23.6a).

Kokkinopilos lies only 3 km to the south of Asprochaliko. Artefacts were collected from red beds from the 1960s onwards. Recent interpretations have highlighted the point that the Kokkinopilos collections need not come from a short timespan, but might be spread out over a longer period (Bailey *et al.* 1992). Nevertheless, a plot of length of sidescrapers (racloirs) from Kokkinopilos shows a similar distribution to that of scrapers from the Asprochaliko basal Mousterian (Fig. 23.10). There appear to be more fine 'classic' specimens from Kokkinopilos, and a slightly higher proportion of long pieces. The Kokkinopilos material differs from Asprochaliko in two major respects:

- facetted butt flakes are very common at Kokkinopilos, but are seen on less than 1 per cent of Asprochaliko flakes (although on more of the large specimens);
- at Kokkinopilos there is a component of bifacial

pieces which are not handaxes, i.e. leafpoints. There is nothing strictly comparable at Asprochaliko, although a few artefacts were diagnosed as limaces, and some of the thinner cores might be regarded as bifacial pieces.

Similar bifacial pieces have been recognized elsewhere in Greece as part of the Middle Palaeolithic (Dakaris *et al.* 1964). Runnels (1995, 711–14) gives a review of material both from the later Lower Palaeolithic and from the Middle Palaeolithic, showing the fairly wide scatter of sites which can attributed to the Mousterian. Few of these can be dated accurately enough, or have full enough collections, to allow detailed comparisons.

The relationship between Asprochaliko and Kokkinopilos is thus of central interest. Higgs & Vita-Finzi (1966) noted the possibility of functional variants in different local environments. Similarities between Asprochaliko and Pantanassa, however, suggest that a similar adaptation might sometimes be used in a rockshelter site and on an open site. Functional differences do not easily explain the differences between Asprochaliko and Kokkinopilos. Different toolkits might be required in these two situations, but it seems unlikely that a single group would vary their knapping practice as much as the range of tool-types. In fact, the dominant sidescrapers are fairly similar on the two sites, whereas the technology of working — both in platform facetting and the bifacial element at Kokkinopilos — separate them.

Since these features do not occur at Asprochaliko from 100,000 to 40,000, there is some case for arguing that most of the Kokkinopilos material may be older.

Comparisons across the Mousterian world

Middle Palaeolithic technology now appears to have a time-depth from as much as 300,000 years ago down to about 40,000 BP in Europe. It appears to be both more variable than was once appreciated, and at the same time more similar in general pattern across the continents of Europe, Asia and Africa than old classifications permitted to be seen.

Initially, Asprochaliko was noted for its place in site catchment studies, but later studies have tended to place more emphasis on culture-history. Where did the blade industry, and the later Middle/Upper Palaeolithic transition, fit in the grand scheme of European prehistory, and the replacement of the Neanderthals? Present consensus is that a lithic industry with an early blade component such as in the basal Mousterian allows us to say nothing about the species or variety of hominid maker. Among the flake industries in the late Lower/early Middle Palaeolithic, the production of elongated flakes appears to have arisen on a number of occasions. Early examples at *c.* 200,000 BP are known from Europe (e.g. Belgium) and from Africa (e.g. the Kapthurin Formation), and from Israel (e.g. Tabun: Bar-Yosef *et al.* 1992; Mercier *et al.* 1995). Some of these are likely to have been associated with early moderns, others with Neanderthals.

The Asprochaliko basal Mousterian is roughly contemporary with the Neanderthals of Krapina, and with the early moderns of Skhul and Qafzeh in Israel (Stringer *et al.* 1989; Valladas *et al.* 1988). As there is no evidence of early moderns in Europe until 40,000 years ago (e.g. at Mladec), Neanderthals seem more likely to have been the makers. The Neanderthals are associated with a certain image of 'otherness', for example by Stringer & Gamble (1993), but debate about their cultural standing appears to be developing rapidly. The discovery of a four-hole flute on a Mousterian site in Slovenia may give some support to the arguments put by other authors that Neanderthals may well have possessed the abilities of other hominids of the period (*cf.* Hayden 1993; or Jameson *et al.* 1994 for arguments concerning resource exploitation in Greece).

At Asprochaliko we have only the assemblage of stone artefacts, and rather general faunal associations. It seems evident, however, that the local pattern may be different from that of other areas of the Balkans, of Italy, and central Europe.

In Italy a recent study of the Pontinian poses interesting contrasts (Kuhn 1995). Here it would appear that there was raw material 'stress' with only very small pebbles available for tool-making. Similar circumstances may appear on much earlier sites in Europe, such as Bilzingsleben, and later at Erd in Hungary (Gabori-Csank 1968; Mania 1995). Asprochaliko provides a counter in demonstrating the extent to which small artefacts may have been made by choice, even when materials were available for making larger artefacts. In the Pontinian, lamellar flaking increased from about 50,000 BP, whereas at Asprochaliko it was used early on and then disappeared together with the larger tools.

A thorough review of this period in central and eastern Europe has been presented by Allsworth-Jones (1990), with particular reference to the Szeletian. This shows the scarcity of dated evidence to compare with the early levels of Asprochaliko. There is, however, some evidence suggesting that leafpoints occurred not just in the later Szeletian, but further

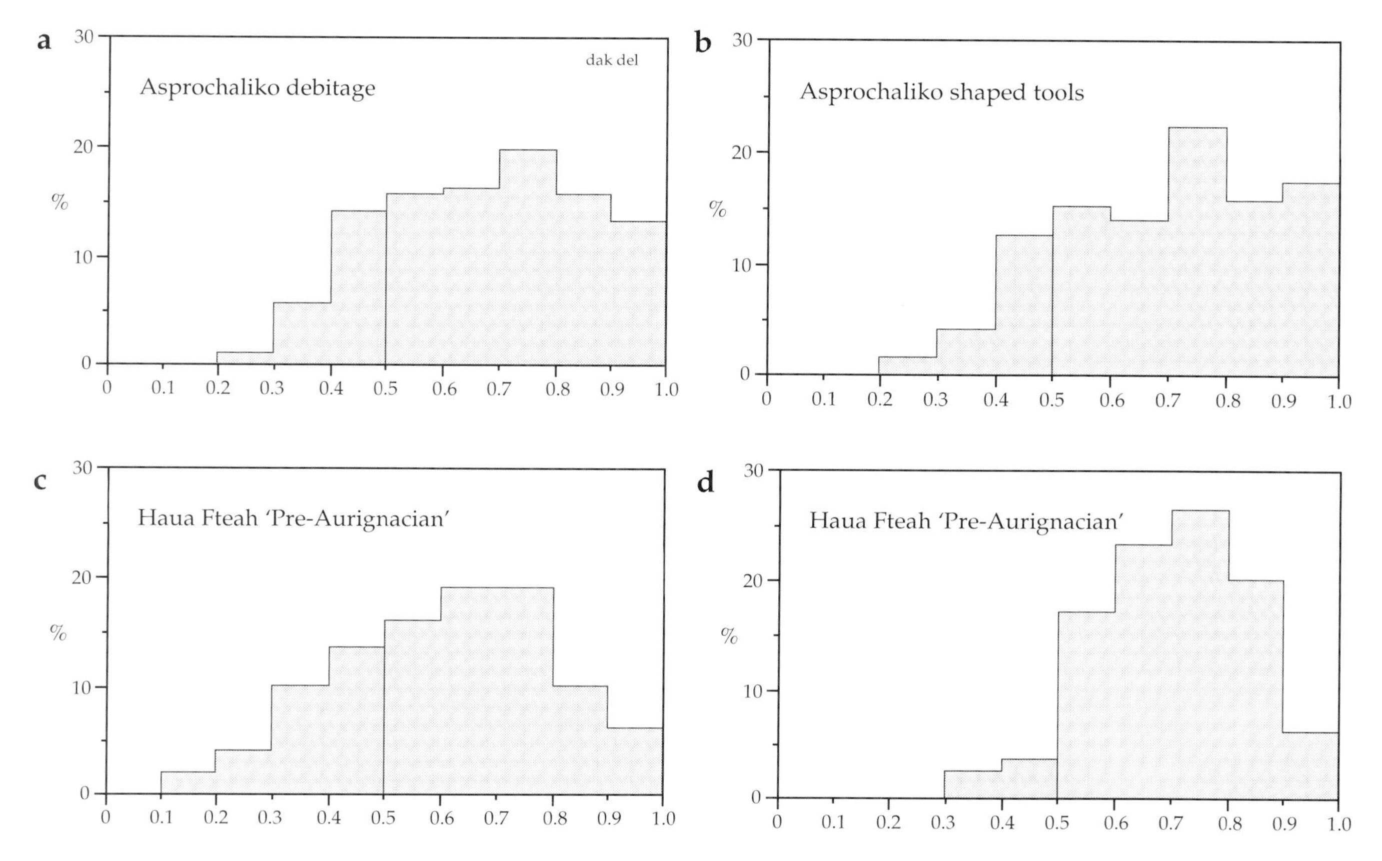

Figure 23.11. *Breadth/length proportions of flakes and shaped tools from the Asprochaliko basal Mousterian, compared with samples from the Haua Fteah, Cyrenaica. (After McBurney 1967.) (Asprochaliko debitage sampled from bags A9-33, 67 and 68.) Artefacts to the left of the vertical line at 0.5 are more than twice as long as broad. There appears to be no significant difference (i.e. selection) between the Asprochaliko flakes and the shaped tools. Both include more elongated specimens than the Haua 'typical' Mousterian, but also more specimens where length approximates breadth.*

back towards the Last Interglacial. Allsworth-Jones argues for their presence in the Upper Remete cave in Hungary, where Layer 4 appears to span the period from the Last Interglacial to early Würm (Gabori-Csank 1983). He also sees Levallois characteristics pointing towards an affinity with the Mousterian of southeast Europe (see also Iwanowa 1979). The helpful information here is the testimony that leafpoints may have existed at 100,000 BP or earlier (as also in Africa). This helps sustain the idea that some of the Kokkinopilos finds could be older than any of the Asprochaliko sequence, but does not prove it.

A site quite close to Asprochaliko which deserves mention is Samuilitsa in Bulgaria (Allsworth-Jones 1990; Sirakov 1983). Out of 82 cores Allsworth-Jones classified 43 as disc cores, and 17 as Levallois, suggesting some similarity with the Asprochaliko basal Mousterian in flaking patterns. A few leafpoints were found at various levels. Also in Bulgaria Mousterian assemblages have been described from levels 14–11 of Bacho Kiro Cave (Drobniewicz *et al.* 1982; Iwanowa 1979). Here again both Levallois and disc core elements are present, and some smaller disc cores suggest that small flakes were desired. Assemblage compositions are similar to Asprochaliko, except that notches appear to be scarcer.

The site of Karaïn in southern Turkey presents some parallels with Asprochaliko (Otte *et al.* 1995), also encompassing a similar date range (*c.* 60–140 ka). Size spectra of flakes are comparable (Otte *et al.* 1995, table 5) and there appears to be a similar series of long sidescrapers, coupled again with a mixture of Levallois and disc-core working. Here too there is a near-absence of Mousterian points; there are possibly more denticulates than at Asprochaliko and fewer notches.

On a broader scale of interpretation, interest in classic typology has waned. In southwest Europe the dominant ideas in literature in English are now those of Rolland and Dibble, who suggest respectively the great importance of raw materials in determining form (Rolland 1986; 1990), and a lack of intentional pattern in the shaping of tools (Dibble 1988; 1989). It is argued that retrimming of tools is often responsible for the apparent variety of size and forms, which were formerly characterized in typological terms into excessive numbers of categories. Similar suspicions of the Bordes typology were expressed long ago by C.B.M. McBurney (1967), and most would now agree that, for example, a mechanical division into many scraper classes presents an artificial picture.

Even so, Asprochaliko seems to present a different picture from that argued for southwest Europe: the analyses demonstrate that the shaped tools were predominantly worked on blanks that were selected for their large size — particularly in the case of scrapers. Similar observations have been made for the African Acheulean (e.g. Isaac 1977). It would be very hard to argue that most of these pieces had been extensively retrimmed, because the debitage simply does not offer a background of larger pieces to start from.

Recent work on the Mousterian in the Near East is relevant to Asprochaliko because of problems which can be considered on a common basis. At Kebara, Levallois technique was very common, and the cores were often managed through unidirectional striking — rather similar to that in the larger cores at Asprochaliko. But this was deliberate: 'in spite of the availability of other flaking methods, such as the preferred-flake method or radial or bidirectional reduction, the local artisans made a clear choice' (Bar-Yosef *et al.* 1992, 516). We see similar choices made at Asprochaliko, according to the desired endproduct. At Kebara too doubts were expressed about whether different strategies of flake-production were linked in a single core-reduction sequence, or whether they co-existed as different core-reduction strategies (see cores above).

Conclusions

The reanalyses of the Asprochaliko basal Mousterian allow two major conclusions:

- there was a great emphasis on small cores used to make small flakes;

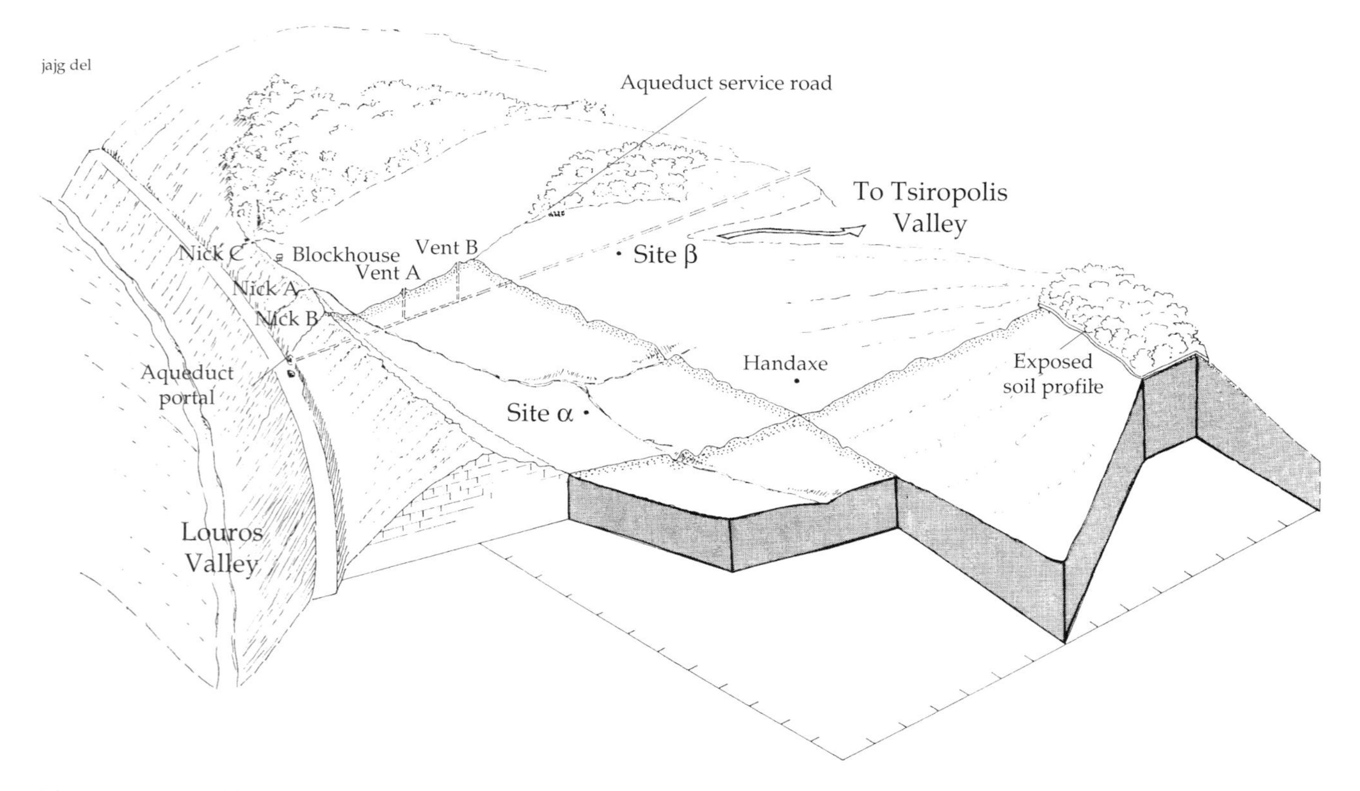

Figure 23.12. *Oblique view of the sediments at Kokkinopilos, seen from the north. (Based on a survey by D.A. Sturdy, C. Sturdy and J.A.J. Gowlett.) Artefacts were widespread in this area. Sites α and β of the original investigations are indicated, and H represents the approximate position of a handaxe found by Runnels & Van Andel (1993a). Base grid marked at 10 m intervals. The Roman aqueduct followed the Louros Valley, leaving it at the portal, and travelling underground towards Tsiropolis.*

- there is in the debitage a numerically small component of large flakes which were used for making a high proportion of the retouched tools, especially scrapers.

We turn now to considering possible answers to some of the questions posed above.

What artefacts were early humans seeking to produce at Asprochaliko? Evidently the makers had a variety of goals, needing not just different finished tools, but probably different (although related) routines of blank striking. Their technological goals were to produce many small sharp flakes, and to produce some much larger flakes which would be used as Levallois knives or for retouched tools. Their pattern of production was largely consistent through different levels, particularly for the element of small tools, but it seems possible that the larger tools were made or used in fewer episodes, concentrated at certain levels. The general pattern of the assemblage resembles that from many other Mousterian sites, including its elements of both Levallois and disc cores, but the range of shaped tools is fairly limited, and if there is equal preference for very small flakes on other sites, this is not always emphasized in the literature.

Within site, the basal Mousterian is distinguished from the upper Mousterian by having the element of larger tools and Levallois cores, but otherwise perhaps merely by negative factors, such as the lower frequency of retouched pseudo-Levallois points.

Is there information that is relevant to recent research on other sites? Probably yes. Both the aspects of reduction sequences and the questions raised by large numbers of small artefacts are relevant to the issues now treated in the Middle Palaeolithic of the Near East, particularly the matter of hafting. These seem far from the issues of retrimming raised in discussions of the Mousterian of southwest Europe, but Asprochaliko lies in the middle geographically, and perhaps also in its problems.

Is there convincing economic evidence about why people used the site? Here the assemblage is probably of less help than the site catchment studies. Higgs & Webley (1971) suggested that the site was well-positioned for the hunting of red deer in the nearby wooded vales of the Louros, both to the north and south where the valley opens up. It also had easy access up a side valley to the neighbouring plateaux (see Sturdy *et al.*, Chapter 30). In this case it would be logical to see the site in several roles: as a hunting station suitably distanced from prey that might otherwise be disturbed; as a monitoring position for observing animals that did pass through the valley; and arguably as a well-placed manufacturing and repair site, especially for projectile shafts and tips. Although there is no direct evidence for spearthrowers in this period, their use cannot now be ruled out, given the emphasis on lightweight sharp flakes.

Finally, how clearly different is the Mousterian adaptation from that visible in Upper Palaeolithic rockshelters such as Klithi? Asprochaliko is perhaps the best earlier analogue that we have in Greece, although its regional setting and economy is different. It lies at a lower altitude than Klithi, in a through-valley, and with access to a greater variety of environments (see Sturdy *et al.*, Chapter 30). Larger animals and greater species variety were thus available, as the faunal remains testify, although we have no proof that these were hunted. Traditionally, the difference of the Neanderthals from modern humans would be emphasized through both technology and economy: cruder flake tools, a mixed bag of fauna. At Asprochaliko the faunal range in the Middle Palaeolithic is not much greater than in the Upper Palaeolithic (Sturdy *et al.*, Chapter 30). The toolkit also shows decided aspects of specialization. If these factors speak for continuity, any gulf between the epochs will need to be measured in other ways.

Acknowledgements

Many people have worked on Asprochaliko since the 1960s excavations. We thank A. Douzougli and K. Zachos of the Archaeological Ephoreia at Ioannina for much help and support; also our colleagues E. Adam and V. Papaconstantinou; the 1980 analysis was carried out by us working with David Bannear, who assigned the Bordes categories. The basal Mousterian tools were drawn then by J.A.J. Gowlett: the figures are reproduced as drawn, although in some cases a different orientation has been preferred (general convention now insisting that flakes should be portrayed with the bulb at the bottom). The analysis of the debitage took place in 1989, with much assistance from S. Crowe, R. Jameson and C.A. Gowlett. We thank Helen Higgs and members of the Oxford Radiocarbon Accelerator Unit (see Chapter 2) for help in radiocarbon sampling and analysis, and Joan Huxtable in particular for her TL analyses. Gowlett thanks the British Academy and the Leverhulme Trust for his Senior Research Fellowship, during which diagrams were completed; and G.N. Bailey for help with the electronic preparation of some figures.

Chapter 24

The Middle Palaeolithic Industries of Epirus

Vangelis Papaconstantinou & Dimitra Vassilopoulou

During the last 30 years, surveys and excavations have established numerous traces of Mousterian or Middle Palaeolithic industries in many parts of Greece. However, for a number of practical reasons, mainly the rarity of long sequences in excavated sites, the period is poorly known. Published discussions suffer from a paucity and poor quality of data, as well as from the imposition of preconceptions or outdated working hypotheses.

Only the Asprochaliko rockshelter has provided a stratified sequence of Middle Palaeolithic industries (Higgs & Vita-Finzi 1966; Gowlett & Carter, Chapter 23). Some evidence of a Middle Palaeolithic occupation has also been reported from Franchthi Cave (Perlès 1987), from the base of the sequence at Kephalari Cave (Felsch 1973) and more recently from Theopetra Cave in Thessaly (Kyparissi-Apostolika 1994) and Kalamakia Cave in the Mani Peninsula (Darlas 1994). Elsewhere, material comes from open-air sites in Epirus, the Pelopponese, Thessaly and the Ionian Islands (Chavaillon *et al.* 1964; 1967; 1969; Darlas 1985; Kavvadias 1984; Leroi-Gourhan 1964; Leroi-Gourhan *et al.* 1963a,b; Lumley & Darlas 1994; Milojčić *et al.* 1965; Pope *et al.* 1984; Runnels 1988a,b; Sordinas 1965; 1970; 1983; Theocharis 1967). Although this material has been assigned a broadly Middle Palaeolithic age on the basis of geological and typological arguments, it consists for the most part of surface finds. This, together with the apparently heterogeneous character of the collections, raises serious doubts about the age and integrity of the material. In addition, the publications are usually 'preliminary' reports and do not present sufficient evidence to enable the reader to evaluate independently the authors' conclusions. This can create confusion, well illustrated by the case of the Micro-Mousterian. As we shall demonstrate in more detail below, this label has come to be used to characterize a variety of collections, regardless of any formal or technological similarities, and often without even the support of metrical data. The reader thus has to take on trust the interpretations of the author, and it becomes difficult to distinguish evidence from hypothesis, and science from fiction.

In what follows we shall present some new evidence on the Epirus Mousterian, together with a re-evaluation of existing evidence. Since the Epirus data dominate the discussion of the Middle Palaeolithic in Greece more generally, we intend to highlight a number of practical and theoretical problems that affect the general study of the Mousterian in this part of the world. Rarity of dates or associated faunal, floral, geological or anthropological evidence means that we must of necessity concentrate on the flint artefacts. We shall place particular emphasis on the limitations which constrain interpretation of the lithic evidence. This may not seem a very interesting task, but unfortunately a consideration of methodological issues is rarely given the proper attention it deserves. We shall draw on a detailed analysis of the Asprochaliko industries, particularly the so-called Micro-Mousterian, as well as observations on the material from surface and open-air sites scattered widely in the Epirus region. The latter material is subject to numerous uncertainties of dating and sampling (Bailey *et al.*, Chapter 27). Therefore we shall not attempt an exhaustive site-by-site inventory, but rather concentrate on highlighting major issues of general interest, emphasizing the larger collections.

The Mousterian in Greece

The initial hypothesis of Middle Palaeolithic industrial variability in Epirus, which has dominated all subsequent discussion, was proposed by Higgs in 1966 (Higgs & Vita-Finzi 1966). Using the data from extensive surveys in northern and western Greece, the results of excavations at Asprochaliko and Kokkinopilos, and some information from Thessaly (Milojčić 1965) and the Peloponnese (Chavaillon *et al.* 1964; Leroi-Gourhan *et al.* 1963a,b), he proposed three distinctive facies (types of industries): a classical Levallois-Mousterian; a Micro-Mousterian; and a Mousterian with bifacial leafpoints. The type localities which exemplified each facies were, respectively, the lowest levels of Asprochaliko, the upper (pre-Upper Palaeolithic) levels at Asprochaliko, and the Kokkinopilos 'red-beds'. The evidence of the Asprochaliko stratigraphy and the finds in the Peloponnese were used to argue for a geographically extensive Micro-Mousterian facies, younger than the Levallois-Mousterian. The chronological relationship of the bifacial Mousterian was less clear, because of unresolved uncertainties about the dating of Kokkinopilos. This left open the possibility that some of the variability might be 'functional' rather than 'temporal' in nature: the absence of bifacial leafpoints at Asprochaliko in contrast to Kokkinopilos might reflect differences of function between contemporaneous sites, rather than having chronological significance. This three-part classification was used to order the remaining surface material in Epirus, at sites such as Karvounari, Morfi and Agios Georgios.

It is important to note here that the only available published data to substantiate the above hypothesis were: a typological study of a sample of surface finds from Kokkinopilos (Mellars 1964); a typological study of surface finds from the Peloponnese (Chavaillon *et al.* 1967; 1969); some typological and technological comments about the Asprochaliko industries and the surface finds in the Peloponnese and Thessaly; and metrical data on only 400 implements from Asprochaliko, Kokkinopilos and surface findspots nearby (Higgs & Vita-Finzi 1966).

After 1966 more surface finds were discovered but no detailed or quantified data were published. There was also little detailed examination of technological factors beyond noting the presence or absence of 'classical Levallois cores', 'disc cores', 'flakes' and 'blades'. Thus it is not surprising to find that the Higgsian hypothesis has remained unchallenged. On the contrary, the new data have been fitted into the existing Epirus scheme with only minor modifications. Micro-Mousterian, classical Levallois-Mousterian, and Levallois with bifacial leafpoints have been reported from several localities (Pope *et al.* 1984; Runnels 1988a,b). The methods proposed by Higgs have continued to be used without question (Kourtessi-Philippakis 1986). Large and small, Levallois and non-Levallois, many tools and few tools, upper layer and lower layer — these survive as supposedly meaningful contrasts for assessing the significance of Middle Palaeolithic industrial variability.

The earlier work should clearly not be criticized for a failure to apply methods and concepts that were not available at the time. Nevertheless there has been a tendency for Palaeolithic interpretations in Greece to mimic concepts and categories applied elsewhere, under the influence of what might be described as scientific colonialism. In spite of the flimsy data available — few absolute dates, only two typological studies, comparisons based on *'fossiles-directeurs'*, and a failure to specify the definition of industrial types — the Greek Middle Palaeolithic has been subdivided into various groupings as if this was an unproblematic exercise. Thus the information potential of the stone industries has been misunderstood or over-simplified (see Perlès 1986 for further discussion). By examining some of the deficiencies of earlier interpetations, and by contrasting simple answers with complicated questions, we hope to contribute to a better understanding of Middle Palaeolithic industrial variability.

Limitations of the Epirus data

It is necessary, first of all, to appreciate the sampling biases introduced by the methods of data collection. Methods of sampling are rarely mentioned in the publications so that it is often difficult to determine the degree of bias.

At Asprochaliko, which is usually considered to provide the most reliable collection of material, the site was excavated in horizontal 15 cm spits. Although excavation also took account of geological layers, these are quite steeply sloping in some areas of the site, so that some material cannot confidently be assigned to a single stratigraphic unit. In addition there are local areas of disturbance caused by major rock falls and unresolved stratigraphic problems (Bailey *et al.* 1983b). Finally there are problems of curation (lost pieces, contradictory notes). Thus only a sample of the finds can be provenanced with confidence and the relationship of this sample to the total of excavated material is difficult to establish. It should also be noted that in some areas of the site excavation did not reach sediments with Middle Palaeolithic material. For all these reasons interpretations of vertical and horizontal variability should be treated with caution.

The surface finds are from two different phases of survey. The first is the collection of material made from 1962 onwards under the direction of Higgs. This includes material from Karvounari, Morfi, Agios Georgios, Voulista-Panagia, Gortses, Stefani, and Paramythia. In addition, artefacts from about 40 other sites were collected, but because of the small samples or undiagnostic character of the material, these were not referred to in the original publications. We have examined this latter group of material as part of the present study.

The main difficulty in assessing the Higgs surface collections is the lack of detailed information about collection methods. In the case of some of the sites, the presence of cores, common flakes, retouched tools, fragments and occasional eoliths suggests that everything was collected. At other sites, in contrast, there are high proportions of retouched tools, and very few cores, common flakes or broken pieces, and it is not possible to determine whether these are representative samples or result from collecting bias.

The second phase of survey took place from 1983 onwards as part of the present Klithi project. In this case the surveys were oriented towards resolving geological and palaeogeographical questions, rather than towards systematic survey for archaeological sites. Flints were only collected in cases where there were risks of immediate destruction or reburial, and the emphasis was on the collection of informative pieces such as cores, retouched tools and predetermined flakes, which could provide a basis for the planning of future work.

It follows that the totality of material has to be used with considerable reservation, and our aim will be to use it as a basis for formulating working hyotheses rather than as a data base from which one can draw firm and detailed conclusions.

The Asprochaliko industries

The importance of this site needs no emphasis. It is in fact the only Greek site with a long sequence of Middle Palaeolithic industries, with a time span from *c.* 100 ka to 35 ka (Huxtable *et al.* 1992; Gowlett & Carter, Chapter 23). It has been the main support for interpreting the Epirus Mousterian and has also been the main point of reference for all comparative studies on the Greek Mousterian. Only short notes were published on the industries in the original publications (Dakaris *et al.* 1964; Higgs 1963a,b; 1965a,b; 1966; 1967; 1968a,b,c; Higgs & Vita-Finzi 1966; Higgs *et al.*, 1967; Higgs & Webley 1971), and some additional information was added in 1983 (Bailey *et al.* 1983b). The Mousterian sequence was divided into two main units: a basal unit, consisting of Layers 16 and 18, and containing a Levallois-Mousterian industry; and an upper unit, mostly Layer 14, containing the Micro-Mousterian. This subdivision was based mainly on the material from the TRB trench and Rectangles 2, 3 and 42. The basal industry was characterized by a Levallois element, with quantities of blades, many D-shaped scrapers and large implement size. The Micro-Mousterian was characterized by lack of Levallois technology, rare blades, small points and some endscrapers, generally small implement size, and a more intensive use of raw-material.

In 1984, we undertook a fresh study based on 15,000 artefacts, which has led to a detailed re-evaluation (Papaconstantinou 1988). This reveals rather more uniformity between the two types of industries in a number of respects than was previously supposed, as well as some fresh contrasts. Throughout the Middle Palaeolithic sequence there are some impressive continuities. The raw materials used remain unchanged throughout, according to macroscopic observations, whether in terms of type of flint, provenance, quality, or size of primary nodules. Also the proportions of cores, primary, common and predetermined flakes, retouched tools, microchips and fragments remain fairly constant throughout the sequence. In terms of typology also the similarities are more striking than the differences. Scrapers, usually of the single lateral type, together with partially retouched flakes, constitute the dominant element in all units examined. Upper Palaeolithic tool-types are always very rare. The most important point of similarity, however, is in terms of implement size. In all the units examined retouched tools have a mean length of 35 mm and are longer on the average than unretouched flakes. Mean flake size is 30 mm. There are no sharp discontinuities, gradual changes or fluctuations of size (Fig. 24.1).

There is, however, a radical technological change, which coincides with the stratigraphic boundary between the lower and upper industries, i.e. the upper spits of Layer 16. Products that one would identify as Levallois, in the classical sense, disappear quite abruptly, and throughout Layer 14 there is not a single flake or blade that can be attributed to the classical Levallois method. In their place, 'pseudo-Levallois' points become the dominant element. Analysis of cores, flakes and retouched tools shows that these pseudo-Levallois points were produced systematically by careful core preparation to predetermine the shape of the flake. Nodules, cortical flakes and common flakes were all used as cores, with flakes being the most common. In the case of a flake used as a core the procedure for producing a 'pseudo-Levallois point' was as follows. First a striking platform was prepared by direct retouch. From this partially or totally prepared platform a Kombewa flake was struck, i.e. a flake presenting two bulbar surfaces. Then a second flake was struck from the

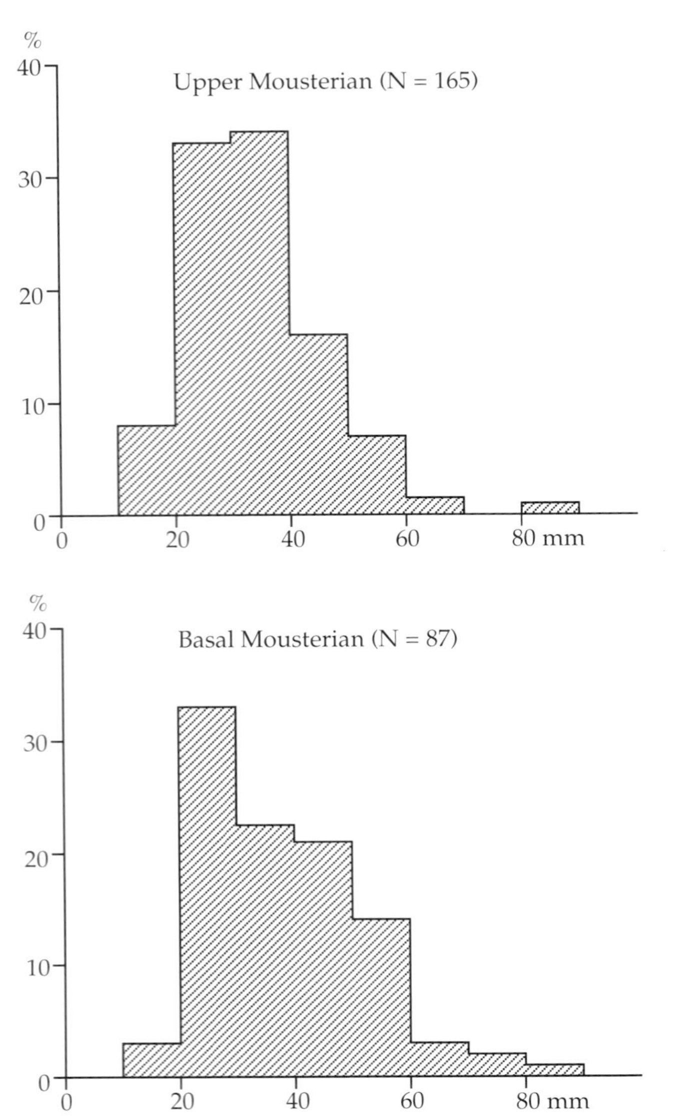

Figure 24.1. *Comparison of length of retouched tools from the Upper Mousterian and the Basal Mousterian at Asprochaliko. (Data from Papaconstantinou 1988, tables 47–62.) All measured specimens are from trenches TRB, Rectangle 2 and Rectangle 3. The Basal Mousterian specimens are from Layer 18 and from Layer 16, spits 24–28. The Upper Mousterian specimens are from Layer 16 spits 15–23. (Compare Fig. 23.4.)*

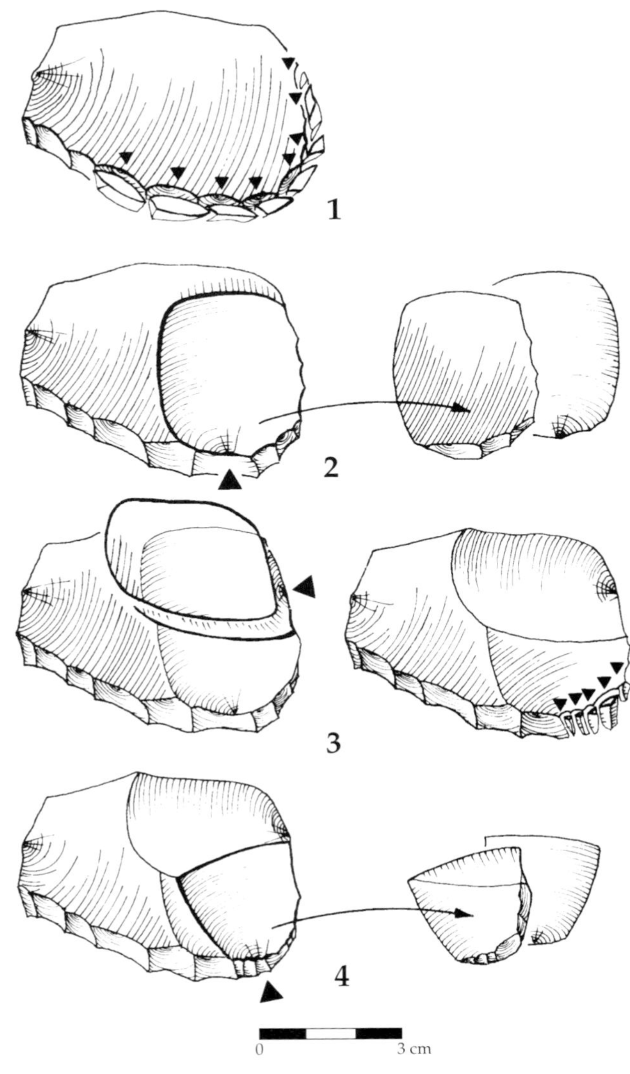

Figure 24.2. *Knapping sequence showing the various stages in the production of an Asprochaliko flake.*

same striking platform at right angles to the axis of the previous removal. These two flake removals provide the necessary and sufficient conditions for the removal of a third flake of pointed type. To obtain such a flake the knapper had to prepare a new striking platform with direct retouch and finally strike a blow tangential to the core and perpendicular to the main scar created by the first two flake removals. A similar procedure was used when the core was a nodule and not a flake, the main difference being the absence of Kombewa flakes. In either case the typical endproduct has a maximum length of 30 mm or less, is relatively thick — *c.* 5–8 mm — and typologically-speaking is a pure 'pseudo-Levallois point' (Fig. 24.2).

The method described above has the advantage that it allows successive removals of pointed flakes without further core preparation. The removal of each pointed flake automatically prepares the way for the next. Reducing a core in such a way, one finally ends up with disc cores. However, at Asprochaliko these byproducts, though present, are rare. Most of the cores are abandoned after one or two flake removals and are thus rather informal in shape. Boëda (1988a,b) has proposed two distinct terms in the study of Levallois methods. The term 'recurrent' is used to describe Levallois production resulting from surfaces prepared in such a way as to ensure a succession of flake or blade removals rather than a single removal. This is contrasted with 'lineal' production, in which the Levallois method is used in such a way as to produce a single flake from each prepared surface. The method described here is recurrent in Boëda's terminology, at least potentially so and according to knapping experiments. Since most of the Asprochaliko cores were abandoned after just one flake removal, however, more data will be needed to confirm the above interpretation.

At any rate this method has no known parallels elsewhere. It is quite distinctive and falls somewhere between the commonly recognized Levallois techniques, combining both an element of predetermination and a discoid 'Mousterian' method. For this reason we have named it the 'Asprochaliko method', and the resulting products 'Asprochaliko flakes', to distinguish them from the formally identical pseudo-Levallois points produced by quite different processes (e.g. Boëda 1986; Bordes 1953; Kelley 1957).

These 'Asprochaliko flakes' were an important source of blanks for production of retouched tools — about 30 per cent of the retouched tools were made on such flakes. Apart from pieces showing only slight traces of retouch, 'flakes' were mostly transformed into offset (*déjeté*) scrapers and transverse scrapers — about 56 per cent of these scraper types were made on 'Asprochaliko flakes' (Fig. 24.3).

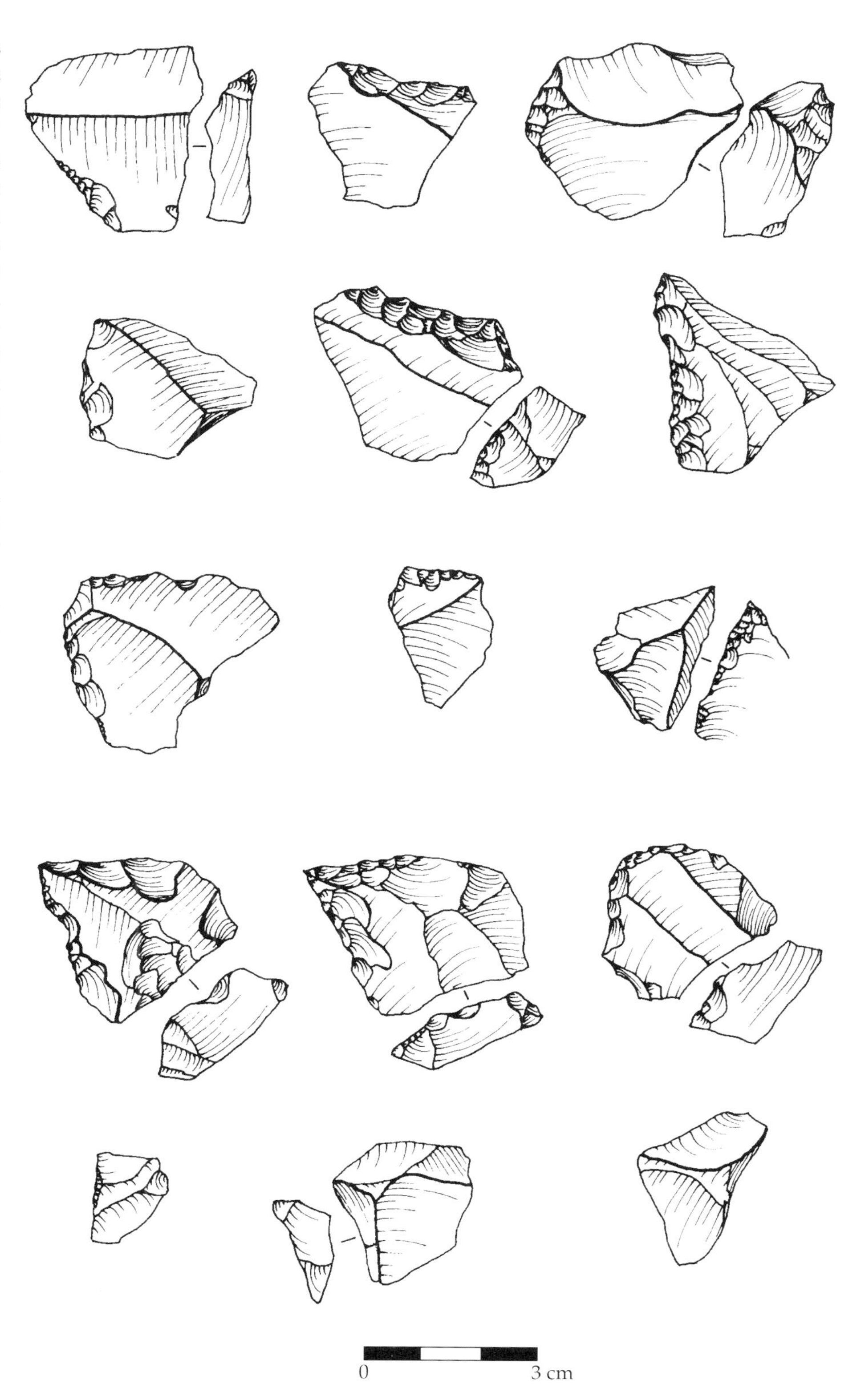

Figure 24.3. *Asprochaliko flakes from Asprochaliko, Rectangles 2 and 3, Layer 14, Spit 19.*

Mousterian points proper are in fact very rare. It should be emphasized that 'Asprochaliko flakes' tend, by the nature of the method by which they are produced, to be short and thick, whereas the blanks in the basal Mousterian are produced by recurrent unipolar and centripetal Levallois methods which tend towards the production of elongated flakes or blades (Gowlett & Carter, Chapter 23). This is the only contrast between the two industries which has size implications, and in reality the main tool-type in both cases is the simple lateral scraper, usually made on a primary flake, and these are identical in size in both industries.

The open-air sites

For the purposes of this discussion we have treated as Middle Palaeolithic any collection with lithic material which does not contradict the general expectations of Middle Palaeolithic industries.

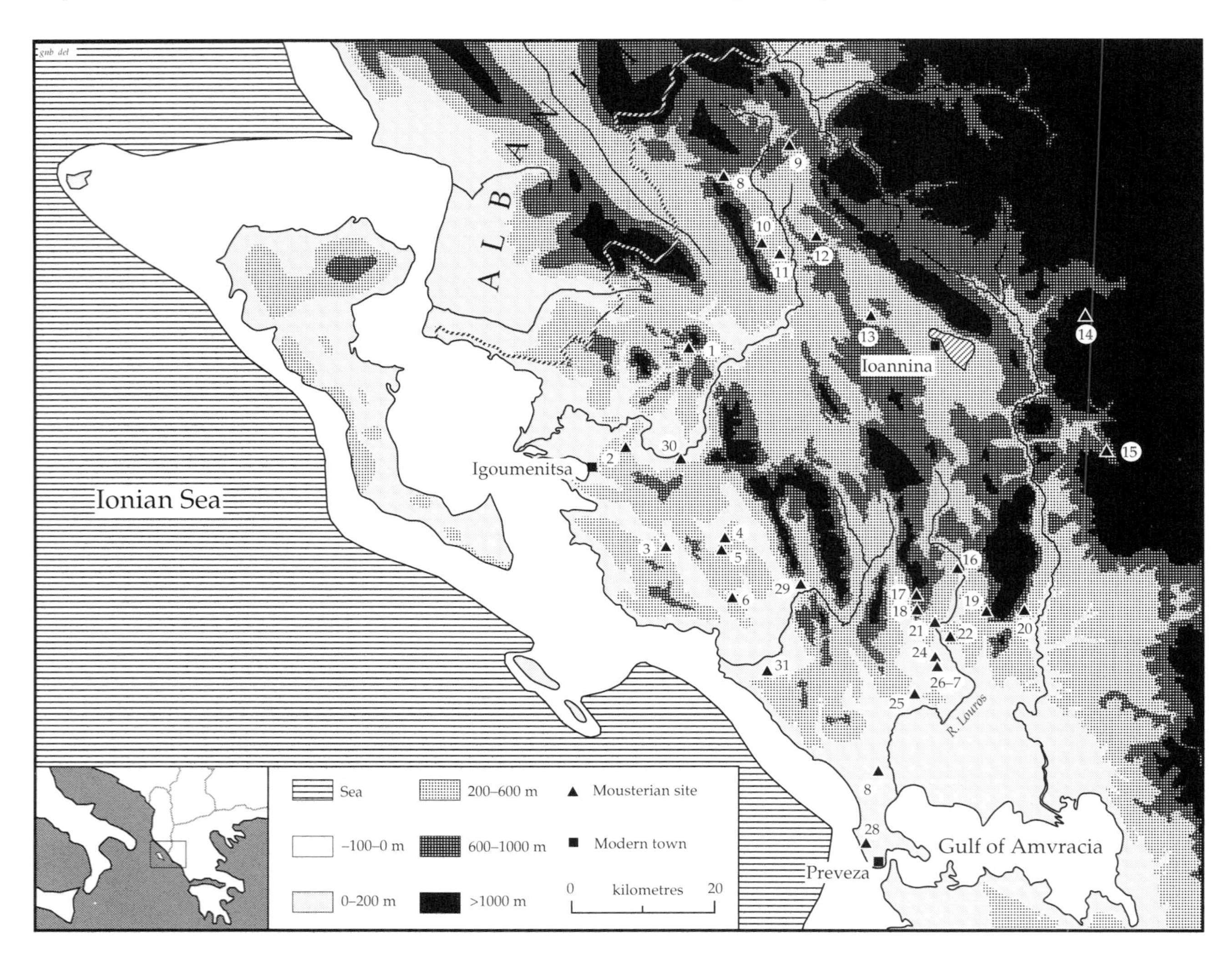

Figure 24.4. *Map showing location of Middle Palaeolithic sites discussed in the text. Gortses (24) is near Kokkinopilos, probably in the same location as Chilia Spitia (see Note 1):*
1) Pogoniani; 2) Parapotamos; 3) Chiliomodi; 4) Micro Karvounari; 5) Megalo Karvounari; 6) Morfi; 7) Sampsous; 8) Tseravinas; 9) Ano Ravenia; 10) Kouklii (Agii Anargyri); 11) Riachovo; 12) Negrades; 13) Rodotopi; 14) Megalo Peristeri; 15) Pramanda; 16) Voulista Panagia; 17) Tsouka Modi; 18) Chilia Spitia; 19) Gymnotopos; 20) Meliana; 21) Asprochaliko; 22) Agios Giorgios; 24) Kokkinopilos; 25) Stefani; 26) Tsiropolis; 27) Ziros; 28) Preveza; 29) Glyki; 30) Neochori; 31) Tsouknida.

We have also included some typical isolated finds such as diagnostic cores and retouched implements, and some poor assemblages with non-diagnostic tools, albeit with more reservations. In the absence of stratigraphic, geological or radiometric data, we are forced to rely on typological and technological criteria, and our assessment of what constitutes Middle Palaeolithic material is therefore necessarily provisional in many cases. At some sites the presence of diagnostic tool types from more recent periods (Upper Palaeolithic or later) may make it possible to exclude a Middle Palaeolithic presence. However, the reverse does not follow. We cannot assume that a collection lacking later tool-types such as bladelets and arrowheads is by definition Middle Palaeolithic, although the degree of patination may help in some cases. We still know too little about the Greek Palaeolithic to be sure that industries with Middle Palaeolithic characteristics may not in fact belong to much earlier periods appropriate, say, to the Middle Pleistocene, or indeed to later periods — early Upper Palaeolithic or even historical periods. In addition, the geographical position of Greece suggests the possibility of interaction between populations of Neandertals and *Homo sapiens sapiens*, for which labels such as Middle and Upper Palaeolithic would be quite misleading. We are also cautious of using the Asprochaliko sequence as a basis for generalization. The two major industries present there do seem to form a temporal sequence, but in no way a 'progressive' trend leading up towards the Upper Palaeolithic! The sequence also does not extend back beyond 100 ka. Because of uncertainties about the status of much of the open-air material we shall concentrate on the larger collections in what follows, incorporating some of the smaller collections and more isolated finds as appropriate. The material can be grouped into three main geographical areas: coastal Epirus; the Louros Valley; and the Epirus hinterland (Fig. 24.4), and we shall consider each in turn.

Coastal Epirus

Sites are distributed throughout the coastal region from north of Igoumenitsa to the vicinity of Preveza, and include some of the largest collections.

Parapotamos

About 40 pieces were collected. Levallois flakes are the most common element. These are much larger than at Asprochaliko, with a mean maximum dimension of *c.* 60 mm, and indicate the application of a recurrent Levallois method. Simple lateral scrapers are common. The artefacts are made on a red flint of good quality which is very common in the area and on the Ionian islands. Unfortunately there are no cores (Fig. 24.5).

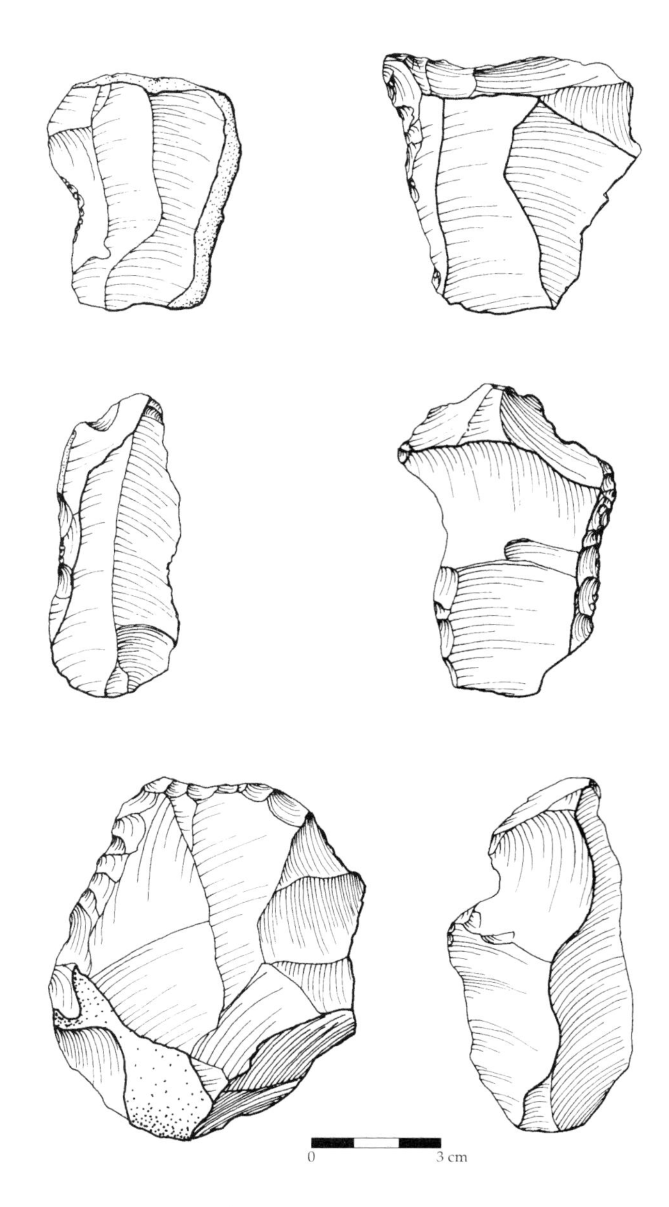

Figure 24.5. *Artefacts from Parapotamos.*

Chiliomodi

Here there is a similar industry with a dominant Levallois element, and with a marked tendency towards the production of elongated flakes and blades. There is a notable absence of retouched tools in a collection of about 30 pieces. Large, good-quality nodules of flint are exposed in abundance on the surface of the mid-Jurassic beds at this site (Fig. 24.6).

Micro and Megalo Karvounari

There are about 150 artefacts at Micro Karvounari. All are heavily patinated, with the exception of two or three unpatinated fragments with parallel scars. The collection contains only two small Levallois tortoise cores. Both indicate that a single rounded flake was removed from each after core preparation. There are about 10 retouched tools, mainly single lateral convex scrapers and three elongated Mousterian points. Flakes with discontinuous or minor retouch are also present. Many Levallois flakes indicate a core reduction sequence proceeding by centripetal removals, a fact that justifies the presence of the tortoise cores. However, there are also many elongated flakes 70–80 mm long that could have resulted from a recurrent, possibly unipolar, method, although cores of this type are absent. The industry seems to be very close to the basal Mousterian industry at Asprochaliko (Fig. 24.7). Megalo Karvounari has produced similar evidence. There are about 1000 pieces. These include occasional blades with parallel scars and light patination which could be relatively recent in date. Otherwise the collection is dominated by patinated flakes (Fig. 24.8). Although these are elongated and co-exist with some genuine blades, thus indicating an industry aimed at producing long, thin blanks, the existing cores indicate the production of rounded flakes, struck after core-production based on centripetal removals. Flakes of this type are indeed present in the collection. There are also indications of an occasional discoid debitage in the form of three pseudo-Levallois points and one flake reworked as a core by centripetal flake removals. These could indicate the presence of the 'Asprochaliko method' since the core is a typical example of an Asprochaliko core. Tools include, as usual, single lateral scrapers, some of Quina type, and two examples of Mousterian points (Fig. 24.9).

Morfi

The collection is of similar size to the Karvounari finds and is evidently a mixture, since it contains many Middle Palaeolithic artefacts, bladelets and bladelet cores, flakes in fresh condition (possibly of Holocene age) and typical Upper Palaeolithic burins. There is also a broken, partially bifacial implement which does not seem to belong to the Middle Palaeolithic series since it lacks the typical heavy patination. The striking element here is the presence of many good examples of Levallois flakes produced from tortoise cores. Tortoise cores themselves are also present. The tendency towards the production of elongated flakes and blades is also marked. There are no examples of cores to demonstrate the presence of a recurrent Levallois method, and it is perhaps risky to infer this method from the flakes and blades alone, given that an Upper Palaeolithic industry is also present. There are two good examples of disc cores, but only one pseudo-Levallois point, a fact that excludes affinities with the Asprochaliko industry. Apart from two very large naturally backed knives, the only interesting feature of the tools is the presence of double convergent scrapers and of Mousterian points. A limace is also present (Fig. 24.10).

Sampsous

The collection here is obviously a mixture since pottery is also present. Among the flints there are pieces that would not be out of place in a Mousterian context. However, from the technological point of view, there are very few diagnostic pieces. The cores are of discoidal type, although not typical. There is also a Levallois tortoise core made on a small flake. Pseudo-Levallois point and typical examples of Levallois flakes are absent. Some single lateral scrapers and a notch are the only retouched tools (Fig. 24.11).

Between the coastal region and the Louros Valley there are some smaller findspots with material that might be broadly grouped in the same family of industries as the large sites already discussed. These include Glyki and Neochori, where Levallois-like blades were found; Tsouknida, with large flakes and an offset scraper on a pseudo-Levallois point; Kipourja; and finally Preveza, where Levallois material is present.

The Louros Valley

The picture presented by the sites from this area is more complicated. Only two sites have resulted in large and diagnostic collections, namely Stefani and Kokkinopilos. Otherwise the collections lack diagnostic pieces or are characterized by considerable heterogeneity.

Kokkinopilos

At least 20 findspots have been located in the gullied red sediments of this area, producing over 5000 artefacts in total. The key point about this material is that even the finds of obviously Middle Palaeolithic character are very variable, offering such a variety morphologically and technologically as to provide the basis for a veritable Middle Palaeolithic technical dictionary. When the site was first excavated (Dakaris *et al.* 1964), attention was focused on distinguishing Middle Palaeolithic from Upper Palaeolithic finds. As a consequence, all the artefacts considered to be of Middle Palaeolithic type were grouped into the single category of the 'Kokkinopilos industry', supposedly characterized by the association of bifacially worked points with Levallois cores and blades. However, no convincing arguments or evidence were ever presented in support of this association. Mellars (in Dakaris *et al.* 1964) likewise based his technological and typological

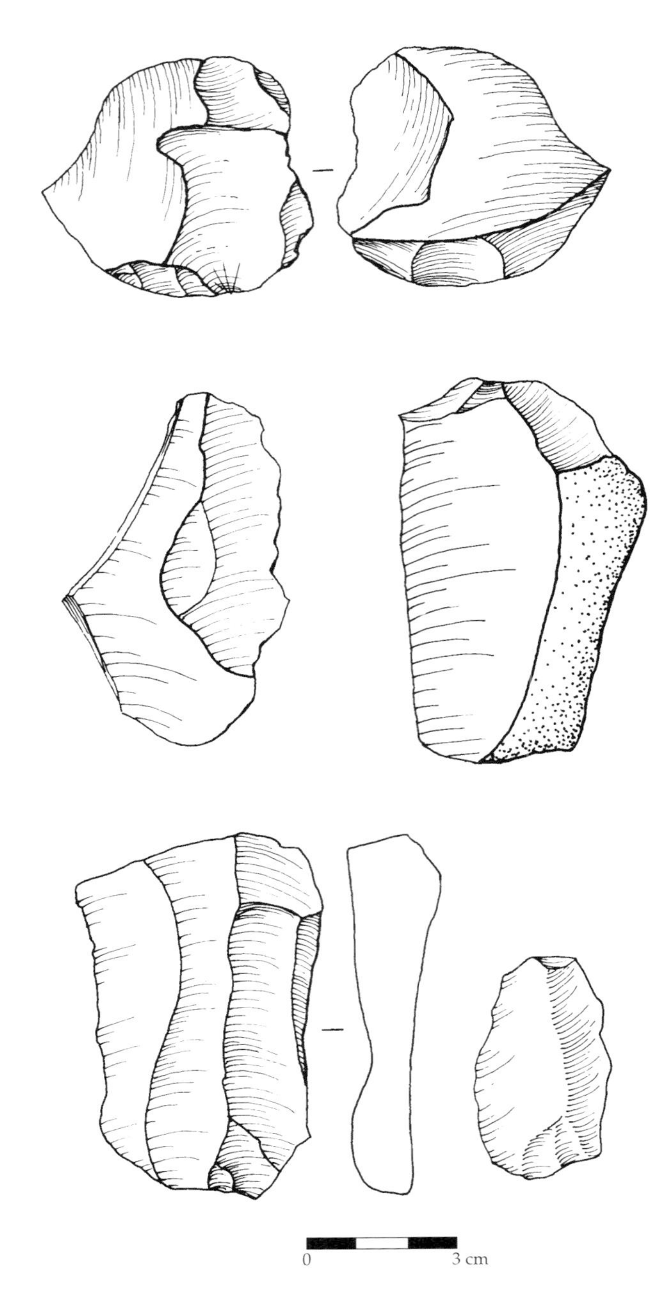

Figure 24.6. *Artefacts from Chiliomodi.*

conclusions on the assumption that the material belonged to a single industry. The only evidence mentioned at that time in favour of such an assumption was the degree of patination on the artefacts, but even this characteristic was used primarily as a means of differentiating Middle Palaeolithic from Upper Palaeolithic material. Mellars (pers. comm.) has recently confirmed that there is no reason to treat all the artefacts as a single industry and that Kokkinopilos is better viewed as a sort of 'two-dimensional Combe-Grenal'.

We were only able to make a brief examination of about 5000 artefacts, and we think that a more detailed analysis should be undertaken to provide a definitive description of this prolific material. Our brief study suggests the following conclusions. From the typological point of view there is little to add to the

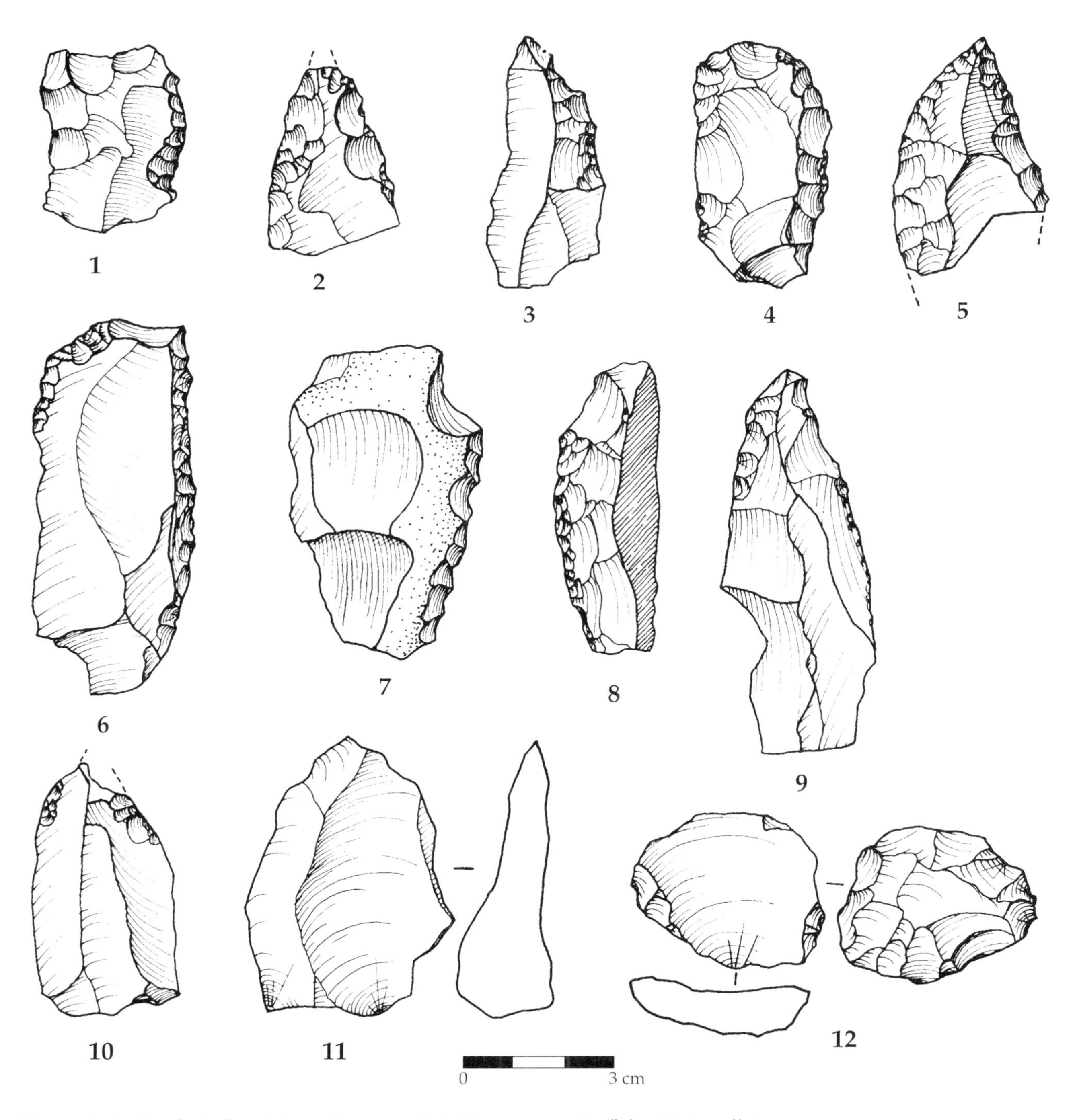

Figure 24.7. *Artefacts from Micro Karvounari: 1–10. scrapers; 11. flake; 12. Levallois core.*

description of the retouched tools presented by Mellars (in Dakaris *et al.* 1964). From the technological point of view, there is great variability, with cores of every type present, including tortoise cores, cores indicating a recurrent Levallois method oriented towards the production of elongated flakes and blades, disc cores, cores reminiscent of the 'Asprochaliko method', Clactonian cores, and amorphous cores. Similar variability can also be observed in the flakes and blades. It is clear that Kokkinopilos is an important site, with a considerable aggregation of Middle Palaeolithic material. For the moment, however, we have no means of subdividing this material.

Levallois blades like those found at Kokkinopilos and in coastal Epirus generally are also present at Tsiropolis and in the gravels of the southwest shore of Lake Ziros. At Ziros a bifacial implement was found as well as large Levallois flakes (Fig. 24.12).

Stefani

The collection comes from several findspots and includes about 200 pieces. It is a relatively homogeneous collection in the sense that tools of Upper Palaeolithic type, or unpatinated flints of more recent origin, are rare. The site could be described as

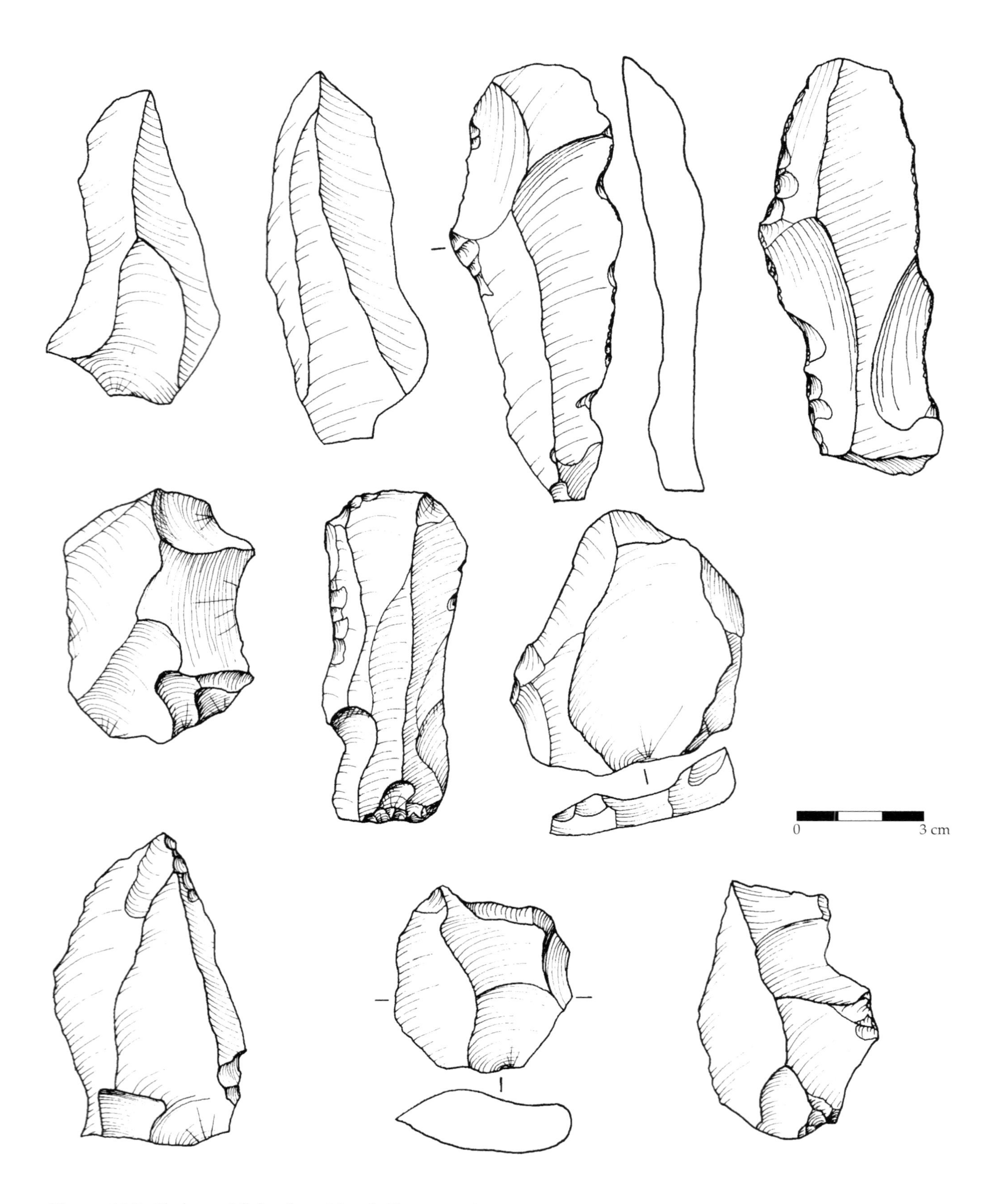

Figure 24.8. *Blades and flakes from Megalo Karvounari.*

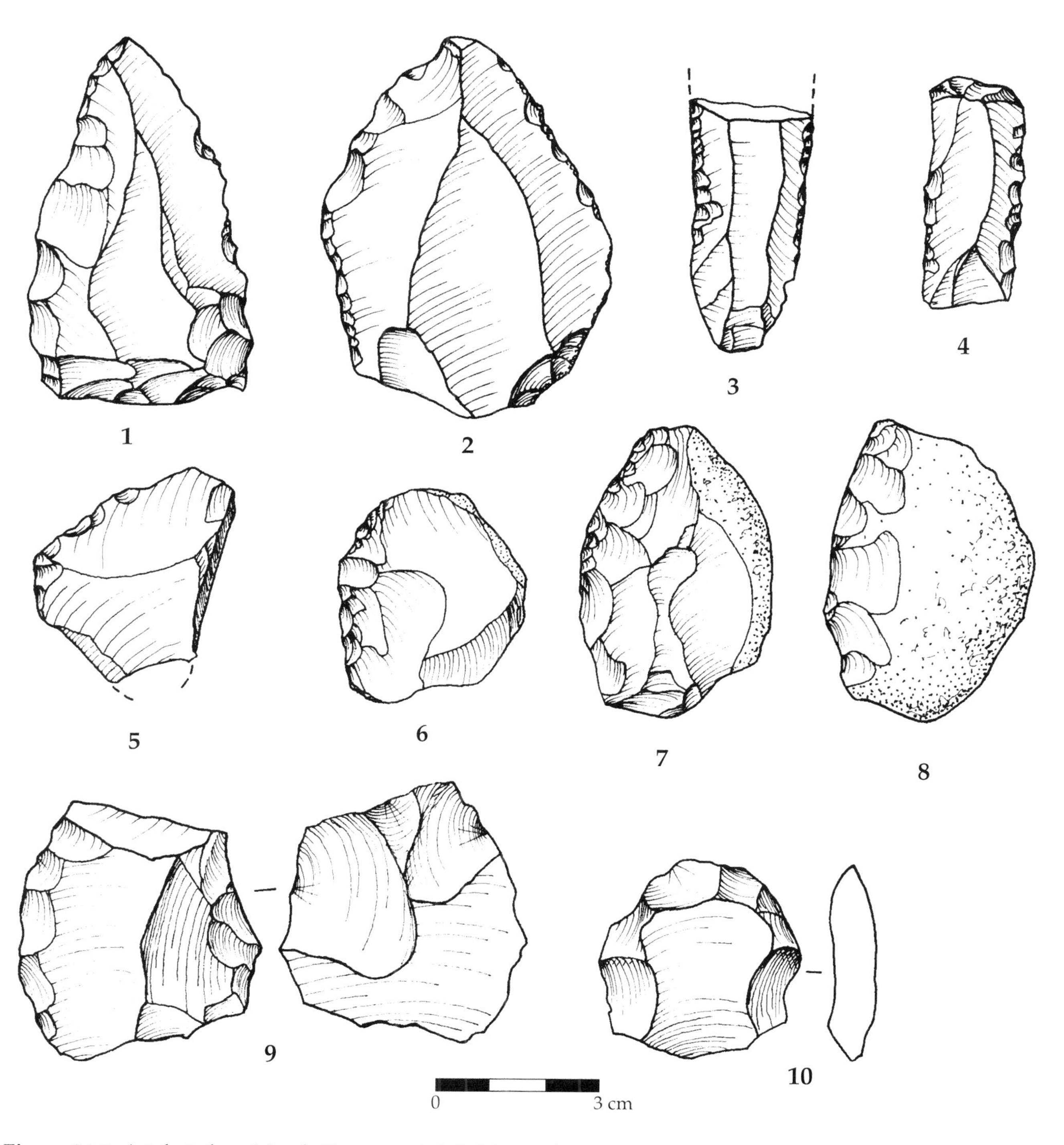

Figure 24.9. *Artefacts from Megalo Karvounari: 1–2. Mousterian points; 3–4. retouched blades; 5. Asprochaliko flake; 6–8. Quina scrapers; 9–10. cores.*

Levallois-Mousterian in the traditional sense, with examples of tortoise cores, amorphous core and disc cores. The flakes are generally small (30–40 mm in the maximum dimension). While there are some examples of elongated flakes and broken blades that could have resulted from a recurrent unipolar Levallois method, most of the flakes show radial scars and indicate the practice of a disc debitage, or a Levallois debitage oriented towards the production of a single rounded flake. There are also 6 pseudo-Levallois points, 2 of them retouched as *déjeté* scrapers, but this does not constitute enough evidence to identify the presence of the 'Asprochaliko method'.

Other sites near Asprochaliko

Small flakes associated with disc cores and occasional Levallois

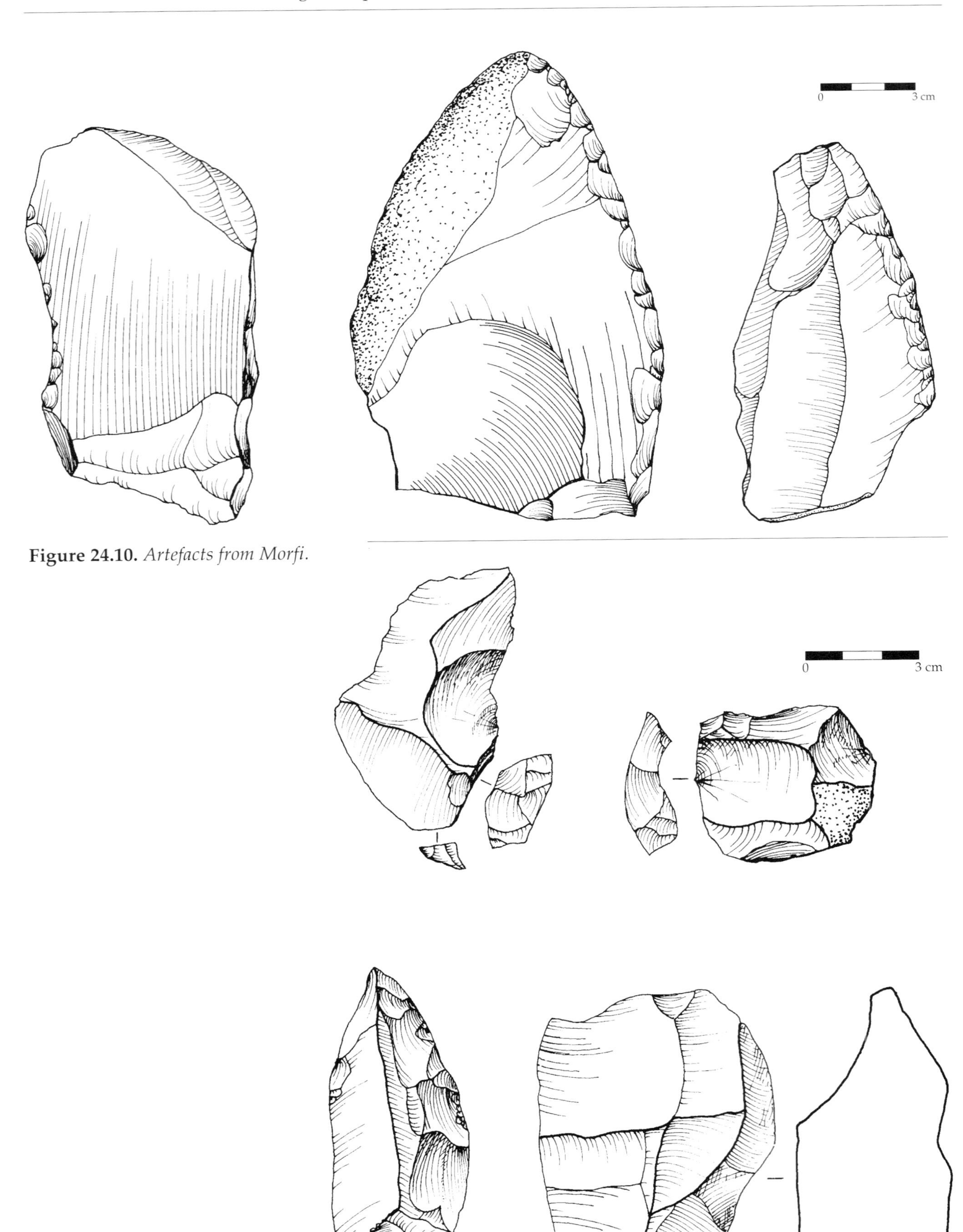

Figure 24.10. *Artefacts from Morfi.*

Figure 24.11. *Artefacts from Sampsous.*

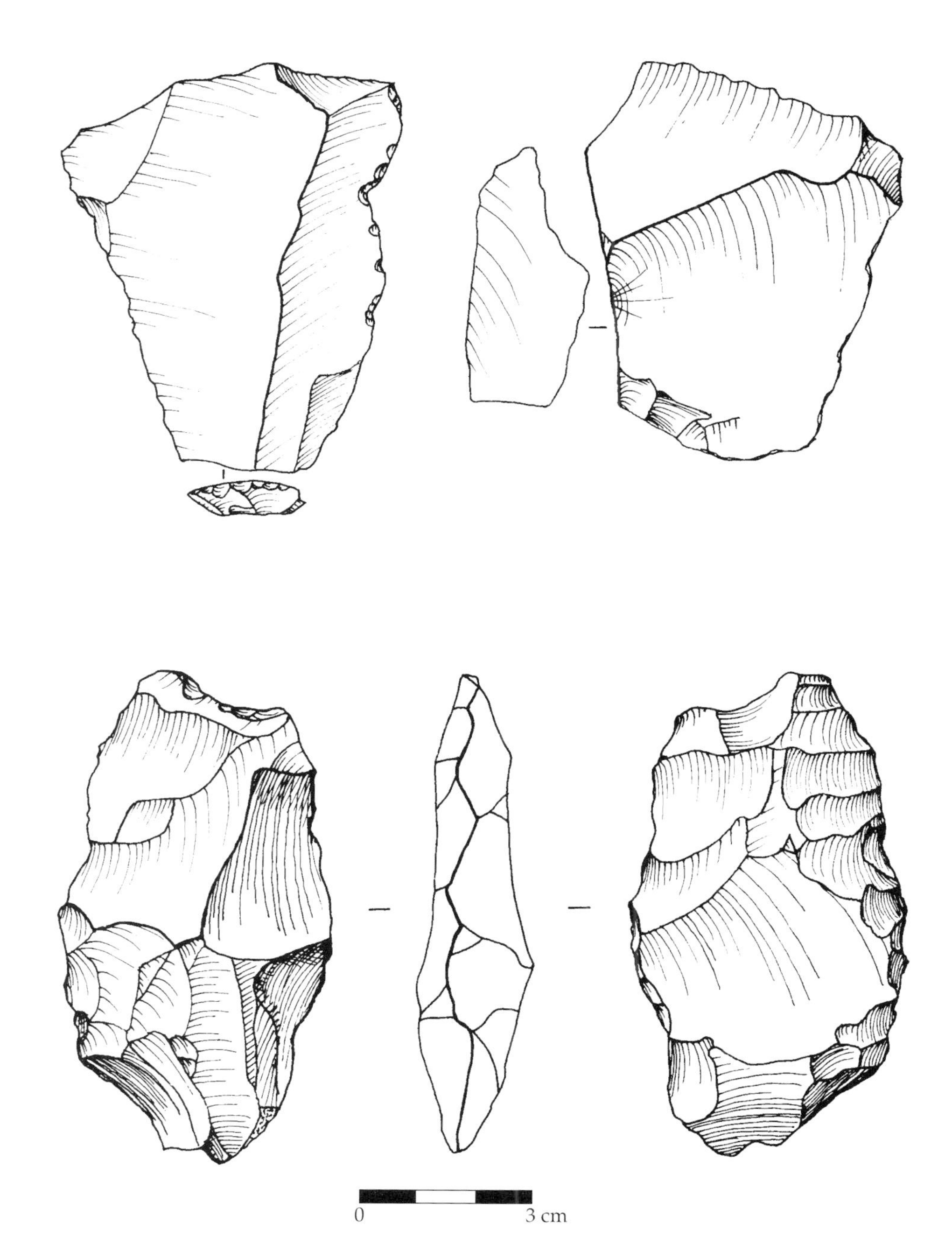

Figure 24.12. *Artefacts from the vicinity of Lake Ziros.*

tortoise cores were found at Agios Giorgios, OldAgios Giorgos, at localities near Gymnotopos and Gorgomylos east of Asprochaliko, and at Meliana to the north. At Chilia Spitia and Tsouka Modi, 3 km northwest of Asprochaliko, there are disc cores and small flakes (20–30 mm), heavily patinated, mixed with Holocene flints and pottery. At all these localities pseudo-Levallois points occur from time to time, and single lateral scrapers are the most common type of retouched tool (Fig. 24.13).

Gortses[1]

This site above Asprochaliko deserves special attention since it is a collection of 630 pieces which provide a good example of an incoherent assemblage. Apart from some apparently recent flints (bladelets, end-scrapers and completely unpatinated flakes), it is clear that the Middle Palaeolithic pieces are extremely heterogeneous. Most are small flakes (20–30 mm) with only two or three flake-removal scars, and are clearly produced from the irregular, polyhedric type of core, with many striking platforms, that predominates in this collection. Another group of cores can be assigned to the spectrum of Levallois techniques. Two of these show the recurrent unipolar technique, one was prepared by radial flake removals so as to produce single rounded flakes, and another core is similar to the Asprochaliko type. There are also two very well made classical Levallois points, but no accompanying cores of the appropriate type. Pseudo-Levallois points are rare and atypical. Most of the Levallois flakes are elongated with more or less parallel flake scars, and are the predominant category amongst the patinated pieces. Of particular interest is the fact that the retouched tools, mostly scrapers and points, are usually made on these Levallois blanks. There is also a smaller number of ordinary flakes, which are larger on the average than other flake products in the collection, and which are either unretouched or show slight retouching (Figs. 24.14 & 24.15).

Voulista Panagia

This is the last of the large collections from this area, with about 200 artefacts. The majority of the pieces are small as at Gortses, and are associated with a non-systematic debitage. There are rare pseudo-Levallois points which could indicate the presence of a discoidal technique. Retouched tools are rare and as elsewhere are mostly lateral scrapers. There are also some thick double scrapers. On the whole, the impression is of an assemblage produced by breaking flint into small pieces without sophisticated methods.

The Epirus hinterland

Here we are mainly concerned with isolated finds or mixed collections with no more than about 15 to 20 artefacts with a few heavily patinated pieces of Middle Palaeolithic aspect (Fig. 24.16). Near Pogoniani a typical tortoise core was found with ordinary flakes. At Riachovo, between Mazaraki and Lithinon, there is a disc core and some small patinated flakes. About 20 artefacts of possible Middle Palaeolithic type were collected at Ano Ravenia, and a similar collection, including also some more recent-looking pieces, was made around the shores of Lake Tseravinas. A good Levallois flake was found near Negrades and an isolated bifacial leafpoint at Kouklii. At Rodotopi, northwest of Ioannina, is a rather undiagnostic collection similar to the Tseravinas one, and at Pramanda, southeast of Ioannina, three patinated retouched tools including a double scraper with inverse retouch, were found. Finally, East of Ioannina, at Megalo Peristeri, 11 undiagnostic pieces were found including a bladelet core.

Problems of classification: the Micro-Mousterian illusion

The persistence of the Micro-Mousterian concept, although perpetuated to some degree by cross-referencing between the Epirus industries and the Elis industries in the Peloponnese, is primarily due to problems of classification. Choice is, of course, necessary in the construction of classes and the selection of attributes, both of which are in principle limitless. It is not possible to say that some choices are 'better' than others, but it is possible to examine critically the coherence of the foundations on which a classificatory scheme is based, and the relationship between the classes so formed and the interpretations subsequently built around those classes. Thus there is no doubt that one can classify the Epirus material in terms of artefact-size, frequency of retouched tools, or frequency of the Levallois technique. However, assigning cultural or temporal significance to the categories formed by these criteria requires explicit justification, since a variety of processes may give rise to the same formal characteristics in a flint assemblage.

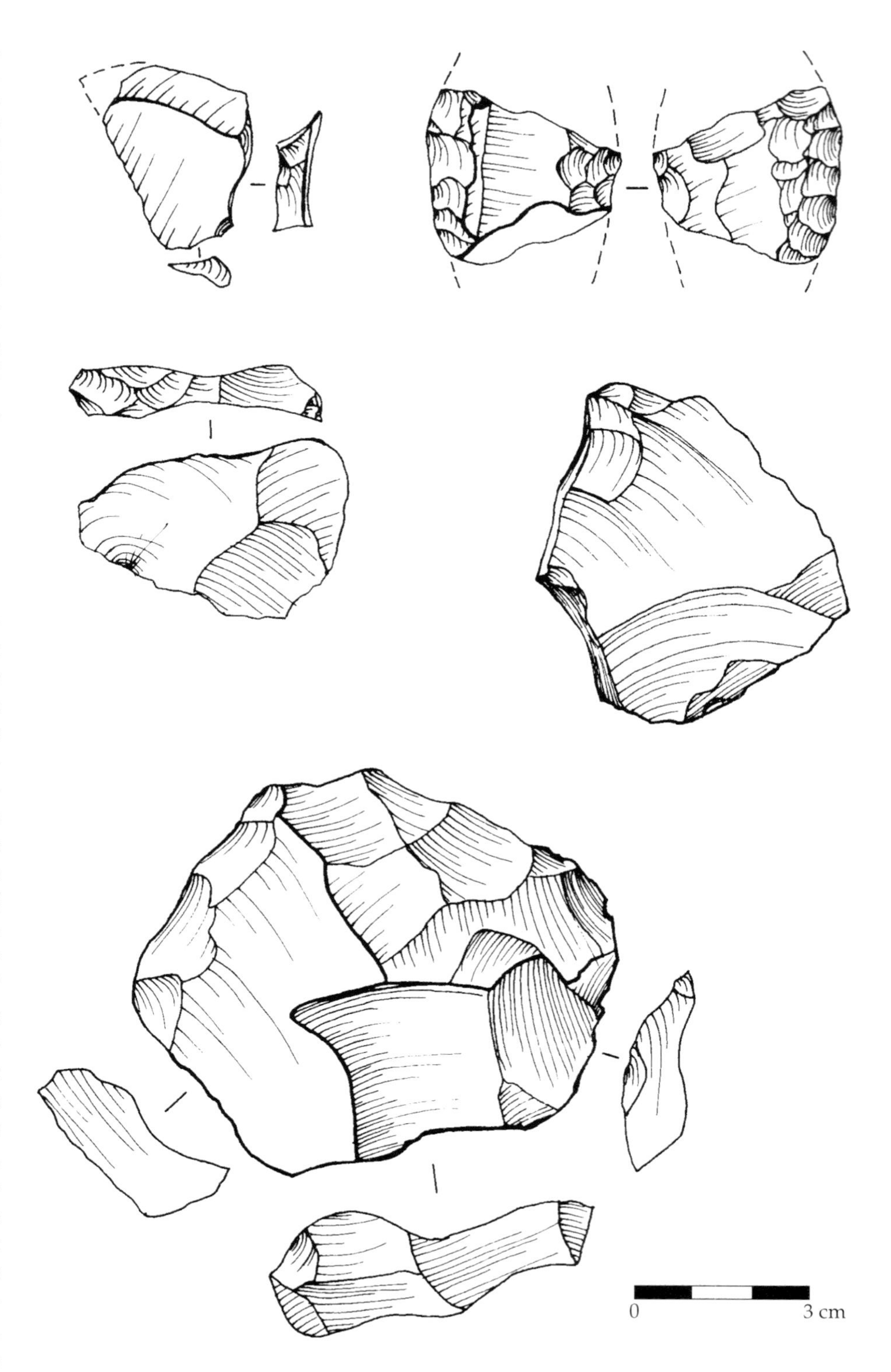

Figure 24.13. *Artefacts from Chilia Spitia.*

Our analysis of the upper industry at Asprochaliko shows that small artefact size was an intentionally sought-after characteristic. Flakes were frequently used as cores, thereby consciously

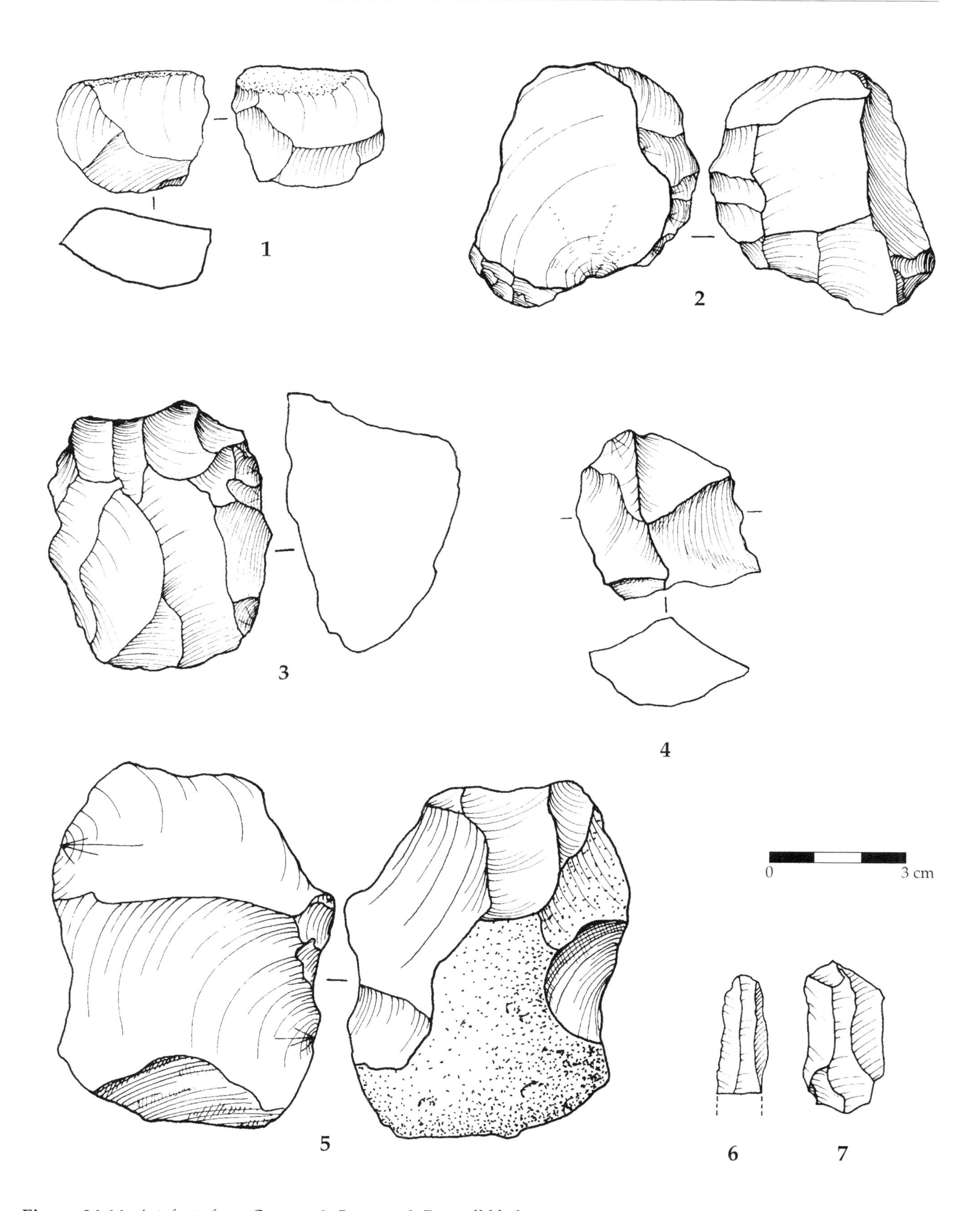

Figure 24.14. *Artefacts from Gortses: 1–5. cores; 6–7. small blades.*

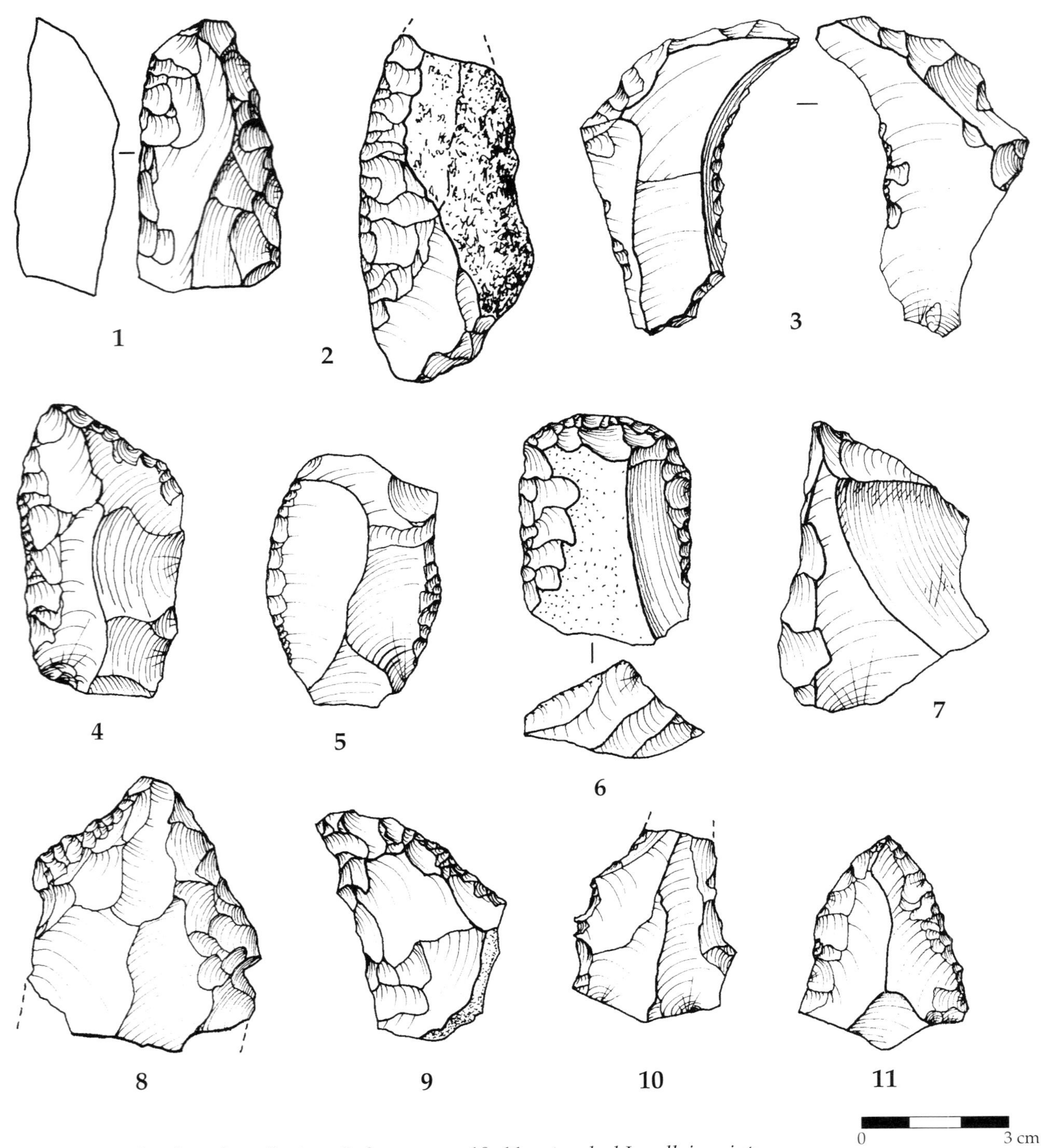

Figure 24.15. *Artefacts from Gortses: 1–9. scrapers; 10–11. retouched Levallois points.*

reducing the potential size of the subsequent flake removals. Cores on flakes, prepared so as to yield a small Asprochaliko flake, are quite common in the assemblage. This selection for small size is demonstrably not the result of constraints imposed by the small size of the available raw material, since there are numerous sources of good quality raw material including large-sized nodules close to the site. The basal Mousterian industry at Asprochaliko is also made on the same types of raw material but lacks the obvious selection for small implement size. We should also re-emphasize that this selection for small size in the upper industry was only applied to certain kinds of end-products. Other artefacts, for example the single lateral scrapers, were made on larger flakes.

At present there is no known parallel for this 'Asprochaliko method' of debitage elsewhere in Epirus or Greece, so that it is not possible to consider small size as a defining characteristic of a technical and cultural tradition. For example, it might be that the selection for small implements is related to the function of the site within a given subsistence system. Whatever the particular explanation in the case of Asprochaliko, it is clear that small artefact size, whether intentional or dictated by such factors as the time available for the procurement of raw material, can result from quite different technical processes of artefact manufacture. For example, the sites in the Peloponnese have small-sized implements produced by a Levallois method which focuses on the production of a single flake from a core prepared by a series of radial flake removals. These cores are made on small pebbles (Chavaillon *et al.* 1967). At other sites near Asprochaliko, such as Voulista Panagia and Gortses, small flakes were produced from disc cores, or by the non-systematic debitage method *'au fil du nucleus'* (Tixier *et al.* 1980). Other industries which have been attributed to the Micro-Mousterian facies because of the small size of the artefacts — the Pontinian in Italy, or industries from Jabrud in Syria, Crvena Stijena in Yugoslavia or Gasr ed Dauum in Tripolitania, can also be shown to have important technological differences (Kuhn 1995; Papaconstantinou 1988).

It appears then that similarities of small artefact-size, which have led to the grouping of diverse industries into the Micro-Mousterian category, are quite superficial, and mask a variety of distinctive

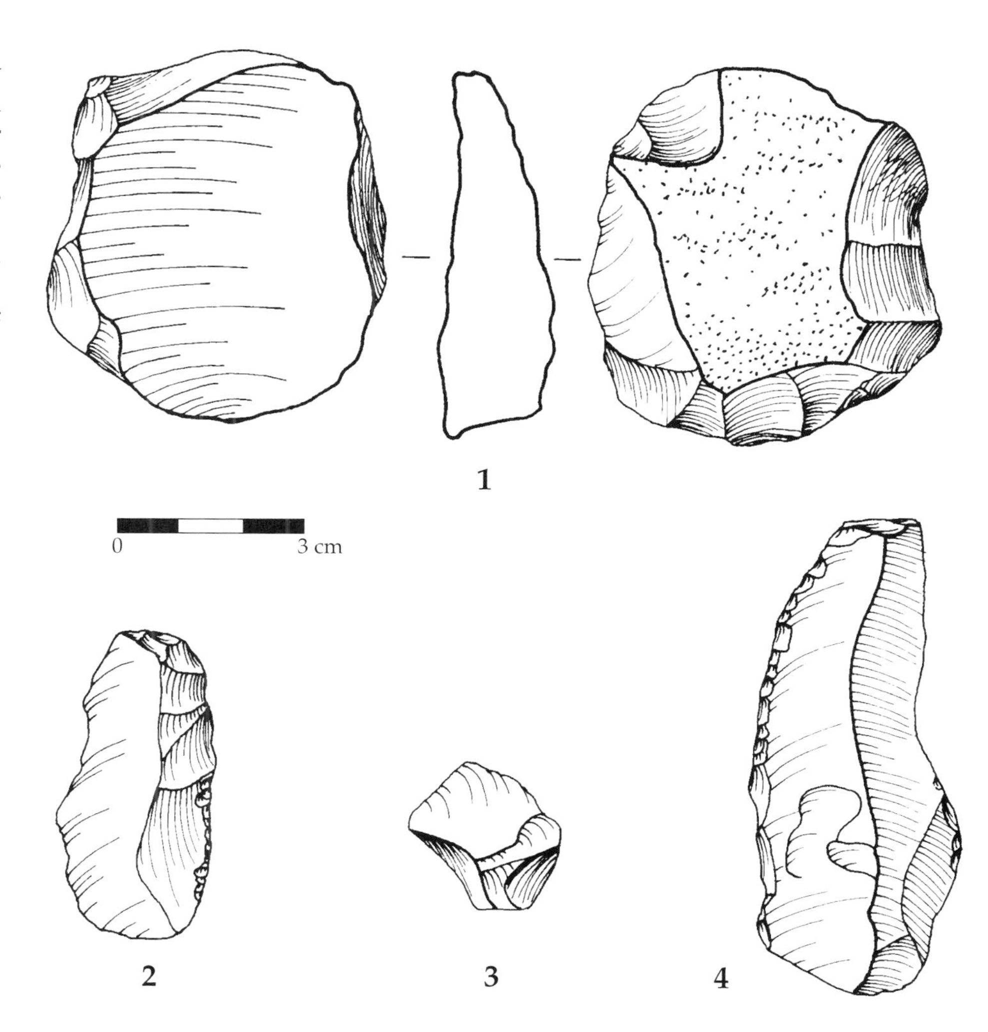

Figure 24.16. *Artefacts from inland Epirus: 1–2. Pogoniani; 3–4. Riachovo.*

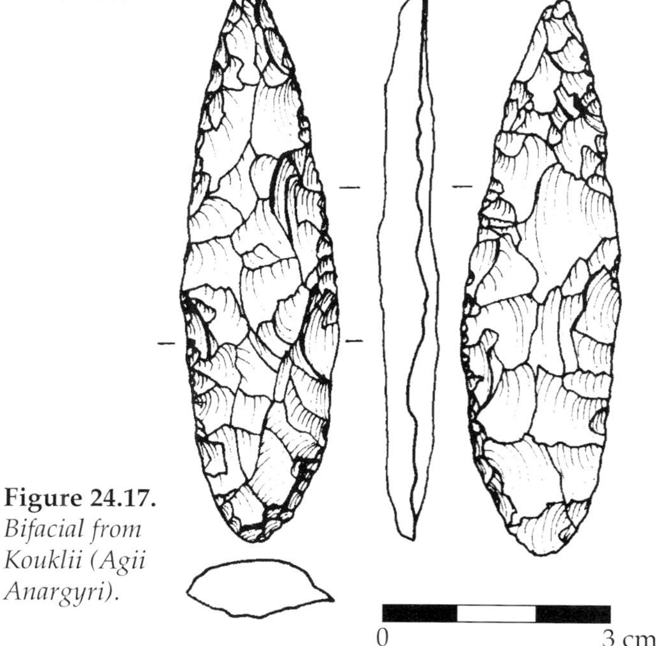

Figure 24.17. *Bifacial from Kouklii (Agii Anargyri).*

technological processes and endproducts. Typological and technological differences between industries are the norm not only in the Greek 'Micro-Mousterian' but also in sites elsewhere in the Mediterranean attributed to the Micro-Mousterian. While there is no doubt that 'cultural tradition', 'time' and 'site function' all contribute to the type of core reduction sequence practised and the technological intentions that shape it, we cannot assume that the simple effect of small size can differentiate Palaeolithic cultures. It follows that the concept of the Micro-Mousterian as a cultural horizon must be rejected. The material from open air sites in Thessaly (Runnels 1988a,b) or the Peloponnese (Pope *et al.* 1984) must also be ruled out as having any affinities with the pre-Upper Palaeolithic Mousterian industry at Asprochaliko.

Other industrial characteristics used to identify cultural or temporal groupings within the Middle Palaeolithic are equally suspect. Levallois technology, for example, is not a uniform category, but a general term which covers a variety of different flaking methods, as already indicated above. It is worth noting here that the Asprochaliko method, although not obviously recognizable at first sight as a pure Levallois method, is much closer to recurrent Levallois methods than to any other debitage method, while its relationship to the family of disc-core methods remains at present an unresolved issue. There is of course the further problem that the categorization of an industry as Levallois or non-Levallois is usually based on the percentage of Levallois products, and this figure is likely to be extremely unreliable when derived from surface collections.

The use of frequencies of retouched tools presents similar difficulties. The frequency of retouched tools may vary according to the function of a site, or even within different sectors of an excavated site, according to the availability of raw material, and over time, to say nothing of sampling biases. Comparison in these terms between caves, rock-shelters and open-air sites will be especially problematic. At Parapotamos and Chiliomodi, for example, the industries are technologically very similar with an emphasis on the production of elongated flakes and blades. At Chiliomodi, however, there are no retouched implements, and we might be tempted to assign this industry to a different Levallois facies. However, Chiliomodi is situated next to an important source of raw material, and it could equally well be argued that this is a factory site from which the retouched tools, or the blanks for making tools, have been removed elsewhere.

Problems of time and form

Several hypotheses have been advanced to place Middle Palaeolithic industries in Greece in some chronological order, in spite of the rarity of absolute dates. These hypotheses are usually based on formal comparisons between selected tool types found elsewhere in dated contexts and their formal equivalents in Greece, and necessarily depend on implicit assumptions about the relationship between artefact form and chronology, although efforts have also been made to associate surface material with dated geological sediments.

The first point to emphasize about the Epirus data is that none of the open-air sites are associated with absolute dates. The complexities of the geology do not yet allow artefacts to be dated by association with the geological formations in which they occur. Kokkinopilos is instructive in this context. In spite of attempts at radiometric dating by Uranium-series and thermoluminescence techniques, no acceptable dates have yet been produced, and there is continuing controversy about the geological processes by which the red sediments were formed and their age. It has also been established that the Middle Palaeolithic artefacts are in gully fills representing redeposited sediments, so that they cannot strictly be said to be *in situ* (Bailey *et al.* 1992; Runnels & Van Andel 1993a).

Radiocarbon dates from Asprochaliko raise other problems. Only one date that can be considered as viable is associated with the peculiar industry described above — sample I-1957 in Layer 14 with a reading of >39,900 (Bailey *et al.* 1983b). Recent TL dates from Layer 18 give a more definite value, with several readings converging on a date of *c.* 100 ka (Huxtable *et al.* 1992).

These recent dates undermine the hypothesis of a relatively recent age for the Greek Levallois-Mousterian. Reisch (1982) has suggested that only one Greek assemblage dates back to the Last Interglacial, namely the material found in a Eu-Tyrrhenian beach terrace at Elaea in the Peloponnese. According to Reisch the artefacts are 'archaic', although it is not possible to establish from the published illustrations or descriptions in what respect the material is archaic, except perhaps in terms of the mediocrity of the raw material. Reisch has also used faunal data to question the Last Interglacial date originally attributed by Milojcic and his team to the Levallois-Mousterian found in Thessaly (Milojčić *et al.* 1965). Runnels (1988a,b) has gone further and concluded that the Greek Middle Palaeolithic is generally more recent than 70 ka, with a time span from 50 to 40 ka. The industries from the southern Argolid in the Peloponnese are attributed to a date of *c.* 40 ka on the basis of Uranium-series dates (Pope *et al.* 1984). The authors consider that this material has close affinities with the Asprochaliko pre-Upper Palaeolithic Mousterian, although in fact there is no typological or technological similarity. In Thessaly Runnels has estimated the age of the surface material attributed on typological grounds to the Middle Palaeolithic as being between about 45 and 35 ka, on the basis of C14 and Thorium-Uranium dates. According to Runnels, the Thessalian industries contain Levallois-Mousterian and Aurignacian elements, and he groups these with a family of Balkan and southeast European Mousterian industries, linked to the Szeletian because of the presence of bifacially worked leaf points. He has also linked the Thessalian Mousterian to the Asprochaliko industry on the basis of similarities in small size.

These arguments are based on formal comparisons. Such arguments are appropriate for certain purposes (we have used them ourselves), but they also require a degree of 'retouching' for other purposes. Prehistoric archaeology is still strongly influenced by an evolutionist perspective with its notions of progress, stability and tendency. This may be acceptable in some cases, but in others it is highly inappropriate, notably for the Greek Middle Palaeolithic, where there is no clearly established pattern of relationship between dates and formal, technological or typological features of the flint industries. Of course the notion of a gradual and relatively synchronous passage of all humanity from pebble tools to microliths via flakes and blades is no longer taken seriously, but more subtle historical or evolutionary assumptions continue to pervade discussions of formal variability in stone artefacts.

Various authors have used the presence of bifacially worked points to assess the cultural and temporal relationships of the Greek Levallois-Mousterian. Runnels (1988a,b) has proposed similarities between the Hungarian Szeletian and the Greek Levallois-Mousterian, based principally on the assumed similarity of the Greek industries and the presence of bifacially worked points. As we have emphasized above, however, the Greek industries are a very variable group, and the Epirus sites alone show little in common with the Peloponnese sites either in technological or typological terms. Bifacial points are also a doubtful common denominator. Runnels admits that he is using an 'interpretation based upon the presence or absence of type fossils' (1988b, 278), but he also states that bifacially worked points are very variable typologically and do not constitute a reliable type-fossil (1988b, 287). In any case it is hard to see why the Greek Levallois-Mousterian should be considered closer to the Szeletian than any other type of industry solely because of the bifacial leafpoints. We might as well say that the Greek Levallois-Mousterian was closely related to the French Mousterian becauses of the Levallois flakes! In addition, the Greek leaf points come from open-air sites and apparently mixed collections without reliable context, so that it is not possible to say whether these points are associated with Mousterian or Aurignacian industries, or indeed anything else. The Morfi specimen referred to earlier is unpatinated and may be much more recent.

Similarly, the 'Asprochaliko flakes' cannot be used as type-fossils, since, when found in isolation, they are simply pseudo-Levallois points, and we have indicated above that these can be produced by a variety of different technical processes. Therefore we cannot say, from the presence of two or three such points at a given site, that it therefore has affinities with Asprochaliko. Other type-fossils, such as the offset scraper, are similarly unreliable. We have shown (Papaconstantinou 1988) that this tool type is very common at Asprochaliko, where it is usually made on 'Asprochaliko flakes'. However, while there is 'culture' in the know-how of the 'Asprochaliko method' and its products, we cannot be sure that the offset scraper at this site represents anything more than a functional requirement. Many sites all over the world have produced offset scrapers in varying quantities; many of them are in the Balkan peninsula and the Mediterranean region. None of them, however, as far as we know, are made on 'Asprochaliko flakes'.

In order to avoid confusion in these sorts of discussion, we suggest that a distinction be drawn between a *cultural marker* and an *industrial marker*. A cultural marker refers to technological products or morphotechnological features which can be demonstrated to have cultural significance in a particular context, for example the products of the 'Asprochaliko method'. We reserve the term industrial marker for distinctive features that are prominent in a lithic assemblage, but which are not demonstrably cultural markers. We include in this category the offset scrapers and the bifacially worked leaf points.

Attempts to combine time and form are further subverted by the Asprochaliko sequence as a whole, which fails to show any clear indication in the Mousterian industries of progressive tendencies with time.

Thin and long Levallois artefacts occur early in the sequence and are replaced by thick and small Asprochaliko flakes in the more recent industry. The latter industry contains no blades at all, and tools of Upper Palaeolithic form are no more numerous here than in the basal industries dated to 100 ka. Either preconceptions about the character of the relatively young Middle Palaeolithic industries are wrong, or Asprochaliko is an exception to the general rule in which late industries are expected to show more signs of Upper Palaeolithic technical features. If Asprochaliko is an exception, then one is left with the difficulty of establishing what is the norm. Many Greek Middle Palaeolithic assemblages have been regarded as late in date simply because of the presence of some end-scrapers and blade cores. However, the chronological implication of an association with Upper Palaeolithic features has to be proved and not simply assumed. As Braidwood observed over 40 years ago: '. . . to assume that we have dated Mount Carmel by calling it simply Levallois-Mousterian is meaningless, as the latter is not a term with primarily chronological meaning' (cited in Daniel 1967, 271).

Finally, there is often a presumption in the literature on the Greek Palaeolithic that one of the opportunities provided by the Greek material is to cast new light on the transition from Middle Palaeolithic to Upper Palaeolithic, with the implication that transitional industries might be discovered. If the Middle Palaeolithic and Upper Palaeolithic, respectively, represent huge blocks of homogeneity punctuated by some short-lived transitional event, that event will be exceedingly difficult to identify, given that most archaeological data represent gross aggregations of many behavioural events, a blurred pattern representing some average tendency over many millennia. Conversely, if Middle and Upper Palaeolithic mask a much greater variability than the labels imply, this greatly complicates the task of identifying what is transitional. Either way, any attempt to identify temporal trends or patterning in the Middle Palaeolithic is quite futile in the absence of a more detailed framework of absolute dates and far better contextual control over the material. For the moment, and given the problems of interpretation posed by open-air sites such as Kokkinopilos, we think it is over optimistic to claim that in various locations in Thessaly (Runnels 1988b; Theocharis 1967) and the Peloponnese (Chavaillon *et al.* 1969; Leroi-Gourhan 1964; Pope *et al.* 1984), archaeologists have discovered sites where the transition from Middle to Upper Palaeolithic has been fossilized on the ground surface. In our opinion, this is a good illustration of 'historical' thinking, that is the expectation that short-term events can be discerned in prehistoric data, and one that is unlikely to facilitate understanding of the Palaeolithic.

Achronous signatures and space

In the absence of better chronological data, we have to accept for the time being that the Middle Palaeolithic industries of Epirus cannot be dated to a resolution of better than about 65 ka, i.e., taking the Asprochaliko sequence as a reference point, they may lie anywhere between 100 ka and 35 ka. In effect, all the material must be treated as contemporaneous. This may seem an odd use of the term 'contemporaneity', but contemporaneity is a relative term in archaeology — that is, it is relative to the chronological resolution available (Papaconstantinou 1986). We use the term to indicate a stability in the essential features which govern the patterning within a given period of time. A more detailed framework of dates in future, together with a rejection of the methodological preconceptions that underpin the very concept of a 'Middle Palaeolithic period', may show this assumption to be wrong. But, for the present, we must be content to treat the Middle Palaeolithic material as a whole as an achronous data set, and to inspect the data for other dimensions of patterning. We shall therefore focus on patterning in the material as a whole, and on features related to environmental and spatial variation within the regional landscape.

The most striking geographical pattern within the region is the concentration of large sites near the actual Ionian coast or at low altitudes (not greater than 100 m above modern sea level), with industries dominated by production of blades and thin, elongated flakes. Flakes were mainly removed by recurrent Levallois methods based on unipolar or centripetal flaking, at least according to the pattern of flake scars on the flakes and blades themselves. However, the actual cores that one might expect to find associated with these methods are rare. On the contrary, the dominant core type is the classical tortoise core with its radial preparation. At first sight this seems strange, since there are no archaeological parallels or experimental evidence to suggest that a recurrent method of flake removals switches to a linear method (aimed at producing a single flake removal from a surface) in the final stage of core reduction. One might expect the reverse sequence to be more likely, but the size of the blades compared to those of the tortoise cores, which are often small and occasionally made on flakes, suggests that this is unlikely in the Epirus case. Further technological analysis will be required to solve this problem. The Epirus sites are characterized by the presence of various Levallois methods, indications of a disc debitage, and perhaps in some cases of the Asprochaliko method. However, it is not yet clear whether all the various types of cores and intentionally predetermined flake and blade products come from different stages of a single *'châine operatoire'*, whether they represent independent technical processes designed for quite different purposes, or whether they indicate some kind of stratigraphical and technical mixture.

These blade-like industries in the coastal region also present some interesting differences in tool frequencies (for example the contrast between Chiliomodi and Parapotamos) and tool-type inventories. Bifacial points, whatever their age and significance might be, are found in some of these collections.

Kokkinopilos, Tsiropolis and Ziros are the nearest parallels inland from the coast for these Levallois blade-like industries and bifacials are also present at Kokkinopilos and Ziros. Further afield, in Acharnania, a site on the southern shore of Lake Amvrakia has yielded a collection of Levallois blades and flakes and bifacials.

The sites on the Louros and in the vicinity of Asprochaliko show a different picture. With the exception of Kokkinopilos, the sites have generally produced only small numbers of artefacts. What is relatively surprising is that the Asprochaliko type of industry seems to be quite isolated, occurring only at Asprochaliko itself. There are possible parallels at some of the other sites, where there are occasional pseudo-Levallois points and disc cores, which could suggest affinities with Asprochaliko. However these occur in poor and highly mixed collections, so that it is impossible for the moment to say whether they indicate real cultural and technological similarities, or merely formal convergence. Nevertheless it is interesting to note that these artefacts all occur in localities very close to Asprochaliko (Gorgomylos, Agios Giorgios). In general the main point about the Louros valley is that the industries, whether they involve the Asprochaliko method of flake production or a classical discoid technique, are predominantly non-Levallois and non-blade-producing, and therefore form a clear contrast with the coastal sites. It appears, then, that we may have evidence for two geographically distinct traditions. How to fit Kokkinopilos into this picture remains uncertain. Given that it seems to contain the full range of technological and typological variation recorded in Epirus, it is tempting to see it as representing a location on the boundary between two geographical provinces.

Not much can be said about the character of Middle Palaeolithic settlement in the hinterland and at altitudes above 150 m (amsl), given the few finds. In the regions already examined (the coast and the Louros valley), there are a few small sites above 150 m — only Chilia Spitia, Tsouka-Modi and Gorgomylos approach 600 m. Since these areas have been more thoroughly explored than the hinterland, there is reason to think that the general rarity or absence of Middle Palaeolithic sites at higher altitude is a reality rather than a function of sampling error.

The general pattern of Middle Palaeolithic settlement is, then, quite different from the Upper Palaeolithic pattern, which shows more intensive use of the hinterland (see also Bailey *et al.*, Chapter 27). Whether it was climatic conditions or other factors which inhibited Middle Palaeolithic use of the Epirus hinterland, is difficult to say. Evidence from elsewhere in Greece strongly suggests a general Middle Palaeolithic preference for lowland settlement. Sordinas (1983) has discovered Levallois-Mousterian industries in Corfu which he has attributed to the early stages of the Last Glacial, and has suggested that a land-bridge between Epirus and the Ionian islands was available for the first time at this period. Middle Palaeolithic industries in the Peloponnese and Thessaly have so far been discovered at low altitude and near the modern coastline, and the same is the case for Aetolia and Acharnania according to provisional surveys in this area (Papaconstantinou 1988).

Conclusions

It should be clear from the above that there are still large areas of uncertainty in our understanding of the Epirus Middle Palaeolithic. If the nature of the Asprochaliko sequence and its industries, and the geographical distribution of material, offers some clear patterning, many other problems remain, and it is worth emphasizing two points in conclusion. First, it is important to note that not a single Middle Palaeolithic industry in Epirus to our knowledge is made on raw materials of poor quality. Grey flint and jasper are the most common materials, while coarse-grained material such as quartz or quartzite is very rare or not used at all. The abundance of large nodules of flint in the coastal region might explain the larger size of the artefacts found there, but raw material constraints are not sufficient to account for the variability of the Epirus industries. The case of Asprochaliko, where two quite different industries were produced from the same variety of raw materials, is ample demonstration of that point. The small artefact size that characterizes the upper Mousterian industry at Asprochaliko and a number of other sites in the Louros area, must be the result of other factors.

A second point concerns the retouched tools. If we take the most numerous tool-type, then at Asprochaliko as at other sites, the collections are dominated by artefacts with slight or irregular retouch, which do not represent standardized tool forms. For standardized types, the commonest tools are scrapers of various kinds. Borers, end-scrapers and burins are extremely rare. Pointed types, such as the Mousterian point, are also rare, and are found only in the larger assemblages such as Morfi, Karvounari and Kokkinopilos. Bifacial implements and bifacial retouch are also rare. Offset and transverse scrapers are relatively common in Epirus, especially at Asprochaliko and in the Louros region. For all the above types, size standards are difficult to establish. In most sites, as at Asprochaliko, it seems that size standards can only be established for particular categories of artefacts. For example, simple convex scrapers and Mousterian points are essentially bigger than offset scrapers in all sites examined. A similar point can be made for the unretouched, predetermined flakes and blades produced by the various Levallois and non-Levallois methods. For example, flakes produced by the recurrent Levallois method are larger than those produced by the Asprochaliko method. However, this sort of difference may be specific to Asprochaliko because of factors such as site function, and we do not think it can necessarily be generalized to all such cases. There is ample evidence from the surface material that Levallois flakes were sometimes removed by a linear method of debitage from very small cores made on flakes, while 'huge' Asprochaliko flakes may be discovered in the future. Thus many factors may affect artefact size, including locally variable factors such as availability of raw material. Size is thus an unsuitable variable on which to rely in formulating hypotheses about cultural and technological similarities and differences between assemblages.

The industrial sequence observed at Asprochaliko, that is a classical Levallois-Mousterian followed by a distinctive industry founded on the systematic production of small 'Asprochaliko flakes', also raises some further questions. To what extent does this sequence represent a temporal patterning applicable more widely in Epirus, as opposed to a site-specific pattern produced by purely local factors? Whatever the case may be, it is clear that several methods of systematic debitage were practised in Epirus, including Levallois and Asprochaliko methods, discoidal debitage and non-systematic debitage. In almost all sites Levallois flakes and blades are found alongside pseudo-Levallois points and other products of Asprochaliko or disc flaking methods, together with flakes produced without predetermination of their form. A more detailed technological analysis of the material from these open-air sites needs to be undertaken. But in the meantime we suggest that in all cases we have evidence of several technical traditions, the relationship between which is not at all clear. This variability may reflect stratigraphic, cultural, or anthropological mixture, functional or economic differences, or indeed some other factor or factors. Kokkinopilos provides an extreme example of this problem, but a similar patttern is present even at quite small and humble sites such as Gortses. We suggest that most of the known sites are indeed 'two-dimensional Combe-Grenals', and that solving the problem of Middle Palaeolithic variability in Epirus raises issues essentially similar to those presented by the problem of Mousterian variability as a whole.

Note

1. The location of this site is uncertain. The context in which it is referred to in Dakaris *et al.* (1964, 214) suggests that it is a small patch of red deposit above Kokkinopilos. There is no village of Gortses in the vicinity, and this may be a misprint for Galakas, a village near the red bed northwest of Kokkinopilos which was re-examined in the 1980s and named Chilia Spitia.

Acknowledgements

We are grateful to the Ioannina Museum for permission to examine their collections and in particular to Elias and Ioanna Andreou for their assistance and hospitality. The ideas presented here have benefited from discussion with E. Adam, G. Bailey, E. Boëda, P. Carter, G. Chourmouziades, C. Doumas, J. Gowlett, A. Holl, C. Perlès, A. Sordinas, D. & C. Sturdy and J. Tixier.

Chapter 25

To Know and To Have: Raw Material Availability and Upper Palaeolithic Stone Assemblage Structure in Epirus

Eugenia Adam

In this chapter I present a general comparative study of the Upper Palaeolithic (UPL) lithic assemblages from Asprochaliko, Kastritsa and Klithi. The presentation focuses on raw materials and knapping techniques, and includes the results of experimental knapping of locally available flints in the vicinity of each site. Observations on the prehistoric material concentrate on Asprochaliko and Kastritsa. For comparison with Klithi, I refer to Roubet's detailed analyses (Chapters 8 & 9). Since our methods are not exactly comparable, I have also made use of the small sample that I examined in my original study (Adam 1989, 224–47). Full supporting details are in Adam (1989). Here I focus on the availability and properties of the raw material, and on the ability of the knappers to control and exploit it, emphasizing the versatility, adaptability and skill indicated by the stone industries.

All the Upper Palaeolithic assemblages discussed here are made on various types of flint and most of them have as their main endproduct the creation of tool inventories dominated by bladelet tools, particularly backed and retouched bladelet types. All assemblages are dominated by flakes, a result of the flaking techniques involved in the manufacture of laminar blanks, and they include practically all stages of flint knapping: *in situ* exploitation attested by the presence of primary debitage and cores of most raw materials, core reduction, blank production and secondary modification. Stages of tool maintenance and discard are also present, albeit to varying degrees. Differences are observed in the means by which the desired endproducts are obtained as well as in the spectrum of raw materials employed at each site and the techniques involved in handling them. Some of these differences reflect variation in the nature of the locally available raw materials, but others reflect variation in the preferred techniques of tool production and most probably differences in the types of activities practised at each site and its role within the wider use of the landscape, as well as general time trends.

Sites and samples

The sites are not easily comparable because they occupy different environmental niches within the wider Epirus area, different periods of the local UPL, and have yielded very different quantities of material. Asprochaliko remains the sole rockshelter with an early UPL occupation in Epirus, while Kastritsa possesses an Upper Palaeolithic sequence not so far encountered in other Epirotic sites. No doubt continuing research will provide more data to help establish how far each site is typical of occupation within the local environment, or represents a specialized facet of local exploitation activities as is clearly the case at Klithi, where the archaeological record of the site itself as well as the information provided by the other Voïdomatis rockshelter deposits clearly confirm its specialized character (Parts III & IV).

The samples selected for analysis from Asprochaliko and Kastritsa are from distinct archaeological units as defined by Bailey *et al.* (1983b) and comprise a total of 3318 and 17,232 artefacts, respectively (Table 25.1). The small sample size at Asprochaliko reflects the relatively small size of the assemblages available from the undisturbed Upper Palaeolithic layers, but even allowing for that disturbance it is worth adding that the UPL deposits at Asprochaliko are much thinner than the MPL ones (Gowlett & Carter, Chapter 23). A small sample of 4806 artefacts from Q26 at Klithi (Table 25.2) is also included here. This sample was originally selected for study in 1984, because it came from a well dated and undisturbed context. Subsequent analysis and interpretation has shown that this sample straddles a variety of provenances (Bailey & Woodward, Chapter 4; Roubet, Chapter 8). Nevertheless I consider it to be a useful sample for comparative purposes, particularly with respect to the dominating influence of the local raw material on the character of the Klithi industry, and bearing in mind the rather uniform nature of the lithic assemblages at Klithi as suggested by Roubet's more detailed qualitative and quantitative analyses (Chapters 8 & 9).

Raw materials

The dominant rock is flint collected in the form of pebbles from river gravels, and in the form of nodules from primary contexts, or more commonly from secondary deposits. Flint is abundant in Epirus and northwest Greece in general, and comes in a wide variety of colours and grains and is the dominant raw material in all Palaeolithic industries so far discovered in the area. Radiolarite and jasper cannot certainly be excluded although their presence in the worked industries has not so far been confirmed.

The characterization of raw materials was done macroscopically in artificial light; colours were determined according to the 1975 edition of the Munsell Soil Color Chart. Texture and condition of natural surfaces were also recorded. Materials were classed as either fine- or coarse-grained; natural surfaces were classed as chalky, weathered chalky (smooth and thin film of cortex), patinated, or river-rolled. Table 25.3 shows the quantitative representation of flint types (based on colour). Grey, white, brown and reddish brown flint are quite common; yellow, reddish yellow, dusky red, grey brown and most of the remaining flint types are less common, while olive grey and olive brown flint is mainly confined to Kastritsa. These colour categories are not directly comparable to those defined by Roubet (Chapter 8) and Sinclair (Chapter 21), since they were defined according to independent criteria devised for the full range of material examined here. Artefacts made of flint of two or more colours are rare, although the exact representation of this type is difficult to assess because, as flaking experiments on these rocks have shown, these nodules when flaked often produce artefacts of individual colours that cannot be traced back to the original multi-coloured blocks.

Each site has a flint inventory that mostly reflects the types and qualities of locally available flint. In addition each site also shows a range of non-local types, usually represented by already prepared cores and the resulting debitage, tools, and tool manufacture and maintenance pieces (spalls, retouch and resharpening chips and by-products). In contrast to

Table 25.1. *Sample provenance, size and date of studied assemblages.*

Stratigraphic unit	Sample size	Radiocarbon date
Asprochaliko		
Layer 4	1983	–
Layer 10	1335	26,100 ± 900
Total	**3318**	
Kastritsa		
Stratum 1	3844	13,400 ± 210
Stratum 3	9344	–
Stratum 5	2346	19,900 ± 370
Stratum 7	770	20,800 ± 810
Stratum 9	928	20,200 ± 480 & 21,800 ± 470
Total	**17,232**	
Klithi		
Stratum 7 & 6	4806	14,060 ± 200 & 14,200 ± 200

Table 25.2. *Bagnos and provenances of the lithic material studied from Q26 at Klithi.*

Bagno	Miniquad	Spit	Context	Stratum
B5200	–	–	–	20
B5201	B	13	3001	20
B5202	A	12	3001	20
B5203	C	12	3001	20
B5204	D	12	3001	20
B5205	A	13	3004	7
B5206	B	13	3004	7
B5207	C	12	3004	7
B5208	D	13	3004	7
B5209	C	13	3004	7
B5210	C	13	3004	7
B5211	B	13	3004	7
C5220	C	14	3011	6
C5221	C	14	3013	6
C5222	A	13	3004	7
C5223	A	14	3004	7
C5224	B	13	3004	7
C5225	D	14	3004	7
C5226	B	14	3004	7
C5227	B	14	3011	6
C5228	D	14	3014	6

Table 25.3. *Percentage representation of flint types present in the UPL Epirus assemblages. * = Voïdomatis flint.*

	Asprochaliko		Kastritsa					Klithi
Flint colour	10	4	9	7	5	3	1	Q26
Grey	23.0	21.0	32.3	26.9	26.8	24.9	28.5	71.9*
Black	0.8	0.5	5.1	2.3	1.9	1.3	0.9	6.8*
White	5.4	22.3	10.3	16.5	20.7	16.7	18.8	2.1*
Pink	0.6	4.1	0.7	2.6	0.4	1.7	1.1	0.5
Red	7.0	6.9	7.3	3.9	3.7	3.8	4.8	2.6
Brown	20.3	19.2	2.2	4.9	5.6	5.1	4.4	6.3
Yellow	0.4	0.1	0.7	0.3	1.4	0.9	1.0	0.1
Dusky red	3.9	2.0	3.7	3.9	3.6	4.2	4.8	0.3
Two colours	3.9	1.3	–	1.0	0.2	0.8	1.4	0.8
Multi-coloured	0.8	0.1	–	–	–	0.1	0.08	–
Grey brown	7.0	5.2	5.9	4.9	7.5	6.5	6.6	1.5
Red grey	6.2	3.1	4.4	3.2	2.5	2.2	1.9	1.9
Red brown	15.5	11.0	6.6	10.4	6.5	9.0	9.0	4.9
Red yellow	5.0	2.7	0.6	1.4	1.7	1.9	–	0.3
Pale brown	–	–	14.0	12.3	11.9	15.1	10.7	–
Light brown	–	–	6.6	4.9	5.4	5.9	4.7	–
Olive grey	–	0.2	–	–	–	0.03	0.3	–
Olive brown	–	–	–	–	–	0.07	0.3	–
Total (N)	**1335**	**1983**	**928**	**770**	**2346**	**9344**	**3844**	**4806**

the two main sites, Klithi relies almost exclusively on the locally available *Voïdomatis flint*. This is grey to black, often banded or patinated, very fine-grained and soapy in texture, and differs from the black and grey types encountered in the other two assemblages. Grey and black flint is widely available in Epirus, but the Voïdomatis variety is distinguishable from the rest by its grain size, lustre, cleavage planes, inclusions and weathered outer surface. All authors who have examined the Klithi industry stress these distinctive characteristics (Moss, Chapter 11; Roubet, Chapter 8; Shawcross & Winder, Chapter 10; Wenban-Smith, Chapter 5). Voïdomatis flint is absent from Asprochaliko but, interestingly enough, is present at Kastritsa from Stratum 5 onwards.

The presence of different types of raw materials often contributes to variability in lithic assemblages, affecting tool size and manufacturing techniques as has been clearly demonstrated, for example, in the case of the Spanish Solutrean (Straus 1980, 71). The coexistence of local and non-local raw materials is also evidence of knowledge of wider areas or contacts. At Temnata cave in Bulgaria, raw material sources can be traced over distances of hundreds of kilometres, including even northern Greece (Pawlikowski 1992, 286), and in the Romanian Gravettian good quality flint from the Prut River circulated over the entire east Carpathian area (Chirica 1989, 139). If the procurement of local raw materials is considered as part of a daily routine, the systematic acquisition of non-local materials must indicate an organized plan either for the procurement of the material itself as the main objective, or in combination with other activities (hunting, investigation of resources) as a complementary activity, or through exchange.

Asprochaliko

The majority of the flint employed is fine-grained with few inclusions. Most nodules collected for experimental purposes in the vicinity of the site were small in size, of reddish brown, red, black, brown and white colours. Black flint is available locally but is not very common. Flint was collected for experiments from the nearby Louros and from a small tributary stream that runs near the site. The most interesting aspect of the raw material collected and knapped experimentally is its smallish size. This, combined with inclusions and cleavage planes, caused frequent changing of the flaking direction in order to economize on good quality raw material. This trend was also noticed in the UPL assemblages, though these do not include as many primary pieces with river rolled outer surfaces as one might expect given the proximity of the river. On the contrary, primary surfaces are mostly of chalky cortex. Grey, brown, white and reddish/brown flint are the dominant varieties (Table 25.3) and are represented by all stages of manufacture, while black, pink, yellow, dusky red, olive grey and flint with two or more colours are only represented by debitage and tools and in much smaller quantities than the rest, suggesting that they were not systematically exploited but were introduced either as blanks or as finished tools.

Flint was also almost exclusively employed in the Middle Palaeolithic (MPL) industries of Asprochaliko, albeit in different ratios: grey flint dominates (*c.* 60 per cent), brown is consistently present (*c.* 30 per cent), and red, pink and yellow varieties are rare, while multi-coloured pieces are few. No significant differentiation is recorded within the MPL industries as far as flint varieties are concerned (Papaconstantinou 1988, 86–7; Chapter 24). Primary surfaces present a similar variety to that already observed in the UPL assemblages: nodules were collected from river banks and surface exposures, though chalky cortical surfaces seem to be less numerous in the MPL assemblages than in the UPL ones (Adam 1989, 63, 71, 79, 87). Another difference lies in the fact that grey and brown flint are present in smaller quantities in the UPL industries (22.0 per cent and 19.7 per cent respectively) than in the MPL ones. There is no noticeably poor quality material in either industry at Asprochaliko and I tend to agree with Papaconstantinou (1988, 98) that the availability, quality and size of the nodules remained fairly stable for a very long period of time.

Kastritsa

Kastritsa presents a wider range of flint types than Asprochaliko, and a marked contrast with the dominance of a single flint type at Klithi. The very location of the Kastritsa site may account for these differences, though the provenance of the flint present in the Kastritsa assemblages is difficult to assess. Whereas Klithi is located near the Voïdomatis River, and Asprochaliko is equally close to a river and within a gorge rich in flint, Kastritsa is isolated on a ridge by a lake at some distance from flint-bearing formations and with no nearby source of river gravels bearing flint nodules. This is reflected in the industries. Rolled surfaces on primary artefacts and cores are rare, and the commonest natural surfaces are chalky cortex in various stages of weathering, suggesting the nodules were not necessarily collected from an *in situ* vein of flint or primary deposit, but were rather found as secondary deposits. On the other hand, the constant presence of primary artefacts in all strata, and on most flint types, and the fairly stable diachronic representation of the main flint types throughout the sequence, indicate that lithic resources were within reasonable reach, ensuring a constant and predictable supply of raw material. Kastritsa probably had a wider catchment for the collection of flint than the other sites, partly because of the site location itself and partly because of the resource procurement and exploitation strategies followed by the inhabitants of the site.

The flint used in the Kastritsa industries is mostly fine-grained and easily flaked. So far no preferential use of particular types has been observed. Strata 3 and 1 exhibit the widest range of raw material types (Table 25.3). Throughout the sequence grey flint predominates followed by pale brown and white varieties, with most of the remaining categories in similar qualities, all fully exploited. Yellow, reddish brown, olive grey and olive brown flints are less common and represent isolated cases.

Exploitation of yellow flint *in situ* is suggested only in Stratum 3, where there are 3 cores and core tablets. Otherwise this flint variety is represented only by debitage in all the other strata and by tools only in the upper deposits (Strata 5 to 1). The situation is similar in the case of reddish yellow flint, which is totally absent from Stratum 9, exploited *in situ* for certain only in Stratum 1 (2 core tablets), and represented in the other strata (5 to 1) by debitage and tools. Olive grey and olive brown flints are only present in the two upper strata and mostly in the form of debitage and tools.

The presence of Voïdomatis-type flint is a notable feature from Stratum 5 onwards, with quantities increasing in Stratum 3 and decreasing again in stratum 1. A total of 103 artefacts in this material was recorded from Strata 5, 3, and 1. The presence of 13 cores and tablets indicates that the material was worked *in situ* from Stratum 5, an observation reinforced by the presence of 55 debitage products, and by one case of refitting, comprising two opposed-direction flakes on a core (see Fig. 25.6:5a,b). Voïdomatis flint is also represented by 35 tools including backed bladelets (17 pieces), retouched bladelets (5 pieces), 2 notches, 2 truncated bladelets, 2 micropiercers, 3 microburins (2 of which are of the Krukowski type), 1 burin, 1 piercer, 1 shouldered point and 1 microgravette. It should be said that this flint is present in the form of cores, core tablets, debitage and tools in all strata, reflecting equal treatment of the material through time. Examination of an even larger sample is expected to increase the number of observations. The flint macroscopically identified as of Voïdomatis type was analyzed in the laboratory along with modern samples collected from the Voïdomatis and the two groups produced similar spectra, thus confirming the original classification (Maniatis *et al.* 1988, 655–7). The presence of this flint type in Kastritsa does not necessarily imply a direct or indirect relation to the Voïdomatis area and consequently to Klithi, since it is not certain that the flint was confined to a single area or distributed by a single river system (i.e. the Voïdomatis and its tributaries). The issue of inter-site relations, which forms one of the focal points of the present volume, would benefit from further field work on the location of flint sources combined with laboratory analyses.

Klithi

The bulk of the flint employed at Klithi was collected from the adjacent Voïdomatis River gravels. Primary deposits of this flint have been located a few kilometres upstream from Klithi (Bailey *et al.*, Chapter 16; Woodward pers. comm.) but it is not certain whether this is the only such area. This flint variety is easily distinguishable from the grey and black flint common in the other two industries, as stated earlier, being more fine-grained and shatter-prone. Banding is a common feature of the local flint along with cleavage planes and impurities. The river nodules are usually rounded and less often tabular, almost entirely decorticated, their original natural surface eroded away by water action. The ridges are rounded and battered, and the size is generally small, as indicated by the experimental collection (Adam 1989, 225). Roubet (Chapter 8) gives a fuller account of raw materials employed at Klithi based on a much larger sample. The information presented here refers exclusively to the Q26 sample.

Systematic collection of pebbles from the river gravels near the site revealed that the quantity of raw material varies according to the time of the year and the amount of water in the river. Besides, not all available pebbles are suitable for flaking since the material has frequent internal weaknesses that cannot be detected by inspection of the outer surface. The proximity of raw material is thus counteracted by the erratic flaking quality of the pebbles, a weakness overcome by the technological skill of the knappers.

The pieces that I collected rarely exceeded 6 cm. The majority of the nodules was decorticated with rolled and battered surfaces and ridges rounded to the point of forming natural 'crests' as a result of water action. The colour of the flint ranges from light grey to black; brown lumps are rare, while patinated pieces are few.

Red, yellow, pink and other coloured varieties present in the archaeological assemblage were absent from the river gravels and were probably introduced to the site in the form of retouched tools which were subsequently resharpened or otherwise modified as indicated by the retouch chips recorded by Newcomer (Bailey *et al.* 1986a, 14). This original observation was further supported by the fact that yellow and dusky red flint are only present in the analyzed sample in the form of non-primary chips, suggesting that they were imported in the form of blanks or finished tools that were retouched and/or resharpened on the site. Reddish grey flint is present in the form of debitage and tools, very few of which are primary, while brown flint is represented by 3 cores and tablets as well as primary debitage, suggesting *in situ* working of a raw material that could well be found locally, albeit in small quantities, judging by the experimental collections of Adam (1989, 225) and Moss (Chapter 11). Most tools from the Q26 sample were manufactured on local flint, an observation that applies equally to cores, technical pieces and debitage.

Experimental knapping of the raw material confirmed my original impressions about the impact of a hard-to-control, shatter-prone and cleavage-ridden material upon the final qualitative character of the industry at hand. The experimental collections reflected faithfully the archaeological material recovered at the site. In brief, the experiments showed that the quality of the raw material influences the products of debitage and, consequently, the whole of the industry. The local raw material requires a certain level of technological skill to conform to the knapper's intentions, which were the production of elongated, preferably straight pieces (Adam 1989, 239).

The small dimensions of the artefacts are most probably the result of the original size of the nodules employed. The effect of the raw material is also evident in most technological aspects of the industry.

The flaking qualities of the materials employed at the Epirus sites are broadly similar, but there are also some differences. At Klithi the raw material nodules are of small size and have frequent impurities and weaknesses that require the consumption of a large number of river nodules and painstaking concentration while knapping. Asprochaliko flints also present weaknesses but to a lesser degree. The impression at Asprochaliko is that material was in short supply while at Klithi the impression is of a raw material that was of inadequate quality.

One could conclude that the Voïdomatis Gorge sites (Klithi, Megalakkos, Boïla) exploited the local flint varieties because their inferior flaking qualities were compensated for by their abundance and easy availability. On the other hand, the Asprochaliko UPL assemblages, in spite of the location of the site in a river gorge, exploited fewer river pebbles, judging by the poor representation of rolled and battered surfaces indicative of intensive and prolonged water action, and mostly relied on flint from secondary deposits, judging by the predominance of smooth and eroded chalky cortex on natural surfaces. This could be the result of the unsuitability or poor availability of river nodules in the Louros River, or the result of a more discriminating strategy of raw material selection. The Voïdomatis Gorge sites, and in particular Klithi, seem to have relied on the local flint because it was available in considerable abundance. Intensive exploitation of local resources is also reflected in the faunal remains at Klithi (Gamble, Chapter 12) and the bone artefacts (Adam & Kotjabopoulou, Chapter 13), and consequently in the function of the site. Asprochaliko in contrast exhibits a wider range of faunal resources (Bailey *et al.* 1983b, 37, 40) and is usually interpreted as a more general-purpose site than Klithi (Bailey 1992, 26). Of the three main sites, Kastritsa exhibits the highest presence of chalky surfaces, both fresh and weathered, and a limited use of river pebbles. The variety of flint types and of natural surfaces and their diachronic representation indicate access to and knowledge of areas beyond the immediate site vicinity.

The industries

Asprochaliko

The UPL industries from Asprochaliko represent the earliest such assemblages from Epirus so far known. The minimum date for the industries is 26,100 ± 900 bp and refers to Layer 10, present only in the western part of the site (see also Adam 1989, 59–102).

Layer 10 is a flake dominated assemblage with more bladelets than blades (Tables 25.4 & 25.5; Figs. 25.1 & 25.2). The flakes are mostly of hard hammer mode with non-parallel lateral edges (Fig. 25.3:5–6) and the bulb away from the main ridge(s). Changing of the flaking direction is suggested by the dorsal scars on the flakes, the presence of core direction change pieces (Adam 1989, 48), and the cores themselves. Cresting is only present in three cases and the cores bear few traces of preparation. The bladelets are mostly of soft hammer mode and non-straight in profile. There is only one bidirectional core, and bidirectional scars are rare on the dorsal surfaces of debitage, suggesting very limited use of this technique, a technique which ensures the production of straight pieces.

Tools comprise 3.5 per cent of the industry. Flakes are prefered to blades as blanks for the manufacture of non-bladelet tools (Fig. 25.3:13–14). Bladelet tools predominate (Table 25.6; Figs.

Table 25.4. *General composition of the Asprochaliko assemblages.*

Category	Layer 10 N	Layer 10 %	Layer 4 N	Layer 4 %
Tools	47	3.5	105	5.3
Cores	17	1.3	29	1.5
Tablets	4	0.3	19	0.9
Flakes	746	55.9	1138	57.4
Blades	28	2.1	23	1.1
Bladelets	117	8.7	145	7.3
Chips	216	16.2	261	13.2
Microburins	–	–	1	0.05
Burin spalls	–	–	3	0.1
Debris	160	12.0	259	13.1
Total	**1335**	**100.0**	**1983**	**99.9**

Table 25.5. *Complete debitage at Asprochaliko by layer.*

Category	Layer 10 N	Layer 10 %	Layer 4 N	Layer 4 %
Flakes	242	44.8	393	48.9
Blades	17	3.1	11	1.4
Bladelets	84	15.5	88	10.9
Chips	37	6.8	52	6.5
Knapped debris	35	6.5	96	11.9
Pot-lid debris	112	20.7	103	12.8
Natural debris	13	2.4	60	7.51
Total	**540**	**100.0**	**803**	**99.9**

25.3:15–16 & 25.4) and backed bladelets account for 38.3 per cent of the tool inventory, while endscrapers are the next most numerous tool group (Fig. 25.3:12–14). There are no backed bladelets with inversely retouched ends. Most backed bladelets are made on non-primary blanks with one dorsal ridge and straight profiles. All but one are backed by direct abrupt retouch.

Layer 4 is also a flake-dominated industry with bladelets outnumbering blades and a tool percentage of 5.3 per cent, higher than in Layer 10. Cores show limited preparation, frequent change of flaking direction (Fig. 25.5:1–2) and limited maintenance. As before, flakes are prefered to blades as blanks. The tool inventory is dominated by bladelet tools (Table 25.6; Fig. 25.4), mostly backed bladelets. This layer differs from Layer 10 in that backed bladelets with inversely retouched ends (Fig. 25.5:9–10) make their first appearance, but is otherwise similar.

Kastritsa

All strata are dominated by flakes with the exception of Stratum 9 which is dominated by debris. Blades are more numerous than bladelets in Strata 9 and 7, about equally represented in Strata 5 and 3, and less numerous than bladelets in Stratum 1 (Tables 25.7 & 25.8). The site shows more intensive use during Stratum 3 resulting in larger assemblages rich in tools and debitage. Refits are common in the upper strata and far less in the lower ones. The industries exhibit diachronic technological and morphological differentiation (see also Adam 1989, 104–222).

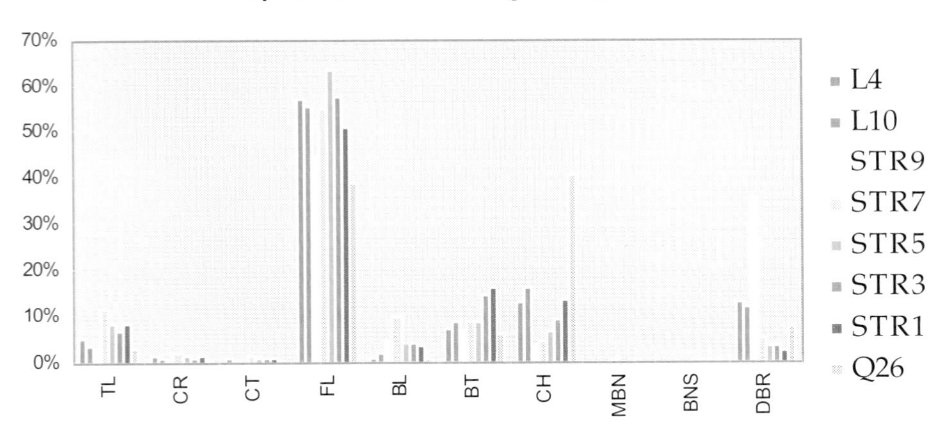

Figure 25.1. *Graphic representation of assemblage composition at Asprochaliko, Kastritsa and Klithi.*

Stratum 9. Natural debris (DN) outnumbers all other categories (Table 25.8; Fig. 25.2) and many artefacts bear severe edge damage. This is a characteristic not encountered in any other stratum. These are indications of natural action, possibly by water due to the fluctuations of the level of the lake (Bailey *et al.* 1983b, 26).

Flakes have large butts, very few traces of platform abrasion and are of hard hammer mode. Blades are mostly of soft hammer mode with small butts. The same applies to the few bladelets. Cores and technical pieces are very poorly represented in this stratum.

This stratum yielded relatively few tools (3 per cent: Table 25.7; Fig. 25.1). The tool inventory comprises few types and contrary to the other strata is not dominated by bladelet and backed tool types but by

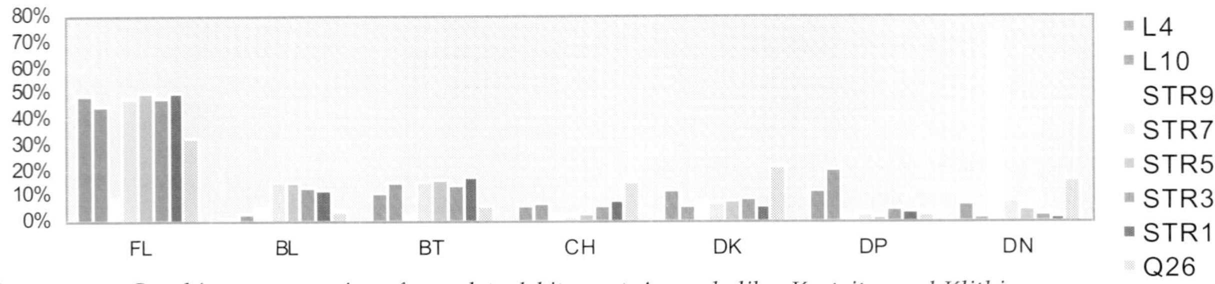

Figure 25.2. *Graphic representation of complete debitage at Asprochaliko, Kastritsa and Klithi.*

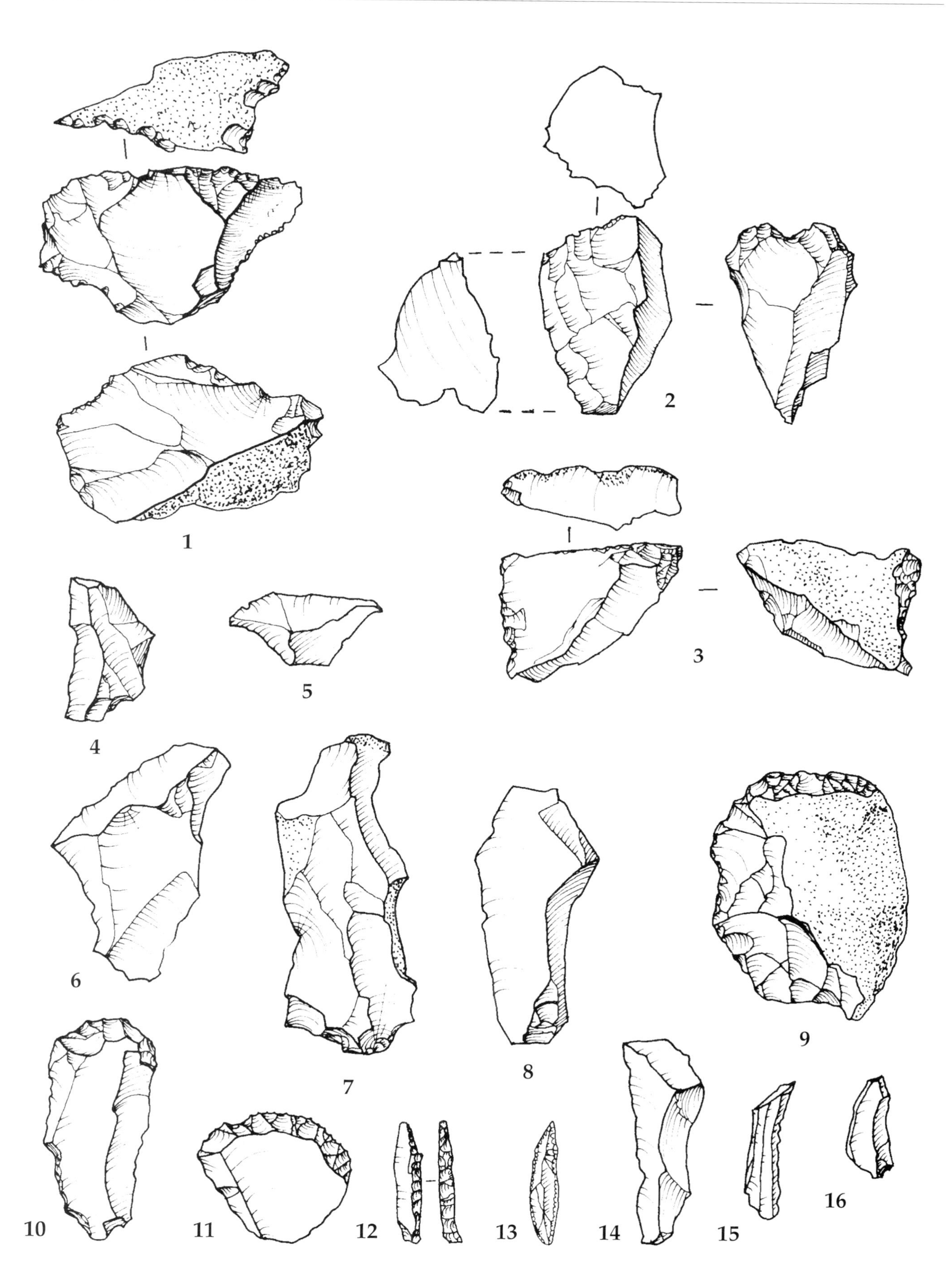

Figure 25.3. *Asprochaliko Layer 10: 1–3. cores; 4–6. flakes; 7–8. blades; 9–11. endscrapers; 12. backed bladelet; 13. microgravette point; 14–16. bladelets. Full size.*

endscrapers (Fig. 25.6:1). Burins, burin spalls, microburins, gravette points and microgravettes as well as shouldered points are absent from this stratum. Truncated pieces, Aurignacian blades and sidescrapers are present in small numbers compared to the other strata. Most blanks are non-primary and straight with unidirectional dorsal scars and more than one ridge.

The backed bladelet types (Fig. 25.6:2) are represented by very few examples including backed bladelets with inversely retouched ends. There is no evidence for the practice of the microburin technique, the sole example of this class being a Krukowski microburin, which is not the result of intentional segmentation. Bladelet tools in Atratum 9 are outnumbered by tools made on flakes or blades.

Table 25.6. *Percentage representation of tool groups in Epirus UPL assemblages.*

Tool group	Asprochaliko 10	4	Kastritsa 9	7	5	3	1	Klithi Q26
Endscrapers	16.9	12.4	25.0	7.7	9.4	3.0	3.1	14.6
Composite tools	2.1	1.9	3.6	1.1	2.0	0.4	0.9	0.6
Piercers	–	0.9	3.6	1.1	1.6	2.2	3.1	–
Burins	–	–	–	3.3	9.6	6.6	9.1	3.6
Backed tools	2.1	–	–	1.1	1.6	5.2	2.8	1.2
Truncations	–	6.7	10.7	8.8	4.7	4.0	2.8	4.2
Retouched blades	6.3	5.7	14.3	2.2	4.7	3.8	0.6	0.6
Notches	2.1	3.8	10.7	3.3	3.1	2.5	2.8	0.6
Bladelet tools	55.1	60.2	21.4	57.1	51.0	62.1	66.0	66.6
Varia	12.7	8.6	10.7	14.3	12.5	10.2	8.5	7.8

Stratum 7. Both flakes and blades have plain butts and are mostly detached by hard hammer. Bladelets are mostly of soft hammer mode with traces of core platform preparation. Bladelet cores outnumber flake cores and usually have a single platform. Core platforms are plain, and cores were turned during flaking. There are no blade cores. Stratum 7 is richer in tools (11.8 per cent: Table 25.7; Fig. 25.1) and presents a wider range of types. Burins make their first appearance (all on truncations) along with bladelets with semi-abrupt retouch. The backed bladelet types (Fig. 25.6:4) are enriched by the introduction of pointed backed bladelets, backed bladelets with opposed retouch and bilaterally backed bladelets. There are no true microburins (only Krukowskis), gravette points or microgravettes, and no shouldered types. Notched bladelets, sidescrapers, totally or partially

Table 25.7. *General composition of the Kastritsa assemblages.*

Category	Stratum 9 N	%	Stratum 7 N	%	Stratum 5 N	%	Stratum 3 N	%	Stratum 1 N	%
Tools	28	3.0	91	11.8	192	8.2	637	6.8	319	8.3
Cores	3	0.3	17	2.2	43	1.8	122	1.3	60	1.6
Tablets	1	0.1	12	1.5	27	1.1	75	0.8	44	1.1
Flakes	418	45.0	426	55.3	1498	63.8	5413	57.9	1964	51.1
Blades	43	4.6	77	10.0	101	4.3	402	4.3	134	3.5
Bladelets	67	7.2	67	8.7	217	9.2	1373	14.7	633	16.5
Chips	33	3.6	38	4.9	164	7.0	910	9.7	536	13.9
Microburins	1	0.1	2	0.3	2	0.1	20	0.2	27	0.7
Burin spalls	–	–	1	0.1	17	0.7	52	0.5	26	0.7
Debris	334	36.0	39	5.1	85	3.6	340	3.6	101	2.6
Total	**928**	**99.9**	**770**	**99.9**	**2346**	**99.8**	**9344**	**99.8**	**3844**	**100.0**

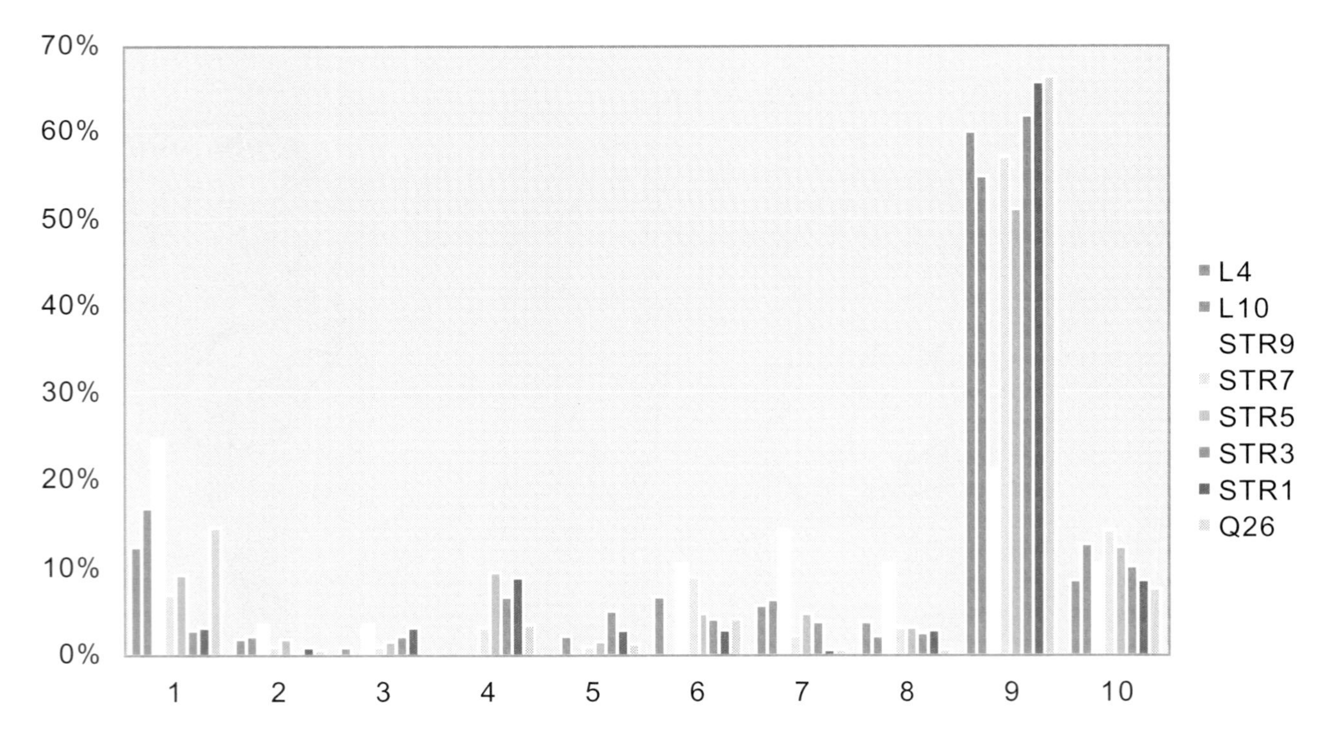

Figure 25.4. *Graphic representation of tool groups at Asprochaliko, Kastritsa and Klithi.*

retouched pieces and truncations are more numerous than in Stratum 9.

Stratum 5. From here onwards assemblages become larger indicating denser site use and a wider range of activities. Flakes are the dominant artefact while blades and bladelets are present in roughly equal numbers. Flakes have plain proximal parts and are of hard hammer mode. Blade butts are smaller than in previous strata and of soft hammer mode; a fair number have facetted proximal parts. Blade cores make their first appearance along with bidirectional scars on the dorsal surfaces of the blades (Fig. 25.7:4). Bladelets (Fig. 25.7: 2–3) are mostly extracted from single platform cores and, contrary to blades, they are predominantly of soft hammer mode with plain proximal parts. A clear, major, technological break is attested in this stratum in the form of systematic blade production, a change accompanied by an equally important change in the tool inventory, which makes up 8.2 per cent of

Table 25.8. *Complete debitage at Kastritsa by stratum.*

Category	Stratum 9 N	Stratum 9 %	Stratum 7 N	Stratum 7 %	Stratum 5 N	Stratum 5 %	Stratum 3 N	Stratum 3 %	Stratum 1 N	Stratum 1 %
Flakes	36	*8.9*	101	*48.3*	281	*50.4*	935	*48.2*	403	*49.8*
Blades	20	*5.0*	320	*15.3*	84	*15.1*	261	*13.5*	102	*12.6*
Bladelets	10	*2.5*	33	*15.8*	91	*16.3*	279	*14.4*	141	*17.4*
Chips	3	*0.7*	4	*1.9*	18	*3.2*	123	*6.3*	62	*7.7*
Knapped debris	34	*8.4*	15	*7.2*	43	*7.7*	186	*9.6*	52	*6.4*
Pot-lid debris	4	*1.0*	6	*2.9*	14	*2.5*	93	*4.8*	33	*4.1*
Natural debris	296	*73.5*	18	*8.6*	26	*4.7*	61	*3.1*	16	*2.0*
Total	**403**	***100.0***	**209**	***100.0***	**557**	***99.9***	**1938**	***99.9***	**809**	***100.0***

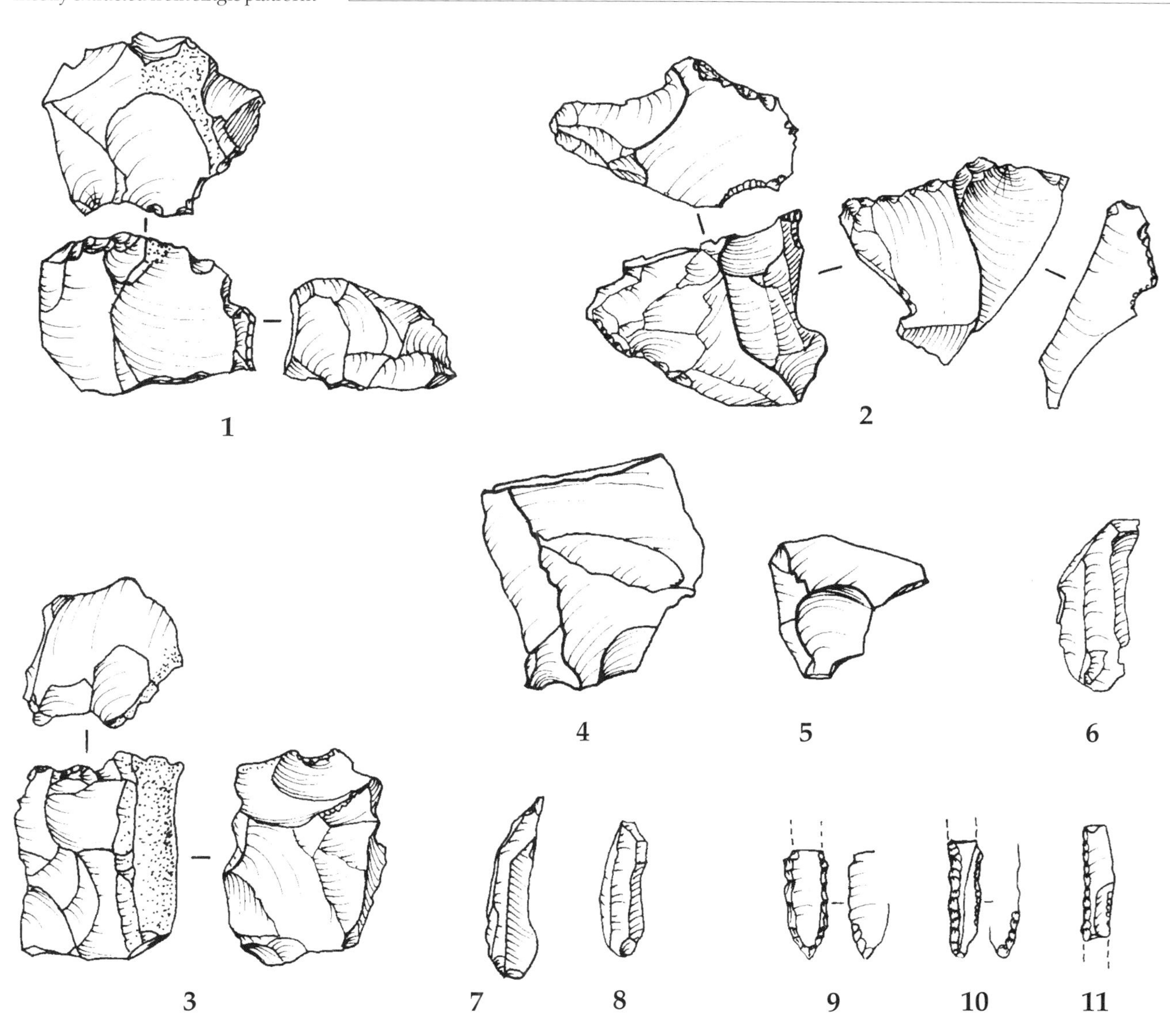

Figure 25.5. *Asprochaliko Layer 4: 1–3. cores; 4–5. flakes; 6–8. bladelets; 9–10. backed bladelets with inversely retouched ends; 11. backed bladelet, plain. Full size.*

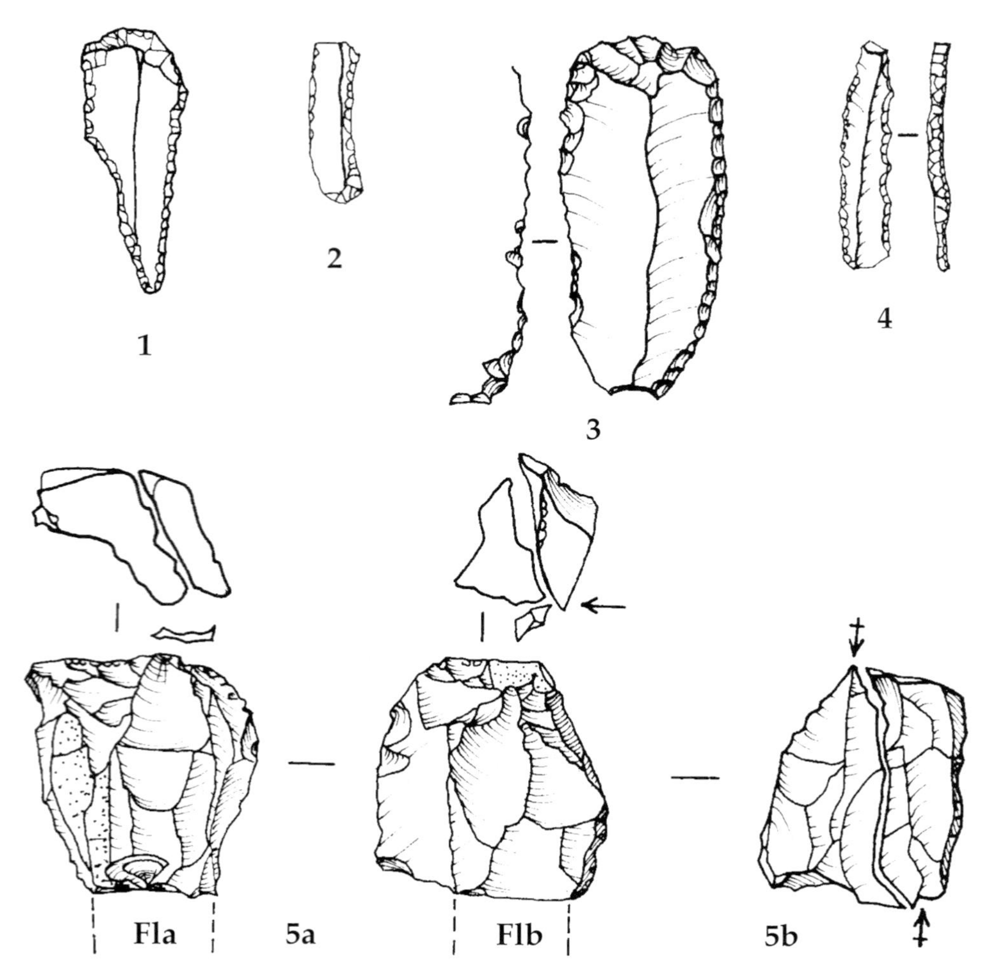

Figure 25.6. *Kastritsa Stratum 9: 1. endscraper; 2. backed bladelet, plain. Stratum 7: 3. end–scraper; 4. backed bladelet. Stratum 3: 5a. Voïdomatis flint core with refitted flakes; 5b. refitting flakes, removed from opposed alternate platforms. Full size.*

the assemblage (Table 25.7; Fig. 25.1).

Piercers, dihedral burins and burins on breaks now appear in large numbers; microgravettes, shouldered points (Fig. 25.7:6), shouldered pieces and dufour bladelets first appear here in very limited numbers. The number of all non-bladelet tools increases as well. Endscrapers (Fig. 25.7:5) are present in equal proportions to burins. The burin class is dominated by truncation burins. Bladelet tools comprise more than half of the tool inventory with a predominance of backed bladelets of various types, the commonest being the plain unilaterally backed bladelet, followed by truncated, bilaterally backed types, backed bladelets with opposed retouch and with inversely retouched ends. The manufacture of backed bladelets results in a number of Krukowski microburins. Sidescrapers and totally or partially retouched pieces are present in equal numbers.

Stratum 3. Flake butts are smaller than previously. Blades have small butts, are often of hard hammer mode and have mostly plain proximal parts. Bladelets have small butts, unidirectional dorsal scars, are of soft hammer mode and have a considerable number of facetted proximal parts, contary to the blades. Straight bladelets were selected for tool manufacture.

Most of the cores are bladelet cores (Fig. 25.8:2–3) followed by flake and very few blade cores (Fig. 25.8:1). A considerable number have two opposed platforms and are flaked bidirectionally, a technique ensuring better control for the production of straight and long blanks. Core platforms are often facetted, mostly those of the bladelet cores. In Stratum 3 the previously favoured flaking technique of turning the core around while flaking is replaced by bidirectional flaking with more elaborate core preparation and maintenance. The results of this technique can be seen on the cores, the debitage and on the very blanks chosen for tool manufacture.

Blades (Fig. 25.8:4–5) are prefered to flakes as blanks. Most non-bladelet blanks are straight in profile with the exception of piercers, which tend to be made on twisted or curved blanks that support the intended movement of the tools as required by the function of the implement. Primary blanks are also used in small numbers, a trend common throughout the sequence. Bladelet blanks are regularly non-primary (a reflection of the flaking strategies for bladelet manufacture as noted on the cores), straight, with unidirectional dorsal scars and a single dorsal ridge. Bladelets with two dorsal ridges are usually backed by anvil retouch, being thicker and less prone to breakage under the bipolar strain this technique implies. Several of the surviving proximal parts of the bladelet blanks are facetted.

A major technological innovation in Stratum 3 is the technique of fragmentation of blanks, expressed in two ways, firstly by the appearance (though limited) of the microburin technique and secondly by the practice of intentional breakage of retouched and plain blades. The tools most commonly affected by the latter technique are sidescrapers and Aurignacian blades, both fragmented after retouch. The intentional fragmentation of the tools might reflect an attempt to multiply the number of available straight elements or to increase the number of suitable retouched edges by dividing an accommodating tool.

The tool inventory for this stratum (6.8 per cent) is very rich both in numbers and in types. The dominant tool types are those made on bladelets and mostly the backed types. The commonest backed bladelet type is the plain, unilaterally backed bladelet (Fig. 25.8:13), followed by those with inversely retouched ends (Fig. 25.8:14), those with semi-abrupt retouch, the truncated and bitruncated types, the backed bladelets with opposed retouch, and the pointed unilaterally backed types. The number of bilaterally backed bladelets drops dramatically and pointed or bipointed types of this variety are absent. Notched, truncated and dufour bladelets are few, while bladelets with inverse retouch are practically absent.

Sidescrapers are the largest group of non-bladelet tools, followed by burins (Fig. 25.8:8). Multiple burins appear here for the first time, and burins on breaks increase in number. Totally or partially retouched pieces, truncations, backed blades, Aurignacian blades and notched pieces are present in increasing numbers. Microgravettes (Fig. 25.8:11) and shouldered points (Fig. 25.8:9–10) and pieces are more numerous. Endscrapers decrease in number while micropiercers make their first appearance and are usually made on twisted or curved bladelets. The number of piercers increases.

Stratum 1. The flake butts are often larger than in Stratum 3 and the bulb is usually away from the main dorsal ridge(s). There are fewer blade cores than in Stratum 3 and change of flaking direction (Fig. 25.9:2) is again prefered to bidirectional flaking, hence the location of the bulbs away from the main ridge. Flakes and blades are equally used as blanks, contrary to the preference for blades observed in the previous stratum; twisted and curved blanks are used as supports for piercers and micropiercers. Microburins are present in greater numbers and the microburin technique seems to replace the habit of thinning the ends of bladelets by inverse retouch, with a concomitant decrease of this tool class. Gravette points and backed blades disappear, while shouldered points (Fig. 25.9:10–11), bilaterally backed bladelets (no more pointed varieties) and microgravettes are present in smaller numbers.

Backed bladelet tools are dominated by unilaterally backed types, mostly plain, followed by truncated, bitruncated and pointed (Fig. 25.9:16–18) and bipointed types. There is also a decrease in the frequency of fragmentation of retouched or plain blanks.

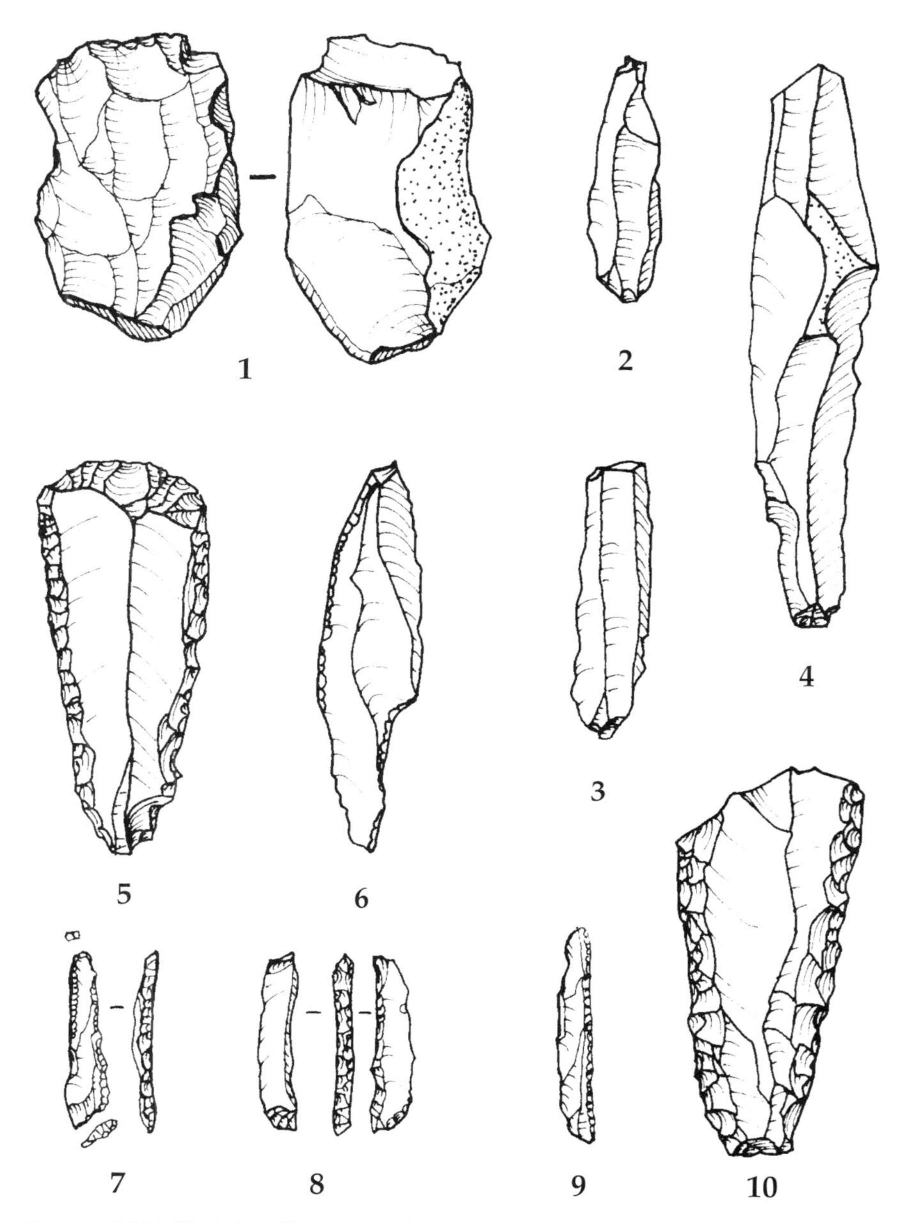

Figure 25.7. *Kastritsa Stratum 5: 1. core; 2–3. bladelets; 4. blade; 5. endscraper; 6. shouldered point; 7–9. backed bladelets; 10. Aurignacian blade. Full size.*

Klithi

Human presence at Klithi overlaps with the later occupational phases at Kastritsa. Unfortunately there are insufficient radiocarbon dates from Kastritsa to be precise about the degree of overlap (Table 25.1), but occupation at Klithi is certainly contemporaneous with Stratum 1 at Kastritsa, almost certainly with Stratum 3, and probably with at least the upper part of Stratum 5 though this is less certain.

The general composition of the Q26 samples is summarized in Tables 25.6, 25.9 and 25.10, and the analysis was supplemented by experimentation on

Table 25.9. *General composition of the Klithi sample from Q26.*

Category	N	%
Tools	165	3.4
Cores	22	0.4
Tablets	18	0.4
Flakes	1870	38.9
Blades	58	1.2
Bladelets	312	6.5
Chips	1952	40.6
Microburins	8	0.2
Burin spalls	14	0.3
Debris	387	8.0
Total	**4806**	**99.9**

Table 25.10. *Complete debitage for the Klithi sample from Q26.*

Category	N	%
Flakes	312	33.1
Blades	40	4.2
Bladelets	56	6.0
Chips	148	15.7
Knapped debris	205	21.7
Pot-lid debris	25	2.7
Natural debris	157	16.6
Total	**943**	**100.0**

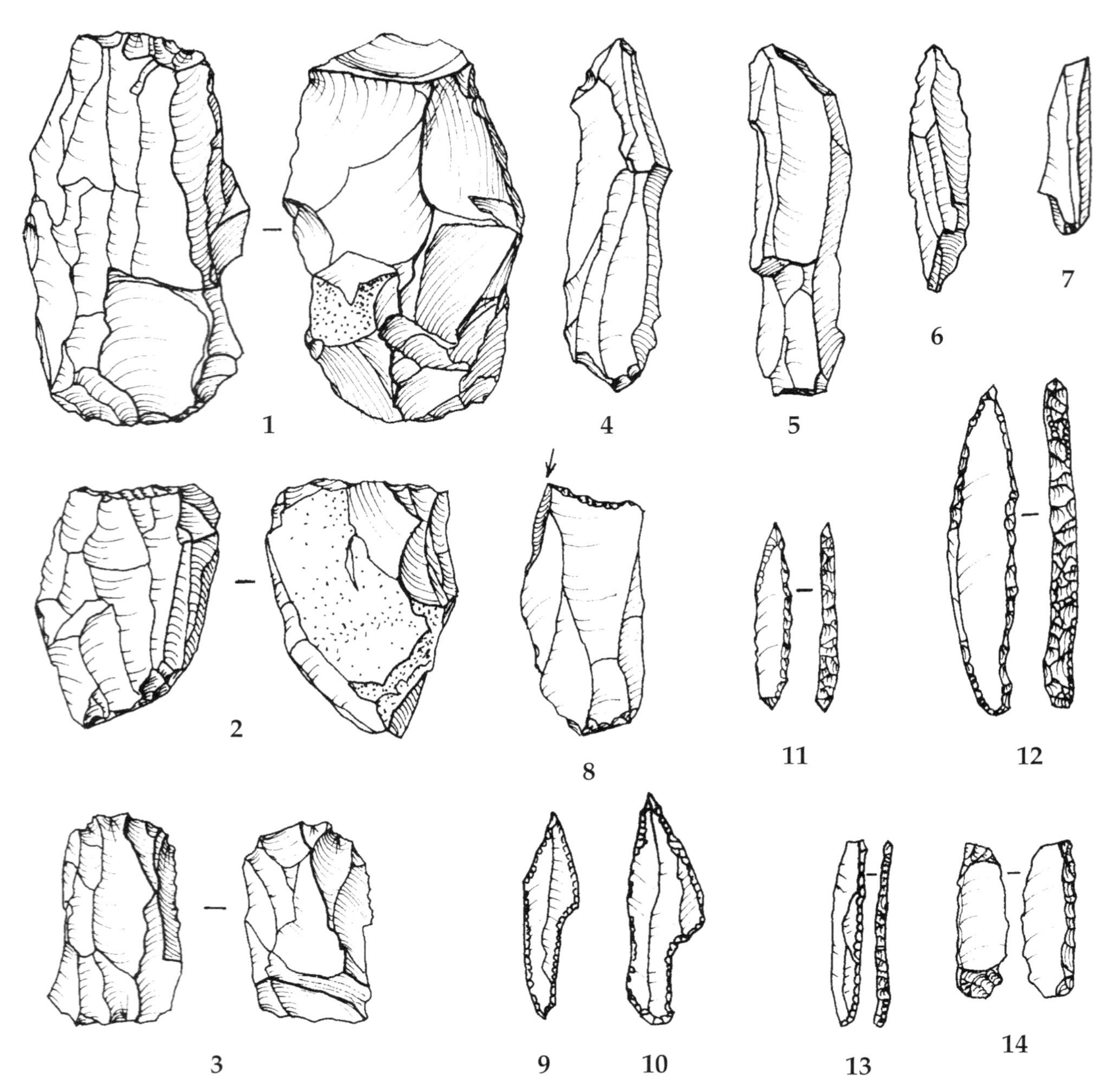

Figure 25.8. *Kastritsa Stratum 3: 1–3. cores; 4–5. blades; 6–7. bladelets; 8. simple truncation burin; 9–10. shouldered points; 11. microgravette; 12. gravette point; 13. unilaterally backed bladelet, plain; 14. backed bladelet with inversely retouched ends. Full size.*

the flaking qualities of the local raw materials (Adam 1989, 225–8).

Klithi is a flake-dominated assemblage with a tool inventory dominated by backed bladelets, and its main characteristics can be summarized as follows:

- The desired end-products were long and narrow pieces, i.e. bladelets for bladelet tools and laminar blanks for most other tool types (see also Roubet, Chapter 8; Shawcross & Winder, Chapter 10). Most of the debitage with the exception of bladelets was carried out with hammerstones. Blanks are mostly non-primary; core tablets and crested pieces are used as blanks in a few cases, possibly as a result of the shortage of suitable blanks caused by the weakness of the raw material. Tools are made almost exclusively on local flint, though the larger samples analyzed by Roubet (Chapters 8 & 9.1)

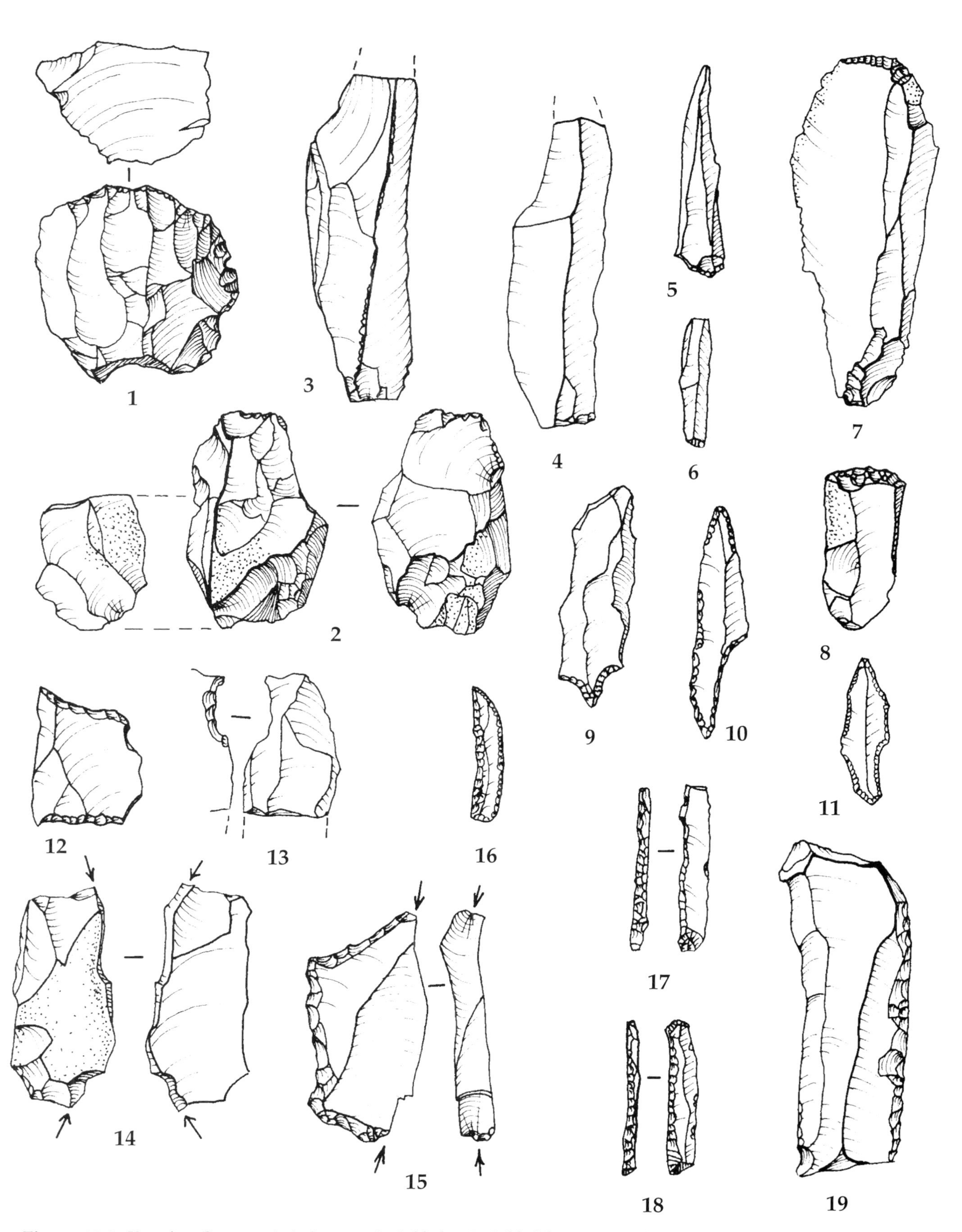

Figure 25.9. *Kastritsa Stratum 1: 1–2. cores; 3–4. blades; 5–6. bladelets; 7–8. endscrapers; 9. piercer; 10–11: shouldered points; 12. double truncation; 13. notched piece; 14–15. multiple burins; 16–18. backed bladelets with retouched ends; 19. sidescraper. Full size.*

show that non-local flint also plays a small but important role in tool production.

- The lack of elaborate core preparation — limited and mostly partial cresting and minimal shaping of the back of the cores — is seen as the result of the erratic nature of the raw material (see also Roubet, Chapter 8). Core preparation is restricted to the creation of the striking platforms, while the back and the sides of the cores are rarely affected. Traces of platform abrasion are rare. Core platforms are facetted in very few cases, often primary, and platfrom maintenance seems confined to tablet removals.
- Flaking strategy includes the creation of a striking platform, followed by the removal of the flawed exterior surface of the nodules, and finally by the extraction of debitage. This strategy is deduced from several characteristics of the industry: a point of percussion on most non-primary debitage which lies behind the main dorsal ridge or between the two main dorsal ridges; the presence of chips produced during blade/bladelet removals (Fig. 25.10:5–6); the existence of partially crested pieces used to correct the core front; the presence of opposed platform bidirectional cores indicating maximum exploitation for the production of straight blanks (Fig. 25.10:2); and debitage which follows the longest axis of the nodules. The alteration of the flaking direction on the cores (Fig. 25.10:1) indicates maximum exploitation of the usable pieces and points to an economy of raw material imposed not so much by the quantity of the locally available flint as by its quality. The majority of the cores were abandoned either when the platforms were crushed or when the core front was beyond repair.
- Laminar blanks are favoured for most tool-classes. Straight, non-primary bladelets are chosen for backing, which is usually done by direct abrupt retouch, in some cases abrupt on anvil (Fig. 25.10:15) reaching 16.3 per cent. Plain, unilaterally backed bladelets are the most numerous type (Fig. 25.10:15–16), while truncated (Fig. 25.10:18) and pointed varieties are few. Bulbs are usually removed by inverse invasive retouch and less frequently by fragmentation (for a global approach on this issue see Chapters 9.1 and 9.2). Endscrapers are the second most numerous group (Fig. 25.10:13–14), followed by varia, truncations (Fig. 25.10:19) and burins (Fig. 25.10:21). There are no geometric microliths, while shouldered pieces are rare, represented in Q26 by a single broken example, Fig. 25.10:20). The fragmentation of laminar blanks, plain or retouched, is also practised but to a lessser degree than in Stratum 3 at Kastritsa.

Comparisons

Comparisons between the units described above can only be partial, since the earliest Asprochaliko phases are not represented at Kastritsa, while Klithi overlaps only with the upper part of the Kastritsa sequence.

The industries from Layers 10 and 4 at Asprochaliko are not differentiated on technological grounds, i.e. with respect to raw materials, core preparation and exploitation, blank selection and modification. The main differences are morphological and restricted mostly to the bladelet tool group. The Asprochaliko industries lack burins, gravette points, shouldered points or pieces, backed blades, and have fewer bladelet types than the later industries.

The study of cores, technical pieces and debitage shows a limited capacity for the production of laminar blanks, notably frequent change of flaking axis, location of the bulb away from the main ridge, multidirectional dorsal scars, and non-straight profiles, in contrast to the later assemblages. The choice of blanks varies, too, in that flakes are more often preferred than blades or laminar pieces as blanks for the non-bladelet tool types. Another feature consistent with the early date of the industries is the presence of twisted bladelets — a feature already observed by Perlès for the Franchthi phase I industries (Perlès 1987, 96); interestingly enough, these twisted bladelets are never used for the manufacture of bladelet tools at Asprochaliko and are in general rarely retouched, straight bladelet blanks being preferred for the latter purpose.

In contrast to Asprochaliko, the Kastritsa industries exhibit a clear knowledge of and capacity for laminar blank production, even from the earliest phases.

The earliest industries (Stratum 9) are characterized by very few traces of *in situ* core exploitation and a limited tool inventory with endscrapers outnumbering bladelet tools, in contrast to the later industries from the site, and a strong presence of retouched blades, notched and truncated pieces. The industries suggest limited use of the site in the form of short visits; the fluctuating levels of lake Pamvotis around 20,000 BP (Bailey *et al.* 1983b, 29) may have restricted access to Kastritsa and have probably affected the archaeological record from these layers.

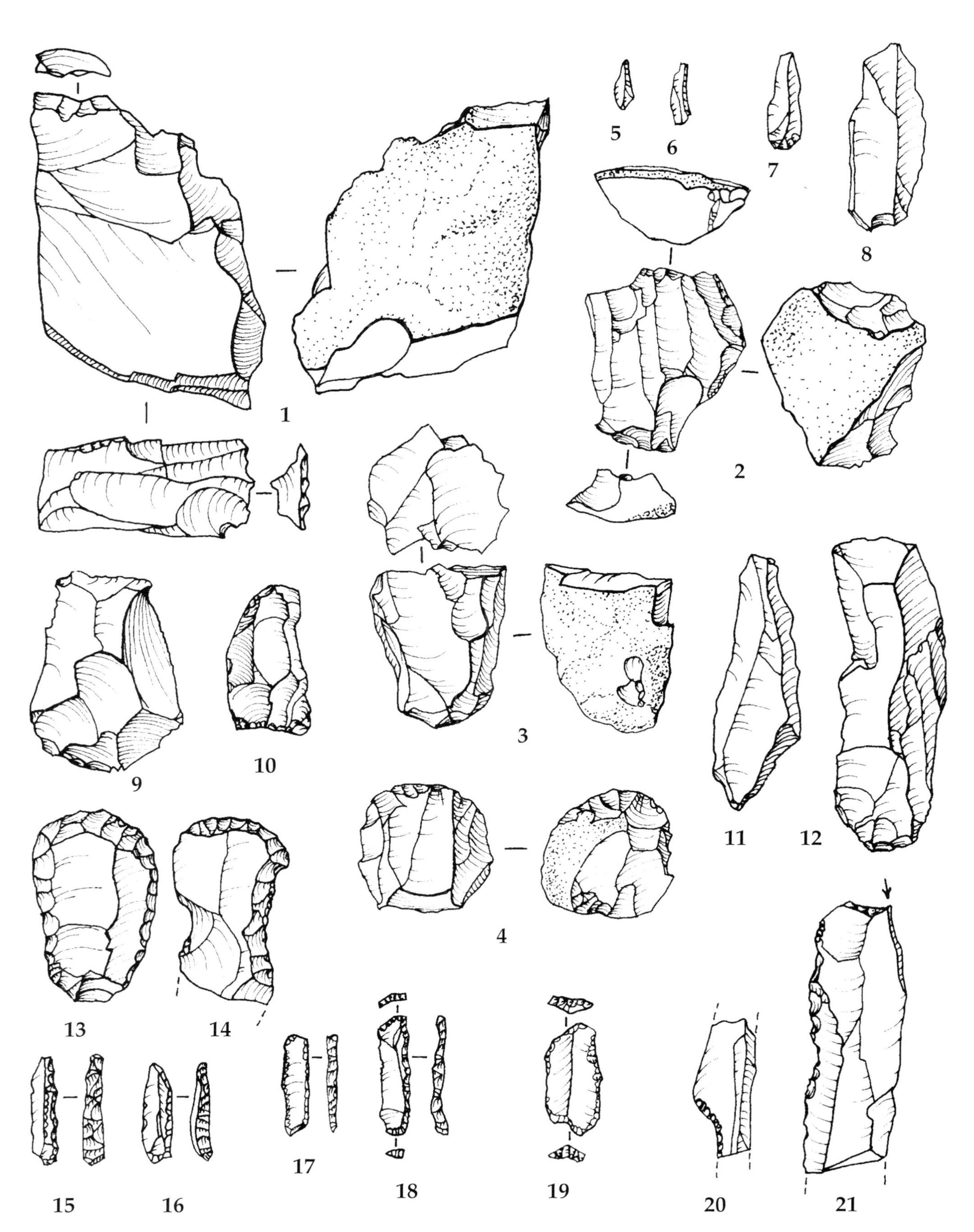

Figure 25.10. *Klithi Q26: 1–4. cores; 5–6. debitage chips; 7–8. bladelets; 9–10. flakes; 11–12. blades; 13–14. endscrapers; 15–18. backed bladelets; 19. double truncation; 20. shouldered piece; 21. burin on truncation. Full size.*

Starting with Stratum 7 and especially Stratum 5 the site was used more intensively. The long UPL sequence of Kastritsa allows us to pinpoint both technological and morphological changes, evident in the interchange of different techniques for the exploitation of cores and modification of blanks. It is clear that the catchment area of the shelter included adequate quantities of good quality flint (better quality and more abundant than at Asprochaliko and Klithi) and other natural resources, including a wide variety of prey. Hunting is attested by the presence of a complicated lithic toolkit. Shouldered points and backed bladelets modified for hafting appear early in the sequence and continue into the latest phases, and there is also a large series of bone and antler points (Chapter 13). The industries suggest the wide practice of non-hunting activities as well, such as the systematic manufacture and maintenance of stone tools, the production of organic artefacts (few needles, points, awls, pierced deer canines etc.) and the processing of various materials.

The dates from Klithi suggest an overlapping with the two upper strata of Kastritsa (3 and 1); the technological differences between Stratum 3 and Klithi, though, cannot be interpreted as a mere result of the different raw materials employed at the two sites. Klithi is much closer on technological grounds to Stratum 1, with its preference for changing the flaking direction on the cores, and for debitage oriented towards the production of bladelets. The observed differences in tool types may be due to the function of the sites: the much weaker presence of shouldered pieces and points at Klithi may be connected to differences in prey species between the two sites, while the smaller number of burins and piercers at Klithi may reflect the more limited production of organic artefacts. Klithi is much more easily compared to the other excavated Voïdomatis gorge sites, which seem to share a more homogeneous environment (see Sinclair, Chapter 21; Kotjabopoulou *et al.*, Chapter 22). The strongest characteristic of the Klithi industries is their laminar character. This feature, combined with the versatility in blank selection — flakes and laminar blanks for non-bladelet tools, bladelets and small flakes for backed pieces (Roubet, Chapters 8 & 9.1) — allowed the prehistoric knappers to overcome the difficulties imposed by the local raw materials.

Acknowledgements

I wish to thank Geoff Bailey for his rigorous comments on this chapter and for his unfailing attention over years of research, Judy Ogden for making the illustrations presentable, and Colette Roubet for exchanging information on the Klithi industries. Responsibility for the final verison, and for any remaining errors, is of course mine.

Appendix 25.1. *Tool types. (For definitions see Adam 1989, 39–55.)*

Tool groups	Tool type
1. Endscrapers (nos. 1–4):	1. Simple endscraper; 2. Atypical endscraper; 3. Double endscraper; 4. Endscraper on retouched flake or blade.
2. Composite tools (nos. 5–6):	5. Endscraper/burin; 6. Endscraper/truncation.
3. Piercers (nos. 7–9):	7. Piercer; 8. Atypical piercer (bec); 9. Micropiercer.
4. Burins (nos. 10–16):	10. Simple dihedral burin; 11. Multiple dihedral burin; 12. Simple truncation burin; 13. Multiple truncation burin; 14. Simple burin on break/natural surface; 15. Multiple burin on break/natural surface; 16. Mixed multiple burin.
5. Backed tools (nos. 17–22):	17. Gravette points; 18. Microgravette; 19. Shouldered point; 20. Shouldered piece; 21. Totally backed blade; 22. Partially backed blade.
6. Truncations (nos. 23–4):	23. Truncated piece; 24. Bitruncated piece.
7. Retouched blades (nos. 25–7):	25. Piece with continuous unilateral retouch; 26. Piece with continuous bilateral retouch; 27. Aurignacian blade.
8. Notches (no. 28):	28. Notched piece.
9. Bladelet tools (nos. 29–45):	29. Truncated bladelet; 30. Bitruncated bladelet; 31. Unilaterally backed bladelet plain; 32. Unilaterally backed bladelet with opposed retouch; 33. Unilaterally backed bladelet pointed; 34. Unilaterally backed bladelet bipointed; 35. Bilaterally backed bladelet plain; 36. Bilaterally backed bladelet pointed; 37. Bilaterally backed bladelet bipointed; 38. Backed bladelet with inversely retouched end(s); 39. Truncated backed bladelet; 40. Bitruncated backed bladelet; 41. Denticulate bladelet; 42. Notched bladelet; 43. Dufour bladelet; 44. Bladelet with inverse retouch; 45. Bladelet with semi-abrupt retouch.
10. Varia (nos. 46–9):	46. Sidescraper; 47. Totally or partially retouched piece; 48. Endscraper/notch; 49. Miscellaneous.

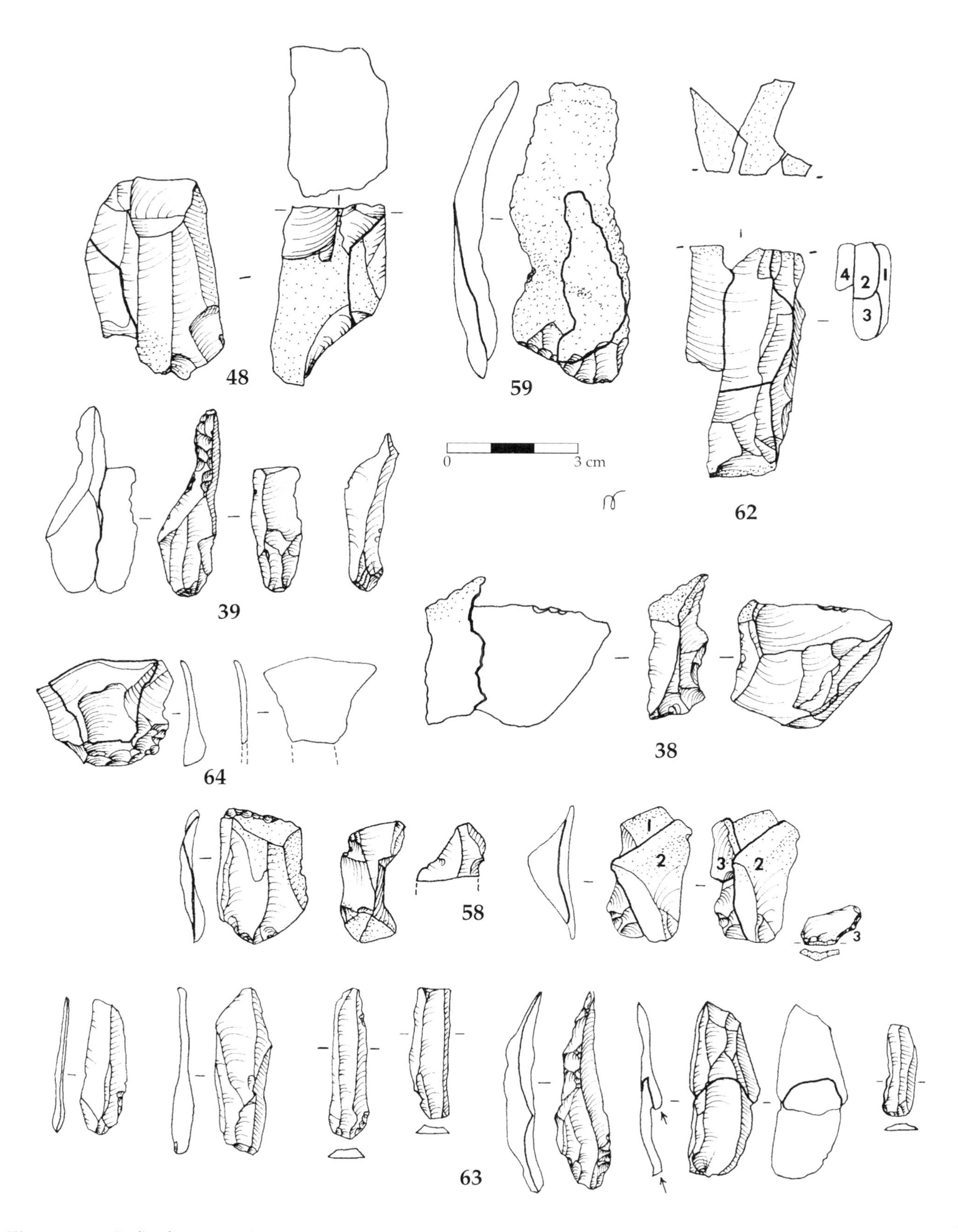

Figure 26.6. *Refits from Kastritsa Stratum 5 (Y14–15). Refit numbers correspond to the list in Appendix 26.1.*[5]

Figure 26.7. *Refits from Kastritsa Stratum 5 (Y14–15). Refit numbers correspond to the list in Appendix 26.1.*[5]

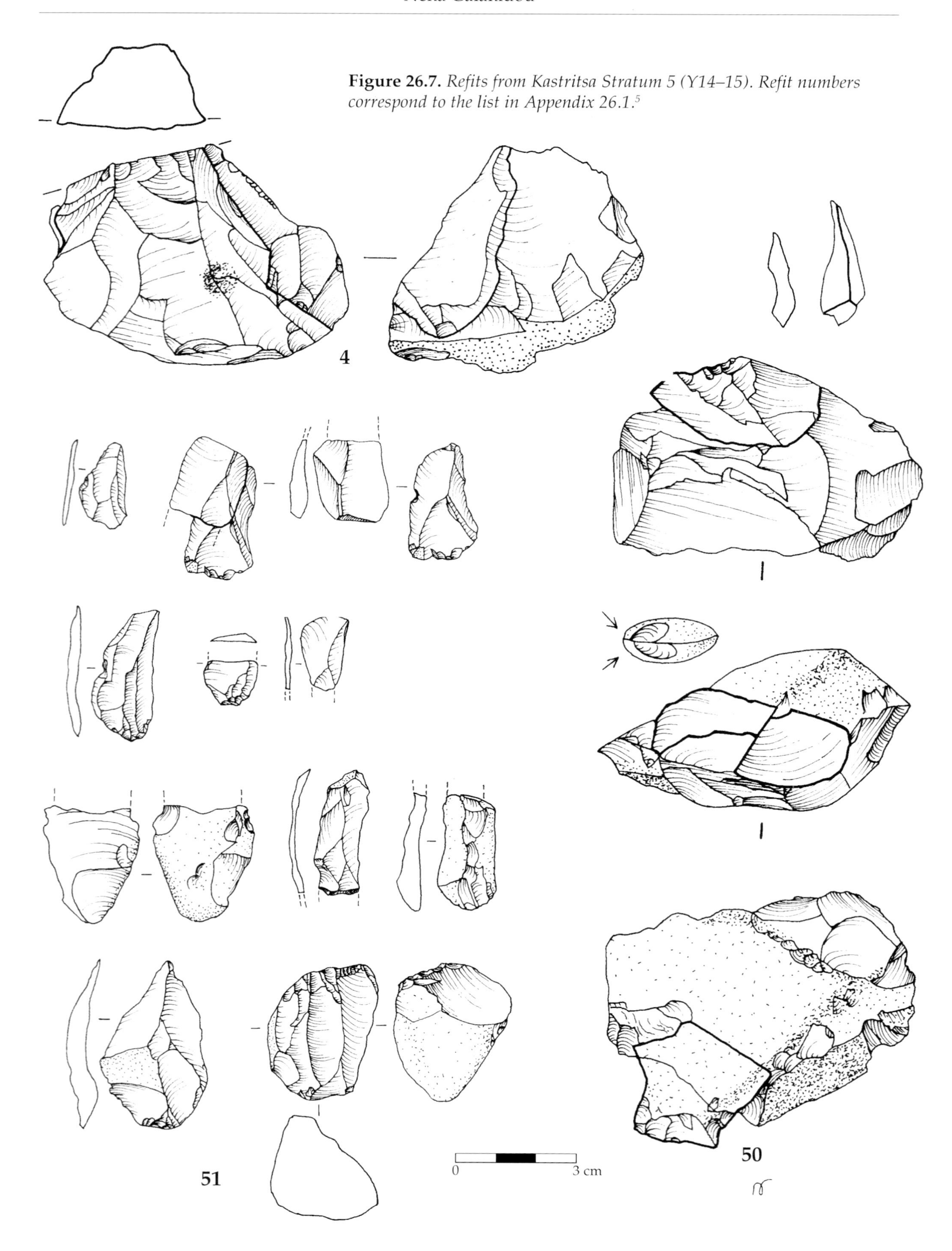

decortification stage is predominant, and use of both soft and hard hammers at later stages is evident.

Taphonomic issues

The great number of specimens apparently originating in the same reduction sequence, but lacking their preceding and succeeding artefacts, is remarkable. This observation, which independently confirms that chipping floors were correctly identified during excavation, deserves further consideration. It is possible that some of the missing pieces were deliberately taken away as blanks for secondary retouch, or for use as tools, but the refitted groups point to a more random representation of specimens. It therefore seems reasonable to argue that site-formation processes have also contributed to this pattern. Even if during some future study the missing links are found in layers and rectangles that were not included in the sample, horizontal or vertical disturbance on a small scale is indicated.

The horizontal separation between refits cannot be measured with precision because the minimum provenance units are so large.[3] In 5 and 3 instances in Y14 and Y15 respectively refits cross rectangle boundaries. Given the size of the rectangles, however, the horizontal separation of these refits may have been less than the distance between other refits from within a single rectangle.

Given the size of the spits excavated, the finest vertical resolution possible is to within 10 cm. Refitted objects are vertically separated by a maximum distance of 60 cm in Y14, and by a maximum distance of 40 cm in Y15 (Table 26.3). Refits crossing the Y14–15 stratigraphic boundary are separated by a maximum distance of 50 cm. Y15 has greater spatial integrity than has Y14. This pattern may be attributable to a high lake level in Y14A, which may have contributed to partial mixing of the deposits.

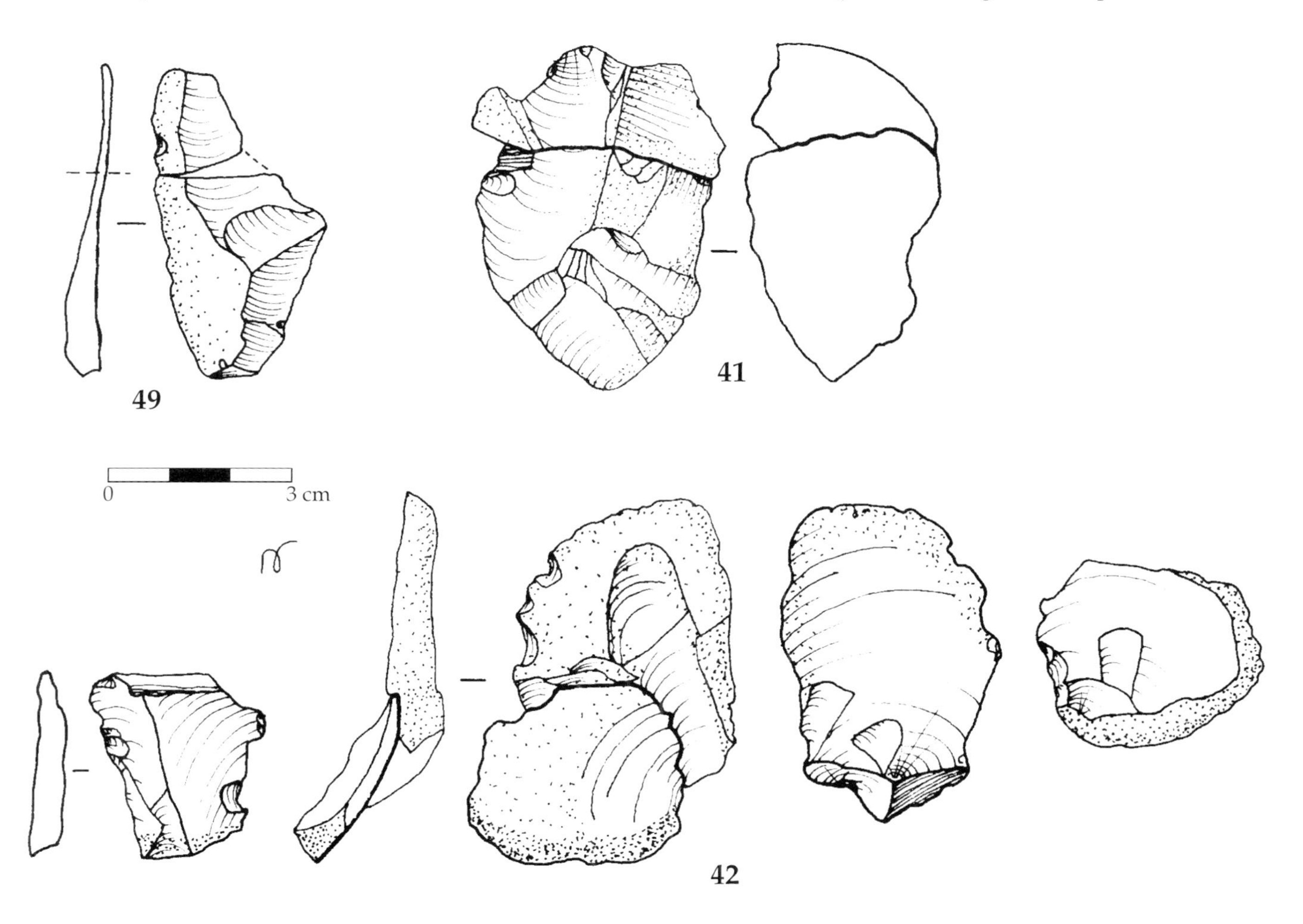

Figure 26.8. *Refits from Kastritsa Stratum 9 (Y21–5). Refit numbers correspond to the list in Appendix 26.1.*[5]

Stratum 5 has produced the longest series of refitted sets. Y14 has yielded a smaller number of refitted sets but with longer refitted sequences, whereas Y15 has yielded more refitted sets but with shorter sequences (Table 26.2). The maximum number of conjoined successive removals, i.e. refits of type (C), is 3 each for Y14 and Y15, while 4 at most cross the stratigraphic boundary between the two. The number of specimens found from the same reduction sequence ranges between 2 and 13 in Y14, and between 2 and 6 in Y15. The figures are considerably lower for Y21–3 and Y24, where only 2 successive removals of specimens were conjoined, and where only one instance of 4 specimens from the same reduction sequence was observed.

In Stratum 5 individual reduction sequences are well bracketed within each layer, with the exception of 7 refits (9.46 per cent) that cross the Y14–15 stratigraphic boundary. As the sample derives from the 1967 excavation, during which stratigraphy was recorded with precision, these 7 cases should help us to assess the integrity of Y14 and Y15 as discrete units of deposition of archaeological material during one or more episodes of occupation. In 4 out of the 7 instances the specimens derive from the junction between two different layers, i.e. from contexts that are assigned to Y14–15 and from the immediately overlying or underlying area of Y14 or Y15. At junctions between layers and on the surfaces adjacent to them some degree of mixing is to be expected. I would therefore argue that these 4 cases do not constitute strong evidence for lack of spatial coherence, but rather indicate a pattern of local mixing at the junction between layers. The remaining 3 cases are a join and two brief conjoins, each consisting of only two artefacts. They derive from contexts which are separated vertically by maximum distances of 20, 30 and 40 cm, and make up approximately 4 per cent of the refits in Stratum 5. The relative shortness of these conjoined sequences and the little distance separating their components argue for limited vertical, interlayer movement by relatively few pieces; the evidence is thus not really sufficient to cast doubt on the stratigraphic integrity of Y14 and Y15.

Table 26.3. *Minimum and maximum extent of vertical separation between refit sets, by stratum. (Nr = number of refit sets.)*

min.–max.	Stratum 5					Stratum 9				Rect. 16 L2
	Y14	Y15	Y14–15	Total		Y21–3	Y24	Total		
cm	Nr	Nr	Nr	Nr	%	Nr	Nr	Nr	%	N
0–10	13	32	1	**46**	*62.16*	1	2	**3**	*60*	1
0–20	3	3	0	**6**	*8.11*	0	0	**0**		0
0–30	0	3	0	**3**	*4.05*	0	0	**0**		0
0–40	1	1	0	**2**	*2.7*	0	0	**0**		0
0–50	5	0	1	**6**	*8.11*	0	0	**0**		0
0–110	0	0	0	**0**	*0*	2	0	**2**	*40*	0
10–20	1	1	1	**3**	*4.05*	0	0	**0**		0
10–30	0	0	1	**1**	*1.35*	0	0	**0**		0
20–30	1	1	2	**4**	*5.41*	0	0	**0**		0
30–40	1	0	1	**2**	*2.7*	0	0	**0**		0
50–60	1	0	0	**1**	*1.35*	0	0	**0**		0

The stratigraphy of Stratum 9 is rendered complex by the intermingling of beach and cultural deposits. A considerable number of objects, though not all of them, have rounded and dulled edges resulting from the action of water. A low degree of spatial integrity is therefore to be expected, with refits absent. Not only were refits present in the upper series (Y21–3), however, but they were also found in Y24, though absent from Y25. This suggests that the water that entered the site when the lake was high either left at least some of the primary deposits of material in the upper layers intact or redeposited material that refits. The types of refit found, all three groups being represented, and the number of specimens involved (Table 26.2) suggest that both assumptions are plausible. The two refits whose components seem to have been separated vertically by a maximum 110 cm were discovered in bags containing material from Spits 60–71, Y21–23, that had not been separated during excavation. This contextual information is, of course, not particularly helpful in tracing vertical displacement. It is, however, significant that no refits cross anything that was identified as a layer during excavation. Moreover, an additional incidental join (Appendix 26.1: refit 49) from Rectangle 5, Y21, not included in the quantitative analysis, demonstrates that the layers associated with early occupations retain more potential to yield artefacts that refit than has hitherto been thought (Adam 1989, 204).

In Rectangle 16, despite the considerable number of specimens examined, only one refit was observed, suggesting that the material on this margin of the talus has undergone a lot of mixing.

Concluding comments on refitting

From a diachronic perspective, there is variation in refitting patterns through time. Stratum 5 has been more fruitful than Stratum 9, although the latter has produced a number of interesting refits. The lower proportion of refits in Stratum 9 (4 per cent) than in 5 (6.88 per cent) confirms that the latter has the higher spatial integrity (Table 26.2). Within Stratum 5 refitted sets are more numerous, and those in Y15 are separated by smaller vertical distances than those in Y14 (Table 26.2). This pattern suggests that the original deposits in Y14 have undergone more severe disturbance than those in Y15, probably due to the presence of a beach which limited living space.

Within Stratum 9 the number of refits is higher in the more recent layers.

From a synchronic perspective, the rectangles within the cave and near the southwest wall were more prolific of refits than were those on the margins of the talus (Fig. 26.9). The dearth of refits in Rectangles 51, 52, 61 and 62 may be attributed to their marginal location, combined with the overall low densities of artefacts. The exceptionally high proportion of refits in rectangle 42, Y15 attests to the preservation of deposits with little disturbance. The distribution of tools and of different stages in the reduction sequences appears to be spatially homogeneous. It gives no indication that any of the three areas studied ought to be associated with any specialized activity. Artefacts related to the manufacture of blanks, to secondary retouch and to use of tools are all found in the same rectangles. This lack of spatial separation is encountered in both Stratum 9 and Stratum 5.

The refits at Kastritsa are proportionally more numerous (5.66 per cent) than those at Klithi (1.72 per cent) (Appendix 5.1). The picture changes, however, when the comparison refers to number of refits per size of area examined rather than per total number of artefacts examined. The average number of refits per square metre at Klithi is 19, while that at Kastritsa, excluding the marginal rectangles, is 3.6. These figures are influenced considerably by the fact that the contexts examined for refitting at Klithi yielded high densities of material over a limited area, while those examined at Kastritsa yielded medium to low densities over a larger area. Inter-site comparisons based on the qualitative differences between the two sites are therefore more informative than any based upon quantitative differences. The Kastritsa refits are more diverse than those at Klithi (where refits are predominantly joins of broken artefacts) and involve longer series of conjoined artefacts. The low overall percentage of refits crossing stratigraphic boundaries, 7 out of 80 (8.75 per cent), and the small vertical distances that separate them, suggest that the stratigraphic units examined at Kastritsa, especially Y14 and 15, have greater coherence than those studied at Klithi, where 19 out of 48 refits (39.6 per cent) cross stratigraphic boundaries (Table 5.2).

The refitting results at Kastritsa suggest two conclusions. The first is that some areas have not been subjected to much disturbance. The second is that medium densities of artefacts were probably found in Y14 and Y15 not because material had been removed from the site, but because a correspondingly moderate number of lithic artefacts had been deposited in the first place. We already know that the area at the mouth of the cave has yielded the highest densities of material (Bailey *et al.* 1983b). If a global view of patterns in the horizontal distribution of refits is to be acquired, it is essential that the refitting project should in future encompass these high-density areas. The lower densities of material yielded by the layers in Stratum 9 may be related to disturbance when the lake was high. Comparatively speaking, these earliest episodes of occupation must have been infrequent and brief.

The refitting study has resolved the problem of analytical units at Kastritsa as far as the limitations of the available data allow. On the whole layers seem to contain sufficient information to be treated as independent units of spatial analysis, and had the excavations permitted it would have been preferable to run the following analysis on individual layers. Spatio-temporal resolution is fairly high in the layers examined, especially those in Stratum 5. No refits cross stratum boundaries, but this observation

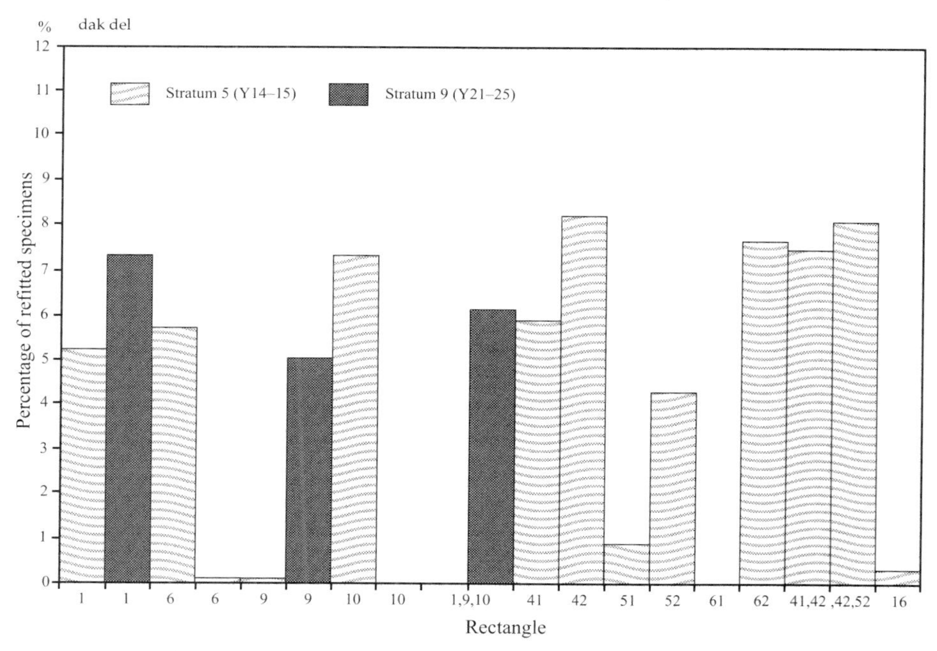

Figure 26.9. *Bar chart showing percentage of refitted specimens per rectangle.*

requires further exploration, since the two strata selected were not adjacent to each other. The refits from Kastritsa rule out a 'many-to-one' relationship between layers and episodes of occupation, since there is little evidence that specimens resulting from discrete knapping events cross layer boundaries. Each layer encompasses an unknown but probably small number of episodes of occupation. Unsurprisingly, the evidence cannot tell us conclusively just how many. Lithic artefact refitting cannot really be expected to offer any such certainty. The relationship of layers to episodes of occupation, and the contemporaneity or otherwise of features within a stratigraphic unit or of layers in different areas of a site, cannot be clear until the results of refitting are combined with studies of seasonality, microstratigraphy, sediment formation and the orientation of specimens. More refitting and future work on patterns of seasonality should advance our understanding, but in the absence of any refined excavation strategy at Kastritsa the relation between stratigraphic units and episodes with behavioural significance is bound to remain obscure.

The spatial distribution of lithic artefacts

The units of observation

The same principles have been applied as at Klithi (Galanidou, Chapter 15), although as no analysis of usewear has yet been attempted tools have here been grouped according to their morphological categories. I have also used one additional size group, since I expected to find greater variation in size at Kastritsa than at Klithi (Table 26.4).

Frequency variation

Examination of the total numbers of lithics found in different areas of the site reveals an interesting pattern. In Stratum 5 (Y14–15), two modes and three outliers with high totals may be observed (Figs. 26.10 & 26.11). The area immediately outside the shelter (rectangles 2, 12 and 13) has yielded the highest number of lithics. Lower numbers were yielded by the adjacent rectangles, and particularly low numbers were found inside the shelter in rectangles 1 and 9, and in rectangles 32, 42, 52, 62, 15 and 17.

In Stratum 9 (Y21–6), analysis of the variation in the total numbers of lithics shows that the cave and rectangles 3 and 6 have yielded few artefacts overall, while rectangles 2, 4 and 5 have yielded larger numbers of artefacts (Figs. 26.12 & 26.13).

Unconstrained cluster analysis

In analyzing the data from Kastritsa I have chosen not to perform any smoothing, since the grid cells are so large (2 m × 1.5 m) (see discussion in Chapter 15). Given the uncertainty about the exact depth of each layer, I have analyzed lithic frequencies rather than densities. To reveal any local patterns in the assemblage composition, I have evaluated the proportions of each artefact class within each rectangle and clustered the rectangles using Ward's method.

Stratum 5

All lithic categories[4]

Suggested cluster solutions: 2 or 4 (Fig. 26.14). Optimal: 4 (Table 26.5 & Fig. 26.15). Clusters have the following characteristics:

- Cluster 1 (18 grid cells): contiguous block across entire area excavated, including part of cave. All stages of reduction sequence and all tool types present. Highest mean proportions of burnt debris, backed bladelets and notched/denticulates.
- Cluster 2 (3 grid cells): two rectangles on northwestern margin of site and a rectangle in sheltered part. Nodules, technical pieces, burin spalls, burins, shouldered pieces and Aurignacian blades absent. Highest mean proportions of cores,

Table 26.4. *Variables in the lithic assemblage.*

Lithic categories	Lithic size
Nodule (i.e. raw material brought onto the site for knapping)	A<=1 × 1 cm
Core	B<=1.2 × 2.5 cm
Primary piece (i.e. more than 10 per cent cortex)	C<=3 × 3 cm
Debitage (i.e. flake, blade and bladelet)	D<=1.8 × 5 cm
Technical piece (i.e. related to the production of blank, e.g. core tablet, crested piece, diagnostic product of accident)	E<=5 × 5 cm
Knapping debris	F>=5 × 5 cm
Burnt debris	
Edge-damage piece	
Burin spall	
Burin	
Backed bladelet	
Shouldered piece	
Scraper (i.e. endscraper, sidescraper)	
Piece with linear retouch	
Notched/denticulate	
Borer (i.e. bec, piercer)	
Aurignacian blade	
Other (e.g. *pièce esquille*, microburin)	

Table 26.5. *Means and standard deviations of relative frequencies of all lithic categories by cluster for 4 clusters (Stratum 5, Y14–15).*

Lithic category	Cluster 1	Cluster 2	Cluster 3	Cluster 4
Nodule	0.80 ± 0.12	0.00 ± 0.00	0.00 ± 0.00	0.00 ± 0.00
Core	1.77 ± 0.78	9.25 ± 7.91	0.00 ± 0.00	0.00 ± 0.00
Primary piece	7.13 ± 2.18	6.76 ± 3.19	50.00 ± 0.00	14.29 ± 0.00
Debitage	68.24 ± 6.60	72.08 ± 16.58	50.00 ± 0.00	42.86 ± 0.00
Technical piece	2.62 ± 1.08	0.00 ± 0.00	0.00 ± 0.00	0.00 ± 0.00
Knapping debris	9.13 ± 6.29	10.83 ± 6.43	0.00 ± 0.00	38.10 ± 0.00
Burnt debris	11.03 ± 5.10	1.08 ± 1.86	0.00 ± 0.00	4.76 ± 0.00
Edge-damage piece	8.63 ± 3.58	13.75 ± 6.96	0.00 ± 0.00	50.00 ± 0.00
Burin spall	11.24 ± 4.96	0.00 ± 0.00	0.00 ± 0.00	0.00 ± 0.00
Burin	3.46 ± 3.09	0.00 ± 0.00	0.00 ± 0.00	0.00 ± 0.00
Backed bladelet	26.17 ± 7.10	14.58 ± 8.32	0.00 ± 0.00	0.00 ± 0.00
Shouldered piece	0.73 ± 1.20	0.00 ± 0.00	0.00 ± 0.00	0.00 ± 0.00
Scraper	7.79 ± 4.01	21.67 ± 2.89	0.00 ± 0.00	0.00 ± 0.00
Linear retouch	17.86 ± 4.77	28.75 ± 7.81	0.00 ± 0.00	0.00 ± 0.00
Borer	4.50 ± 3.26	1.67 ± 2.89	0.00 ± 0.00	0.00 ± 0.00
Notched/denticulate	14.50 ± 8.65	12.92 ± 11.20	100.00 ± 0.00	0.00 ± 0.00
Aurignacian blade	2.00 ± 1.72	0.00 ± 0.00	0.00 ± 0.00	0.00 ± 0.00
Other	3.10 ± 2.54	6.67 ± 11.55	0.00 ± 0.00	50.00 ± 0.00

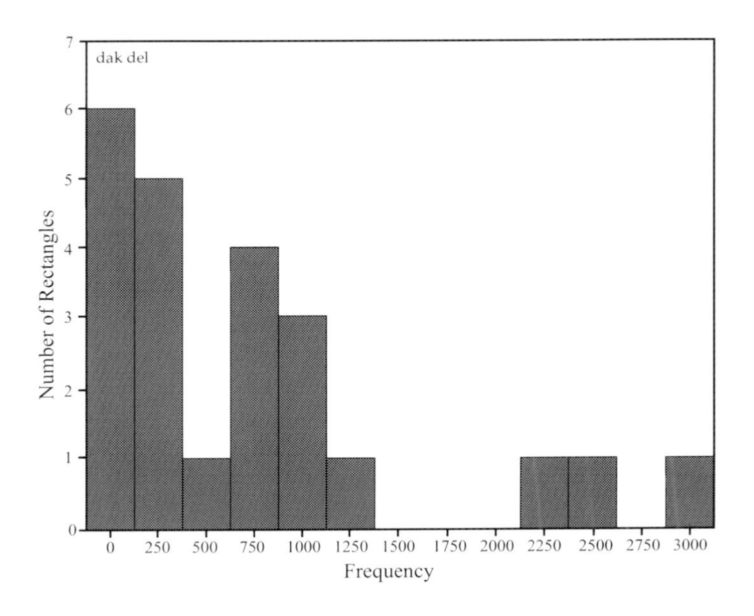

Figure 26.10. *Histogram of lithic artefact frequency, Stratum 5 (Y14–15).*

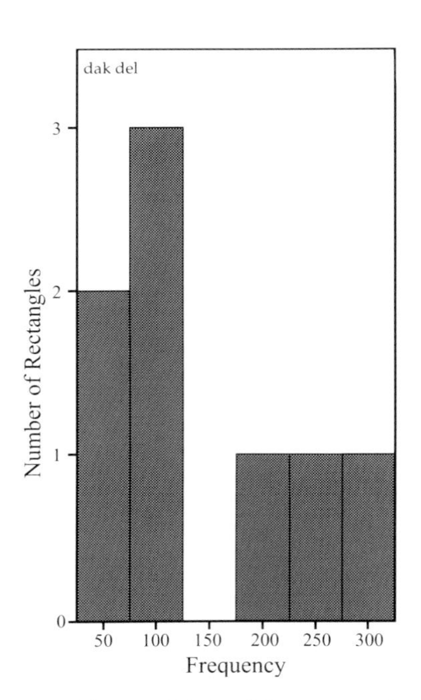

Figure 26.12. *Histogram of lithic artefact frequency, Stratum 9 (Y21–6).*

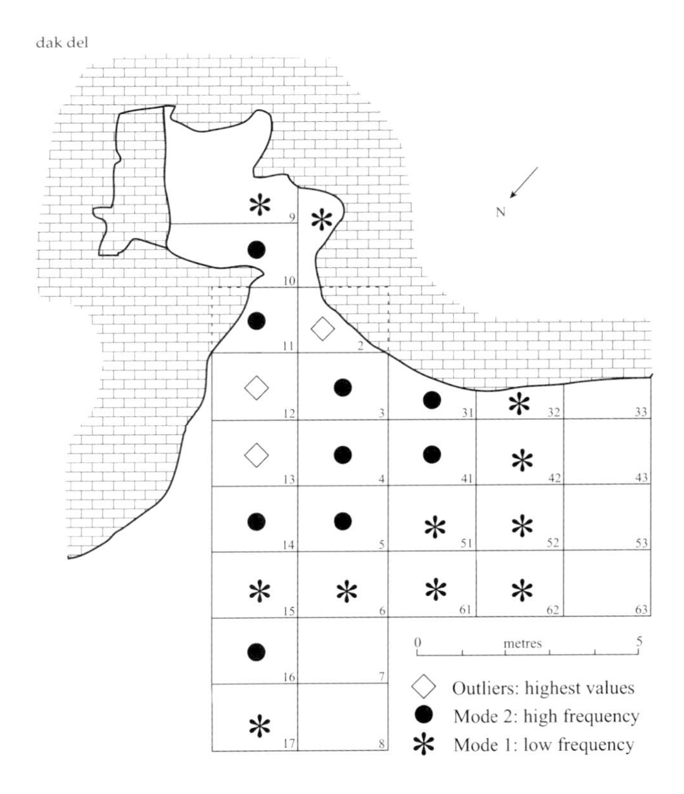

Figure 26.11. *Frequency of lithic artefacts, Stratum 5 (Y14–15); modes and outliers from Figure 26.10.*

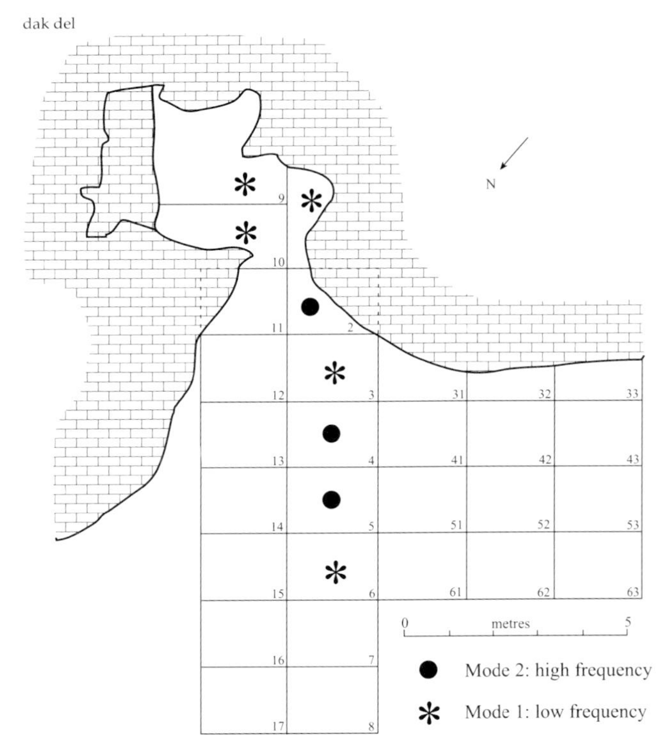

Figure 26.13. *Frequency of lithic artefacts, Stratum 9 (Y21–6); information from Figure 26.12.*

debitage, knapping debris, pieces with edge damage, scrapers and pieces with linear retouch. Note that these are low-count rectangles: absence of some tool types may merely reflect size bias.
- Cluster 3 (1 grid cell): Rectangle 15. Very low count of artefacts. Contains only primary pieces, debitage and notched/denticulates. As the low count may be the result of sampling biases, this rectangle will be excluded from consideration.
- Cluster 4 (1 grid cell): Rectangle 62. Technical pieces, nodules, cores and most types of tool absent.

High proportions of backed bladelets, notched/denticulates and burnt debris mark the same cluster, but an overall homogeneous distribution of technological and typological categories has been observed.

Lithic size

Suggested cluster solutions: 2 or 5 (Fig. 26.16). Optimal: 5 (Table 26.6 & Fig. 26.17). Clusters have the following characteristics:
- Cluster 1 (8 grid cells): scattered in cave, in its mouth and in northeastern area. Highest mean relative frequencies of sizes C, D, E and F. Lowest mean relative frequencies of sizes A and B.
- Cluster 2 (7 grid cells): Rectangles 3–6, 16, 17 and 61. Highest mean proportion of size A. Relatively high mean proportions of sizes C and E.
- Cluster 3 (1 grid cell): Rectangle 15. See comment on Cluster 3 in previous analysis.
- Cluster 4 (6 grid cells): extends over most of northwestern trench. Highest mean relative frequency of size B. Relatively high proportion of size A.
- Cluster 5 (1 grid cell): Rectangle 62. Size A absent.

Clusters 1, 2 and 4 are spatially contiguous. A pattern appears in which the proportion of small artefacts found gradually increases from the eastern to the western part of the site, while the proportion of larger specimens found decreases. Cluster definition is thus based upon gradation.

Synthesis of Stratum 5

In general there is little variation in assemblage composition from one area of the site to another, in high-count and low-count rectangles alike. This may be a genuine pattern reflecting human behaviour and/or post-depositional processes, or it may be a result of the fact that large provenance units permit only low resolution which masks local variation in artefact composition. The most spatially extensive cluster, which contains more grid cells than any other, reveals a pattern in which high proportions of burnt debris are associated with high proportions of backed bladelets and notched/denticulates. Higher proportions of large specimens have been yielded by the cave than by other parts of the site. Rectangles containing hearths are not necessarily characterized by high proportions of small specimens. At Klithi, by contrast, variation in the distribution of lithic specimens of different sizes is detected mainly in relation to hearths, with higher densities of small lithic specimens marking the areas around the hearths and high densities of large lithic specimens present in the talus.

Table 26.6. *Means and standard deviations of relative frequencies of size groups by cluster for 5 clusters (Stratum 5, Y14–15).*

Size	Cluster 1	Cluster 2	Cluster 3	Cluster 4	Cluster 5
A	8.50 ± 2.12	17.79 ± 4.15	33.33 ± 0.00	11.09 ± 2.79	0.00 ± 0.00
B	29.40 ± 3.21	28.75 ± 4.89	0.00 ± 0.00	37.56 ± 3.24	43.48 ± 0.00
C	35.04 ± 2.97	33.23 ± 3.33	0.00 ± 0.00	28.90 ± 3.33	26.09 ± 0.00
D	9.97 ± 1.83	5.45 ± 0.91	0.00 ± 0.00	6.41 ± 1.33	13.04 ± 0.00
E	14.95 ± 3.55	13.98 ± 4.95	66.67 ± 0.00	13.63 ± 4.78	8.70 ± 0.00
F	2.14 ± 0.87	0.80 ± 0.64	0.00 ± 0.00	2.41 ± 1.06	8.70 ± 0.00

Stratum 9

All lithic categories

Suggested cluster solutions: 3 or 5 (Fig. 26.18). Optimal: 3 (Table 26.7 & Fig. 26.19). Clusters have the following characteristics:
- Cluster 1 (3 grid cells): Rectangle 6 and large part of cave. High mean relative frequencies of cores, primary pieces, debitage, technical pieces, edge-damage pieces and pieces with linear retouch. Burin spalls, burins and Aurignacian blades absent.
- Cluster 2 (4 grid cells): contiguous group scattered over mouth of cave and through part of talus. High mean relative frequencies of debitage, knapping debris, burnt debris and backed bladelets. Hearths have been excavated in two of the rectangles in this group.
- Cluster 3 (1 grid cell): Rectangle 10. Very few artefacts. Quite similar in composition to other rectangles inside cave, but differentiated from them by absence of nodules, burnt debris, edge-damage pieces and notched/denticulates.

Lithic size

Suggested cluster solutions: 2 or 4 (Fig. 26.20). Optimal: 2 (Table 26.8 & Fig. 26.21). Clusters have the following characteristics:
- Cluster 1 (3 grid cells): in sheltered area. High mean proportions of sizes E and F. Low mean proportions of sizes A and B. As shown by previous analysis, Cluster 1 groups rectangles which have predominantly yielded artefacts related to the manufacture of blanks.
- Cluster 2 (5 grid cells): scattered through mouth of cave and talus. Highest mean proportions of sizes A, B and C. Lowest mean proportions of sizes E and F. Overlaps with Cluster 2 from analysis of all lithic categories.

Synthesis of Stratum 9

The present-day cave has yielded notably low counts of artefacts. It is differentiated from other areas by containing higher proportions of material from technological categories related to the

Table 26.7. *Means and standard deviations of relative frequencies of all lithic categories by cluster for 3 clusters (Stratum 9, Y21–6).*

Lithic category	Cluster 1	Cluster 2	Cluster 3
Nodule	0.31 ± 0.54	0.09 ± 0.17	0.00 ± 0.00
Core	6.43 ± 5.95	0.52 ± 0.67	5.00 ± 0.00
Primary	15.52 ± 5.83	10.03 ± 3.75	17.50 ± 0.00
Debitage	65.72 ± 12.99	61.41 ± 4.79	67.50 ± 0.00
Technical piece	4.21 ± 1.65	1.66 ± 1.44	2.50 ± 0.00
Knapping debris	4.35 ± 4.25	10.10 ± 4.76	7.50 ± 0.00
Burnt debris	3.46 ± 5.99	16.18 ± 4.85	0.00 ± 0.00
Edge-damage piece	23.81 ± 5.46	5.27 ± 7.26	0.00 ± 0.00
Burin spall	0.00 ± 0.00	0.96 ± 1.92	10.00 ± 0.00
Burin	0.00 ± 0.00	4.55 ± 1.50	0.00 ± 0.00
Backed bladelet	14.29 ± 10.71	19.97 ± 15.80	20.00 ± 0.00
Shouldered piece	0.00 ± 0.00	0.00 ± 0.00	0.00 ± 0.00
Scraper	7.14 ± 12.37	6.70 ± 3.31	30.00 ± 0.00
Linear retouch	34.52 ± 8.99	41.37 ± 27.16	30.00 ± 0.00
Borer	0.00 ± 0.00	0.00 ± 0.00	10.00 ± 0.00
Notched/denticulate	13.10 ± 12.54	13.62 ± 11.86	0.00 ± 0.00
Aurignacian blade	0.00 ± 0.00	0.96 ± 1.92	0.00 ± 0.00
Other	7.14 ± 7.14	6.58 ± 6.91	0.00 ± 0.00

Table 26.8. *Means and standard deviations of relative frequencies of lithic size groups by cluster for 2 clusters (Stratum 9, Y21–6).*

Lithic size	Cluster 1	Cluster 2
A	2.93 ± 0.98	14.79 ± 2.72
B	9.76 ± 6.25	32.05 ± 5.23
C	31.94 ± 8.92	32.68 ± 2.74
D	10.56 ± 5.50	8.45 ± 1.52
E	34.07 ± 9.52	11.11 ± 5.12
F	10.74 ± 2.40	0.92 ± 0.98

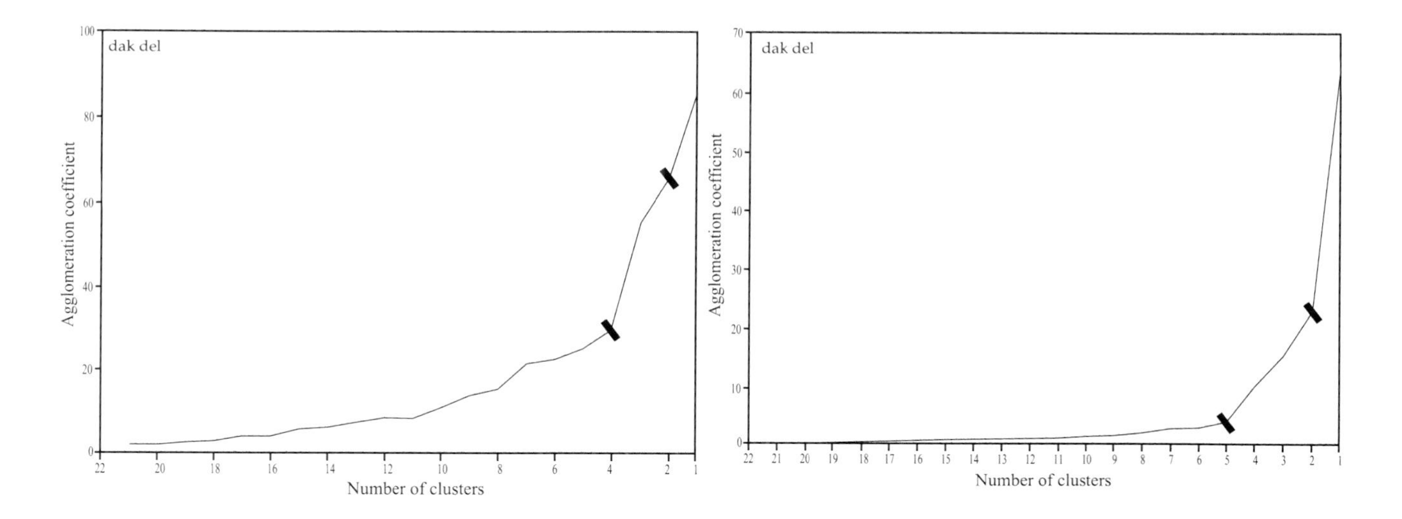

Figure 26.14. *Plot of the agglomeration coefficient against number of clusters for all lithic categories in Stratum 5 (Y14–15).*

Figure 26.16. *Plot of the agglomeration coefficient against number of clusters for lithic size in Stratum 5 (Y14–15).*

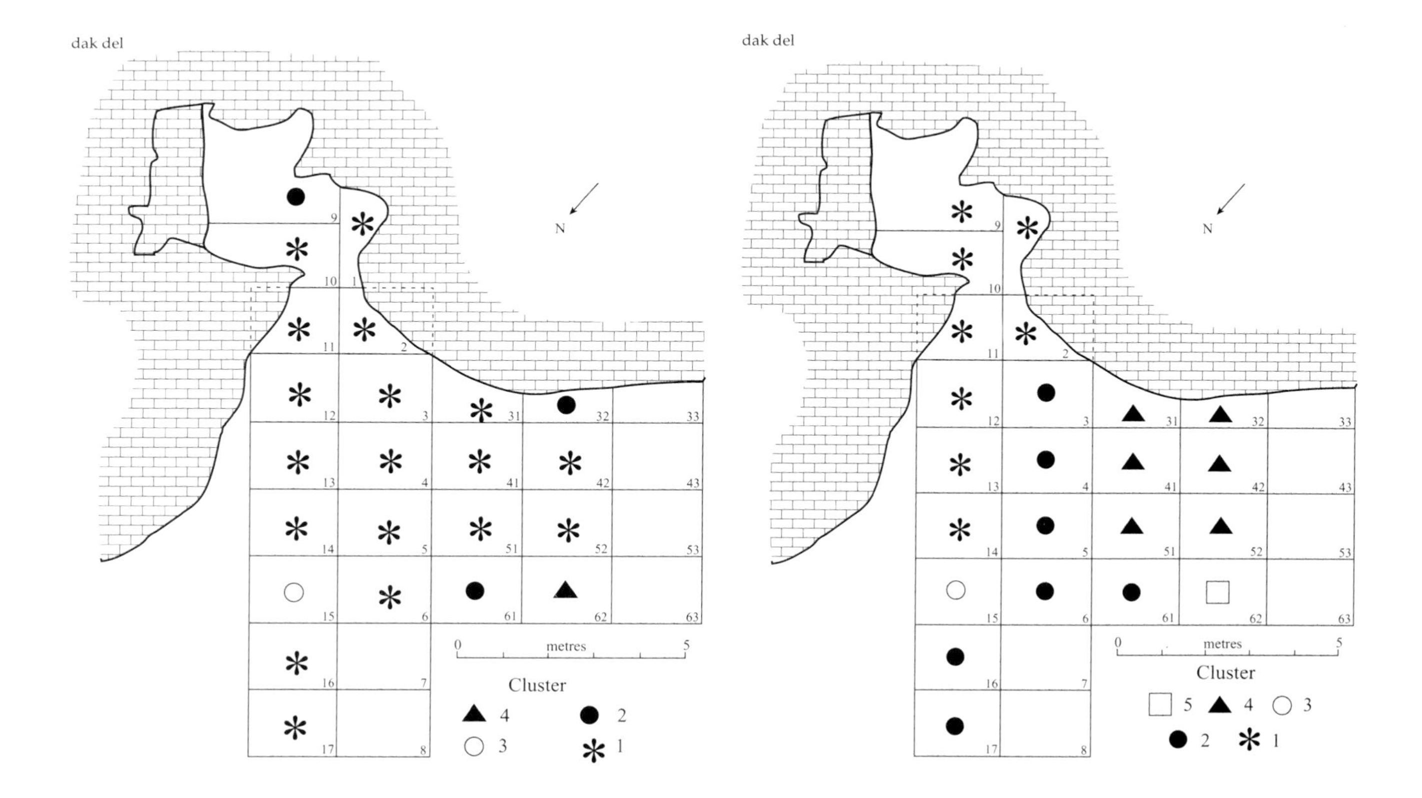

Figure 26.15. *Distribution of 4 clusters on site plan for all lithic categories in Stratum 5 (Y14–15).*

Figure 26.17. *Distribution of 5 clusters on site plan for lithic size in Stratum 5 (Y14–15).*

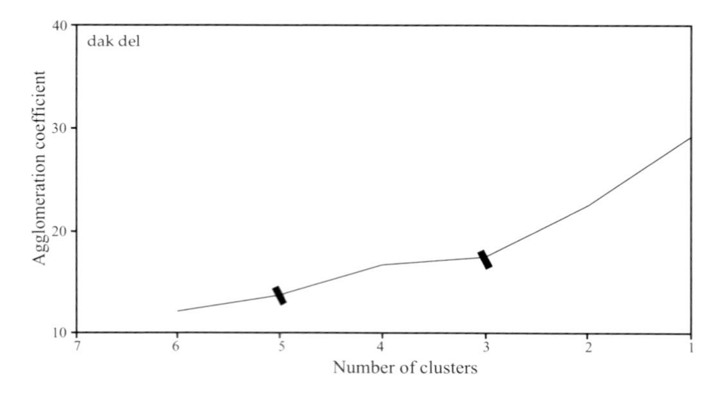

Figure 26.18. *Plot of the agglomeration coefficient against number of clusters for all lithic categories in Stratum 9 (Y21–6).*

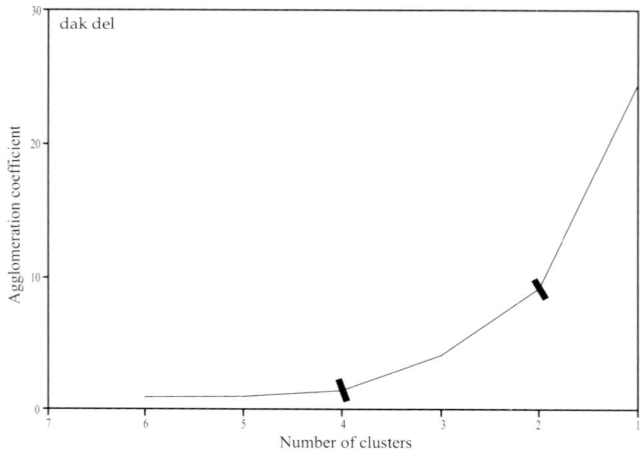

Figure 26.20. *Plot of the agglomeration coefficient against number of clusters for lithic size in Stratum 9 (Y21–6).*

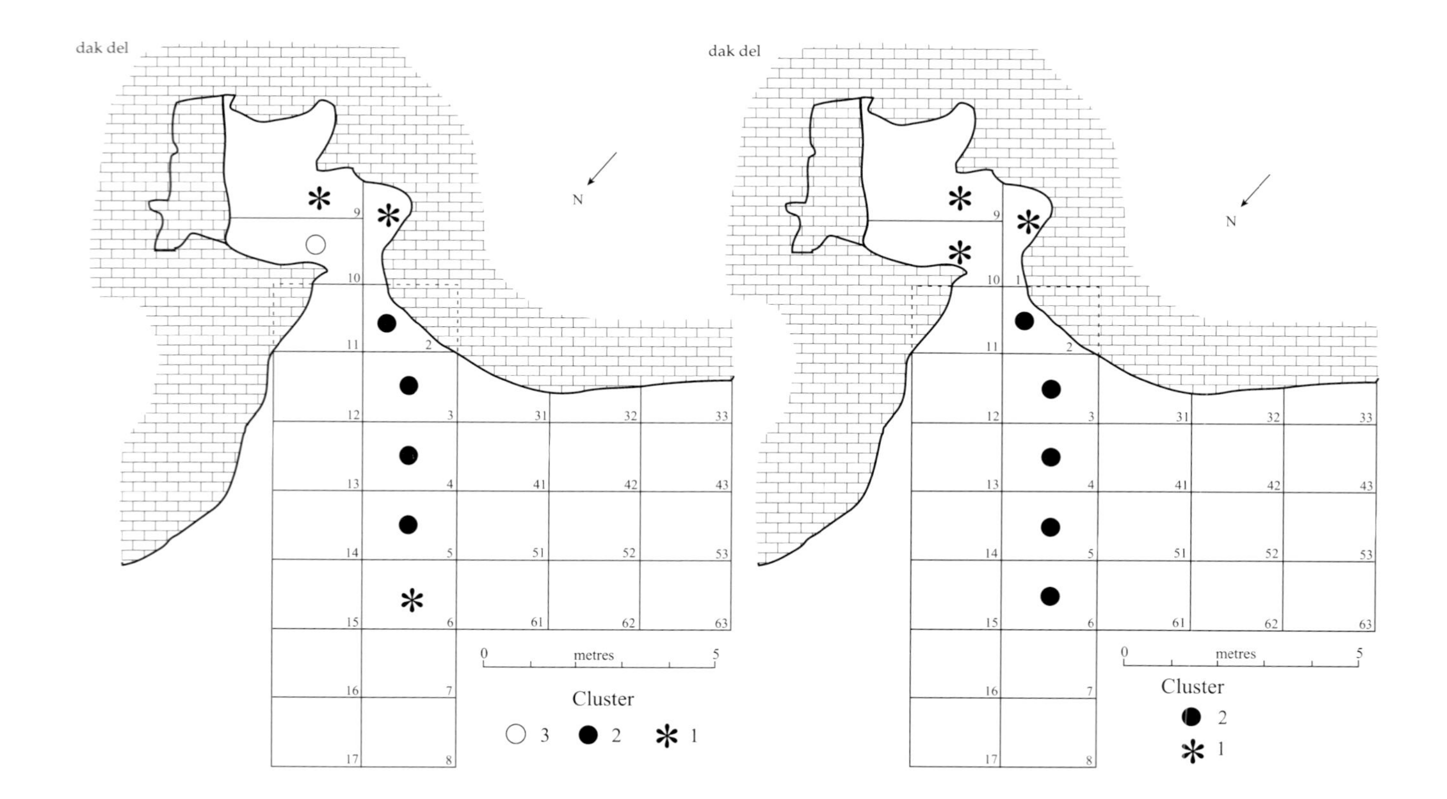

Figure 26.19. *Distribution of 3 clusters on site plan for all lithic categories in Stratum 9 (Y21–6).*

Figure 26.21. *Distribution of 2 clusters on site plan for lithic size groups in Stratum 9 (Y21–6).*

production of blanks. High frequencies of burnt debris and backed bladelets mark the area outside the cave. The data to hand suggest that during the early phases of occupation most human activity took place in the entrance of the cave. This was usually the area in which hearths were created and in which activities relating to backed bladelets occurred. The absence of shouldered pieces from Stratum 9 is a temporal pattern. High proportions of large specimens characterize the cave, while in the entrance and the talus there are markedly higher proportions of small (sizes A and B) artefacts. The variation observed in the distribution of size groups may be partly attributable to the action of water. When the lake was high, water may have picked up some of the smaller specimens inside the cave, which are lighter and thus more easily displaced, and redeposited them towards the entrance and outside. According to the refitting evidence, most of the detectable large-scale disturbance occurred in Y25. Natural agents, then, are not a sufficient explanation for the variation in size that we observe; we must also look for cultural causes. The hearths found in Rectangles 2 and 3 suggest the possibility that here (as is the case at Klithi, but not in Kastritsa Stratum 5) small artefacts are associated with hearths.

Discussion of spatial distributions

The foregoing cluster presentation shows that the lithic assemblage in Stratum 5 (Y14–15) appears to be distributed more homogeneously throughout the site than is the assemblage in Stratum 9 (Y21–6). In the former there is a slight difference between the edges and the rest of the site; in the latter the cave yielded higher proportions of specimens related to the manufacture of blanks than did the mouth and the talus, which yielded higher proportions of burnt debris and backed bladelets. This difference between the two strata demonstrates that spatial patterns can be identified at Kastritsa despite the large provenance units used. It also backs up my earlier suggestion that the lack of spatial variation in Stratum 5 need not necessarily be a mere side effect of the size of the provenance unit. A redundant pattern emerges, more clearly in Stratum 9 and less so in Stratum 5, whereby rectangles characterized by high proportions of backed bladelets are also marked by high proportions of burnt debris. Another pattern appears in that the cave contains fewer lithics and higher proportions of large artefacts than any other area of the site.

The overall low numbers of artefacts in Stratum 9 (Y21–6), and the little energy invested in making the hearths, which are simple ashy lenses, suggest that a few brief visits were made to a minimally furnished site during the early phases of occupation. The extent of the camp at this stage is uncertain, as the evidence we have is a sample from Stratum 9. During this phase hearths were invariably built in what is now the entrance to the cave, and this practice was repeated during almost every subsequent occupation (Strata 7–1), though new fireplaces were also created elsewhere. In purely functional terms this was the optimal location for a hearth, since during the period before the major rockfalls took place the area must have been well sheltered as well as offering good views of the lake. The hearths in Rectangles 2 and 3 appear to have functioned as a kind of threshold separating the inner and outer parts of the cave, the inner cave (Rectangles 9 & 10) containing particularly low counts of artefacts. There is no burnt debris in the inner cave; this waste material is distributed around the hearths and towards the lake shore, showing that its movement, whether natural or deliberately effected, has in general been roughly from southeast to northwest. In Stratum 9 high proportions of small specimens, debitage, knapping debris, burnt debris and backed bladelets characterize the hearth areas and their neighbouring rectangles.

In Stratum 5 (Y14–15), although the simple type of hearth is also found, the greater energy invested in building some stone-lined hearths may suggest longer stays than those represented in Y21–6 (Figs. 26.22 & 26.23). Hearths were usually aligned along the shelter wall on a northwest axis, but were also set up on the talus and in the inner part of the cave (Table 26.1). It should be noted that the presence of so many hearths in so limited an area is partly a side effect of grouping together Layers 14 and 15. It nevertheless remains interesting that even when hearths are sought in each layer separately there is no consistency in where they are located, as there is at Klithi (Figs. 26.22–26.24). Given that the rockshelter is of medium size, even if some hearths were used contemporaneously for different purposes (for example cooking or sleeping beside), or to accommodate the needs of separate family units, the number and the close proximity to one another of these hearths point to some temporal variation in their use, probably during different episodes of occupation.

The lack of significant spatial variation in the lithic assemblage distribution in Stratum 5 is depicted with uncompromising clarity by the clustering result, which has defined one major group of 18 rectangles (i.e. Cluster 1) and three smaller, insignificant ones. The entire lithic assemblage, with markedly high proportions of burnt debris, backed bladelets and notched/denticulates, is represented in this group. The refitting study has shown that archaeological material in certain areas of Y14–15 has not undergone any severe disturbance, confirming that homogeneity in assemblage composition need not imply disturbance of archaeological deposits. A homogeneous distribution of archaeological material may merely represent a way of using space

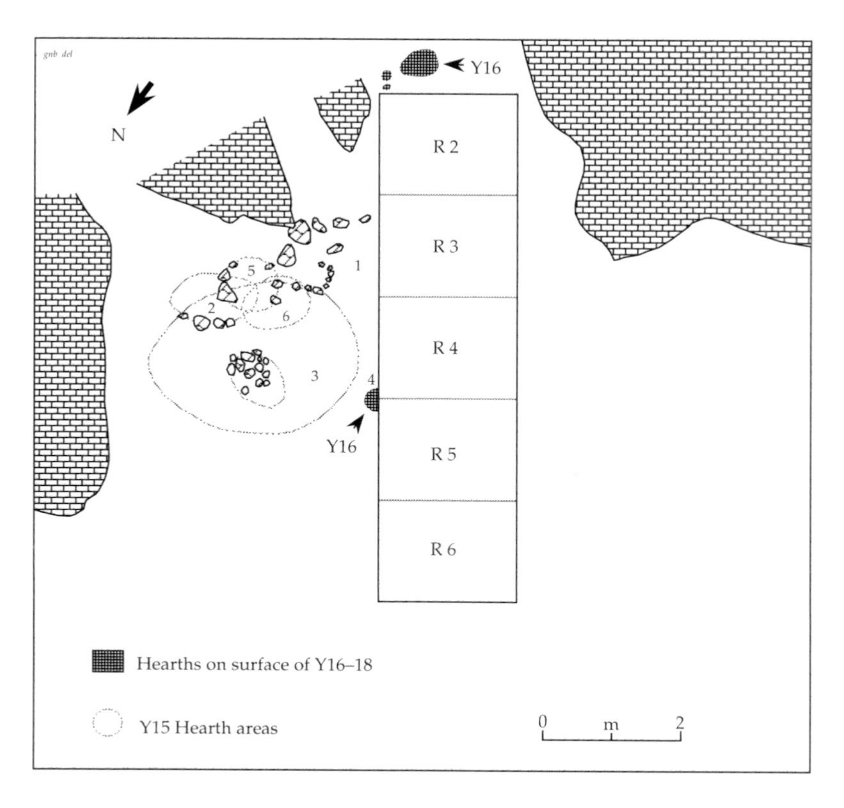

Figure 26.22. *Kastritsa 1967: hearths on surface of Y16-18 and some hearths in Y15.*

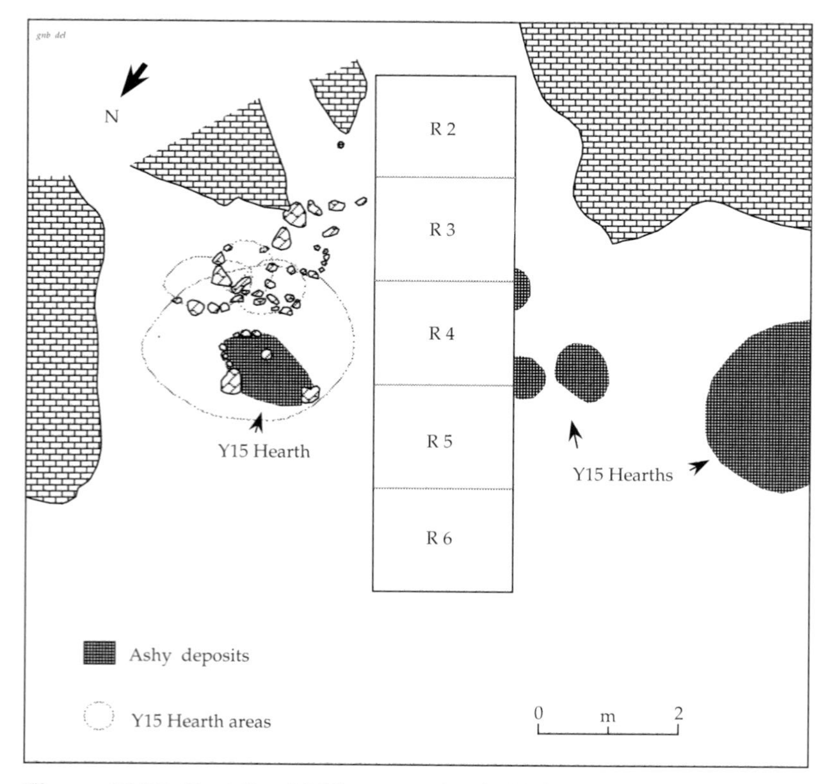

Figure 26.23. *Kastritsa 1967: occupation in Y15.*

similar to that found in Australian aboriginal campsites in the Western Desert, where all activities are carried out within the confines of family camps, no specialized areas being set aside for stone-chipping, butchering, etc. (Gould 1977, 33). The close proximity to one another of the hearths (and consequently of the hearth-related distributions of cultural debris) within the confined space of Kastritsa partly accounts for the lack of spatial variation in the composition of the assemblage. As the perimeter of one hearth-related distribution typically intersects that of another, the existence of numerous hearths in a confined area obscures any possible differences in assemblage composition (Fig. 26.23). There is a clear contrast here with the site structure and spatial distribution of lithics both at Klithi and in Stratum 9 at Kastritsa, where hearths have fixed locations. This contrast may be said to support the view that where many hearths are found close together differences in assemblage composition may be masked that would be evident if separate hearth-related distributions were being examined. It should be added that the greatest weakness of Unconstrained Clustering is that it is unable to decipher this sort of overlapping distribution of material (Blankholm 1991; Whallon 1984). We might, of course, have pictured Kastritsa quite differently if the minimum provenance unit had been smaller, since it might then have been possible to explore the boundaries of hearth-related distributions analytically.

To summarize, there are three possible explanations for why there appears to be no spatial variation in the composition of the lithic assemblage in Stratum 5 (Y14–15):

- there was no such variation in the first place, because the site was never divided into areas apportioned to different domestic activities;
- variation did exist, but it is now masked by the way in which the hearth-related distributions of

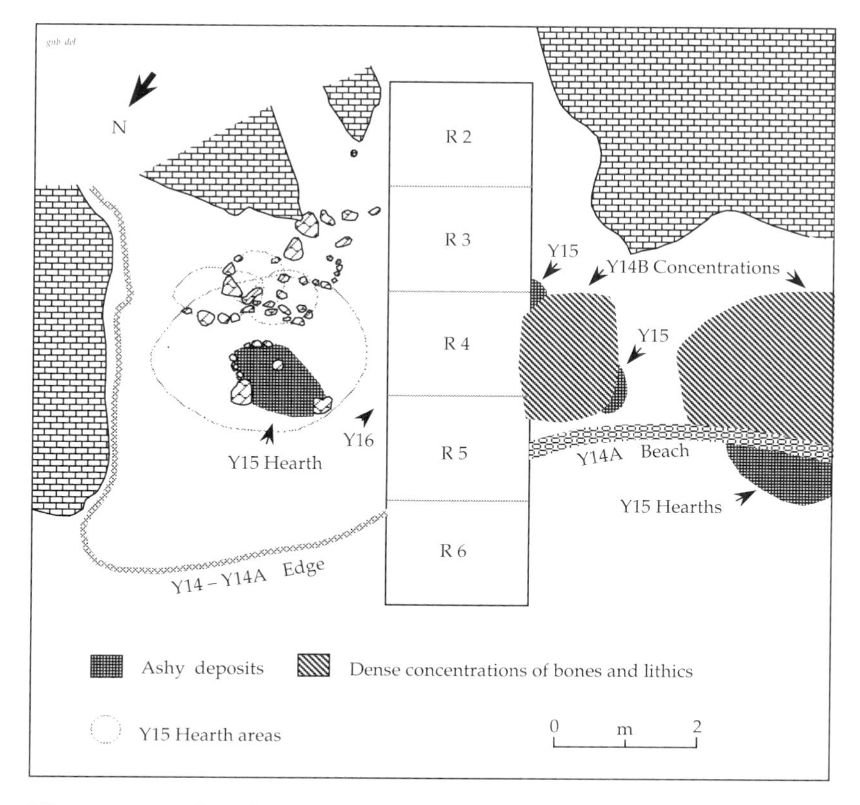

Figure 26.24. *Kastritsa 1967: occupation in Y14 and Y15.*

cultural material overlap horizontally, an obstacle with which my quantitative technique cannot deal efficiently;
- variation existed prior to excavation, but it has been obscured by the fact that the minimum provenance units used are so large.

It is clearly extremely difficult to evaluate these hypotheses, since we are currently stuck with our large minimum provenance units and have no way of knowing what degree of contemporaneity may have existed between the hearths found. I have no doubt that our understanding of this issue and many others will eventually be greatly improved by refitting lithics and bones using high-density rectangles, and by studying seasonality in the faunal assemblage. The evidence from Kastritsa as it stands does, however, permit another aspect of site structure to be addressed: intensity of occupation.

The variation in frequency of the cultural material in Stratum 5 (Y14–15) (Fig. 26.11) bears some relation to how intensively different areas of the site were used. Human activity seems to have taken place first and foremost at the present entrance of the cave, with the areas to the north and west running it a close second; less use seems to have been made of the inner cave and the edge of the site on the shore side. During the occupation recorded in Stratum 5 the cave's present entrance (i.e. Rectangles 2, 3, 11 & 12) was under cover. High frequencies may be found in the mouth of the cave either because this was a much-used area in which a lot of primary refuse was discarded, or because this was where secondary deposition of most of the debris resulting from the occupation took place. The presence of hearths in all three high-count rectangles (i.e. 2, 12 & 13) offers some support for the former assumption. People may have slept on the inner side of the hearths in what is now the cave. This hypothesis is supported by the fact that few lithics were found here. Although most of the artefacts found are large, they were fairly widely dispersed over the surface and would therefore not have caused discomfort. The fall-off in frequency of cultural material along the west part of the site (Rectangles 32, 42, 52 & 62) indicates that the remains of the occupation extend no further in this direction. It remains unclear how far the archaeological sediments to the east and northeast extend, however, and any future excavation of the site should pursue this point.

Concluding remarks

It is evident that, despite the pooling of data inevitably imposed by the coarse-grained units of analysis, certain interesting patterns have emerged. These clearly reveal differences between the two strata in the ways in which the site was used and archaeological deposits were formed.

Stratum 9 records brief occupations, with little in the way of evident features. The hearths found here are simple ashy layers in the present-day entrance of the cave. Latent structures have been discerned both in lithic artefact refits and in variation in assemblage composition. The latter, identifiable between the inner and outer areas of the cave, has resulted from a combination of the actions of natural agents (i.e. high lake levels) and human behaviour. Hearths are associated with small lithics, burnt debris, backed bladelets, debitage and knapping debris.

Stratum 5 records the first extensive occupation of the site, marked by the appearance of stone-lined hearths alongside open ones. Latent structures have been detected mainly in artefact refits rather than in local differences in the composition of the lithic assemblage. The arrangement of a large number of hearths in close proximity to one another in Y14–15 suggests either that these hearths were used contemporaneously by discrete social units or for discrete purposes, or that they were used at different times, probably during separate episodes of occupation. If the latter explanation is true, Y14–15 represents a horizontal as well as a vertical palimpsest of episodes of occupation. In other words, our horizontal view of site structure, typically represented by a site plan, leads us to see the remains of numerous non-contemporaneous and partly overlapping events of occupation arranged side by side. Despite the palimpsest effect of the multiple hearths in these layers, spatial integrity is manifested both inside the cave and outside it along the western wall in the number of artefacts that can be refitted. This raises two possibilities: either there never was any spatial variation in the composition of the assemblage, or variation did exist, but is now obscured by the coarse units of analysis. Variation in the frequency of the cultural material found is probably linked to more intensive use of the present cave entrance than of the other areas of the site.

When we turn to a comparison between Klithi and Kastritsa, it is clear that any interpretation of spatial patterning must take account of important variations between the two sites in terms of taphonomic histories and different methods of excavation and recording, as well as the within-site variability identified at Kastritsa. Klithi has higher densities of material than Kastritsa, and loose deposits that are more liable to encourage post-depositional horizontal and vertical displacement of material (Bailey & Woodward, Chapter 4). Both these factors might be expected to blur spatial patterning. Conversely the provenance units at Kastritsa are much coarser. Notwithstanding these sources of ambiguity, there are clearly striking differences in spatial organization between Klithi and Stratum 5 at Kastritsa, which must be the result, at least in part, of differences in site use. The number and the condition of both evident and latent features at Kastritsa point to greater spatial integrity and less intensive site use than at Klithi. The well preserved stone-lined hearths, the caches of tools, and the refitting results are all consistent with this observation. A form of site maintenance different from that employed at Klithi may partly account for this pattern. Kastritsa has yielded numerous hearths at various locations within individual layers. Klithi, by contrast, though it is by far the larger site, has fewer site features, just one or possibly two hearths being located by the north wall throughout the sequence, resulting in more intensive use of the space around them and probably in recurrent clearing out of material and extensive mixing. At Kastritsa the dispersal of hearths in a variety of locations, regardless of whether they were contemporaneous or not, has resulted in less intensive maintenance of the surrounding space.

It seems reasonable to conclude that a greater variety of activities probably took place at Kastritsa than at Klithi, but that Kastritsa was not necessarily used by more people, or for more prolonged visits. Indeed, the greater spatial integrity of the pattern found at Kastritsa, at least in Stratum 5, might encourage us to suppose that the site was used by fewer people, or for shorter visits. It would, however, be unwise to suppose any such thing. To begin with, the greater spatial integrity of Stratum 5 may to some extent reflect less localized and less intensive patterns of site maintenance, resulting from the fact that the hearths in this stratum were set up in a number of different places. The higher rates of sedimentation at Kastritsa, and the greater protection from post-depositional disturbance afforded by the more compacted sediments, may also have resulted in greater integrity. It is, moreover, easier to identify refits in a lithic assemblage in which (as at Kastritsa) there is a greater variety of raw materials. The difficulty of disentangling the various taphonomic and behavourial factors that may have affected spatial patterning here is clearly a considerable hurdle in the way of any further refinement of our interpretation. Kastritsa, however, could easily have been written off as an 'old' excavation, excavated and recorded using methods entirely inadequate to the answering of 'modern' questions. In the event, a great deal of valuable information has been obtained by returning to this site. There are certainly grounds for hoping that more detailed interpretations may be possible at a later stage, when all of the faunal and artefactual material has been examined in more detail and integrated more fully with studies of spatial structure.

Acknowledgements

I would like to express my gratitude to the Hellenic Foundation, London, and Clare Hall, Cambridge, for assistance with funding, and to the staff of the Archaeological Museum of Ioannina for their generous assistance in facilitating access to the material. Many thanks are also due to Geoff Bailey, Clive Gamble, Antikleia Moundrea-Agrafioti and

Catherine Perlès for their useful comments on an earlier draft of this chapter.

Notes

1. Since there are no section drawings for Rectangle 16, which was excavated in 1966, it has proved difficult to assign layers to the 1967 layering scheme. This rectangle was included in the sample in order to see whether refitting might clarify the stratigraphy. I have retained the layer description (L2) according to the 1966 scheme.
2. Information on recent breakages may be useful in forming an estimate of the impact of recovery methods on the preservation of artefacts. At Kastritsa the high degree of cementation necessitated the use of hard tools (e.g. chisels and hammers) during the excavation. This must presumably have had a serious effect upon the integrity of the specimens recovered, but at this stage we are unable to quantify it.
3. For this reason, no plans showing the horizontal distribution of refits have been produced.
4. Percentages are evaluated in relation to two totals: all lithics excluding tools, and tools only.
5. All the artefacts illustrated in this chapter were drawn in the field by the author and re-inked for publication by Judy Ogden.

Appendix 26.1. *Refitted lithic artefacts from Kastritsa Strata 5 and 9. Type: b: join, c: conjoin, d: same reduction sequence.*

Refit No.	Rectangle	Spit	Layer (Y)	Stratum	BagNo	Type				Total
						b	c	d		
19	1	55–7	14	5	7-3897	2	–	2		4
7	1	59	15	5	7-3960	2	–	–		2
46	6	66	14	5	C-1223	2	–	–		2
47	6	66, 65	14	5	C-1129, C-1105	2	–	4	flakes	6
43	6	70	15	5	C-2779	2	–	–		2
44	6	69	15	5	C-2725	2	–	–		2
45	6	69	15	5	C-2725	3	–	–		3
26	9	60–71	21–3	9	7-3878	2	–	–		2
22	10	55–9	14	5	7-2406	2	–	–		2
35	10	55–9	14	5	7-2406	2	–	–		2
12	10	61	15	5	7-2409	2	–	–		2
24	10	61	15	5	7-2409	2	–	–		2
25	10	61, 60–61	15	5	7-2409, 7-3945	2	–	–		2
16	10	63, 62	15, 15	5	7-3896, 7-3901	2	–	–		2
17	10	63, 62	15, 15	5	7-3896, 7-3901	2	–	–		2
8	41	65	15	5	7-2552	2	–	–		2
9	41	65	15	5	7-2552	2	–	–		2
10	41	67	15	5	7-3253	2	–	–		2
13	41	65	15	5	7-2283	2	–	–		2
15	41	65	15	5	7-2552	2	–	–		2
69	41	67	15	5	7-3253	2	–	1	distal part of cortic. bladelet	3
72	41	64	15	5	7-3503	2	–	–		2
74	41	67	15	5	7-3253	2	–	–		2
55	41	64, 63	15, 14	5	7-3503, 7-3509	2	–	–		2
60	42	64	14	5	7-3528	2	–	2	1 cort. flake, 1 blade	4
73	42	65, 66	14, 14–15	5	7-3100, 7-3589	2	–	–		2
68	42	66–8	15	5	7-3412	3	–	–		3
71	42	66	15	5	7-2405	2	–	–		2
30	51	68	14	5	7-1709	2	–	–		2
29	62	71	15	5	7-2367	2	–	–		2
70	31–41	66	15	5	7-2519	2	–	–		2
3	16	69	L2		C-677	2	–	–		2
49	5	75	21	9	C-2257, C-2720	2	–	–		2
48	1	61, 62	15	5	7-3985, 7-3906	–	2	–		2
27	1	60–71	21–3	9	7-3762	–	2	–		2
4	6	65	14	5	C-1150	–	3	–		3
20	10	55–9	14	5	7-2437	–	2	–		2
37	10	55–9	14	5	7-2437	–	3	–		3
39	10	55–9	14	5	7-2437	–	2	1	bladelet	3
6	10	60	15	5	7-2402	–	2	–		2
38	10	60	15	5	7-2402	–	2	–		2
40	10	61	15	5	7-2409	–	2	–		2
5	10	5–9, 57–8	14, 15	5	7-2437, 7-2365	–	2	–		2
14	41	65	15	5	7-2552	–	2	–		2
58	41	65, 63, 64	15	5	7-2283, 7-3676, 7-3503	–	3	3	flakes	6
52	41	67	15	5	7-3253	–	2	–		2
67	41	67	15	5	7-3253	–	2	–		2
59	41	65, 63	15, 14	5	7-2283, 7-2482	–	2	–		2
61	42	64	14	5	7-3528	–	2	–		2
64	42	64	14	5	7-3528	–	2	3	broken flakes	5
65	42	66	15	5	7-2405	–	2	–		2
66	42	66–8	15	5	7-3412	–	2	–		2
62	42	63, 66, 66	14, 15, 14–15	5	7-2951, 7-2405, 7-3589	–	4	–		4
41	1, 9, 10		24	9	7-3755	–	2	–		2
42	1, 9, 10		24	9	7-3755	–	2	1	flake	3
63	41–2	63	14	5	7-3275	–	2	4	2 bldlts, 1 blade, 1 crested blade	6
50	41–2, 42, 42	63	14	5	7-3275, 7-3671, 7-3133	–	3	–		3
51	42, 41–2	64, 63	14	5	7-3528, 7-3275	–	2	9	8 flakes, 1 core	11
53	42, 42–52	66, 66–8	15	5	7-2405, 7-3694	–	2	1	flake	3
56	42, 41, 42	65, 64–3, 63	14, 14–15, 14	5	7-3100, 7-3503, 7-3509, 7-3133	–	4	2	1 cort. flake, 1 flake	6
54	41	65	15	5	7-3499	–	2	–		2
57	42	66	15	5	7-2405	–	2	2	cort. flakes	4
110	1	60	15	5	7-3908	–	–	2		2
116	1	60	15	5	7-3908	–	–	3		3
115	1	64	21	9	7-2575	–	–	4		4
119	1	59, 57, 54–7	14	5	7-2442, 7-2443, 7-3893	–	–	6		6
118	6			5	C-1150	–	–	3		3
112	10	54, 55	14	5	7-3967, 7-3968	–	–	4		4
117	10	54–7	14	5	7-3893	–	–	4		4
114	10	55, 58	14	5	7-3968, 7-3758	–	–	2		2
113	10	55–7	14	5	7-2439	–	–	3		3
108	41	64	15	5	7-3503	–	–	2		2
102	41	65	15	5	7-2552	–	–	6		6
104	41	65	15	5	7-2552	–	–	3		3
109	41	66	15	5	7-2520	–	–	2		2
107	42	63	14	5	7-3275	–	–	13		13
101	42	64	14	5	7-3528	–	–	2		2
106	42	66	14–15, 14	5	7-2943, 7-1625, 7-3100	–	–	4		4
111	52	67, 66–9	15	5	7-3900, 7-3849	–	–	3		3
105	41, 41, 42	64, 64, 66	14, 15, 14–15	5	7-3235, 7-3503, 7-2943	–	–	4		4
103	41–2	63	14	5	7-3275	–	–	3		3

Chapter 27

Rockshelters and Open-air Sites: Survey Strategies and Regional Site Distributions

Geoff Bailey, Thomas Cadbury, Nena Galanidou & Eleni Kotjabopoulou

Regional interpretations of Palaeolithic settlement and land use in the Epirus landscape have been dominated by a small number of excavated sites. The original Higgsian model of seasonal mobility was based on just two rockshelter sites (Asprochaliko and Kastritsa) and a single species (red deer), and assumed that these sites were sufficiently representative to form the basis for generalization to the wider region. The more varied information from subsequent excavations at Grava and the Voïdomatis basin has introduced greater variability into the picture, resulting in multi-site and multi-species models (see in particular Sturdy *et al.*, Chapter 30). Attention has naturally focused on the Epirus rockshelters because they are stratified sites with detailed information about on-site activities and relatively precise chronologies. Nevertheless the sample of excavated sites remains small, especially in relation to studies of hunter-gatherer archaeology in many parts of the world, which emphasize the number and variety of locations in the landscape used for different purposes by mobile populations. This raises the question of how far the Epirus rockshelters are representative of prehistoric settlement and subsistence activities, and how far they are merely the byproduct of fortuitous conditions of preservation or discovery.

Our aim in this chapter is to examine the survey strategies by which Palaeolithic sites have been, or can be, discovered, and to evaluate the results of the successive surveys carried out in Epirus in the 1960s and during the course of the current project. We consider how far the distribution of open-air sites revealed by these surveys generates useful information about prehistoric settlement and land use in comparison with the results from the excavated rockshelters. We concentrate in particular on the contrasts and continuities between the Middle and Upper Palaeolithic, and we take as a point of reference two hypotheses that emerged from the 1960s work: (1) that Middle Palaeolithic sites are predominantly open-air locations confined to lower altitudes nearer the coast; (2) that Upper Palaeolithic sites are more obviously confined to rockshelters, and signify a shift of settlement strategies to include greater emphasis on the Epirus hinterland.

Nature of the problem

In spite of over thirty years of survey and investigation in the Epirus region, the number of Palaeolithic sites which have undergone systematic excavation and produced stratified and dated evidence is just eight. Six of these are rockshelter sites. Three of these (Klithi, Megalakkos and Boïla) are located within a radius of 2 km in the same valley. The remaining sites are widely scattered — Kastritsa on Lake Pamvotis near Ioannina, Asprochaliko in the Louros Valley, and Grava on the island of Kerkyra, all discovered and excavated in the 1960s. Of the two open-air sites, Kokkinopilos, near to Asprochaliko, is the subject of ongoing controversy about the stratigraphic associations and dating of the artefacts (Bailey *et al.* 1992; King *et al.*, Chapter 28; Runnels & Van Andel 1993a), while the other is represented by just six artefacts and a red deer mandible recovered from a section through river sediments immediately downstream from the Boïla rockshelter (Bailey *et al.*, Chapter 16). When we turn to the analysis of regional settlement patterns, the question inevitably arises as to how representative these sites are of the wider pattern, concentrated as they are in just four localities and dominated by rockshelter deposits. Are the rockshelters few in number because other rockshelters have yet to be discovered and excavated? Is it because most settlement activity occurred in open-air locations? Is it possible that rockshelter sites were only occasionally resorted to, for temporary shelter, for example, or during climatic extremes, and that the concentrations of surface finds that occur in many parts of the landscape are the only remaining clues we have to the existence of the major residential bases of the Palaeolithic?

What of the open-air sites? Compared to the excavated rockshelters, there are large numbers of these, most of them surface finds. We have compiled a data base of 484 find spots of worked flints from published and unpublished records (including the excavated sites). Of these, 58 lie outside the Epirus region, comprising locations recorded during the Higgs surveys of the 1960s, or sites recorded by Hammond (1967) in Albania. Of the remaining 426, the great majority are poorly stratified or surface finds in open-air locations. These are widely scattered across the landscape and seem likely to give a more representative geographical coverage than the few excavated sites, but they pose their own problems and potential biases. First and foremost, they are very difficult to date except at the coarsest scale. Some are certainly post-Palaeolithic and others may be. Excluding these leaves us with 95 locations in Epirus which can be attributed with some confidence to the Palaeolithic era. Of these, 16 cannot be dated with further precision, while the remainder have been assigned to Middle Palaeolithic, Upper Palaeolithic or Mesolithic periods, some to more than one period. Even at this level of resolution, sites are very difficult to evaluate in terms of the types and frequencies of activities they represent, especially if they are known only from small numbers of surface finds which may represent a mere fragment of the original site. Almost none, apart from the excavated sites, can be dated more precisely. In addition, because of complex taphonomic histories, faunal remains are almost never recorded in open-air deposits, and this seriously hampers evaluation of variability in land-use strategies. Open-air sites are also, like the rockshelters, subject to their own vagaries of differential survival, visibility and detection, and require a good understanding of Quaternary geomorphology to evaluate the likelihood of site destruction or exposure.

Regional analysis of Palaeolithic settlement distribution across the Epirus landscape thus poses something of a paradox. On the one hand are stratified sites, mostly in rockshelters, with detailed dating and subsistence information. But these are few in number and possibly quite unrepresentative of the wider pattern of land use, although they must represent preferred locations, repeatedly used over long periods. On the other hand are the open-air sites, which seem to offer a more representative sample of areas utilized, but less information about the activities carried on at each location and much poorer chronological control. Many have yielded very few finds and appear to represent quite transient occupation. These two types of evidence appear to be inherently incommensurate, as discussed earlier (Bailey, Chapter 1; Papaconstantinou & Vassilopoulou, Chapter 24), and the confounding problem (Winder, Chapter 6) looms large at the level of inter-site comparison because of the very considerable potential biases of differential preservation, visibility and recovery. Nevertheless it is clear that these two classes of data must be brought into some sort of relationship if questions about Palaeolithic land use and settlement are to be addressed.

This task is less problematic than might at first seem to be the case if we recall that all Palaeolithic sites in this region represent palimpsests. This is as much true of the rockshelter sites (Galanidou, Chapters 15 & 26) as it is of the open-air sites. The distribution of sites in the regional landscape is no more and no less of a palimpsest than is the distribution of artefacts within a site, with occasional glimpses of more highly resolved pattern here and there on the regional scale, just as there are on the intra-site level.

Moreover, the ease of locating rockshelters and the likelihood of finding stratified deposits and good conditions of preservation has tended to highlight rockshelter sites as a distinctive category in contrast to open-air sites. This contrast, however, is probably over-exaggerated, and it is more realistic to treat these two categories as points on a continuum, offering a balance of advantages and disadvantages rather than as mutually exclusive types. We make this point both in relation to the potentialities offered for the prehistoric occupants, and in relation to site taphonomy and depositional history.

Rockshelters offer the advantage of some natural enhancement of shelter, warmth and protection. But this is not a sufficient or a necessary reason for human occupation. The postholes at Kastritsa (Galanidou, Chapter 26) suggest that some additional artificial modifications were necessary to make the site comfortable. By the same token they show that by the Upper Palaeolithic period people were clearly capable of making artificial shelters, and we see no reason to deny this capability to the Middle Palaeolithic inhabitants of Epirus.

On the debit side, rockshelters have the disadvantage of a fixed location, which may not be the ideal one for access to resources. We certainly see no reason to equate superior qualities to one type of site over the other, or to equate one with residential bases and the other with temporary or task-specific activities. It seems quite possible that at least some of the rockshelter sites are locations for specialized or task-specific activities rather than residential bases, in spite of the large number of finds recovered from excavation; conversely some of the open-air sites could represent substantial occupations, perhaps even residential bases. Similarly, we acknowledge the manifest advantages of many rockshelter sites for trapping stratified sediments and preserving organic remains and dating materials. But we also note the complex palimpsest of activities that tends to result from repeated occupation of a confined area with slow rates of sedimentation, and the vulnerability of some rockshelter deposits to post-depositional disturbance and erosion — witness, for example, the complex discussions about the Asprochaliko stratigraphy (Bailey *et al.* 1983b; Higgs & Vita-Finzi 1966). Conversely, open-air sites, though they are sometimes subject to dramatic episodes of erosion, as at Kokkinopilos, offer the possibility of greater vertical and spatial separation of discrete occupation events, and can under favourable circumstances provide good conditions for stratification, dating and organic preservation, as with the open air deposits adjacent to the Boïla rockshelter.

Thus, the distinction betwen highly resolved and accurately dated rockshelters on the one side, and poorly resolved and poorly dated surface sites, on the other, is in fact somewhat arbitrary, and it is preferable to take each site on its merits, rather than to assume in advance that one type of site will be more advantageous than another, whether for the prehistoric occupants or the modern archaeologist. Our aim, then, must be to look for broad scale patterns of redundancy or underlying structure, making the maximum use that we can of all the available data, avoiding preconceptions about the suitability or otherwise of some categories of evidence, and taking account as far as is possible of potential biases.

Survey strategies

An extensive literature exists on sampling methods in archaeological site survey (e.g. Cherry *et al.* 1978; Mueller 1975). Many of the methods and principles that have been devised apply to relatively recent archaeological periods where an interest in settlement patterns, and an abundance of surface finds and features, guarantee the discovery of sites and indeed demand the application of systematic sampling procedures because of the large number of find spots. Many studies offer detailed prescriptions for the systematic coverage of areas that are very small in relation to the likely annual territories of mobile Palaeolithic peoples, and are of questionable relevance to Palaeolithic objectives. On the other hand, Palaeolithic investigations are less often accompanied by such rigour, largely because the effects of geological changes make the discovery of sites and the interpretation of site distributions a much more haphazard undertaking. Because of the much greater time spans involved and the need to establish chronological controls, Palaeolithic research strategies are also more strongly dominated by the search for individual sites with deep stratigraphy, rather than the analysis of site distributions. Thus, much Palaeolithic site survey might best be described as an exercise in 'geological opportunism', with the discovery of even a single site with *in situ* material counting as a success, and excavation of the 'type site' as the ultimate goal. Opportunism and chance discoveries have often, therefore, played an important part, at least in the initial exploration of a region.

Nevertheless the general principles of sampling apply with equal force, though they need to be adapted to the particular circumstances of Palaeolithic archaeology. Where, as here, the interest is not simply in establishing the industrial sequence, but in examining the geographical expression of Palaeolithic settlement and activity on a regional basis, the nature of the survey strategies used to find sites, and the reliability of the resulting site distributions, becomes a more pressing issue. Two factors stand out as critical in the design and interpretation of regional site survey: (1) the interplay between geomorphological change and site visibility; (2) the problem of dating and establishing contemporaneity between sites. Also, as in the case of sampling at smaller scales of analysis (Winder, Chapter 7), the sampling paradox applies with equal force to regional survey: until one knows what sorts of locations and geological formations are likely to yield artefacts, it is difficult to formulate sensible targets for sampling strategies. Until one finds sites, one doesn't know where to look for them.

Epirus surveys

Four episodes of site survey have been carried out over the past 30 years in Epirus. The first survey was conducted by Higgs in 1962, with a permit to range over the whole of Epirus, as well as western Macedonia on the eastern side of the Pindus Mountains (Dakaris *et al.* 1964). Survey methods were necessarily extensive in nature, and carried out with only small-scale maps (1:250,000) as a guide. Coverage appears to have been confined to areas accessible by road and to have been undertaken in an opportunistic fashion with the straightforward objective of finding sites, particularly rockshelters, and collecting the artefacts visible at each find location. Documentation about survey areas and survey methods is limited, but the network of roads negotiable even by landrover was limited in the early 1960s, and survey appears to have been limited to the Ioannina basin, the Louros and Thesprotikon valleys and adjacent coastal areas, and the Acheron basin, with only occasional forays beyond these areas, notably into the lower Arachthos basin (Fig. 27.1). The discovery of Kokkinopilos led to a predictive strategy: similar 'red-bed' deposits were systematically targeted in the expectation that they too would yield Middle Palaeolithic artefacts, an expectation largely borne out in the areas investigated. Some of these sites were revisited on subsequent occasions, resulting in large collections of material. In 1979 many of these locations were revisited and material from them re-examined.

In the later 1960s a second episode of survey was undertaken to test the hypothesis of seasonal transhumance between Kastritsa and Asprochaliko. The most obvious animal migration routes between the two sites were systematically covered, resulting in

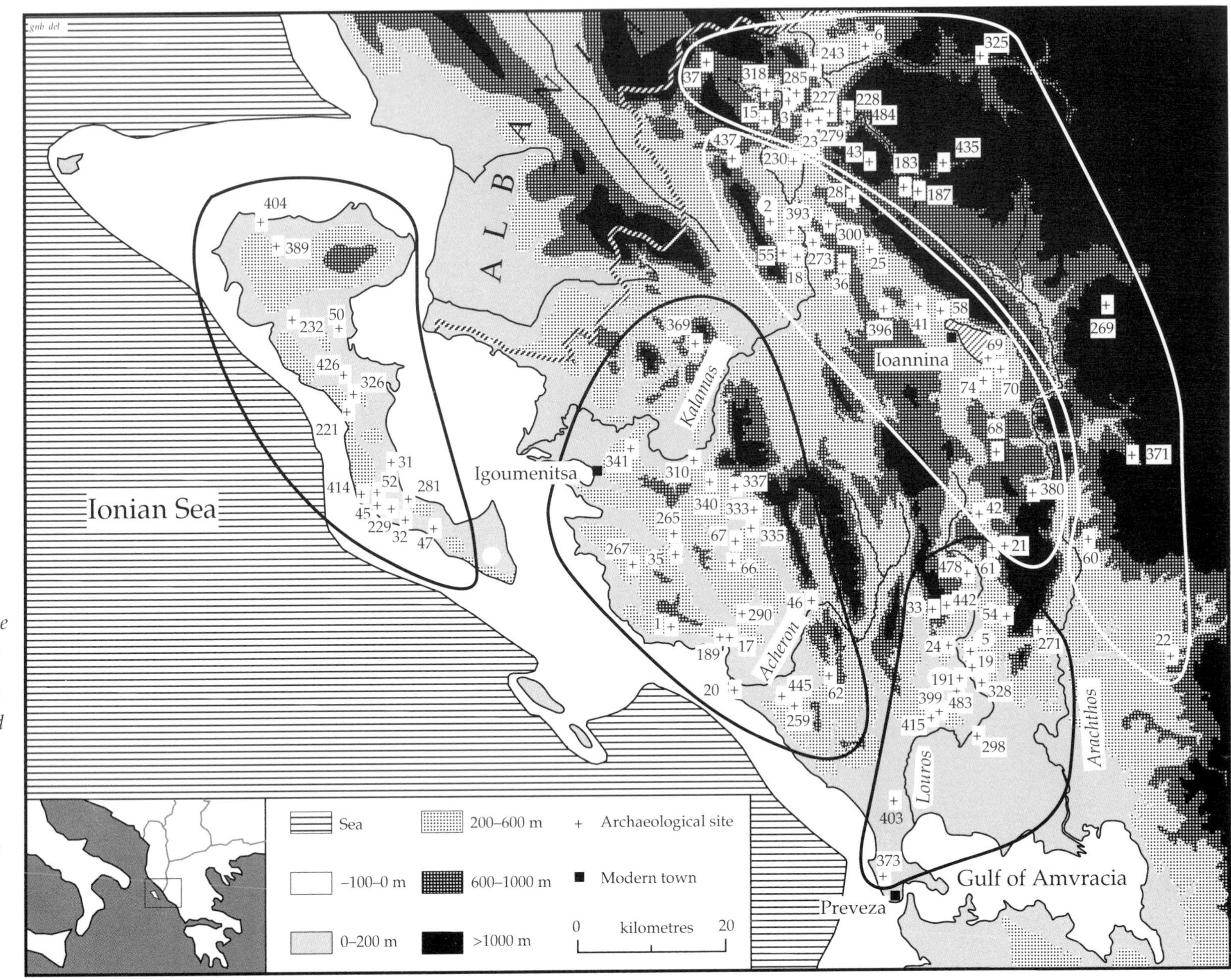

Figure 27.1. *General distribution of sites discussed in the text, showing geographical features and areas used to subdivide sites in to sub-regional groupings. Site numbers correspond to those shown in Appendix 27.1. The West area comprises the lower Kalamas and Acheron basins, the South area the Louros basin, the East area the Ioannina basin, and the High Pindus the area to the north and east of the Arachthos River. The Kerkyra area comprises those sites on the island of Kerkyra.*

the discovery of a number of open-air sites. The adjacent valleys of the Arachthos and the Thesprotikon were also searched as a negative test, and the absence of sites there seemed to confirm the transhumance hypothesis (Sturdy 1969; pers. comm.). Searches were also made further to the west in the expectation that a similar transhumant route would be found between the rockshelter sites at the mouth of the Voïdomatis and the coastal region near Parga. A number of rockshelter sites are known in the Parga area but none has produced unequivocal or datable evidence of occupation.

A more limited survey was undertaken in 1987 in the northern region of Epirus to the west of Klithi, in the Konitsa, Kalamas and Gormos basins and the coastal region extending towards Igoumenitsa, following geological and palaeogeographical survey and the identification of areas of potential attractiveness to Palaeolithic populations. This survey covered an area of Epirus that was largely complementary to that examined in the 1960s, and extended along a transect from the hinterland to the coast and across a range of geologies and areas of varying attractiveness to Palaeolithic populations. Sampling was directed by the needs of palaeogeographical survey (Sturdy *et al.*, Chapter 30), but included areas where sites were expected as well as areas where they were thought likely to be absent. By this stage of research a clear contrast had been established between limestone and flysch areas (Sturdy *et al.*, Chapter 30) both in terms of potential attractiveness to human populations and recovery of archaeological sites. Removal of artefacts at each find spot was restricted to diagnostic material, in order to establish future potential, rather than to effect a comprehensive and systematic collection.

Finally in 1992 a more detailed but more geographically circumscribed survey was undertaken in the Kalamas–Gormos basin and the Voïdomatis basin to test systematically some of the hypothesized associations between site location and landforms (see Bailey *et al.*, Chapter 16 for details of the Voïdomatis basin). The area was stratified into sub-areas on the basis of geographical features, such as upland valleys, river gorges and lowland basins, and of geological variations, notably between limestone and flysch areas. Even in these more limited areas not all targeted locations of interest could be systematically field-walked, because of limited time and resources, difficulties of access, and lack of good topographic maps of 1:50,000 scale or smaller. Sample areas were selected for a combination of reasons: principally ease of access, proximity to previously known sites, or lack of previous finds.

Sampling strategies

From the experience of these various surveys it is possible to identify and comment on at least three levels of consideration in Palaeolithic site survey: (1) the size of the survey area and the sampling procedure to be used in the survey area as a whole, in other words how to select the types of locations to be visited, whether at random, or by stratifying the area into different types of geological and geographical features, or by some other means; (2) the sampling strategy to be employed within each type of location (whether random, systematic or judgemental) so as to maximize the chances of finding material within the constraints of time, money and personnel (assuming that the general area of survey is too large to allow all targeted locations to be visited); (3) the intensity with which the ground is to be covered at each sample location, and the sampling procedures to be employed in collecting surface material.

As far as the first level is concerned, river catchments, or parts of river catchments which form well-defined catchment basins, are a convenient minimal unit of study, and broadly three sampling strategies can be employed within them. First, one can target those geological features in the landscape which, because of geological conditions of sediment accumulation and erosion, are most likely to offer good visibility of Palaeolithic stone artefacts: caves or rockshelters, eroding fan and alluvial sediments ('red beds'), and sections cut in river terraces. Secondly one can identify those areas which one might expect to be most attractive to Palaeolithic activity, given some behavioural model of human movements over the landscape in relation to the monitoring and exploitation of animals or other resources. Ridges with commanding views of grazing basins, and saddles or river-crossings which form intermediate points on the seasonal migration routes of animals between known areas of Palaeolithic occupation, are obvious examples. The transhumance hypothesis provided just such a set of expectations in the 1960s and more detailed modelling exercises have provided a new set of expectations to guide the analysis of existing material and future survey (Sturdy *et al.*, Chapter 30; Winder, Chapter 31). Thirdly one can target those 'negative' areas which are not expected to yield finds, either on geological or behavioural grounds. The discovery of sites or finds in areas where they are not expected is, in itself, an extremely useful type of information. So too is the absence of finds in areas where they have been predicted. Ideally survey strategies should be designed so as to test both types of predictions.

Each of these strategies has its advantages and problems. Targeting geological features has the virtue of providing a systematic framework for survey, but also the potential vice of systematically biasing the results in favour of geological deposits with fortuitously good conditions of site visibility. On the other hand, if it turns out that not all such deposits produce archaeological evidence, this may give important clues about behavioural factors affecting choice of site location. For example, the repeated association of Middle Palaeolithic artefacts with eroding red sediments in lowland areas of Epirus breaks down when one moves into the Epirus hinterland, where similar deposits are equally extensive but rarely yield flint artefacts. Similarly, rockshelters offer (at least in broad terms) a higher probability of preserving sediments and archaeological materials than open-air locations, and hence a systematic target that may reveal cultural preferences in favour of some locations at the expense of others, or geological variables that have potentially removed or obscured cultural evidence.

The apparent rarity of rockshelter deposits with evidence of Palaeolithic occupation is a notable feature, and does not at first sight seem to be attributable to lack of exploration or to the lack of suitable geological and topographic conditions. Limestone rockshelters abound, and many appear to be potential candidates for occupation even though they are empty of deposits, or have deposits lacking in surface indications of prehistoric activity. On the other hand, it is possible that in the complex topography of the Epirus landscape there are some areas that have not yet been visited or searched intensively, where rockshelter sites may lurk undetected. It is also conceivable that in a highly active geomorphological environment rockshelter deposits have been removed by erosion or obscured from view by roof collapse. Even such a rich site as Asprochaliko apparently gave no surface indications of Palaeolithic occupation and was inspected and rejected as a potential site on several occasions before the decision was taken to excavate (P. Carter pers. comm.).

Discovery of sites by predictive modelling can provide a useful test of the underlying behavioural model. But much depends on the quality of the 'test' data. Some of the sites discovered by this means in past surveys have consisted of one or two surface finds of flint artefacts or undiagnostic material. Since flint was widely used in later prehistoric periods, and indeed right up until historical times, it may be difficult to date isolated finds unless they are very distinctive pieces with characteristic shapes, technical features or secondary retouch. Moreover, in an area where flint is widely available, it may even be difficult to say with confidence whether an isolated find of undiagnostic debitage is a genuine artefact, as opposed to a piece produced by natural or accidental agency. Absence of finds in places where they are predicted can also be difficult to assess, since this may indicate lack of preservation or visibility, rather than lack of prehistoric activity.

Negative areas, that is areas lacking in finds, pose particular problems, especially the flysch basins which form very extensive tracts of terrain in parts of Epirus. A variety of geological and archaeological considerations suggest that these basins were unattractive to human occupation during the Palaeolithic period (Sturdy *et al.*, Chapter 30). They are intrinsically infertile from the point of view of soil nutrients for animal grazing; they are also subject to very rapid erosion and creation of badlands landscapes because of the combination of soft bedrocks, tectonic instability and reduced vegetation cover (King *et al.*, Chapter 28; Turner & Sanchez-Goñi, Chapter 29). Previous surveys have failed to locate significant finds, but the rapid erosion may have removed or buried the evidence.

As for the intensity with which the ground is covered at specific locations, systematic guidelines are difficult to lay down, because the discovery of a flint artefact sitting on a surface or eroding from a sediment depends so much on chance, intuition, experience and expectation. Some individuals have a good 'eye' and some do not. Even experienced observers can miss evidence, and there are several examples on record from past work in Epirus of locations that were repeatedly visited before the existence of artefacts or cultural deposits was established. Ground cover and visibility can change over time with changes in land-use, weather or vegetation. Reduced grazing pressure in recent years in many parts of Epirus has allowed the regeneration of scrub vegetation and in some cases of impenetrable bramble thickets which seriously hamper field survey, while new road cuttings or other engineering works have exposed previously inaccessible deposits. Even the discovery of rockshelters is not as easy as might be expected. Many informed observers walked past Megalakkos over a six-year period before it was recognized as containing prehistoric deposits. Ideally sub-surface test excavation should also accompany the discovery of surface finds, but permit restrictions in Greece currently do not allow excavation to be carried out concurrently with survey. All of this underlines the point that successful survey in a region is likely to require long-term involvement and repeated visits.

Given the manner in which the various Epirus surveys have been carried out and the difficulties of locating or recognizing sites, it would be rash to assert without qualification that the known site distribution is representative of the prehistoric settlement pattern. The sample of sites at our disposal can only be described, at best, as a grab sample. On the other hand, the distribution of sites is the result of cumulative investigations that have stretched over several decades. They have covered a variety of different geographical and geological areas, produced nearly a hundred find spots which can be assigned with some confidence to the Palaeolithic and Mesolithic periods, and generated hypotheses of prehistoric settlement distributions to focus subsequent investigation. Concurrent geological investigations have also given us a good insight into the effects of geomorphological change on site visibility, and some means of assessing their effects, notably through sampling of areas with equivalent geological histories but different archaeological expressions of prehistoric activity. It should be possible to evaluate general trends in such data, to assess potential biases in the light of the above discussion, and to identify hypotheses in need of further testing.

Limitations of the Epirus data and methods of presentation

The sites discussed here are based on a variety of published sources (Dakaris *et al.* 1964; Hammond 1967; Higgs & Vita-Finzi 1966; Sordinas 1969; 1970a). Unpublished sources include the original field notes and records of the 1960s material, including examination of the material recovered by the various surveys and now housed in the Ioannina Museum, and the observations undertaken as part of the Klithi project. Most of the finds are surface sites and comprise flint artefacts, but ceramics have also been identified in some cases. Much of the data is difficult to evaluate, either because the original descriptions are inadequate, or because the finds are so few, and we have therefore had to group data into some fairly simple categories.

Any find of artefacts is taken here to represent a site, using the term in a very general sense to include any manifestation of human activity, from a single worked flake at one extreme to a stratified site with hundreds of thousands of artefacts at the other. We exclude from further consideration those find spots that are obviously or probably post-Palaeolithic, that is to say sites with diagnostic flints or ceramics of Neolithic or later date, but we include Mesolithic sites where these have been identified as such.

The remaining sites, totalling some 95 find spots (Appendix 27.1; Fig. 27.2), are further classified into four broad chronological categories on the basis of their flint artefacts: sites of Palaeolithic date, but not datable to a finer resolution — these are sites which might include Middle Palaeolithic or Upper Palaeolithic material or both (P); sites with diagnostic Middle Palaeolithic material (MP); sites with diagnostic Upper Palaeolithic material (UP); and those with diagnostic Mesolithic finds (MESO). Mesolithic sites form such a small category that we do not offer detailed discussion here, though we shall comment later on the reasons for their apparent rarity, and the greater part of our analysis and interpretation refers to the Middle and Upper Palaeolithic periods. We further assume that the distribution of sites in this period was constrained by glacial climatic conditions that prevailed, albeit with some fluctuations, throughout this period.

We further group sites into three categories according to their size: (1) major sites, where the number of finds or the area over which they are distributed suggest a major focus of activity; (2) intermediate sites where the number of finds is sufficient to

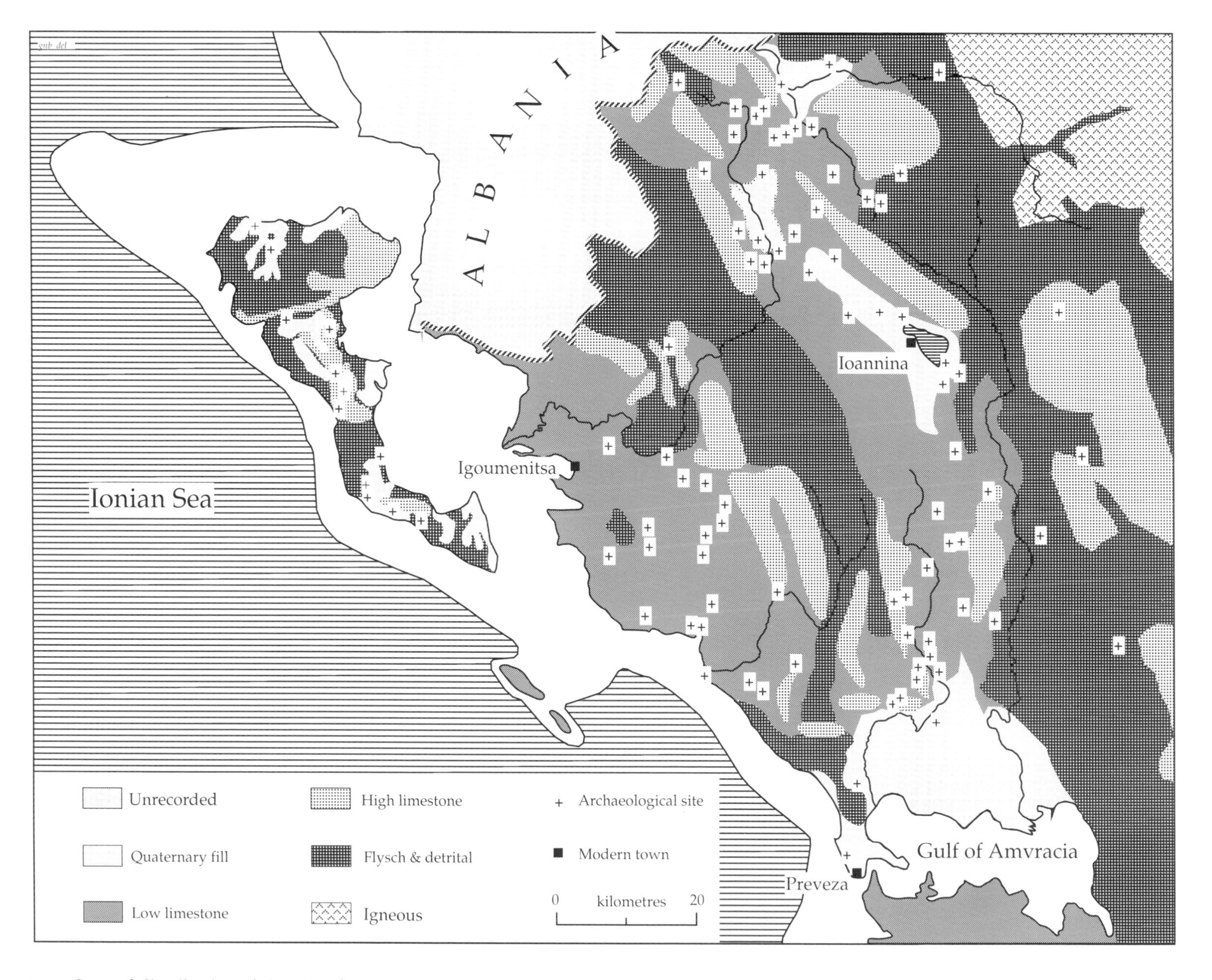

Figure 27.2. *General distribution of sites in relation to major geological categories. (For further discussion of geological categories, see Bailey* et al., *Chapter 16; King* et al., *Chapter 28; and Sturdy* et al. *Chapter 30.)*

suggest repeated occupation or activity, without necessarily implying the specific type of activity or site function; (3) isolated finds with one or a very small number of flints. Sites of category (1) are fairly obvious, where the number of artefacts may run to many hundreds or thousands, although it should not be assumed that such sites necessarily equate with residential bases. Category (3) sites at the other extreme are also obvious, many consisting of just one worked flint. We define category (2) sites as those which have yielded numbers of artefacts ranging between about 20 and 100. Obviously these distinctions are rather arbitrary, and the attribution of sites to one or other category may be influenced by the collection policy and search intensity at the time when the site was discovered.

We have also grouped sites by their altitudinal zone in order to give some general measure of their seasonal potential. As a general rule, we treat finds located between sea level and 200 m as lowland sites, potentially usable at any time of year, and those between 200 m and 600 m as representing sites that could have been used in any season, although this may vary according to local circumstances. Sites in the higher altitudinal zones must in general represent locations of summer or specialised activity; the higher the altitude, the more likely this is to be so.

Another indicator of seasonal potential is distance inland from the coastline. Sites that are far inland, even if they are at relatively low altitude, are more likely to have been avoided in winter than those at comparable altitude nearer the coast. For this purpose we have grouped sites into five areas: Kerkyra; Western Epirus, representing the lower parts of the Kalamas and Acheron River catchments and the area between them; Southern Epirus, representing the Louros River basin and the adjacent coastal lowlands; Eastern Epirus, representing the Ioannina and Doliana basins and the high ground on the catchment boundary between the Ioannina and Louros basins; and the High Pindus, an area comprising the foothills and slopes of Nemertzika on the Albanian border, the Konitsa basin and the catchments of the Aoos and Voïdomatis Rivers, and the upper reaches of the Arachthos catchment (Fig. 27.1). In general, the first three areas (Kerkyra, West and South) fall into the coastal and lowland categories, while sites in Eastern Epirus and the High Pindus should be treated as inland, upland sites in areas unlikely to have been available for use in winter, especially during periods of glacial climate.

Epirus site distributions

General features

If we first examine the distribution of sites as a whole, there are some striking patterns. First, there are concentrations of sites, as well as some quite extensive gaps in distribution (Fig. 27.1). The major concentrations are in the northern part of Eastern Epirus, in the Louros basin, and to a lesser extent in Western Epirus and on Kerkyra. It is natural to attribute this in part to the concentration of search activity in the areas close to the major excavated sites, particularly Klithi and Asprochaliko. This cannot be the whole story, however, since there are substantial numbers of sites in areas that have not been the focus of excavation, notably in the Western group. Ease of accessibility and visibility of sites may be suspected of influencing the pattern, and certainly this must be a factor for some parts of the distribution, the absence of sites in lowland Albania being an obvious case in point. Here too, however, it cannot be the whole story, because we know that some of the empty areas have been extensively surveyed, notably the areas of central Epirus between the Western and Eastern groups, and parts of the Arachthos basin.

Geological factors certainly play an influential role, since the distribution of sites at the gross scale corresponds very closely to the distribution of limestone areas, whereas the empty areas are dominated by flysch or flysch-like bedrock (Fig. 27.2). As mentioned above, and as is discussed in detail later (Sturdy *et al.*, Chapter 30), these latter areas are of intrinsically lower economic potential and attractiveness and are likely to have been much less frequently visited if at all during the Palaeolithic era. Only three sites in our sample (all Category 3) are located well within flysch areas (Fig. 27.2), Palaiosellion (Site 325), with just two worked flints, both described as Epipalaeolithic, Kalentini-Graikikon (Site 60), discovered in 1962, which yielded some flakes and a Levallois core, and Ano Kalentini (Site 22) with some flakes and a blade core. Two sites are in relatively narrow flysch zones between areas of more favourable geology, while the third is close to an upland area of limestone (Figs. 27.1 & 27.2). It may be that these represent routes of travel between relatively attractive areas of high altitude exploitation and concentrations of settlement at lower altitude. Elsewhere the flysch areas are notable for the absence of sites, even though they have been criss-crossed by competent observers, and even when they are close to limestone areas with concentrations of sites, as in the north of our study zone in the upper Kalamas and *individual earthquakes that are the local expression of crustal deformation. Greece is tectonically one of the most active regions in the world and an investigation of the regional tectonics is fundamental to an understanding of land use in Epirus, setting the scene for other sorts of environmental processes, and affecting human activities at a variety of scales. At both extremes, the very small scale short-term on the one side, and the very large scale long-term on the other, tectonic activity appears mostly destructive from the human point of view, destroying whole villages in a single earthquake at one extreme, and whole landscapes at the other. One interesting point made in this chapter, however, is that at intermediate time-scales of relevance to the Palaeolithic period, tectonic activity may in fact be constructive, creating and sustaining stable local landscapes that are particularly attractive for human settlement.*

Another important point concerns the relationship between erosion and land use. Many of the badlands landscapes visible today are often blamed on over-exploitation by domestic goats — goats, as it were, are seen as the cause or the trigger of overexploitation. A long-term perspective informed by tectonics, however, suggests that the badlands landscapes are primarily the result of underlying tectonic instability and that goat grazing is a response to an already degraded landscape that cannot be made use of in any other way — in effect it is the erosion that 'causes' the goat grazing.

Chapter 29 looks at the contrasts and comparisons between local and regional vegetation histories, using the evidence from pollen cores at Lake Tseravinas in the region of Klithi and Lake Ziros in the Louros Valley near Kokkinopilos. This work extends the temporal and geographical range of the pollen results from Gramousti and Rezina (Chapter 20). As with other sorts of studies, however, the benefits of expanding the range of focus are offset by costs in the form of loss of resolution. Gramousti and Rezina are small basins which give the most locally specific results and the best chronological resolution, and are thus the ones most relevant to human land use within the exploitation territory of Klithi. But by virtue of being small intermontane basins they also have the shortest sequences. The Ioannina Lake diagram, most recently studied by Tzedakis (1993; 1994) is at the other extreme, a large basin with a regional pollen catchment which gives a more generalized picture of regional vegetation and the poorest dating control but by far the longest sequence available in the region. Tseravinas and Ziros are somewhere in the mid-range of this spectrum. One of the most important results of this chapter is to show the considerable geographical variation in vegetational histories within the region. The Ziros diagram, though not well-dated, appears to show that lowland Epirus was more wooded than the contemporaneous hinterland at the time of occupation of Klithi. Another theme touched on in this chapter is the relationship between vegetational history and geological processes of landscape evolution. For most of the Pleistocene, absence of woodland has been the norm in upland Epirus, except in isolated refugia, because of cold and dry climates, and this has been an important factor in the massive erosion of sediments visible as Quaternary fans and river terraces. Erosion on this scale has been the norm throughout the Pleistocene, a fact that puts into perspective modern worries about erosion caused in recent millennia by human deforestation.

Chapter 30 presents a comprehensive application of techniques of site territorial analysis to the principal Palaeolithic sites of Epirus, making use of information on animal behaviour and geological and vegetational change at the local and regional scale, and attempting reconstructions of animal distributions across the whole region as well as locally within arbitrarily defined site exploitation territories. This provides important results on the relationship between local and regional patterns of land use, on the relationship between environments and resources potentially available for use and those actually selected, on issues of site location and selection, on patterns of seasonal movement, and on the likely size of the Palaeolithic population. Seasonal movements of herd animals between coastal lowlands and the upland hinterland emerge unscathed as a primary factor in the regional pattern, much as originally conceived by Higgs et al. *(1967), but the human response to this pattern is shown to involve a greater degree of selectivity than might be implied by a simple notion of environmental determinism. The results also highlight the variability in the size of the human groups and the economic functions associated with the different Palaeolithic sites of the region, as well as pointing to underlying similarities in site selection.*

Chapter 31 brings to the fore the nature of the dynamic relationships between people, animals and plants, combining information on modern behaviour and ecology with computer simulation to model interactions over time. One important result is to show that the risk of overpredation is very low where plants and animals are patchily distributed in a complex topography like that of Epirus. This not only knocks out one of the central props of the Higgsian notion of a 'close man–animal relationship' (Chapter 1), but also suggests that an element of meta-selection (i.e. selection operating on larger entities than that of the individual organism or gene) may be in operation. Such a concept smacks of group selection, anathema to the neo-Darwinian synthesis of evolution (itself a notoriously reductionist theory which makes no concession to differences of scale), but nevertheless emerges as a viable concept on an expanded time-scale. This model is then used to make predictions about the likely responses of regional populations to palaeogeographical and vegetational changes and hence to predict changes in the pattern of archaeological site distributions at different time periods. This highlights the now-submerged coastal plain as a key unknown.

Finally Chapter 32 returns to a theme which was one of the starting points for the original Epirus investigations, the use of modern patterns of seasonal transhumance to interpret Palaeolithic patterns of site distribution (Chapter 1). This chapter highlights political, social and perceptual variables and is written by a social anthropologist who is ipso facto *predisposed to be sceptical about long-term environmental determinism. The proximate stimulus to this investigation was the work of the project on the geological history of erosion and hence an interest in the response of the modern population to a geomorphologically active environment. As recounted here, the modern inhabitants of rural Epirus appear not to recognize or be affected by the badlands erosion that so impresses visiting archaeologists and geologists. Nevertheless their experience, however mediated by cultural and social factors, embodies an awareness of physical factors in the landscape, and interesting continuities do emerge to link the present and the past. These are not so much similarities in patterns of seasonal movement, but are rather similarities in the way in which mobility at a variety of scales acts to maintain continuity in the face of instabilities in the environment, whether physical, social or political.*

Chapter 28

The Tectonic Background to the Epirus Landscape

Geoff King, Derek Sturdy & Geoff Bailey

The subject of Tectonics deals with the deformation of the Earth's crust and mantle and is commonly associated with studies of plate motions at the largest scale — the collision and separation of continents, the creation of ocean basins, and the building of mountains — processes which are generally considered to happen too slowly to have a significant impact on landscape change in the Quaternary period or on the human time-scale. Even the most rapid manifestations of crustal change such as volcanoes and earthquakes are generally treated as having temporary or largely negative or neutral effects on human activity (Hardy *et al.* 1991a,b,c; Moseley 1983; Moseley & Feldman 1988).

We believe that this assumption of a stable landscape, which changes only in response to climatically or humanly induced changes of vegetation and soil cover, is misleading. The rapidly expanding field of 'Neo-Tectonics' has produced a growing body of evidence that uplift or subsidence involving relative vertical displacements of tens to hundreds of metres can occur on late Quaternary and even historical time-scales. Moreover, tectonic movements are not only negative in impact, but can sometimes have beneficial effects, periodically renewing the fertility of volcanic soils in the case of repeated volcanic eruptions, for example, or sustaining fertile sediment basins and barriers to animal movements that can be turned to human advantage in areas of tectonic subsidence or uplift (Bailey *et al.* 1993; King & Bailey 1985; King *et al.* 1994). Such considerations apply with particular force in Greece, which has rates of earthquake activity amongst the highest in the world.

Greece is tectonically active as a result of ongoing plate motions in southeast Europe and the Mediterranean (Fig. 28.1). Most of Greece is undergoing long-term extension and subsidence as a result of subduction along the Hellenic arc, while Epirus is undergoing long-term compression and uplift. Estimates of overall rates of movement vary, but deformation rates of 3–4 cm yr^{-1} occur, comparable to strike–slip movement in California. This large-scale deformation associated with repeated movements on faults results in relative vertical displacement, with areas of uplift adjacent to subsidence, at all scales, from the very local (a single earthquake can result in a vertical displacement of 1 m or more on either side of a fault extending over a horizontal distance of some kilometres) to the regional scale (the system of mountain ridges and valley basins that characterizes the regional topography). In much of the Aegean the major faults are either nearly east–west, creating features such as the Gulf of Corinth or Euboea, or more north–south to produce the fingers of the Pelopponese or Chalkidiki. Motion on these major features is largely pure extension with little strike–slip motion. In the west, in Acharnania, substantial right lateral strike–slip appears which continues northwards into Epirus. The region of Epirus, however, is compressional.

It is these tectonic processes that have shaped the long-term geological evolution of the region, and which are responsible for the topographic complexity and spatial diversity of the regional landscape. They also create an inherent instability in the landscape, which can initiate erosion, or accentuate climatically or humanly induced tendencies to erosion on relatively short time-scales and in relatively restricted localities.

Our aim in this chapter is to outline the tectonic processes which have operated in the past and which continue to operate today on what is now the central and eastern Mediterranean to produce the landscapes from which prehistoric humans had to obtain their living.

Issues of scale

Tectonic processes can be examined at a series of different scales. At the largest scale we discuss the whole Mediterranean region. In Triassic times, 200 million years ago, the Atlantic Ocean did not exist — or was a very narrow seaway — and the Tethyan Ocean, more than 4000 km from north to south, lay between land areas that are now parts of Europe and Africa. Limestones, a major rock-type, found throughout the Mediterranean were deposited in shallow regions of this ocean and were uplifted to form land as the Tethyan Ocean slowly closed and Africa and Europe converged. At a smaller scale, more rapid motion has taken place, with some small plates moving at speeds exceeding 10 cm yr^{-1}. Many of these smaller plates in our region can be viewed, rather simplistically, as squeezed between the larger plates of Africa and Europe, with relatively complex motions as a result. The compression of the Epirus mountains or the stretching of the Aegean basin result mainly from motion at this secondary smaller scale. Rapid uplift and subsidence of land are also related to motion of the smaller plates. Elevation of land above sea level initiates erosion, and detritus is deposited in the surrounding seas. This is the origin of the flysch, which, uplifted in its turn, forms the second ubiquitous rock type of the Mediterranean. We shall see that the distribution of limestone and flysch has a major influence on potential land use.

At a smaller scale again, local landscapes can be influenced by tectonic activity, particularly in plate boundary regions. At scales of 5 to 50 km, motion can be very rapid, and uplift or subsidence of 100 m is possible within historic times. It is easy to see that tectonic uplift can destroy an environment by triggering erosion but active deformation is by no means always negative in effect. Tectonic subsidence can create well-watered sediment traps and the accumulation of fertile soils. Uplift and subsidence also create natural barriers to animal movement that can be exploited by humans. It is interesting to note that many early prehistoric sites are in regions of tectonic activity; the East African Rift Valley, North Africa, the Levant, and Sub-Himalayan India are obvious examples. There is a discovery factor here. Tectonically

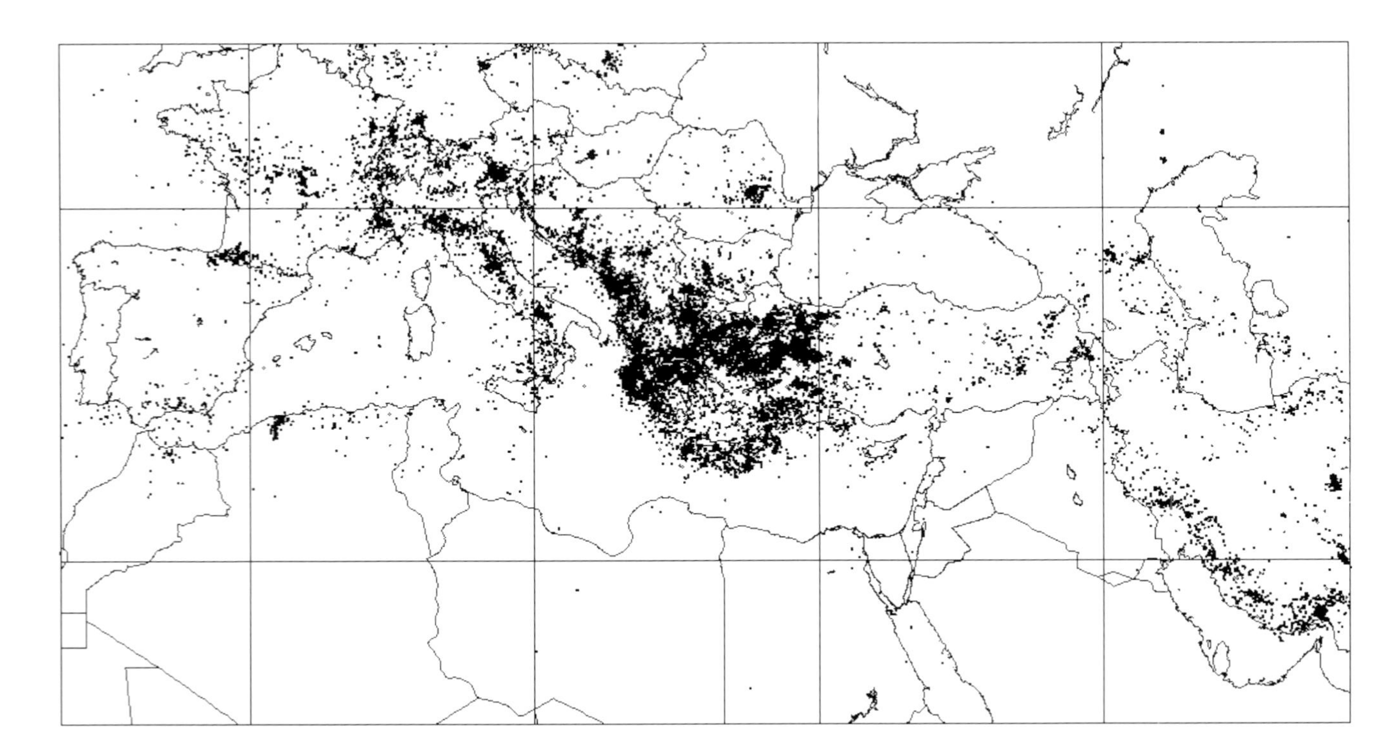

Figure 28.1. *Seismicity map of the Mediterranean region plotted from data compiled by the National Earthquake Information Center of the US Geological Survey, showing all events above magnitude 4 between 1970 and 1989. Since small earthquakes are only reliably located where there is a good network of local stations, the total number of epicentres does not necessarily reflect activity. Thus France, where a large number of small events are well located, is not more active than East Africa, where no small events are well recorded. Nevertheless, seismicity does indicate on-going tectonic deformation, and any region where epicentres appear certainly experiences deformation with rates that may be archaeologically significant.*

active areas are often those most likely to develop thick, rapidly formed sequences of terrestrial sediments in which conditions for both fossilization and discovery of early archaeological sites are favourable. But sometimes the reverse is true, and tectonically active regions ensure the destruction or burial of human evidence within a few centuries at most. In our discussion of Epirus, we shall touch on some of the reasons why a correlation between tectonic activity and landscapes attractive to early prehistoric human settlement is to be expected.

The closure of the Tethyan Ocean

Figure 28.2 outlines the evolution of the Mediterranean. The upper figure corresponds to Triassic times about 200 million years ago, the central figure to the Eocene about 50 million years ago and the lower figure to the present. The location of pieces of the present coastline at earlier times provides a guide to relative motions and rotations. The sections of coast are fragmentary because in many places so much deformation has occurred that the relationship between past and present coastlines is unidentifiable. No part of the Greek coast, for instance, could be identified 200 million years ago. The present day configuration of smaller plates is shown in the lower figure. The boundaries of small plates at earlier times are hard to identify unless they were associated with subduction. Subduction is the process that occurs when an oceanic plate collides with a continental plate. The oceanic plate consists of denser rocks which are dragged beneath the continental crust and sink back into the underlying mantle. When continental plates collide, neither can be fully subducted and their edges crumple. The subduction process is important in Mediterranean tectonics because it appears to be forces associated with subduction that drive the motion of the smaller plates.

Detail in Figure 28.2 is locally speculative but the broad features are correct. In the Triassic, land areas of the European plate lay to the north and land associated with the African plate to the south. Parts of the intervening region consisted of shallow sea floor upon which limestone was deposited, and a few small areas above sea level shed material that formed detrital rocks. The region that was destined to become Greece was partly attached to southern Europe and partly to what is now the Adriatic and surrounding areas. The creation of the Tethyan Ocean effectively ceased around Triassic times, though spreading at a mid-ocean ridge is possible. The subduction of ocean crust and associated vulcanism and mountain building was certainly occurring near to the northern boundary of the ocean at this time.

For the rest of the Mesozoic and into the early Tertiary, limestones continued to be deposited in shallow parts of the Tethyan Ocean but subduction processes and the emergence of land above sea level, particularly in the northern part of the ocean, resulted in increasing amounts of flysch deposition. Over what is now northwest Greece, limestone was deposited until about the end of the Eocene. A knowledge of the origin of the rocks can help us to understand the nature of their modern erosion products. On the limestone today, small pockets of red beds, apparently composed of wind-blown material of African origin, have perplexed workers in this region and elsewhere in the Mediterranean. There are serious difficulties with assuming that these deposits arrived as recent (Quaternary), wind-borne dust, not least because of the amazing selectivity with which the air-borne particles seem to have landed only upon the limestone. This difficulty disappears if we recall that it is not only today that

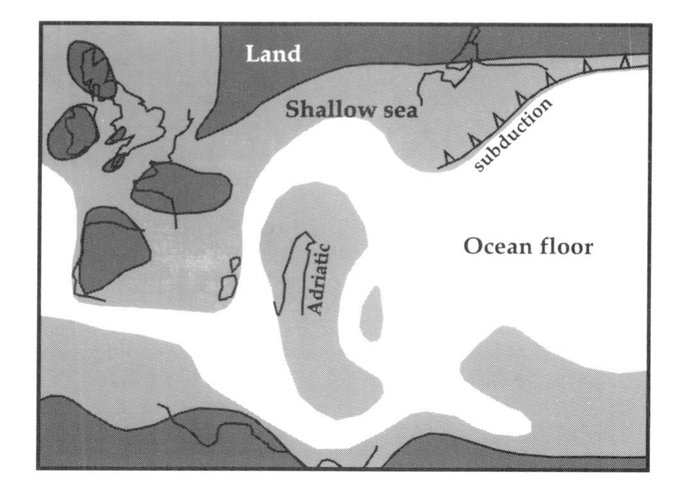

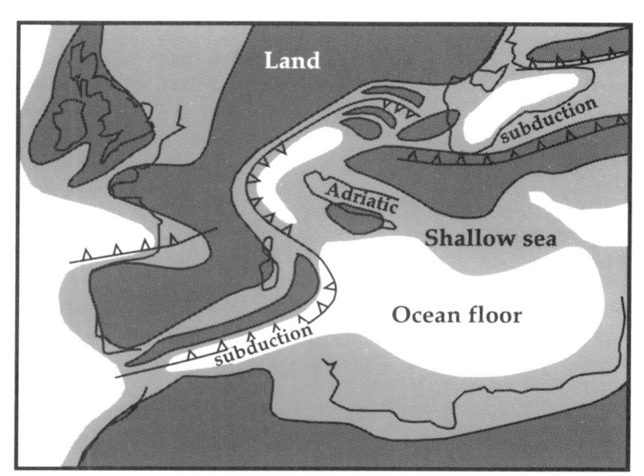

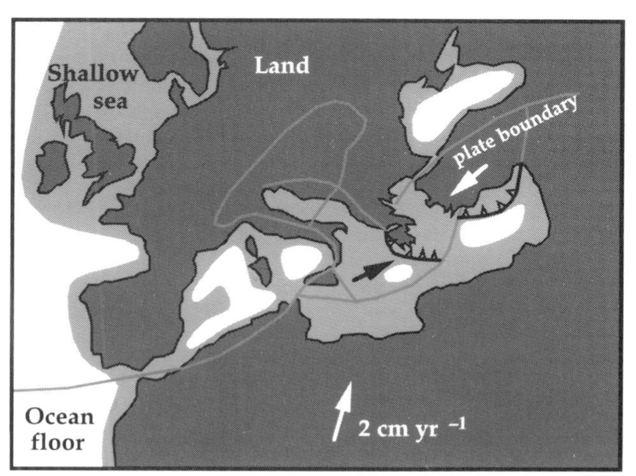

Figure 28.2. *The evolution of the Tethyan Ocean. Land areas are shown dark, deep ocean floor white, and shallow water or continental shelves are given light shading. Upper: 200 million years ago. Middle: 50 ma. Lower: present-day. (Simplified from Biju-Duval* et al. *1977.)*

wind-borne dust occurred. Over the large period of time when the Tethyan Ocean floor was accumulating limestone, its surface would have received air-borne particles which would eventually become embodied in the ooze, exactly as in parts of the modern oceans (Pye 1987, 171). When the limestone dissolves during modern weathering, this insoluble residue reappears, and forms a component, and in some places the major component, of the red beds.

By 50 million years ago the geography had changed substantially. The land mass of Europe still lay to the north and Africa to the south, but the total area of ocean floor was substantially reduced. Apparently by this time all of the original ocean floor of the Tethyan Ocean had disappeared by subduction. The area of new ocean floor between Africa and the rotated Adriatic unit was created by sea floor spreading in the preceding 150 million years ago. Small areas of deep water persisted north of this unit and separated it from the European land mass. The deposition of limestone was still widespread but with the emergence of more land and associated sub-aerial erosion, flysch was becoming more prevalent, notably in the area that was to become Greece. The flysch now found in northwest Greece is of early Tertiary age and reflects the change from an oceanic to a continental margin position, and detrital rocks continued to form in shallow seas close to the land margins through the Neogene. Subduction systems operated in a number of places adding volcanic and plutonic material.

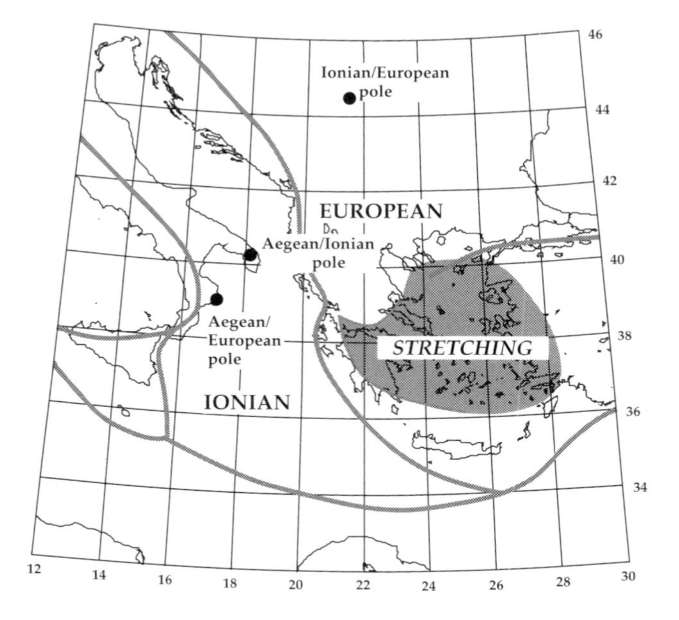

Figure 28.3. *Plate boundaries and poles of rotation for the central Mediterranean. Plate boundaries are shown as narrow zones but can be wider whereas the zone of stretching in the Aegean is actually composed of many localized stretching features. The poles shown are those relevant to motion at the plate boundaries of northwest Greece.*

Active deformation of the Central Mediterranean

The trends of the last 200 million years continue today. Limestone sedimentation still persists but many marine areas are within reach of sediments of terrestrial origin. In this chapter, following King *et al.* (1993), we describe the current active tectonics in terms of the movement of small plates and interactions at their boundaries. This approach is by no means universally accepted under all circumstances and not all authors consider the boundaries between small plates to be well enough defined for a plate description to be useful. For example, stretching in the Aegean can be viewed as a broad zone of diffuse deformation. However, closer examination shows that deformation is concentrated on the boundaries of several smaller blocks. Often apparently diffuse motion on a large scale can be resolved as plate or block motion on a small scale and thus the distinction between the two is a secondary effect of the scale at which the deformation is examined. For the purposes of relating tectonics to archaeological problems in northwest Greece such interesting questions are not of major importance; a plate description is adequate and has the virtue of clarity.

The motion of a plate in two dimensions can be considered descriptively to have two components. One is the displacement of one plate relative to another plate, and the other is the rotation of a plate about an axis. Both these concepts can be handled by one convention, that of a single pole of rotation located either within or outside the plate. Known as Euler's theorem, this is the correct general way to describe the motion of a plate or cap restricted to move on the surface of a sphere. Three poles are shown (Fig. 28.3): the Aegean–Ionian pole, the Aegean–European pole, and the Ionian–European pole.

In Figure 28.4, we show the significance of these poles for the areas of the plate boundaries. The Aegean–Ionian boundary (28.4a) is associated with very active subduction; rates range from some 3 cm yr^{-1} near Levkas to 6 cm yr^{-1} south of Crete. The Aegean–European boundary (Fig. 28.4b) is more diffuse, and is extensional, with a rate of movement of about 2.5 cm yr^{-1} near the entrance to the Gulf of Corinth and 5 cm yr^{-1} towards western Turkey. Motion in northwest Greece is defined by the Ionian–European pole and, at the longitude of the entrance to the Gulf of Amvracia, its rate is some 1.5 cm yr^{-1}. The variation in rates is clear from a consideration of the suggested geometry of the poles of rotation.

The tectonic style of the various regions is a corollary of the type of motion. Subduction of the Ionian plate beneath the Aegean plate is associated with rapid local uplift in areas such as Levkas, Kefallinia, Zakinthos and Crete, quite sufficient to create major changes in historical times. Other symptoms of the collision process are major earthquakes on reverse faults (vertical fault motions associated with compression of the crust) and seismicity related to the slab of old Ionian ocean floor which descends, at about 45°, nearly as far as the region of Athens. The active volcanoes of the Aegean area all represent light elements that have abandoned the subducted slab as it heats up in the mantle, and have risen to the surface. In the Aegean basin, the compression near the arc gives way further north or east to extension as an expression of the relative Aegean–European motion. The Gulf of Corinth and the Gulf of Euboea take up this motion as major rift features. Substantial uplift and subsidence have occurred in these regions in historical times. In western Greece near the Gulf of Amvracia, a strike–slip component (horizontal fault motions) appears, so that the structures do not have a simple character. In northwest Greece, the focus of study in this book, the main component of the motion is compressional but there is a substantial element of strike–slip motion.The Gulf of Amvracia lies at the junction of three plates, the European, Ionian and Aegean, and it is this location at a triple junction that explains its character and morphology — and its potential importance to humans and herbivores at various stages of the past (Sturdy *et al.*, Chapter 30).

south of our study area and is undergoing long-term extension rather than compression, but the principles remain the same.

Gulf of Corinth

As a result of the 1981 earthquake sequence much is known about the eastern Gulf of Corinth (see Vita-Finzi & King 1985 and references therein). Three events with magnitudes greater than six produced vertical motion over a wide region, one of the most spectacular being the subsidence of a chapel on the Perachora peninsula. At the time of the Corinth earthquake this part of the coast sank by 1.0 m. Dramatic vertical movements can happen quickly with potentially dramatic impact. Changes of this sort that have affected the archaeological and historical record have been documented by Vita-Finzi & King (1985). At a longer time-scale we now have good geological data on the series of natural erosional terraces on the south side of the Gulf of Corinth studied most recently by Armijo *et al.* (1995) from

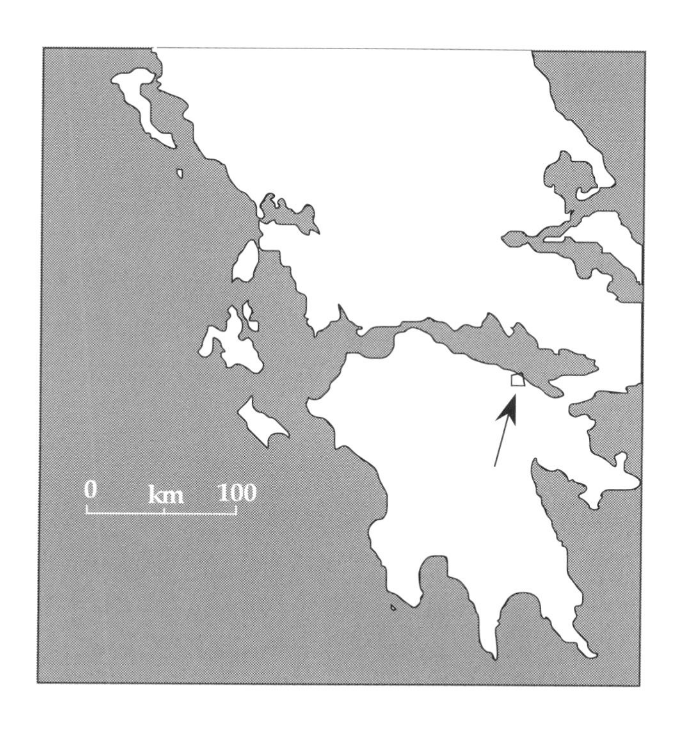

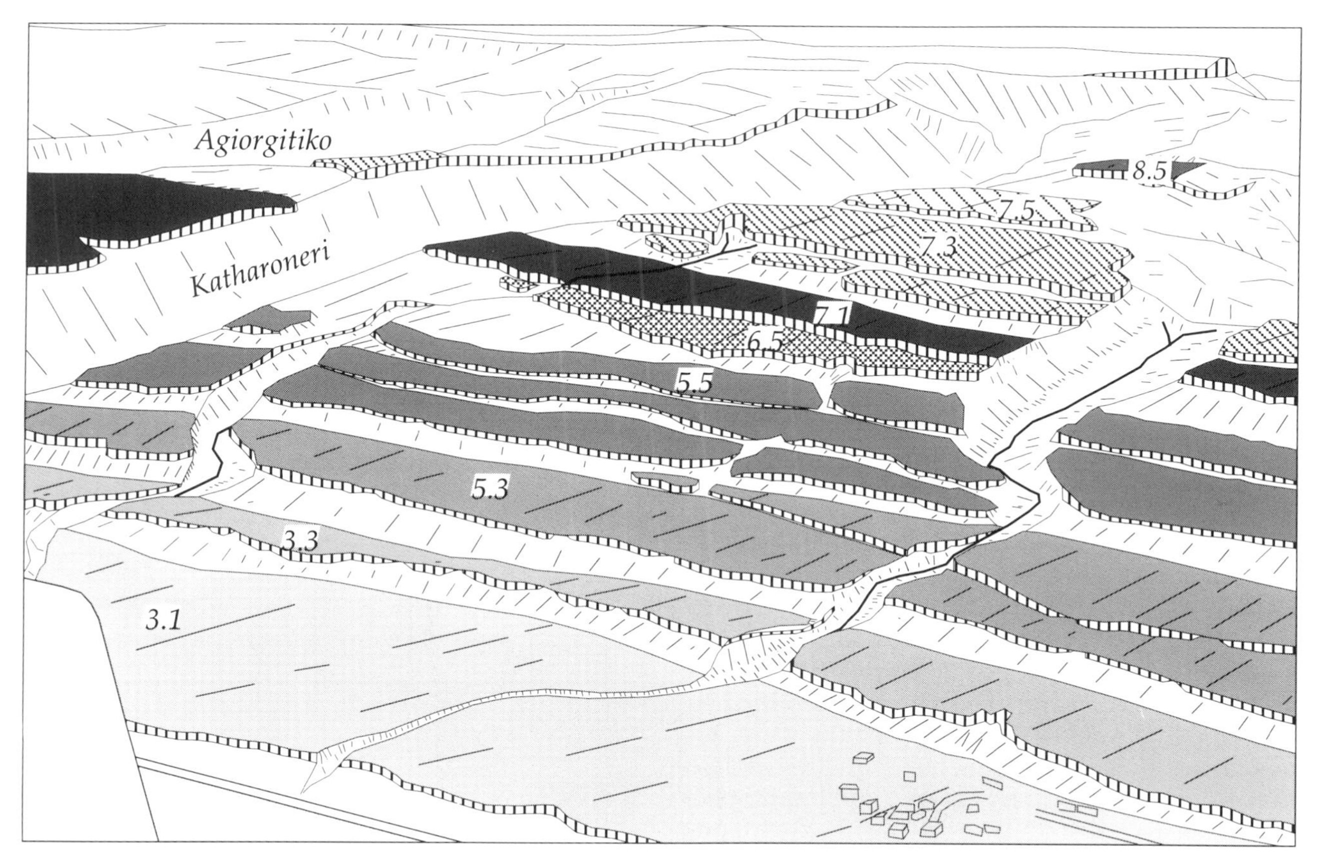

Figure 28.8b. *An interpretation of Figure 28.8a with the terraces identified (after Armijo* et al. *1996). For location in the Gulf of Corinth, see arrowed box in inset (above).*

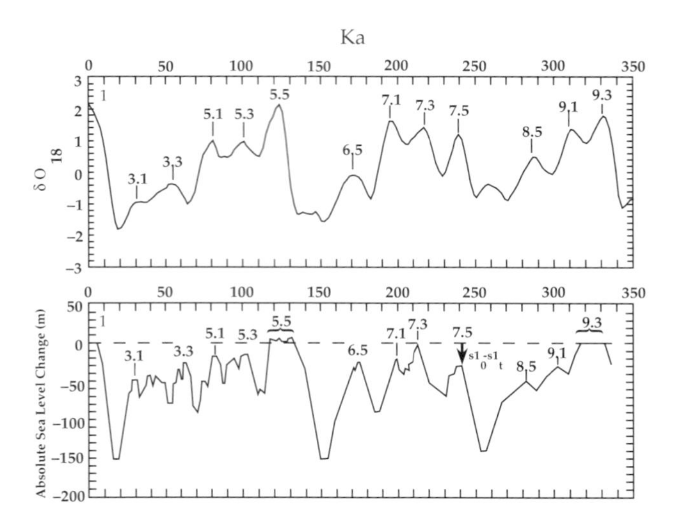

Figure 28.9. *Oxygen isotope series for ocean cores together with associated sea levels and Corinth terraces. (After Chappell & Shackleton 1986.)*

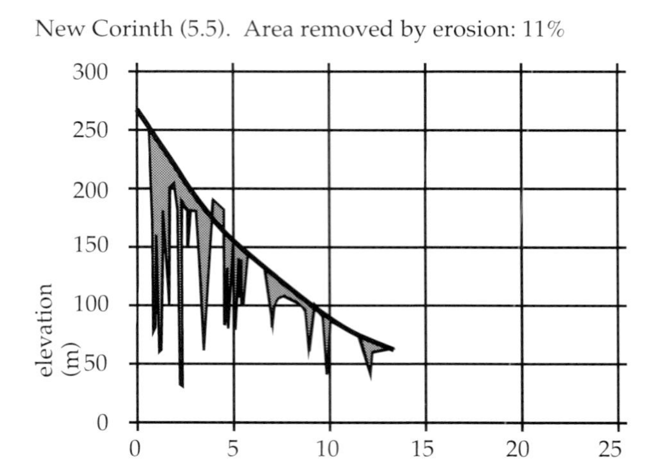

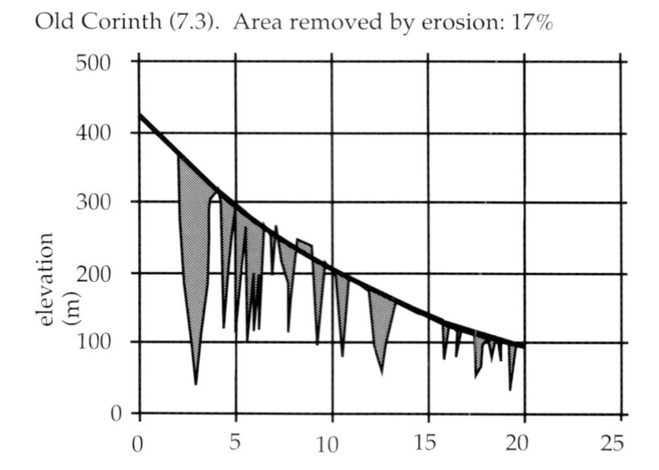

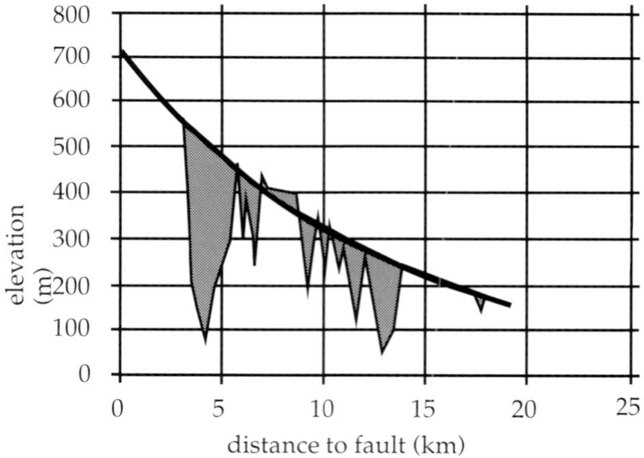

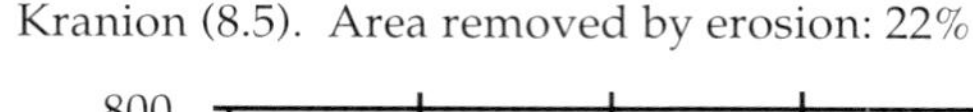

Figure 28.10. *Degrees of erosion for terraces of different ages. This ranges from 22 per cent for the Kranion terrace with an age of 280 ka to 11 per cent for the New Corinth terrace with an age of 120 ka.*

which the following description is adapted. These have been formed at successive periods of high sea-level. Because the area is undergoing progressive uplift associated with the faulting on the south side of the Gulf, the shelves created at each successive period of high sea-level form a staircase (Fig. 28.8). This sequence can be calibrated by comparison with the dated sequence of sea-level stands produced by Chappell & Shackleton (1986) from radiometric dates on uplifted terraces on the Huon peninsula in New Guinea in conjunction with the independently dated deep-sea oxygen isotope record (which is, in effect, a record of relative sea-level change) (Fig. 28.9). The resulting rate of cumulative uplift is about 1.5 mm yr^{-1}, and the fault rate, allowing for isostatic effects (that is the relative displacement of blocks on either side of a fault, allowing for subsequent readjustment as a result of the delayed response of the underlying mantle) is about 1 cm yr^{-1}.

In this region of the Gulf of Corinth uplift rates are consequently known with considerable accuracy. In Figure 28.8, the steep downcutting in many places, associated with dramatic gullying and destruction of agricultural land, is precisely correlated with uplift over the last 300 ka. This can be quantified in detail and Figure 28.10 shows the amount of erosion for terraces of different ages. It is unquestionable that all the land degradation and rapid and spectacular erosion is directly associated with active faulting. Where there is no active faulting, landscapes are stable. There is no circularity in this argument for the Corinth region, since the nature and the rate of tectonic motion is not inferred from the active erosion.

Tectonics and erosion in Epirus

In Epirus the relationship between tectonic movement and erosion is less clear-cut, because the active fault structures that have been mapped are largely identified by mapping areas of active erosion, using such evidence as recent landslides, uplifted river terraces, and the like, evidence that can in theory be attributed to non-tectonic processes such as climatic change or overexploitation by human economies. There is thus a risk of circular argument, in which tectonic activity is identified by the presence of erosion (or sedimentation), which in its turn is attributed to the tectonic activity. This problem arises because the major active fault structures in Epirus are associated with deformation distributed by multiple faulting and folding across uplifted and unstable ridges typically 3 to 5 km wide. Simple single fault strands accommodating all or most of the deformation cannot be found. Small active faults can be located, but their relation to overall deformation across the major features is obscure. Furthermore, in an uplifted and uniformly erosional environment little is available to record and date displacements. The fault structures that are easily visible at the surface today, and which abound on the published geological maps, are easily identifiable precisely because they represent a much more ancient pattern of tectonic activity — one which may differ from the Quaternary or recent one — and have become visible because the overlying deposits have been stripped away by erosion.

Disentangling alternative hypotheses of landscape change is of vital importance not only to the reconstruction of the Palaeolithic landscape but to an understanding of the dynamics of landscape change and their impact on land use at all periods including the present day. It is tempting, for example, to attribute the extensive badlands erosion in the flysch basins to overgrazing by domestic goats in the Holocene, and thus to suppose that in the Pleistocene period there existed uneroded grazing basins much more attractive to animals than today. If, however, our reconstruction of tectonic processes is correct, the badlands erosion of the flysch basins would have been as much a feature of the Pleistocene as of the present day, and the presence of goats there in recent periods is not the cause of the erosion but an adaptation of the animal economy to an area which cannot be used for food production in any other way. Distinguishing between tectonics, climate and humans is made more complicated by the fact that these three variables may interact with each other. Tectonic activity, for example, may create an underlying instability which is triggered or accentuated by climatically-induced or humanly-induced tendencies to erosion, such as a reduction in tree cover (Turner & Sánchez-Goñi, Chapter 29).

Two ways of breaking out of the potential circularity of argument noted above have been applied; large-scale modelling of tectonic processes and small-scale detailed geological analysis of specific localities. The modelling, described in more detail below, makes use of known constraints, such as the expected regional consistency of plate motions and the readily mapped geometry of major structures (to some extent identified by active erosion) to predict the location of secondary areas of uplift and secondary areas of subsidence, the latter particularly amenable to dating (King *et al.* 1993). It produces patterns that are close to those identified on the ground. Were the erosional features used to identify active structures distributed randomly, or in relation to factors other than tectonics, there should be no such correspondence.

The geological approach focuses on particular localities of erosion in detail, using a variety of geological and dating techniques, in order to distinguish between alternative hypotheses of erosion and to give greater precision to estimates of rates of change. The most promising areas for this purpose are the middle Kalamas basin (which includes the Doliana basin and Lake Tseravinas in the northern area), and the Kokkinopilos area in the middle Louros Valley (which includes the adjacent Ziros Lake and the Tsiropolis deposits). Both areas are close to key Palaeolithic sites, and have been the focus of intensive geological and palynological investigation, some of the results of which are reported here (see also Turner & Sánchez-Goñi, Chapter 29).

Modelling active deformation

Simple extension and contraction can explain some features of northwest Greece but others cannot be explained so simply. The Gulf of Amvracia is hard to account for as a simple transition between primarily compressional and extensional regimes, and the contractional limestone ridges of Epirus are not continuous, but are punctuated by local regions of extension and subsidence (Fig. 28.6). Our interpretation of these structures in the field is that they accommodate strike–slip motion as well as regional compression or extension, and that this explains why there is a correlation between offsets in the major features and local areas of vertical motion.

The relationship between plate motions, structures, and areas of uplift and subsidence observed in the field, can be modelled using a technique developed by Bilham & King (1989). King *et al.* (1993) show the detailed results of this new modelling method for northwest Greece. Here we offer a simplified account, which concentrates on the results rather than the steps taken to achieve them. Two preliminary points should be emphasized.

The modelling technique applied here excludes from its output the features entered as input. This prevents cluttering the results with information which we already know. When, for example, we inform the model that there is a large compressional structure, such as one of the Epirus mountains, this does not appear in the model's output, which reveals only the effects of the combinations of the structures on the areas outside the input features. The second is that the modelling does not provide accurate estimates of actual uplift or subsidence rates. On the models, the intensity of dark/black shading (subsidence) and of light/white shading (uplift) is not corrected for isostatic effects, notably the effects of erosion or accumulation of sediment. However, Bilham & King (1989) show how the rates can be expected to approximate to adjacent fault slip rates. Since many of these exceed 5 mm yr^{-1} and some exceed 10 mm yr^{-1} it is not surprising that so much change has occurred in historic times and that the changes during and since the Palaeolithic period may be very substantial. We shall first consider the Epirus region and then the Gulf of Amvracia, the southern boundary of Epirus.

In Epirus the features to be modelled are rather small in area in relation to the total landscape because the uplift and subsidence observed in the field outside the main mountain ranges are localized, though spectacular. Figure 28.11 shows the structures from Figure 28.6 represented as simple white lines, with field observations of uplift shaded white and of subsidence shaded dark. We need to bear in mind that uplift or subsidence in the field can only be identified if reasonably unequivocal evidence is available in the form of morphological phenomena. In the confused surface morphology and stratigraphy of the flysch basins, for instance, such unequivocal evidence is likely to be hard to come by. Areas of uniform grey on Figure 28.11 do not, therefore, necessarily indicate stability as a first glance at this figure might suggest. We shall briefly discuss here two examples of localities where good information on vertical motions is available, from the middle reaches of the Kalamas River (between letters A and F in Fig. 28.11), and from the Acheron River at the Gliki gap (between letters Y and X in Fig. 28.12).

The middle Kalamas contains a region of rapid uplift and associated river down-cutting (near letter D in Fig. 28.11). The Kalamas cuts through sediments to leave a 30–40 m terrace, whose upper sediments are of Holocene date according to the evidence of contained pottery and TL and C14 age determinations. The youngest dates suggests an uplift rate approaching one metre per century if we assume that the vertical displacement of the river is wholly due to tectonic movement. The terrace sediments were deposited in slow or still water but the modern river below the terraces has a steep gradient and flows in a series of rapids and waterfalls. This is one of the most spectacular examples of rapid tectonic change in Epirus. The river then flows between two ridges which rise to over 1200 m, Kasidiares and Kourenton (respectively lettered C, D, E and G, H in Fig. 28.11), using a natural gap containing local sediment fill, the Soulopoulou offset (lettered F in Fig. 28.11). This gap is not erosional, for the anticlinal structures to the north and south plunge beneath the sediments. This area is of central importance to an understanding of the regional tectonic history. It is also an area of potential significance to the Palaeolithic inhabitants of Klithi, for whom the area would have looked quite different from its modern appearance (Sturdy *et al.*, Chapter 30). We present the observed morphology briefly in order to highlight the comparison with the results of the modelling.

Our second field example is the Gliki gap, where the Acheron river flows west through a defile in the Souli and Paramythia ranges (this is the course of the Acheron between structures W–Z, and V–X in Fig. 28.11). At first sight, the behaviour of this river is even more singular than that of the Kalamas through the Soulopoulou gap, because there is a perfectly good valley running due south from the bend where it turns to the west (between letters W and Z in Fig. 28.11) from which it is blocked only by a slight uplift of soft flysch. Again terraces, here with the more modest height of 18 m and containing pottery, at the entrance to the defile through the mountains, provide valuable clues. Like the Soulopoulou gap, the Gliki gap is not erosional, and down-dropped blocks on the edges of the gap suggest it is not at all a conventional karstic gorge.

Figure 28.12 shows the areas of uplift and subsidence predicted by the modelling, which correspond well with the observations of Figure 28.11, and indicate some additional areas where field observations have either not been made or have not been possible. To the south of the figure, the two main structures trending south–southeast have been continued indefinitely to prevent bogus results caused by artificially terminating structures to fit the edge of a diagram. This means that the model cannot predict the uplift shown east of letter S on Figure 28.11, for instance. This area is modelled in the Gulf of Amvracia region discussed below.

The coincidence of areas in Figure 28.11 (field observations) and Figure 28.12 (predictive model) justifies our view that local subsidence may reasonably be expected in a region which, though broadly contractional, includes strike–slip motion, and that equally not all uplift in such a region may be attributable only to contractional processes. King *et al.* (1993) give simplified diagrams of why this should be so, since the modelling process itself gives no intuitive understanding of this particular aspect.

The conclusion from this modelling is that the uplift in the middle Kalamas basin is mainly the result of attenuation in the strike–slip component of motion on the Kasidiares structure from south to north. We should take this opportunity to observe that this corrects the view of Sturdy & Webley (1988), who correctly identified the Doliana uplifts as associated with strike–slip motion, but whose explanatory diagram incorrectly suggested changes in fault strike as the cause of the uplifts. The Soulopoulou and Gliki gaps are explained as down-drops caused by the interaction of oblique motion across structures and their offsets. The interesting point which arises from the total of the predictions against the observed field phenomena, of which only examples have been given here, is that a good fit is only possible in this case when the regional slip vector is tightly constrained within a few degrees. In the Epirus case, the modelling requires relative plate motion close to, but slightly north of, 275° East. A full discussion of the slip vectors, fault geometries, and modelling sensitivity is given by King *et al.* (1993), who conclude that a regional slip vector of 276° across Epirus gives the best fit. They show that this figure cannot be increased or decreased by more than 10°, without violating field evidence or producing models which do not bear any resemblance to modern Epirus. Slip vectors are illustrated in Figure 28.13, which shows how relative motion is accommodated by the structures of Epirus. Figure 28.13 is, of course, just a different graphical representation of the same basic calculations that produced Figure 28.12. The northeast corner of the diagram is taken as fixed and this may result in some distortion in this corner, though as the length of the arrow tails shows, this is not significant.

Figure 28.14 shows the region of the Gulf of Amvracia; the 100 metre contour approximately delineates the area of accumulation of Younger Fill (Vita-Finzi 1969; 1978) — that is, fills of historical date, though not necessarily of one episode — and the present sea. The area enclosed indicates roughly the area of subsidence. The Preveza peninsula provides a local exception on the western edge of the gulf. It is a local narrow area of uplift which produces the constricted entrance to the Gulf itself. The main structural features shown are identified by solid lines. The grey box outlines the area of the model of Figure 28.15. It will be seen

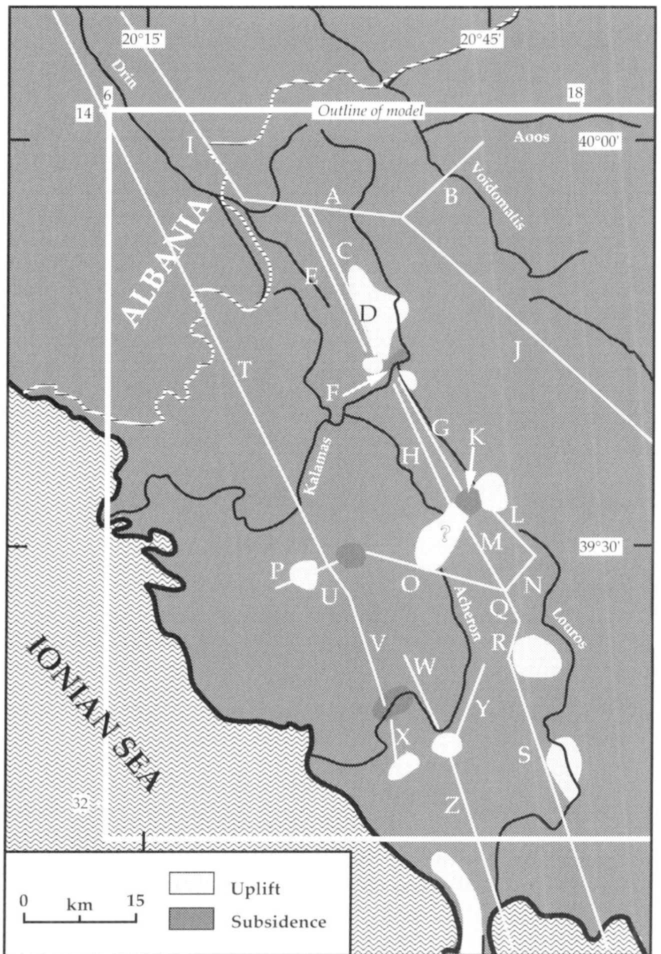

Figure 28.11. *Field observations of non-mountainous uplift and subsidence in Epirus.*

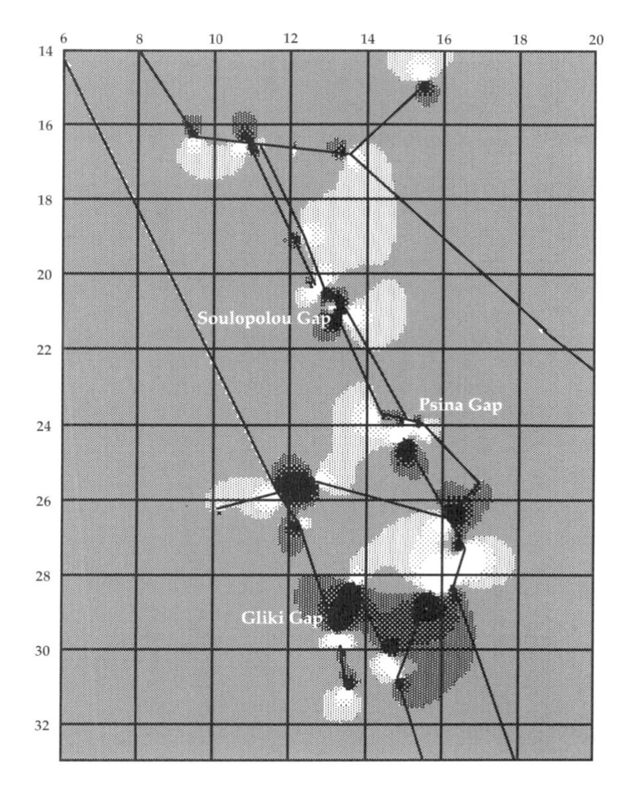

Figure 28.12. *Model of Epirus for the structures of Figure 28.5 and a regional slip vector of 276°E. White shading: predicted uplift. Dark shading: predicted subsidence.*

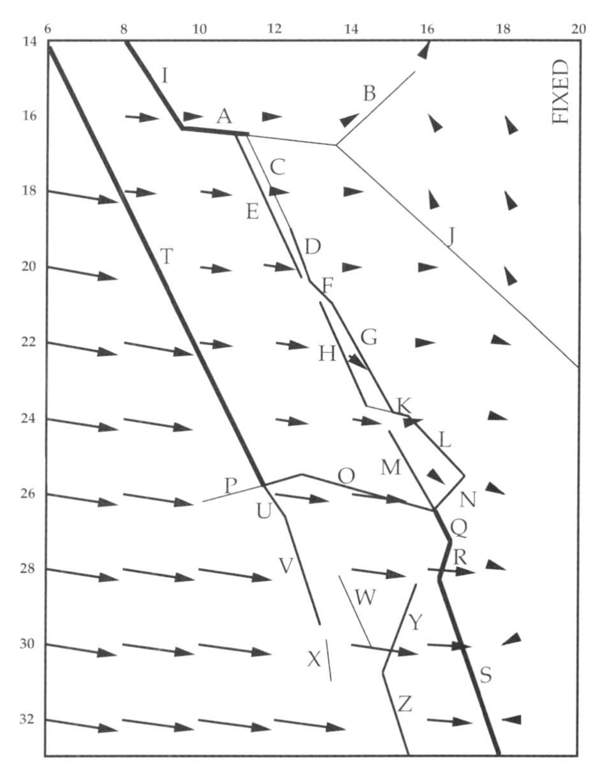

Figure 28.13. *Model of Epirus slip vectors. Data exactly as in Figure 28.12. Direction of arrows gives the direction of the slip vector. Length of arrows gives the slip vector rate (expressed as displacement per unit time). Thickness of lines delineating structures is proportional to motion accommodated.*

that four structures extend out beyond this box. Two of them, labelled Souli-Thesprotika and Pente Dendra on Figure 28.14, represent the structures from Epirus which enter the Gulf region and for the purposes of this discussion can be considered as one 'Epirus' structure. The three external faults are then the 'Epirus', Aetolia and Levkas West structures and they provide the numerical input to the model.

The Gulf of Amvracia lies at a triple plate junction as indicated earlier, and King *et al.* (1993) show how data from other workers can be combined with our results in Epirus to suggest the locations and powers of poles of rotation which describe the relative plate motions. They also tabulate directions and rates of motion of the three plates in the region of the Gulf of Amvracia, derived directly from the postulated locations and powers of the poles. We apply this numerical data to the three major faults discussed above. In this simple arrangement, the combined 'Epirus' faults take up Ionian–European motion, the Aetolia fault takes up Aegean–European motion and, completing the triangle, the Levkas West fault takes up the Ionian–Aegean motion. The other faults mapped on Figure 28.14 are, except for the Levkas North fault, recorded from field observations, and in the model we allow them to slip freely — that is, to do what the combinations of the external structures and their own inter-reactions mathematically determine. Clearly a test of this kind of model is not only that uplift and subsidence are correctly predicted but that the calculated fault motions are entirely consistent with field observations — a normal fault in the field should not, for instance, be represented by a reverse fault in the model.

The general outline of the subsidence of the Gulf of Amvracia and its northern plain predicted by the model (Fig. 28.15) is consistent with the physical data. Although small areas of light and dark shading along the Arta–Amphilochia feature (identified on Fig. 28.14) are products of the simplified method of delineating the faults, the general uplift east of the feature is significant in the modelling and real on the ground. The fit is certainly good enough to move with confidence to Figure 28.16, where again the same calculations are represented graphically as slip vector arrows. The reason for the existence of the Gulf of Amvracia can be identified from this figure. Although there is a slight southward motion of western Epirus into the Gulf, this is much less than the southward movement of Acharnania away from it. A gap inevitably forms to create the Gulf and this also explains the sudden termination of the mountains of Epirus at the northern edge of the Gulf region. The Gulf region, unlike most of Epirus, is therefore a large sediment trap as the accumulations of historical fill show; but the plate motions which create this trap have been in existence from long before the Palaeolithic period, so that the tendency for this region to accumulate sediments has always existed on the human time-scale.

The middle Kalamas

The middle Kalamas basin, referred to above, is particularly instructive, and worth further comment. It appears to have undergone at least two major episodes of uplift and erosion. During the early Pleistocene the basin was filled with a lake, and fragments of these old lake sediments are identifiable at a number of localities within the Kalamas basin and to the north at Farangi. Preliminary interpretation of pollen data from these sediments suggests a Middle Pleistocene date (at least 250 ka and possibly older) (Turner & Sánchez-Goñi, Chapter 29). Then tectonic movement, involving strike–slip motion and uplift of the Kasidiares mountain ridge along the western edge of the basin, opened up the Soulopoulou gap at the southern end of the basin, draining the lake. In recent millennia the river Kalamas has begun to cut down deeply through its pre-existing bed and the underlying lake sediments to a depth of 30 m, with a dramatic steepening of its profile, between Mazaraki and Lithinon, and indeed to re-excavate a deep and narrow limestone gorge that it first created at a much earlier stage in the evolution of the landscape (presumably some time in the Tertiary).

One possible explanation for such a change in stream behaviour is climatic change leading to increased stream competence. In the nearby Voïdomatis river valley, intensive geological investigations, have identified river terraces which reach comparable heights — up to 20 m in places — above the modern stream bed. These have been dated to the latter part of the Last Glacial period (*c.* 25 ka to 14 ka) by a combination of TL, C14 and ESR dating techniques (Macklin *et al.*, Chapter 17). In this case a climatic explanation for aggradation and subsequent incision has been proposed. Reduced precipitation and increased erosion from treeless slopes during the glacial period resulted in aggradation, while rapid reafforestation at the end of the glacial period, and increased precipitation, resulted in downcutting (Macklin *et al.*, Chapter 17). However, since the valley is crossed by two major normal faults at least one of which is known to be active (Waters 1994), underlying tectonic movements may also be implicated.

A climatic explanation, however, is inherently implausible for the high aggradation terraces of the Middle Kalamas because they are of much more recent date. An initial T/L date of 4.2 ± 0.6 ka (BM ref DOL26) (Appendix A) was subsequently confirmed by C14 dates (OxA-3942 6240 ± 70, and OxA-3943 9160 ± 80 some 5 m below DOL26), and pottery sherds are also present in the silty gravels which form the upper deposits in the terrace. Climatic changes on a scale that might account for such a sharp change of stream behaviour simply did not occur within the Holocene, while the likely direction of change resulting from increased human impact, if any, would have been towards reduced tree cover, and hence reduced stream competence and aggradation, rather than the other way about.

All indications point inexorably to tectonic uplift as the cause of river downcutting in this instance, and this is consistent with evidence which suggests that downcutting and headward erosion has continued apace within living memory — a water mill (now in ruins, but with some traces of machinery surviving to within living memory) that is now perched some 10 m above present stream level, below the village of Kataraktes, and deep, steep-sided cracks up to 40 m deep into Plio-Pleistocene gravel deposits, with resulting reworking of gravelly material that has almost buried a farm building on a small basin of Holocene fill near Riachovo and is threatening to engulf the adjacent farm land. The postulated uplift that has altered the river profile has also tilted the Doliana basin immediately to the north, resulting in the ponding back of sediment from numerous slope failures around the basin, the filling of the basin with these recent sediments, and in recent decades the development of drainage schemes and an intensive agriculture. The present-day features of the basin are thus the result of recent tectonic activity producing an environment substantially different from that in the Palaeolithic.

The Kokkinopilos area

Kokkinopilos is undoubtedly the most enigmatic of the Epirus sites and has been a source of controversy ever since it was first discovered in 1962 (Fig. 28.17). The red beds are a striking feature of the present-day landscape. They are silty red sediments up to 40 m thick, with little cover of vegetation, and are heavily dissected with especially deep and steep-sided gullies at the southern end, representing a dramatic example of badlands erosion on a local scale. They have attracted attention not least because of their archaeological associations. Palaeolithic artefacts have been found on the surfaces and eroding out of gully sections. Two locations, Site α and Site β (Fig. 28.17) were excavated by Higgs in 1963 and 1964 (Dakaris *et al.* 1964), while artefacts of later prehistoric and historical date are also scattered on the surface, notably of Bronze Age and Roman date. The aqueduct built by the Romans after the battle of Actium to bring water from the springs of Agios Giorgos, just 1 km to the northeast of Kokkinopilos, to the coastal city of Nikopolis also tunnels beneath the deposits, and remains of the ventilation shafts (*spiramina*) built by the Romans are still visible. In 1991 a complete thick-butted bifacial handaxe with an elongated point was found in a gully section (Fig. 28.17) by Runnels & Van Andel (1993a), stimulating a new round of investigation and discussion.

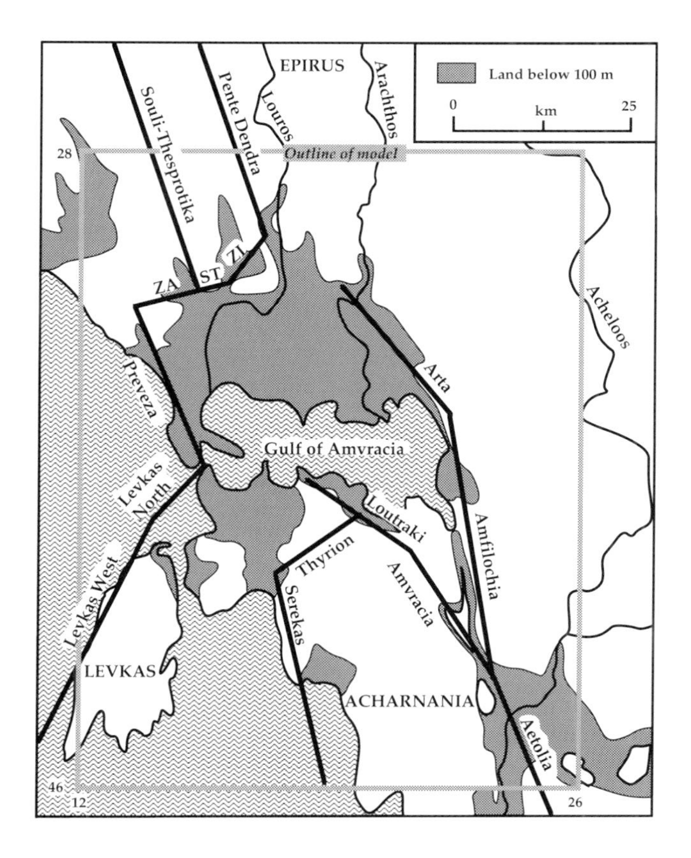

Figure 28.14. *Simplified map of the Gulf of Amvracia region. Structures from Figure 28.5. The grey rectangle indicates the area of Figure 28.15.*

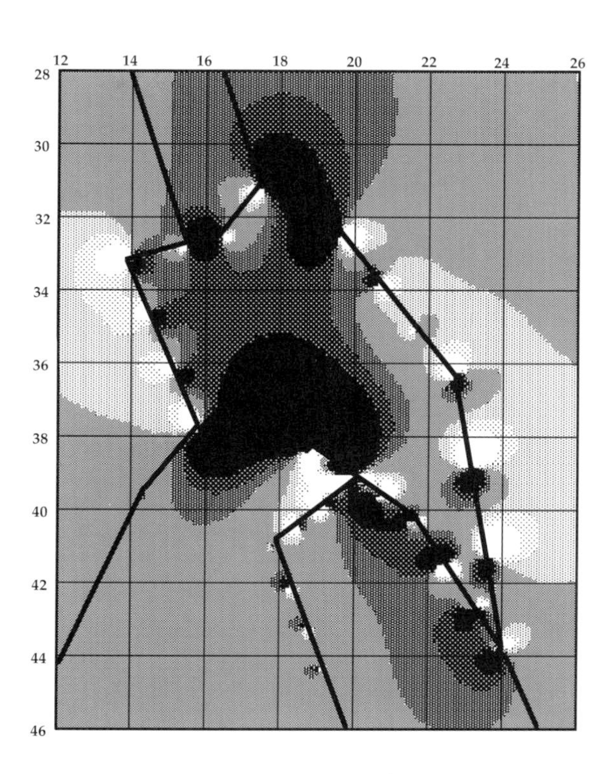

Figure 28.15. *Model of the Gulf of Amvracia for the triple plate boundary shown on Figure 28.3. White shading: predicted uplift. Dark shading: predicted subsidence.*

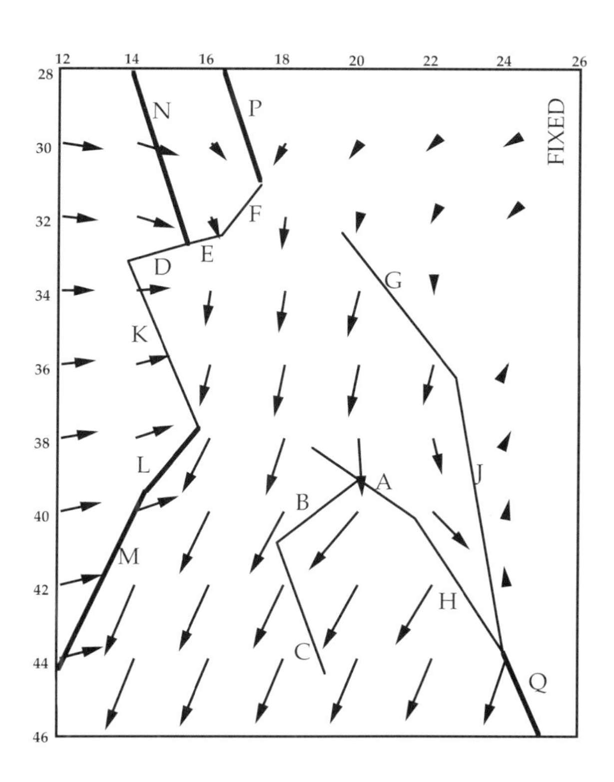

Figure 28.16. *Model of Gulf of Amvracia slip vectors. Data exactly as in Figure 28.10. Direction of arrows gives the direction of the slip vector. Length of arrows gives the slip vector rate (expressed as displacement per unit time). Thickness of lines delineating structures is proportional to motion accommodated.*

The red sediments have given rise to a variety of hypotheses about two issues: (1) the date and process of their original deposition; and (2) the date and causes of the subsequent spectacular erosion and deposition (Bailey *et al.* 1992; Dakaris *et al.* 1964; Harris & Vita-Finzi 1968; Higgs & Vita-Finzi 1966; King & Bailey 1985; Runnels & Van Andel 1993a). Geological investigations are ongoing and neither issue can be said to have been unequivocally resolved as yet. Descriptions of the sequence of sediments and palaeosols are given in Runnels & Van Andel (1993a) and Bailey *et al.* (1992). Lake Ziros, one of our principal pollen-bearing localities, is located just to the south of Kokkinopilos, and additional descriptions of the surrounding geology are given in Chapter 29.

With regard to origin, an aeolian deposition was originally favoured for three reasons: (1) the Palaeolithic artefacts found within the Kokkinopilos sediments suggested a relatively recent age geologically speaking, i.e. Middle and Upper Palaeolithic

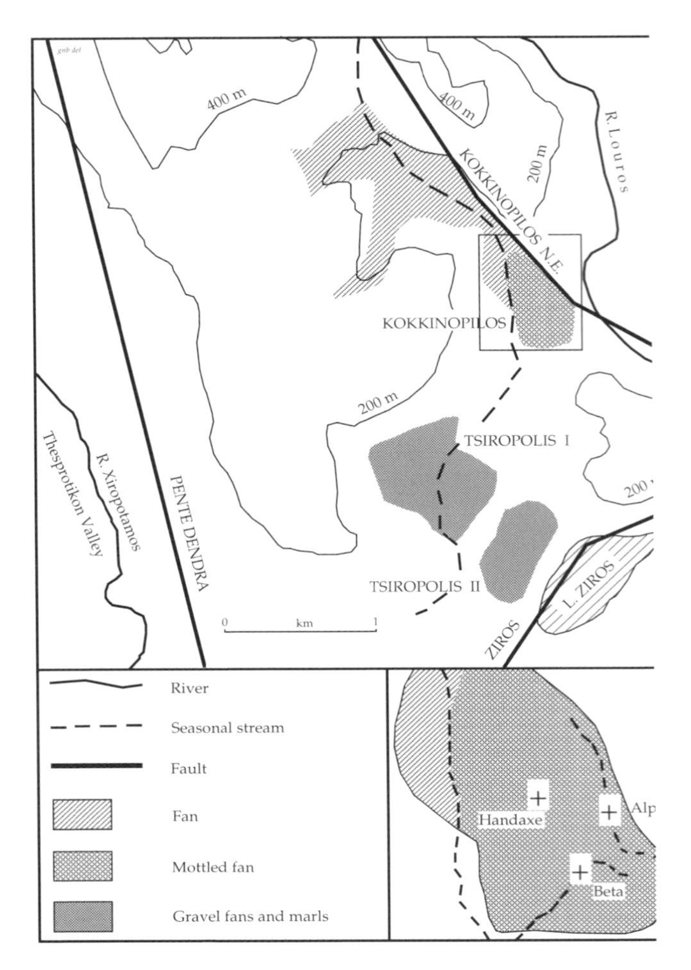

Figure 28.17. *Kokkinopilos in its local context showing distribution of deposits, location of archaeological sites and major faults.*

artefacts of broadly Last Glacial age; (2) the age of the deposits as suggested by their contained artefacts gave insufficient time for the creation of sediments from the surrounding limestone; (3) the position of the deposits on an interfluve perched above the adjacent valley systems of the River Louros and the Thesprotikon is inconsistent with water-laid deposition: in the present-day landscape, gravity and the action of water would carry away fine-grained sediments from the area as fast as they were brought in.

Although not all workers are agreed on details, and unequivocal evidence is still far from being established, the following consensus seems to be emerging. Firstly, the sediments include features typical of water-laid deposition, notably interfingering of coarser gravel material at the edges of the basin (Higgs & Vita-Finzi 1966), that make an hypothesis of a wholly aeolian deposition difficult to sustain. The fine-grained nature of the sediments indicates deposition in low energy conditions, probably as a lake or marsh rather like the nearby edge of the Arta plain, which represents a more recent manifestation of a similar process, and perhaps subject to seasonal drying out, with the addition of colluvial material at the distal edge of fans derived from adjacent slopes.

Secondly the sediments are probably of much greater age than originally believed, although absence of organic preservation and difficulties of radiometric dating preclude firm statements. This is suggested by a series of soil horizons throughout the sequence which show progressive post-depositional alteration with increasing age over a time span very considerably greater than the 100 ka of the Last Glacial, while TL dating indicates an age of greater than 150 ka (Bailey *et al.* 1992; Appendix A). Bailey *et al.* (1992) have also suggested that the artefacts recovered from the Higgs excavations of the 1960s are not genuinely *in situ* within the sediments, but were dropped on the surface after deposition had ceased, and have subsequently become incorporated in sediments because of gullying and slumping of deposit or creation of solution hollows by karstic processes.

Runnels & Van Andel (1993a) in contrast have claimed, on the basis of later discoveries and observations, that some artefacts including their handaxe find are genuinely *in situ*. These artefacts, however, are restricted to the upper levels of the sediment, and in any case it is now widely accepted that Middle Palaeolithic industries in Europe may extend back to about 200 ka, while the handaxe elements present in the collections including the complete specimen discovered by Runnels & Van Andel (1993) might fall within the range of the Middle Palaeolithic or conceivably be earlier. At any rate the notion of a greater age for the bulk of the sediments is not really affected by the issue of whether the artefacts are *in situ* or not, and with a greatly expanded chronology the problem of how to generate sufficient sediment from limestone bedrock is removed.

Finally, there is the role of tectonics both in the formation of the original deposit and in its subsequent uplift and erosion. The creation of the Kokkinopilos basin as a sediment and water trap by the uplifting anticlinal ridge of the Kokkinopilos Northeast fault follows naturally from the tectonic history outlined earlier. Continued tectonic movement has also been invoked as the underlying cause for the transformation of the basin from a sediment trap to a zone of instability and erosion.

When the transition from sediment accumulation to gullying and erosion took place is unclear. Some gullying was taking place as early as the Upper Palaeolithic, since Site α of the Higgs excavations clearly consists of unpatinated Upper Palaeolithic artefacts buried on the floor of a gully by slumping of deposit. This is consistent with Runnels & Van Andel's (1993) claim of *in situ* Mousterian artefacts near the top of the deposit. The Middle Palaeolithic artefacts at Site β also appear to have been disturbed. At the time of excavation the artefacts were found in what was believed to be an *in situ* position at the junction between a reddish lower sediment and an upper yellow sediment. Over 20 years later continued erosion, no doubt accelerated by the effect of the archaeological excavation, has greatly deepened the gully to reveal a near-vertical boundary between the red and yellow deposit. We suggest that this results from disturbance of deposit by a solution cavity which could have been caused by sub-surface karstic solution processes even while Kokkinopilos was still a basin of accumulating sediment, and that the true nature of the boundary was unclear to the original excavators because of the relatively small scale of the excavation. TL dates of >150 ka (Appendix A) offer at best some indication of a minimum age, but in any case Site β offers no clear evidence for or against the view that gullying had already begun at the time when Middle Palaeolithic artefacts were being discarded on the site, nor evidence for or against the belief that Palaeolithic artefacts elsewhere in the Kokkinopilos deposit are *in situ*.

The dramatic gullying at the southern end must post-date the construction of the aqueduct, otherwise the Roman engineers would have built their ventilation tunnels in the bottom of the gullies rather than at the tops of the adjacent ridges. Higgs (in Dakaris *et al.* 1964) refers to a local account that the major gully at the southern end had been formed within living memory, but we have not been able to corroborate this claim. Similarly we have not been able to corroborate our earlier claim (Bailey *et al.* 1992) that Kokkinopilos was used for cultivation and that erosion was inhibited by protective dams and terraces until the widespread depopulation of rural areas in the 1950s and abandonment of land used for dry cultivation. Equally there is no evidence that erosion and gullying have been caused by over-intensive land-use practices, which in any case seem an improbable cause of disturbance in Upper Palaeolithic times.

Whatever the proximate triggers of erosion — whether mechanical disturbance caused by the tunneling activities of Roman engineers, or changes of climate or of human activity — it is difficult to account for the scale of the resulting erosion without also invoking an underlying tectonically-induced vulnerability. Equally in a deposit that has been subject to prolonged tectonic disturbance and karstic activity, and slumping and gullying of deposits from a variety of causes, we think it unlikely that geological studies will provide an unequivocal stratigraphic framework for the interpretation of the archaeology. The use of the artefacts to date the geology is even less promising. At any rate, the creation of the Kokkinopilos basin as a sediment and water trap follows naturally from the tectonic history outlined above, and it is clear that the sequence of geological events cannot be understood without reference to an underlying tectonically-induced vulnerability.

Conclusions

From this overview we draw the following conclusions:

- The smaller the temporal and spatial scale of observation, the less predictable the impact of the tectonics on erosion and landscape change. On the largest scale, let us say on a time scale of millions of years for the whole of Epirus, the pattern of tectonically induced erosion is essentially stable, uniform and predictable. Mountain ridges are pushed up in the hinterland, soil is eroded from their slopes and eventually carried via a series of intermediate basins and valleys out to sea, where it forms the raw material for the uplifted mountains in the next stage of the cycle. On the smaller scale of hundreds of thousands of years in particular sub-regions, we observe divergent but generally predictable patterns due to the variation in tectonic activity in different parts of the Epirus landscape. Both the Kalamas basin and the Ioannina basin, for example, were major lakes in the Middle Pleistocene. However, whereas the Ioannina basin has remained a lake, the Kalamas lake basin has been drained and transformed into a very different landscape because of the effects of strike–slip motion in that part of the Epirus landscape. On a smaller scale again, ranging from tens of thousands to thousands of years in individual basins, we observe increasingly divergent and less easily predictable patterns, subject to multifarious causes including climatic and anthropogenic interactions. For example, within the past one to two millennia, the Doliana basin was filling up with sediment while the Kokkinopilos basin was being subjected to rather dramatic episodes of erosion.
- The impact of uplift and erosion may have positive effects on human settlement. When one thinks of erosion, whether it is tectonically induced or otherwise, it is natural to emphasize the negative aspect. However, in the complex topography of an area like Epirus, a complexity that is itself a product of the tectonic history, soil that is removed from one area is often trapped and concentrated in adjacent fault-bounded basins or river floodplains where it can be turned to human advantange. Thus one person's erosion is another person's accumulation of sediment. Many of these sediment traps are the major areas of irrigation agriculture today, and some would have been of importance to Palaeolithic patterns of land use. Tectonic activity also creates and sustains barriers and enclosed basins on both a regional and a local scale which provide opportunities for the human control and manipulation of mobile animal resources.
- The relationship between tectonics and uplift is particularly clear in areas such as Epirus and the Gulf of Corinth where tectonic activity is very marked. But it does not follow that tectonics is the only factor contributing to landscape change, or that in areas where tectonic activity is less marked, there is not also a tectonic factor contributing to patterns of erosion. In Epirus the tectonics creates an underlying instability, which makes some parts of the landscape especially vulnerable to erosion. Within these actively deforming areas it is impossible to predict precisely when and where erosion will take place, since on this local scale erosion is a stochastic process. Eventually one locality or another within these actively deforming areas will undergo dramatic erosion and degradation, but the final trigger that tips the balance from stability to erosion may be very small. Changes of land use or climatic change are superimposed on this pattern, and may accelerate erosion in these areas or inhibit it for a time through protective measures such as increased vegetation cover or construction of dams and terrace walls. Elsewhere, erosion may be accelerated in steeper terrain by climatic changes, for example in the upland interior under Last Glacial climatic and vegetational conditions, or by tree clearance for pastoral or agricultural purposes (Macklin *et al.*, Chapter 17; Willis, Chapter 20; Turner & Sánchez-Goñi, Chapter 29). In general, however, the primary underlying cause of many of the most dramatic and large-scale examples of erosion is tectonic. The potential impact of tectonic disturbance may be no less in areas of lesser tectonic

activity, since it is the effect of disturbance, as much as the rate of displacement or of cumulative uplift, that is relevant, and this has generally been ignored in less active areas because the rates of change are small and difficult to measure, and because it is less easy in such circumstances to disentangle the effects of the tectonics from other causes of erosion. Even in these areas of lesser activity, however, the cumulative effect of small changes may be considerable, given sufficiently long time spans.

As far as the reconstruction of Palaeolithic landscapes is concerned, the further back in time the archaeological sequence extends, the greater the likelihood of tectonically induced landscape change. In Epirus the tectonic history of the region has produced landscape changes relevant to archaeological interpretation at two scales. At the larger scale there is the creation of limestone plateau areas which are separated from each other by regions less attractive to humans and animals — either steep, narrow mountains or the potential badlands of the Epirus flysch. These features were already largely in place early in the Pleistocene and have changed little during the period of human occupation. At this larger scale there are also major areas of subsidence such as the Gulf of Amvracia which have persisted as sediment sinks throughout the period of interest to us, and which have sustained conditions of sedimentation independently of climatic changes.

At a smaller scale there are more local features alongside the major structures which are liable to changes over shorter time spans. In some cases repeated tectonic activity associated with these local features has transformed the local landscape from a zone of sediment accumulation to one of uplift and erosion, as is manifestly the case at Kokkinopilos, or has resulted in a repeated cycle of sedimentation and erosion as in the complex tectonic environment of the upper Kalamas basin. In other cases local activity has sustained areas of subsidence and sedimentation, or alternatively uplift and the formation or accentuation of local barriers useful in the control of animal movements, and has thus helped to create stable conditions for particular forms of economy, reflecting on a smaller scale the juxtaposition of the large-scale barriers and sediment basins that define land-use potential on a regional scale. Such changes at the local scale have profound implications for potential land use, including present-day and future agricultural prospects, and the implications for Palaeolithic land use at this local scale will be considered in more detail in Chapter 30.

Acknowledgements

We thank IGME for the issue of fieldwork permits and the ARCHAEOMEDES Project (funded by Directorate General XII of the Commission of the European Union, contract EV5 V-0021), the U.S. Geological Survey in Golden, Colorado, and the Institut de Physique du Globe, Paris, for provision of support and facilities.

Chapter 29

Late Glacial Landscape and Vegetation in Epirus

Charles Turner & Maria-Fernanda Sánchez Goñi

In this chapter we examine the vegetational history of Epirus at a variety of spatial and temporal scales with three objectives: (1) to clarify the degree of geographical variability in the vegetational record in different parts of Epirus on spatial scales that have relevance to the distribution of animal and other resources of interest to the human population of the region; (2) to focus on the patterns of change in the Late Glacial period of particular relevance to the occupation at Klithi; and (3) to examine the interplay between vegetational change and other manifestations of landscape change, notably erosion. We present new evidence from two localities, Lake Ziros in southern Epirus and Lake Tseravinas, which lies close to the site of the former Lake Gramousti (Willis, Chapter 20). Lake Ziros is of particular interest because of its position on the edge of the lowland region nearer the coast, whereas Lake Tseravinas, although in the same area as Lake Gramousti, has a longer sequence which extends well back into the Late Glacial. We draw on the results of Willis from the small basins of Rezina and Gramousti (Chapter 20) and of Tzedakis (1991; 1993; 1994) from the larger basin of Ioannina, but our perspective is both geographically more extensive than that of Willis, and chronologically more closely resolved than that of Tzedakis.

In particular we are concerned with factors affecting the balance between forested landscapes and those dominated by herbaceous or even more open types of vegetation. Evidence to be discussed below will show that open vegetational environments have in fact characterized the area for much of the past 2 million years. Over a variety of scales, both in time and in space, we have to consider how the balance between forested and more open vegetation types has been affected by the following factors: climate, the activity of humans, perhaps the activity of wild animal species, and tectonic disturbance. Even to approach this we need to be able to reconstruct detailed palaeoenvironmental and palaeoclimatic records for different areas of Epirus.

Palaeoclimatic studies in Epirus

In continental areas the potential for reconstructing Quaternary climatic and environmental conditions depends very largely on the diversity and extent of the stratigraphic record. Since erosion is the predominant process, that record is generally fragmentary, in contrast to the long continuous sedimentary records of the deep ocean which have provided a global framework for our knowledge of Quaternary and earlier palaeoclimatic change.

Greece, as a result of its geological setting and tectonic history, possesses an abundance of Quaternary alluvial and colluvial deposits, particularly of well-developed alluvial fan sequences grading into fluvial terrace systems. High mountain areas were glaciated during the cold stages of the Quaternary and retain traces of glacial sedimentation (Macklin *et al.*, Chapter 17). In closed basins lacustrine deposits may accumulate, and it is in this respect that Epirus is highly favoured, since fault-bounded intermontane basins have permitted the development of persistent, deep lakes in which sediments have been laid down throughout long periods of the Quaternary.

The most obvious example is the Ioannina basin, a completely closed catchment which has retained to the present day a large lake, although somewhat reduced in area by drainage in the last 150 years. Extensive exposures of marly lacustrine sediments in other areas of Epirus, including the Kalamas basin to the northwest of Ioannina, the area on the west side of the Louros Valley around Filipiada, and the vicinity of ancient Nikopolis, north-east of Preveza, provide evidence for older lakes of large extent, drained probably in the Lower and Middle Pleistocene as a result of downcutting and tectonic movements. Elsewhere there are smaller basins, only a few hectares in size, formed by tectonic processes or by karstic solution, occupied by lakes which nevertheless yield sedimentary records for the latest part of the Quaternary. These can yield a particularly valuable palaeoenvironmental record. The relatively high rainfall in Epirus means that lakes and their surrounding marshes tend to remain wet throughout the drier summer months. This favours the preservation of organic sediments — peats, detritus muds, gyttjas — which elsewhere in Greece are usually prevented from forming by desiccation and oxidation.

The importance of these lacustrine sediment sequences in Epirus is that they provide not only long but also more or less continuous records of detailed changes in the biological and physical environment covering considerable time spans. They complement the generally shorter and less complete records available from cave sediments, which also yield evidence on (different) aspects of faunal and climatic change (Gamble, Chapter 12; Woodward Chapters 18 & 19).

The principal available biological indicators in the lacustrine sediments are pollen, diatoms, ostracods, freshwater molluscs and plant macrofossils. Pollen analysis is of particular value, as it provides a picture of the wider terrestrial environment, rather than just of the palaeoenvironments of the water body itself. Furthermore, as more palynological information becomes available for the area, spatial as well as temporal patterns of environmental and climatic change can be inferred.

A number of pollen analytical investigations of Late Quaternary lacustrine deposits in Epirus have already been carried out. The sites are shown in Figure 29.1. Bottema (1974) studied cores from Lake Ioannina (Lake Pamvotis) and obtained a vegetational record covering the Holocene and the last glacial/interglacial cycle. Recently this record has been extended by Tzedakis (1991; 1993; 1994) to cover a series of glacial/interglacial cycles back an estimated 423 ka to the latter part of the Middle Pleistocene.

Lake Ioannina, which lies at *c.* 470 m above sea level, is about 5 × 11 km in extent, which means that its pollen catchment is extremely large, and dominated by regional and far-travelled sources. In other words, the vegetational record obtained integrates much of the vegetation of Epirus from the peaks of the Pindus mountains in the east to the sea coast in the west.

In order to avoid this effect, Willis (1992a,b,c and Chapter 20 of this volume) examined cores from two smaller lakes, both less than 300 m in diameter. Both these sites are in northern Epirus and about 18 km apart. Rezina Marsh, a small basin, lying at an altitude of about 1750 m in the northern Pindus mountains, yielded a pollen diagram extending back to about 10,000 radiocarbon years BP. Lake Gramousti, drained in 1961, is, by contrast about 400 m above sea level (not 285 m, as previously published), and is situated on the northeastern margin of the Doliana basin. It appears to have formed within a complex karstic solution hollow overlying Triassic sediments, which contain bands of gypsum. The radiocarbon dating scale applied to the pollen diagram (Willis 1992a; Gowlett *et al.*, Chapter 2) covers the period approximately 13,000 BP to 1000 BP, but, because of ambiguous radiocarbon dating characterizing the core, it is not really certain how much of the Late Glacial and the Holocene is represented. The pollen results described later, which we have obtained from Lake Tseravinas only 8 km distant, lead us to think that a hiatus is present in the Gramousti sequence.

During the course of the present project, palynological investigations were carried out on two further relatively small lake sites which had been cored in 1986. The results of this work, particularly the pollen analyses carried out by M.-F. Sánchez Goñi, are presented here for the first time. Lake Tseravinas lies about 8 km due west of Lake Gramousti, on the northwestern margin of the Doliana basin, at an altitude of about 450 m and Lake Ziros, nearly 80 km further south, in southern Epirus, about 16 km northwest of Arta. Lake Ziros occupies a small basin adjacent to the outcrop of the Kokkinopilos red beds, at a much lower altitude than the lake sites further north — just below 50 m above sea level. The site lies about 20 km from the modern coastline.

Returning to the older Pleistocene record, there occur in various parts of Epirus thick sequences of lacustrine deposits from lake basins that have been drained long ago and subsequently exposed and dissected. Some of these have also been sampled during the course of wider regional surveys carried out in association with the Klithi project. Only preliminary results are so far available, but are sufficient to give an indication of age. For example, megasporangia of the stratigraphically significant water fern *Azolla filiculoides* have been found in sections of lacustrine deposits near Filipias, a plant believed to have become extinct in Europe during the Riss/Saalian glacial period towards the end of the Middle Pleistocene. Near the top of the lacustrine infill of the Kalamas basin, pollen assemblages occur with abundant representation of *Pterocarya* and *Abies*, thus implying an age older than that of the base of Tzedakis' core 249 from Ioannina, but still of Middle Pleistocene age

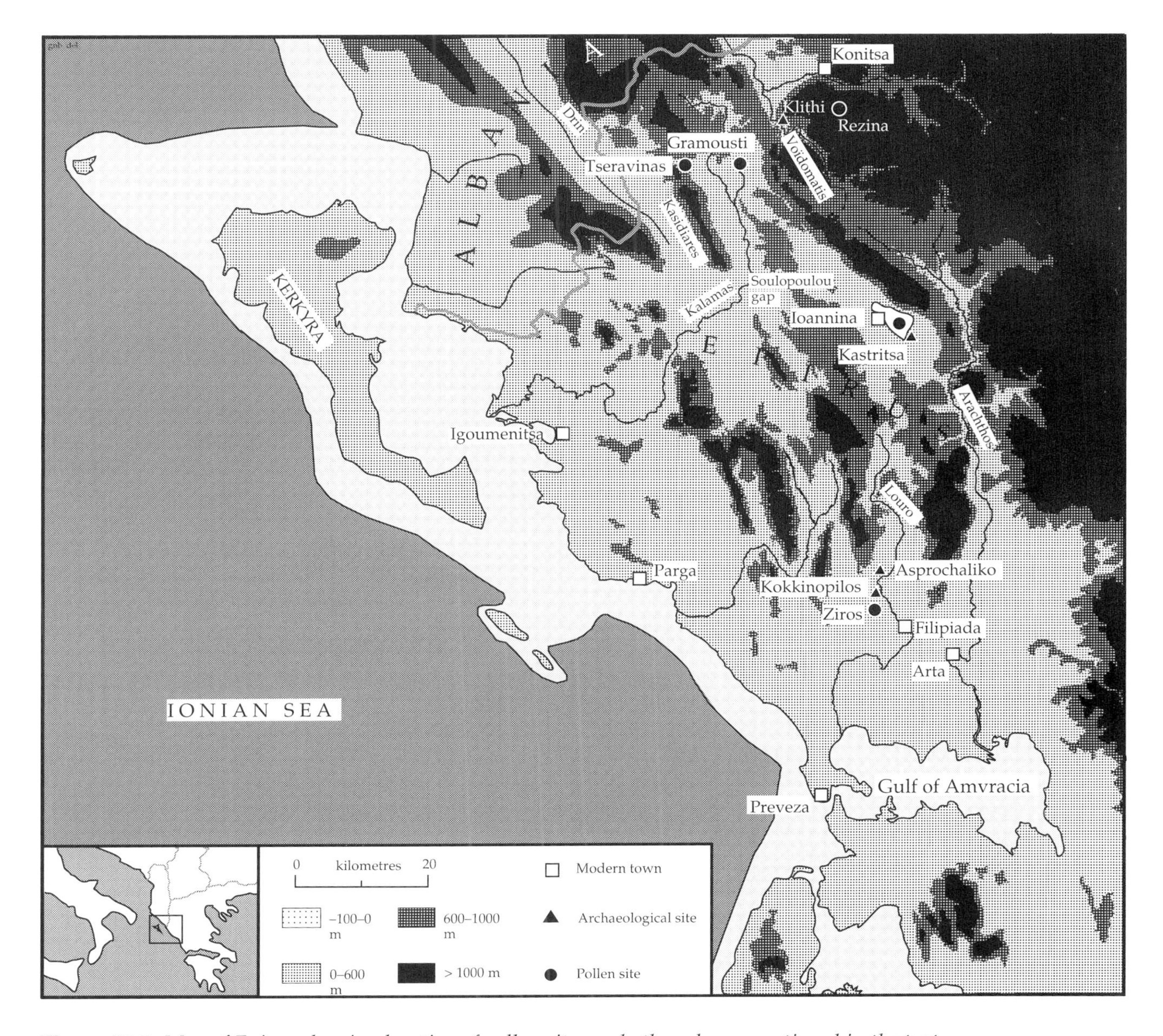

Figure 29.1. *Map of Epirus showing location of pollen sites and other places mentioned in the text.*

since the assemblages lack any of the characteristic Lower Pleistocene pollen types.

In summary, well-developed pollen diagrams are available from a number of different sites in Epirus. These differ in their geographical location and their altitude, with one site at a comparatively low altitude in southern Epirus, three sites between 400–500 m in northern Epirus, and a further site in the northern Pindus mountains at about 1750 m. These sites have strikingly different pollen catchment areas, yielding information about either local or regional vegetation patterns. They also have a very different stratigraphical coverage. The smaller lakes have provided records covering the Holocene and, to some extent, the Late Glacial period, though in some cases deeper boreholes (using mechanically rather than manually driven coring equipment) would certainly have taken the record much farther back in time. Sedimentation rates were quite high and the cores themselves were studied for the most part at closely spaced intervals. On the other hand the core from Ioannina represents a very much longer period of Quaternary time and sampling has been more widely spaced, with the investigation detecting major vegetational patterns rather than detailed changes. Other older Pleistocene deposits are recognized but not yet fully investigated.

Vegetation cover and landscapes during Pleistocene climatic cycles

The pollen diagrams from Lake Ioannina (*alias* Lake Pamvotis), particularly that from the deep borehole (No. 249) investigated by Tzedakis (1991; 1993; 1994) (Fig. 29.2), show a sequence of vegetational fluctuations which are clearly the equivalent of the glacial/interglacial or interstadial succession well-known from other parts of Europe, and, indeed, a sequence which can also be correlated with the oxygen isotope stratigraphy of the deep oceans. The base of Tzedakis' diagram is interpreted by him as being the equivalent of stage 12 in that stratigraphy, which is the basis for an age estimate of 423 ka.

The pollen assemblages of the interglacial stages are dominated by arboreal pollen, particularly of oak species, both deciduous and evergreen *Quercus*, species of hornbeam *Carpinus* and *Ostrya*, elm *Ulmus*, beech *Fagus* and fir *Abies*, together with smaller percentages of other temperate trees, such as hazel *Corylus*, lime *Tilia*, ashes *Fraxinus* spp., *Pistacia* and *Phillyrea*, the two latter genera essentially characteristic of Mediterranean-type vegetation. Within the interglacial stages there is clear evidence for progressive changes within the forest vegetation, similar to those recognised within interglacial vegetational successions in northwestern Europe and there used by Turner & West (1968) to subdivide interglacial periods. This is of particular interest in that normally such changes are in part ascribed to differing rates of immigration of tree taxa from their refugia in southern Europe, yet the same features can now be detected within the heart of what itself was undoubtedly just such a refugial area. Evidence for vegetational regression at the end of interglacial periods is rather different in northern Europe, since *Betula* was very sparse, whilst *Pinus* expansions were less marked.

More interesting, in its implications for the present project, is the confirmation that Epirus, like virtually the whole of the Mediterranean basin, was covered in what can best be described as an open steppe-type vegetation during the cold stages of the Quaternary, that is in fact for about 70 per cent of the last 2 million years. The characteristic taxa are *Artemisia*, grasses Poaceae, Chenopodiaceae and different groups of Asteraceae. The shrub *Ephedra* occurred sparsely. Much reduced percentages of oak, pine and fir indicate that these trees persisted albeit in small quantity somewhere within the Ioannina pollen catchment, whereas very much smaller traces of pollen of other deciduous tree taxa are here interpreted by both Bottema and Tzedakis as evidence for very restricted refugia for such species, probably in mountainous areas, particularly the Pindus.

Tzedakis has demonstrated how the cold stages, though interrupted by interstadial fluctuations (i.e. minor climatic amelioration), show vegetational development with temperate forest vegetation being replaced by steppe forest, then by grassland steppe and finally by desert steppe. Tzedakis has also prepared pollen concentration diagrams for the Ioannina sequence which give an even more rigorous picture of this contrast between interglacial and cold stage vegetational conditions. During the cold stages the percentage pollen diagrams exaggerate even the limited importance of oak and pine, whose pollen productivity was in fact very greatly reduced, compared to their interglacial fecundity. On the other hand, non-arboreal pollen productivity was no greater during the cold stages than during the temperate stages, despite the dominance of the vegetation by grasses and other herbs. This implies that biomass production during the cold stages was very low indeed.

Despite the fact that this steppe vegetation has been widespread in the Mediterranean basin not just during most of the last cold stage of the Quaternary, the Würmian or Weichselian, but also during previous cold stages, it has to be acknowledged that no modern analogue for this vegetation apparently exists today, although some measure of comparison may be made with steppic vegetation in mountainous areas of western Iran (Wright *et al.* 1967) or perhaps with areas of central Asia such as parts of Tsinziang in western China. To make comparisons more difficult, the main pollen taxa of these cold stage assemblages cannot be identified to species level. We suspect that the *Artemisia* species involved was or were herbaceous wormwoods or mugworts rather than woody species of the same genus, such as the American sagebrushes. The family Chenopodiaceae includes a large number of species and genera that today enjoy open-ground, ruderal habitats or are halophytes. Grasses are of course ecologically very diverse. There remains a slight chance of achieving some identifications through plant macrofossils, but if suitable sites were found (in Greece or elsewhere) recovery of bulk samples from depth would probably be necessary.

Despite the lack of modern analogues, the pollen evidence makes clear that the environment of Epirus during the cold stages, and in particular during the Würmian, was arid, treeless except in very favoured areas, with a mosaic of grassland and more

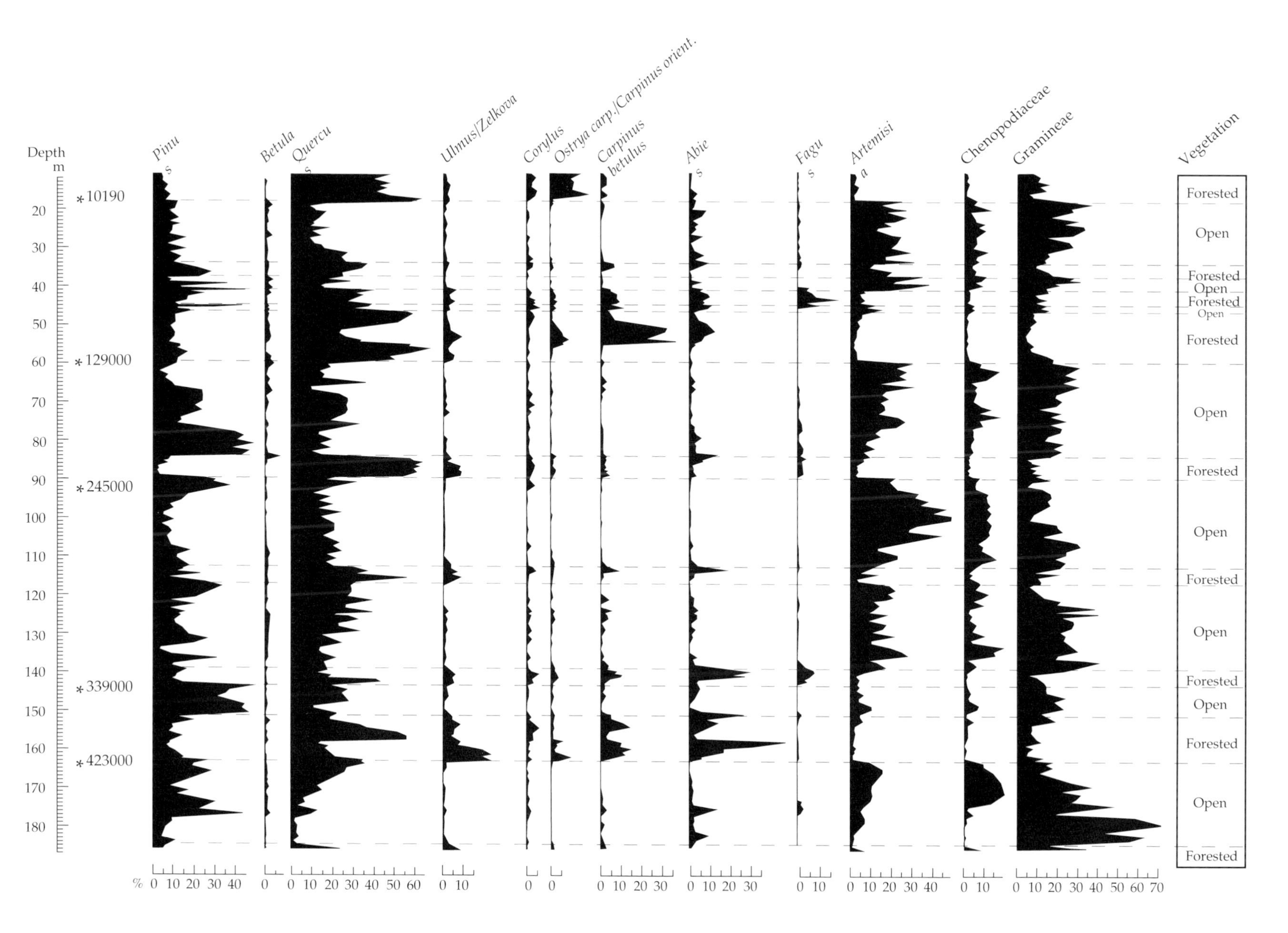

Figure 29.2. *Summary diagram of the Ioannina pollen sequence. The uppermost date is the radiocarbon date from Bottema's (1974) core. The other dates are based on correlation with the deep-ocean oxygen isotope record. (From Tzedakis 1993; 1994.)*

open vegetation and, at least seasonally, with a fair amount of bare ground and by implication unstable slopes and poor soil development. There is still uncertainty as to how cool summers might have been at this latitude, though winters are likely to have been cold. There is equally debate about whether the aridity was the result of generally low rainfall or of strong seasonality.

However, the pollen evidence for an open, unstable landscape predominating in Epirus during the Quaternary is reinforced by geological evidence. The upper Kalamas basin, immediately west of the Ioannina basin, bounded on the west side by the Kasidiares mountain range and extending from Doliana in the north to Palinouri in the south, contained in Early and Middle Pleistocene times a large lake, certainly larger than the greatest extent of Lake Ioannina, which was finally drained through the Soulopoulou gap, following tectonic movements in this southwestern part of the basin. Palynological evidence suggests that this occurred during the Middle Pleistocene. Even whilst the lake was extant, large alluvial fans from Kasidiares and from a lesser range to the east (separating the Kalamas and Ioannina basins) impinged on the lake and formed an interdigitating fan and lacustrine stratigraphy. After the draining of the lake, fan deposits continued to accumulate. Uplift, particularly of Kasidiares, was no doubt the impetus for fan development, and the demonstration of episodes of recent fan activity there in late Holocene times (Bailey *et al.* 1993; King *et al.*, Chapter 28) is one of a number of lines of evidence for the continuing importance of active tectonic movements in the Epirus landscape. However, fan formation on the massive scale seen all along the margins of the basin can really only be envisaged as occurring under open vegetational conditions. The stratigraphy of these alluvial fan deposits is complex, though it may be possible to distinguish fans of different ages in terms of weathering of the sediments. Thermoluminescence has been attempted of some of these deposits, but most results are beyond the range of the dating technique, with the exception of a fan deposit near Mazaraki which has given a date of 51 ± 14 ka (DOL3, Appendix A). In general they must be regarded as representing sedimentation during the cold stages of the Quaternary. They may well have still been active during the Late Glacial, at the time of occupation of Klithi. Reactivation of fans in the late Holocene will have been favoured by deforestation and other disturbance induced by human activities, particularly pastoralism.

Palaeoenvironmental change during the Late Glacial and Holocene

The long sequences from Lake Ioannina have given a broad picture of palaeoenvironmental change over a substantial period of the Quaternary, but, because of the size of the lake basin, they are incapable of providing a detailed picture of local vegetational change. To try to provide such a local environmental picture of Epirus landscapes at the time of the occupation of Klithi, it was clearly necessary to concentrate further on smaller lake basins and to try to reinforce and extend back in time the observations of Willis (1992a,b,c and Chapter 20).

Lake Ziros

Geographical, geomorphological and geological setting

Geographically, Lake Ziros lies just within the Nomos of Preveza, about 15 km northwest of the town of Arta, 4.5 km north-northwest of the village of Filipiada and barely 1 km west of the river Louros and the main Arta–Ioannina road, from which it can be approached by an untarmacked by-road. Its altitude is just below 50 m above sea level. The Palaeolithic archaeological site of Kokkinopilos lies 2 km to the north.

The setting of the lake is extremely unusual, as it occupies a small elongate enclosed basin *c.* 1.3 km in length within and cutting across the north–south trending range of higher ground that separates the Louros Valley to the east from the Stephani basin and Thesprotikon Valley to the west (Fig. 29.3). The origin of the Ziros basin is clearly related to a southwest/northeast-trending fault which cuts through the range, with downthrow to the southeast.

To the north of Lake Ziros the high ground forming the interfluve between the Louros Valley and the Thesprotikon Valley consists of fine-grained early Jurassic (Lower Lias) limestone. This forms an impressive fault scarp on the northwest margin of the lake with cliffs rising to a height of about 60 m (*c.* 100 m asl) above the water level and, behind that to the summit of Xerovouni at 260 m a.s.l. To the north of Xerovouni occurs a depression in the surface of the Lias limestone, infilled by up to 30 m of reddish and red-brown silts, the Kokkinopilos deposits. Runnels & Van Andel (in prep.) have suggested that this depression is a polje formed by karstic solution on a tectonic fault (see also King *et al.*, Chapter 28). To the south of Lake Ziros the range of higher ground west of the Louros Valley decreases in height and consists of Triassic dolomitic limestones, often very brecciated

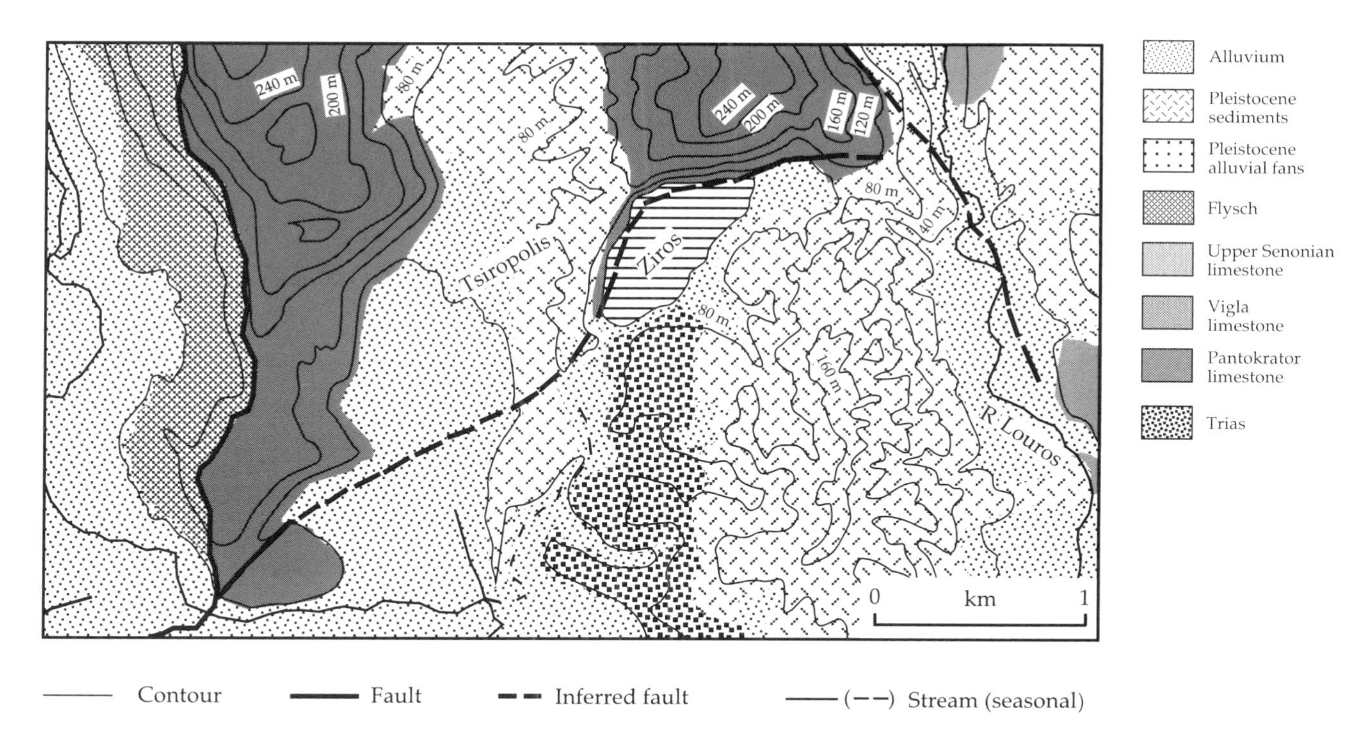

Figure 29.3. *Location map of Lake Ziros. (Information from IGRS 1969.)*

and continuing layers of gypsum. On the eastern (Louros) side of this range and, indeed, forming the western margin of the Louros Valley, a thick and complex series of fluviatile gravels and lacustrine silts and marls overlie the Triassic strata. These are referred to the Plio-Pleistocene on the geological map, but according to preliminary pollen analyses, are probably of Pleistocene age. The western end of the Ziros basin is formed by a low ridge of poorly consolidated coarse gravels and reddish sands, which extends about 2 km northwards towards Tsiropolis, where there is a further series of reddish silts (similar to those of Kokkinopilos) and white lacustrine marls which have yielded a sparse vertebrate fauna (*Ursus cf. deningeri* and *Rhinoceros* sp.). The geological map represents these Pleistocene deposits separately from those on the eastern flank of the ridge.

The lake itself closely infills its basin and is elongate in shape, 1 km in length and 450 m across at its widest point. A small patch of alluvium to the east of the present lake is occupied by the grounds of a former youth residential camp, used in 1992 to house Albanian refugees. On the southern margin a very minor intermittent stream emerging from a short valley has built up a small delta, which, it will be shown, extends into the lake. This is at present the only visible inflow into the lake, though at some time in the past there may have been an inflow at the eastern end, where the youth camp is now sited. Nevertheless, the lake generally maintains a remarkably constant level (only falling 1 m after the very dry winter and spring of 1991–92). Local opinion is that the lake is fed by submerged springs. Construction of a gravelled road parallel to the southern margin of the lake and at a height of several metres above lake level, whilst partly blocking the inflow stream, seems to have provided a further catchment area, gathering water and channelling it into the lake at the inflow point of the stream, whenever heavy rains occur.

Vegetation

The area around Lake Ziros is an unusual and attractive one and the vegetation has been both modified and conserved as a result of human activity. The slopes surrounding the lake are mostly steep and quite well wooded. However, on damp marshy ground at the lake edge grow *Salix* spp., with branches sometimes festooned with the liane *Periploca graeca*, the colourful shrub *Vitex agnus-castus*, often with its roots in the water. A few stands of common reed *Phragmites australis* and bulrush *Schoenoplectus lacustris* are present.

There is a strong contrast in species diversity and composition between the quite well developed woodland growing on both the rather acid Triassic strata and cherty siliceous gravels on the slopes to the south and west and the steep limestone fault scarp immediately north of the lake (see Fig. 29.3). On the acid soils *Quercus pubescens* is the dominant tree with *Carpinus orientalis* frequent, but as an undershrub. There is a sparse but distinctive ground flora, and bracken *Pteridium* flourishes in clearings and on open ground. Only at the woodland edge and beside the road do the typical pseudomacchie trees or shrubs, such as Kermés oak *Quercus coccifera*, *Phillyrea* and the viciously spiny Christ's thorn *Paliurus spina-christi* occur. The tree flora of the highly calcareous limestone slopes is much more varied and there are signs that this has been more prone to grazing, despite the very steep slopes. There is no dominant tree or shrub but manna and common ash *Fraxinus ornus*, and *F. excelsior*, olive *Olea europaea*, the evergreen oaks *Quercus ilex* and *Q. coccifera*, Judas tree *Cercis siliquastrum*, *Pistacia terebinthus*, and fig *Ficus carica* are all present together with shrubs such as the tall heather *Erica arborea* and a shrubby sage *Phlomis fruticosa*.

Some planting has taken place, particularly of *Pinus* and *Cupressus*, not native to the immediate area, probably associated with the residential camp site, which has been present for many years. There are a couple of small cultivated fields in a minor valley to the south of the lake.

Bathymetry

In August 1992 two traverses were made using a small boat, taking soundings at estimated 40 m intervals. Traverse A was sited along the major southwest–northeast axis of the lake, and Traverse B at the widest point of the lake at right angles to Traverse A (Fig. 29.4).

The maximum depth of water recorded in this survey was 59 m, but unconfirmed verbal reports from IGME suggest that depths of up to 70 m have been recorded. The greatest depths noted were in the southeastern and central areas of the lake, showing that a deep trench exists, presumably along the fault zone, sited between the central line of the lake and its steep northwest margin. Two relatively shallow areas, at the northeastern end and close to the road on the southern shore, were revealed, where small deltas have been built out into the lake. In general, however, the lake is comparatively deep with steeply sloping margins. In Traverse B the northern flank of the trench was shown to have the astonishing gradient of 1 in 1 (45 degrees) and the southern flank 1 in 2. The longitudinal transect, in particular, which ran along the southern slope of the trench rather than along its bottom, suggests an irregular floor that has probably been affected by slumping.

During the bathymetric survey samples of surface sediments from the lake floor were collected using a frozen finger sampler. Samples I and III came from the northeast end of the lake at depths of 10 m and 20 m. Both consisted of fine grey calcareous silts, rich in organic matter and with abundant small intact molluscs and fragmentary shells.

Sample II, from a depth of 15 m and at a site about 80 m from the southeast shore, close to the line of Transect B, consisted unexpectedly of medium to fine angular gravel and large plant detritus, including leaf fragments, set in a grey calcareous silty matrix. The presence of relatively coarse-grained and clearly inwashed material at such a depth and distance from the shore indicated previously unsuspected extensive and active transport processes affecting sediments on this part of the lake floor. In this area, where formation of a delta has probably been associated with a small side-valley, inwash into the lake is probably now accentuated and perhaps controlled by the presence of the gravel-surfaced road running here close to the southeast shore of the lake. In winter, or at other times of heavy rainfall, this road may act as an inflow conduit.

Lake Tseravinas

Geographical, geomorphological and geological setting

This lake is situated about 10 km west of Kalpaki, on the south side of the main road from Kalpaki to the Albanian border at Kakavia. Lake Tseravinas itself is approximately circular in outline and about 700–800 m in diameter, the lake surface being at about 450 m a.s.l. (Fig. 29.5). The lake lies in the middle of a small depression, partially filled by alluvial sediments, which is bounded on the north by the Doliana strike–slip fault (the *'décrochement de Delvinaki'* of the geological memoir IGR/IFP (1966)), which forms the northern boundary of the Doliana basin. On the west and southwest it is bounded by alluvial fans descending from the Kasidiares mountain range and, on the southeast, by low hills of Triassic strata interspersed with smaller depressions also filled with alluvial sediments that connect the Tseravinas depression with the main central depression of the northern Doliana basin.

Geologically speaking, the Doliana fault separates an upstanding ridge of Lower Jurassic (Lower Lias) limestone (Siniais Limestone) to the north, from Triassic dolomitic limestones and breccias, with well-developed beds of gypsum. Many of the smaller

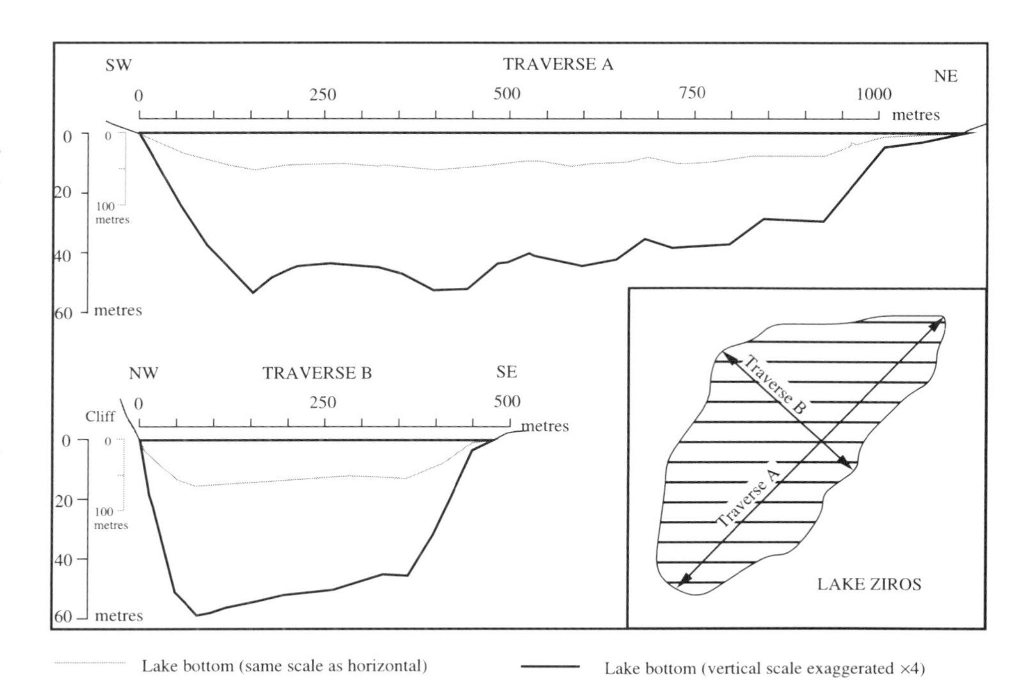

Figure 29.4. *Bathymetric traverses across Lake Ziros.*

depressions in the area are dolines resulting from the solution of gypsum. An essentially similar situation is found 8 km to the east around Lake Gramousti, where the Doliana fault separates a Cretaceous Senonian limestone ridge to the north from Triassic deposits of this kind to the south, and where, indeed the basin of Lake Gramousti itself may have a solutional origin.

In the case of Lake Tseravinas, however, the origin of the basin seems more likely to be tectonic than solutional, since the Kasidiares range, formed of a Middle to Late Jurassic limestone (the Vigla Limestone) is also bounded by an active and complex fault zone on its eastern flank. At Tseravinas this north–south-trending Kasidiares fault zone abuts the east–west-trending Doliana fault (Bailey *et al.* 1993), and modelling of tectonic activity of the whole of Epirus and adjacent regions suggests that this particular part of the Doliana basin should be undergoing subsidence (King *et al.*, Chapter 28).

Unlike Lake Ziros, Lake Tseravinas does not at present occupy a closed basin. Two or three small intermittent streams carry in water during the winter and early spring or at times of sudden storm rainfall, and an outflow stream exists taking water via the small River Nezeros into the River Kalamas. It is not quite certain whether this is a natural outflow, or the result of a drainage scheme.

Although there are now only scattered farms in the vicinity of the lake, during the time of Turkish occupation there was a hani, a small inn or staging post on the road past the lake, where in the early nineteenth century the English artist and writer Edward Lear stayed and sketched (Lear 1851). John Cam Hobhouse, later Lord Broughton, accompanying his friend Lord Byron on his travels, also visited the area and left an interesting account (Hobhouse 1813).

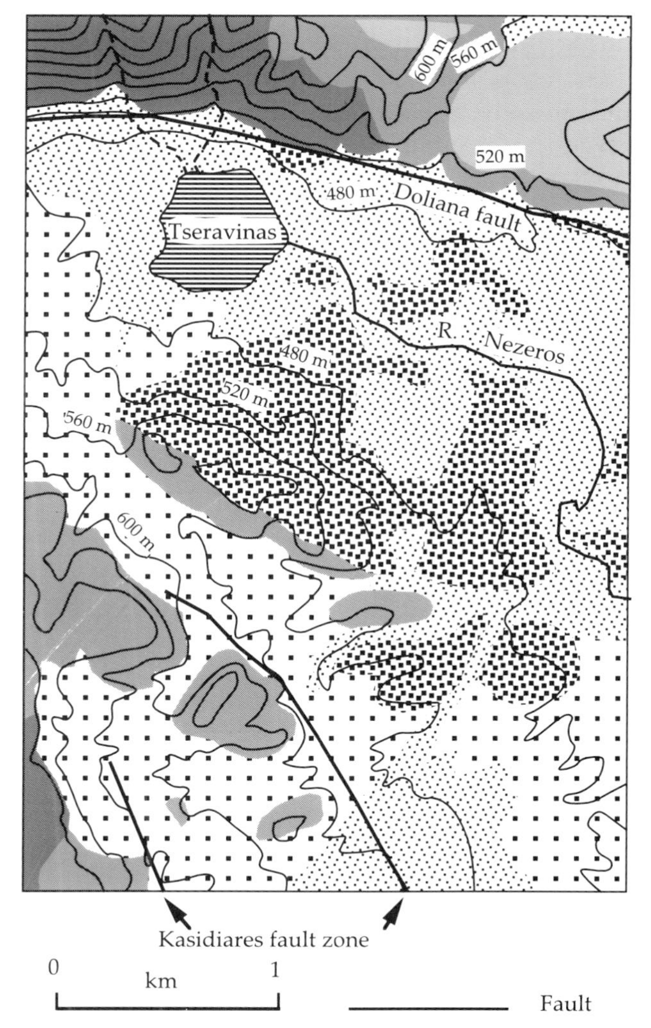

Figure 29.5. *(below) Location map of Lake Tseravinas. See Figure 29.3 for key to sediment types. (Information from IGRS 1968.)*

Vegetation

Parts of the perimeter of Lake Tseravinas are fringed with reedswamp, consisting principally of common reed *Phragmites communis* and occasionally bulrush *Schoenoplectus lacustris*. A belt of reedswamp, 4–5 m wide, is particularly developed along the western margin of the lake, beyond which are grazed pasture and a small arable enclosure covering a large flat alluvial area, which was presumably once part of the lake basin but has been infilled by alluvial and lacustrine sediments. Woodland occurs both on low ground, virtually reaching the shore, and on higher slopes to the south and southwest of the lake (Fig. 29.5). The soils, as around Lake Ziros, are derived from Triassic rocks and cherty siliceous gravels. On the northern side, beyond the road, on the steep slopes of the Siniais Limestone, rather more varied woodland occurs, apparently growing up after reduction of grazing. At a distance the fans and flanks of the Kasidiares ridge are also well-wooded. As might be expected from an area which has a permanent water resource, both the open-ground herb and grassland plant communities and the woodland scrub show evidence of long-term grazing pressure by goats and sheep. The woodland edges are dominated by pseudomacchie trees and shrubs such as the prickly Kermés oak *Quercus coccifera*, Christ's thorn *Paliurus spina-cristi*, *Phillyrea media*, oriental hornbeam *Carpinus orientalis*, pear *Pyrus* sp., hawthorn *Crataegus monogyna* and thorny climbers, roses *Rosa* spp., *Asparagus*, *Smilax*, and brambles *Rubus fruticosus agg.* Once again there is a strong contrast in tree species diversity and composition between the woodland on different soil types. On the more acid soils where the woodland is dense and mature, the deciduous oak *Quercus pubescens* dominates with occasional specimens of the semi-evergreen *Q. trojana* and Turkey oak *Q. cerris*. *Carpinus orientalis* occurs in the understorey. Occasionally, particularly where stream gullies have dissected the hillsides, individual specimens of more unusual trees occur such as the maple *Acer obtusatum*, lime *Tilia* sp. and service tree *Sorbus torminalis*. On the limestone slopes, there are no real tree dominants. Even the older trees are multi-stemmed, providing evidence of grazing pressure in the past, and many spiny shrubs and herbs are still present and some grazing is still taking place. Tree species include *Quercus pubescens*, *Q. frainetto*, *Fraxinus excelsior*, *Carpinus orientalis*, *Pistacia terebinthus*, *Celtis australis* and *Cercis siliquastrum*. The ground flora is much more diverse than on the acid soils.

As an indication of the natural richness of the local vegetation, even more diverse tree communities occur in sheltered wooded valleys in the limestone hills to the north of the lake and in the steep and virtually inaccessible gorge of the River Gourmos only 2 km to the east, which appears to have been largely spared sheep and goat grazing pressure.

Bathymetry

This lake is also steep-sided close to its margins, but it differs substantially from Lake Ziros both in its nearly circular shape and in having a broad almost flat floor at a depth of *c.* 28–31 m (Fig. 29.6). Deep sequences of soft muds are accumulating all over this floor and so, in contrast to Lake Ziros, sediment focusing is probably relatively unimportant. The sediment samples, recovered using a not entirely satisfactory frozen-finger sampler, consisted of fine black muds, highly anoxic and unconsolidated. However, the sampler tended to penetrate deeply into these muds and it is doubtful whether the frozen sections brought up and collected actually represent the uppermost surface samples. It was, however, extremely instructive to

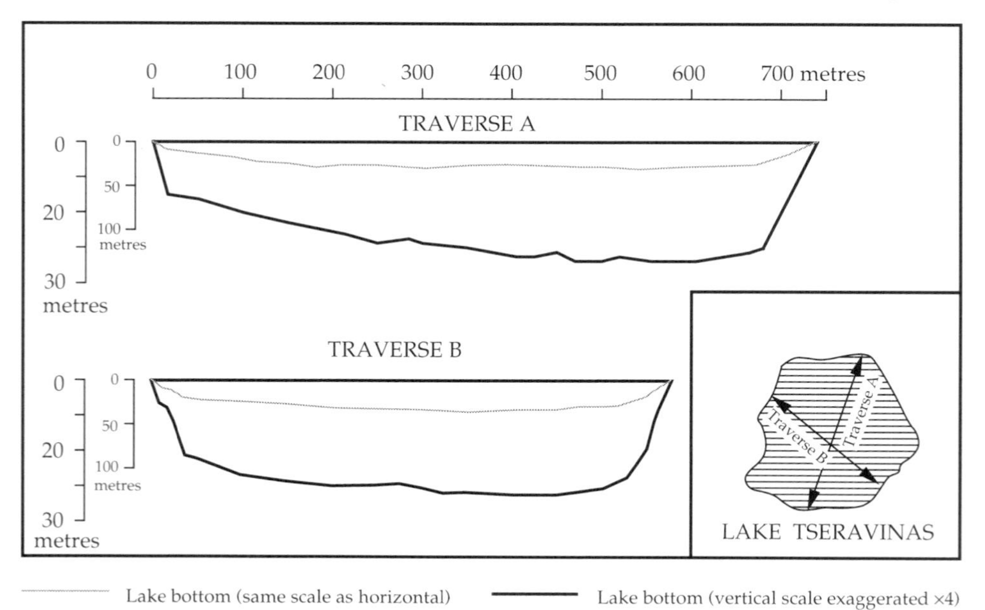

Figure 29.6. *Bathymetric traverses across Lake Tseravinas.*

obtain sediment samples from depth and to note the differences between the sediment lithology and texture here and at comparable depths in Lake Ziros.

Field and laboratory study of cores from Lake Ziros and Lake Tseravinas

Coring

Ideally we would have liked to have cored Lake Ziros using drilling equipment mounted on a raft. However, not only was such equipment not available to us at the time, but the depth and configuration of the basin would anyway make the site difficult to core satisfactorily. In many parts of the basin the lake floor slopes so steeply that slumping is likely to have taken place, especially given the likelihood of ongoing tectonic activity in the basin. Nevertheless, it was possible to penetrate a reasonable thickness of marginal sediments in at least one area. In August 1986 a hand-driven borehole was put down using a 5 mm diameter modified Livingstone corer at a point on the northeast shore of Lake Ziros just above lake level. Coring reached a depth of 13.29 m and augering extended the depth of the hole to 13.68 m. Core samples were recovered between 1.60–13.29 m and bag samples taken above and below.

At Lake Tseravinas, too, our only option was to core at the margin of the lake, rather than through deep water in the centre of the basin. The site selected was within the reedswamp on the western side of the lake, where we knew from trial borings that a thick sediment sequence was present. Again a modified Livingstone hand-operated corer was used. Coring proceeded satisfactorily down to a depth of 14.6 m, but below this depth recovery proved difficult. Though some cores were taken, it was then also necessary to utilize a gouge sampler. The lowest samples recovered came from 16.55 m.

At the time of coring in 1986, the surface of the reedswamp was at approximately lake level, but in 1992, after an exceptionally dry winter and spring, this surface stood at least 50 cm above that of the lake. Clearly it was not expected that current and very recent sedimentation would be well represented at this site in view of these changes in the water level. However, one of the surprises of the bathymetric survey here was that, even at the very edge of the reedswamp, the lake floor descended abruptly several metres (Fig. 29.6). This raised questions as to how and why such a thickness of sediment had accumulated to this level along the western margin of the lake, and we have concluded that at one time a small delta was building out into the lake basin at this point, a conclusion conformable with the sediment record described below. We assume that human activities, including modification and diversion of an inlet stream here, effectively halted the formation of this delta in the relatively recent past, and that its surface close to the lake became colonized by reedswamp. We very much hope that at a future date we may be able to core the central part of the lake, where sediment accumulates regularly over a gently sloping floor, but at a depth of 20–30 m below the lake surface. Such a core might yield a pollen record from the present day through the Late Pleistocene, perhaps back into the Last Interglacial or beyond. Such a core would give an invaluable local record of environmental change to compare with the regional record from Lake Ioannina.

Radiocarbon dating

Virtually all the carbonaceous organic material that has been recovered from sediment cores from Lake Ziros appears to originate from submerged aquatic plants. These, having grown in an environment rich in bicarbonate ions, are unsuitable for radiocarbon dating because of potential hard-water error. To date, regular sampling of the core has failed to produce even small wood fragments sufficient for radiocarbon dating by the AMS method.

Organic detritus of terrestrial origin is also very sparse in the Tseravinas core, but particularly from the lower sections, for which dating was most desirable. Eventually a small number of nutlets of *Carex* were extracted from certain horizons, but since these were insufficient in volume even for AMS dating, further very small particles, preferably of wood but where necessary of charcoal, were sought out and separated from small core samples washed and sieved in distilled water and then examined under a low-power binocular microscope. Great care was taken to exclude any non-woody organic detritus. Eventually four samples of organic material, collected from critical horizons in the Lake Tseravinas core at 622–5 cm, 966–70 cm, 1377–81 and 1572–6 cm were submitted to the Oxford Radiocarbon Accelerator Unit for AMS dating. A further wood sample from 468 cm was sent for dating to Geochron, which proved to require AMS measurement (Table 29.1).

Sediment magnetic susceptibility

Measurements of magnetic susceptibility of the sediment were made using a Bartington metre with a MS1A sensor (Thompson & Oldfield 1986) at 2 cm interval profiles of uncalibrated volume susceptibility. This analysis was primarily applied in order to provide an indication of increased inorganic components in the sediments, which could indicate inwash of clastic material or reworking of soil material. Secondly, an attempt to correlate both Ziros and Tseravinas magnetic susceptibility curves has been made.

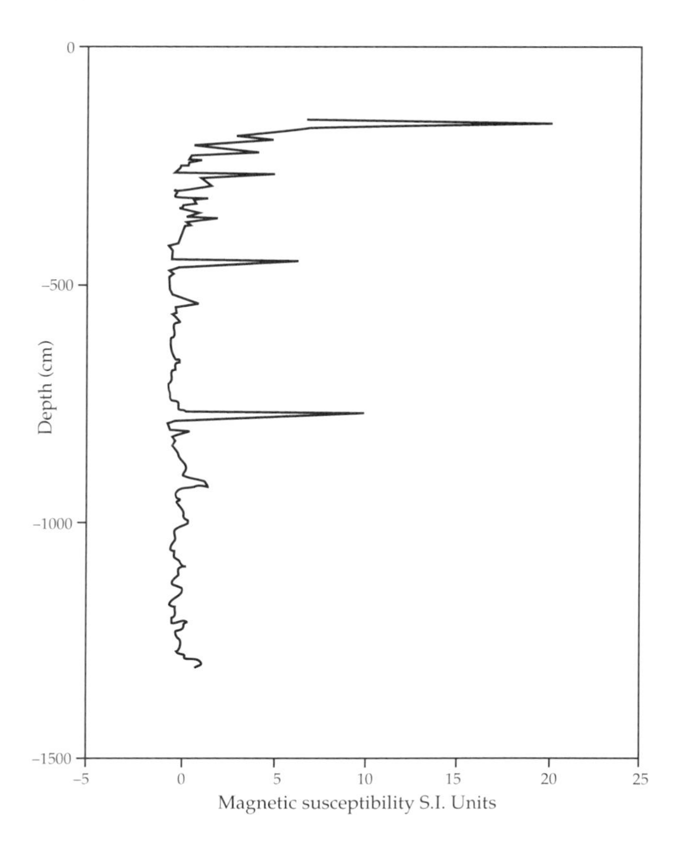

Figure 29.7. *Magnetic susceptibility curve from the Lake Ziros core.*

Table 29.1. *Radiocarbon dates from Lake Tseravinas. (See also Gowlett* et al., *Chapter 2.)*

Depth (cm)	Sample no.	Materials	$\delta^{13}C$ values	Uncalibrated radiocarbon date (yrs bp)	Calibrated dates (yrs BP)
468	GX-20030	wood	–26.6 per mil	3825 ± 72	4217 +98/–126
622–5	OxA-4860 TS/I/622	*Phragmites* rhizomes	–25.5 per mil	6635 ± 75	7512 +25/–116
966–70	OxA-966 TS/I/622	charcoal	–26.6 per mil	13,530 ± 130	16,203 +169/–175
1377–81	OxA-4862 TS/I/1377	*Carex* nutlets and wood	–26.4 per mil	14,930 ± 150	17,843 +207/–163
1572–6	OxA-4863 TS/I/1572	*Carex* nutlets and charcoal	–28.5 per mil	15,300 ± 160	18,221 +152/–159

Pollen analysis

A brass sampler with a circular cross section was used to take calibrated samples of sediment, 2 cm^3 in volume, for pollen analysis (Birks 1976). Sixty-one samples from the Lake Ziros borehole were taken at intervals of 10 cm from the lower part of the core (1352–790 cm) and at 50 cm intervals from the upper part (790–200 cm). From the Lake Tseravinas borehole, 57 samples were obtained at intervals of 10 cm and 20 cm in the lower part of the core (1650–870 cm) and at 50 cm intervals nearer to the top (850–50 cm). Sampling intervals reflect our main purpose, which was to study the environments of the Late Glacial and Holocene. Clearly the later Holocene could and should be studied here in more detail.

The preparation treatments involve decalcification with 7 per cent HCl, boiling in 10 per cent NaOH, microsieving through 10 mm monofilament mesh, flotation in $ZnCl_2$, and acetolysis according to Erdtman's method. Pollen residues were mounted in silicone oil. The use of hydrofluoric acid has been deliberately avoided. Tablets containing exotic *Lycopodium* spores were added to measured volumes of sediment, so that it has also been possible to calculate pollen concentration changes through the sequence.

Over 100 different pollen and spore taxa are recorded in both the principal pollen diagrams from Ziros and Tseravinas (Figs. 29.8 & 29.11). These have been calculated on the basis of percentages of total land pollen with pollen sums greater than 300 grains. In the Tseravinas diagram, a few samples are based on pollen sums ranging from 100 to 300 grains and only three (samples 1070, 1045 & 960) were so poor in pollen that pollen sums ranging from 73 to 100 grains had to be used. The categories 'indeterminable' and 'undifferentiated' include grains so corroded, folded, crumpled or badly situated on the slide that they were unidentifiable.

Concentration pollen diagrams have been generated for selected taxa from the Lake Tseravinas sequences (Fig. 29.12) and for *Quercus* from Lake Ziros (Fig. 29.9).

The pollen diagrams have been subdivided into a series of pollen zones to facilitate description and understanding of the vegetational succession. Boundaries of the zones were defined empirically on the basis of significant changes in pollen percentages for particular taxa or groups of taxa. Such pollen assemblage zones follow the definition of biozones established by Hedberg (1976). In the context of this definition, a pollen zone is a group of strata unified by its pollen content and thus differentiated from adjacent strata. These zones are numbered from the base upwards and prefixed by the site designation. The vegetational interpretation of these zones is based on studies of modern pollen rain (e.g. Bottema 1974; Bradshaw & Webb 1985; Wright *et al.* 1967).

Since both the Ziros and Tseravinas boreholes have been put down near the lake margin, they are both likely to yield evidence of lake-level fluctuations and also changes in the concentration of nutrients (Harrison & Digerfeldt 1993). Consequently, particular attention has been paid to the identification of aquatic plants and certain indicator microfossils.

Results from Lake Ziros

Sediments

The outline stratigraphy is as follows:

0.00–1.60 m	coarse gritty sand and angular limestone pebbles, sometimes with a matrix of clayey silt
1.60–1.75 m	grey silty clay
1.75–2.15 m	grey-brown organic silty clay, passing into:
2.15–2.68 m	grey to grey-brown marl with shell fragments and thin lenses of fine detritus mud
2.68–2.95 m	blackish brown organic detritus mud
2.95–3.50 m	as 2.15–2.68
3.50–8.90 m	pale grey to white fine-grained marl with occasional shell fragments
8.90–10.15 m	olive-brown to grey fine-grained marl
10.15–12.05 m	grey, grey brown to whitish marls with shell fragments and some fine organic material
12.05–13.29 m	faintly laminated white to grey-brown marl with shells and organic detritus
13.29–13.68 m+	fine angular limestone gravel with a silty, marly matrix.

A major component of the marls appears to be fine irregular crystals of $CaCO_3$, secreted by species of the green algae *Chara*. Oospores of *Chara* are abundant or frequent in sediment samples from almost all levels below 4.90 m. Also present are shell fragments of molluscs, both freshwater gastropods and bivalves, usually finely comminuted and including the distinctive opercula of the gastropod *Bithynia*. Macrofossils of higher plants that have been recovered during preparation of pollen samples include fruits of the submerged aquatics *Naias marina*, and water crowfoot *Ranunculus*, subgenus *Batrachium*.

Magnetic susceptibility

Three major sections of positive magnetic values were recorded in the Ziros sequence (Fig. 29.7) at 782–768 cm, 464–456 cm and 252–160 cm. Five others (1304–1276 cm; 932–910 cm; 546–542 cm; 384–318 cm and 300–268 cm) show minor positive values ranging from 0 to 2 (S.I. Units). All these sections correspond to clayey horizons and suggest periods with allogenic inputs (Oldfield 1991). These inputs can be explained by episodes of erosion produced during a period of sparse or disturbed vegetation cover caused mainly by climate or human activity.

Palynology and vegetational history

The description of the percentage pollen diagram from Lake Ziros (Fig. 29.8) is based on a series of pollen zones, ZI 1 to ZI 6. Because of the relatively small size of Lake Ziros, the vegetation recorded in its pollen sequence must mainly correspond to local lowland vegetation (Jacobson & Bradshaw 1981). Since there is, at present, no absolute dating information for the Lake Ziros core, the chronology of this sequence and its zones is discussed after description of the Lake Tseravinas succession.

Zone ZI 1 (1352–1275 cm)

Quercus pubescens-type pollen, the most abundant taxon in this zone, shows a decline from the base of the diagram from *c.* 45 per cent to 30 per cent. Significantly, *Abies* is consistently present, though its values also fall from 7 per cent to 2 per cent. *Pinus* and *Corylus* are present at low values, but also decline. Herbaceous pollen types are well represented, particularly *Artemisia* (10–15

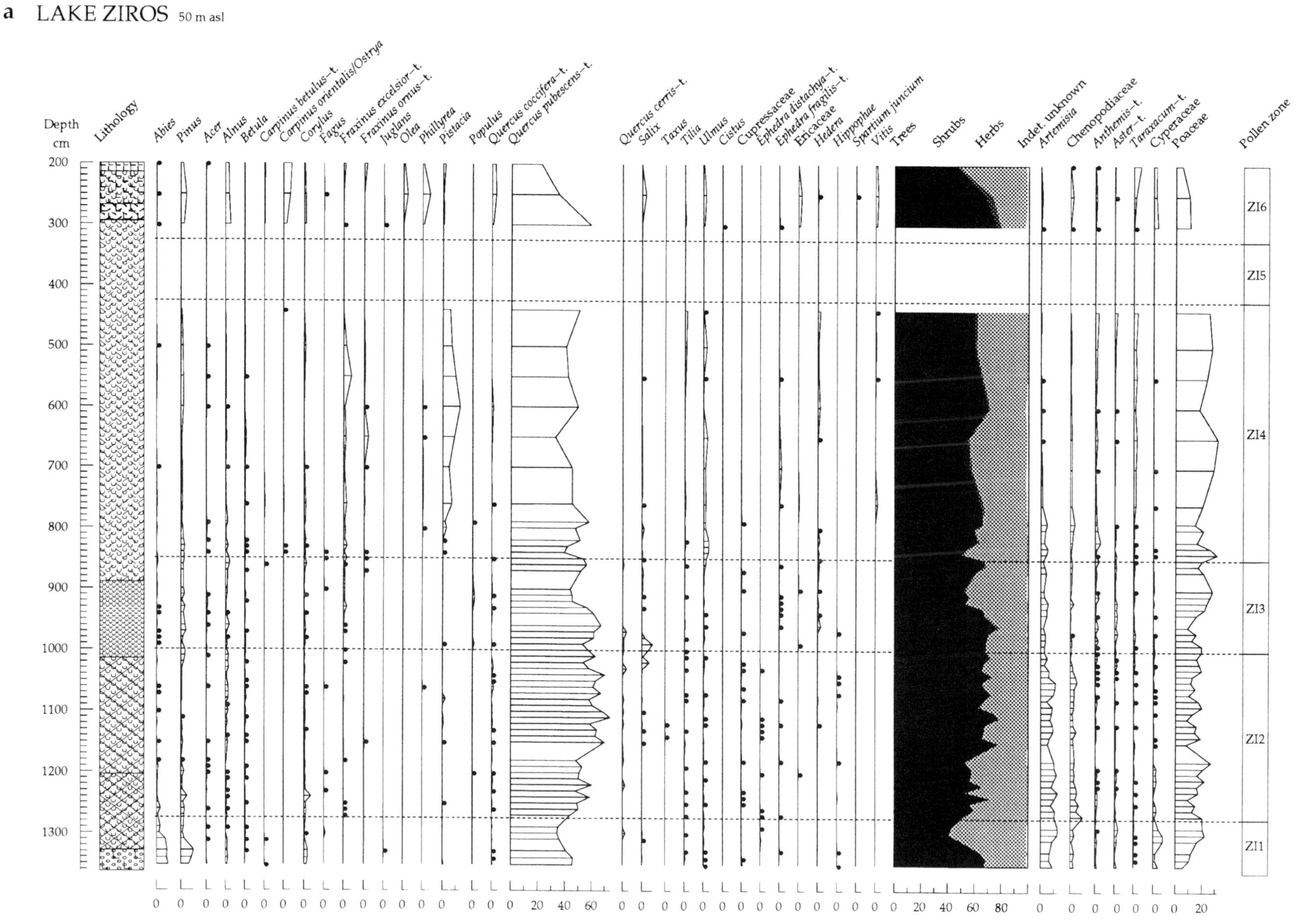

Figure 29.8. *Pollen diagram from the Lake Ziros core, analyzed by M.-F. Sánchez-Goñi. Frequencies expressed as percentages. (See section on Sedimentology for explanation of the lithology.)*

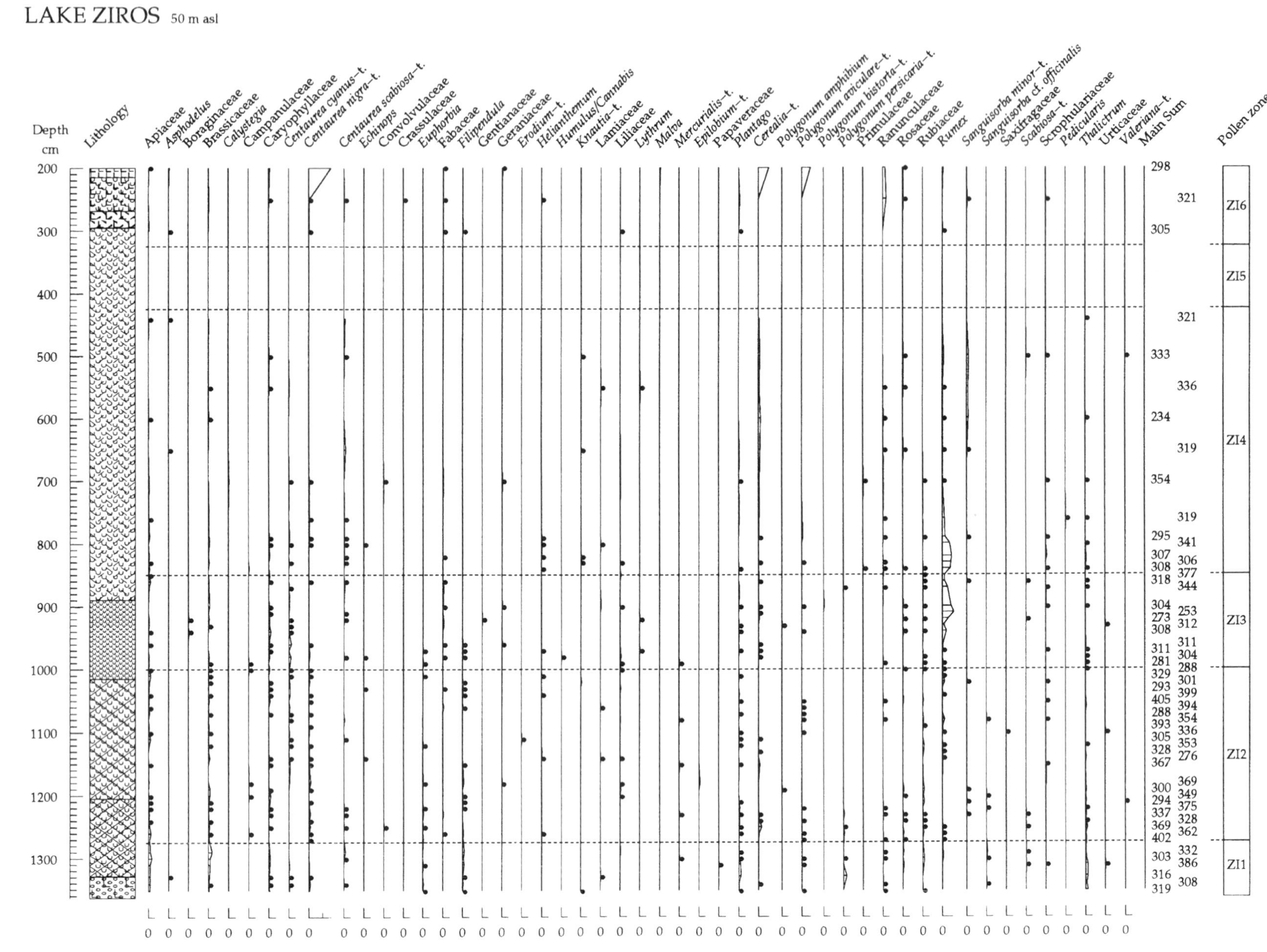

Figure 29.8. *(continued).*

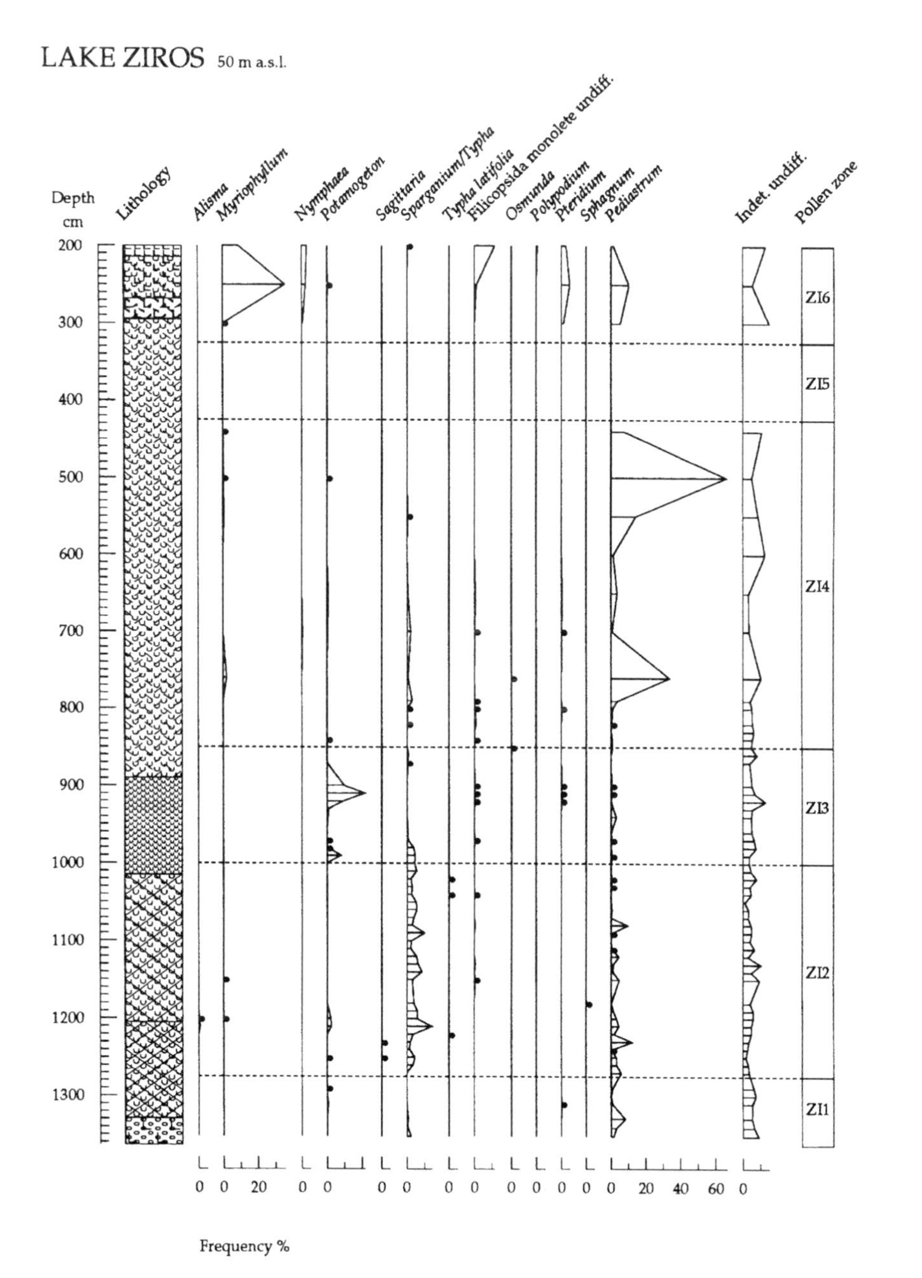

Figure 29.8. *(continued).*

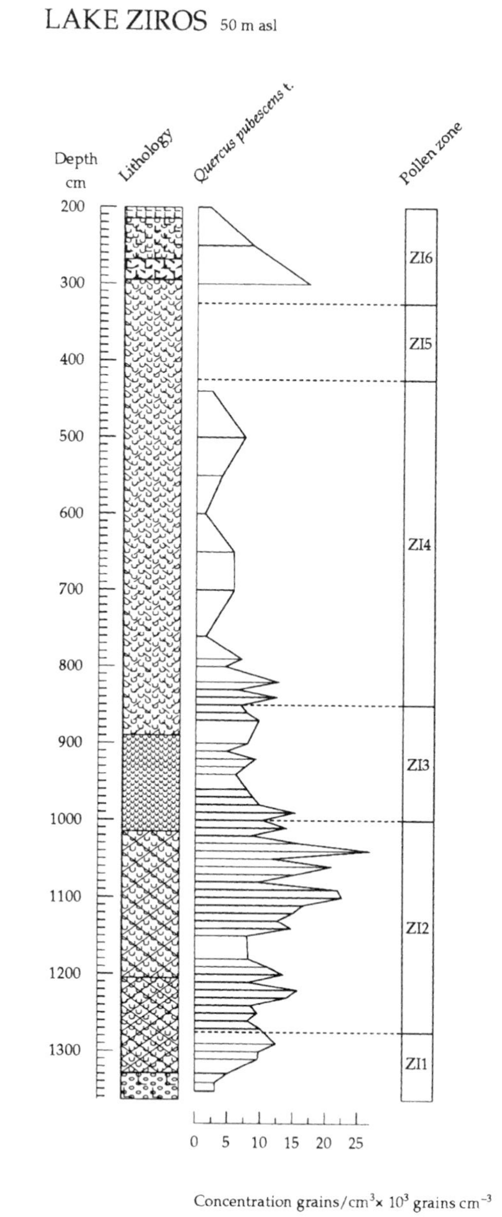

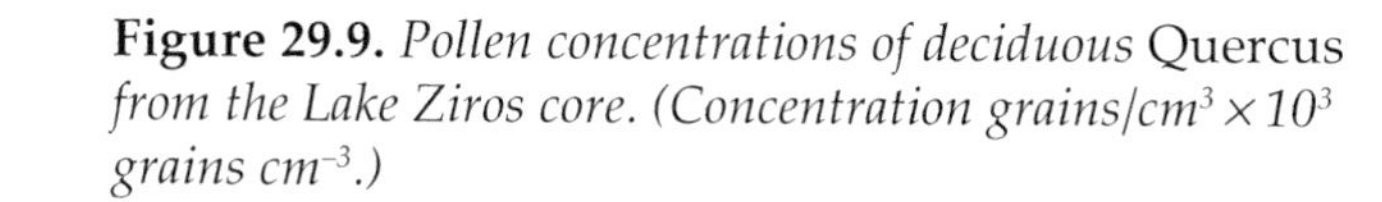

Figure 29.9. *Pollen concentrations of deciduous* Quercus *from the Lake Ziros core. (Concentration grains/cm³ × 10³ grains cm⁻³.)*

per cent), Chenopodiaceae (3–5 per cent) and Cyperaceae (2–7 per cent), also Brassicaceae, *Filipendula*, *Plantago*, *Sanguisorba officinalis*-type, *Thalictrum* and Apiaceae.

At first sight these results suggest a mixture of open-ground steppe communities and of oak-dominated woodland. However, pollen concentration data for this zone (Fig. 29.9) show that the actual amount of *Quercus* pollen, essentially that of deciduous oaks, produced during this zone was an order of magnitude less than in all subsequent zones. This suggests that despite their apparent abundance from the percentage data, oaks were in fact quite sparse, though certainly present and forming scrub or copses in climatically favoured localities. What the pollen diagram in fact is recording is the very low pollen productivity of the steppe vegetation, which must nevertheless have been dominant over wide areas, a feature also demonstrated by Tzedakis (1994) from the Ioannina core. This implies low biomass and low biological productivity. The upper part of this zone corresponds to a minor peak of positive magnetic values again indicating a poorly vegetated area with exposed ground permitting inwash of clastic sediment.

Zone ZI 2 (1275–1000 cm)

This zone shows a curious combination of features: high *Quercus* pollen values (50–75 per cent), including *Q. pubescens*, *Q. coccifera* and *Q. suber* types, together with significant amounts of *Artemisia* (5–10 per cent) and Chenopodiaceae (1–5 per cent). Other deciduous forest trees are sparse or absent. *Betula*, *Alnus*, *Ulmus*, *Fraxinus excelsior* and *Corylus* occur at very low frequencies. At the end of this zone *Salix* pollen increases from *c.* 1 per cent to 5 per cent, reaching its maximum value. At the same time, the frequencies of pollen of open water and marsh plants such as *Potamogeton*, *Sparganium* and *Typha latifolia*, as well as the percentages of the algae *Pediastrum*, decrease and then fall to zero.

The sharp rise in pollen concentration values of *Quercus* at the beginning of this zone indicates with certainty the establishment of quite well developed oak forest or woodland, comprising largely deciduous oaks, but with some semi-evergreen and evergreen species. However, in Greece and throughout the Mediterranean area, these *Artemisia* and Chenopodiaceae are generally associated with arid, steppe-like conditions during the Late Würmian (Bottema 1974; Magri & Follieri 1992; Perez Obiol & Julià 1994; Reille 1990; Van Campo 1984), so a mosaic of forest and steppe, probably conditioned by soil type and aspect, must be envisaged.

Close to the site itself, *Salix* was spreading around the margins of the lake. The magnetic susceptibility values suggest an absence of allogenic sediment input which seems to confirm absence of erosion in the Ziros basin as a result of a well established forest cover.

Zone ZI 3 (1000–850 cm)

The decrease in the pollen values of *Artemisia* (2–5 per cent) and Chenopodiaceae (1–3 per cent) is associated with an increase in those of grasses Poaceae (20–30 per cent) and *Rumex* (2–7 per cent). At the same time, thermophilous pollen types such as *Acer*, *Fraxinus excelsior*, *Ulmus* and *Hedera* are more abundant than in any other zone but the percentages of *Quercus pubescens*-type pollen decrease (40–65 per cent). A very small increase in *Pinus* pollen percentages may indicate its expansion in distant habitats.

The former oak-dominated woodland had at this time diversified to form a deciduous forest with a broad range of tree taxa. Poplar *Populus* was present in this zone, probably growing in damp woodland close to the lake. Steppe communities had largely disappeared but low frequencies of grass pollen suggest that open areas were still present and may even have increased slightly. The low allogenic input indicated by the magnetic susceptibility curve between 932 cm and 910 cm suggests a well developed vegetation cover. Among the aquatic plants only the submerged pondweed genus *Potamogeton*, was frequent. Other aquatic plants virtually disappeared from the pollen record.

Zone ZI 4 (850–425 cm)

Pollen assemblages from this zone are dominated, as in the previous zones, by *Quercus pubescens*–type with values ranging of 35–60 per cent. Other forest trees present were ashes *Fraxinus excelsior* and *F. ornus*, elm *Ulmus*, maple *Acer*, hazel *Corylus*, and lime *Tilia*. However, the most characteristic feature is the expansion of *Pistacia* with maximum values of *c.* 15 per cent associated with the maximum values in *Sanguisorba minor*-type and Poaceae pollen.

Expansion of *Pistacia* is also recorded, although with lower percentages, in other pollen sequences in Epirus during the Early Postglacial (Bottema 1974; Willis 1992a,b). Today two species occur in the region, *Pistacia lentiscus*, a rather shrubby species which is largely confined to the coastal Mediterranean vegetation zone, and *P. terebinthus*, a tree that occurs widely below 1000 m. It is not really possible to separate the pollen of these two species reliably, though some authors have attempted to do so. Given the well established, severe under-representation of *Pistacia* in the pollen rain (Bottema 1974; Wright *et al.* 1967), this zone suggests a very open deciduous oak forest providing suitable habitats where *Pistacia* and, in open glades, grasses and *Sanguisorba minor* might flourish. *Pinus* pollen only occurs at such low values that long-distance transport is probable, though pine and also silver fir *Abies* might have been present nearer to the site in very small quantity. Among the aquatic organisms, the algae *Pediastrum*, characteristic of open water environments, and pollen mainly from floating-leaved and submerged plants (*Myriophyllum*, *Nymphaea*, *Potamogeton*) are well recorded in the diagram. At the end of this zone, positive magnetic susceptibility values confirm the existence of open habitats.

Zone ZI 5 (425–325 cm)

Pollen assemblages from this section of the stratigraphic sequence were very corroded and it has not yet been possible to obtain satisfactory counts. The marls here have a very bleached whitish appearence. It is suggested that oxidation may have taken place, perhaps associated with a fall in lake level and consequent desiccation. Hilton & Lishman (1985) suggest that magnetic susceptibility generally decreases with oxidation. Nevertheless, sediments of this zone, though oxidized, show positive magnetic susceptibility values, suggesting an input of allogenic material. Probably, in such a closed basin, this input results from the erosion of the very steep, sparsely vegetated slopes surrounding Lake Ziros.

Zone ZI 6 (325–200 cm)

This zone is affected by perturbations in the rate of sediment accumulation and preservation. In marginal areas of the lake, and particularly at this sampling point, it seems probable that sediments had built up to a level where wave action permitted resuspension of sediment and redeposition in the centre of the lake (sediment focusing). Therefore the record is very incomplete. Above 200 cm this wave action has resulted in the development of marginal beach gravels. The three pollen assemblages available from this zone differ considerably, but seem to represent a very condensed sequence of Late Holocene vegetational development, already known from other sites. Our current interpretation is that a temperate forest dominated by deciduous oak (*Quercus pubescens*-type pollen), also with hazel *Corylus*, lime *Tilia* and elm *Ulmus*, was invaded by oriental hornbeam *Carpinus orientalis* and by sclerophyllous trees such as *Phillyrea*, olive *Olea* and Kermés oak *Quercus coccifera*. The latter trees were associated with *Pistacia*, *Cistus* and *Spartium junceum*, suggesting the establishment of an eu-mediterranean evergreen forest close to this lake. This vegetation now occurs mostly as fragmented and much modified stands from sea level up to 400 m in areas of Epirus that are frost-free throughout the whole year (Bottema 1974), including the environs of Lake Ziros. The top of this zone shows a further decline in oak and though grasses generally decrease there is a definite expansion of cereal-type pollen and species of open ground (*Taraxacum*-type and *Centaurea nigra*-type). Following Bottema (1974) and Bottema & Woldring (1990), these can be recognized as indicators of human activity, both agricultural and pastoral. Likewise, the assemblage indicates a rise in pollen of *Asphodelus*, *Polygonum aviculare*-type and vine *Vitis* as well as the presence of walnut *Juglans*. The data are at present too sparse to allow confident interpretation of these events in any detail. The sediments of this zone show the highest magnetic susceptibility values of this sequence, which corroborate the existence of open habitats, probably associated with crops such as *Vitis*, cereals, and maybe *Olea*, and by relatively strong erosion of adjacent slopes.

Grass percentages, generally over 20 per cent, and a range of herbaceous pollen types suggest that open habitats were present and persisted throughout the period, and therefore certainly throughout the Holocene.

Lake levels
The variations in the percentages of aquatic plants can indicate lake level fluctuations (Bottema 1974; Harrison & Digerfeldt 1993). Thus, zones ZI 1 and ZI 2, containing the highest frequencies of *Sparganium* and *Typha latifolia* marsh plants within this sequence, suggest periods of low lake level, whilst the high percentages of the pollen of open water plants (*Potamogeton*, *Myriophyllum* and *Nymphaea*) and of the algae *Pediastrum* suggest that zones ZI 3, ZI 4 and ZI 6 correspond with high lake levels.

Results from Lake Tseravinas

Sediments
The sedimentology indicates that the sampling point overlies the delta of a minor stream prograding into the lake. The low ground on this side of the lake has been drained and converted to pasture and arable, and the stream long ago diverted, so that further sedimentation has long ceased at the coring site, even though marginal reedswamp persists close to the lake. An outline stratigraphy of the core is given below.

0.0–0.6 m	brown silty sand and grit with modern organic root detritus
0.6–1.4 m	brown silty clay with modern roots and organic detritus
1.4–2.0 m	dark brown peaty detritus mud
at 2.0	thin bed of small pebbles
2.0–2.1 m	pale grey shelly marl
2.1–4.15 m	dark grey to grey silty clay mud with calcareous nodules, root concretions and occasional shell fragments
4.15–5.7 m	dark brown coarse peaty detritus mud, with wood fragments at 4.6 m
5.7–5.8 m	grey silty marl with organic seams
5.8–5.9 m	peaty detritus mud passing into:
5.9–6.7 m	stiff grey clay-mud
6.7–8.4 m	alternating bands of grey or white marl and dark brown detritus mud, the organic seams thinning below
8.4–14.0 m	grey to greyish white or white marl, sometimes laminated organic detritus, interrupted by thin organic seams or thin beds of detritus mud, both marls and detritus mud often extremely shelly, and in places the marl coarse and sandy to the touch
14.0–14.6 m	shelly grey clay-mud
14.6–16.5 m+	grey or white marls, shelly, the calcareous marl coarse to the touch. This deposit not bottomed.

Magnetic susceptibility
At Tseravinas, six major positive magnetic sections can be observed in the magnetic curve (Fig. 29.10) at 1572–1504 cm, 1440–1348 cm, 684–516 cm, 474–180 cm and 160–50 cm. Two minor peaks (0–4 S.I. Units) are recorded at 1004 and 976 cm and 844–838 cm. As in Ziros, these peaks are related to inwash of magnetic mineral into the lake. They are no doubt related to the gradual development of the delta, both in response to lake level changes and to disturbance, climatic or human, of the hinterland which was drained by the now defunct inflow stream.

Palynology and vegetational history
The Tseravinas percentage pollen diagram (Fig. 29.11) has been subdivided into five pollen zones. The same zonation scheme is applied to the pollen concentration diagram (Fig. 29.12).

Zone TS 1 (1650–1350 cm)

This zone is dominated by non-arboreal pollen taxa (NAP 80–95 per cent). Among these, the most important are Poaceae (15–30 per cent), *Artemisia* (5–18 per cent), Chenopodiaceae (2–6 per cent), Asteraceae (5–35 per cent) and Caryophyllaceae (1–4 per cent). *Filipendula* (1–5 per cent), *Sanguisorba officinalis*-type and *Plantago* reach their maximum values. *Quercus pubescens*-type (0–5 per cent) is very poorly represented while *Abies* (2–8 per cent) and *Pinus* (5–15 per cent) show relatively high percentages.

Considering the underrepresentation of *Abies* in modern pollen spectra (Bradshaw & Webb 1985; Willis 1992b), silver fir may have occurred in small quantity near the lake. The low pollen values of *Pinus*, in contrast, suggest that it was not present locally. Oaks also seem to have been virtually absent. These pollen assemblages, therefore, suggest a steppe-like landscape, very characteristic of Late Würmian vegetation in many other areas of the Mediterranean basin (Van Campo 1984; Bottema 1974; Magri & Follieri 1992; Perez Obiol & Julià 1994; Reille 1990). The positive magnetic susceptibility values support the existence of an open landscape which favoured the deposition of allogenic material within the lake, although in the middle part of this zone a stabilization of the slopes is suggested.

Zone TS 2 (1350–1000 cm)

This zone is characterized by a progressive increase in *Quercus pubescens*-type to *c.* 50 per cent and by minimum values of *Pinus* (3–9 per cent) and *Abies* (0–1 per cent). By contrast, *Betula* (2–15 per cent) and *Corylus* (1–5 per cent) record their highest frequencies in the diagram. *Salix*, *Alnus*, *Ulmus*, *Fraxinus excelsior*-type and *Quercus coccifera*-type are relatively well represented. At the beginning of this zone the steppe taxa, *Artemisia* (7–38 per cent) and Chenopodiaceae (2–10 per cent) reach their greatest percentages, but then decline dramatically. Similarly there is a noticeable collapse in Cyperaceae and Asteraceae values. A characteristic feature is, however, low but persistent presence of

Rumex (0–2 per cent)

These changing pollen assemblages suggest that during this zone the steppe landscape was progressively colonized by a succession of tree taxa, *Betula/Quercus/Corylus*. The end of this zone records a deciduous forest, dominated by oak but mixed also with *Fraxinus* and *Ulmus*, though a few patches of steppe still persisted. This zone corresponds with authigenic sedimentation, mainly of marl and thin beds of detritus mud. This is reflected by the negative magnetic susceptibility values. Tree colonization stabilized the slopes, precluding erosion.

Zone TS 3 (1000–930 cm)

This thin zone is characterized by a sudden increase in *Pinus* to 35 per cent, with a rapid decline in *Quercus* to 15 per cent and in Poaceae to 5 per cent. With the exception of *Acer*, which reaches its maximum frequency (2 per cent), all the deciduous trees are very rare or virtually disappear and a return to high values of *Artemisia* (13 per cent), Chenopodiaceae (12 per cent) and Asteraceae (30 per cent) is recorded. Pollen concentration curves (Fig. 29.12) follow the same fluctuations as the percentage curves. A disintegration of the deciduous forest, leading to its replacement by pine woodland and open habitats, appears to have occurred at this period. This interpretation is supported by the minor positive peak in the magnetic susceptibility recorded between 1004 cm and 976 cm.

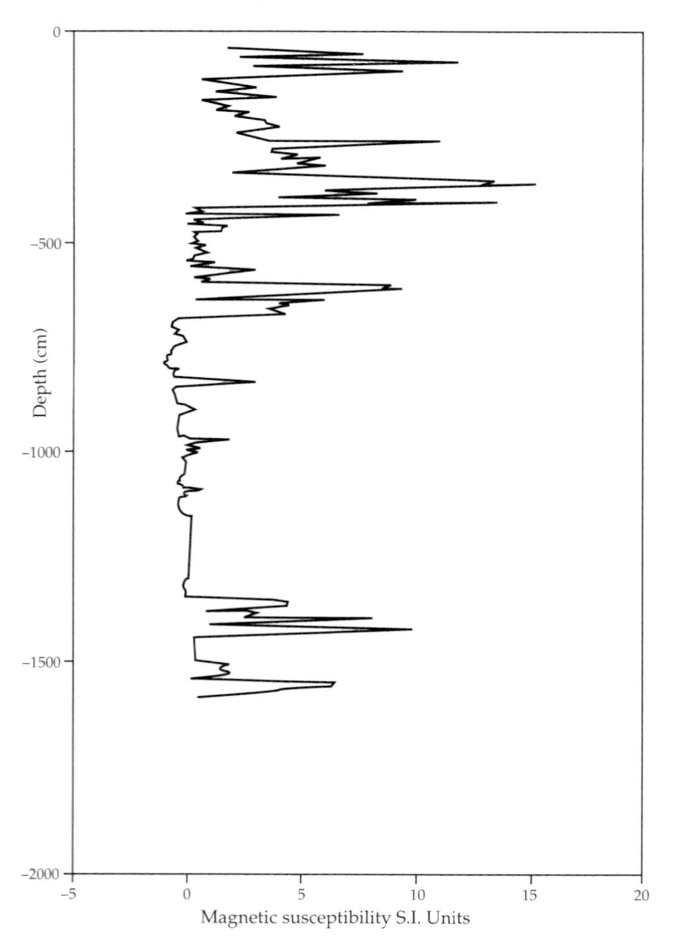

Figure 29.10. *Magnetic susceptibility curve from the Lake Tseravinas core.*

Zone TS 4 (930–650 cm)

In this zone, *Quercus* rises again to 70 per cent before decreasing progressively to 15 per cent. At the end of the zone *Abies* rises sharply to 7 per cent. *Tilia* (2–9 per cent), *Pistacia* and *Sanguisorba minor*-type show their maximum values, associated with an increase in Poaceae to 30 per cent.

On the basis of the poor dispersion of *Tilia* pollen and its consequent under-representation, the pollen assemblages suggest the existence of an open oak–lime co-dominant forest near the lake. Again we have to postulate the presence of patches of *Pistacia* and open glades or an open forest floor with *Sanguisorba minor*. When *Quercus* starts decreasing, above 850 cm, an episode of mineral magnetic input into the lake is recorded. Probably, at that moment, the opening of the oak forest allowed *Tilia* to become established in the area. In the transition between TS 4 and the following zone, high positive magnetic susceptibility values suggest an important change in the vegetation cover.

Zone TS 5 (650–50 cm)

This zone is characterized by a reduction in *Quercus* from 25 to 4 per cent and likewise in some other deciduous trees. However, for the first time, *Carpinus orientalis*-type (1–4 per cent) appears consistently. A sudden increase in grasses to 75 per cent occurs in the lower half of this zone. The size and morphology of the Poaceae pollen suggest that the majority belongs to *Phragmites*, growing on the fringe of the lake as at the present day. The upper part of this zone is dominated, like the lower part, by herbaceous taxa, but here Cyperaceae (5–55 per cent), Asteraceae (2–25 per cent), *Polygonum aviculare*-type (0–25 per cent), *Plantago* (0–5 per cent) and *Centaurea nigra*-type (0–3 per cent) dominate the pollen. The curve for *Pteridium* spores shows a very notable increase (1–15 per cent). If one assumes that the increased Poaceae and Cyperaceae pollen actually reflect taxa associated with marginal aquatic vegetation and then recalculates the pollen diagram to exclude them from the pollen sum, nevertheless the percentages for *Quercus* (20–55 per cent) still show a marked decrease in comparison with those of the previous zone. In fact, pollen concentrations of *Quercus* in this zone, excluding the level at 150 cm, show low values (Fig. 29.12).

This zone can, therefore, be interpreted as demonstrating the presence of open vegetation associated with grazing, as indicated not only by Poaceae pollen but particularly by other herb types, especially *Plantago* and by the great development of *Pteridium* bracken (Bottema 1974; Bottema & Woldring 1990). The presence of Chlamydospores in pollen preparations from this zone indicates, according to Van Geel *et al.* (1989), the occurrence of erosion at this time, which fits well with the reduction in the arboreal cover as well as with the highest values in the magnetic susceptibility curve. Fine charcoal fragments are abundant in washings from the pollen samples within this zone, suggesting burning of vegetation, but it should be noted that charcoal was also present in small quantity in older levels (e.g. see Table 29.1).

Lake levels

Pollen of open water aquatic plants is remarkably sparse from this site. Small amounts of Nymphaeaceae, *Potamogeton* and *Myriophyllum* are recorded during zones TS 1–3, *Myriophyllum* being a little more abundant in zone TS 3, but in the succeeding zones TS 4 and TS 5 they virtually disappear. In fact, because of the morphology of the lake basin (Fig. 29.6), the shallow water zone where such plants could root is extremely restricted. The planktonic green algae *Pediastrum* spp. are abundant in zone TS 1, still frequent through most of zone TS 2 but absent from the

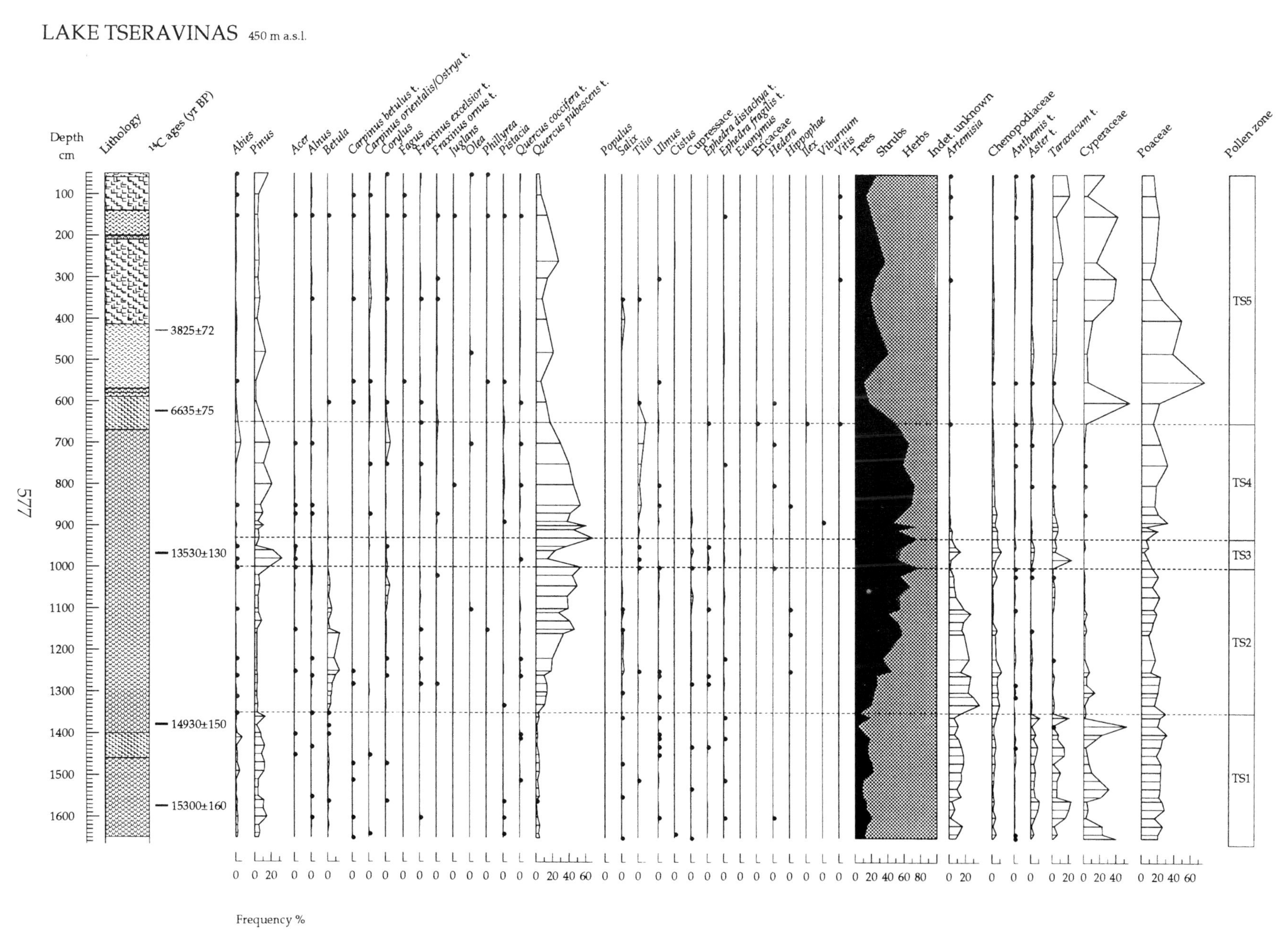

Figure 29.11. *Pollen diagram from Lake Tseravinas, analyzed by M.-F. Sánchez-Goñi. Frequencies expressed as percentages. (See section on Sedimentology for explanation of the lithology.)*

b LAKE TSERAVINAS 450 m a.s.l.

Depth cm
Lithology
^{14}C ages (yr BP)
3825±72
6635±75
13530±130
14930±150
15300±160

Apiaceae, Asphodelus, Boraginaceae, Brassicaceae, Calystegia, Campanulaceae, Caryophyllaceae, Spergularia t., Centaurea cyanus t., Centaurea nigra t., Centaurea scabiosa t., Echinops, Epilobium t., Erodium, Euphorbia, Fabaceae, Filipendula, Geranium, Helianthemum, Humulus/Cannabis, Knautia t., Lamiaceae, Liliaceae, Linum, Lythrum, Malva, Mercurialis t., Papaveraceae, Plantago, Plumbaginaceae, Cerealia t., Polygonum, Polygonum aviculare t., Polygonum persicaria, Primulaceae, Ranunculaceae, Rosaceae, Rubiaceae, Rumex, Sanguisorba minor t., Sanguisorba cf. officinalis, Scabiosa t., Scrophulariaceae, Solanaceae, Thalictrum, Urticaceae, Main sum

Pollen zone: TS5, TS4, TS3, TS2, TS1

Frequency %

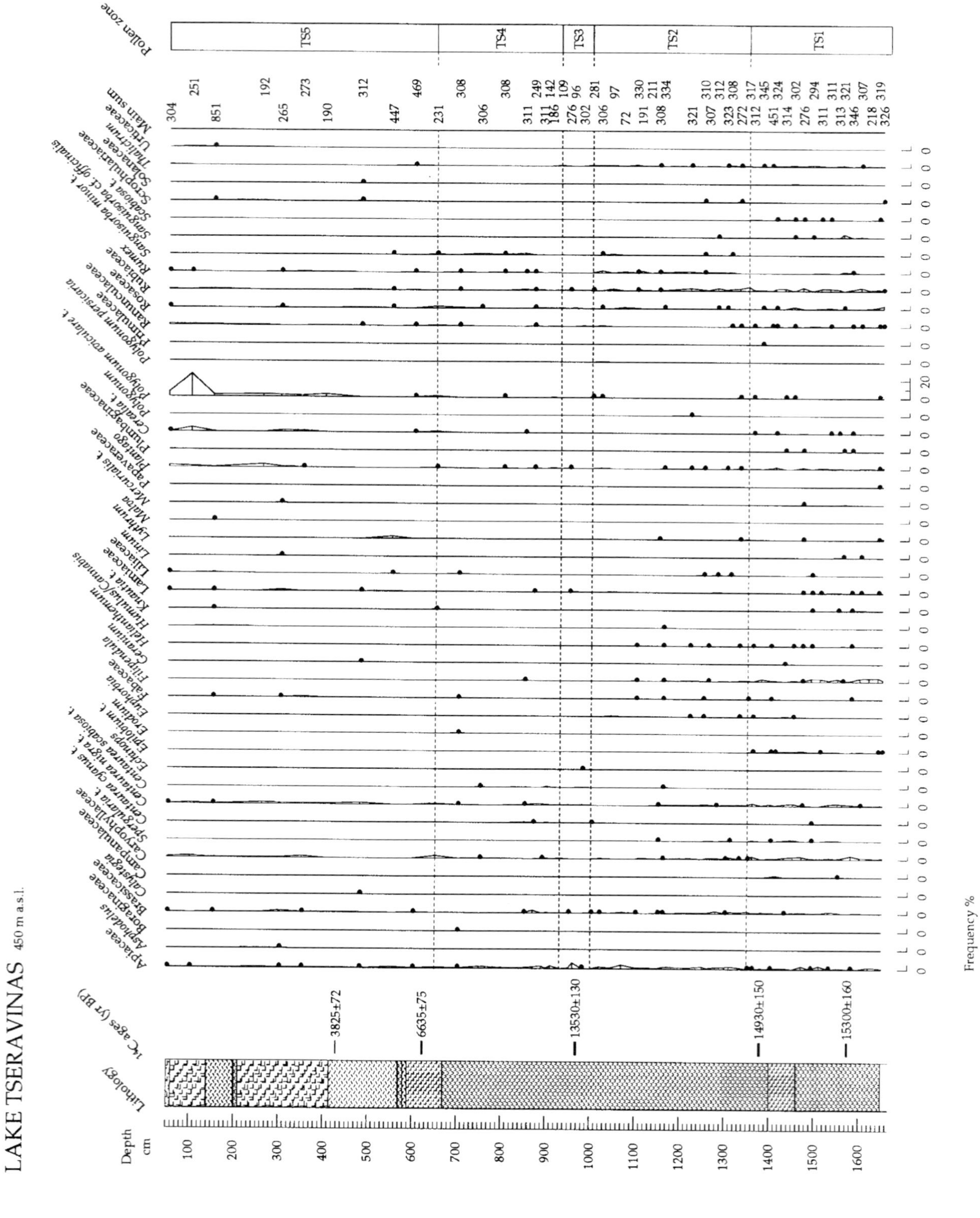

Figure 29.11. *(continued).*

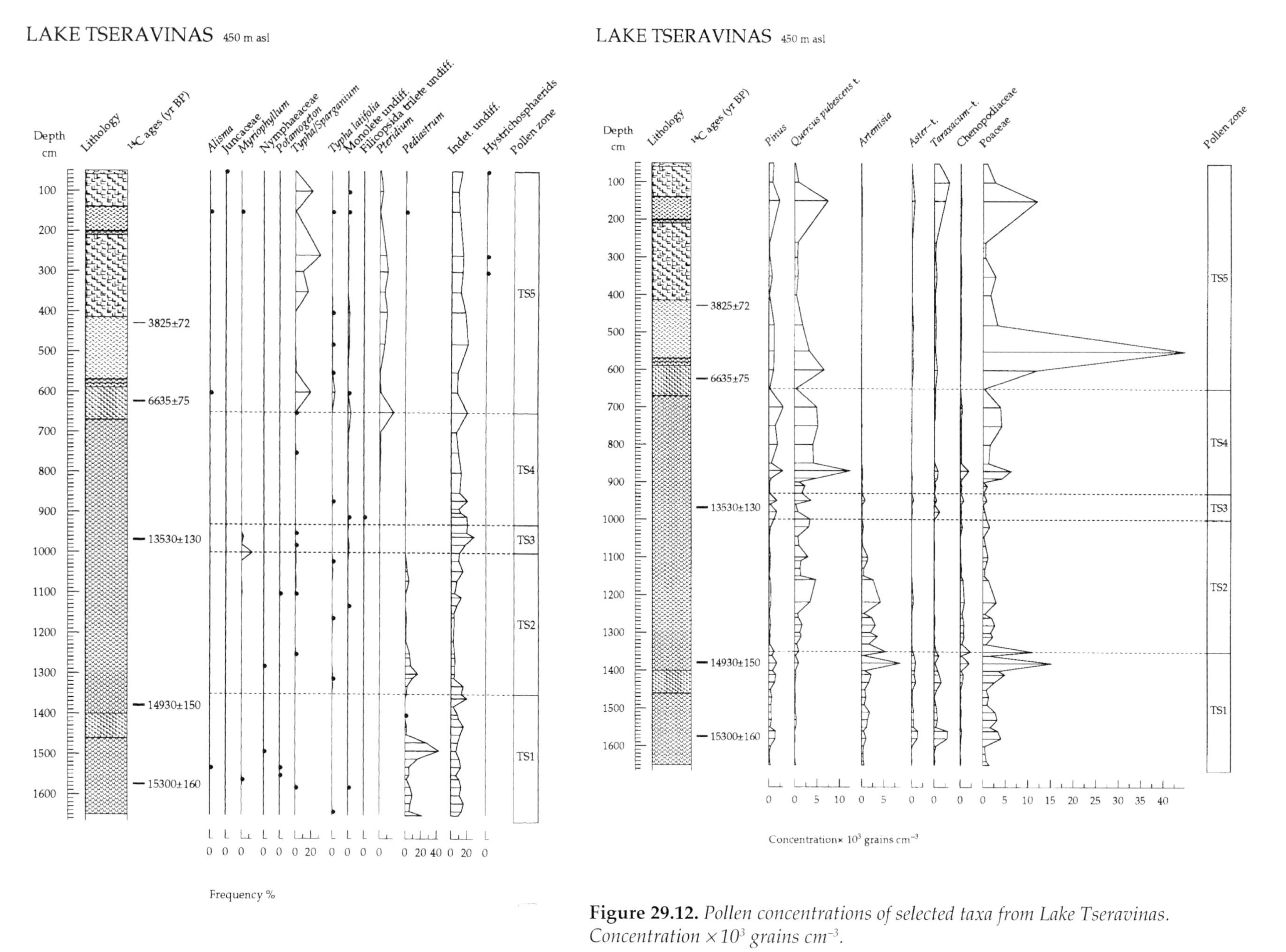

Figure 29.11. *(continued).*

Figure 29.12. *Pollen concentrations of selected taxa from Lake Tseravinas. Concentration $\times 10^3$ grains cm^{-3}.*

upper parts of the core. This probably reflects changes in the nutrient status of the lake waters and perhaps deserves further consideration.

Plant macrofossils, however, augment the picture of shallow water and marginal vegetation. The marl-forming alga *Chara* was particularly abundant during zones TS 1–3, with the submerged aquatics horned pondweed *Zannichellia palustris* and water crowfoot *Ranunculus* sp., *Batrachium* sp. and marginal sedges *Carex* spp. in zone TS 1. Other aquatics such as marestail *Hippuris vulgaris* and pondweeds *Potamogeton* spp. and again *Carex* spp. occurred in zone TS 2.

In contrast, during the later zones the pollen percentages of fringing marsh plants increase significantly (*Sparganium*, *Typha latifolia*, *Lythrum* and perhaps *Polygonum aviculare*-type). This may be due to a rise in lake level in the later part of the Postglacial, or more probably to local vegetational changes associated with the growth of the marginal delta.

Vegetational changes at Lake Tseravinas, their chronology and correlation with Lake Ziros

Radiocarbon dating of the lower part of the Tseravinas core has profound implications for the interpretation of vegetational change in northern Greece during the critical transitional period between the Late Würmian and the Holocene. The story is not yet fully developed, and further radiocarbon dates would clearly be useful. All dates quoted refer to uncalibrated radiocarbon years BP, though calibrated dates are also shown in Table 29.1. Provisional correlation of the Tseravinas and Ziros vegetational sequences is presented in Figure 29.13.

Zone TS 1

At Tseravinas, zone TS 1 represents a steppe-grassland landscape in which not only *Artemisia* and Chenopodiaceae, but also grasses and particularly herbs such as different groups of Asteraceae, *Filipendula* and *Rumex* were important. Oaks were probably present but only in very sparse quantity. However, a distinctive feature of this zone is the presence of fir *Abies*, a low pollen producer, which must have been locally present, probably together with pine. This *Abies* peak is a very useful marker in the Late Würmian of Epirus. It is clearly also present in both Bottema's and Tzedakis' pollen diagrams from Ioannina. It is also the key feature which allows us to correlate this zone at Tseravinas with zone ZI 1 of the Ziros core. The two dates obtained for this zone, 14,930 ± 150 BP for its top and 15,300 ± 160 BP about 2 m lower in the core confirm its Late Würmian age and that it pre-dates the conventionally accepted Late Glacial climatic amelioration.

An important result of the correlation of zones TS 1 and ZI 1 is that it provides good evidence for

ZIROS zone	ZIROS pollen	ZIROS vegetation	TSERAVINAS vegetation	TSERAVINAS zone	TSERAVINAS pollen	Provisional dating uncalibrated radiocarbon years BP
ZI 6	*Quercus* (*pubescens* and *coccifera*-types), *Carpinus orientalis*-type, *Phillyrea*, *Olea*, *Vitis* *Juglans*, Cerealia	crops open-forest				
ZI 5	POOR IN POLLEN	open-forest	open-forest grazing	TS 5	*Carpinus orientalis*-type, *Quercus pubescens*-type *Plantago*, *Polygonum aviculare*-type, Poaceae, *Taraxacum*-type, *Pteridium*	
ZI 4	*Quercus pubescens*-type *Fraxinus* (*excelsior* and *ornus*-type), *Tilia*, *Ulmus* *Pistacia*, *Sanguisorba minor*-type	open-forest	open-forest	TS 4	*Pinus*, *Abies*, *Quercus pubescens*-type *Tilia* *Pistacia*, *Sanguisorba minor*-type	6700
ZI 3	*Quercus pubescens*-type, *Pinus* *Acer*, *Fraxinus excelsior*-type, *Hedera* *Artemisia*, Chenopodiaceae, Asteraceae, *Rumex*	forest-steppe	forest-steppe	TS 3	*Pinus*, *Quercus pubescens*-type *Hedera*, *Artemisia*, Chenopodiaceae, Asteraceae	10,000
ZI 2	*Quercus* (*pubescens*, *coccifera* and *suber*-types) *Betula*, *Alnus*, *Corylus*, *Ulmus*, *Salix*, *Artemisia*, Chenopodiaceae	forest-steppe	forest-steppe	TS 2	*Quercus* (*pubescens* and *coccifera*-types) *Betula*, *Corylus*, *Salix*, *Fraxinus excelsior*-type, *Artemisia*, Chenopodiaceae, *Rumex*	11,000 ? (or 13,500)
ZI 1	*Abies*, *Pinus*, *Quercus pubescens*-type *Artemisia*, Cyperaceae, Chenopodiaceae, Poaceae *Filipendula*, *Plantago*, *Sanguisorba officinalis*-type *Thalictrum*, Apiaceae, Brassicaceae	scrub steppe	steppe	TS 1	*Abies*, *Pinus* *Artemisia*, Cyperaceae, Chenopodiaceae, Poaceae, *Filipendula*, *Plantago*, *Sanguisorba officinalis*-type, Asteraceae, Caryophyllaceae, Rubiaceae	15,000

Figure 29.13. *Pollen-stratigraphic correlation between the Lake Ziros and Lake Tseravinas sequences.*

human-induced clearance in the Holocene differ in detail. During Glacial periods large quantities of coarse limestone debris were moved downslope by freeze–thaw action, whereas Holocene erosion resulted in erosion of silty-clay sediments which often provided an agriculturally attractive cover over the coarse gravel valley fills accumulated during the Pleistocene (Lewin *et al.* 1991; Macklin *et al.*, Chapter 17).

Acknowledgements

Dr M.-F. Sànchez Goñi was supported in 1992–94 by the ARCHAEOMEDES Project, funded by DG XII of the European Commission as part of the Environment (Desertification) Programme under contract EV5V-0021. Both authors are grateful to Professor R.G. West and Dr P.L. Gibbard for the use of laboratory facilities in the Department of Plant Sciences, University of Cambridge. In Greece invaluable help and cooperation were provided by Dr Chrysanthe Ioachim and Mr Giorgios Kolovos of IGME, and by Mr I. Petrou of IGME, who provided the use of his boat and skilled assistance in making the bathymetric surveys of Lakes Ziros and Tseravinas. The owner of Lake Tseravinas, Mr. Panagiotis Mentzos, kindly gave us permission to make boreholes. The arduous task of putting down boreholes to considerable depths manually at various sites was greatly lightened by the assistance of Geoff Bailey, Charlie Batho, Meurig Horton, Chrysanthe Ioachim, Eleni Kotjabopoulou, Roark Mühlen-Schulte, Peter Newcomer, Peter Peacock, Derek Sturdy and Derrick Webley. Steve Burgess assisted with the vegetation surveys.

Chapter 30

The Palaeolithic Geography of Epirus

Derek Sturdy, Derrick Webley & Geoff Bailey

The main objective of this chapter is to reconstruct the Palaeolithic landscape in terms that have relevance to the Palaeolithic economy by mapping the prehistoric distribution of plants and animals. Our maps take account of what is known or can be extrapolated about habitat requirements in relation to topography, soils, vegetation and snow cover, adjusted of course to take account of climatic, vegetational and geological changes. We concentrate on those larger land mammals known to have been exploited, or likely to have been available, because these are the resources for which we have the best evidence. We produce reconstructions at two geographical scales: an Epirus-wide reconstruction; and a more localized and detailed reconstruction in the vicinity of those sites which have yielded on-site evidence of prehistoric subsistence, mainly animal bones, namely the four rockshelter sites of Klithi, Asprochaliko, Kastritsa and Grava.

Given the uncertainties that attach to much of the data available to us, we concentrate on simple questions: what economic options were open to the Palaeolithic inhabitants of Epirus; and which options were selected?

Since the reconstruction of resource distributions is obtained largely independently of the archaeological evidence for site distributions and contents, we expect to gain some insight into the relationship between environmental determinants and economic choices and thus to throw some further light on the nature of the interactions between them. Circularity of argument is, of course, an ever-present hazard in such an approach. If cattle bones are present in a prehistoric site we shall naturally tend to look for cattle habitat in the neighbouring landscape. We have also tended to examine in greater detail landscapes near known archaeological sites. We can, however, minimize the risks of circularity by being consistent in the definition and application of the criteria by which we place animals in the landscape, by looking at the region as a whole (and not just the local areas around known archaeological sites), and by looking at the proportional representation of animal habitats and their relative distances from individual archaeological sites in comparison with the proportional representation of animal taxa in the excavated bone remains, across a range of case studies. The reconstruction of potential land use categories is, therefore, based on evidence which is essentially independent of the archaeological evidence for palaeoeconomy.

Most of our data comes from the landscape itself. Broadly speaking, we call this our physical data. Much of it is not realistically quantified. The chemical analysis of modern subsoils described later can use figures accurate to several places of decimals, but when we discuss the water retentiveness or edaphics of Late Glacial subsoils we use broad classifications such as 'good, fair, bad, awful' rather than figures of, say, evapo-transpiration in microlitres per second. Similarly we grade slopes as 'flat/gentle, moderate, rough/steep' rather than giving angles, because of data which suggest that slope angles are locally changing even over the time scale of <100 ka with which we are concerned. Highly active geomorphological and tectonic processes would make the apparent accuracy of modern measurements potentially bogus.

We also have modern data about species represented in the sites, which might be more accurately described as our preconceptions about plants and animals. Some of these preconceptions are examined in more detail below, but it is worth emphasizing at the outset that the placing of plants and animals into the prehistoric environment is not nearly as straightforward as we might hope for (see also Winder, Chapter 31). The behaviour and habitats of plants and animals today is not necessarily an accurate guide to their behaviour in the past, especially where the past environments have no precise modern analogue. Shackleton & Van Andel (1986) have attempted a somewhat similar exercise with the reconstruction of molluscan habitats at different sea level stands adjacent to Franchthi Cave and a comparison with the molluscs brought back to the site by the prehistoric inhabitants. Even organisms with such specific habitat requirements as intertidal molluscs, however, pose formidable uncertainties of interpretation (Thomas 1987), and this study well exemplifies the difficulties as well as the potential of the sort of approach attempted here.

Landscape classification and animal distributions

Criteria

At first sight placing animals in the prehistoric landscape might seem to require little more than the application of modern data on large mammals to a Last Glacial scenario. Couturier's (1938; 1962) classic studies of Alpine ibex and chamois, and the long series of studies of red deer in Scotland (Clutton-Brock & Albon 1989; Clutton-Brock *et al.* 1992; Darling 1956) provide useful information for two taxa that predominate in our archaeological samples, while Lovari (1985) offers a range of studies of chamois. The behaviour of modern animals, however, in environments which are different from those which we try to assess can be misleading. The habitats of many species including deer and wild caprids have greatly altered in recent millennia in response to expanding agricultural economies; red deer in particular are capable of adapting to a wide range of conditions from Scottish moorland to dense lowland forest, while chamois and ibex have been restricted to mountain fastnesses by the expansion of domestic stock. Varying ecological interactions with humans and with other predators, competitors and parasites further back in time may also have altered habitat distributions (see Winder, Chapter 31). Hence some sorts of information about animals (the nature of their stomachs or feet, for example) are highly relevant, and provide a secure basis for extrapolation into past environments, whereas other variables will only emerge from further analysis.

Table 30.1 lists the most common five herbivores found in Epirus, and grades them against six criteria. The species in question are *Bos primigenius, Equus hydruntinus, Cervus elaphus, Capra ibex,* and *Rupicapra rupicapra,* which, for convenience, we refer to as cattle, horse, red deer, ibex and chamois respectively. The criteria are themselves ranked according to our evaluation of their reliability.

Feet

This criterion measures the ability to negotiate ground of increasing ruggedness. This is very much a function of the morphology of the legs and feet and needs little discussion, as fortunately physiological changes in limb-bones over the last 18 ka are not substantial. The deer lie between the mountain-negotiating abilities of horse and cattle on the one hand, and goats and chamois on the other, and this is completely obvious. However, this is a good stage at which to note that the equivalence of goats and chamois with rugged terrain does not necessarily mean their equivalence with mountainous terrain. It is perfectly true that today ibex and chamois have a purely montane distribution. It is also true that the morphology of their limbs and feet shows that they are well suited to mountain crags. This does not lead to the inevitable corollary that they have always been mountain dwellers. We suggest that we restrict our thoughts on these two species' feet to their ability to negotiate rugged terrain; that we note that rugged terrain includes, but by no means to the exclusion of other landscapes, mountains; and that we are aware of the strong possibility that today's montane distribution of ibex and chamois is a Holocene phenomenon resulting from competition with other animals, especially domestic goats. In particular, we feel that chamois and ibex are well suited to exploit 'angry' karst and scree-riddled country, which even deer would not risk their legs over and which cattle and horses would venture onto

Table 30.1. *Criteria for drawing animal dispersal maps.*

Criterion	Ranking of criterion	Grading	Cattle	Horse	Red deer	Ibex	Chamois
FEET	good	1=least rugged	1	2	3	5	4
WATER	good	1=most dependent	1	2	3=	5	3=
BROWSE/GRAZE	fair	1=most graze	2	1	3=	5	3=
EXPOSURE	fair	1=least rugged	1	2	3	4=	4=
PARASITES	poor	1=most sensitive	4=	3	1	4=	2
TERRITORY	bad	1=most territorial	4=	3	1=	4=	1=

FEET: Grades the ability of the animal to negotiate country of increasing ruggedness. Ruggedness correlates with steepness but also with 'angry' karst, heavily gullied landscapes, etc., which may appear flat plateaux at large scales.

WATER: Grades dependence on water, both for quantity per day and frequency of visits to actual water.

BROWSE/GRAZE: Grades from graze to browse through herbivorous omnivory.

EXPOSURE: Grades ability to withstand exposure (temperature+wind). Not a particularly sensitive feature.

PARASITES: Grades the sensitivity to parasite build-up.

TERRITORIALITY: Grades the apparent adaptability of the animals to changes in their territoriality. Least reliable criterion of these six. Probably heavy Holocene changes with domestication, etc.

only at their peril. 'Angry' karst can be, from a distant viewpoint, completely flat, and indeed it is only the intra-karst relief of the most striking 'angry' karst in Epirus that makes it so difficult to cross. The Badanj site in Herzegovina, where chamois are associated in the Late Glacial with extensive areas of 'angry' karst plateaux, is a good parallel to draw (Miracle & Sturdy 1991). Similarly, there are some areas where substantial amounts of scree cover are interspersed with good browse or graze. These would be accessible to goats and chamois but not to deer, horse or cattle. Such areas, again, may not be strictly montane, particularly with the cold conditions of Last Glacial Epirus. A good example is the Aristi–Papingon area near the Klithi site, where thin tongues of flysch appear likely to have been partly covered by, and partly interspersed with, lobes of scree, some of which, usually cemented, remain today.

Water

Here the criterion is the daily amount of water that is required by individuals of each species and the frequency with which they must have it. The goat is the clear winner on drought resistance, requiring only about 2–3 litres per day, much of which can often be obtained from the vegetation, and needs to drink only every second day unless the weather is very hot. Cattle are most dependent on water, and although we should not use modern figures for cows giving large amounts of milk, there is no doubt about their dependence on large daily quantities of water. We are short of data on the chamois, as so often with this animal. Because water is not usually a problem in its modern mountainous retreats, we cannot be too sure of the middle-ground status we assign to it.

Browse/graze

Studies of a wide range of ruminants have shown that there is a close correlation between the structure of the stomach and feeding style across a spectrum which ranges from selective feeding on concentrated foodstuffs at one extreme, broadly equivalent to browsing on leaves and woody materials of trees and shrubs, to non-selective bulk intake of grass and roughage at the other (Hofman 1973; 1985). Muzzle width in deer species also varies according to the preference for browse or graze (Putnam 1988). Strictly speaking these morphological classifications express a contrast between selective feeding on concentrated foods, whether from trees and shrubs or from herbs and grasses, and non-selective bulk intake of cellulose, rather than a straightforward contrast between woodland and grassland. This is an important distinction because of the tendency to equate simplistically certain species with woodland environments.

On these criteria roe deer lie at the selective end of the range and cattle at the other extreme. Red deer, goats and chamois are more opportunistic feeders. They have an ability to combine browse and graze according to varying circumstances of season and habitat and are thus intermediate between these two extremes. To this extent the criterion of browse/graze is a little more susceptible to post-Pleistocene changes. Red deer, for example, will take grasses, herbs and forbs when they are green and succulent, and are happy to rely on browse in the winter months (Putnam 1988). They are 'picky' feeders (selective without obvious, immediate rationale). It is not sensible to be over-dogmatic about their favourite food as it appears to change, for even one individual, from day to day. The range is wide, and the one fairly certain fact is that deer vary their intake, if they can, both in terms of what they eat and where they eat it.

Unfortunately, the equation of red deer with 'woodland' has become widespread in the literature, despite the fact that, of the two large populations of modern European red deer, one, the Central European, lives largely in woodland while the other, the Scottish, lives largely in open conditions, both habitats being, for their two areas, the marginal ones. At two of our sites with good bone data in Epirus, Kastritsa and Asprochaliko, the red deer are considerably the most abundant animal. At the same time, the pollen data show little evidence for woodland, especially in the hinterland (Turner & Sánchez-Goñi, Chapter 29) and we can only postulate the likelihood, at best, of gallery woodland down watercourses (for example, from the presence of beaver in the Klithi and Kastritsa fauna). Since pollen data are unlikely to under-represent tree cover, we believe that the equation of red deer with woodland is simply wrong for Epirus and that the modern equation occurs for exactly the same reasons as the equation of ibex and chamois with mountains. Deer will make use of woodland, particularly in winter, when it seems that woodland may be as useful in providing shelter or cover as much as food. Even those deer species such as the roe deer which are more specialized in their feeding adaptations and concentrate on woodland browse are capable of thriving in the open agricultural landscapes of Europe with little access to woodland or scrub for food or shelter (Putnam 1988). In the absence of tree cover, then, deer, and especially red deer, can still do very nicely, as their faunal associations in Last Glacial Europe elsewhere show quite clearly. Scrub for winter browse, however, might have been available in some parts of Epirus and the position of red deer in the graze/browse ranking is not altered by this discussion.

Chamois and ibex in their alpine habitats today tend to avoid competition by occupying different altitudinal ranges: ibex move to higher altitude, up to the snowline, in summer, whereas chamois move lower into forest cover in winter. This reflects both the greater agility of the ibex and the more selective feeding adaptation of the chamois, which are happy to browse on trees in winter. How far either species might might have made greater use of browse, particularly in winter, in the absence of competition with domestic goat and sheep is uncertain. Modern goats have notoriously catholic tastes and an ability to convert the most improbable materials into food. A predilection (in the folklore) for washing hanging on lines may, of course, tell us more about the hardships of life for goats in urban backyards than it does about real food preferences, and if life is sufficiently difficult, goats will eat everything from prickly Kermés oak leaves to cement bags. Nevertheless, the ability to convert improbable twigs into useful food does not seem likely to be a purely Holocene phenomenon.

The horse stomach is particularly well adapted to grass; it is a wonderful converter of cellulose. Unless it cannot get good grazing, the horse will rarely browse. Cattle, which are also well able to convert large amounts of grass into energy, are not able to graze very short grass usefully. There is a minimum stem length below which they are physically unable to graze. Although not as consistent browsers as, say, deer in winter, they will browse at any season, particularly if they have, or are allowed, no grazing. This tendency was probably exaggerated in Last Glacial Epirus, because their dependence on water would keep them close to the gallery woodland along water courses, which is the only woodland which appears, as we have already noted, to be likely, and even that not to any real extent until the Late Glacial.

Exposure

This and the next two criteria offer grounds for comparison which are much less firm. 'Exposure' attempts to rate the tolerance of each species to cold, windy and wet conditions — the relationship between the three being close. Since aridity seems to have prevailed in our period in Epirus, cold and wind are probably the factors we must consider. Knowing little about the horses except that they appear to be closer to *Equus hydruntinus* than to the highly cold-adapted *E. przewalski* we still feel some justification for putting the steppe ass near the bottom of the tolerance scale. Whether the cattle should fit between horse and deer or, as we have them, as the least tolerant of exposure, is not easily resolved and we do not put great importance on this distinction.

Parasites

With this criterion we are also on difficult ground because tolerance to parasitic infection is both vital and, with our present archaeological techniques, impossible to measure. It is also liable to vary according to population density and degree of contact and cross infection between different ungulate species. Modern studies of deer, chamois and ibex are of animals that overlap in their range with domestic stock (Balbo *et al.* 1985; Holt 1976; Schröder & Kofler 1985) and thus introduce factors that may not apply to the prehistoric situation.

It is perfectly possible that 'domestication' concentrates on certain limited species, among many other reasons, because they are more tolerant to the increased risk of parasite infestation which the close proximity of domestication imposes. By this criterion, cattle and goats should be the most tolerant and deer, which are not successfully domesticated as herds but only as individuals, should be the least, and that is how we rate them. But we cannot prove it, and some modern studies of deer living in close proximity to domestic stock and exposed to comparable risk of parasitic infection suggest the reverse (Holt 1976). Unfortunately, the criterion is a most important one because on it, as much as on any other, depend both animal densities and the extent, patterns and distance of their annual migrations. By modern data, we believe our ranking to be appropriate and again it is left to the expertise of individuals to decide whether they believe that the resistance to parasite infestation among the Cervidae, particularly, is likely to have decreased or increased in the Holocene. It is also true that we expect the winters, during our periods, to have been sufficiently harsh to have assisted in breaking the parasite cycles of most of the intestinal parasites which would affect the herbivores, provided that they made seasonal migrations between discrete grazing areas. The importance of parasite cycles as a contributory factor in herbivore migration is often ignored, and it is essential at least to try to take it into account. It is largely true that, not even excepting the 'domestic' animals, herds which stay in the same place all year are either much less dense than their food supply often warrants, or do not survive without medicaments, as modern farmers know to their cost.

Territoriality
Finally, and most contentiously, we would like to include the concept of 'territoriality' in our criteria. But we are even more ignorant about the territoriality of Pleistocene herbivores than about their other attributes. Because territoriality is clearly a matter of behaviour more than physical morphology, it is peculiarly vulnerable to the criticisms we have made of applying modern ethology to late Pleistocene herbivores. Would red deer today be so territorial if they had not been pushed into the margins by sheep and cattle? Certainly today, the territoriality of red deer is an effective obstacle to very close man–animal relationships and particularly to herd domestication, except in conditions such as deer-parks or the island of Rhum, where deer movements are heavily circumscribed by humans or the sea. If late Pleistocene red deer were the same, the sort of close human–deer relationship at which Higgs *et al.* (1967) more than hinted is a pipedream only. Our position is similar to that which we take up on the issue of the parasites. We suggest that the Holocene has probably exaggerated an existing tendency and that today's ranking of territoriality would probably have obtained in the late Pleistocene; the difference, however, between the not very territorial goats and highly territorial red deer would probably have been much less.

Palaeogeographical categories

The principal palaeogeographical categories are: position of the coastline and of winter and summer snowlines for modern, Late Glacial and Last Glacial Maximum conditions; relative edaphic conditions, based on the nutrient properties of bedrock and overlying deposits (limestone, flysch, older fans, active fans, alluvium); terrain; and water retentiveness of land surfaces. We have further evaluated our assessment of relative edaphic properties by analysis of available phosphate and mineral content of a large series of soil samples from different bedrock and sediment types. These categories provide the basis for mapping likely animal distributions and seasonal movements. The maps of animal distribution are simplified to the extent that we associate one or two species with particular blocks of landscape. This does not mean that we believe these were the only animals to feed in that part of the landscape, rather that these were the species most likely to have been found there.

Our most detailed archaeological evidence comes from the latter part of the Last Glacial, broadly from 20 ka to 10 ka, a period which witnessed a change of climate from one of the coldest periods in human history to practically modern warmth. In order to track these changes we use two reconstructions for two rather loose periods: the period immediately after the Last Glacial Maximum at 16 ka, the very first apparent signs of amelioration after the maximum cold (between about 20 ka and 16 ka); and the 'Late Glacial' period, at around 13 ka, when we should expect some form of warming.

Coastlines
The western boundary of our area is set by the coastline, which would have changed with eustatic changes in sea-level. We use the sea-level curves of Chappell & Shackleton (1986, see also Fig. 28.10), and Van Andel (1989; 1990; Van Andel & Shackleton 1982). These cannot cannot be fitted absolutely unquestioned to the coasts of Epirus because of the tectonic effects discussed earlier (King *et al.*, Chapter 28). Figure 30.1 shows the –100 m and –200 m contours off the coast and reveals that, except around the islands of Paxos and Antipaxos south of Kerkyra, there is not much to choose between them. We can take the suggested figure of –130 m for the Pleniglacial sea level depression with confidence, because the amount of land revealed by getting sea level wrong by 30 m, provided we are still bracketed between –100 m and –200 m, is not very great. The picture is different when we consider the rise in sea level after the maximum of the Last Glacial. According to eustatic curves of global sea level change (Fairbanks 1989; Van Andel 1990), sea level would still have been at about –100 m through until the beginning of our Late Glacial period at about 13 ka. The major reduction in the amount of coastal plain around Kerkyra would have occurred between 13 ka and 10 ka, when sea level rose from about –100 m to –50 m. By the end of this period Kerkyra would have approximated more closely to its present configuration, and would probably have been separated from the mainland by a very narrow and shallow strait at its northeastern corner (Fig. 30.1).

Snowlines
To the north and east, snowlines are important determinants (Table 30.2). They are specifically drawn to give an indication of snowline behaviour at mean

Table 30.2. *Suggested snowlines in the late Upper Palaeolithic of Epirus.*

Period	Winter	Spring	Early summer	High summer
18–13 kyr	450 m	700 m	1000 m	1700 m
13–10 kyr	700 m	1000 m	1300 m	2000 m

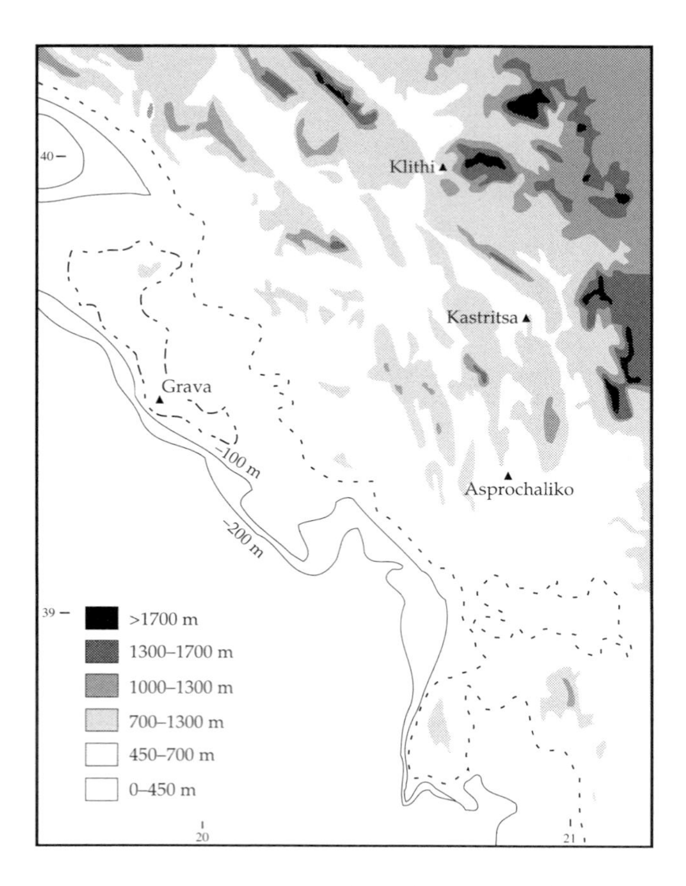

Figure 30.1. *Base map of Epirus showing coastlines and snowlines under different climatic conditions.*

heights. Hence the 'contours' marked at, say, 1000 m dip down by varying amounts on the north side of hills and in gullies that receive little sun, and rise by varying amounts on south-facing and insolated slopes. Roughly speaking, on west and east facing slopes, the contours drawn correspond to the physical contours on the ground.

Interpretation of these snowline maps depends on a base calculation of the Last Glacial Maximum snowline. The moraine data is our best current guide. Moraines in the Pindus are frequently found at heights of 1400 m and even below, where they appear to be the result of (mainly) lobes of local ice-sheets or (less often) of valley glaciers, rather than of extensive Alpine-style glaciation. Their discontinuity shows that the typical height indication of 1400 m is not a snowline height, but a point reached by ice lobes. Moraines rather more indicative of mountain glaciation on Astraka above the Klithi site are well-preserved at about 1700 m. Small cirque moraines are found in the Gamila at varying heights above this, including 1900 m. We have no evidence that mountain glaciation other than lobes or individual glaciers reached any lower than 1700 m. Mountain slopes between 1300 m and 1700 m are characterized by distinctive geomorphological features such as doline fields and 'angry' karst which suggest, at best, 'periglacial' conditions at this altitude rather than permanent glaciers. We therefore take the Last Glacial Maximum permanent snowline for Epirus as around 1700 m, which may mean 1800 m on some south-facing slopes, and 1600 m on some north-facing slopes.

For the modern position of the permanent snowline, we take the 2400 m contour as our guide. Small mountain blocks have higher permanent snowlines than large, because the small area of permanent or long-lasting snow has less of a local cooling effect through the albedo factor. Only very small areas of Epirus lie above 2500 m. At that height on the Smolitsas range, north-facing gullies can retain snow in August, and Rackham (1983, 306) notes in Boeotia that Parnassus, which is 2457 m high, 'just has permanent snow'. If there was enough land at >2400 m today, it would probably carry permanent snow, and this figure of 2400 m is a realistic modern basis for snowline calculations. The Pleniglacial snowline depression was then some 700 m.

We suggest, on very limited evidence, that our 13 ka figure for the permanent snowline might be placed mid-way between Last Glacial Maximum and modern figures, perhaps with a slight low bias, say at 2000 m, a depression of some 400 m.

Present-day winter snowlines in Epirus for the months of January–March lie at around 1100 m. This is variable, year by year, as everywhere else. But if we apply a similar snowline depression of 700 m, we would have a winter Last Glacial Maximum snowline at around 400 m and a Late Glacial winter snowline at around 700 m. Figure 30.1 shows the effect of snowlines at 450 and 700 m, which should give an indication of winter and spring conditions during our first, immediately post-Pleniglacial period. The 700 m and 1000 m snowline contours similarly should give an indication of winter and spring conditions in our second period, the Late Glacial.

Although browsing is possible under all but the heaviest snowfalls, feeding would not be easy above the snowlines, even if there was not much snow. Vegetation would have been ice-encrusted and there would have been relatively little browseable scrub in comparison with lower altitudes nearer the coast (Turner & Sánchez-Goñi, Chapter 29). We therefore suggest that the snowlines we have drawn reflect the winter distribution of the majority of the herbivores.

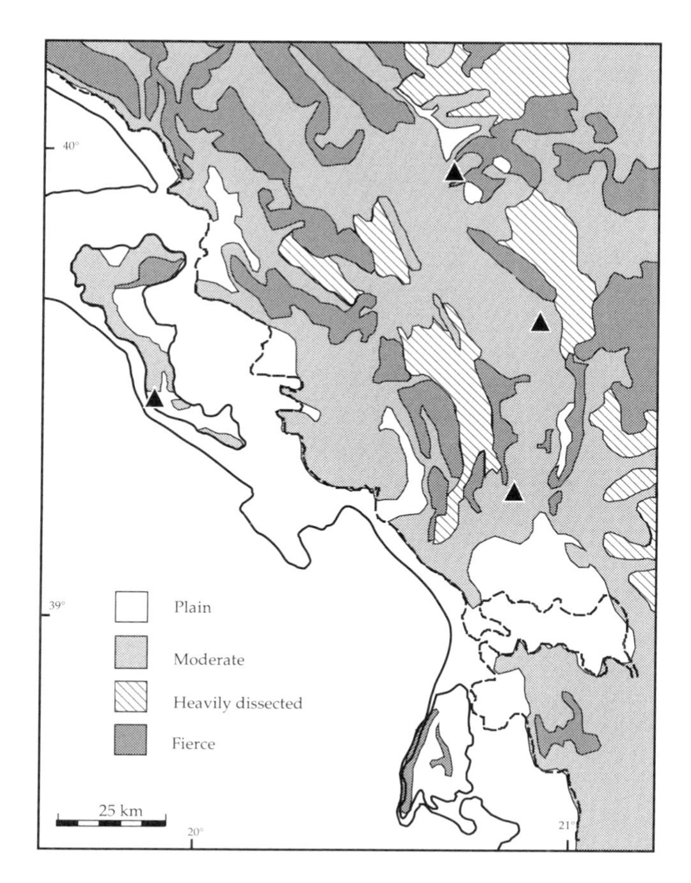

Figure 30.4. *Base map of Epirus showing principal terrain categories used in palaeogeographical reconstruction.*

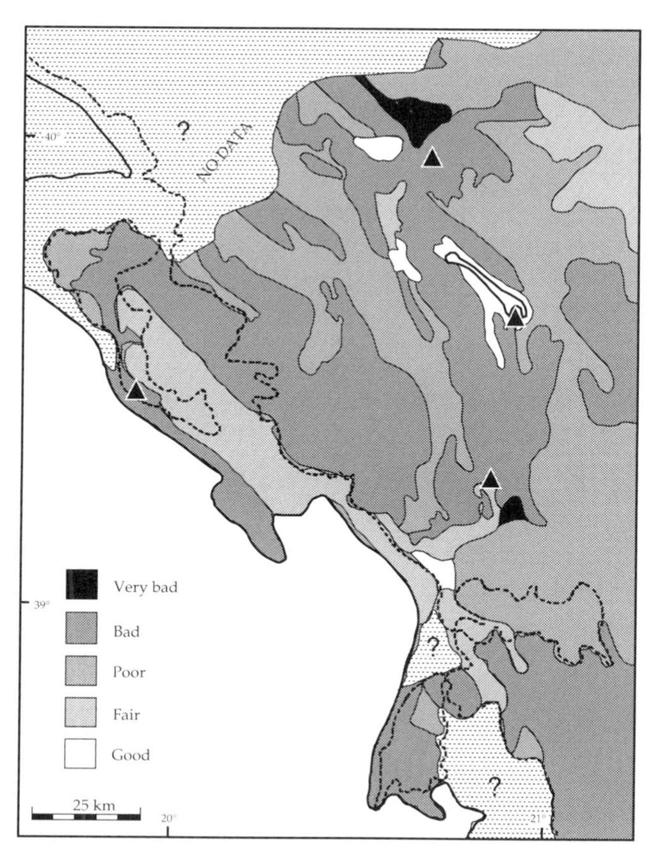

Figure 30.5. *Base map of Epirus showing distribution of water retentive soils used in palaeogeographical reconstruction.*

5. Fair — fans and lake marls of Plio-Pleistocene date, e.g. the pre-Holocene fill of the Doliana basin;
6. Good — pure lake marls, and thick clays or loess.

Landscape units

In the analysis and comparison of different areas of the landscape, we divide each area of interest into sub-areas, which we describe as *landscape units*. Each landscape unit is defined in terms of relatively homogeneous conditions as regards our main palaeogeographical categories. We give a weighting to each landscape unit using the relative rankings of Table 30.4, and sum the rankings for each category to give an overall figure. Thus a landscape unit consisting of rough terrain, poor edaphics and good water retentiveness would achieve a rating of 8, and this is further adjusted to take account of seasonal factors and altitude using the weightings and formula of Table 30.4. For a landscape unit of rough terrain, poor edaphics and good water retentiveness at 700 m in summer, say, the rating is 8. For a landscape unit with the same characteristics at, say, 300 m the rating is 16 for use in summer and 32 for use in winter. We use this simple system of weighting to allow systematic comparisons of the relative productivity of different areas of the landscape. In

Table 30.4. *Relative ranking of landscape units by edaphics, water retentiveness, terrain and season.*

	Edaphics	Water	Terrain	0–400 m	400–800 m	>800 m
Relative ranking[1]						
Very bad	0	0	–	–	–	–
Bad (fierce)	1	1	1	–	–	–
Poor (rough)	2	2	2	–	–	–
Fair (moderate)	3	3	3	–	–	–
Good (gentle)	4	4	3	–	–	–
Seasonal weighting						
Winter/spring	1	1	1	4	0	0
Spring/summer	4	2	1	1	1	1
High summer	2	4	1	0.5	1	2
Autumn/winter	1	3	1	1	1	0

[1] Descriptions in brackets refer to the terrain classification.

The overall numerical weighting of a Landscape Unit (LU) is obtained by the formula LU=A [ES + WS + T] where:

A = Numerical weighting of altitude by season
ES = Edaphics classification adjusted for season
WS = Water retentiveness classification adjusted for season
T = Terrain classification

Table 30.5. *Distribution of animal taxa according to landscape categories for Last Glacial Maximum early summer conditions. Figures are numbers of animals per 100 hectares.*

	Terrain/ Edaphics	Taxa: *Rupicapra*	*Capra*	*Cervus*	*Equus*	*Bos*	*Capreolus*	*Sus*
Limestone	Rough	–	10	–	–	–	–	–
	Moderate	–	5	5	–	–	–	–
	Gentle	–	–	10	–	–	–	–
Flysch	Rough	–	–	–	–	–	2	–
	Moderate	–	–	–	–	–	4	–
	Gentle	–	–	–	–	–	4	–
Older fans	Rough	–	8	–	–	–	–	–
	Moderate	–	4	4	–	–	–	–
	Gentle	–	–	4	4	4	–	–
Pliocene lake	Rough	–	8	–	–	–	–	–
	Moderate	–	4	4	–	–	–	–
	Gentle	–	–	4	4	4	–	–
Loess	Rough	–	10	–	–	–	–	–
	Moderate	–	5	5	–	–	–	–
	Gentle	–	–	4	4	4	–	–
Triassic	Rough	–	5	–	–	–	–	–
	Moderate	–	3	3	–	–	–	–
	Gentle	–	–	3	3	3	–	–
Alluvium	Rough	–	–	–	–	–	–	–
	Moderate	–	–	–	–	–	–	–
	Gentle	–	–	–	–	1	5	1
Active outwash	Rough	–	–	–	–	–	–	–
	Moderate	–	–	–	–	–	–	–
	Gentle	–	–	–	5	–	–	–
High limestone	Rough	2	2	–	–	–	–	–
	Moderate	3	3	–	–	–	–	–
	Gentle	4	4	–	–	–	–	–
Limestone/ flysch	Rough	3	3	–	–	–	–	–
	Moderate	4	4	–	–	–	–	–
	Gentle	5	5	–	–	–	–	–

general, the higher the overall rating the more productive the landscape unit. Summing the ratings for all landscape units within a given area gives us an overall rating for the area, and we use these figures to compare the exploitation territories of our major rockshelter sites and in particular to bring out the the potential for use at different seasons.

Animal habitats

Combining our assessment of animal behaviour with landscape categories we place the various taxa in the landscape as in Table 30.5. The table shows both those taxa that we expect to predominate in particular types of landscape and an assessment of animal densities for early summer grazing conditions. For the latter we take a figure for red deer of 10 animals per 100 hectares in the best grazing conditions, namely gentle limestone by analogy with average red deer densities in Scottish conditions, and a figure of 10 ibex per 100 hectares for what we consider to be the best summer grazing conditions for this species, namely rough limestone.

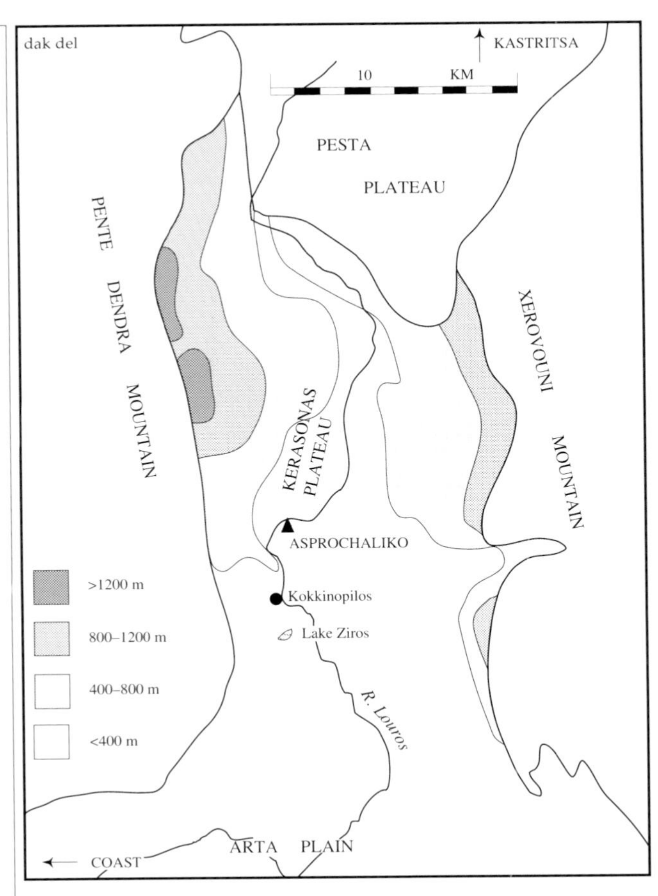

Figure 30.6. *Asprochaliko territory showing altitudinal variation.*

Site exploitation territories

Site territorial analysis by convention examines the area within a 10 km radius to focus attention on the immediate environmental setting of a site. But this is essentially an arbitrary limit and may exclude more distant areas which are nevertheless of importance in understanding the relationship between individual site locations and mobile resources. It may also mask the importance of local features near the site. We therefore start with the local drainage basin as a guide to the area to be examined in detail, not least because the watershed is often delimited by natural barriers, and consider the general features of the area so defined as well as the specific features in the immediate vicinity of each site. The question of what constitutes a barrier to animal movements will depend, of course, on the species in question and seasonal factors. Chamois and ibex are capable of crossing steep or broken ground that would deter other species. A river that acts as a barrier to cattle may be easily negotiable by deer, while a river in

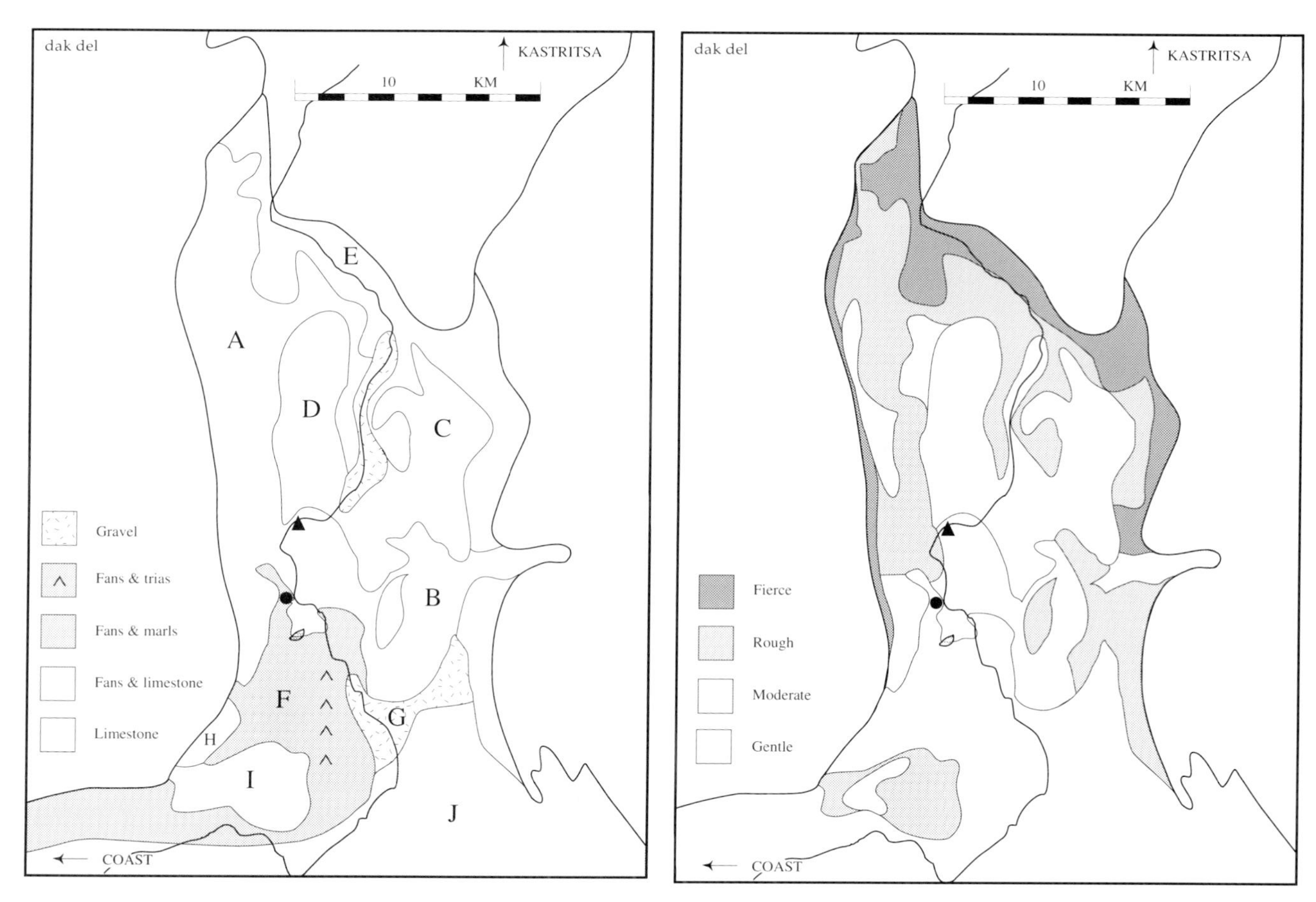

Figure 30.7. *Asprochaliko territory showing variation in geological categories. Landscape units A–J are those used in Table 30.7.*

Figure 30.8. *Asprochaliko territory showing variation in terrain categories.*

seasonal spate with meltwaters may hinder the passage of all animals, except at well-defined crossing points. Winter snowlines will impose seasonal barriers of their own for most animals, as discussed earlier, and extensive areas of swamp or marsh may act as barriers to deer in summer because of insect pests. In the complex topography of Epirus it is not difficult to find topographic barriers that set realistic limits to the area that needs to be examined for individual sites, and we shall consider these for each site in turn. The question of how topographic barriers closer to individual sites might have constrained animal movements, or indeed have been actively exploited to manipulate those movements and facilitate hunting success is quite another matter. As we shall see, such considerations are central to the understanding of all four sites analyzed below.

Asprochaliko

We delimit the margins of the territory to west and east by reference to the steep limestone ridges and associated flysch of Pente Dendra and Xerovouni, to the north by the closure of the Louros Valley by steep cliffs and the higher ground of the Pesta plateau, and to the south by the northern margins of the swampy basin of the Gulf of Arta (Fig. 30.6). Topographically the area grades from higher slopes in the north which would have been under snow in winter to lowland in the south. In terms of geology it is dominated by limestone (Fig. 30.7) which grades from rough or steep terrain in the north to gentle or moderate terrain in the south (Fig. 30.8), and which we rate overall as the best substrate edaphically though nowhere really good (Fig. 30.9). A series of fans and marl deposits are found in the southern part of the area, notably in the vicinity of Kokkinopilos, which have relatively good water retentiveness (Fig. 30.10). Apart from the limestone, scree, alluvium and older fans account for most of the remainder of the territory (Table 30.6).

In terms of our main variables the territory is a transitional one — between cold and warm, steep and gentle terrain, and drier and more water retentive soils — and this is how we interpret the territory in terms of seasonal movements of the large herbivores, as a spring and autumn area between summer grazing to the north and wintering areas to the south and west (Fig. 30.11). As our analysis of landscape units indicates (Table 30.7), the overall potential of the territory is highest in the late-winter, spring and early summer period.

During the Upper Palaeolithic period, deer (mostly red deer but also including some fallow deer, *Dama dama*) (Bailey *et al.*

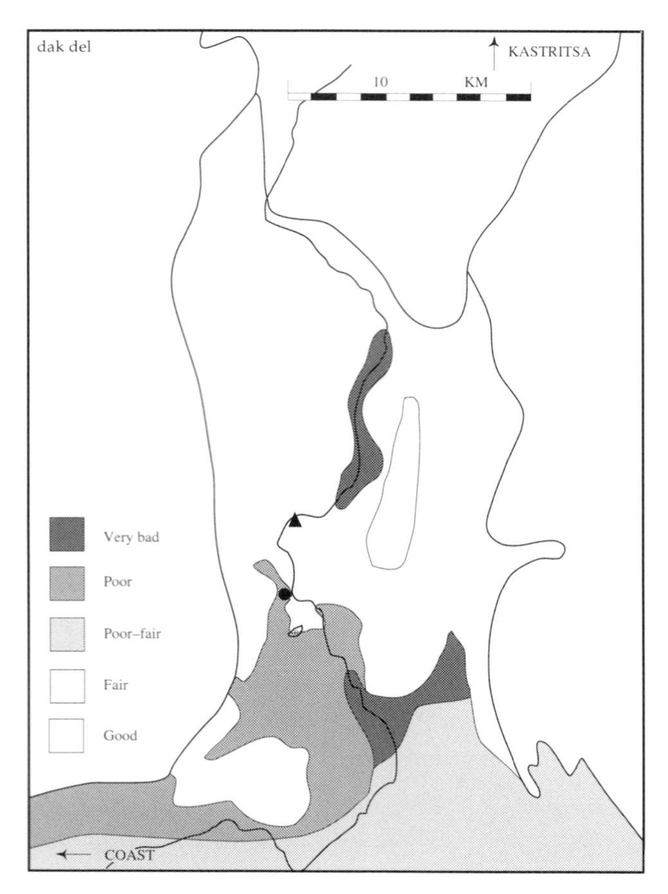

Figure 30.9. *Asprochaliko territory showing variation in edaphic categories.*

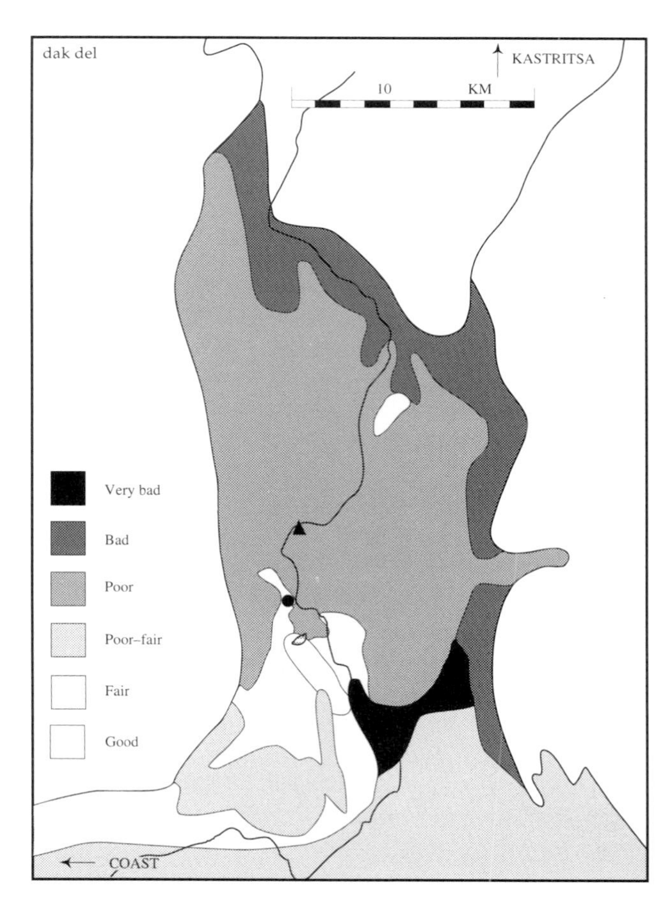

Figure 30.10. *Asprochaliko territory showing variation in water retentiveness categories.*

Table 30.6. *Distribution of edaphic/terrain categories at Asprochaliko (spring).*

	Terrain			
	Rough (ha)	Moderate (ha)	Gentle (ha)	Total (ha)
Edaphics				
Scree (barren)	3763	0	0	**3763**
Limestone	3356	3620	3956	**10,932**
Older fans	88	350	1606	**2044**
Pliocene lake	0	0	188	**188**
Triassic	0	0	306	**306**
Alluvium	0	0	2188	**2188**
Active outwash	0	0	987	**987**
Total	**7207**	**3970**	**9231**	**20,408**

Table 30.7. *Ranking of landscape units in the Asprochaliko territory. (See Table 30.4 for method of calculation and Figure 30.7 for location of units.)*

Landscape unit	Winter/ Spring	Spring/ Summer	High Summer	Autumn/ Winter
A Pente Dendra	0	18.25	24.5	5.5
B Ammotopos plateau	30	18.5	8.25	11.5
C Gorgomylos plateau	0	21	18	12.5
D Kerasonas plateau	16	19	17	12
E Xerovouni slopes	0	15.5	17.25	7.5
F Kokkinopilos–Filipiada Pliocene	32	17	9.5	14
G Kambi outwash gravels	12	3	1.5	3
H **Name??**	32	19	8.5	12
I Ronkia mountain	29	18.25	8	11.25
J Arta plain	32	18	9	13
Total	**183**	**167.5**	**121.5**	**102.25**

Table 30.8. *Numbers of animals per taxon in Asprochaliko territory (spring), using animal densities as in Table 30.5, compared with the representation of taxa in the excavated faunal remains.*

Taxon	Territory N	Territory %	Site fauna N	Site fauna %	Deviation
Rupicapra	0	*0*	0	*0*	0
Capra	538	*34*	36	*36*	0
Cervus	672	*43*	53	*53*	+
Equus	130	*8*	0	*0*	–
Bos	103	*7*	0	*0*	–
Capreolus	109	*7*	7	*7*	0
Sus	22	*1*	4	*4*	0
Total	**1574**	***100***	**100**	***100***	

1983b) and ibex are the principal taxa represented in the faunal remains, and this corresponds to our palaeogeographical analysis, which indicates that these should be the predominant animals within the site exploitation territory (Table 30.8). Cattle and horse are not represented at all on the site, although the palaeogeographical reconstruction indicates that both would have been available in the wider territory. Their absence may reflect the small size of the Upper Palaeolithic faunal sample but minor taxa such as roe deer and pig are represented in small numbers both on-site and off-site, so that it appears that cattle and horse were disregarded in spite of their apparent availability. Conversely deer are somewhat better represented on-site than might have been predicted from their availability in the local environment.

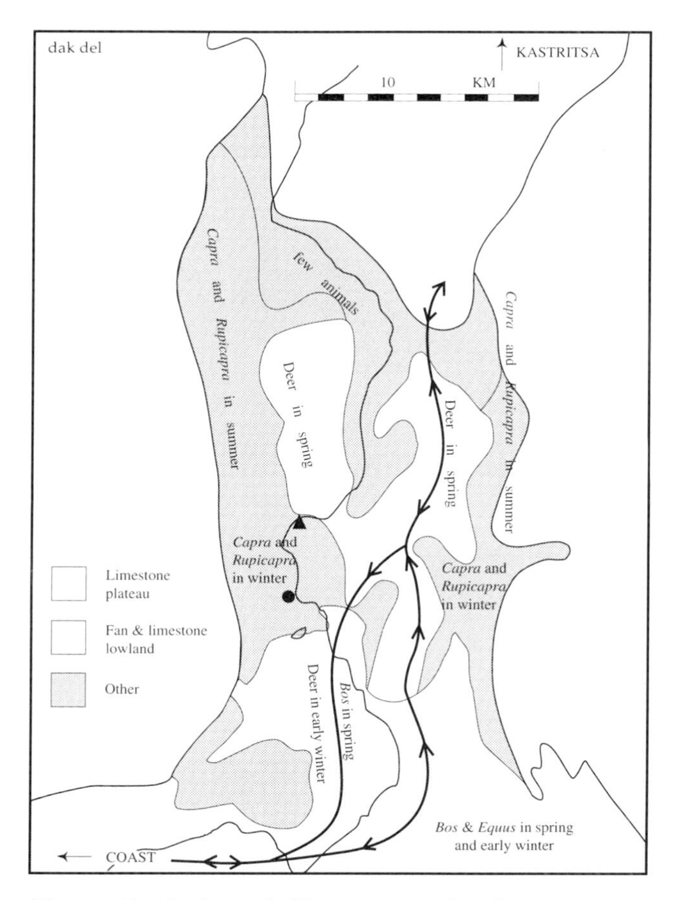

Figure 30.11. *Asprochaliko territory showing distribution and seasonal movements of principal animals.*

Asprochaliko itself is not a migration site in the sense that it lies directly on the main routes of animal migration, since the preferred routes of seasonal movement at least for deer and horse and probably also for cattle would lie on the gently graded limestone plateaux some 4 km to the east of Asprochaliko, though cattle with their greater dependence on water might be expected to keep closer to the course of the river. Ibex and chamois would likewise pass close to the site in their more localized seasonal movements between summer pastures on Pente Dendra and winter pastures in wooded low lying areas to the south, but would not be constrained to pass immediately in front of it. But the site does have local features that would facilitate control and capture of animals. It is in a short section of limestone gorge and it would be a relatively simple matter to encourage some animals to divert through the gorge, which acts as a potential funnel both for animals moving north in spring and for animals returning southwards from the hinterland in autumn. We suspect that the possibilities for trapping animals near the site, or controlling their movements, would be better in spring. Seasonal meltwaters would make the river more difficult to cross at this season, and the funnelling effect of the gorge might be more easy to exploit, particularly for ibex and deer, both of which might be attracted through the gorge to reach early spring and summer grazing to the northwest of the site.

The possibilities for exploiting deer are of particular interest because of the location immediately to the north of the site of the Kerasonas plateau. This is a localized area of gentle relief surrounded by steep slopes and forms a sort of natural corral which would offer particularly attractive grazing to deer in spring and summer. Such a location, in combination with the funnelling effect of the Asprochaliko gorge, offers obvious possibilities for selective diversion of some animals and corralling of them in a location where they could be left to feed undisturbed and to improve their condition before being killed for consumption at a later date.

The site thus offers a number of potential advantages to the monitoring and control of animals. It is at the intersection of two distinct migration routes, a short distance ibex/chamois one, and a long distance deer-cattle-horse route, thereby combining in one location the opportunity to exploit two distinctive groups of species. While being close to these major migration routes, it is not directly on them, and therefore creates the possibility of monitoring seasonal herd movements while also being discreetly located so as to minimize disturbance of the animals. The gorge location offers the possibilities of trapping animals, while a more subtle strategy focused on the deer might involve encouraging some animals through the gorge and up on to the adjacent Kerasonas plateau. The grazing potential of this area would have persisted throughout the summer (Table 30.7), and any animals attracted here would be easy to control and to cull for human consumption at a later date. Many more deer would have ranged more widely into the hinterland in summer, and similar possibilites exist for diverting them into this corral on their return during the autumn although the water retentive soils to the south of the site would have offered more attractive grazing by this time (Table 30.7).

These local features suggest a reason as to why deer were preferentially exploited at Asprochaliko. It seems that the site was used to target quite specifically those animals whose exploitation was most easily facilitated by using to the full the opportunities of the local topography, at the expense of other species which were nevertheless available in the general vicinity.

Geological changes that would affect our interpretation are relatively slight and localized. Some of the water retentive sediments in local basins have undergone uplift and erosion since the time of their initial deposition, as at Kokkinopilos, where the process was already underway by the Upper Palaeolithic period (King *et al.*, Chapter 28), and which might have reduced their water retentive properties to some degree. The Louros River has undergone cycles of aggradation and incision comparable to those experienced by the Voïdomatis (Higgs & Vita-Finzi 1966). Those sections of the river that are currently aggrading today with well-watered alluvial sediments, notably to the north of Asprochaliko, were probably gravel streams of poor edaphic potential and water retentiveness, especially during the Last Glacial Maximum. As suggested above, the river probably played more of a role as a seasonal barrier than as a feeding area. Scree formation was presumably more active, particularly on steeper slopes in the northern part of the territory, and would have reinforced the barriers to movement imposed by the basic topography, and the supply of coarse material to the Louros stream bed. According to the pollen evidence from Lake Zirós (Turner & Sánchez-Goñi, Chapter 29), there was a substantial oak woodland in the area during the Late Glacial, which probably reflects both the more moderate climate in the southern part of Epirus, compared with the region nearer to Klithi, and the presence in the lake vicinity of the water retentive sediments of Kokkinopilos and similar localities. Roe deer and pig are both present thoughout the Asprochaliko sequence in small numbers, suggesting the persistence of some tree cover.

How far the opportunities for controlling animal movements in the immediate locality of the site were realized in the Middle Palaeolithic is difficult to judge. Deer (*Cervus* and *Dama*) are more common in the Middle Palaeolithic levels, roe deer and pig

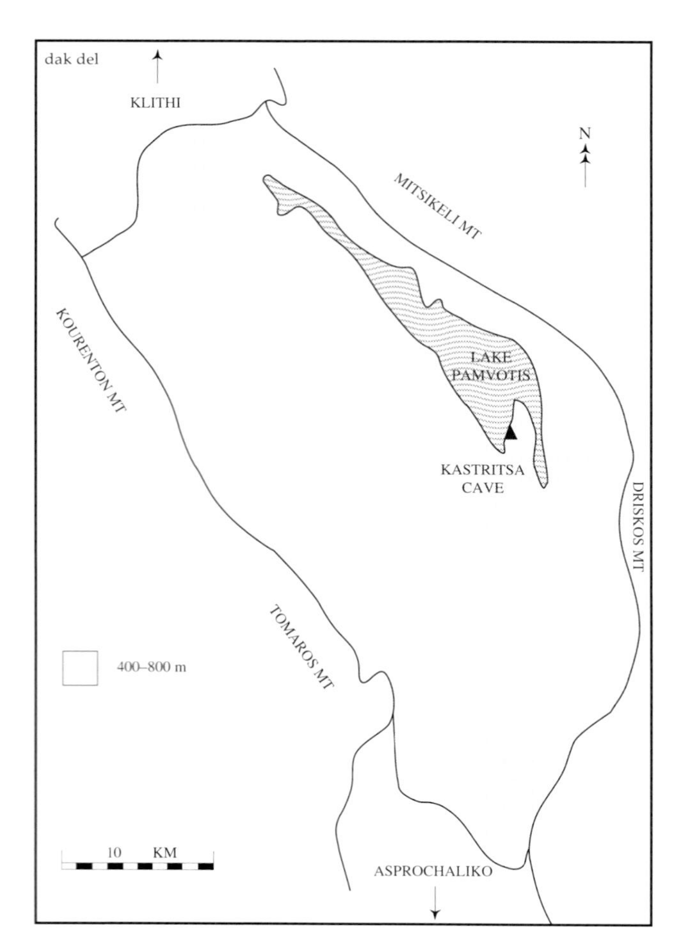

Figure 30.12. *Kastritsa territory showing altitudinal variation.*

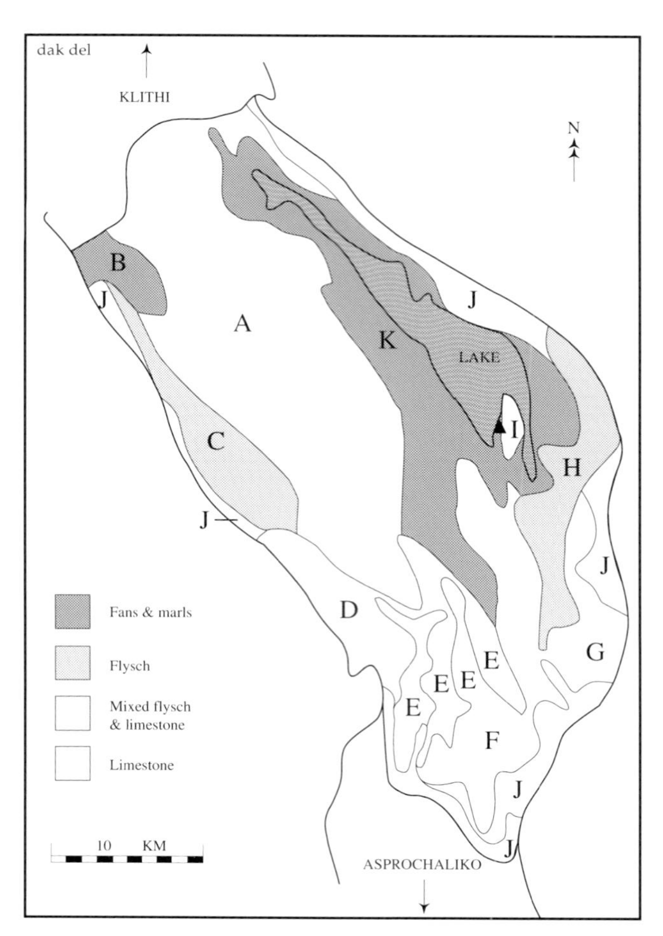

Figure 30.13. *Kastritsa territory showing variation in geological categories. Landscape units A–K are those used in Table 30.10.*

are also present throughout the Middle Palaeolithic levels, though no more so than in the Upper Palaeolithic levels. Ibex bones are notably rare in the Middle Palaeolithic faunal sample which might reflect higher snowlines and more distant habitats. Horse bones are completely absent, which in these earlier periods might simply reflect the local disappearance of their habitat under more wooded conditions, but cattle bones are present in small numbers. If one removes the effects of environmentally-induced changes, the faunal spectrum gives the impression of being slightly broader in comparison with the Upper Palaeolithic levels, but the differences are quite small, and it is not possible to make any definitive statement about how far if at all Middle Palaeolithic strategies of local landscape use differed from later ones.

Kastritsa

To the north and east, the crests of limestone ridges backed by the flysch of the Arachthos basin set an obvious natural limit, and a similar sort of barrier marks the western edge of the territory. To the northwest and the south there are no sharp topographic barriers, and we place our boundaries on the more broken limestone topography which marks the watershed at its most constricted point between the Ioannina basin and the adjacent drainage basins — the Louros to the south and the Kalamas to the northwest.

There is little altitudinal variation within the territory so defined and the present lake level lies at about 470 m a.s.l. (Fig. 30.12). Limestone areas of gentle or moderate terrain predominate (Figs. 30.13 & 30.14; Table 30.9), which as before we rate as the most attractive areas from an edaphic point of view (Fig. 30.15). The other notable feature of the territory is the extensive fans and lake marls around the expanded Ioannina lake, which we rate quite highly in terms of their water retentiveness though rather less highly in edaphic terms (Fig. 30.16). Patches of water retentive soils are also present on the western boundary of the basin, particularly on the fans and marls in the northwest, and to a lesser extent on the mixed flysch-limestone areas to the southwest.

The Ioannina pollen core (Bottema, in Higgs *et al.* 1967; 1974; Tzedakis 1993; Turner & Sánchez-Goñi, Chapter 29) suggests that the basin would have been dominated by grasses and steppe plants with few trees during glacial periods. Small numbers of roe deer and pig are present in the faunal remains of the site, and beaver is also present, but significantly these taxa are better represented in the most recent (Late Glacial) deposits, when climatic amelioration might be expected to have caused some woodland expansion, and they are never common. As at Asprochaliko, we infer from the faunal spectrum the presence of at least scattered tree cover. In winter, however, the basin would have offered few attractions, except perhaps to chamois and ibex descending from

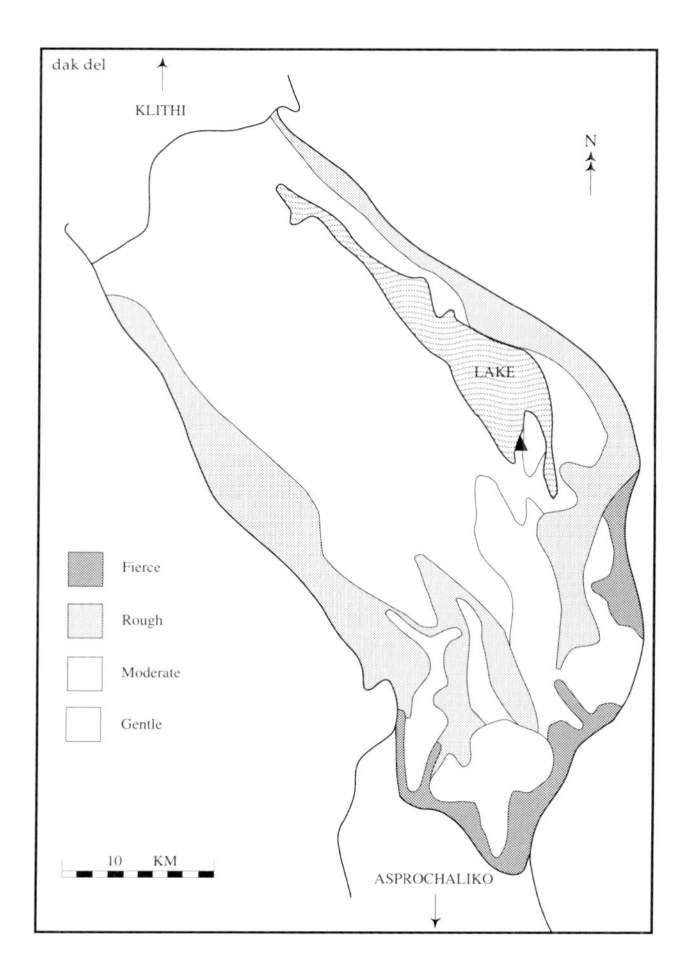

Figure 30.14. *Kastritsa territory showing variation in terrain categories.*

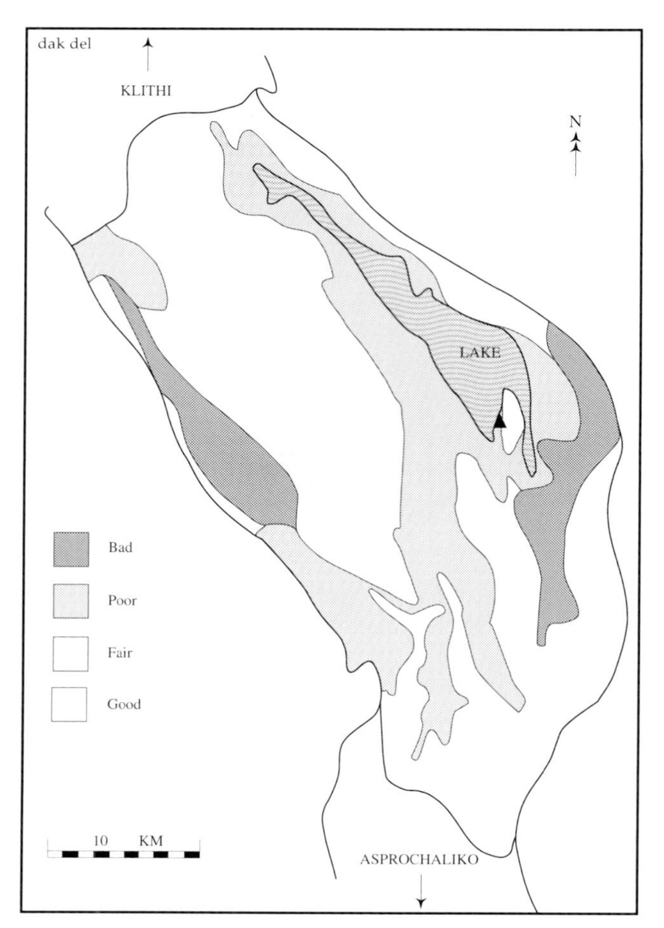

Figure 30.15. *Kastritsa territory showing variation in edaphic categories.*

higher ground, especially if we bear in mind that the area would have been surrounded by snow-covered mountain slopes, with cold-air sinkage, ice-frosting of vegetation, and very limited browse, with the attractions of the lower and warmer Louros basin just a short distance south across the watershed, or the lower lying parts of the Kalamas basin to the northwest. The analysis of landscape units (Table 30.10) shows that the highest potential of the territory is over the summer period.

Deer, cattle and horse should all be well represented within the exploitation territory, with some ibex on the steeper and rougher ground around the territory margins (Fig. 30.17). We further suggest that deer would move across the central limestone plateau in spring and early summer when the limestone grazing would be at its most attractive, returning in autumn along the western margins where the more water-retentive soils are to be found. We concentrate cattle on the well-watered lake margins, and horse on the better-drained gravel facies of the lake-edge fans. As at Asprochaliko, the faunal spectrum recovered in excavation reflects in a general way the availability of resources within the site territory but with some evidence of selectivity — deer and horse seem better represented than their presence in the local environment would warrant, while ibex are much less well represented (Table 30.11).

The question of geological changes in the landscape since the time of Upper Palaeolithic occupation at the site centres principally

Table 30.9. *Distribution of edaphic/terrain categories at Kastritsa (summer).*

	Terrain			
	Rough (ha)	Moderate (ha)	Gentle (ha)	Total (ha)
Edaphics				
Scree (barren)	3634	0	0	**3634**
Lake (barren)	0	0	5796	**5796**
Limestone	10,148	13,823	27,313	**51,284**
Flysch	3960	4464	1649	**10,073**
Older fans	88	241	15,507	**15,836**
Pliocene lake	31	209	728	**968**
Triassic	0	0	81	**81**
Alluvium	0	0	1932	**1932**
Active outwash	0	0	0	**0**
Total	**17,861**	**18,737**	**53,006**	**89,604**

on the extent of the lake. Following Vita-Finzi (Higgs *et al.* 1967, 5), we show an extended area of lake for the glacial period, based on the presence of beach deposits containing freshwater mollusc shells dated to *c.* 20 ka in the Kastritsa cave at a level originally reported as 3.2 m above the present water level, but later shown to be as much as 6.4 m higher than present (Bailey *et al.* 1983b, 29). Much attention has been devoted to the reasons for this raised level — reduced evaporation, increased input of meltwaters (Higgs 1978) or indeed tectonically induced variations in

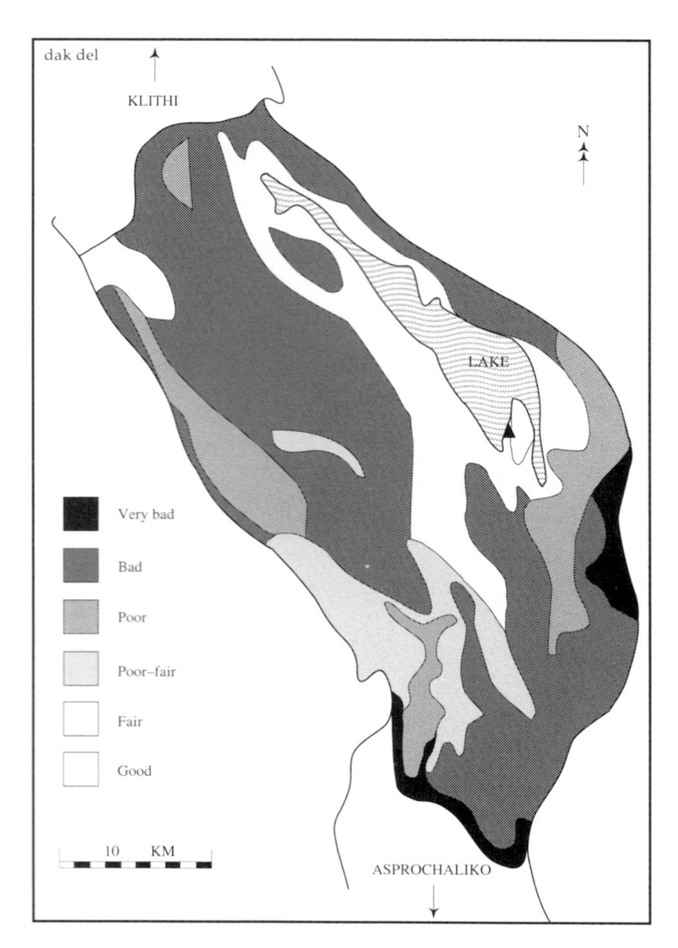

Figure 30.16. *Kastritsa territory showing variation in water retentiveness categories.*

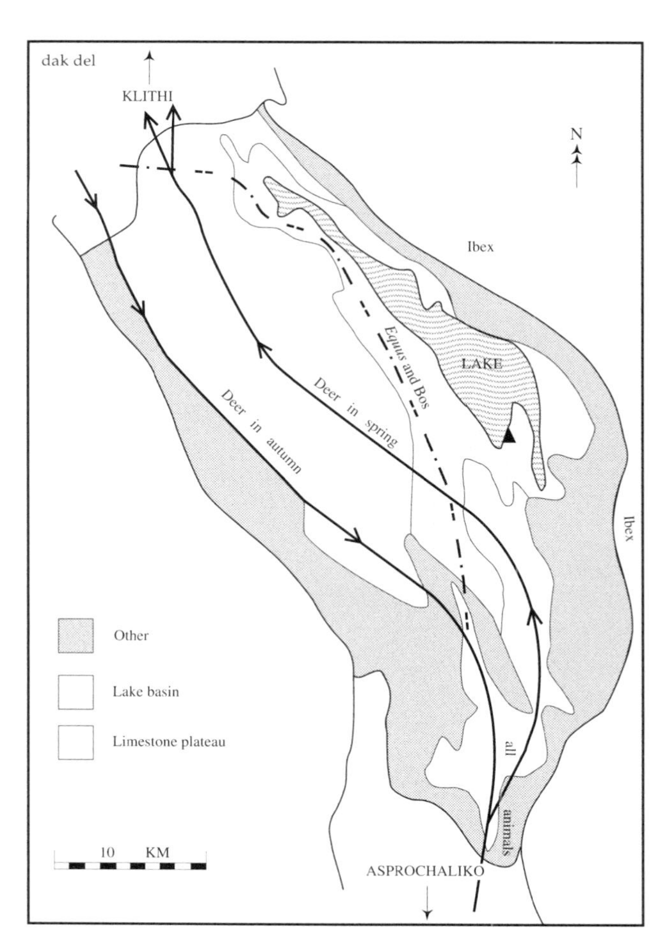

Figure 30.17. *Kastritsa territory showing distribution and seasonal movements of principal animals.*

Table 30.10. *Ranking of landscape units in the Kastritsa territory.*

Landscape unit	Winter/ Spring	Spring/ Summer	High Summer	Autumn/ Winter
A Ioannina basin limestone	0	17.5	14	9.75
B South Kalamas basin	36	19	11.5	17
C Smolitsas Valley	0	11	12.5	9.25
D Tomaros slopes	0	15	16	11.5
E Xerovouni slopes	0	17.5	17.5	12.5
F Louros watershed	0	17	13	9
G Pesta plateau	0	17	13	9
H Aetorraki high plateau	0	10	12	9
I Kastritsa hill	0	16	12	8
J Steep slopes	0	16	12	8
K Ioannina basin marls and fans	0	17	23	14
Total	36	173	156.5	117

Table 30.11. *Numbers of animals per taxon in Kastritsa territory (summer), using animal densities as in Table 30.5, compared with the representation of taxa in the excavated faunal remains.*

Taxon	Territory N	Territory %	Site fauna N	Site fauna %	Deviation
Rupicapra	0	*0*	0	*0*	0
Capra	1733	*23*	71	*1*	–
Cervus	4092	*54*	6796	*77*	+
Equus	652	*8*	1260	*14*	+
Bos	671	*9*	466	*6*	0
Capreolus	420	*6*	115	*1*	–
Sus	19	*0*	103	*1*	0
Total	**7587**	***100***	**8811**	***100***	

drainage — and to the modelling of climatic parameters on the assumption of increased lake levels (Prentice *et al.* 1992). The geological evidence for raised lake levels, however, is in conflict with the pollen evidence which suggest a lake level no higher than the present (Bottema 1974; P.C. Tzedakis, pers. comm.). One way of resolving the conflict would be to suppose that the small limestone hill in the side of which the Kastritsa cave is located has undergone some further uplift since the time of Palaeolithic occupation. However that may be, it is not unreasonable to postulate a more extensive lake during the Last Glacial, even without a rise in lake level, if only because much of the present-day lake margin has been subject to recent sediment infill and subsequent drainage. At any rate it seems likely that the lake edge would have converged on the base of the Kastritsa hill much closer to the cave than is the case today, and that if we shrink the area covered by the lake in the Last Glacial (as compared with that indicated in the figures) we should nevertheless postulate a concomitant increase in the extent of marshy ground around it.

The configuration of the lake margin close to Kastritsa is of some importance because it appears that, as at Asprochaliko, the site is located well to the side of the main routes for animal movement, but with an immediate environment that offers possibilities for diverting, funnelling, trapping and corralling some of the animals. At Kastritsa the funnel is created by the convergence of the lake edge and the Kastritsa hill, while the natural corral lies to the east of the site, and its potential in this respect would be enhanced to some degree if the lake were more extensive than today.

Klithi

The boundaries of the Klithi territory are defined by the Kasidiares–Kourenton mountain ridge to the west, and by the slopes of the Pindus to the east, reinforced by glaciers in the nearer vicinity of Klithi. The southern boundary is the watershed with the Ioannina basin, while to the north we take as our boundary the low hills to the north of the Konitsa basin, which is backed by the Sarandaporos flysch basin, with the steeper slopes of the Nemertska mountain further west (Fig. 30.18).

Substantial geological changes affecting the land-use potential of the territory have taken place since the Pleistocene, on the higher slopes of the Voïdomatis catchment, in the Konitsa basin, and in the Gormos–Kalamas basin. The Voïdomatis and Konitsa basin areas are in close proximity to the site and need correspondingly careful consideration, while the geological changes further west are on a relatively large scale. Since the geological changes in these areas have a major impact on our palaeogeographic assessment, we consider them first.

Our observations on the fills of the Konitsa basin broadly confirm and extend geographically the valley-fill sequence discussed by Macklin *et al.* (Chapter 17). Sections at the mouth of the Voïdomatis and on the Aoos River near Konitsa show that both rivers were aggrading their beds with a coarse sediment of boulders, cobbles and gravel in a sandy matrix up to a maximum height of some 7 m above the present river level.

Woodward *et al.* (1994) have discussed pedogenic weathering of soil profiles on Last Glacial alluvial units, notably the Aristi Unit, dated by TL and ESR to between 28 ka and 24 ka, and have shown that a soil is present on this unit at the mouth of the Voïdomatis Gorge where the river enters the Konitsa basin, which they believe to be evidence of a stable land surface with soil development during the Late Glacial (see also Macklin *et al.*, Chapter 17). The dating of this soil is problematic, however, to the extent that the uppermost member of this unit in the same location, consisting of sandy slack-water sediments, is radiocarbon-dated to about 12 ka, in which case significant soil development would post-date the main Palaeolithic occupation in the area (notably at Klithi). Even if we accept the earlier dates, the relative thinness of the Late Glacial soil, and its absence elsewhere on the Konitsa plain in spite of extensive survey, suggest that its impact on the water retentive potential of the Konitsa basin at large, and the capacity for supporting vegetation was little affected. We do not, therefore, regard the presence of this soil as sufficient to modify our assessment of land-use potential.

After this period of Late Glacial aggradation, both rivers then cut down through their beds leaving benches on which flints and pottery of Neolithic or later date are sometimes found. In the later Holocene, within the last millennium, the central area of the basin was covered with silts and clays resulting from erosion of material from the surrounding hill slopes, which created a present-day landscape attractive to modern farmers. During Upper Palaeolithic times the basin was thus covered in gravels and sands subject to heavy seasonal flooding. Little vegetation would have been supported except in very restricted areas, and we rate the grazing potential of the area as being very low, until downcutting and confinement of the river channel, and soil development, made the area more attractive in the Late Glacial. A flush of scattered grasses and forbs might have attracted a few animals in spring, but the two rivers would have been hard to ford at this season, posing awkward barriers to movement of animals and people.

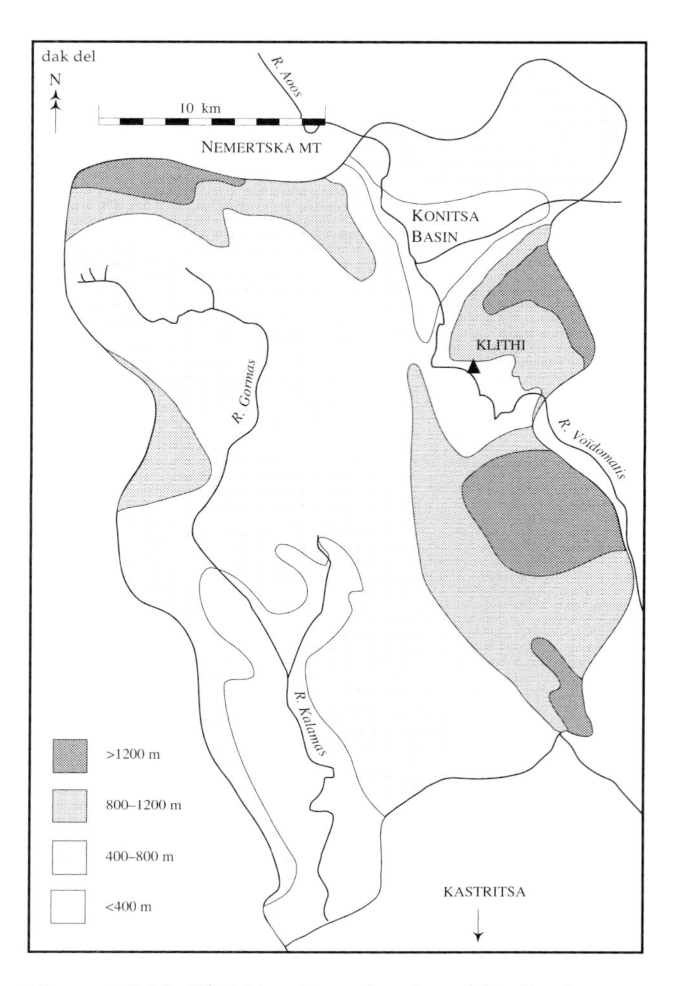

Figure 30.18. *Klithi territory showing altitudinal variation.*

The Kalamas basin has undergone major transformations since the Pleistocene. Today the basin is divided into three zones: a northern zone (which we refer to as the Doliana basin) in which recent Holocene sediments have drowned a gently dissected landscape of old fans and Triassic limestone; a central area of jumbled river gravels, alluvial and colluvial fans and remnants of old lake marls, heavily eroded and dissected; and a southern area of gentle relief in which the modern river is cutting through Middle Pleistocene lake marls. Neither the northern nor the central zone offer substantial areas of good grazing under modern conditions: the northern zone is a closed basin with cold-air sinkage and frost conditions, and would support wet woodland or marsh of little interest before modern drainage and mechanized agriculture, while the central zone is too heavily eroded.

We believe, however, that these conditions are the result of recent tectonic movements which have created a restraining rise between the northern and central zones, causing ponding back of Holocene sediment in the northern zone and downcutting and erosion in the central zone (King *et al.*, Chapter 28). Palaeolithic humans and animals saw a very different basin, not divided as today but forming a single and fairly uniform zone with a gently sloping surface, and composed of a detailed mosaic of Triassic breccias with local brown soils, Jurassic limestones with *terra rossa* soils of varying thicknesses, alluvial and colluvial fans of varying degrees of water retentiveness, and highly water-retentive

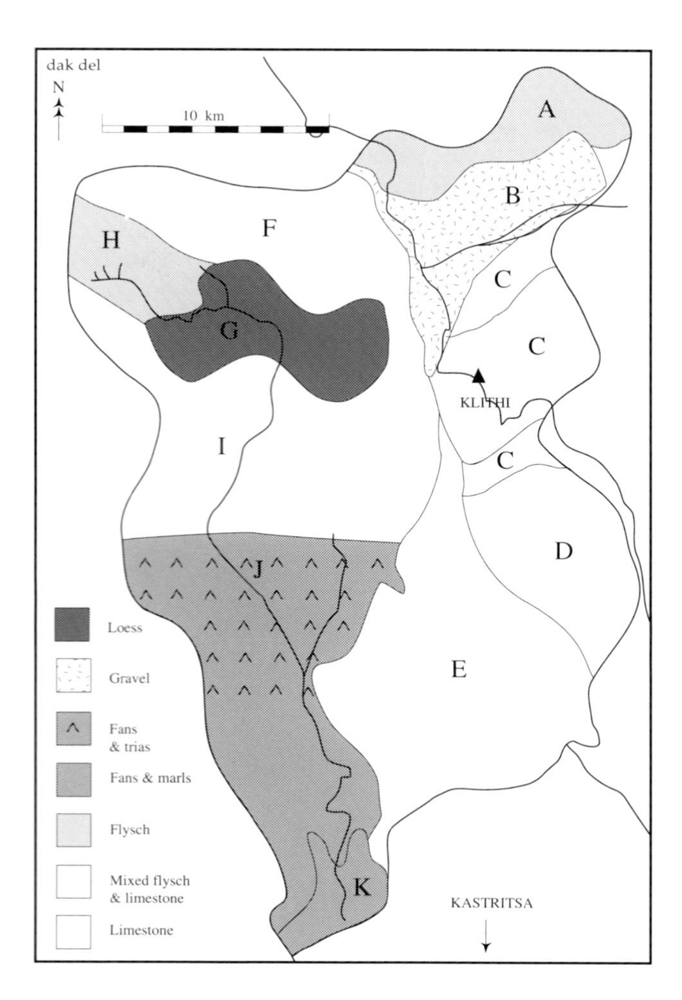

Figure 30.19. *Klithi territory showing variation in geological categories. Landscape units A–J are those used in Table 30.13.*

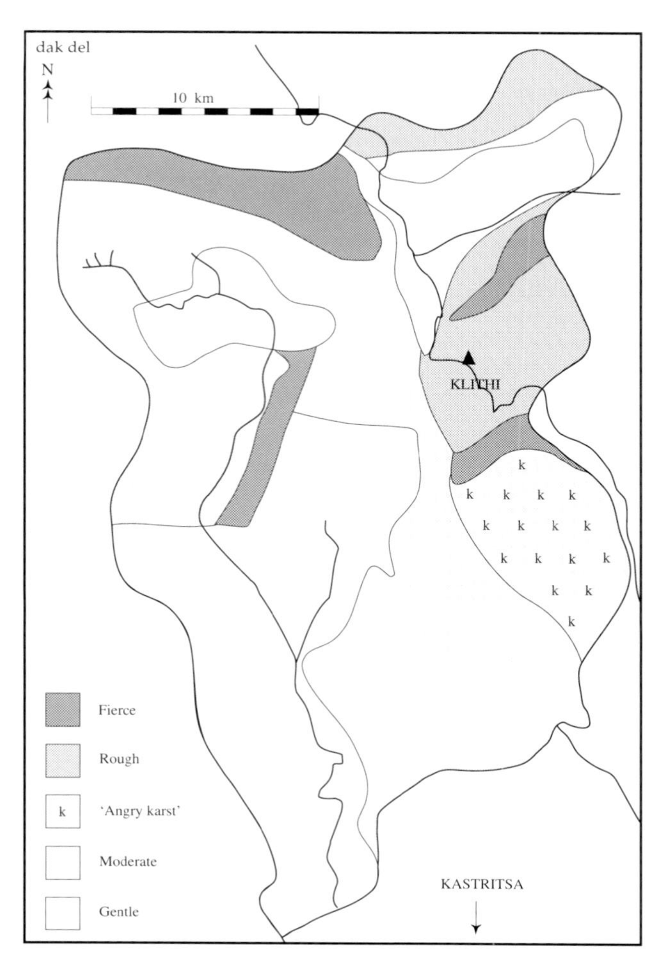

Figure 30.20. *Klithi territory showing variation in terrain categories.*

Table 30.12. *Distribution of edaphic/terrain categories at Klithi (summer).*

	Terrain			
	Rough (ha)	Moderate (ha)	Gentle (ha)	Total (ha)
Edaphics				
Klithi West				
Scree (barren)	1656	0	0	**1656**
Lake (barren)	0	0	19	**19**
Limestone	3491	7670	3260	**14,421**
Flysch	859	1875	279	**3013**
Older fans	0	1116	7278	**8394**
Pliocene lake	0	131	525	**656**
Loess	0	1116	2747	**3863**
Triassic	0	0	894	**894**
Alluvium	0	0	301	**301**
Active outwash	0	0	413	**413**
Sub-total	**6006**	**11,908**	**15,716**	**33,630**
Klithi East				
Scree (barren)	735	0	0	**735**
Limestone	5760	5109	1141	**12,010**
Flysch	900	2103	342	**3345**
Older fans	36	85	1697	**1818**
Alluvium	0	0	72	**72**
Active outwash	0	0	3201	**3201**
High limestone	0	2542	0	**2542**
Limestone/flysch	1531	354	0	**1885**
Sub-total	**8962**	**10,193**	**6453**	**25,608**

old lake marls and their soils. This would have offered much more attractive grazing conditions with patchworks of plant communities. The northern zone would not have been a local frost trap as today and would have offered a more attractive wintering ground for ibex and chamois. To the north on the Gormos plateau were loess soils up to 1 m thick (Appendix A) providing well-drained but water-retentive soils particularly attractive as late summer grazing for animals such as deer.

The main impact of geological changes associated with glaciation in the upper Voïdomatis catchment (Macklin *et al.*, Chapter 17) would have been to remove large areas of high altitude as potential grazing, to reinforce natural barriers to the east of Klithi, and to accentuate meltwater conditions in spring and early summer.

In the following assessment, we have made adjustments to incorporate the geological changes identified above. Geologically speaking, the territory is highly varied, with limestone topography ranging from steep and rough slopes or angry karst plateau areas in the vicinity of Klithi to gentle or moderate terrain to the west and south (Figs. 30.19 & 30.20). As always the gentler limestone terrain forms our best edaphic category (Fig. 30.21), while the complex series of fans on the Triassic limestone in the southern part of the Kalamas basin, though edaphically poorer, have relatively good water retentive properties (Fig. 30.22). We also rate the Gormos plateau very highly in terms of water

The movements of ibex and chamois are likely to have covered smaller distances and we show the likely movements in the vicinity of the sites discussed earlier. Horse and cattle are likely to have had closely related movements as complementary grazers, and cattle in particular are quite water-dependent. Thus we concentrate them in the Ioannina and south Kalamas basins in summer, on the margins of the Ioannina Lake in autumn, and in the lowlands of the Arta basin and the coastal areas and the now-submerged Kerkyra plain in winter.

For the deer we propose movements up the eastern side of the Louros, on the lower flanks and plateau of Xerovouni, in spring, with diversion of some animals onto the Kerasonas plateau north of Asprochaliko; through the gentler limestone topography of the Ioannina basin for the early summer flush of grazing; onto the flanks of the Nemertska mountain in high summer, with a concentration on the Gormos plateau with its water retentive loess and red bed formations during the rutting season; a return migration down the western fringe of the Ioannina basin in autumn to exploit the browse of the flysch fringe; and a scattering throughout the lowland region in winter in areas of oak scrub.

Ibex and chamois exploiting the high slopes of the Mitzikeli and the slopes above Klithi we place in the southern Kalamas basin in winter, while the animals summering on Pente Dendra we imagine moving to lower ground in the lower Louros basin.

The distribution of seasonal terrain and edaphic factors, combined with the large-scale natural barriers created by the tectonic features discussed above, form what we refer to as the Epirus 'horseshoe'. The western arm of the horseshoe comprises the rolling limestone terrain of western Epirus, considerably extended at lowered sea levels. This area is a prime candidate for use as a winter grazing area but could have been used at other seasons also. The eastern arm is the limestone hinterland of moderate terrain which extends from Asprochaliko to Klithi, with the Ioannina basin situated midway between them. This area is rather neatly controlled by our three main rockshelters. Factors of altitude, snowcover, and enclosure by high mountain ridges make this ineligible for use except as as a summer grazing basin. To the south, linking the two arms of the horseshoe, is the major sediment sink represented by the Gulf of Arta. This area, together with other areas of water retentive soils in the western arm of the horseshoe, would have formed a potentially important source of winter grazing or browse, and perhaps also areas of summer grazing for some animals, depending on the height of the water table, the nature of the sediments and the species in question. Deer, for example, tend to move away from swampy areas in summer because of insect pests.

The overall distribution of archaeological sites at a regional scale has been discussed in detail by Bailey *et al.* in Chapter 27. Problems of dating and potential biases are discussed in detail there. But it is worth noting two points of particular relevance to the present discussion: firstly, the close correlation between site locations and the edaphically favourable limestone areas; and secondly, the association between the site distribution and the routes of animal migration around the Epirus 'horseshoe'.

The question of closure to the north requires further comment because the location of the Albanian border has tended to impose an arbitrary barrier in our earlier syntheses (Bailey *et al.* 1986a; 1993; Sturdy & Webley 1988). The Drin Valley clearly provides a major potential routeway northwestwards out of Epirus to the extensive lowlands on the Albanian coast, and provides another potential axis of seasonal movement between winter grazing areas on the coast and the summer grazing areas west of Klithi. It is worth noting, however, that the upper Drin runs through rugged terrain, and that the distance to the coast is rather greater than by the route that runs south from Klithi around the Epirus horseshoe. Restrictions on movement northwards along the coast, even at periods of lowered sea level, have already been noted. Movement southwards would also have had the virtue of increasing the likelihood of encounter with more moderate climatic and perhaps more attractive vegetational conditions, as compared with movement northwards along the Drin. We therefore consider that the pattern of movements indicated in Figure 30.25 would have been the preferred pattern for the large herbivores, although we do not exclude the possibility of movements to and from the north.

Individual site selection and local features

Within the overall regional pattern, individual sites are clearly located to take advantage of local features, but their location and pattern of use are also influenced by a regional perspective. The three rockshelter sites for which we have most information, and which appear to have been most intensively and consistently used, are clearly interlinked, and neatly control the margins of the hinterland basin that forms the eastern arm of the horseshoe. Within this regional perspective, each site controls different local resources and emphasizes unusual features. Asprochaliko is on the margin between the more wooded coastal lowland and the hinterland steppe environment. It offers a good view of the main migration routes whithout being so close as to cause disturbance, and controls local environments that would facilitate access to some animals, such as deer on the Kerasonas plateau. Kastritsa is on the margin between limestone and flysch regions, and controls the Kastritsa peninsula into the lake while minimizing lake-side disturbance, the lake-side being a key resource. Klithi is on the margin between useable and unuseable areas of limestone terrain, offers easy access to a good view of both ibex (or chamois) and red deer migration routes, is well away from the red deer rutting area, and controls local environments within the general area that would have most facilitated access to the ibex and chamois.

The resources exploited at each site reflect these local features in broad terms. Thus ibex is the dominant taxon on-site and off-site at Klithi, while red deer is clearly dominant both on-site and off-site at Kastritsa and Asprochaliko. There is, however, preferential selection for, or avoidance of, the secondary species. At Klithi there is a selective preference for chamois and a selective avoidance of red deer; at Kastritsa a selective avoidance of ibex and a selective preference for horse and cattle; and at Asprochaliko a selective preference for ibex and selective avoidance of horse (Fig. 30.26). Thus, where the palaeogeographical analysis shows that a particular resource was equally available at two locations, the archaeological analysis often shows a selection, and it is the secondary resources that are subject to this selection. In other words, at the local level, there is economic specialization with respect to the resources locally available, and a clear selection for those activities that are most easily performed at the site in question, at the expense of those that are best performed elsewhere.

Water-retentive areas are also vital to the reconstruction of the Palaeolithic landscapes, but are not immediately reflected by site distributions and locations. Both Klithi and Asprochaliko have access to areas of improved water retentiveness but neither is located in the key areas in question. Similarly Kastritsa is tucked away at one remove inside a key water retentive area. Thus water retentiveness adds to the general attraction of an area but is not the controlling factor in individual site locations. From the above features we conclude that the Upper Palaeolithic economy was founded on a regional integration of resources, involving a considerable degree of human and animal mobility, rather than a series of local economies tied to local resources and opportunities, and to local constraints.

Human population estimates

In an earlier assessment (Bailey *et al.* 1986a), we suggested that the total human population that could be supported in the eastern hinterland of Last Glacial Epirus could have been as low as 50 people. No attempt was made at that time to incorporate the resources of the western plateaux and coastal lowlands. In the light of the more detailed data presented here, it is possible to re-assess the figures. For calculation of total biomass and human population, we use the data of Tables 30.15 and 30.16. The results indicate a regional population of 616, which we may take as representing a range of say 500 to 1000, allowing for additional contributions from minor resources, and the inherent uncertainties in this sort of calculation. This suggests that our previous figure was a considerable underestimate, mainly because it took no account of the extensive coastal lowland region of western Epirus. Even so the figure, while higher than before, is consistent with the notion of the Epirus region as being occupied by a single social and economic unit or 'mating network', and gives further support to our belief that we should think in terms of a regional integration of resources by a single palaeoeconomic unit, involving a considerable degree of human and animal mobility, rather than the co-existence of sub-regional populations pursuing essentially independent economic strategies tied to local resources and opportunities. Even if some humans and animals remained in the region of western Epirus throughout the year, the resources available in the eastern hinterland could only have been exploited by groups moving seasonally inland from the coastal areas.

We can refine these notions further by estimating in the same way the likely size of human group present in the vicinity of Kastritsa and Klithi (Tables 30.16 & 30.17). Using the same methods of calculation and the same set of assumptions we arrive at surprisingly different figures for the two sites. At Klithi the data suggest a resident group of just 6 people, at Kastritsa a group of 98 people, an order of magnitude difference. We would of course arrive at a much higher figure for Klithi if we were to include in our estimates the resources of the wider region including the Klithi West territory. But since the herds of deer, cattle and horse in the latter area would

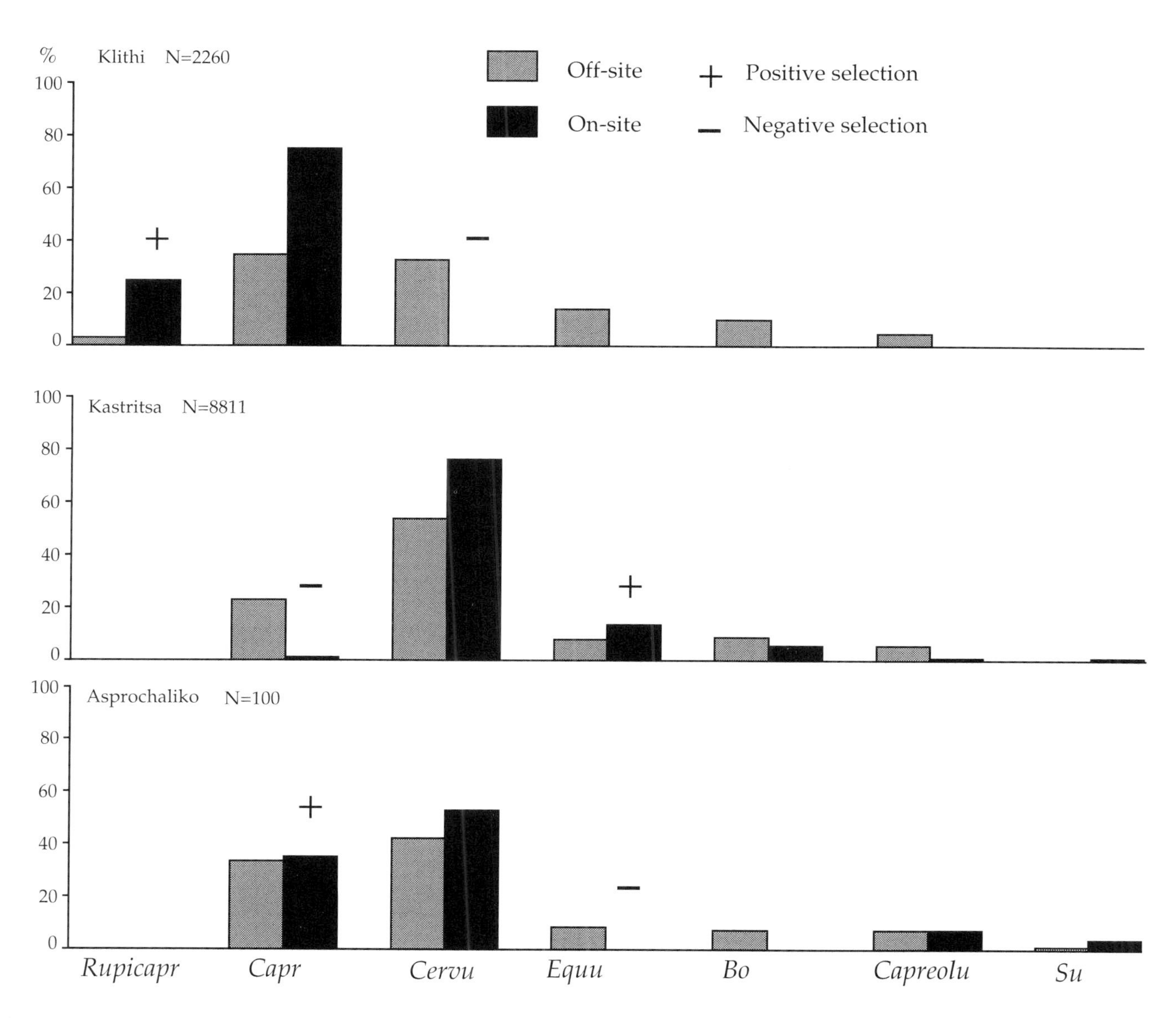

Figure 30.26. *Comparison of off-site and on-site faunal data, showing selective preference for (+) or avoidance of (–) secondary taxa. N refers to the number of identified specimens used for on-site estimates.*

Table 30.15. *Numbers of principal prey animals that can be supported in the region of Epirus shown in Figure 30.25.*

	Inland population Summer N	Inland population Summer %	Inland population Winter range ha	Coastal population Winter range ha	Coastal population Winter range %	Coastal population Animals N	Regional total N	Extracted total N	Usable meat kg	Meat weight kg	Calorie yield kcal	Human population N
Deer	5797	*70*	115,940	99,966	*30*	4999	10,796	864	165	142,560	213,840,000	188
Cattle	1192	*14*	13,420	116,627	*35*	5831	7023	562	375	210,750	316,125,000	278
Horse	1349	*16*	26,980	116,627	*35*	5831	7180	574	165	94,710	142,065,000	125
Ibex	–		–	–	–		4083	327	55	17,985	26,977,500	25
Total	**8338**		**166,760**	**333,220**		**16,661**	**29,082**	**2327**		**466,005**	**699,007,500**	**616**

These figures assume that deer, cattle and horse herds comprise a population that summers in the inland grazing basins controlled by Kastritsa and Klithi (Figs. 30.17 & 30.23), and a population that summers on the coast or elsewhere (the coastal population), and that animal densities in summer are 1 per 10 hectares and in winter 1 per 20 hectares. The numbers of deer, cattle and horse that spend the summer inland are taken from Tables 31.8, 31.11 and 31.14 . The number of ibex in these tables are summed to give the figure for the regional total. The numbers of deer, cattle and horse in the coastal population are estimated by taking the total winter grazing area available at a sea level of –100 m, subtracting the area required as winter range by the inland population, and arbitrarily weighting the proportions of taxa towards open-terrain animals such as cattle and horse. We further assume an extraction rate of 8 per cent of total animal numbers, a yield of 1500 kcal per kg of usable meat, and a daily calorie requirement for a human group consisting of 4.5 equivalent adults of 14,000 kcal. For weights of usable meat per animal we use the figures of Clark 1983, 103, taking the lower end of his range of figures for cattle and horse, and the upper end for deer and ibex (viz. 375 kg, 165 kg, 165 kg and 55 kg respectively). (See Bailey *et al.* 1986b for further discussion.)

Table 30.16. *Numbers of animals available as food, meat and calorie yields, and supportable human population for the territory of Kastritsa, rescaling animal numbers in proportion to on-site taxonomic representation.*

	Territory	Site	Territory rescaled	Extracted	Meat		Human population
	N	%	N	N	kg	kcal	N
Chamois	–	–	–	–	–	–	–
Ibex	1733	*1*	53	4	220	330,000	<1
Deer	4092	*77*	4092	327	53,955	80,932,500	71
Horse	652	*14*	743	59	9735	14,602,500	13
Cattle	671	*6*	319	26	9750	14,625,000	13
Roe	420	*1*	53	4	64	96,000	<1
Pig	19	*1*	53	4	660	990,000	1
Total	**7587**		**5314**	**424**	**74,384**	**111,576,000**	**98**

Table 30.17. *Numbers of animals available as food, meat and calorie yields, and supportable human population for the territory of Klithi (east), rescaling animal numbers in proportion to on-site taxonomic representation.*

	Territory	Site	Territory rescaled	Extracted	Meat		Human population
	N	%	N	N	kg	kcal	N
Chamois	136	*25*	325	26	468	702,000	<1
Ibex	974	*75*	974	78	4290	6,435,000	5.6
Deer	4441	*0*	–	–	–	–	–
Horse	228	*0*	–	–	–	–	–
Cattle	69	*0*	–	–	–	–	–
Roe	119	*0*	–	–	–	–	–
Pig	1	*0*	–	–	–	–	–
Total	**1968**		**1299**	**104**	**4758**	**7,137,000**	**6**

have been the same animals that had previously passed through the Ioannina basin, their contribution is already accounted for in the population estimate for Kastritsa. In any case there is no evidence that the people who stayed at Klithi made use of any other than the locally available ibex and chamois while present at Klithi itself, though other parties of people may have been exploiting other resources not so far away, for example red deer from Boïla (Kotjabopoulou *et al.*, Chapter 22). Equally it does not necessarily follow that all the people who could have been supported by the resources of the Kastritsa territory were present on the site at the same time. Nevertheless the results reinforce the contrast already noted in other respects (Chapters 13, 25 & 26) between Klithi and Kastritsa, suggesting that Klithi was a highly task-specific site used by a small group, whereas Kastritsa could have been used by a larger group for a wider range of activities.

One other implication of these results is that the numbers of people that could be supported in the Epirus hinterland is quite a small proportion, about 17 per cent, of the estimated total regional population, which strengthens the case for treating the eastern hinterland as a rather specialized area visited seasonally by relatively small groups of people who were based on the coastal lowlands where they formed part of larger social groupings.

individuals with well-adapted mutation rates.

The presence of these genes means that PALECO is a member of a class of models known as *genetic algorithms*. The principal advantage of genetic algorithms is that individuals are subject to a form of natural selection that winnows the range of values adopted by the genes until a range of values is manifest that is viable given the nature of the model ecosystem in which they must operate. This means that PALECO is a self-organizing model that will spontaneously search for configurations that are consistent with the rules governing the model ecosystem. The same basic PALECO model can be used to investigate a range of types of ecosystem and ecosystem configurations. In the study at hand we need an overkill ecosystem, so it remains to find a set of rules that simulate the overkill hypothesis.

Translating the overkill hypothesis into birth and death rates

There are three types of individual to consider, plants, herbivores (HERB) and carnivores (CARN). Each individual is dependent on a suite of resources and the availability of those resources is expressed as a carrying capacity, CARRY, which gives the number of individuals that could be supported in a given patch. Some individuals are also subject to predation and the predation pressure at a given patch is expressed as a variable, PRESS, that gives the number of individuals required to sustain the predators indefinitely. The carrying capacity and predatory pressure encountered at a given patch will be shared among all similar individuals. The number of individuals currently at a given patch is held in a variable, LOAD.

If LOAD is greater than CARRY, no individual can breed and some individuals may starve. If CARRY is greater than LOAD, there are sufficient resources for breeding to be possible. Similarly, if PRESS is greater than LOAD, predation pressure cannot be sustained and there is a chance that the prey population will dwindle. If LOAD is greater than PRESS, predators will not prevent populations from growing. Given PRESS, LOAD, CARRY and RECUR (the genetically controlled recurrent death rate) we can calculate the probability that an individual will survive a given cycle.

$$\text{SURV} = (1.0 - \text{RECUR}) \times (1.0 - \text{PRED}) \times (1.0 - \text{STARVE}) \quad (1)$$

If LOAD is greater than CARRY then

$$\text{STARVE} = (1.0 - \text{CARRY}/\text{LOAD}) \quad (2a)$$

Otherwise $\text{STARVE} = 0.0$ (2b)

Similarly, if PRESS is greater than LOAD then

$$\text{PRED} = (1.0 - \text{LOAD}/\text{PRESS}) \quad (3a)$$

otherwise $\text{PRED} = 0.0$ (3b)

The basis for calculating reproduction probabilities is similar, but not quite identical.

$$\text{BORN} = \text{SURPLUS} \times \text{SAFETY} \quad (4)$$

If CARRY is greater than LOAD then

$$\text{SURPLUS} = (1.0 - \text{LOAD}/\text{CARRY}) \quad (5a)$$

otherwise $\text{SURPLUS} = 0.0$ (5b)

Finally, if PRESS = 0.0, then

$$\text{SAFETY} = 1.0 \quad (6a)$$

If LOAD is greater than PRESS

$$\text{SAFETY} = (1.0 - \text{PRESS}/\text{LOAD}) \quad (6b)$$

otherwise $\text{SAFETY} = 0.0$ (6c)

Thus an individual can die out because of its recurrent death rate OR because of starvation OR because of over-predation and can only reproduce if it has access to sufficient resources AND experiences a sustainable level of predation.

This approach to births and deaths is based on the presumption that there is a local carrying capacity and a sustainable predation level that can be calculated for any patch at any instant. However, it does not presume that carrying capacities are fixed parameters, but allows them to vary with variation in soil and climate and with the age profile of the ensemble of individuals currently in residence. The term individual is being used here in a deliberately arbitrary manner. In some cases, an individual in the model may actually map onto a discrete organism, in others (particularly plants) it may represent a mob of organisms all genetically similar, of approximately uniform age, all occupying the same trophic level.

The use of equations (1) to (6) ensures that PALECO is not a deterministic model. Different runs of PALECO with different random number streams could result in different results.

Calculating carrying capacities

Let every patch have a nominal carrying capacity of 50 plants. The carrying capacity for herbivores can then be set arbitrarily to the standing population of plants and that of carnivores to the standing population of herbivores.

$$\text{CARRY(PLANT)} = 50 \quad (7)$$
$$\text{CARRY(HERB)} = \text{LOAD(PLANT)} \quad (8)$$
$$\text{CARRY(CARN)} = \text{LOAD(HERB)} \quad (9)$$

Thus, if we were to consider the effects of food supply alone, we would expect the model to be at demographic equilibrium when the number of plants herbivores and carnivores in each patch approaches 50. The effect of equations (7) to (9) is to ensure that predators which are occupying a patch containing at least as many prey as predators will not die of starvation in the short term.

Calculating predatory pressure

The predation pressure on plants is nominally set to the size of the total herbivore population multiplied by some constant greater than 1.0.

$$\text{PRESS(PLANT)} = \text{OVERKILL} \times \text{LOAD(HERB)} \quad (10)$$

Similarly

$$\text{PRESS(HERB)} = \text{OVERKILL} \times \text{LOAD(CARN)} \quad (11)$$

but, as carnivores have no predators

$$\text{PRESS(CARN)} = 0.0 \quad (12)$$

OVERKILL is a direct index of the amount of disequilibrium in the ecosystem. The fact that OVERKILL is greater than 1.0 means that a population of predators which is running at near its local carrying capacity (defined using equations 7 to 9) will, (by equations 10–12) be subjecting local prey populations to an unsustainable level of predation. Whenever this happens, prey (plants or animal) may die and predators will eventually be forced to move on or face starvation.

Plants can only disperse immediately after 'birth'. Animals can disperse in any cycle provided they have survived the effects of starvation and predation. A migrating individual will choose that patch which maximizes the sum SURV + BORN as calculated in equations (1) and (4) at the instant migration decisions are made.

Investigating resilience under the overkill hypothesis

Sometimes a loosely defined concept enables one to discuss imperfectly understood aspects of complex systems. The concept of ecological resilience is a case in point. A *resilient* ecosystem is one which tends to be buffered against the effects of disturbance in the sense that relationships between system components tend to persist despite changes in the state variables (Holling 1973, 17). Resilience clearly has profound implications for humans since a human population in a resilient ecosystem is less likely to drive any species within that system to extinction. In a resilient ecosystem there will usually be a wider range of sustainable human subsistence strategies than in a fragile ecosystem.

In practice, definitions such as this can easily give rise to tautological pseudo-explanations. 'Why did populations become extinct?' 'Because the ecosystem was fragile.' 'How do you know the ecosystem was fragile?' 'Because populations became extinct.' Despite this objection, anyone who has seen old garden plots revert to rough scrub in a few years will recognize intuitively that some ecosystems are inherently resilient while others are fragile and transient. The present report is concerned with a model of a three-level food web. If the model food web is resilient, one would expect it to persist for a long time with all trophic levels represented throughout. The length of time a model can be run without losing one or more trophic levels can be taken as a crude index of ecological resilience.

Resilience is a concept which allows archaeologists to use ecological insights as the basis for predictions about the archaeological record without resort to crude environmental determinism. If an ecosystem is resilient, it means that certain predator–prey interactions can be sustained or repeated over an appreciable period of time. One can easily conceive of circumstances under which broad spectrum feeders (like humans) would have a wide range of possible feeding strategies with varying degrees of sustainability. Suppose, for example, that the effect of intensive ibex hunting was to drive ibex to the verge of extinction. There is no reason to believe the fragility of the ibex population would prevent humans from this course of action but there *is* reason to believe the action could not be repeated very frequently. Large dumps of ibex bones are only likely if the exploitation of ibex is repeated. Consequently, if ecological theory predicts that ibex populations were fragile but we discover large dumps of ibex bone in the archaeological record, there is something wrong with our theory.

OVERKILL and resilience

It is intuitively obvious that the OVERKILL variable, as a measure of inherent disequelibrium, will have an impact on resilience. If the OVERKILL variable is set high, prey populations will be in constant danger of extinction and the system will be fragile. If it is low, the model will be dynamically sluggish because it will take many time-cycles before predators exert significant pressure on their resource base to make the system resilient.

In order to select a suitable value for OVERKILL, PALECO was configured with 20 patches, each of which has a carrying capacity for plants of 50 and is seeded with an initial population of 640 plants, 270 herbivores and 80 carnivores. For the first six cycles, all organisms (including plants) were allowed to disperse freely among patches, protected from all mortality and prevented from breeding. In this way, each organism was given the chance to find the most favourable location for its own survival and reproduction. After this warm-up period, organisms were allowed to die, breed and migrate in the normal way.

Thirty model runs were undertaken, each with a different value of OVERKILL. Each run differed from all the rest only in the value assigned to OVERKILL. The starting configuration, warm-up period and founding populations were identical. OVERKILL values in excess of 1.2 always resulted in the extinction of one or more trophic levels. Values between 1.00001 and 1.2 were sustainable for at least 200 subsequent cycles. High OVERKILL rates tended to produce generally wilder fluctuations and, by implication, more fragile simulated food webs than lower values. When OVERKILL was close to 1.0, PALECO exhibited remarkably stable behaviour with all groups running very close to their local carrying capacities.

A fragile ecosystem was required for the exercise at hand. Accordingly, OVERKILL was set to 1.2 in both the simulations to be described below. Once again, both runs were given the same (6 cycle) warm-up period and the same founding population.

Experiment 1: 20 patches

PALECO was run with 20 patches, each with a nominal carrying capacity of 50 plants. Once again, the system was seeded with a founding population of 640 plants, 270 herbivores and 50 carnivores and allowed to warm up for 6 cycles. Figure 31.1 shows the number of plants through simulated time. Note that the plants run through a series of 'boom and bust' cycles as the trophic level expands and contracts. Figures 31.2 and 31.3 show similar time series data for herbivores (HERB) and carnivores (CARN) and portray similar dynamic behaviour. Herbivores eat plants and carnivores eat herbivores. Plants are dependent on the carrying capacity of the soil. It is natural to ask how much of the dynamic behaviour of each level can be attributed to a given feeding relation. In Figure 31.4 the number of plants and herbivores are plotted against each other. Note that for most of the simulated time, PALECO is running with between 800 and 1000 plants forming a more or less horizontal scatter. This suggests that the size of these levels is not intimately coupled throughout their dynamic range. Is it possible that plants and herbivores have negotiated a *donor-controlled* relationship? Certainly we get a very different picture if we plot herbivores against carnivores (Fig. 31.5). Here there is a clear, almost linear relationship between the two; the carnivore and herbivore levels are intimately coupled, suggesting that the relationship between carnivore and herbivore is of the *active-predator* type. In Figure 31.6, the number of carnivores is plotted against plants and the pattern is broadly similar to that of Figure 31.4; the carnivore and plant levels are not intimately coupled.

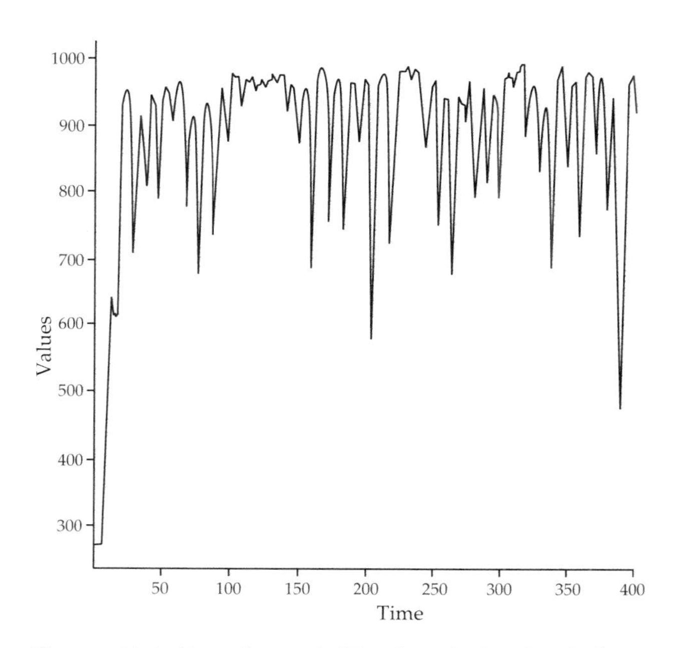

Figure 31.1. *Experiment 1. Number of simulated plant populations through time.*

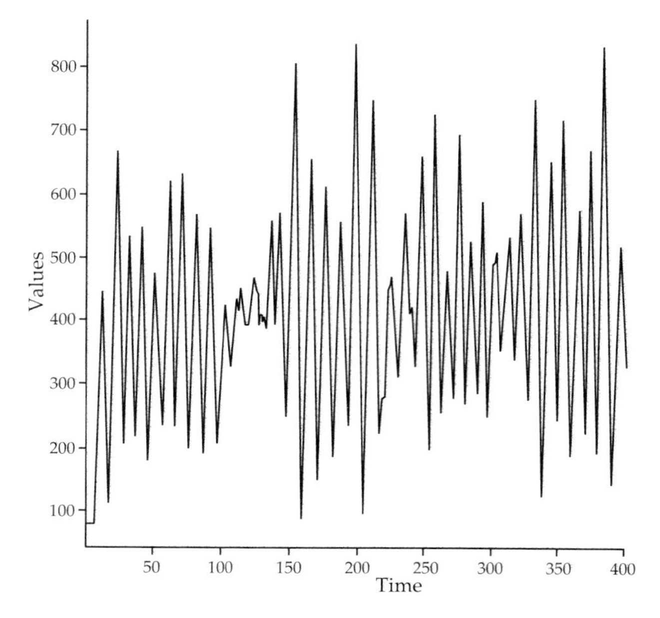

Figure 31.2. *Experiment 1. Number of simulated herbivore populations through time.*

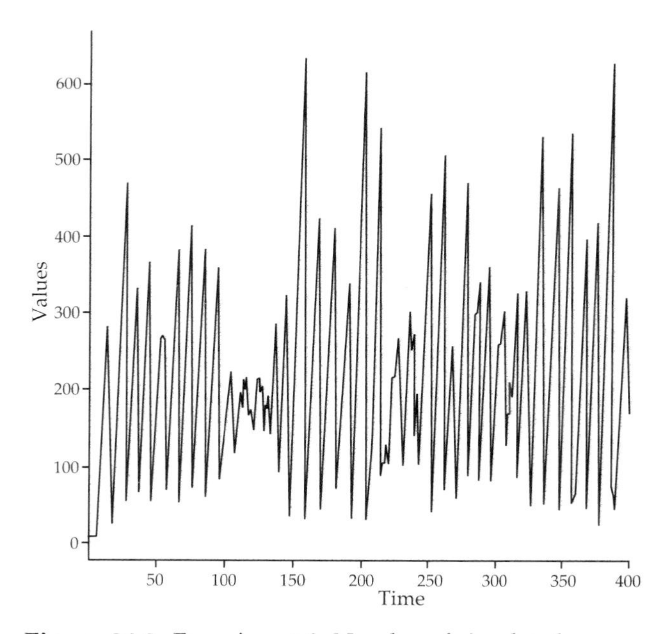

Figure 31.3. *Experiment 1. Number of simulated carnivore populations through time.*

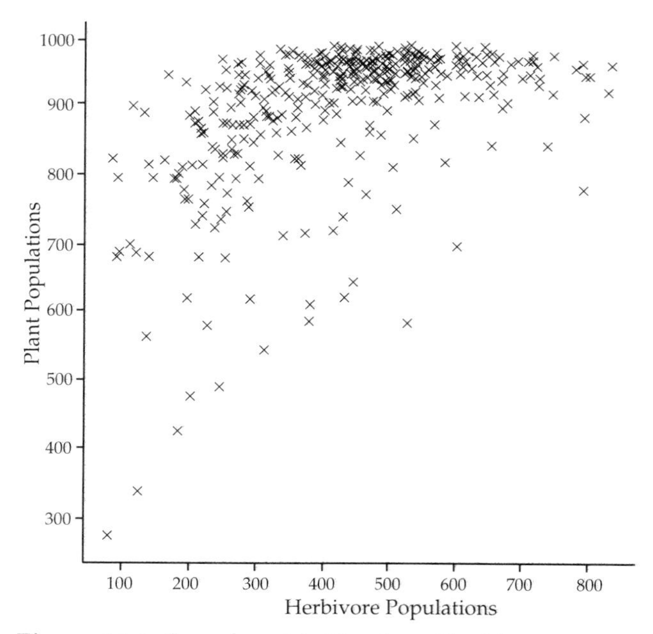

Figure 31.4. *Experiment 1. Number of herbivore versus plant populations.*

It would be natural, then, to suppose that PALECO was exhibiting the behaviour of a simple 'cascade model' (Cohen & Newman 1985) which predicts that plant populations are unchecked by herbivores because these are held in check by carnivores. However, Figure 31.4 has deep troughs as well as peaks. The depth of these troughs varies randomly and cannot be explained by variation in carrying capacity since this is constant (in PALECO). Therefore, herbivores must occasionally be precipitating crashes in the plant population despite the effects of carnivores.

It is likely that some of the couplings between trophic levels will be lagged. The number of carnivores today may be coupled to the number of herbivores tomorrow, for example. Figures 31.7 to 31.9 display the correlation coefficients calculated between each level at a range of positive and negative time lags. Thus Figure 31.7 shows the lagged correlations between plants and herbivores. Large correlation coefficients associated with positive lags suggest that the size of the plant level can be used to predict that of the herbivore level some cycles later. Large correlation coefficients associated with negative lags suggest that the

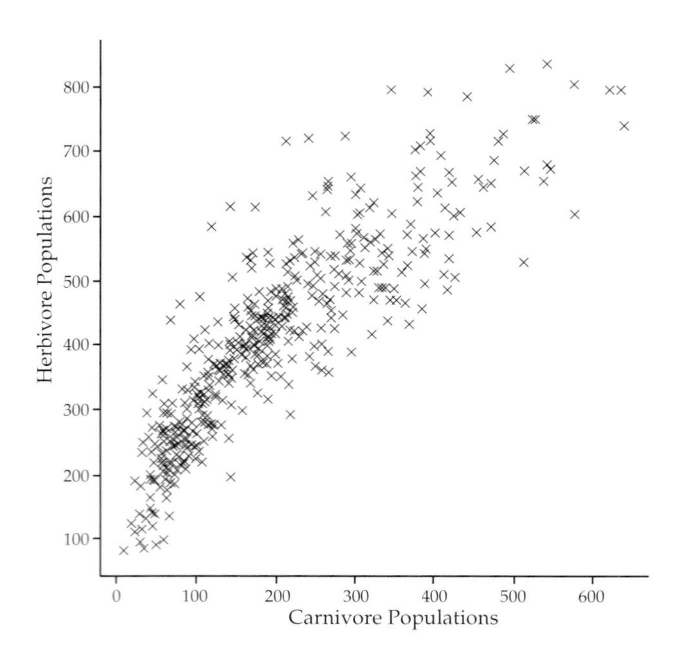

Figure 31.5. *Experiment 1. Number of herbivore versus carnivore populations.*

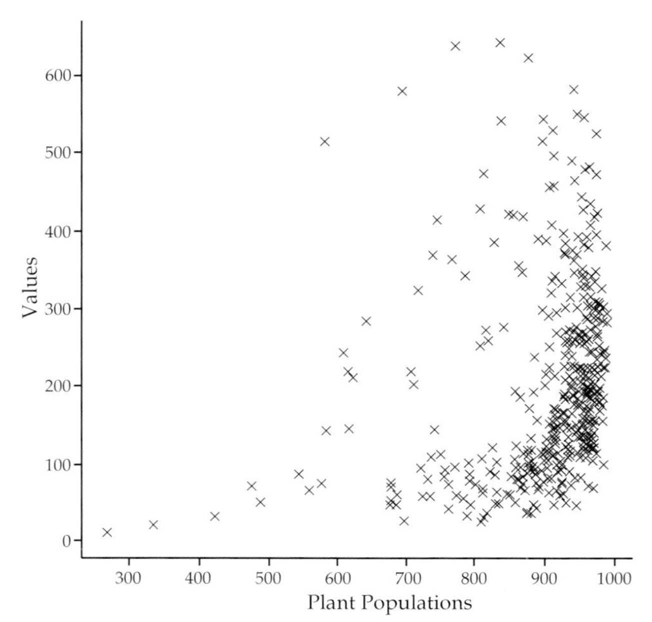

Figure 31.6. *Experiment 1. Number of carnivore versus plant populations.*

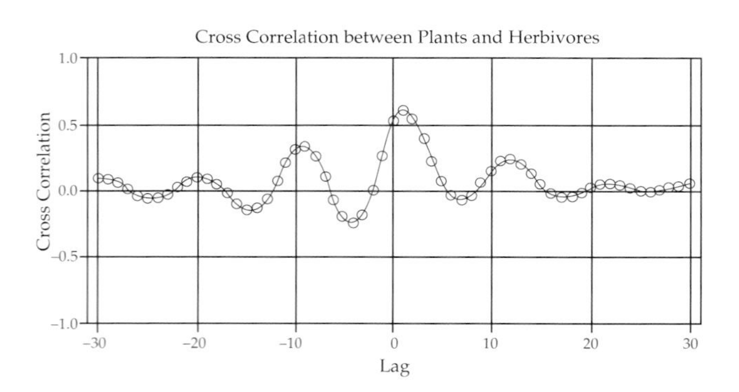

Figure 31.7. *Experiment 1. Lagged correlations between plants and herbivores.*

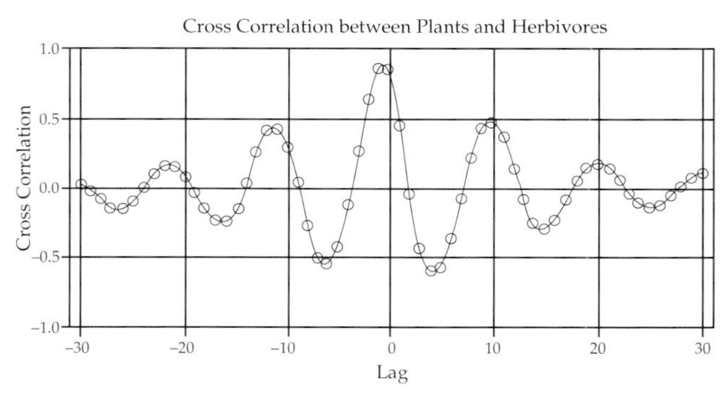

Figure 31.8. *Experiment 1. Lagged correlations between herbivores and carnivores.*

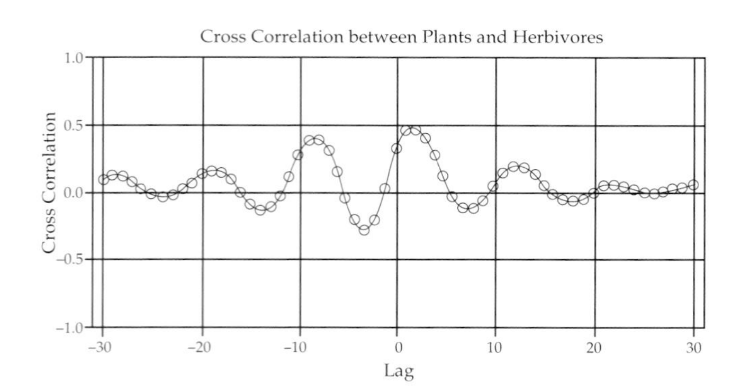

Figure 31.9. *Experiment 1. Lagged correlations between plants and carnivores.*

size of the plant trophic level can be used to 'predict' that of the herbivore level some cycles earlier. If one accepts the orthodoxy that causes can only have effects at the present or in the future, the former case suggests that the size of trophic level for plants may be causally related to that of herbivores while the latter suggests that herbivores may be conditioning the size of the plant level. High coefficients symmetrically distributed at positive and negative lags suggest that the levels involved may have become locked into a series of coupled oscillations with a more or less fixed period.

The relationship between carnivores and herbivores most clearly exhibits the characteristics of coupled oscillations. Not only is there a high correlation between the number of herbivores and carnivores in the current cycle (Fig. 31.5) but the lagged correlations (Fig. 31.8) suggest that the two populations may be locked into a series of coupled oscillations with a period of about ten cycles. As one might expect, the number of herbivores in the present cycle is a rather good predictor of the number of carnivores in the next. The situation with plants and herbivores (Fig.

31.7) is less clear cut. The number of herbivores in the current cycle has a weak negative correlation with the number of plants 4 cycles later and a weak positive correlation with the number of plants 10 cycles later. The number of plants is a moderate to good predictor of the number of herbivores in the next cycle. However, the number of herbivores is a very poor predictor of the number of plants five cycles later and relatively poor as a predictor of the number of plants 10 or 11 cycles on. The relationship between plants and carnivores (Fig. 31.9) is similar to that between plants and herbivores.

Interpreting experiment 1

Plotting time series for plants, herbivores and carnivores provides only limited information about the dynamic interaction of the three levels. Plotting the correlation coefficients for a range of time lags gives much more information about the qualitative relationships between them. From such plots as these we can work out the general, statistical behaviour of the PALECO model, though it would be impossible to divine the mathematical rules that govern its detailed behaviour. The data indicate that herbivores and carnivores have become locked into a series of coupled oscillations with a period of approximately 10 cycles. The plant population rises and crashes periodically. The crashes correspond to the peaks of the herbivore cycle. Once herbivores (and carnivores) have crashed, their impact on the size of the plant level is negligible and plants re-expand to the carrying capacity within a couple of cycles. It takes the herbivores approximately 8 cycles to outrun the carnivores and precipitate another crash. During the 8 recovery cycles the relationship between herbivore and carnivore is of the *active-predator* type while that between herbivore and plant is *donor-controlled*. During the crash, the ecosystem changes configuration. The relationship between herbivore and plant is of the *active-predator* type with some over-predation resulting in a crash both of herbivores and plants. The relationship between carnivores and herbivores remains in the *active-predator* mode so that the herbivores crash faster than the plants they feed on. The plants recover to slip once more into a *donor-controlled* configuration for the next 8 cycles when another crash occurs.

If we look at time series data for the plants, herbivores and carnivores from one of the twenty patches alone (Figs. 31.10, 31.11 & 31.12) we see broadly similar boom and bust cycles to those observed in the whole ecosystem. However, when we consider one territory in isolation, the local extinction of herbivores and prey is a routine occurrence. Clearly, not all patches experience these local extinctions at the same time; at least some patches will have both predators and prey at all times. The overkill hypothesis, coupled with the fact that the ecosystem is large in comparison to the dispersal abilities of individuals, introduces a degree of patchiness into spatial distributions in times of stress which maintains ecological resilience.

Experiment 2: de-spatializing the model

Suppose we now re-run the PALECO model with exactly the same founding populations but only one patch, this time with a carrying capacity of 1000 plants. The only difference between this model and that described in the previous section is that the model has no spatial differentiation and organisms can no longer migrate. The dynamic trajectories of plants, herbivores and carnivores are represented in Figures 31.13, 31.14 and 31.15. The plant population expands for about 15 cycles and is then checked by the herbivores. These are in turn checked by the carnivores after about 20 cycles. The herbivore and carnivore populations then crash because herbivores cannot emigrate to avoid predation and carnivores cannot emigrate to search for food. After about 25 cycles, both animal populations have been driven to extinction and the ecosystem contains only plants. Note that the theoretical carrying capacities of these two ecosystems are identical. The warm-up period and overkill rate does not vary between the two. The genetic makeup of the founding populations is identical in all respects yet the model with 20 patches each with a carrying capacity of 50 plants persists for more than 400 cycles while that with only one territory collapses after 26.

It is interesting to compare the time series data for plants, herbivores and carnivores in Experiment 2 with the equivalent time series for a single patch of Experiment 1 (Figs. 31.10, 31.11 & 31.12). Note that herbivore and carnivore populations crash repeatedly,

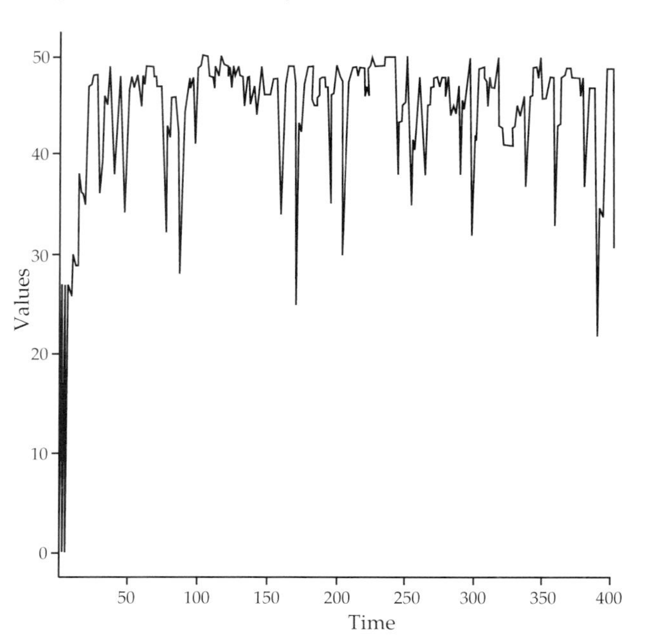

Figure 31.10. *Experiment 1. Number of simulated plant populations on a single patch.*

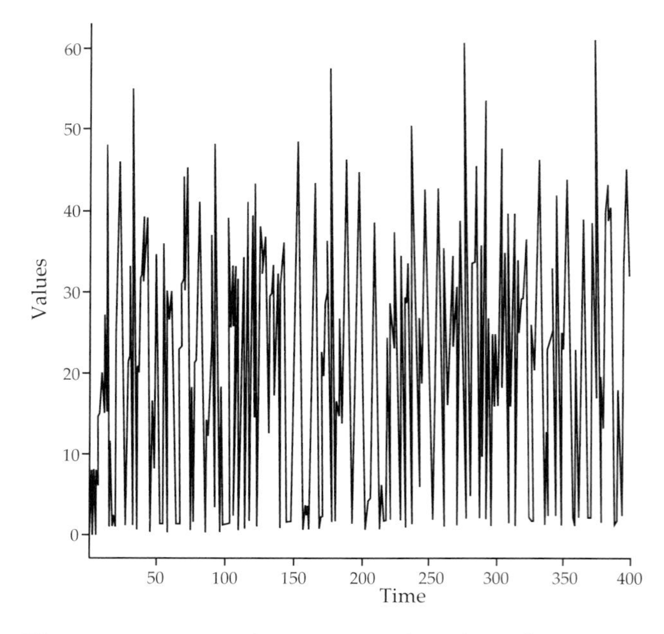

Figure 31.11. *Experiment 1. Number of simulated herbivore populations on a single patch.*

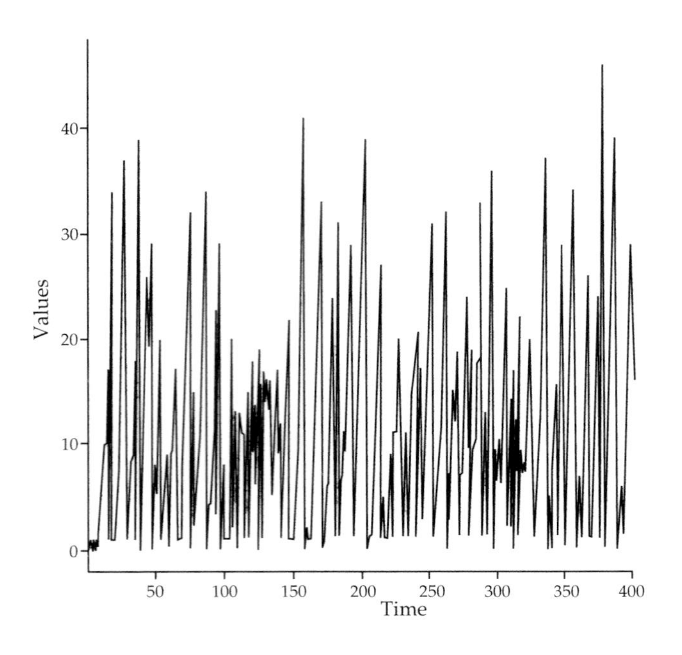

Figure 31.12. *Experiment 1. Number of simulated carnivore populations on a single patch.*

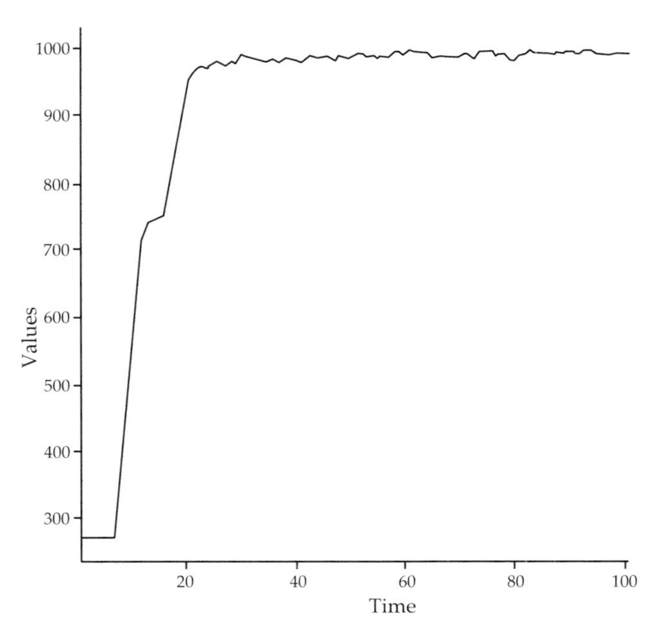

Figure 31.13. *Experiment 2. Number of simulated plant populations through time.*

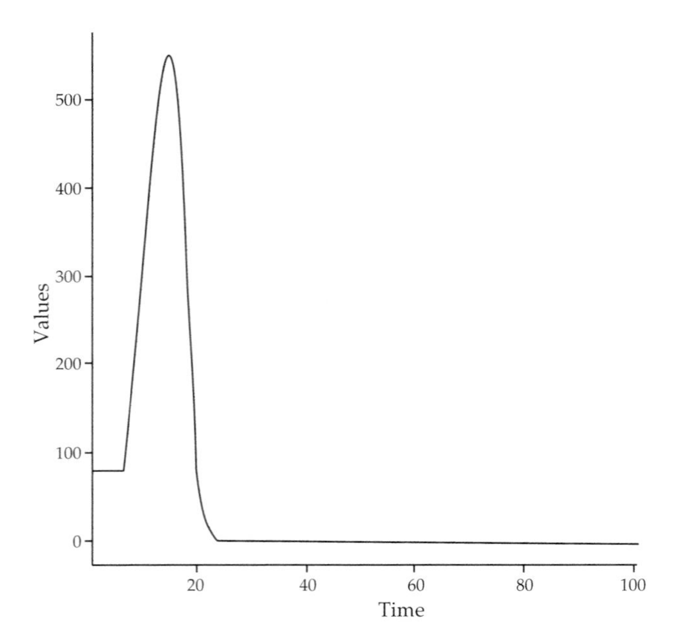

Figure 31.14. *Experiment 2. Number of simulated herbivore populations through time.*

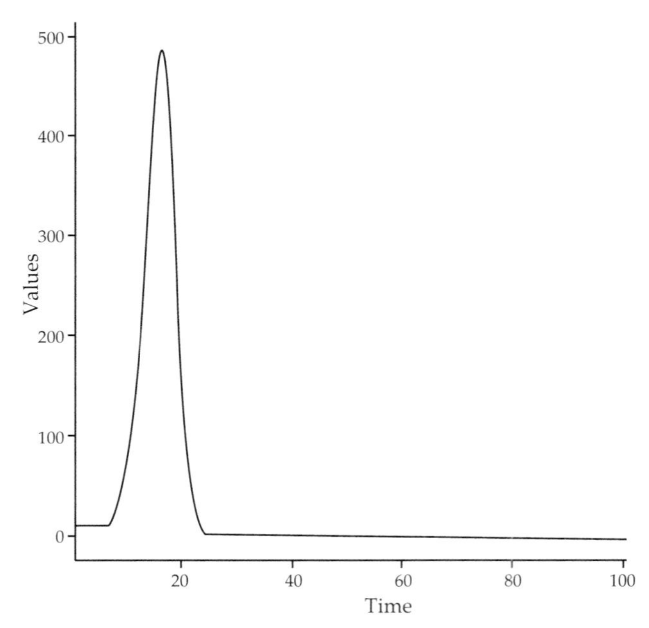

Figure 31.15. *Experiment 2. Number of simulated carnivore populations through time.*

often becoming locally extinct. However, they never become totally extinct in Experiment 1 because there is always a refugium in the form of other patches in which small populations of predator can find food and small prey populations can hide in times of stress. These are not *simple refugia*, areas where prey can hide from predators, but *statistical refugia*, areas where both predators and prey alike can persist by dint of their patchy distribution patterns.

Spatial differentiation, dispersal and refugia

The sole difference between the two PALECO runs just described is that the latter has no spatial structure and any predator can reach all available prey instantly. Because of the overkill hypothesis, this de-spatialization guarantees fragility. The former is subdivided into spatial locations and predators can only reach that proportion of the prey that is geographically close to them. The effect of this spatialization is to introduce time lags into predator–prey relationships that create regional variation in predation pressure. This in turn creates refugia in times of stress that have two effects on the model. Firstly, it makes it very difficult for starving predators to exhaust prey stocks completely and secondly, it provides small pockets of prey that reduce the probability of predator extinction. Thus, it is clear that a large carrying capacity is not, of itself, sufficient to create refugia. The prerequisite for refugia is that a balance be established between dispersal mechanisms and carrying capacity that allows predators and prey to play 'hide and seek' indefinitely. Presumably, dispersal mechanisms are subject to some natural selection that in turn creates an ecosystem in which animals and plants are distributed unevenly.

Many ecologists have noted that real ecosystems are often internally patterned. For example, Watt (1947) in an influential pre-computer study intended to 'apply dynamic principles to the elucidation of the plant community itself' presented evidence to support his claim that 'patchiness' (i.e. spatial pattern) was an almost universal property of plant communities, each of which was characterized by a cycle of 'upgrade' and 'downgrade' development. During the upgrade phase there is a net build-up of plant material, during the downgrade there is a net break-down. Watt clearly recognized the importance of patchiness when he wrote (Watt 1947, 17)

> The widespread occurrence of patchiness is of interest in itself, but the persistence of the patch in time under normal conditions is itself fundamental. Why, for example, starting with a set of patches, do we not get a general blending of the whole with the vegetation of every square foot a replica of every other?

Watt went on to answer this question in terms of small edaphic discontinuities, disturbances and inherent time lags created by restricted opportunities for colonization and implied that patchiness in vegetation was almost universal. Subsequent research on patchiness has stressed the role of 'disturbance' in maintaining spatial pattern though this has obliged some authors to define the term somewhat broadly;

> A disturbance is any relatively discrete event in time that disrupts ecosystem, community, or population structure and changes resources, substrate availability, or the physical environment. (Pickett & White 1985, 5)

According to this definition, inherent predatory overkill is a form of 'disturbance'. The senescence of a cohort of plants with limited life spans must be treated as a form of 'disturbance' because it produces clearings. Even pedogenesis and the gradual leaching of soil nutrients are forms of 'disturbance'. Whether one accepts this as a reasonable definition of the term, the fact remains that patchy distributions are common among plants and we know a great deal about the sorts of factors likely to maintain patchiness. Similar observations are commonly made for animal populations from insects to ibex and it seems reasonable to argue that patchiness or spatial pattern is manifest in all ecosystems. One of Watt's stated aims was to generate ecological laws and, although he did not present this observation as such, he clearly felt that patchiness was crucial to the understanding of ecological dynamics. Accordingly, we may define *Watt's law* as stating that *ecosystems tend to be persistently patchy*.

Gause's 'immigrants' and simple refugia

Early work on Lotka-Volterra models of predator-prey systems suggested that predators and prey should enter a series of coupled oscillations of the sort generated by the first PALECO run above. Coupled oscillations would provide a very convenient explanation of persistent patchiness; ecosystems are patchy because different regions are being sampled at different stages in the oscillatory cycle. Unfortunately, the prediction of coupled oscillations was at variance with laboratory evidence, most of which suggested that micro-predators and their prey commonly competed to extinction. Early population ecologists found themselves on the horns of a dilemma. On the one hand they had a family of elegant mathematical models that predicted coupled oscillations and explained patchy distributions. On the other hand, they had a considerable body of microcosm experiments that resulted in extinction. Unless one could show that coupled oscillations could occur in the laboratory, it was difficult to justify the use of Lotka-Volterra equations.

Two early studies found that the key to generating coupled oscillations in a laboratory was to provide refugia. In the first of these, Gause (1934) used a *Paramecium* as a prey species and a predatory protozoan grown in centrifuge tubes. Although the predator usually exhausted the prey in these conditions, Gause was able to produce coupled oscillations by monitoring predator numbers and adding a few Paramecia when the predator was nearly extinct. These immigrants grew away faster than the predators, which subsequently recovered and destroyed the population once again. A new inoculation of immigrants at the critical point in this process allowed the cycle to be repeated. In effect, Gause provided his microcosm with a simple refugium that increased the resilience of the system.

Huffaker's oranges and statistical refugia

In a later study Huffaker (1958) was able to dispense with the simple refugium by designing his microcosm in such a way that extinctions were avoided. Huffaker used a herbivorous mite that fed on oranges and a carnivorous mite which was capable of completely eradicating the herbivore in laboratory experiments. Huffaker devised a microcosm in which oranges and rubber balls were spaced out on trays and separated from each other with barriers of Vaseline which the predators found difficult to cross and an arrangement of wooden posts and air currents that allowed prey to disperse. After many experiments a configuration was found in which coupled oscillations could be maintained; Huffaker had managed to adjust relative dispersal rates so as to produce a statistical refugium in a tray of oranges.

Coupled oscillations, patchiness and overkill

Both Gause's and Huffaker's experiments are commonly interpreted as evidence that Lotka-Volterra processes may, under certain circumstances, describe real predator–prey interactions. This evidence is often used to justify the application of Lotka-Volterra models to predator–prey relationships. However, the fact that real predator–prey systems *can* act like Lotka-Volterra equations does not prove that Lotka-Volterra equations constitute an appropriate model. The Lotka-Volterra equations may be exhibiting the right dynamic behaviour for the wrong reasons. Nevertheless, these microcosm experiments undoubtedly demonstrate that the distribution of prey and predator through space may have a profound impact on their ability to co-exist and it is this aspect of the experiments we will concentrate on here.

Modelling Huffaker's microcosm

Huffaker's experiment, in particular, has received considerable attention from ecological modellers and is now very well understood. The potential ability of predators to destroy prey in this case is well established and it remains to construct and analyze a mathematical model of the hide and seek behaviour Huffaker facilitated. Maynard Smith (1974) built a transition-matrix model of Huffaker's microcosm from which he deduced that permanent coexistence is favoured in the following conditions.

1. Prey have a high capacity for migration.
2. There is cover for prey that enables them to survive the extinction of the predator.
3. Predator migration is restricted.
4. There are many patches.

In a separate modelling exercise Hilborn (1975) took a different approach to the Huffaker system, using a gridded numerical simulation which showed that the key to persistence of a predator–prey system was the relative dispersal rates of predator and prey.

Two years later Hastings (1976) built a differential equation model of the same system which was manipulated analytically to show that high mobility in predator or prey can have the effect of stabilizing the system. This is an interesting point because it illustrates that the prerequisite for co-existence is that prey and predators keep their distance. It does not matter whether it is the prey or the predator that moves on as long as the prey get a chance to recover. One of the strategies that can have this effect is where the predator–prey relationship shows an *aggregation effect* by which predators tend to disregard small patches of prey. These are left to grow undisturbed and so act as the refugia which sustain the predators at a later stage in time. Attempts to model patchy ecosystems phenomenologically have shown that aggregation effects can enhance the stability of arthropod predator–prey systems where predatory overkill is commonly assumed (May 1981, ch. 6).

Slobodkin (1961) has noted that some *prudent predators* concentrate on killing old, very young or sick prey and seldom attack reproductively active, healthy individuals. This selective killing would have the effect of ensuring that predators move on before the ability of a prey population to recover has been jeopardized. A prudent predator is one which has opted for a *donor-controlled* relationship with its prey.

PALECO and Huffaker's microcosm

The PALECO model described above was not built primarily to simulate Huffaker's microcosm but has produced similar results in a three-level food chain. (Huffaker ensured that exhausted oranges were replaced so there was no need for Maynard-Smith, Hilborn or Hastings to model plant growth.) Furthermore, the PALECO experiment shows that these regularities can emerge spontaneously when trophic levels made up of individuals with different life expectancies and migratory behaviour are subject to natural selection. Under these circumstances, patchiness occurs *spontaneously* and is maintained by natural selection. *Watt's law is a corollary of the overkill hypothesis*. Indeed, we can turn this observation into a criterion for testing the overkill hypothesis. Given an ecosystem which receives few immigrant predators or prey, the lack of spatial pattern may be taken as a refutation of the overkill hypothesis. The converse is not necessarily true. Patchiness can be imposed on an ecosystem by an underlying patchiness in the distribution of resources, particularly for sedentary organisms such as plants, or by social organisation. However, whenever a prey organism exhibits a patchy distribution pattern one would expect a degree of spatial pattern in the distribution of its predators. If pockets of prey are difficult to locate, one would expect predators which overkill to be at a competitive advantage with respect to those which do not, *provided that they have a good chance of finding another patch*. It is quite possible, therefore, that patchiness in the resource base may be one of the factors determining the initial resilience of the 'overkill strategy'. Once the overkill strategy is established it will in turn impose spatial pattern on the distributions of all species involved, regardless of the underlying resource distribution.

This computer experiment illustrates two corollaries of the overkill hypothesis. Firstly, that a predator whose powers of dispersal give it free access to all pockets of prey will be operating in an extremely fragile ecosystem where the probability of prey extinction and subsequent starvation is high. Secondly, a prey organism which is widely distributed relative to the dispersal powers of its predators is unlikely to be driven to extinction, even under the overkill hypothesis. Prey and predator will then coexist in a resilient ecosystem which manifests the characteristic patchiness of many real ecosystems.

Maynard-Smith (1974) devoted some of his chapter on migration and local extinction to the evolution of migratory behaviour. In it he argued that the selective advantage of migration in transitorily patchy environments was obvious; organisms dependent on disturbed earth, dung, corpses etc. must migrate to persist. Indeed, even when patches are long-lasting compared to the life cycle of the individual, some readiness to migrate will be favoured by natural selection, at least if local extinctions are likely. In continuous environments short-term, diffusive migration is unlikely to be advantageous although very long-distance migration may be favoured that allows individuals from populations of peak size 'to cross barriers not crossed in normal diffusion movements' (1974, 84).

The PALECO model presented above does not contradict Maynard-Smith but provides a slightly different perspective on migratory behaviour. Firstly, it suggests that ecological discontinuities are not solely functions of the distribution of natural resources but may arise spontaneously as a result of local predatory overkill. When overkill occurs, predators and prey will experience a selection pressure that will sometimes permit long-term co-existence. This often results in the characteristic hide and seek predator–prey system which imposes a degree of patchiness on the ecosystem, hence Watt's law. The reason Gause's and Huffaker's experiments required such ingenuity was that the microcosms were too small to manifest the characteristic patchiness that facilitates co-existence in the wild. Gause, for example, was working with planktonic organisms which tend to manifest spatial patterning on too large a scale to be accommodated in any laboratory microcosm (Steele 1978).

I have already suggested that a balance between relative powers of dispersal and overkill may emerge under the effects of natural selection. However, the process by which this takes place may not conform to the textbook model of natural selection. According to this model each individual has a genetic makeup or *genotype* and a morphological and behavioural expression of the genotype, the *phenotype*. Classical evolutionary theory has natural selection acting to determine the probability that a given *individual* will breed or die. The effect of this is to reduce the relative abundance of certain phenotypes. I will refer to the classical form of natural selection at the level of the individual as *proximate* natural selection below.

Consider a new, aggressive predator that has been suddenly introduced into an otherwise resilient ecosystem. This predator will begin to establish feeding relations with a range of prey species and will compete with other predators. Prey populations will come under stress as the invasive population expands. Under natural selection, this growth phase will favour predators that maximize their immediate breeding success; this is not a situation that leads to low relative rates of dispersal, aggregation effects and prudent predation. However, prey and competing predators will experience selection pressures in favour of dispersal and defence strategies that either eradicate the immigrant or enable them to coexist with it. If coexistence strategies are achieved, some predator–prey links involving the immigrant will persist. If, however, no linkages are stabilized, the immigrant will become extinct (possibly taking other species with it). Thus, an immigrant predator will be subject to proximate selection pressures that will ensure its own extinction *unless* those species with which it interacts find effective strategies for co-existence. The immigrant predator experiences no proximate selection pressure in favour of prudence though it may have prudence thrust upon it.

Selection and meta-selection
None of this denies that the proximate effect of natural selection is to impose differential survival and breeding rates of individuals, neither does it imply that prudent predators can only emerge as a result of group selection acting on the predator population. However, it does imply the existence of a further, meta-selection that favours certain types of feeding relationship and dispersal mechanisms. The consequence of this meta-selection is that fragile feeding relations will tend to disappear in the longer term (sometimes taking a predator or prey species with them). Under meta-selection, ecosystems will take on self-organizing properties that facilitate persistent feeding relationships (resilience).

The mechanism for this meta-evolutionary process will differ from that of proximate natural selection in that organisms locked into fragile feeding relations may be expected to cycle from one demographic catastrophe to another until the link breaks completely or a more 'prudent' configuration is achieved. Once the link breaks, the feeding relation has clearly 'died'. However, if the link becomes resilient, the feeding relation can be seen to have adapted to the constraints imposed by meta-selection. Meta-selection, like cultural evolution, may be a Lamarckian process.

Hierarchy theory and Watt's law

Recent years have seen a widespread interest in the implications of formal hierarchy theory on scale and rates of ecological processes (for reviews see Allen & Starr 1982; O'Neill *et al.* 1986; O'Neill 1989) and there are clear resonances between the results of the PALECO simulations above and some of the concepts of hierarchy theory. The PALECO model has itself a hierarchical structure. Genes are nested into individuals, aggregates of individuals form patches and so on. When the program is run, the rules that govern feeding behaviour, migration, birth and death spontaneously impose a natural selection which acts at the level of the individual to change the gene pool. This does not merely change the frequencies of different types of genes, it determines the combinations of genes that make up a viable individual. In the terms coined by Koestler (1967) the individual is a holon (*cf.* taxon), a spontaneously generated, self-perpetuating entity. Some types of holon can exert profound influences on the properties of others. Predatory holons are connected to prey holons, for example. The nature of these connections is such that some possible holons become extinct simply because they share the ecosystem with another type of holon. A predator that disperses widely will prevent the establishment of poorly dispersed prey. However, the same prey species could establish perfectly well in an ecosystem that lacked the aggressive predator.

I have used the results of simulation experiments to argue for a further, meta-selection pressure. This implies the existence of a meta-population of feeding relations within which this meta-selection is manifest. This second level in the ecological hierarchy (above the individual) is made up of more or less persistent, spontaneously generated, self-perpetuating entities; these must be holons too. Some feeding relations are inherently fragile and will fail to persist in the long term. Yet others are resilient or become resilient under the effects of proximate selection pressure and will persist.

This short (two level) hierarchy that has individuals as one holon and feeding relations as another exhibits an important property of hierarchy theory *sensu stricto*. Firstly processes occur on longer time scales at higher levels; individuals are responding to a proximate and rapid natural selection pressure whilst the feeding relations respond to a slower process of meta-selection. The PALECO model is not strictly hierarchical in this sense. Genes may change under mutation as often as once every reproductive event, individuals change their genotypes once a lifetime so the second level changes slower than the first. The third level, the patch, on the other hand, may change under the effects of migration and death throughout the simulation, possibly as many as several hundred times per cycle.

Now let us move beyond the PALECO model and into an hypothetical region where the PALECO-like ecosystems really occur. Each ecosystem would map onto an ensemble of feeding relations located in some geomorphological space. All ensembles would be subject to the same thermodynamic laws. Suppose there are rare occasions when individuals migrate between these ecosystems. If the migration results in a loss of resilience, each migration event will trigger corresponding shifts and adjustments in the ensembles, each of which will then be subject to a selection pressure in favour of a resilient configuration. If there are configurations of ensembles that are less prone to suffer a severe loss of resilience under recurrent immigration, one would expect ensembles that find such a configuration to be more persistent than others. This implies the existence of a meta-meta-selection pressure to favour ecosystems which remain resilient under conditions of low-level migration.

We may speculate about what these configurations would be. A resilient ecosystem might reject the immigrant by strenuous competition and the introduction of barriers to reproduction. Alternatively, both ecosystems might operate in a similar configuration at the meta-level so that an immigrant is likely to find predator–prey relations in the new ecosystem that are broadly equivalent to those it exploited in the last. When this occurs, an immigrant will appear *pre-adapted* to life in the new ecosystem. An ecosystem which suffers a severe collapse under the effects of low rates of migration may come to be colonized by immigrants from neighbouring ecosystems which happen to be pre-adapted to each other. In this way, different ecosystems will come to display some redundancy in the *types* of meta- and meta-meta-configurations that persist in the very long term.

Because of the decrease in response rates of holons at higher levels in the system, the strength of constraints imposed on lower holons by those at a higher level will decline as the hierarchical distance between them increases. No amount of meta-meta-selection pressure will overcome the proximate selective advantage of continuing to breed and feed. However, in the very long term one would expect meta-meta-selection to favour those organisms whose feeding and dispersal behaviour is sufficiently plastic to enable them to adapt spontaneously to factors that one might expect to result in a dramatic loss of resilience. The ease with which humans adopt new distribution and feeding strategies and the human capacity for abstract thought and symbolic manipulation may have emerged as a consequence of hierarchically nested meta- and meta-meta-selection pressures.

Taken to its logical conclusion this hierarchical view of natural selection can appear heretical although it undoubtedly makes sense of a number of striking biological observations. It is commonly observed, for example, that vegetation can be classified on the basis of the plant species it contains. Indeed, the discipline of phytosociology is founded on this observation (for a textbook review see Mueller-Dombois & Ellenberg 1974). Clearly, some combinations of taxa work particularly well together and tend to recur over wide areas. It is conceivable that resilient plant associations could occasionally emerge by natural selection at the level of the individual but their commonness in nature must surely be a response to meta-selection pressures acting over very long time-scales.

Textbooks of speciation generally agree that the establishment of barriers to reproduction among related taxa is crucial to the process. Two types of speciation are recognized. *Allopatric* speciation occurs when two related populations are isolated by appreciable geographical barriers and respond to divergent selection pressures. *Sympatric* speciation occurs when the populations diverge in the same environment. Most agree that the genetics of sympatric speciation is problematical and some geneticists (for example, Mayr 1964) question whether sympatric speciation occurs at all.

However, there is another way of considering the problem. Suppose two populations were truly allopatric, what selective advantage would be achieved by the development of barriers to reproduction? It is possible that local selection pressures might favour divergence that makes inter-breeding difficult but if the two populations never come into contact, there is virtually no selective advantage in the establishment of barriers to reproduction. Reproductive barriers are only likely to be advantageous when divergent populations encounter each other from time to time. Indeed, there is now appreciable evidence that such barriers are commoner among sympatric populations (see, for example Shorrocks 1978). It is undoubtedly true that reproductive barriers prevent the emergence of intermediate feeding and distribution behaviours but it is not clear why this should be universally advantageous under proximate natural selection pressure. Is it really the case that hybrids are less fit than their parents, or is it that meta-selection has favoured individuals which do not threaten resilience by exploring new niches?

Convergent evolution also provides strong circumstantial evidence to support the view that hierarchical selection pressure may constrain the range of niches individuals are free to explore. Marsupial and placental moles exhibit striking similarities of form and behaviour though the two groups are not phylogenetically close. Ichthyosaurs and modern dolphins also appear strikingly similar in body form, though one was a reptile and the other a mammal. Less spectacular, but nonetheless striking instances of convergence can be found among the higher plants where a handful of characteristic *life forms* describe virtually all higher plants and appear to cross well-defined biogeographic, taxonomic and, presumably, phylogenetic boundaries (Raunkiaer 1937).

Finally, an alternative source of circumstantial evidence for the hierarchical model comes from the study of contemporary food webs, which has found that three or four trophic levels are a typical maximum number. This begs a question; why not five levels, or six? Traditionally, ecologists have believed that the length of a food chain is constrained by energy flow and the second law of thermodynamics. However, Pimm (1982) has pointed out that if this were so one would expect longer food chains in the tropics than the Arctic and this is manifestly not so. Pimm suggests that longer food chains are inherently fragile because long chains have longer return times and so are more likely to be disrupted by recurrent stochastic perturbation. The PALECO model has no thermodynamic constraints; the carrying capacity of plants is identical to that of herbivores and carnivores. However, a number of attempts to establish a PALECO model with four trophic levels have failed because an intermediate prey organism has become extinct before the system has achieved a resilient configuration. It is possible this problem could be overcome by introducing a fourth trophic level to a pre-existing three-level model but the fact remains that four-level food chains are much harder to establish than those with three, even in model ecosystems with no thermodynamic constraints.

Resilience, long-term climatic change and Epirus

PALECO has confirmed that a predator which moves around and/or feeds too efficiently will drive its prey to extinction and then starve, while one which moves around or feeds too inefficiently will be at a selective disadvantage to more efficient competitors. It seems reasonable, then, to surmise that a resilient ecosystem could become fragile in response to any factor that changed the relationship between the powers of dispersal of its constituent organisms and the size of the ecosystem. Any factor that perturbed the balance between predator–prey dispersal mechanisms established by natural selection in the given environment could be expected to result in a loss of resilience.

The foregoing discussion has ignored the effect of climatic and geomorphological fluctuations on the hierarchy though it is apparent that such factors could reduce the resilience of a previously well-adapted hierarchy by creating artificial barriers to dispersal. In the long or medium term, one would expect selection pressure at higher holonomic (*cf.* taxonomic) levels to drive the system towards a more resilient trajectory. In the short term, however, intense natural selection would be experienced at the lowest holonomic level. By the time higher holonomic levels have responded to meta-selection pressures, certain species (possibly including humans) may have adopted different feeding and distribution strategies or even become extinct.

Redefining systems, sub-systems and patches

One could easily conceive (and implement) a modified PALECO system containing two or more sub-systems, each of which contains an ensemble of patches. Migration would be free within a sub-system but impeded between sub-systems. Each sub-system would behave like a separate PALECO ecosystem in its own right. Given such a model we could experiment with the insertion and removal of barriers to dispersal. The results of these experiments would presumably be consistent with those described above.

Suppose barriers to dispersal within a sub-system were removed so that predators could access the whole prey population instantly. This would simulate the effects of wiping the Vaseline off Huffaker's tray of oranges; it would convert the whole sub-system into a single, closed patch and resilience would be lost. Now suppose we introduce new barriers to dispersal that prevent predators in one patch from seeking new pockets of prey in another. This would be like putting a jamjar over each orange so that no mite can move from one orange to another. Each patch (orange) has become a closed sub-system in its own right. Once again, local extinctions become much more likely and resilience would be lost.

These insights into the likely dynamic behaviour of ecosystems under the overkill hypothesis can now be applied to Upper Palaeolithic Epirus by looking for events likely to turn patches into sub-systems or sub-systems into patches. This requires us to search for a natural way of partitioning the ecosystem into closed sub-systems and patches. We can then look at the palaeoclimatic and geomorphological history of the region to identify factors likely to add or remove barriers to effective dispersal.

Partitioning Epirus into sub-systems and patches

During the period 120,000 to 10,000 years ago, Epirus was subjected to dramatic changes in climate and sea level. Through some of this time, mean temperatures were high and humans would have had access both to plant and to animal resources. During other periods, temperatures were low and humans would presumably have subsisted almost exclusively on animal resources.

The effect of changing sea levels

Modern Epirus is mountainous with only a small area of moisture-retentive lowland near the sea. This was not always the case. Sea levels just after the glacial maximum had fallen to more than 100 metres below their current levels and a large coastal shelf to the west of modern Epirus formed a land-bridge between Corfu and the Greek mainland (Sturdy *et al.*, Chapter 30). This coastal strip extended southwards to the Peleponnese and northwards along the margins of modern Albania. It would have been possible to travel from Epirus first northwards past Albania, then to the west and finally to the south along the Italian Coast without leaving this coastal strip (Van Andel 1989, figs. 1 & 2). Large ice sheets had formed on the high ground inland and to the north so that much of this land above 1000 metres would have been inhospitable to plants and animals alike. Animals in the mountains would not have enjoyed the same ease of movement as those on the plain. In winter ice and deep snow would have blocked the passes and in spring torrential melt waters would have made movement difficult. By about 10 ka the situation was reversed. The sea level was probably less than 50 metres below its current level. Long migration around the coastal plain to Italy was impossible. There would still have been a lot of spring melt water in the gorges and crossing the coastal strip but the glaciers were gone and travel through mountain passes would have been easier.

Plants and climate

The palynological evidence for the Epirus region is patchy and difficult to cross-date. A detailed interpretation of the pollen sequences is presented in Turner & Sánchez-Goñi, Chapter 29. For present purposes a very simplified summary will suffice. During the warmer periods a mixed flora containing trees and herbs had formed. The arboreal component of the pollen sequences ebbs and flows giving way to an open steppe environment containing large amounts of *Chenopodiaceae* and *Artemisia*. For as much as 70 per cent of the last 4 million years there is very little tree pollen. Any trees would have been restricted to those sheltered regions that enjoyed favourable microclimates. Mountain ledges inland have been suggested as suitable environments because they provide water and shelter and are inaccessible to grazers. Any gardener can testify that west facing slopes and walls may be more congenial to plant survival in cold periods than those that face east or south where rapid thawing can damage frozen plant tissues. One would expect more favourable microclimates in Epirus than in eastern Italy or eastern Greece, for example. It is also possible that well-watered lowland regions in the south of our study area contained some trees. In this respect, we should note the presence of pigs and red deer at Asprochaliko and Kastritsa (Bailey *et al.* 1983). Pigs are not well-adapted to open country and usually exploit broken woodland. A similar case can be made for red deer (see below).

Between 16 & 11 ka there was a climatic amelioration and, as the ice sheets retreated, the trees would have expanded their range, beginning in the south of our study area and gradually spreading northwards. It is convenient to split the Late-Glacial period into two sub-periods. The early Late-Glacial (16–13 ka) saw the most intensive occupation of sites in the mountainous hinterland of which Klithi is an example. By the later Late-Glacial (13–11 ka) the intensity of occupation in the hinterland seems to attenuate and appreciable amounts of tree pollen appear in the pollen sequences.

The period between 11 and 10 ka (the Younger Dryas) is interpreted as dry and cold, but not glaciated. Trees retreated once again.

During the Holocene (from 10 ka onwards) there was a general warming. Notwithstanding this, trees appear to retreat again after about 6 ka and the vegetation opens up significantly *c.* 4 ka. This is interpreted as an anthropogenic effect.

Animals

The animal evidence is similarly patchy and locating these animals in the landscape requires a certain amount of guesswork based on their modern distributions (Sturdy *et al.*, Chapter 30). The older the material, the more tenuous the guess. One of the principal problems is that modern populations of large ungulates are relictual and may not exploit the same niches as their ancestors. Furthermore, human expansion may have driven some populations into marginal environments of a type not exploited in the past. Even when this is not the case, many ungulates can exploit a range of niches and it is sometimes difficult to guess which, if any, of the niches exploited by modern populations would have been occupied in the past. In Epirus, for example, there were cattle populations (*Bos* sp.). Were these living on woodland margins (like seventeenth-century Aurochs, *Bos primigenius*) on open plains (like modern *Bison* sp.) or in the mountains (like modern Yak, *Bos grunniens*)?

There were lions, bear, lynx and two canids present in Palaeolithic Epirus. Canids and Felids that can hunt large prey in open country must have had a profound impact on animals living on the coastal strip. Any ungulate living on the coastal strip of Upper Palaeolithic Epirus would presumably have needed some active defensive strategy in order to co-exist with large predators. This might involve the adoption of a close herding strategy or, as is the case with modern rhinoceros, extremely large body size and a somewhat ferocious disposition. These traits can be observed in modern ungulate populations in Africa. For example, Kruuk (1972) describes the defensive strategies of Zebra and Eland under attack from clans of spotted hyaena. Zebra form a tight group of females and young which trot away from the predators while the dominant stallion protects the rear of the group, chasing, biting and kicking the hyaenas. Eland cows, on the other hand, form two groups, one of which surrounds the calves and the other of which face the hyaenas in a line and actively attack them.

Modern *equids* cannot ruminate or browse to any appreciable extent. The equid leg is well adapted for running on flat land and poorly adapted to broken terrain. It seems likely that the Palaeolithic equids were always restricted to open, flat or undulating landscapes where they would have been subject to attacks from hyaena and lion and have had relatively little protective cover. *Pigs* are unable to contend with an open steppe environment and were probably restricted to woodland and the margins of woodland. *Chamois* and *ibex* specialize in the exploitation of mountainous and other severe terrain, often in areas with few woody plants. They rely on their agility to evade such predators as wolves and large cats. Modern *roe* and *fallow deer* can live in open country or in woodland and uplands. However, modern populations do not form large, defensive herds and it seems unlikely that roe and fallow deer would have been able to contend with predators in open country. Young roe and fallow deer are spotted, a trait which is commonly associated with life in the dappled shade of woodland and scrub.

There remain two animal taxa that cannot easily be located in this environment, *red deer* and *cattle*. Both are large ruminant ungulates and both are capable of subsisting in open country *and* on woodland margins. In the open coastal strip, there would be little cover available and one would expect cattle and cervids to form large defensive herds. In the woods and uplands, however, it is possible to use cover and dispersal to minimize predation rates. Studies of African ungulate species suggest that the formation of permanent defensive herds containing males, females and juveniles makes it difficult for animals to feed selectively on highly nutritious plants (Jarman 1974) and such animals tend to be relatively unselective bulk feeders. Thus, if we can establish the feeding preferences of extinct red deer and cattle populations and/or infer their social organization and dependence on cover, we can form educated guesses about where they would fit into this ecosystem.

A valuable study of ruminant feeding preferences (Hofman 1985) has established a consistent relationship between ruminant feeding preferences and anatomy. Hofman argued that concentrate-selectors, which rely largely on the cell contents of highly nutritious plants, have relatively simple guts and relatively narrow mouths to facilitate selective feeding. Concentrate feeders feed frequently and spend relatively little time ruminating, they tend to be dispersed through the landscape for much of the year and to need a relatively small area to subsist. Bulk feeders, on the other hand, must be able to metabolize cellulose effectively and tend to have a large, anatomically complex gut and a relatively broad 'bite'. They feed over a larger area than concentrate feeders and tend to feed relatively few times and to spend considerable time ruminating.

According to Hofman's scheme, all modern domestic cattle are bulk feeders, Eurasian red deer are of an intermediate, or adaptable type while roe deer are specialized concentrate selectors. Hofman's classification has been examined for deer by Putman (1988, ch. 3) who confirms that this anatomical classification 'matches exactly with what is known of the ecology of these various species' (1988, 46).

If we assume that stomach morphology is not going to differ much between ancient and modern cattle, Hofman's scheme suggests that Palaeolithic cattle would be bulk feeders, more likely than red deer to form large herds feeding in open country. Both male and female cattle are horned, a trait which suggests that horns may have been used for defence against predators and were not merely used for male display and competition. Modern cattle populations tend to form herds in which males, females and calves all run together. All these factors suggest that cattle would certainly have been capable of co-existing with large predators in open country.

It has been suggested that red deer might also have lived in open country (Sturdy *et al.*, Chapter 30) and their intermediate feeding strategy and the ability of some modern populations to live in open country adds some weight to this theory. Some cervids, notably reindeer (*Rangifer* sp.) certainly can co-exist with canids in open country. However, reindeer did not extend into Epirus during the Last Glacial, though they did reach Yugoslavia.

It is a useful exercise to compare the natural history of modern reindeer with red deer to see how many of the attributes of open-country animals modern red deer possess. Reindeer must contend with predation from wolves and commonly live in large herds. Both sexes have well-developed antlers. The reindeer rut co-incides with calving, increasing the number of adults available to protect the herd at this time. Reindeer calves do not exhibit the characteristic spotting of woodland animals (Clutton-Brock 1987). That modern red deer differ from reindeer in all these respects seems to suggest that the colonization of open country is a recent adaptation, possibly a response to deforestation and the extinction of macro-predators and other wild ungulates.

Horses have the broad bite of a bulk feeder but cannot ruminate and so must feed for very long periods to win sufficient nutrition from their bulky food. Horses must remain in open ground for long periods, relying on speed and social organization to deal with predators. Modern cattle can move over more broken terrain than equids but cannot run as fast so it is likely that the two populations exploited different regions within the coastal strip. In the presence of cattle and of predators capable of bringing down cattle and horses, red deer would probably have been more secure living in small groups on the margins of open country and in broken woodland.

Beaver live near water either in dams or holes in the bank. They must have access to trees and scrub to survive. Beavers are selective feeders and can have an impact on woodland succession. Furthermore, the tendency of some beaver populations to dam streams can result in the formation of temporary meadows which may carry rich vegetation and attract herbivores.

Sub-systems and patches

The simplified summary of the palaeoecological data for Late Pleistocene and early Holocene Epirus outlined above invites us to divide the region into two sub-systems, open and covered. The *open sub-system* includes the coastal plain and the area between mainland Greece and Corfu at lowered sea levels. The ungulate species exploiting these environments may well have changed through the Upper Palaeolithic. At some times, the open region might have been occupied by rhino, equid and cattle, at others there might only have been equids or cattle. Regardless of the species mix, the ungulates on the plain would have shared certain basic biological attributes. They would either have been very large and aggressive or moderately large and have formed stable herd structures capable of co-existing with large predators in the absence of effective cover.

The *covered sub-system* includes all the mountainous areas except those rendered inaccessible by climatic extremes and some low-lying wetlands to the south of our study area. Some woodland probably persisted in these regions throughout the Middle and Upper Palaeolithic (providing cover for the pigs at Asprochaliko, for example). There would have been much less accessible cover at the Last Glacial Maximum and the Younger Dryas and rather more in the interim. The ungulates exploiting the covered region were those which can use cover, agility and/or dispersal to avoid predators. Once again, the species mix may have varied through time, but the behavioural and biological attributes would persist.

The relative areas of these sub-systems would have changed as sea levels and climate varied through time. During interglacials, sea levels would have been high and the area of open country would have been at a minimum. The open sub-system would presumably have contained rather fewer patches isolated from similar sub-systems to the north and south by sea and by mountain ranges. The climate was generally temperate and the areas of accessible and grazeable covered country would have been maximal. Migration through mountain passes from patches in Epirus to similar patches to the north and south would have been possible. During the run-up to the glacial maximum sea levels and temperatures were oscillating downwards and the area of open country expanded while the covered sub-system contracted.

During glaciated periods, the open region reached its maximum extent and was occupied by a steppe-like vegetation. It would have been possible for open-country ungulates and their predators to migrate very long distances. The covered region, however, was at its minimum extent with relatively little vegetation in the mountainous hinterland. Ungulates dependent on cover would have been living on virtual islands for much of the year with travel from one stand of vegetation to another only possible via the open region. Without large body size and a defensive herd structure, these animals would have been vulnerable to predators in the open and would have had difficulty crossing open plains.

In the early Late Glacial period the area of open country was gradually contracting and the cover was expanding. In the later Late Glacial this process continued so that by about 11 ka glacial conditions would have been reversed. The open region was greatly reduced and very long-distance migration would have been impossible without crossing mountains or passing through woodland. The covered region would have been at its maximum extent and long-distance migration through the hills would have been possible. Small areas of broken woodland could have become established on the coastal strip around stable river beds, extending the area of covered country onto parts of the coastal strip.

During the Younger Dryas, the rapid reduction in temperature would have caused the covered region to contract once again but this time there was no corresponding increase in the coastal area. The early Holocene saw a return to conditions comparable to the later Late Glacial.

The climatic/vegetational trajectory for the region can be summarized in tabular form.

	Dates (ka)	Open country	Cover
Interglacial	120–110	Minimal	Maximal
Pre-Glacial	110–30	?Expanding	?Contracting
Glacial	30–16	Maximal	Minimal
Early Late-Glacial	16–13	Contracting	Expanding
Late Late-Glacial	13–11	Contracting	Maximal
Younger Dryas	11–10	Minimal	Minimal
Holocene	10–0	Minimal	Maximal

Keeping options open: refugia and resilience in Epirus

The chronological resolution of the schema presented above is much poorer for the earlier periods than the later and it is quite likely that climatic cycles which could, in principle, be determined for the earlier periods have been missed or simplified out of existence in this summary. However, it is clear even from this greatly simplified schema that the cycles of expansion and contraction suggested for open country and for accessible cover do not proceed in phase. Sometimes, as at the Last Glacial Maximum, contraction in the available area of broken country coincides with an expansion in the open country and macro-predators have the option of coming down onto the large, resilient coastal ecosystem. At other times (the Younger Dryas, for example) this is not so and both the open and broken sub-systems will be at their most fragile.

It remains for us to work out what this would mean for individuals operating within those ecosystems. The first thing to note is that individual humans are unlikely to take the survival populations of a prey species as the first consideration when deciding a subsistence strategy. The survival of self and immediate neighbours is likely to be the first priority. One would expect humans to focus their attention on the more resilient regions in Epirus and to favour subsistence strategies that minimize the risk of starvation. Occasional forays into less resilient areas are possible but would be less frequent because the fragile regions would take much longer to recover from human disturbance. Therefore, one would expect site density through space and time to be correlated with resilience.

During the warmer Interglacial period, plant foods may have been available in abundance and human populations would have been less dependent on large mammals than during colder periods. It seems reasonable to suppose that at these periods, humans would subsist on a broad spectrum of plants and of ungulates capable of exploiting broken country. The area of open country would have been at its minimal extent and predators exploiting relictual herds of open-country ungulates could easily drive local populations to the verge of extinction. The safest and most resilient sources of animal protein would have come from broken country (upland and wetlands where woods might form) with animals on the plain exploited less intensively.

Between 110 and 30 ka one would expect some exploitation of plant resources and of animals in broken country and the mountainous hinterland. As sea levels fell one would expect more exploitation of the open plain to have been possible. At various points during this period one would expect the widest range of plant and animal resources to have been available with sites distributed through the hinterland and across the available coastal plain.

Between 30 ka and the Last Glacial Maximum there would have been occasions when the exploitation of broken country would have been difficult but the area of open country was opening up. Around the glacial maximum there would have been few plant foods and one would expect humans and other large carnivores to be driven into the open country. As already noted, ungulates in open country tend to be fast and/or ferocious. Presumably humans would have used a range of herding or trapping strategies to drive these animals towards natural obstacles such as dissected river systems, cliffs and gullies. The dissected plains between modern Corfu and Epirus seem an obvious place to hunt these animals and similar areas around the modern islands to the west of Albania and Yugoslavia may be expected to produce further evidence of large ungulate exploitation between 30 and 16 ka.

Between 16 and 13 ka the area of open country would still be considerable and one would expect resilience here to be high. As the ice retreated, one would expect the mountainous hinterland to become accessible and it is at this period we begin to see chamois and ibex exploitation at Klithi and other sites in the hinterland. Chamois and ibex may have been able to sustain predation during this period but can be expected to have been difficult to catch; they are too agile to drive into gullies or deadfall traps. An obvious stratagem for trapping these species would be to wait until valley bottoms were flooded with spring meltwater and drive them gently into these wet areas. Great stealth would be needed to prevent them from panicking and making for high ground and this method would require a well coordinated team of hunters. Once the animals were concentrated on muddy low ground they could be driven into the water and picked off one at a time.

Between 13 and 11 ka the open country would have diminished and one would expect this subsystem to become increasingly fragile. For a while broken country would have been accessible once again though the retreat of the ice sheets could have reduced the amount of spring meltwater and made it harder to catch these animals. The severe 'cold snap' around 11 ka would have reduced resilience in the hinterland and so put an end to this stratagem.

The Younger Dryas is clearly critical because mobility is severely restricted both in open country and in cover and there would have been few plant foods available. There may be isolated simple refugia for plant species but it is unlikely that Epirus would contain sufficient statistical refugia to protect a diverse large mammal population. This is the point at which the overkill hypothesis would predict that large carnivores and possibly large herbivores must either leave Epirus altogether or run a serious risk of starvation. One would expect versatile omnivore populations (like humans) to explore alternative subsistence strategies or get out.

By the Holocene a number of open-country ungulates may have become locally extinct and large predators would once again have become increasingly dependent on species capable of exploiting broken country. Although the species mix has changed and some of the Pleistocene species that survive into the Holocene may be exploiting different foods, the overkill hypothesis predicts a configuration broadly comparable to that of the Interglacial and the late Late Glacial. Humans would be able to exploit plant foods and animals capable of surviving in broken country.

Resilience, site distributions and animal domestication

The view expressed by Crisp in the quotation at the beginning of this report is widely echoed in the archaeological literature, where the realization that local prehistoric sequences can often be resolved into an early, extensive phase with low population densities and a later intensive phase with high densities has stimulated much research. It has long been accepted that agriculture is a prerequisite of the intensive phase and that the first societies to produce solid evidence of demographic runaway were the early cities of the Near East. There is ample evidence that humans have imposed unsustainable pressure on natural communities throughout later prehistory. However, the converse view that pre-urban humans were somehow able to avoid this is a piece of scientific mythology that has no solid supporting evidence. It is quite possible and, indeed, likely that human and other predators contributed to the extinction of wild equids on the coast of Epirus. Small populations of horses would be perfectly capable of living on the modern coastal strip of Epirus but not capable of sustaining *both* impaired powers of dispersal *and* a standing population of macro-predators.

Long-term climatic change may dramatically

alter an organism's power of dispersal, turning the erstwhile patches of a large ecosystem into a series of virtual islands. The overkill hypothesis suggests that this will result in a loss of resilience which may vitiate pre-existing feeding relationships. Meta-selection will favour the re-adjustment of feeding relationships but extinctions are increasingly probable during these periods. Humans, like any other predator, must either negotiate resilient feeding relations within a given ecosystem or face the likelihood of catastrophic extinction. Under certain circumstances there will be no resilient feeding relations available and predators are likely to become extinct, withdraw, or change their feeding behaviour to accommodate the new high-risk environment in which they find themselves.

This is not a simple environmental determinism. It is merely an acknowledgement that, under certain conditions, ecological resilience may collapse, extinctions may become more probable and feeding relations may change. Furthermore, the overkill hypothesis can be articulated with the available palaeoecological data to make empirically testable predictions about the parts of the landscape which humans are most likely to exploit at certain times. In general, one would expect sites to be concentrated in those areas likely to contain resilient sub-systems. It is relatively easy to cast an eye over the palaeoecological data summarized above and work out what to expect in Epirus if the overkill hypothesis is justified and the region has been partitioned into appropriate sub-systems. Clearly, a rash of archaeological sites in the mountainous hinterland during the Glacial Maximum or the Younger Dryas would refute this interpretation. However, one would expect sites and resilient large mammal populations on the coastal strip throughout the glacial maximum (some of these will be inundated by the sea). During the Younger Dryas, one would expect few sites on the coastal strip and any that exist to yield evidence of a range of 'experimental' feeding strategies.

Although the overkill hypothesis has been constructed with Epirus in mind, its corollaries can be applied to other regions and periods without loss of generality. In Epirus there is some evidence of a human withdrawal between 11 and 10 ka. In the Near East, however, the story is different with humans beginning to adopt a fully sedentary life style and feeding on cereals and bovids. At some stage in this process, the cereals and bovids were domesticated, creating an economy that expanded into a wide range of Holocene environments.

The models presented in this chapter contain no attempt to simulate the impact of changes in ecological resilience on human culture at this time though it is clear that this is likely. Clearly, changes in perceptions of ownership and exchange may well have an adaptive significance in a changing ecosystem. Anthropological studies among Peruvian Llama herders (Flannery *et al.* 1989) illustrate the sorts of effects we can envisage. Llamas are upland herbivores with small herd size, the sort of animals I have argued here would be unable to sustain an appreciable human population, yet they do, indeed sustain an appreciable population of herders. The principal killers of llama are human rustlers, puma and mange, all of which show an *aggregation effect*. Llama predators tend to focus on large herds and by-pass very small herds. This means that llama populations are constrained both in their maximum and their minimum group size. Less than four llamas means chance accidents may render the population inviable. More than thirty and the rustlers, puma or mange will get them.

Flannery *et al.* (1989) observed a great deal of ritual gift giving that at first glance seemed to reduce herd viability by reducing herd size. Computer modelling showed that the opposite was true. Without gift giving the long-term survival prospects of the llama were very poor indeed. The results of this study can easily be summarized in the terms of the overkill hypothesis. In owning and hence controlling the dispersal of small herds, herders impose a degree of patchiness on llama distributions that creates statistical refugia when the predators pass through. This does not eradicate the predators, however, so some migration between patches is essential to restock patches where local extinctions have occurred. The principal mechanism for this is ritualized gift giving. Too much exchange of llama would reduce patchiness in the ecosystem and predators (particularly mange) would be able to move freely through the whole population. Too little exchange of llama would cause many patches to disappear for the want of 'immigrants' to make good local predatory overkill. In the long term this would destroy the statistical refugia on which the llama and their herders depend.

By controlling the exchange of llama (or any other ungulate relying on dispersal through broken terrain or vegetation cover) humans can increase their population beyond 'natural' levels whilst maintaining the spatial patchiness needed for resilience in an overkill ecosystem. Animal domestication would, of course, be a prerequisite of this strategy. Classical studies of animal domestication in the 1960s and 1970s tended to focus on the control of animal *reproduction* as the defining feature of 'true' domestication. It may be, however, that the control of animal *distribution* and the maintenance of spatial patchiness is the key to ecological resilience.

Conclusion

Both the biological and the archaeological evidence discussed above are consistent with the overkill hypothesis. The corollaries of this hypothesis are as follows.

- Predator–prey relations must result in spatial patchiness if they are to be resilient. Such spatial patchiness provides either real refugia (areas inaccessible to predators) or statistical refugia (areas where small of pockets of prey escape the attention of predators).
- Stable predator–prey relations emerge under the influence of 'meta-selection', i.e. selection operating at higher levels and over longer time periods than the conventional neo-Darwinian model suggests. This does not deny the primacy of natural selection at the level of the individual, but is an acknowledgement that other selective processes may be nested above it. Meta-selection has the effect of winnowing predator-prey relations established by natural selection at the level of the individual.
- The belief that earlier prehistory was characterized by human strategies that 'imposed no undue pressure on natural communities' is unsupported. While feeding relations will tend towards resilient configurations, resilience is likely to be lost wherever there are changes in the relative powers of dispersal of predators including humans and their prey.
- The dispersal of the principal prey species in Epirus was dramatically affected by the environmental changes of the glacial climatic cycle. Generally speaking reduced powers of dispersal for open-country species resulting from rising sea-level were compensated by improved dispersal and resilience for hinterland species dependent on tree cover for protection. During the Late Glacial stadial periods, however, notably the Younger Dryas, when a climatic downturn coincided with rising sea levels, resilience in both hinterland and coastal regions would have been reduced, representing a critical period of vulnerability for the human population.
- Finally, the overkill hypothesis has implications for the study of early agriculture. Many domesticated animals and plants are native to upland regions and can only sustain long-term human predation if the human population adopts strategies that maintain patchiness. Domestication provides a mechanism for controlling the spatial distribution of plants and animals. Thus the overkill hypothesis draws our attention to the role of culture and social organisation in determining human responses to ecological stress (Green, Chapter 32; Winder 1996).

Acknowledgements

I would like to thank the Leverhulme Trust for financial support, the ARCHAEOMEDES Project, funded by DG XII of the European Commission, for additional support, and my colleagues on the Klithi project for good company and stimulating discussion.

Chapter 32

Interweaving Landscapes: the Relevance of Ethnographic Data on Rural Groups in Epirus for Palaeolithic Research

Sarah F. Green

Origins: from cultural cynicism to material realities

My involvement, as a social anthropologist, with the Klithi project began with Eric Higgs' theory that modern-day transhumant pastoralists were probably following the same seasonal routes as Palaeolithic peoples had done, because the morphology of the landscape and the Epirot climate largely dictated such matters. As Bailey (Chapter 1) has outlined, Higgs was convinced, despite some qualifying remarks, that there was a direct correlation between transhumant routes and Palaeolithic seasonal movements, on the grounds that Palaeolithic hunter-gatherers had probably exploited the same, or roughly similar, 'ecological niche' as modern pastoralists.

Initially, I entirely rejected this notion as being unacceptable environmental determinism: it did not allow any influence of the social, the cultural, the political or the economic to enter into the equation — or rather (and even worse) it implied that these socio-economic conditions were determined by environmental factors. Furthermore, in suggesting a direct link between today's transhumant pastoralists and Palaeolithic hunter-gatherers, Higgs' proposition ignored the millennia of history in between.

I was therefore initially somewhat dubious about a request from the Klithi team, in 1984, that I should carry out some brief ethnographic work amongst the remaining transhumant pastoralists in Epirus, with a view to assessing Eric Higgs' ideas. Any association between the two groups seemed to be a nonsense, and I was encouraged in thinking this by the fact that, for very different reasons, the 1980s archaeological team was also doubtful about Higgs' theory particularly as the archaeological data were still ambiguous on the issue of seasonality (Bailey *et al.* 1983a, 73). Nevertheless, the team wanted more ethnographic information: since the inter-site and regional perspective developed by Higgs remained a central part of the archaeological work in the area, an ethnographic comparison was regarded as worth pursuing. One could at least *compare* the movements of the two groups around the landscape, even if it was impossible to extrapolate any direct causal links between them.

Despite my doubts, I agreed to go and talk to some transhumants. In the short time I had travelling around the Epirus countryside with Geoff Bailey and Derek Sturdy, speaking to various members of the local population, I concluded that there was indeed nothing to compare between these modern-day Epirot transhumant pastoralists, Sarakatsani and Vlachs, with any conceivable activities of hunter-gatherers during the Upper Palaeolithic. Transhumant pastoralism is an economic specialization dependent upon the existence of a market (Chang 1993; Halstead 1987), as well as certain political and social conditions (Khazanov 1984; Nitsiakos 1986). Further, different hunter-gatherer and pastoralist groups vary enormously across the globe (Ingold 1986), particularly in terms of how they organize moving around the landscape. I concluded that the very different ways the Sarakatsani and the Vlachs practised seasonal transhumance in Epirus showed that the 'natural' environment was less important than cultural traditions (Campbell 1964; Makris 1990; Winnifrith 1987). Furthermore, their seasonal routes had more to do with contemporary legal restrictions, issues of property rights and arrangements for leasing grazing land, the existence of metalled roads, concerns about theft of herds, and the location of markets than it did with the geomorphology of the landscape.

These conclusions were how matters remained until 1992, when I began more lengthy ethnographic research in Epirus, which eventually changed my views. Once again the focus was the landscape, though on this occasion I was concentrating more on the peoples involved in a particular area, Pogoni County, rather than on transhumant pastoralists. In light of this research, I now conclude that the geomorphology and climate of Epirus often have a crucial impact on how people use and move through that landscape, even in this day and age of complex market systems, transportation infrastructures and technological solutions to the constraints presented by the local environment. I cannot even argue that perceptions of the Epirot environment are culturally determined in a way that is independent of the physical characteristics of that environment. The ruggedly mountainous character, interspersed with often steep-sided small valleys and the occasional plain, and the wet climate, with blisteringly hot summers and freezing, snowy winters — these things deeply affect people's physical experiences. What people *say or think* about these experiences, if they do say or think anything about them, is undoubtedly a cultural matter; but the fact of the physical experiences (I am not saying 'natural' experiences, as will be explained below), and their importance in people's sense of their world will equally undoubtedly be incorporated as a part of any cultural understanding.

This change in my perspective is due to numerous factors, but none more important than the several years of collaboration with Geoff King during the ARCHAEOMEDES phase of research. Through a series of often lengthy discussions, our ideas about the Epirot landscape and its relationship with the people of the area were mutually formulated, informed by an interweaving of the perspectives of our respective disciplines.

This new conclusion provides the framework for comparing contemporary and Palaeolithic data. Specifically, this chapter is an attempt to get at aspects of the 'interweaving' of Epirot peoples and their environment in terms of the relationship between the landscape and people's movements through it. I will be using two kinds of data to address the question: an analysis of the historical use of the Epirot landscape by a variety of different groups, which shows that all, in one way or another, centrally incorporated regular movements from one place to another in their practices; and, secondly, an analysis of modern day practices within the landscape, which, though far more sedentary, and involving fundamental changes in how the landscape is perceived, continue to incorporate patterns of seasonal movement.

The major argument is that this pattern of mobility, which is clear across all the groups studied, even though each instance varies according to different kinds of social, political and economic conditions, is the result of a process of 'interweaving' of different peoples with the Epirot landscape. Cultural perceptions of the landscape, when articulated explicitly, were an expression of, as well as a part of, this interweaving, rather than *creating* it, as previous culturalist approaches would suggest. The significance of this point will become clearer as I go through the ethnographic data below.

In light of this consistent pattern of mobility, it is not surprising that the archaeological team's material evidence, since work started in the 1960s with Eric Higgs, has persistently pointed to the conclusion that Palaeolithic hunter-gatherers seasonally moved around the landscape. If I disagree with Eric Higgs' original idea that the activities of transhumant pastoralists can be extrapolated directly back to the possible activities of hunter-gatherers using a kind of environmentally determinist logic, I now acknowledge that there was something important in his connection between the possible movements of hunter-gatherers through the landscape and today's movements of transhumant pastoralists (and I would add, others) through that same landscape.

The approach I am suggesting differs from much ethnoarchaeology, which has focused on detailed analysis of the contemporary effects that local human groups have on the environment, in order to compare archaeological findings with historically or ethnographically verifiable information about the impact of certain kinds of human use of the same environment (e.g. Chang & Tourtellotte 1993; Jones 1984; Murray & Kardulias 1986; Nandris 1985; Whitelaw 1991). An underlying aim in such research is that studies of material remains of living groups can help to interpret the remains of groups no longer in existence. This can assist both in resolving questions regarding the origins of certain forms of economic activity, or in drawing parallels between prehistoric and historic groups which pursued the same kind of economic activity, or in considering the processes of change from one kind of economic activity to another.

This chapter does none of this: it is not considering the origins of transhumant pastoralism or other groups, nor considering the materials left by such groups on their travels. It is instead considering the relationship between patterns of mobility and the Epirot landscape, and through that attempting to rethink what these data can say about the Epirot landscape and people's activities within it.

Theoretical background: beyond nature–culture dichotomies

A number of social theorists, both within anthropology and outside it, have recently pointed out that dismissing physical conditions and experience in analyzing social life is a form of ethnocentrism which perpetuates the nature-culture, mind–body dichotomy (see, for example, Crary & Kwinter 1992; Horigan 1988; Ingold 1992a,b; MacCormack & Strathern 1980). This is not the place to review the full complexity of the argument, which has involved various attempts to get beyond disagreements about which side of the nature–culture dichotomy has the biggest role in causing things to happen in the social world. Suffice it to say that one strand of more recent social theory argues for a kind of 'folding' or 'interweaving' of the 'natural' and the 'cultural'. Within this perspective, nature and culture should neither be considered as an oppositional dichotomy, nor as distinctly separate in any meaningful way. The underlying idea of this approach, as described for example by Ingold (1992a), is that people act in the world as much, or perhaps even more, through direct experience as they do through *thinking* about that experience and defining it in some cultural way.

A distinction has now been drawn within this perspective between two forms of human thought and activity, which had previously been assumed to be the same. The first involves reflexive thought, a process of coming to an understanding of the world through consciously or otherwise thinking about it, using culturally-defined structures of meaning. The second involves a direct experience of the world, in which practice and performance, rather than cognition alone, define the interactions between people and their surroundings. This second form of bringing people and their environment together, through analyzing performance rather than cultural understanding, blurs the distinctions between human agency and that environment, and in so doing also blurs the distinction between 'nature' and 'culture'.[1]

This suggests that the physical world cannot be depicted as being either 'passive nature', a kind of backdrop to human actions in the world, nor 'created by culture', the result of applying cultural understanding to both perceiving and altering the world. Instead, people act in the world as a part of that world, and therefore their experience, as mentioned above, involves a continual interweaving or folding of both cultural and physical experience. Therefore, the assumption that dealing with the (natural) environment *necessarily* involves 'dominating' or 'controlling' it (culturally), rather than interacting with it in a way that affects both, is regarded within this perspective as a misunderstanding of people's existence in the world. This is both because it distinguishes between nature and culture in a clearly ethnocentric manner (Cartesian dualism, etc.), and because it overemphasizes the influence of the cultural at the expense of the physical experience of the world.[2]

This approach can be usefully employed to look at what the findings of anthropologists and archaeologists can say to one another. Instead of suggesting that there is any direct causal link between the constraints of 'nature' on peoples both past and present, and therefore concluding that both are at the beck and call of 'nature' until such a time as they subdue 'nature' with modern-day technology, the approach could be revised thus: given that similar physical conditions existed for the different groups living in Epirus, in what ways did these different groups practice this 'interweaving' of their actions and their environment?[3]

The Pogoni case study: land degradation and mobility [4]

Pogoni County (Figs. 32.1 & 32.3) lies in the northwest of Epirus on the Albanian border, to the West of the Zagori where Klithi is located, and to the north of Ioannina, the capital of Epirus; to the southwest lies Thesprotia Prefecture, the other county in Epirus which borders Albania, and which includes a considerable length of southern coastline around the Igoumenitsa area, traditionally used by transhumant pastoralists for winter grazing land. Pogoni County is an area of relatively low mountains interspersed with small valleys, and is bordered to the west by the Doliana plain, and to the east by the Drinos plain (Fig. 32.3). The central mountain of the area is the Kasidiares, which is steep-sided, long and narrow, and separates the Doliana from the Drinos plains.

There are 32 villages and one municipality (Delvinaki) within Pogoni's administrative borders, the majority of which are located in hilly or mountainous areas, the significant exceptions being a small area located at the northeastern foot of the Kasidiares on the edge of the Doliana plain (Fig. 32.3). Other than this area, Pogoni generally speaking has relatively low quality soils, with a high proportion of flysch, and because none of its mountains reach above 1300 metres, Pogoni does not have the highest quality high mountain summer grazing land.

In sum, the Pogoni County is a rural mountainous

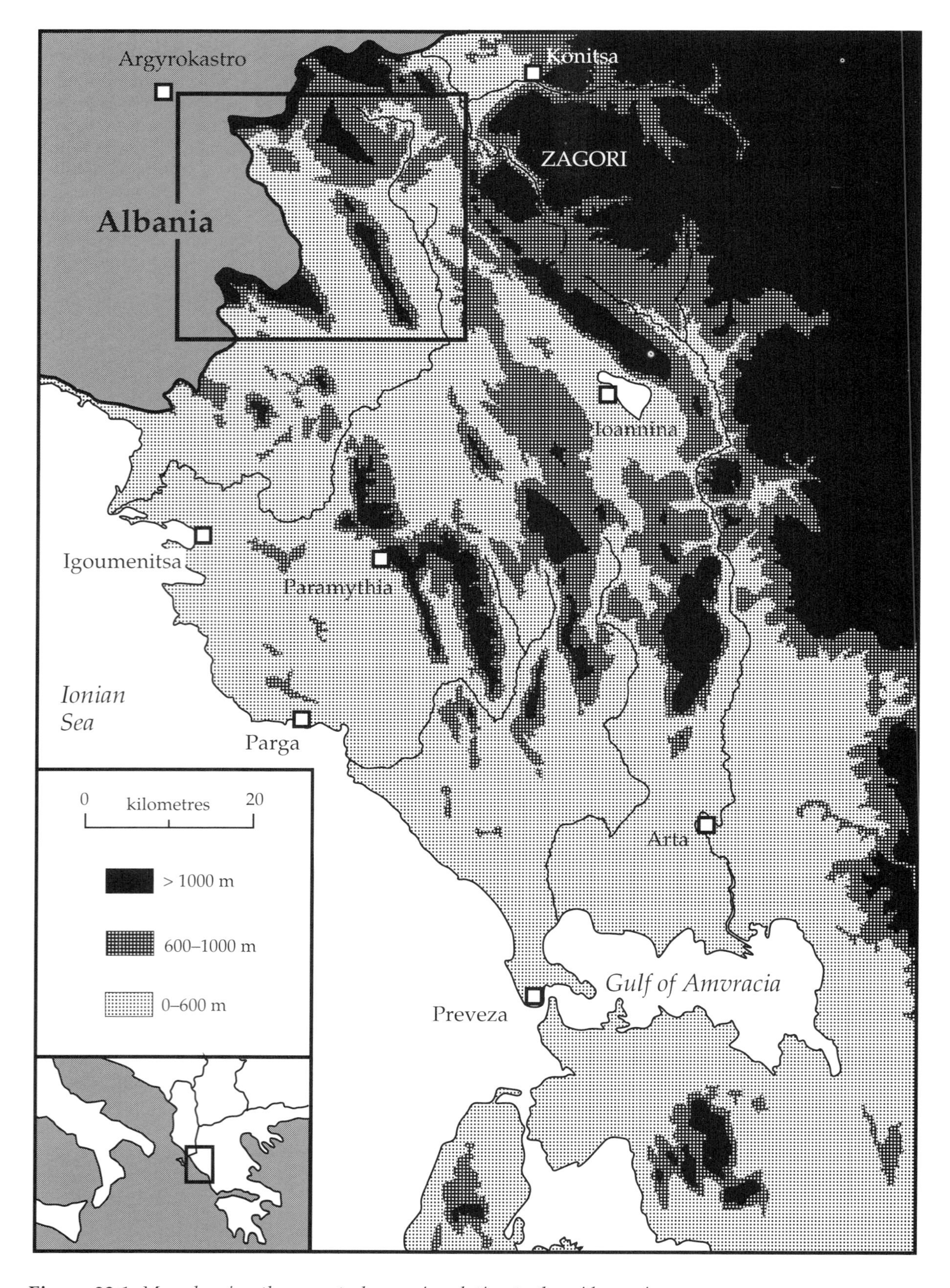

Figure 32.1. *Map showing the case study area in relation to the wider region.*

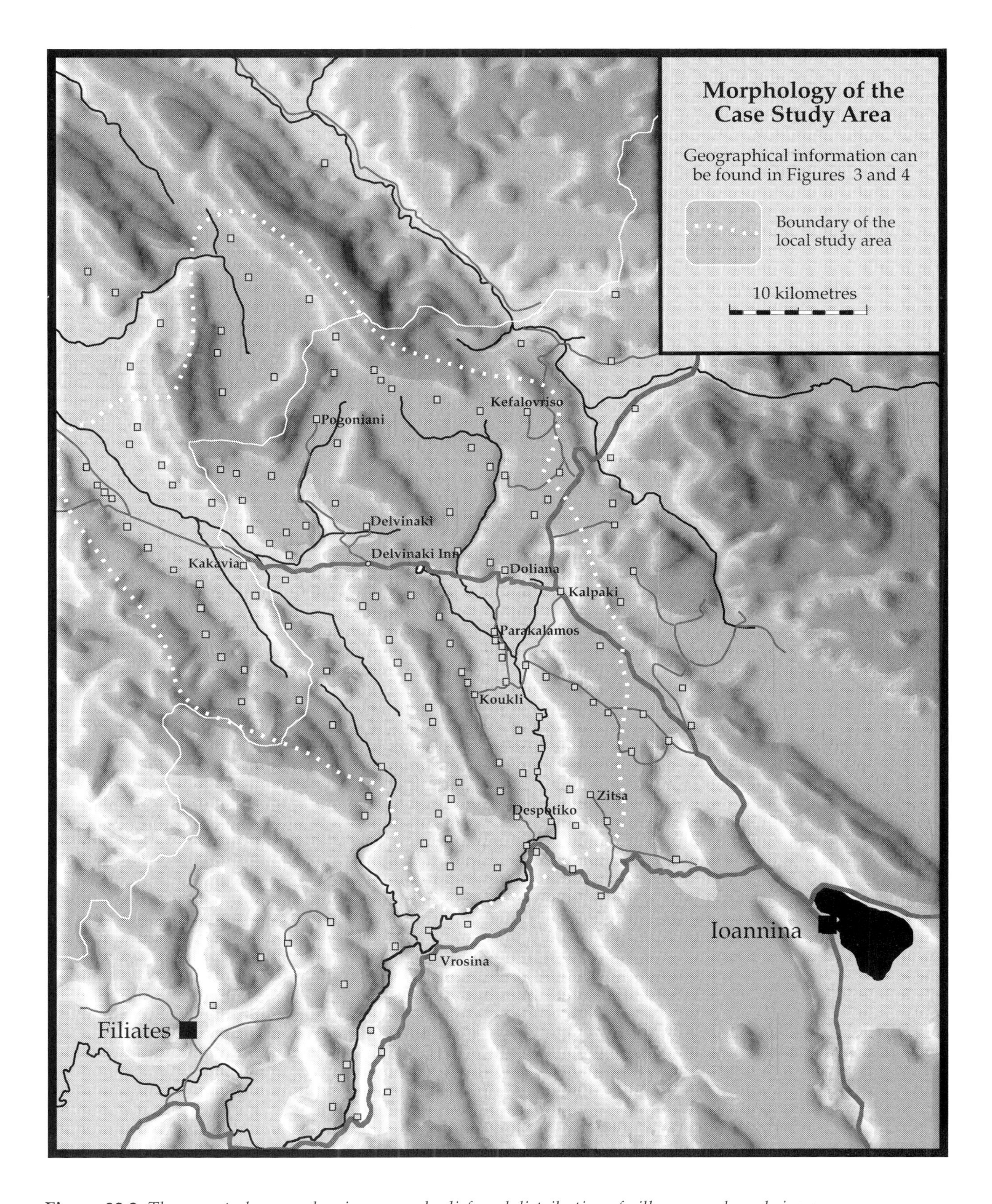

Figure 32.2. *The case study area, showing general relief, and distribution of villages, roads and rivers.*

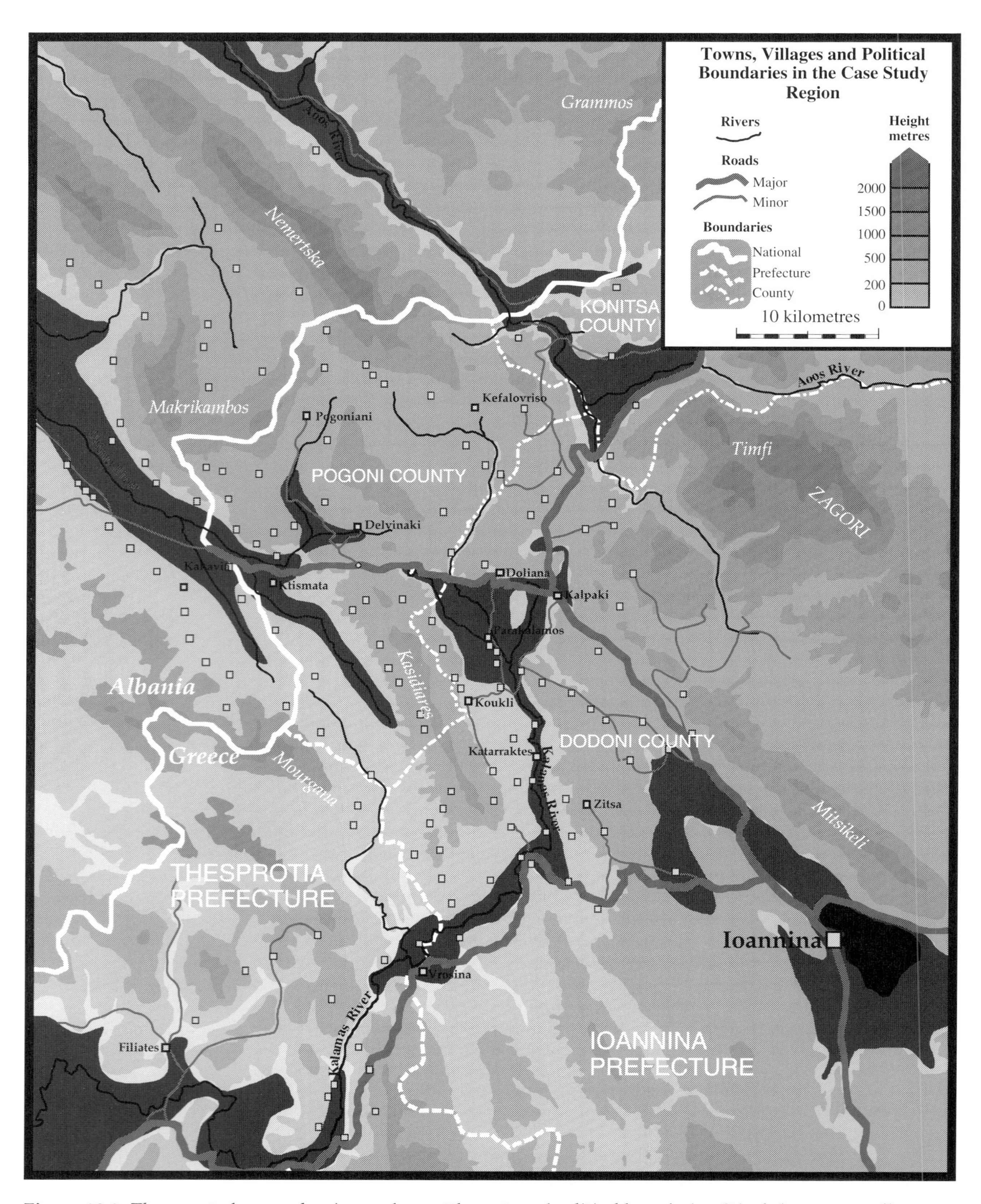

Figure 32.3. *The case study area, showing modern settlements and political boundaries. Stippled areas are valley floors irrespective of altitude.*

region which is neither endowed with the dramatically high mountains of the Zagori, nor with the large fertile plains of areas to the south of Epirus. This makes it a relatively poor and peripheral region. In the past, transhumant pastoralists passed through the region in their bi-annual movements between the high mountains of the Zagori and Konitsa County and the southern coastal areas around Igoumenitsa (Fig. 32.4 shows the routes); they did not linger. I will be focusing on the rural mountainous peoples of Pogoni and on some of the peoples who passed through Pogoni, though more general conditions in Epirus will be mentioned, since Pogoni, as with every other area of Epirus, was part of a regional and inter-regional network of social, political and economic relations (see Fig. 32.2 for the wider case study area).

The research in Pogoni County, piloted in 1992 and carried out during 1993 and 1994, involved investigating local attitudes and actions towards land degradation and desertification, a consistent feature in much of Epirus, and more recently the development of environmental protection projects and of 'agro-tourism'. Again, I worked within a multi-disciplinary team, whose ideas about human behaviour were quite different from my own (Green 1994; Green & Lemon 1996).

The development of badlands erosion is mostly due to underlying tectonic activity, though it may be aggravated by other factors (Bailey *et al.* 1993; King *et al.*, Chapter 28). Although this underlying cause involves long-term processes in human terms, there are continual episodes which visibly affect the surface over short periods, such as sudden cracks appearing over a period of a few months, the slumping of a small area, and the development of badlands in both limestone-based and flysch-based areas.

The badlands often look dramatic to a non-local eye, with those in limestone areas typically appearing as large tracts of bare, dark red 'dunes' and gullies, and those in flysch areas being heavily gullied expanses of grey-brown, dusty and slightly gritty deposits. However, the cracks and slumps in other areas, both flysch and limestone, can also produce a visibly dramatic effect, particularly where they have occurred on cultivated land. It was not uncommon to come across fields where up to half of the area had dropped by as much as two or three meters, or had been entirely lost into a gully.

Given that these episodes are so visible and also frequently affected people's own land, it seemed reasonable to assume that local people would have a great deal to say about them. In fact, local people had few opinions on the matter, and nor did they see these episodes as degradation or soil erosion at all. Despite using every means to encourage informants to discuss these distinctive parts of their landscape, little headway was achieved. Eventually, I actually took informants out to look at an example of badlands, or slumping, or cracking. The most common response at this was to shrug, and say that the feature in question 'had always been like that', and 'had never changed'. On further questioning, however, it turned out that informants had noticed that cracks might widen by as much as half a foot a year, that badlands might rise or drop by as much as several feet, and many had experienced the loss of part or all of their fields through slumping or cracks. But this was nevertheless not considered to be erosion or instability: it had always been like that. I concluded that the explanation must be related to the historical and current relationship Epirots had with their landscape, one which I myself did not share. As I began to talk to locals about their activities within the landscape, I found they continually referred to the past. This was mostly because changes in Epirus since the 1960s meant that most Pogoni locals felt their 'fundamental' relationship with their landscape was rooted in their history, and not in the present. Therefore my research strategy changed and I embarked on an historical investigation of what people actually did within their environment.

Historical groups: transhumants, semi-sedentary groups and long-distance migrants

Most of this discussion focuses on the period before 1913, when Ottoman rule ended in Epirus with the Balkan wars, and the region became a part of the Greek state (Clogg 1992; Hammond 1967), though some of it also applies to the period up to the 1960s. Between 1913 and the 1960s, a series of transitional changes occurred which led to the widespread abandonment of long-range transhumant sheep and goat pastoralism (Campbell 1964; Foss 1978), and the permanent emigration of a good proportion of the rest of the rural population, which moved either to Athens or to a number of large urban centres abroad (particularly in Germany, the United States and Australia; see Green 1994). This affected the rest of Epirus as much as it did Pogoni.[5]

Up until 1913, and to an extent until the 1960s, there were three basic patterns of economic use of the landscape which were practised by people living in the predominantly mountainous areas of Epirus. These were: transhumant sheep and goat pastoralism; long-distance, long-term work migration of adult

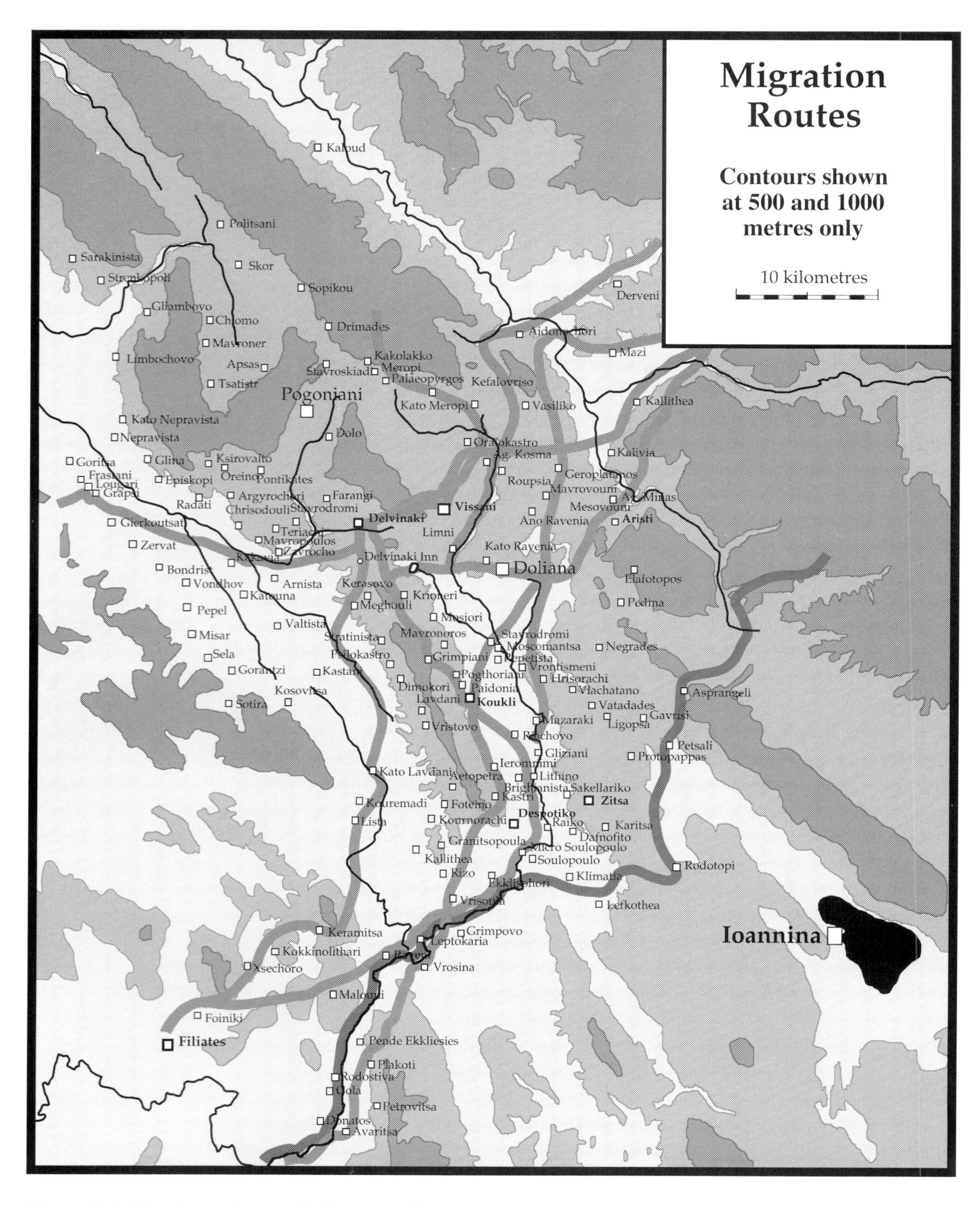

Figure 32.4. *Transhumant routes in the case study area.*

men to distant cities; and semi-sedentary subsistence farming.

The first, transhumant pastoralism, was a specialist activity carried out by two distinct groups — Sarakatsani and Vlachs, with Vlachs dividing into several different social groups (Campbell 1964; Chang 1993; Nitsiakos 1986; Schein 1975). For those passing through Pogoni, it involved long-distance twice-yearly seasonal travel between the high mountainous areas of the Zagori or the mountains of Konitsa County in the summer, and the low coastal areas of Thesprotia, Arta and Preveza in the winter (Figs. 32.3 & 32.4). Generally speaking, both Sarakatsani and Vlachs returned to the same high mountain areas every summer, but would disperse as a community and vary their winter grazing areas, as they had to make annual arrangements to rent grazing lands from local landlords in the coastal areas. The second and third strategies — work migration and semi-sedentary subsistence farming — were mostly carried out together in Pogoni due to the relative lack of large plains and the low quality of the soils.

Many Pogoni villages during the Ottoman period had moved in their entirety on one or more occasions to their current location, either from the bottom of the mountain or from another mid-mountain location. This was reportedly due to three factors: a concern about safety, as during various periods in Ottoman times both irregular militias and various groups of thieves and bandits regularly raided easily-accessible villages; forcible relocation by Ottoman administrators, so that others could be moved into the more desirable areas near plains land and water and wood sources; and being effectively forced to move because of prohibitions on the use of certain essential local resources, such as grazing land, forests for wood-cutting and so on.

Also, unlike their neighbours in the Zagori, Dodoni County and Konitsa County, Pogoni peoples were actively controlled by Ottoman administrators, called aghas, who lived in their villages. These administrators extracted significant proportions of villagers' produce as a tax, and they were also responsible for allocating land to each household to cultivate. In contrast, both Zagori villagers and the transhumant pastoralists who lived above them during the summer had arrangements of self-regulation with the Ottoman administrators, which gave them a considerable level of independence (Campbell 1964). This made it possible for the Sarakatsani, the main group using the Zagori as summer pasture, and the villagers to retain a good portion of their income.

In all these areas and amongst all these people, the main productive activity *within* rural Epirus (i.e. excluding migrant work) was animal husbandry. In Pogoni, the soils available were too poor to rely on cultivation as the main source of either income or subsistence, and in the Zagori, the area was too mountainous to pursue too many other options effectively. While the transhumant pastoralists biannually travelled long distances between very high and very low areas, the villagers of Pogoni located the village half way up the side of a mountain, and travelled up to the top in the summers to graze their animals and to the bottom in the winters. On the Kasidiares, some of the villagers from both sides would go up to the top of the mountain with their animals and sleep there for the summer, also cultivating small amounts in scattered fields. Other villagers would stay in the village, cultivating a few fields scattered around the village and further down below the mountain. The overall experience of the landscape for people in the Pogoni was thus one of moving around it continually, and their major economic resources, their animals, were also mobile. Their fields were a supplement, and of relatively little importance. In Pogoni, apart from small patches of garlic and some other vegetables around houses, most of these fields contained onions, lentils and maize.

Additionally, Pogoni people did not have a strong sense of land as property during the Ottoman period. The village and its surrounding land was administered by one or more *aghas*, who allocated fields to each household. The *agha* could change this allocation at any time if he wished. Families did not therefore own any cultivated land. In fact the process of providing title deeds to villagers following the redistribution of lands after the end of Ottoman rule has still not been completed in parts of Pogoni. As a result, there was no strong personal commitment to particular areas of land; although some lands were repeatedly used by the same families, they were rarely seen as the basis for 'locating' the family within the local social community. They were not the family's property and they were relatively unimportant economically.

The lands which *were* important, the grazing lands, were communally used by all residents — and often different families' flocks were combined together for grazing purposes, so that fewer people were needed to tend the animals. Furthermore, the grazing lands were divided between high and low areas to take advantage of seasonal variations. Thus, the location of grazing lands in themselves was a physical expression of the mobility of the local population.

This brings me to the issue of long-distance, long-term work migration. Given the conditions in Pogoni during the Ottoman period, a strategy developed which can be traced back at least to the seventeenth century, whereby the majority of adult men of a village travelled to distant cities, particularly Constantinople (now Istanbul) and areas in Bulgaria, to work for long periods of time. They would be absent for periods of three to five years, return for two to three months to pass on any saved income and to conceive children, and go out again for three to five years, repeating this cycle until they were too old to continue. The advantage of doing this, as far as Pogoni informants explained it, was firstly that the income from this activity was less accessible to local tax collectors, and secondly that it reduced the population of villages and therefore made it easier to subsist. For the majority of Pogoni villages, and up until the Second World War, almost all the adult men would do this.

This option once again involved periodic movements between places. In Pogoni, everyone[6] who lived in or passed through the area was mobile: twice a year, the transhumant pastoralists passed through with their enormous herds and flocks of animals, following routes made possible by the sub-parallel north–south mountain ranges which created 'avenues' in a roughly northwest to southeast direction; once every three to five years, some men of the village would pass through for a few months; twice a year, some villagers would shift themselves to the tops of mountains and back down again. These were the major movements.

There were also other kinds of movements, as briefly mentioned above: every so often, the entirety of a village would be relocated to somewhere else; the opening and closing of political borders — in recent years, particularly the Albanian border — would cut people off from previous routes and divert them elsewhere. The closure of the Albanian border after the Second World War affected both Pogoni villagers and transhumant pastoralists. Many of the villagers were now cut off from the other half of their communities and from their cultivating land, and a number of transhumant groups who regularly used the southern Albanian coast for their winter grazing lands were diverted to the southern coasts of Epirus.

These kinds of periodic changes and constraints within the landscape, political or otherwise, were not uncommon. For example, McNeill (1992) argues that there have been some relatively recent changes to the physical environment in Epirus and other mountainous areas of the Mediterranean, and suggests that much of the deforestation of the area occurred during the last century or so as a result of increased market integration of peripheral areas such as Epirus, which led to a rise in both human and sheep and goat populations. The relatively poor soils and grazing lands of many areas could not support this increased population, leading to deforestation and degradation of over-cultivated lands. Before this period of expansion, McNeill suggests, there were much larger forests and little soil exhaustion due to overuse. This is one indication of periodical changes not only in the way people moved around and used the physical environment, but also in the environment itself.

Another constraint in the landscape for Pogoni peoples in the past was Thesprotia, which was considered a 'no-go' area for many, because the peoples living in the hills bordering Pogoni had the reputation, as one informant put it, of being 'violent goat-thieves'. Transhumant pastoralists were forced to pass through the area in order to reach the Igoumenitsa winter grazing lands, as they had to cross the Kalamas River at some point and there were few bridges other than in Thesprotia, and they would frequently gather together a large number of transhumant families and their animals in order to produce safety in numbers and have a better chance of passing the area without loss of animals.

Security, theft and predation

This brings up the issue of security, which was a crucial aspect of the landscape in which Epirots lived. Informants continually came back to the issue of the danger of attack as something which vitally affected the way in which they chose to move through the landscape. Stripping away the particular historical contexts, the Epirot environment — in physical and socio-political terms — was chronically dangerous to move through and repeatedly generated protective strategies on the part of groups living there. The area was badly policed until 1937, when Metaxas established a strongly-enforced policy to rid the hinterland regions of numerous bands of thieves, rustlers, bandits and brigands. This point is worth noting, for while archaeologists have spent a great deal of time considering the *hunting* activities of the Upper Palaeolithic peoples, there has been little analysis of the possibility that they might also have been *hunted*, an issue which merits some further discussion before ending the historical section.

The transhumant pastoralists expressed the

strongest views on the threat to their and their animals' security, perhaps unsurprisingly as they made the most frequent long-distance journeys and were constrained to travel on certain routes. However, the way Sarakatsani and Vlach informants spoke about the security issue differs in subtle but important ways. Sarakatsani informants tended to speak about having to be constantly vigilant against attack from many different sources: brigands, rustlers, government forces, irregular militias, hostile villagers — as well as wild animals such as bears and wolves. While the Sarakatsani spoke of how these experiences made them 'tough' in character, the main emphasis was on the idea of *being hunted*, rather than hunting. Vlachs, on the other hand, tended to focus their discussions on the danger of attack from brigands and rustlers; but they also occasionally spoke of Vlachs themselves as brigands and rustlers, sometimes in the kinds of heroic terms described by Herzfeld (1985) for Cretan shepherds. Sarakatsani discussions of their own historical *banditry*, as opposed to brigandage or rustling,[7] tended to be limited to descriptions of having participated as bandits in resistance against Ottoman rule in the mountain hinterlands. Sarakatsani banditry, as it was represented by informants, was politically and not economically motivated, and was therefore morally justifiable.[8]

Campbell records numerous incidents of 'derring do' sheep theft on the part of Sarakatsani men, mostly of one or two animals at a time, and occasionally a larger number (Campbell 1964, 206–9). He goes on to say that these acts were morally justified on the grounds that 'a man could not provide his family with enough food without stolen meat' (Campbell 1964, 207). Although I did not come across Sarakatsani informants who admitted to such economic motivations for theft, the tendency was still to give moral justification for the act. In any event, Campbell does not record any Sarakatsani taking up rustling as their main economic activity as I heard occurred from time to time amongst Vlachs. In certain senses then, while the Sarakatsani represented themselves as having been *hunted*, Vlachs often represented themselves as having been *hunters*, as well as hunted.[9]

An example of the kind of discussion of this issue comes from a conversation I had with Dimitri, the head of a Sarakatsani family now living in Delvinaki. When we sat down to talk, I explained that I wanted to know the details of where his family travelled historically on the way to the southern Albanian coast. All I was expecting was a list of villages and land marks. However, Dimitri began the conversation by looking somewhat dismissively at the map I had brought along with me, and said:

> You mustn't see Epirus as it is nowadays. Today, people can travel in safety around the place — though you should know that because of the Albanians you should never get out of your car between villages.[10] Before, when the Turks were here, there was no security or safety. Thieves and rustlers were everywhere, and the Turkish security was corrupt and did what it liked to us. You had to be careful all the time, every minute. We had men watching the animals day and night — not only because of the wolves, but because of the thieves. A lot of our men were attacked and even killed by thieves who wanted to get our animals.

All the elements of the point being made here are in this quote from Dimitri. Concern over security, and not simply ecological concerns or where was best for the animals in edaphic terms, was a major factor affecting the routes taken across the landscape. Delvinaki was a particularly favoured stop-off point because it was well-hidden: a transhumant group with its animals could not be seen from any direction. It also formed the central point of a host of transhumant routes (Fig. 32.4).

The two other main centre-points were Doliana, to the east of Delvinaki and on the northern edge of the Doliana basin; and the area around Vrosina near the Kalamas River in the south. Doliana, also well hidden from the plain, was a main trading town and was visited for sales of pastoral products, to purchase goods and for administrative purposes. The area around Vrosina, in Thesprotia, provided one of the few routes where one could cross the Kalamas River. Unsurprisingly, rustlers were to be found in large numbers in the hills around Vrosina, and Thesprotia's reputation in the Pogoni area for being 'filled with goat thieves' was probably related to this geomorphological pinch point.

This will be recognized as being reminiscent of what the Klithi archaeologists speculate about Palaeolithic hunting activities. As described at length in this volume and elsewhere (Bailey *et al.* 1983a; 1986; 1993; Sturdy *et al.*, Chapter 30), the idea is that hunters focused their efforts in narrow areas through which migrating animals had to pass, to increase the chances of a successful kill. It seems that Epirot rustlers similarly focused their efforts in attempting to liberate animals belonging to transhumant pastoralists.

That raises three points. First, such physical pinch points in the landscape encouraged searching out other possible destinations so as to avoid the danger every year. For the western Epirus transhumant routes, the obvious alternatives were southern Albania and the route down the Louros towards Arta. The dangers posed by these pinch points in the physical landscape added to the desire to have a range of alternatives. Being able to arrange grazing rights from one year to the next made it possible to choose one of several possible alternative areas to spend the winter; this not only mitigated concerns about overgrazing and secured against possible breaks in social relations in any one area, but also reduced the exposure to rustling.

The second point is the fact that it was the *rustlers*, and not the transhumant pastoralists, who were the 'hunters' in this case. Given that, the focus purely on transhumant pastoralists rather than rustlers in looking for relevant ethnographic information to be used in analyzing the archaeological record might be misplaced. It might prove fruitful to carry out an historical analysis of *rustlers'* use of and movements through the landscape: after all, their focus was 'hunting' animals, and they particularly selected areas of the physical environment that animals would have to cross and from which there was no easy escape route. From what little I know of rustlers' activities from informants, they had regular patterns in some parts of the region and irregular ones in others. Thus, one could guarantee that rustlers could be found around the Vrosina crossing point, but the need to ensure the element of surprise meant that 'hunting grounds' varied from year to year in other parts of transhumant routes.

The third point is the possibility that fear for security (fear of being hunted, if you like), was given by several Sarakatsani informants as a possible contributory factor in the development of long-range transhumant pastoralism. The logic of the argument went as follows: as it was so dangerous moving around in the region, people gathered together in large groups to make their trips; this meant that the number of animals gathered together also became large; although short-range transhumance up and down local mountains could support a small number of animals, few areas could support such large numbers, except in the high mountains in summer and in the low plains coastal areas in winter. Therefore, long-range transhumance developed partly as a result of having so many animals in one place, and that in turn was a response to the insecurity of the area. The argument is interesting not so much because it might be true (there are of course many alternative arguments, e.g. Nitsiakos 1986; Halstead 1987), but because the issue of security was so central to many informants that they became convinced it was a major causal factor in the development of their way of life. In any event, historical records show that just about as far back as pastoralism can be traced in the mountains of Epirus, so can rustling and brigandage (Foss 1978; Hammond 1967). There does not appear to have been a time when the animals of transhumant pastoralists were not 'hunted' in this way.

The degradation puzzle explained

The conditions described above begin to explain something about the attitudes towards soil erosion and degradation which I encountered in Pogoni. The experience of both local residents and passers-through of that landscape was one of regular periodic movements — up, down and across — interspersed with occasional sudden and dramatic changes. Moreover, the lands which Pogoni residents used were also mobile, in a sense: the grazing lands were divided between summer and winter areas, and the fields were scattered in amongst these areas, and could moreover vary according to the whims of the Ottoman *agha*. These fields were anyway relatively unimportant.

Given all of this, the fact that areas of the physical Epirot landscape periodically cracked, slumped or eroded was neither important to local people, nor did it appear anomalous. Stability and lack of change or movement was not something either Pogoni peoples or transhumant pastoralists associated with their landscape in terms of the way they physically used it and moved around it, nor in terms of their social and political experience of it. In terms of pastoralism, if an area of grazing land slumped or dropped into a gully, the animals simply moved elsewhere. For the villagers, since the grazing lands were anyway communal and owned by no one in particular, there was no sense of damage done to a personally owned portion of land. In terms of losing a part of a field through these processes, villagers either cultivated less or opened up another patch of cultivation somewhere else. As these episodes of erosion and degradation were a constant feature of the landscape, and as it was entirely unpredictable where, or to what extent, such episodes would occur, there was nothing to be done about them anyway.

In short, it was not that local people had failed to notice that the landscape was unstable in places, and had a habit of 'moving around', for this approach to the issue carries with it the underlying assumption that physical landscapes ought *not* to crack, slump and move around. For Pogoni peoples, the landscape represented an 'unchanging' condition of mobility, just as the people who lived within it represented an 'unchanging' condition of mobility: the mobility, and the tendency for periodic movements and instabilities was the only aspect of historical Epirot existence which could be said to be 'unchanging'. Given this, it is eminently reasonable to suggest that limestone badlands 'had always been like that' and had 'never changed'.

This description is an example of the 'interweaving' of physical experiences of the landscape with political, social and economic experiences, and cultural perceptions or interpretations. The conditions set by the Ottoman regime were not separated, in practice, from the conditions of the physical environment, or from the way in which different groups physically moved around and used that environment. All of these together constituted the 'landscape' in a particular way, and they culminated together in people's repeated experiences of using the landscape. Despite all the different conditions under which people lived, and the various different strategies they adopted to live, the one thread which connects them all is physical mobility, and it is the one thing they all experienced in different ways. In the historical and modern context, this mobility was, I would argue, the result of the interweaving of all the factors I have mentioned above. The Epirot environment lends itself to possibilities involving mobility, which were taken up in different ways amongst different peoples; once they had repeatedly experienced that mobility, their perceptions of the landscape blended in with their physical experiences of it, and thereby affected how they perceived the future possibilities of the landscape.

This is where the current situation in Epirus comes in. The political, social and economic changes which have occurred during this century and since the collapse of the Ottoman empire have, at first sight, tended towards a much more sedentary, less mobile, pattern of existence. In fact, however, if one looks at the details of the changes, the underlying pattern of mobility has remained, with people relating to Epirus as a place of seasons and periodic visits just as they had done before.

Present-day groups: historical changes and new kinds of seasonal movements

In the period following the end of Ottoman rule (1912–13, which led to continual hostilities between Greece and Turkey until 1923), there were several dramatic political events which had a considerable impact on local populations. These were, briefly, as follows. Firstly, a large-scale exchange of populations between former Ottoman regions, so that there was a greater 'fit' between new national boundaries and the ethnic composition of new nation states (Agelopoulos 1995; Clogg 1992; Kremmidas 1990). The majority of the local Muslim population was moved out of Epirus, and a large portion of ethnic Greeks living in other areas (except for Constantinople, now Istanbul, which was excluded from the exchanges) was moved into Epirus. This led to further restrictions on the ability of Epirots to work in former Ottoman cities for any length of time, which had begun in 1912–13, and so this option was no longer available.

Secondly, there was the Second World War, which not only decimated the livelihoods and populations of various areas in Epirus, it also developed and exacerbated differences between supporters of communist and right wing political factions, which led to divisions within and between groups. And as mentioned above, in Pogoni it led to the closure of the Greek–Albanian border with the communist regime under Enver Hoxja, thus cutting Pogoni peoples off from parts of their communities and parts of their grazing and cultivating lands.

Thirdly, there was the Greek Civil War (1946–49), which was particularly harshly felt in Epirus. Following straight on from the Second World War, this event led to extreme food shortages, considerable loss of population through the fighting, the break-up of many communities over political differences, and the virtual total destruction of most people's source of livelihood, their sheep and goats.

Fourthly, there were various reforms made by a number of Greek governments during this century which vitally affected the ability and attractiveness of various economic strategies in Epirus. For example, in 1938 a reform in rules of residency gave transhumant pastoralists the right to register as residents in the summer villages they seasonally visited, which in turn gave them guaranteed grazing rights there. This countered various earlier reforms which removed these rights and had for a time made seasonal transhumance virtually impossible (Campbell 1964).

Finally, there was the development of various infrastructures in Epirus, most particularly in terms of agricultural technologies: drainage of flood-prone plains, introduction of irrigation systems, tractors and combine harvesters, building of good metalled roads to major markets, and so on. These developed dramatically during the 1967–74 military regime under Colonel Georgios Papadopoulos, who steadfastly followed a policy of 'modernizing' rural Greece in an attempt to stem the continuing flow of population out of rural areas and into urban ones.

The overall effect of all these changes has been the virtual emptying of rural mountain villages of their productive populations, who have been replaced with small populations of pensioners and periodic visits by emigrants during the summer and other celebration periods, particularly Easter. Most of the resident population has now permanently, and as whole families rather than just the adult men, emigrated to major cities both in and outside Greece.

In fact, however, this is not so different from the previous arrangement in terms of the village's experience: at least some members of these families return regularly for village celebrations, and many have built houses to use as summer residences for their holidays, and for their retirement. Just as the migrating men eventually returned to their village when they were too old to continue their travels, so too do many older people now return to the village upon retirement. And these people tend to emphasize the idea that the village is their 'home', rather than their permanent residence in the city, by which they mean that they feel their 'roots', their identity, lie in the village and its landscape. So although local informants tended to say that their village was 'dying', that it was simply a pensioner village where every old person who died was another nail in the coffin of the village's viability, in my experience in many villages, every old person who died seemed to be replaced by a new old person who moved in. The demographics may have changed somewhat; but the pattern of periodic and seasonal movements through the village appears to have remained.[11]

As a result of this demographic change, most of the hill fields and many of the local grazing areas have been abandoned and have become overgrown with prickly oak scrub and small amounts of new forest. The top of the Kasidiares, which used to be virtually bare of vegetation, has now become densely overgrown, with the result that local people joke about it having 'grown hair' (Kasidiares means 'balding' in Greek).

These socio-economic changes have also led to the virtual abandonment of transhumant pastoralism, as already discussed. The few families which still practise it nowadays move their animals mostly by truck along the metalled roads, and the majority of animal husbandry is now operated through farms located along the edges of plains. The animals are still predominantly sheep and goats, but to them have been added pigs, poultry farming and beef cattle. And instead of grazing on the hills and mountains, most now feed on cultivated and stored animal fodder, which are the major cash crops on the plains. The most populated villages are now these farming villages located along the plains, and the market towns, located along major road routes, which service them.

These new farming practices are limited to the major plains, which both provide enough land to make a farming enterprise profitable, and have good access roads to markets. The mountainous areas, where the majority of the population used to live, cannot offer these things. The most rapidly growing source of locally-generated income in these mountainous areas (as opposed to income brought in from cities) is tourism, which is therefore in a sense replacing the old local semi-sedentary animal husbandry.

Leading the way in the development of tourism has been the Zagori, a large portion of which, with its dramatic mountains, the Vikos Gorge, its rivers and forest lands, has been made into a national park. But most other areas in Epirus, including the Pogoni, have been pursuing the development of tourism as a means of revitalizing the stagnant economies of these places. Frequently with EU support, regions such as Pogoni are re-opening old paths through forests and gorges, reconditioning old schools and other buildings into hostels and hotels, building 'modern' style clubs and bars, creating local folk museums and putting on traditional dance and music cultural events.

Tourism is thus once again, in a different form, emphasizing mobility and seasonality in these mountainous areas. Brief visits from tourists during particular seasons leads to the seasonal winding up and winding down of all the services which go with tourism, the moving in of people from elsewhere to run hotels, bars, restaurants, tour guidance, etc., and their moving out again at the end of the season. Moreover, many of the pensioners who live there also practise seasonal movements, spending the harshest winter months in the city (usually Ioannina or Athens, but sometimes further afield, such as in Germany), and the warmer months in the village.

This brings me back to where I started on this case study, with the observation that local informants were continually referring to their past in talking about their experiences of this physical landscape. Both the new demography of these villages (a mostly older, retired population) and the emphasis on tourism tend to encourage the idea of living in the area through past activities and past uses of the landscape. Tourism, both those aspects which emphasize 'cultural heritage' and those aspects which emphasize 'natural heritage', relies strongly on ideas about the history of the landscape and the peoples who used to live within it, rather than the current conditions. The traces of previous cultural forms and communities, of activities and performances, of interactions with the landscape, are used to 'sell' such areas as attractive to tourists. The traces of both the physical interaction with the landscape and the social and cultural interactions which were a part of that are being reinterpreted, and thus in a very real sense contributing to the current day's experience of the landscape.

In today's pattern of mobility through the landscape, therefore, there are numerous repetitions (or reiterations, to use the more accurate term) of previous practices, adjusted to the new economic, social, political *and* physical conditions. But the mobility, and particularly the seasonal mobility, continues.

Conclusion: the relevance for Palaeolithic research in Epirus

It is often difficult to unravel the complexity of modern-day communities — to understand where to start with something such as the insistence that land degradation is not land degradation. The archaeological team, and the other specialists who contributed to their research of the Epirus area, helped in continuously pointing to the physical morphology and climate of the Epirus environment and suggesting that it lent itself to seasonal mobility. Initially in 1984, this seemed to be too environmentally deterministic. But in later ethnographic research, the prehistoric research findings provided me with some ideas which were 'good to think with' in looking for a possible answer to the degradation puzzle. The nature of the mobility of different groups within the case study area, which until recently were connected with animal husbandry and periodic labour migration, was not solely related to differing cultural or socio-economic conditions; it was also clearly patterned by the character of the physical landscape, which was *interwoven* with differing historical conditions: movements across mostly went northwest–southeast along the valleys between the sub-parallel mountain ranges, and movements up and down characterized the seasonal movements; the longer the range of the seasonal movement was, the bigger was the distance between the up (very high mountains in summer) and the down (sea level in winter), and the more concern there was about physical attack, either against the animals or against the people. The only movements which did not follow these kinds of patterns were periodic movements out of the area altogether, which in itself suggests the way in which landscape interweaves with culture and social and political conditions. Moving out altogether may be more influenced by cultural and socio-economic conditions than other things, but that also affects people's physical experience of the Epirus landscape, which feeds back into cultural and socio-economic conditions.

So it is certainly clear that the findings of Palaeolithic archaeologists working in Epirus had something useful to say to me as a social anthropologist in this same area — without there being any implication that people are either 'dictated to' by the constraints of the 'natural' physical environment, or that people 'exploit' (which is to say, dominate or control in some way) particular 'natural' niches because of the 'natural' characteristics of those niches. My argument has been that these 'niches' are both changed by, and in themselves change, people's practices within them, to the extent that distinguishing people, both as physical and cultural entities, from such 'niches', as if one is cultural and the other natural is not terribly helpful. Mobility across and up and down this landscape is a consistent feature of people's practices within Epirus; and that is interwoven with all the other aspects of people's intellectual and physical lives, and appears to be at the root of a lot of people's conscious, reflexive thoughts about their landscape.

As to what this kind of research can contribute towards the Palaeolithic project, perhaps two things could be suggested. Firstly, the data do seem to confirm that looking at the activities of the Palaeolithic peoples in terms of periodic and seasonal mobility is not a bad approach for the Epirus area, so far as comparative historical and contemporary data go. Obviously, this cannot say anything in terms of the actual practices of Palaeolithic peoples, but it does suggest that if these practices did involve a considerable amount of seasonal mobility, it might also have included a variety of different kinds of movements, such as short-range movements versus long-range movements, either practised by the same people or different people, or the same people at different chronological periods. Mobility appears to have been the key in the ethnographic data: beyond that, there was a tremendous amount of variation in practices through time.

Secondly, the approach which suggests an interweaving of physical experiences of the landscape with cultural understandings of it and with socio-economic arrangements within it, all of which make up the physical landscape as it is experienced, might help to modify the still-extant tendency of representing hunter-gatherers as being 'closer to nature' than any other human group, and therefore more subject to the constraints and possibilities of 'unaltered nature' than any other group (see Ingold 1992b; Winder, Chapter 31). This, as outlined in the introduction, tends to perpetuate the nature–culture dichotomy in a way that puts limits on the analysis of the behaviour of people within their landscapes. The 'interweaving' approach could allow Palaeolithic archaeologists to continue to interpret what was going on through looking at the relationship between their material finds and the wider physical context in which they were discovered — for these are evidence of the physical practices of peoples within their landscape. At the same time, it could avoid the conclusion that either these peoples 'exploited' their environment (domination and control of the cultural by the natural) or that they were constrained by it (domination of the natural over the cultural). Instead, one might view the situation as being the following: as soon as people move through a landscape, they will begin to weave their physical experience into other similar experiences (building up an embodied series of memories, which then contribute to future practices and experiences) and into different kinds of experiences (for example, interactions with other people, conscious thoughts about the landscape and so on). The landscape will then come to be an indistinguishable product of that process of physical experience, action, mimesis, reaction, repetition and interaction. One would then be in a position to ask what kinds of landscapes this process might have been likely to produce within a place such as Epirus, and ethnographic data could perhaps contribute some contrastive or comparative material. The analysis of the Pogoni data is one example of what kinds of landscapes are produced by this process.

Put this way, the answer to the question — what kinds of landscapes are produced by this process — would be of significance to Palaeolithic researchers, because it centrally involves actual physical practices and movements through the landscape, rather than cultural, discursive constructions of such practices.

The difference between this approach and the one more frequently pursued within the recent ethnoarchaeological tradition discussed in the introduction is that rather than looking for traces of material remains to compare, to see how different groups affect the 'natural' environment, one could instead look for traces of physical movements and activities to compare, to see how different groups interweave, and thereby create, while being created by, their own landscapes. And this approach might contribute to the work already carried out in tracing the possible uses of the actively tectonic Epirus landscape by Palaeolithic peoples (King *et al.*, Chapter 28; Sturdy *et al.*, Chapter 30). Since it was ideas presented by precisely that kind of research which led me down the route of my own ethnographic research in the Pogoni, I feel pursuing this approach would lead to a satisfying interweaving of intellectual landscapes.

Notes

1. See, for example, Stoller 1995 and Taussig 1993 for discussions of mimesis, and Connerton (1989) for discussions of embodied memory.
2. Theorists such as Bruno Latour even go so far as to argue that apparently inanimate objects (such as a key) have agency, by which he means that they can be regarded as acting in and on the world in a directed way as much as people act in and on the world (Latour 1993; 1994).
3. Incidentally, this approach questions the past habit of many anthropologists and others of depicting hunter-gatherer societies as being 'closer to nature' than any other form of social organization (Ingold 1992b). Within the perspective I am suggesting, both hunter-gatherers and all other groups — particularly, in this case, transhumant pastoralists — are inextricably interwoven with their physical experiences, in a way that neither privileges 'nature' nor 'culture'.
4. This research was part of the ARCHAEOMEDES project (Directorate General XII of the Commission of the European Union, Contract EV5V-0021).
5. These kinds of moments of social and political instability have been a regular feature in Epirus through the centuries (Hammond 1967; Foss 1978; McNeill 1992). The 1913–1960s period is not therefore particularly odd in having been marked by distinct moments, to do with varying socio-economic and political conditions, which vitally affected the local population's existence there, and which often also affected the physical landscape.
6. Women and children of the villages (as opposed to pastoralists) were obviously rather less mobile than the men, but they did still move around the landscape — up and down the mountains with the seasons, visiting markets, and doing odd jobs such as collecting wood for charcoal making.
7. The term 'bandit' is being reserved here to refer to the 'Robin Hood' syndrome: the phenomenon of individuals or groups of people who carry out thefts and other forms of attack, protected by a local (usually peasant) population, and whose acts are popularly justified as having a moral and political motivation against unjust inequalities of a wider economic or political regime. See Herzfeld 1985; Hobsbawm 1985.
8. See also Makris 1990, ch. 2, section 1.
9. See also Chang 1993 and Schein 1975.
10. This was a reference to the flood of illegal immigrants travelling into Greece through Epirus from Albania since the borders were re-opened in 1992, following the death of Enver Hoxja and the collapse of the socialist regime there. During my period of fieldwork, illegal immigrants were seen in many ways as the latest of a continual string of groups identified as 'hunters' of people.
11. It could be argued that as more and more young people grow up in cities with few links with villages, this replacement of old people will stop happening. However, this does not necessarily mean that villages will be abandoned. From current evidence, it seems likely that people will continue to choose to live in such villages, as the attraction of the area for tourists increases, whether or not they have close links with the villages.

Part VII

Conclusion

Chapter 33

Klithi: a Synthesis

Geoff Bailey

The aim of this final chapter is to bring together the results of the various studies that have been carried out under the aegis of the project, to evaluate how far we have succeeded in answering the questions posed at the outset, and to highlight the new questions that have emerged as the work of the project has unfolded. I shall not attempt a comprehensive summary as such because this would be either too lengthy or too uninformative. Nor can this chapter properly be described as conclusive: with such a large range of studies and such a diversity of authors and perspectives, there are many remaining loose ends — work that in retrospect would now be carried out differently, work begun but not yet completed, or work that is still to be embarked on as new questions and new perspectives have come into focus. And while there are many points of convergence between different lines of investigation, there remain unresolved conflicts of evidence and interpretation. In keeping with the general structure of the preceding chapters, I shall begin by focusing on the site of Klithi itself, moving outwards to successively larger scales of comparison and synthesis and to more general issues of interpretation.

Klithi: the site

We can begin with simple questions: over what period of time was the site used; what activities were carried out there, during what seasons, and by how many people? Radiocarbon dates indicate that the main period of occupation is well bracketed between about 16,500 and 13,000 BP in terms of uncalibrated radiocarbon years, perhaps extending at latest to about 12,400 BP, and with traces of re-occupation at about 10,400 years BP. There is some uncertainty about the possibility of earlier and later occupation, in the former case because the windows into the deeper levels of the deposit are very small, namely the drill cores, and in the latter because recent goatherds may have stripped away some of the upper layers of the prehistoric deposit. But it seems clear that the main period of occupation, and certainly the great bulk of the artefactual and faunal evidence recovered in excavation, belongs to a relatively short interval of about 3500 to 4000 years within the Late Glacial, sandwiched between conditions of extreme cold associated with the Last Glacial Maximum on the one side, and the rapid warming of the Bølling/Alleröd interstadials on the other. The trace of later prehistoric re-occupation at the top of the sequence coincides with the brief interval of returning cold associated with the Younger Dryas episode recorded in Northwest Europe at the very end of the Last Glacial climatic sequence, although direct evidence for a comparable climatic shift in the Balkan region is less secure. The uniformity of the lithic assemblages and of the species represented in the faunal assemblages is consistent with this chronology.

Faunal and lithic assemblages

The animal bones are mainly of ibex (*Capra ibex*) and chamois (*Rupicapra rupicapra*). Where the two species can be told apart, ibex is twice as common as chamois. The dominance of these two species is overwhelming, and together they account for over 99 per cent of the total identifiable bone (Gamble, Chapter 12). Kill-off patterns show a concentration on prime-age adults. All parts of the carcass are well represented, and there is very little evidence for differential representation of anatomical elements that might be attributed to natural agents of attrition — traces of carnivore gnawing are notably rare — to the selective importation of some parts of the carcass from distant kill locations, or to selective export for later human consumption elsewhere.

Subtle differences in the anatomical representation of different-aged animals, however, suggest that the Klithi hunters practised variable strategies of carcass transportation to the site: when prime adult animals were killed, some of the less desirable parts of the carcass were removed on the spot before the carcass was carried back to Klithi, resulting in an under-representation of some elements, particularly the heads; when young or old animals were killed, the whole carcass was brought back, either because the poorer condition of the animal placed a higher premium on extracting resources from every part of the carcass, or because the smaller size posed no inconvenience.

The numerous cutmarks and the many split bones suggest intensive rendering down of the carcasses for meat and for bone marrow. Some of the bones were also used to make artefacts such as needles, spatulae and bone points (Adam & Kotjabopoulou, Chapter 13).

It is clear that the main activity of the site was the capture of ibex and chamois, and the transformation of their carcasses into food, bone artefacts and clothing.

The next most common mammalian taxon after ibex and chamois is beaver, although it is represented by only some 42 bones. Some certainly have cut marks, and there seems no reason to doubt that the animals were captured locally, perhaps for their pelts rather than their meat. Their occurrence is also of palaeoenvironmental interest in suggesting the presence of some trees along the river bank. Other taxa represented are birds, some of which may have been brought into the site by non-human predators, lagomorphs, and small numbers of fish vertebrae. Carnivore bones are absolutely rare, just 1 bone of lion, 2 of lynx, 7 of wolf and 1 of fox.

Deer is conspicuous by its rarity. In a collection of nearly half a million bones, just 19 specimens can be attributed to red deer, and 8 of these are pierced canine teeth imported as ornaments, while the other 11 are small bones or bone fragments — phalanges, teeth, and fragments of metapodial and radius — items which could have been carried about for some time and brought in from some distance as marrow snacks, blanks for tool manufacture, gewgaws or incidental items of bric-a-brac, rather than representing food remains of local kills.

The lithic assemblages are similarly dominated by local raw materials and by the production of tools that can be linked to animal exploitation. Flint is available in abundance in the local river gravels but is rarely present in nodules larger than about 7–8 cm in length and is of relatively poor quality, liable to shatter into unusable fragments (Roubet, Chapter 8; Shawcross & Winder, Chapter 10; Moss, Chapter 11; Adam, Chapter 25). Notwithstanding these disadvantages, it is the most abundant raw material represented in the prehistoric assemblages.

The primary aim of core reduction appears to have been to produce long, narrow blanks, which were then transformed into backed bladelets, which are the most common tool type (Roubet, Chapters 8 & 9.1; Adam, Chapter 25). These are mostly straight, pointed at one end and backed along a single edge. Elaborate methods of core preparation making use of cresting and pyramidal core forms are unsuited to the poor quality of the raw material, and not surprisingly are absent from Klithi. More opportunistic but nevertheless highly skilful methods were used to extract the maximum usable material from the available nodules, often resulting in fully worked out and discarded cores. Blank segmentation by the microburin technique is present throughout the sequence (Roubet, Chapter 9.1). This is accompanied by an alternative technique of segmentation identified here for the first time and labelled as the Transversal Klithian Fracture (TKF) technique (Roubet, Chapter 9.1). Observation of the archaeological specimens and experimental replication show that this is an intentional technique involving a transverse blow to create a rectangular blank which facilitates retouch into a truncation (Roubet & Lenoir, Chapter 9.2). The microburin and the TKF technique are well suited to producing either points or truncations respectively, and together represent a flexible combination of segmentation techniques for creating microliths. Geometric pieces such as triangles and lunates are virtually absent, although the technological precondition for their manufacture, namely of bladelet segmentation, is present, and Roubet (Chapter 9.1) considers the industry to be a 'proto-geometric' one.

Flakes were also transformed into tools, notably small endscrapers, which are the second most common tool type. The other main identifiable tool types are notches and denticulates, truncated bladelets, piercers, sidescrapers, burins, and composite tools. Blanks with irregular retouch along the edge are also quite common but opinions differ as to whether this is the result of damage during use or after discard.

All stages of the reduction sequence are well represented, suggesting intensive knapping activity on-site, but nevertheless both refitting (Wenban-Smith, Chapter 5) and metrical studies (Shawcross & Winder, Chapter 10) suggest that many pieces are missing, presumably because they were removed as endproducts and used and discarded elsewhere. Conversely, exotic flints are present mainly in the form of blanks and tools or as tiny flakes removed by edge retouch, and less commonly as cores. Although these exotic raw materials are present in relatively small quantities, their presence is by no means simply the incidental byproduct of visits to the site from further afield. They are usually of superior quality and appear to have been introduced as part of a deliberate procurement strategy aimed at complementing the deficiencies of the local flint, notably for producing longer blanks (blades or laminar flakes), but also for the production of tools made on small flakes and bladelets as well (Roubet, Chapter 8).

Microscopic use-wear studies give further insights into the function of many of the tools and confirm the specialized nature of the toolkit (Moss, Chapter 11). Backed bladelets show traces of impact fractures consistent with use as the barbs of projectiles, while some, notably those with a twisted profile, were used as micropiercers on hide. Endscrapers were used for working hide, and some also show traces of scraping bone or wood. Wood appears to have been a consistent contact material, and traces of its use are found on straight-edged flakes and blades that do not otherwise show secondary retouch. Although it is not demonstrable what the wood was worked for, it would be consistent with the preparation of projectile shafts.

The overwhelming impression given by the lithic assemblages is one of a highly skilful and flexible repertoire of strategies and techniques for the procurement and reduction of raw materials and their transformation into a specialized toolkit suited to the killing of ibex and chamois and the working of hides and bone.

Spatial structure

To what extent did the spatial orientation of the excavation research design and the analysis of intra-site patterning throw light on the interpretation of the site? The prior expectation that is often used to justify intra-site spatial analysis, and one that is implicit in many published studies, is that it will highlight differential patterns in the distribution of the cultural material — localized sets of covarying artefacts that give added insight into the nature and variety of the activities carried out at a site and the function of the site as a whole in a wider context. If that was our expectation at Klithi, then it has been disappointed. There are no localized patterns in this sense, no endscrapers in one corner and backed bladelets and bone tools in another, no piles of cores and primary knapping debris on one side and discarded tools on the other, that might point to the practice of distinctive activities in different parts of the site. On the contrary, all the activities that can be identified from the composition of the bone and flint assemblages seem to be represented everywhere on the site (Winder, Chapter 14; Galanidou, Chapter 15). Indeed it is questionable whether anything other than a general blur of this sort can be expected in a palimpsest of deposits with high densities of finds and repeated re-use of the same confined living space. High-resolution events, such as the preservation *in situ* of adjoining bones from the same joint of the same animal carcass, or the proximity of artefacts representing different stages of the same reduction sequence, are definitely present at Klithi, while localization of some types of artefacts is apparent, notably the bones that have been decorated with linear incised patterns (Adam & Kotjabopoulou, Chapter 13). But these episodes are absolutely rare, and perhaps no more common than one might expect to find by chance in a large sample. In general, there is very little evidence for localization of particular artefact types or faunal elements. Such patterns of covariation as do occur appear to reflect the incidental byproduct of locating activities near hearths (where burnt flints and small specimens such as bladelets and microburins predominate). Or else they may reflect differences in patterns of discard and preservation as between the exposed area of the talus and the more protected inner areas of the shelter (Galanidou, Chapter 15).

This spatial uniformity in the composition of the artefact and lithic assemblages may be considered disappointing or unremarkable, depending on one's preconceptions. But there is patterning of a different sort, and one that emerges strongly from all the spatial analyses (Winder, Chapter 14; Galanidou, Chapter 15), and that is the remarkable redundancy (i.e. lack of change) in the location of the main hearth area, and its dominating effect on variations in the density of finds. Moreover this pattern emerges all the more strongly because of its contrast with Kastritsa, where there appears to be greater spatial integrity, but less redundancy in the location of the hearths (Galanidou, Chapter 26).

What can we learn from these sorts of patterns? The significance of such studies can perhaps best be appreciated by considering the ways in which we might classify sites in terms of their spatial properties. Four separate axes or dimensions of variability can be identified:

- Degree of specialization, a specialized site being one used for a single activity or a limited range of activities with a correspondingly narrow range of artefact types, a generalized site showing greater diversity of activities and materials.

- Duration of visits, varying between short-lived sites used fleetingly for a few days or even a few hours at one extreme, and long-lived sites used as residential bases for longer periods of the year, approaching full sedentism at the other extreme.
- Degree of integrity, varying between sites with artefacts left in primary position and preserving the direct fossilized trace of past activities, and low-resolution sites with blurring and mixing resulting from secondary redeposition, scuffing and disturbance, site cleaning and so on.
- Degree of investment in site 'furniture' or facilities, such as stone-lined hearths, artificial structures, pits for storage or rubbish deposition and so on, and structured deposition of material generally.

Intuitively one might expect a parallel linkage between these four axes, such that sites showing the highest integrity and the least investment in site facilities would be those used fleetingly for highly specialized activities, while residential bases would be those showing the widest range of activities, the least integrity and the highest investment in facilities. The interest of Klithi is that it provides an example of a site that is specialized but with a low-resolution of spatial patterning. Kastritsa, on the other hand, shows higher resolution and integrity in the patterning of artefact distributions and in the preservation of features such as stone-lined hearths, and perhaps greater diversity in its faunal and lithic remains. In neither case can we say much about the duration of visits, although indirect clues considered below suggest that Klithi was probably occupied for months at a time. Neither site, with the possible exception of the lowest layers at Kastritsa, appears to have been fleetingly used.

Superimposed on these patterns of variation is the additional uncertainty of differential taphonomic processes. The slower rate of sediment accumulation at Klithi compared to Kastritsa hints at the possibility that the differences in the integrity of spatial patterning between the two sites may be due, at least in part, to nothing more than the differential rapidity with which material was buried and thus protected from subsequent disturbance.

If these examples do nothing else, they suggest that the relationship between site function, duration and intensity of use, and integrity of spatial patterning, is not straightforward, and that these may vary independently of each other. Here, as in so many other issues, further clarification will come only from extending the range of controlled comparison to include a larger and more diverse sample of sites.

Population size and season of occupation

As for the size of the human group that visited Klithi, both the physical constraints of the rockshelter and the supply of food available within the site exploitation territory argue for a small group of about 5–10 people. This is the number that one might imagine being able to sit and sleep in comfort around the main hearth area at Klithi. If the hints of a second hearth area immediately to the east of the main hearth are to be relied on, and if this second area was used simultaneously with the main hearth, we might double this figure. The number of ibex and chamois that one could reasonably distribute in the vicinity of Klithi under Late Glacial environmental conditions similarly suggests a potential food supply capable of feeding no more than about 6 people on a yearly basis — more of course if one were to reduce the length of occupation: 12 people for 6 months, 24 for 3 months, and so on. Similarly, the detailed analysis of the faunal remains suggests regular visits by an average of 6 people (Gamble, Chapter 12). Notwithstanding the margins of error in all such calculations, both on-site and off-site evidence point consistently to a similar order of magnitude for population size and one that in all probability represents a task force of restricted size engaged in a specialized set of activities, rather than a full residential community. It should be added that some aspects of the faunal data stimulate speculation that food sharing took place between those who hunted and and those who stayed back at camp (Gamble, Chapter 12), and thus hint at the presence of a human group of mixed age and sex and a division of labour.

Seasonal indicators are hard to come by and largely depend on indirect inference from the likely pattern of seasonal animal movements and their accessibility to human exploitation. Occupation in winter can be confidently excluded on climatic grounds, while neonatal bone specimens are sufficiently common to suggest some regular activity in spring. Age composition and anatomical-element representation in general suggest that the site could have been used in spring and early summer when animals would have been in poor to moderate condition. Palaeogeographical considerations, on the other hand, suggest that animals would have been available in greatest numbers in the near vicinity of Klithi in late summer and early autumn (Sturdy *et al.*, Chapter 30) or beginning their descent to lower altitudes, bringing them within easy reach of Klithi. This is also the time of year when the animals and their hides would be in best condition. It is conceivable of course that the site was visited at different seasons in different years, or revisited at different times during the year for different purposes, perhaps with culling of animals concentrated in spring and autumn when the animals would be most vulnerable as they crossed the river during movements between seasonal grazing territories. At any rate, the faunal data suggest regular and repeated annual visits which would have lasted for at least 1–2 months at a time.

The relationship between the on-site faunal data (Gamble, Chapter 12) and the off-site palaeogeographical data (Sturdy *et al.*, Chapter 30) is worth some further comment at this point because the apparent convergence between the two lines of inquiry masks some large margins of uncertainty and some potential discrepancies. Gamble's admittedly speculative interpretation of the faunal data suggests that a group of about 6 people visited for not more than about 2 months at a time and killed perhaps 8–16 animals (Chapter 12). A generous estimate of the minimum number of individuals (MNI) gives a rather smaller figure, about 3 animals per year.[1] The palaeogeographic estimates, on the other hand, suggest that some 104 animals could have been hunted on a regular basis in the vicinity of Klithi without impairing the long-term viability of the herds (Table 30.17). Moreover this number of animals, though capable of feeding only 6 people throughout the year, could support 36 people over a 2-month period. Now there are various ways in which we could account for this discrepancy.

- The palaeogeographic estimates are an order of magnitude too high. This seems unlikely both because the basis for estimating animal numbers is quite conservative, and because it is questionable whether a total herd size of some 100–200 ibex and chamois (the number implied by the bone data as opposed to the 1299 animals suggested by the palaeogeographical estimates) would have been large enough for long-term biological viability.
- The human population culled far fewer ibex and chamois than the number potentially available. This also seems unlikely because it suggests that the human hunters were excessively incompetent (or the prey excessively elusive), both of which are rather weak arguments. The large numbers of prime adults, the technology for despatching animals and exploiting their carcasses, the location of the site in a topographically constrained area which would have facilitated the monitoring and control of animal movements, and the focus on ibex and chamois at the expense of other resources potentially available as suggested by the palaeogeographical analysis, all argue for effective techniques of exploitation. A variety of carnivore competitors were certainly present and may have been an added source of mortality which depressed the numbers of animals available for human predation, but this factor has already been discounted to some extent in the cull rate used to derive the human population size. On the other hand, the sizeable proportions of young and old animals in the faunal assemblage, of less than optimal utility, might suggest that culling rates were perhaps less than the theoretical maximum possible — equally they could suggest some non-selective technique of slaughter such as mass drives, without in any way implying sub-optimal culling rates.
- The numbers of people available for ibex/chamois hunting in summer were far fewer than could be supported, because some other limiting factor was holding down regional human population levels, or because other summer activities diverted personnel elsewhere. Again these seem rather weak objections since regional population estimates (Table 30.15) suggest no shortage of numbers.
- The quantities of bone preserved at Klithi are an order of magnitude less than those originally collected and discarded by the prehistoric hunters. Observations in ethnographic and experimental contexts (Brain 1981; Payne & Munson 1985; Vereshchagin 1967; White 1968) certainly suggest that perhaps as much as 99 per cent of the bones from animal carcasses can be destroyed by post-depositional processes and that the main agent of destruction is the domestic dog, a role equally capable of being filled by wild carnivores in the Pleistocene context. The difficulty with this argument at Klithi is that the bone assemblage shows remarkably little presence of carnivores or surviving trace of carnivore gnawing. It is, however, possible that significant amounts of bone debris were tossed out onto the talus slope, resulting in some under-representation of total bone quantities.
- Klithi was only one of a number of sites used during the chamois and ibex hunting season. Other sites might have been visited by the Klithi group, or by other hunting parties. This is difficult to

discount, given the likely invisibility or lack of preservation of much human activity in the wider landscape, especially if some of the other locations were open-air sites (Bailey *et al.*, Chapter 27). There are, however, reasons for supposing that Klithi was a uniquely attractive base for ibex and chamois hunting, both because of its topographic position and attractive conditions of shelter and warmth, and because the other shelters in the near vicinity, namely Megalakkos and Boïla, show remarkably little evidence of human activity at the period when Klithi was occupied. Megalakkos is such a small site with so little evidence that it can hardly represent a substantial component of any local activity, while Boïla appears to have witnessed its main period of use towards the end of the Late Glacial after occupation of Klithi had largely ceased (Kotjabopoulou *et al.*, Chapter 22). The use of sites further afield should not be ruled out completely, however, in view of the various surface indications in the wider region (difficult to date though they are) and the evidence of use at the Kipi rockshelters, also at present undated (Bailey *et al.*, Chapters 16 & 27).

- Another possibility, which would be consistent with high culling rates but a low resident population, is that much of the meat was filleted and preserved (perhaps by smoking) for consumption elsewhere at a later date. None of the evidence at our disposal offers independent evidence for meat preservation, but such an activity would be consistent with the evidence for the making of clothes in suggesting an emphasis on stocking up for the winter.

The above discussion suggests that we can reconcile the apparent discrepancies between on-site and off-site estimates by fairly modest adjustments to the figures without violating the assumptions on which they are based or appealing to large quantities of now destroyed evidence. A slight increase in the resident population at Klithi and the duration of their visits, say 12 people for 6 months of the year, plus some modest under-representation of activities because of any one of the last three factors listed above, would achieve the necessary reconciliation between the various lines of evidence.

When we first discovered Klithi, the location suggested another summer terminal of a deer transhumance route comparable to Kastritsa (Bailey *et al.* 1983a; Bailey, Chapter 1), while the size and favourable aspect of the shelter opening, the area and apparent depth of the deposit, and the density of the lithic and faunal finds suggested by early indications, all gave us high expectations that we had found the biggest Palaeolithic site in Epirus, with a long sequence and a wide range of finds, perhaps representing an aggregation site at the node of a regional settlement network extending northwest to the coasts of Albania and and southeast to southern Epirus (Bailey *et al.* 1984; Bailey, Chapter 1). Both these predictions have been comprehensively refuted by the final outcome of excavation and analysis. Klithi is emphatically not a base for deer exploitation, whatever else it was used for. And while it is true that the marine shells and the exotic flints suggest contact with a wider area and are in all probability an indication that the people who visited Klithi had come from far afield, all the evidence points to visits by small parties of people for relatively short stays and for a quite limited and specialized set of activities.

Klithi in its local setting

Discussions of seasonality and group size necessarily focus on the wider environmental setting and the presence of other sites. These have already been touched on above and can be considered further in relation to the comparative archaeological data from Megalakkos and Boïla and the palaeoenvironmental sequence.

The excavations carried out at the three rockshelters are not exactly comparable because Megalakkos produced tiny samples of material, in part because much of the deposit has been eroded, while the Boïla site is still under investigation. It is clear, nevertheless, that the lithic and faunal data, though similar in general terms, show subtle but important differences. There are also differences of chronology. Megalakkos and Klithi are essentially contemporaneous, with the bulk of dates and activities in the 16–13 ka period, but with one outlier at Megalakkos of 8.8 ka which may represent sporadic activity at a later period or an anomalous radiocarbon date (Sinclair, Chapter 21). Boïla on the other hand, while it overlaps in time with Klithi, appears to have most of its evidence focused in the period from 14 to 10 ka and perhaps later (Kotjabopoulou *et al.*, Chapter 22) It is notable that within the Voïdomatis catchment there is no certain evidence of activity in any of the three rockshelters before the Last Glacial Maximum, although earlier visits to the mouth of the lower gorge on the edge of the Konitsa basin are indicated by the ESR-dated red deer mandible and associated artefact found in the Aristi Unit just downstream of Boïla (Macklin *et al.*, Chapter 17). Why was Klithi not used before 16–17 ka or after 13 ka, and why was Boïla apparently the preferred base of operations after about 14–13 ka but not much used before?

The absence of occupation before about 16 ka seems most easily explicable by reference to the more severe climate of the Last Glacial Maximum and its impact on the habitat of ibex and chamois. During this period, the presence of a permanent local ice sheet, aridity, lack of tree cover, and scree-covered slopes must have presented a bare and desolate periglacial environment with little attraction to any grazing animals (Macklin *et al.*, Chapter 17). Massive erosion and downslope movement of limestone scree material would have offered further disincentives. The valley bottom itself, though higher and broader than at present, was probably an expanse of exposed gravels and boulders, made more difficult of access by the torrential spring meltwaters. After about 16 ka, the local palaeoclimatic indicators — the sedimentary sequences from Klithi and Megalakkos and the valley-fill sequence — suggest some climatic amelioration, with reduced erosion from limestone slopes, more moisture, and some downcutting and confinement of the river channel.

The pollen data are more equivocal. Only one of the local diagrams, Tseravinas, covers the period of occupation at Klithi, and even then does not appear to extend much before about 16 ka, so that we cannot be sure whether zone 1 at the base of the sequence represents a continuation of vegetational conditions typical of the Last Glacial Maximum or changed conditions appropriate to the period immediately following (Turner & Sánchez-Goñi, Chapter 29). The longer but less detailed sequence from Ioannina, and indeed the classic Tenaghi Phillipon sequence (Wijmstra 1969), nevertheless suggest changes consistent with climatic amelioration at about this time. The percentages of tree pollen at Tseravinas are still relatively low and indicate an overall steppic environment between about 16 ka and 15 ka, though they show a steady and significant rise between 15 ka and 13 ka. This pattern cannot be extrapolated in detail to the vicinity of Klithi because of the impact of varying altitude and aspect on local conditions of tree growth, but the absence of pig and roe deer from the Klithi faunal assemblages, both of which would be expected locally with any significant expansion of deciduous forest cover, suggests that trees were still confined to scattered occurrences along water courses, or on cliff ledges and other inaccessible refuge locations at higher altitude. It thus seems reasonable to argue that the slopes above Klithi offered attractive summer grazing for ibex and chamois, with lower altitude terrain and perhaps more extensive tree cover to the west and south in the Doliana basin providing browse and shelter in winter. Klithi would thus have been on the boundary between seasonal ibex and chamois territories, offering an ideal point for monitoring and exploitation of animals during seasonal moves in spring or autumn.

After about 13 ka, both local and global indicators suggest a further significant amelioration, with tree pollen percentages in the Tseravinas diagram approximating maximum values, and climatic conditions approaching those of the Postglacial. In view of the evidence for the local persistence of tree refugia throughout the climatic extremes of the Last Glacial Maximum, it seems likely that the local vegetational response to this climatic warming would have been almost instantaneous, with tree cover rapidly expanding to blanket many of the slopes around and above Klithi. The tree line, in its turn, and hence the boundary between winter and summer grazing territories, would have shifted to higher altitude and greater distance from Klithi, effectively removing its advantages as a base for ibex and chamois hunting.

The climate of this latest Late Glacial phase, however, was not uniformly warm and wet, and intervals of returning cold have long been identified in the Northwest European pollen sequences, the best known being the Younger Dryas between about 11 and 10 ka. Recent high resolution evidence from the Greenland ice cores (Macklin *et al.*, Chapter 17) demonstrates just how dramatic and rapid were these oscillations between climatic extremes during this period. Whether this sequence can be extrapolated in detail to southeast Europe remains uncertain, but the palaeoenvironmental record of the Voïdomatis offers some local corroboration. A sharp drop in tree pollen is apparent at Tseravinas at about 13 ka, equivalent to the Oldest Dryas, or Heinrich Event 1 of the Greenland ice-core sequence, though there is no sign of a Younger Dryas event in this sequence, apparently because of a stratigraphic discontinuity (Turner & Sánchez-Goñi, Chapter 29), while a Younger Dryas event may be indicated at the base of the Gramousti sequence (Willis, Chapter 20) and perhaps in the sedimentological record of Megalakkos (Woodward, Chapter 19).

Our palaeoenvironmental records are tantalizingly incomplete over this critical period of climatic instability, perhaps precisely because it was a period of rapidly changing conditions which have truncated or obscured the evidence in a number of sedimentary sequences, but there is sufficient direct and indirect evidence to suggest a reversion to cold-climate conditions that may have persisted for up to several hundred years. These must have returned local conditions around Klithi at least some way back towards an open landscape suitable for summer grazing of ibex and chamois, and provide the best explanation for the traces of occupation at the top of the Klithi sequence at 12,300 BP and again at 10,420 BP. Macklin *et al.* (Chapter 17), however, suggest that it may have been the return of extremely cold conditions at about 13 ka, analogous to those that prevailed before 17 ka, rather than the onset of warmer conditions, that terminated occupation at Klithi. There is thus some ambiguity about the interpretation of the climatic record and its impact on human activities, though it seems clear that climatic conditions at either extreme of the range, whether very cold or very warm, would have been inimical to the use of Klithi as a base for ibex hunters. Probably the decisive factor would have been vegetational conditions rather than temperature *per se*, and in this case the local pollen record is more directly relevant than the inferred temperature regime. While the Tseravinas sequence shows a short-lived decline in tree pollen at about 13 ka, the data do not suggest a complete reversion to the steppic conditions that prevailed at the beginning of the sequence. Further interpretation is hampered by uncertainties about the stratigraphic completeness and resolution of this core and by the few radiocarbon dates currently available (Turner & Sánchez-Goñi, Chapter 29).

The onset of a warmer and wetter climate does not necessarily mean the regional disappearance of ibex and chamois, though it would undoubtedly have caused some reduction in the size of their habitat. Summer grazing in particular would have become restricted to areas above the tree line, except to the extent that human groups may have used fire to maintain an open landscape. Nor does the cessation of occupation at Klithi necessarily mean the termination of ibex and chamois hunting. The base of operations might have shifted to locations at higher altitude or involved greater mobility and dispersal of hunting parties. Naturally the chances of identifying these sites are rather small in the absence of suitably located rockshelters. The Kipi sites, situated at the upper end of the Vikos Gorge, are of particular interest in this context. They have given surface indications of human occupation, retain some deposit, and are at a higher altitude and in closer proximity to the highest terrain of the Voïdomatis catchment than Klithi and its neighbouring rockshelters. Excavations at Kipi should help to clarify whether this area was used as a base for caprid hunting after the abandonment of Klithi, as a contemporaneous base used to target ibex and chamois at some other point in their Late Glacial seasonal migrations, or for some other purpose.

Boïla was perhaps less attractive in the 16 to 14 ka period because of its low elevation above the river — during the period of formation of the Aristi Unit the river flowed through the entrance of the rockshelter — and its greater distance from the summer territories of ibex and chamois and their main routes of seasonal movement. It is also a less attractive shelter for occupation during episodes of cold climate, with its northeasterly orientation. After 14 ka, however, the Tseravinas pollen diagram suggests significant expansion of tree cover, while soils had by this time become established over parts of the Konitsa basin following stream incision and the greater confinement of the river channel (Macklin *et al.*, Chapter 17). These factors would have improved conditions for such animals as deer and pig, both of which are present in the Boïla faunal assemblage along with caprids, the deer in significantly greater numbers than at Klithi (Kotjabopoulou *et al.*, Chapter 22). The aspect of the shelter would no doubt have been less of a disadvantage in the warm summers of the Late Glacial interstadials, and indeed perhaps a positive advantage in comparison to Klithi, which in summer with its south-facing orientation becomes unbearably hot during the middle of the day under modern climatic conditions.

Megalakkos seems to be a much less intensively used but more eclectic site, with a wider variety of activities, materials drawn from a larger catchment, and an apparently wider range of dates. This is suggested by the emphasis on exotic raw materials in Unit 6, the red deer bones in Unit 4, the differences in the lithic assemblages between these two units, and the apparent late date of an isolated caprid bone at 8800 BP (Sinclair, Chapter 21). This date seems anomalously late in relation to a proposed interpretation of the overlying scree as of Younger Dryas age (Woodward, Chapter 19), though this discrepancy could perhaps be resolved by supposing that the bone which yielded the date has been displaced from its original stratigraphic position. There are no obvious reasons for rejecting the date on technical grounds (Gowlett *et al.*, Chapter 2), but unfortunately little prospect of finding suitable dateable material for additional checks. Unless we reject the date as an unexplained outlier or one that does not fit our preconceptions, it might conceivably represent some trace of activity in the early Postglacial period, an ibex killed locally in winter, for example, or one killed in summer at a considerably greater altitude, parts of which were brought in from a distance by hunters passing through the Voïdomatis and stopping briefly en route for settlements further to the west.

During the period when Klithi was occupied, it would be natural to suppose that Megalakkos was visited by people attached to the Klithi group, and there are hints of complementarity between the two sites in the predominance of right-handed and left-handed bones, respectively (Gamble, Chapter 12; Sinclair, Chapter 21). If these patterns of differential representation are not simply the result of vagaries of preservation, they could suggest the sharing of carcass parts between the two sites. In any case the small size of the shelter opening, its less favoured aspect, and the small number of finds, strongly suggest that Megalakkos was a site used much less frequently than Klithi. At best it seems to have been a site used fleetingly by people passing through, rather than the base for some local specialized activity.

Although the three sites have certain basic features in common, at a more detailed level they seem to represent three rather different types of activities. Klithi was highly specialized on the exploitation of ibex and chamois and correspondingly vulnerable to shifts in their availability; Boïla had a more generalized location accessible to a wider range of resources and was accordingly adaptable to use in later periods than Klithi; and Megalakkos was a site used more fleetingly and opportunistically, and perhaps in different ways and for different purposes on different occasions. The area of the excavation at Megalakkos was too limited to afford much insight into spatial structure, but it is interesting that the two main assemblages are so distinctively different. This does suggest a greater degree of integrity and differentiation in the patterning of the lithic assemblages than at Klithi, and this is what we might expect from a site used for much shorter visits, and, moreover, a site where occupation surfaces also seem to have been protected by rapid accumulations of sterile silt. Hearth areas have been identified at Boïla, and it will be interesting to see how the final analysis of intra-site patterning compares with the results from Klithi.

Klithi in its regional context

With the shift to a regional focus, we switch to the big issues that have dominated the study of Epirus prehistory: the articulation between the use of different parts of the landscape and the possible similarities between Palaeolithic economic strategies and historical patterns of transhumance; the nature of the determining effect of environment on human strategies of mobility and resource selection; and the evidence for long-term trends and their possible causes.

What new light do the results from Klithi and the new analyses of the older excavations at Asprochaliko and Kastritsa throw on the relationship between these three sites. Are they complementary elements in a single system of settlement and land use as Higgs originally envisaged with his model of seasonal transhumance, and how far is the evidence from these sites typical of the wider Epirus region?

The regional economy

Taking the regional picture first our best indicators come from the palaeogeographic analysis (Sturdy *et al.*, Chapter 30). This offers fairly powerful if indirect support for the view that the hinterland of eastern Epirus was a seasonal territory, subject to an influx of larger game (deer, cattle and horse) in spring and summer, but largely abandoned in winter except for some scattered ibex and chamois. Moreover, estimates of the total regional animal population suggest that it could have supported some 500 to 1000 people on a sustained basis, while the number that could have been supported by the mammalian resources in the eastern Epirus hinterland was no more than about 100. Two conclusions can be drawn from these figures: that the economic potential of the Epirus hinterland was relatively low, perhaps as little as 10 per cent of the regional total; and that the regional human population as a whole was barely larger than the suggested optimal size of a single regional mating network, in Wobst's (1974) terms (see also Bailey, Chapter 1). Both these conclusions reinforce the view that the hinterland of eastern Epirus should be regarded as an integral component of a regional palaeoeconomic system embracing a much wider area, including the western plateaux and coastal lowlands of Epirus, and that the various sites under discussion should be regarded as fragments of a regionally integrated pattern of land use involving a high degree of mobility and in all probability a great many other sites that have not been preserved or discovered. This is consistent with the fact that the largest number of sites at all periods of the Palaeolithic sequence, and some of the biggest sites, are in western Epirus, even though they are mostly stratigraphically disturbed open-air sites, difficult to date, and offer poor conditions of organic preservation (Bailey *et al.*, Chapter 27).

Palynological evidence underlines these

conclusions. Non-arboreal plant biomass was generally very low during the colder climatic stages, at least in the Epirus hinterland, and suggests that animal biomass would have been correspondingly low, especially during the Last Glacial Maximum, except during short-lived seasonal episodes of animal migration. The pollen data also highlight the contrast between an open landscape in the hinterland with very few trees except in scattered refuges and along watercourses, and a more wooded coastal lowland offering browse and shelter in winter (Turner & Sánchez-Goñi, Chapter 29).

One question that arises at this point is how far our palaeoeconomic reconstructions are distorted by the emphasis on land mammals at the expense of plant foods and marine resources. Plant foods are notoriously liable to under-representation because of poor conditions of preservation, and the suspicion that they may be heavily under-represented is sometimes further reinforced by ethnographic analogies drawn from surviving hunter-gatherers. Mason *et al.* (1994) have recently identified charred plant remains from 26,000 year-old deposits at Dolní Vestoniče and have made a case for a significant plant-food potential in the periglacial forest-steppe environments of Europe. Occasional plant remains have been recovered from a number of other Upper Palaeolithic contexts in Europe and the Near East, including Temnata Cave in Bulgaria, based on evidence of lithic use-wear analysis (Kozlowski 1994), Franchthi Cave in the Peloponnese, where carbonised remains of fruits, pistachio and legumes have been recovered in deposits dating from *c.* 13 ka onwards (Hansen 1991), and Ohalo II, a 19,000 year-old lake-edge Kebaran site in Israel with waterlogged deposits and excellent conditions of organic preservation with abundant carbonized seeds of wild barley, fruits, and other cereals, and associated grinding equipment (Kislev *et al.* 1992; Nadel & Hershkovitz 1991).

As far as Epirus is concerned, Klithi failed to produce any evidence of charred plant remains in spite of an extensive programme of wet sieving and flotation designed to check for their presence. Kastritsa, with its lake-side location may perhaps be a better location in which to expect to find relevant evidence, and some flotation work was carried out during the 1960s excavations, but the results have yet to be properly evaluated. Grinding implements, which one might expect to be associated with intensive seed processing, are wholly absent from the Palaeolithic artefact inventory of the region. The backed bladelets, which Clarke (1976) in a famous critique of the meat bias in palaeoeconomic studies suggested were used as knives to prepare plant foods, have been shown in Epirus, at least on the use-wear evidence from Klithi (Moss, Chapter 11), to have been projectile barbs and piercers for skin-working, a point borne out by Adam's (1989, 239) macroscopic study of impact fractures at both Klithi and Kastritsa.

In any case the eastern Epirus hinterland is not the most obvious place to look for plant foods, given the nature of the Last Glacial climate and vegetation, whereas it seems likely, on the evidence of the Ziros pollen diagram, that western Epirus with its more equable lowland and coastal climate offered a more diverse floristic environment with more plant-food potential. It is, however, one thing to say that plant foods were available, quite another to say that they were exploited as food, and quite another thing again to infer from evidence of exploitation a dependency on plant foods as a major staple. It seems not unreasonable to suppose that plant foods were taken advantage of to the extent that they were available, and there is no doubt that there is the need and the scope for further investigation. It would, however, be wildly speculative to invoke heavy dependence on large storable surpluses of plant foods, or to suppose that these could have so overshadowed the role of animal foods as to make animal distributions and seasonal movements irrelevant to patterns of human settlement and mobility. Even the modern Sarakatsani, who make intensive use of naturally-occurring plant foods during the summer season, do not regard these as other than a minor supplement to a way of life that is dominated by animal transhumance (Campbell 1964). The early Mesolithic layers at Franchthi Cave give some indication of the archaeological signature to be expected with heavy dependence on plant foods, with some 28,000 seeds from 27 species, including for the first time cereals, and associated grinding equipment (Hansen 1991). This is vastly more than the plant remains from the final Upper Palaeolithic levels, which have yielded some 700 seeds from fewer species, and which offer a more appropriate guide to what might be expected in the coastal region of Late Glacial Epirus.

As for marine foods, the Mediterranean generally has a rather low potential productivity today in comparison with, say, the Atlantic coasts of Europe, because of limited tidal movement, steep shorelines, and low fertility, and the lowered sea levels of the Last Glacial are unlikely to have greatly altered this picture (Bailey 1982). Even on the surviving shorelines of Mesolithic and later date, shell middens, such as the example from Sidari on Corfu (Sordinas

1969; 1970a), or the shell-bearing deposits of Franchthi Cave (Shackleton 1988) are thin and of limited extent compared to the great estuarine shell mounds of the Ertebølle in Denmark and other comparable coastal areas. As with the plant foods, we are hampered by problems of differential survival of evidence, in the marine case because of loss of potentially early shell middens with rising sea levels; but, as with the plant foods, it seems doubtful that marine foods were ever available or exploited in sufficent abundance to have a significant impact on human population size and settlement patterns during the Palaeolithic period, though some utilization cannot be ruled out.

The general outcome of our regional palaeogeographic and palaeoenvironmental interpretations is to suggest that, in taking Epirus as our regional palaeoeconomic unit, we may be defining an area that is too small rather than too large. The biggest uncertainty is the question of relationships with Albania. It seems likely that the coastal lowlands of Albania to the northwest could have formed another lowland area potentially complementary to the Pindus uplands. It is true that this lowland region is less easily accessible from the Voïdomatis area than the Ioannina basin to the south, and involves negotiating extensive tracts of unattractive flysch terrain and more formidable limestone mountain barriers. Its more northerly position may also mean that it had a harsher winter climate and less tree cover, which would have made it a less attractive winter territory for many of the herd animals. Nevertheless the Drin river offers a potential access route. In the absence of palaeogeographic and archaeological survey, the existence and strength of relationships between the Epirot sites and Albania must remain uncertain. Certainly geographical and climatic considerations argue for obvious and regular links between Klithi and areas to the south and east in the Ioannina and Louros basins.

Inter-site links

In terms of direct archaeological evidence of links between sites, the data are inevitably patchy and open to a variety of intepretations. The marine shells at Klithi certainly suggest contact with the coast, and one marine shell was also recovered from the Kastritsa deposits. Direct evidence of seasonality is still unavailable except at Klithi, and further clues may be forthcoming when more detailed analyses of the faunal remains from Kastritsa and Asprochaliko have been completed. Analysis of growth increments in dental cementum, though still in its infancy and posing many uncertainties of method and intepretation (Lieberman *et al.*, 1990), also offers a potential means of refining estimates of seasonality in the Epirus context.

One of the most suggestive links between Klithi and Kastritsa is the appearance of the characteristic black Voïdomatis flint in the Kastritsa assemblages from Stratum 5 onwards (Adam, Chapter 25). On the other hand, the Kastritsa industries in which this material was first used are technologically distinctive and it is only in the overlying Strata 3 and 1 that technological convergence with the Klithi industries becomes obvious. On these grounds we might hypothesize that the inhabitants of Kastritsa were already making forays into the Voïdomatis region before occupation at Klithi began. This hypothesis is supported by a radiocarbon date at the base of Kastritsa Stratum 5 of 19,900 ± 370 (I-2465), significantly earlier than the earliest date for occupation at Klithi, whereas the base of Kastritsa Stratum 3, by interpolation from radiocarbon dates in other strata, is dated to about 16,400 BP, which is also the effective date of commencement of occupation at Klithi. It is, of course, conceivable that this type of flint may have come from some other region, but the limestone areas within the catchment of the Voïdomatis appear to be the nearest source to Kastritsa.

Conversely, exotic flint raw materials were brought into Klithi from outside the Voïdomatis basin. Some of the flint present at Klithi can be found in the Drin valley to the west, and one of the rare colours shows mineralogical similarities with source material in the Rhodope mountains on the Greek–Bulgarian border (M. Pawlikowski, pers. comm.), but for the most part the sources of origin are unknown. This is the least well-developed aspect of our catchment analyses *sensu stricto* (Bailey, Chapter 1). Some flint types are widely distributed in the Epirus landscape, others may have more than one source, and many of the flint artefacts, particularly from open-air locations and from Middle Palaeolithic or earlier periods, are heavily patinated, all of which poses many ambiguities and uncertainties of intepretation. At any rate a systematic analysis of raw material characteristics, distributions and sources would require a major task of geological survey and analysis and has yet to be undertaken, but the results should throw important light on the potential links between the Epirus sites and indeed between Epirus and regions further afield.

Inter-site chronology

An essential precondition of complementarity between sites is, of course, contemporaneity, and it is instructive to consider the evidence of chronology. If we confine our attention for the moment to the Upper Palaeolithic period, Asprochaliko has the earliest dated occupation with a radiocarbon date for Layer 10 of 26,100 ± 900 BP. The overlying Layer 4 is not dated but its lithic industry is similar to that from Layer 10, and both are technologically and typologically distinctive compared to the industries at Kastritsa and Klithi (Adam, Chapter 25). On these grounds it may be that the whole of the Upper Palaeolithic occupation at Asprochaliko pre-dates the Last Glacial Maximum. At Kastritsa the top of Stratum 9 is dated to about 20,000 years BP, and the earliest occupations must largely pre-date this. The industry in the lowest layers is unlike any others, and is in all probability associated with limited use of the site. The question of earlier occupation at Kastritsa is unresolvable. Some water-rolled artefacts of early Upper Palaeolithic or even Mousterian aspect at the base of the sequence hint at earlier occupation (Galanidou, Chapter 26), but additional evidence of any such use of the cave, if it did occur, has been removed or disturbed by water action associated with high lake levels, which would in any case have made the site unusable until water levels receded after about 20,000 years ago. The overlying strata show a marked increase in the quantity and variety of artefacts from Stratum 5 onwards, a trend under way from as early as about 19,000 BP. From Stratum 3 onwards Kastritsa and Klithi continue in use in parallel until about 13,000 BP, when both sites essentially fall out of use.

The three rockshelter sites thus seem to represent a sequence or cycle of occupations, albeit with some overlap in the case of Klithi and Kastritsa, rather than a series of chronologically parallel ones, representing successively deeper and more intensive penetration of the Epirus hinterland as it opened up to exploitation with changing climatic conditions after the Last Glacial Maximum, and contraction of activity with the further warming and re-afforestation of the Late Glacial after about 13,000 BP. The episodic nature of occupation in the Epirus hinterland becomes even more apparent if we extend our time span to include the Mousterian, which is well represented by abundant remains at Asprochaliko extending back to 100,000 years ago, and probably by earlier material at Kokkinopilos, but is not certainly present at Kastritsa, and almost certainly absent from Klithi.

Evidence of raw material movements, together with other scattered early dates such as the ESR-dated finds of 25 ka at the mouth of the lower Voïdomatis Gorge, suggest that the hinterland may have been visited for exploratory visits long before substantial occupations were established at Klithi and Kastritsa. Hinterland esources may have been too thinly distributed to support other than highly mobile and fleeting trips, but these occasional visits could nevertheless have formed the basis of knowledge for rapidly establishing more settled exploitation of particular localities whenever more favourable conditions permitted. In the coldest phases of the Last Glacial, Asprochaliko may have been the most inland base for exploring and exploiting a hinterland of perhaps quite limited extent and attractions under full glacial climatic conditions. With progressive climatic amelioration, Kastritsa, and later Klithi, became the focal points for more extensive and prolonged exploitation of the remoter inland and upland regions.

Rockshelter deposits, however, do not tell the whole story, and we should distinguish between the particular types of occupation represented at Kastritsa and Klithi from other sorts of activity in the hinterland. The ESR-dated red deer mandible and artefact found on the banks of the Voïdomatis show that at least sporadic visits were being made this far into the hinterland during the period when Asprochaliko was in full use. The Oraiokastro open-air site further to the west, close to the high-summer grazing territories of deer, though not precisely dated, attests to open-air occupation some time during the Upper Palaeolithic period, and most probably to activities very different from those represented at Klithi (Bailey *et al.*, Chapter 27). Even during the Middle Palaeolithic period, when the great majority of evidence is confined to open-air sites at lower altitude in western Epirus and nearer the coast, some finds are present at various locations in the hinterland including the Doliana basin. It seems then that the Epirus hinterland was regularly visited throughout the Palaeolithic sequence, if fleetingly and sporadically at some periods, and that the intensification represented by the later occupations at Klithi and Kastritsa reflects particularly favourable windows of opportunity at particular periods and in particular locations.

Factors in site selection

Climatically driven palaeoenvironmental changes clearly played an important role in determining the availability of some of the hinterland sites for intensive activity, especially at Klithi, and to a lesser extent at Kastritsa. Underlying these temporal trends, however, are spatial factors which make Klithi and

Kastritsa intrinsically attractive bases for exploitation of animals, attractions which they share with Asprochaliko. These factors essentially have to do with the position of each site with respect to topographic features at both large and small scales.

At the larger scale all three sites are located around the edge of a large and virtually enclosed basin that would have confined the summer movements of the larger herd animals — deer, horse and cattle — to predictable areas and facilitated the monitoring and control of their migratory movements. At the local scale, each site is located close to a critical boundary between seasonal grazing territories and to the general routes of seasonal migration between them, but not so close as to disturb the animals or cause them to shift out of range. Each site has a secluded position a little to one side of the main migratory routes, from which they can be monitored and observed from a discreet distance. Moreover, each site controls more localized enclosures bounded by natural barriers — the Kerasonas plateau north of Asprochaliko, the peninsula and arc of land at the eastern end of the palaeolake behind Kastritsa, and the slopes above Klithi. These features are a direct consequence of the complex, tectonically-created topography of the region, and create a landscape which human groups could use to maintain contact with animals, and to predict and control their movements and distribution, without the need for closer methods of control, artificial barriers, or more elaborate technologies of killing at a distance (King *et al.*, Chapter 28).

Notwithstanding the relatively rapid rates of tectonically-induced landscape change, the preferred locations for human activity in the Palaeolithic period were on the edges of fault-bounded basins, where repeated tectonic movements would tend to have renewed or maintained favourable topographic conditions at the local scale, namely uplifted barriers and adjacent water and sediment traps, thereby conferring a measure of insensitivity to shorter-term climatic fluctuations.

Inter-site variability

If the hinterland sites seem to have a number of features in common, it does not follow that they had identical functions, and indeed the on-site evidence provides a number of contrasts, both in the nature of lithic technology and typology, and in the spectrum of faunal resources exploited. Analysis of the lithic industries suggests that three factors contribute to their variability: local raw materials; site function; and time.

The effect of raw materials is most evident at Klithi, where the inadequacies of the Voïdomatis flint have imposed some distinctive constraints on the technology of reduction (Roubet, Chapter 8; Moss, Chapter 11; Adam, Chapter 25). But even here, better quality raw materials were brought in from further afield when needed for particular purposes, and this effect is especially marked at Kastritsa, which seems to lack sources of flint in its immediate vicinity (Adam, Chapter 25). Moreover, the same types of raw materials were clearly capable of being worked in different ways. Throughout all the technological changes witnessed by the long sequence of Middle and Upper Palaeolithic industries at Asprochaliko, essentially the same raw materials were selected for use (Gowlett & Carter, Chapter 23). Similarly, the Voïdomatis-type flint at Kastritsa was thought sufficiently suitable for some purposes to be worth importing from a distance to Kastritsa, though it was probably not the nearest available flint and certainly not of the best quality. Thus the character of the local lithic raw materials can only be regarded as partially determinant of the resulting lithic industries, and was offset by importation of alternative lithic materials from further afield and by skilful manipulation of alternative technologies for core reduction and tool manufacture, depending on the desired end-product.

Similarly, the faunal data suggest that, though the animal species exploited were generally those most abundantly available in the vicinity of each site — ibex at Klithi and red deer at Kastritsa and Asprochaliko, there were definite patterns of preferential selection, and that this selection tended to overemphasize species of secondary abundance within the site exploitation territory at the expense of other species that were equally available but more effectively exploited in greater abundance elsewhere (Sturdy *et al.*, Chapter 30). Chamois were preferred over red deer at Klithi, horse and cattle over ibex at Kastritsa, and ibex over horse at Asprochaliko. As with the flint raw materials, there is clear evidence that local activities were shaped in part by locally available resources, but also by an awareness of alternative resources available elsewhere.

Time trends in lithic assemblage variability are difficult to evaluate, given the small number of deposits available for comparison and the lack of chronological overlap between some of them. They thus pose the same sort of confounding problem on a larger scale that complicates the task of interpreting smaller-scale variations at the intra-site level at Klithi (Winder, Chapter 6), that is the difficulty of deciding whether the differences between assemblages of different date are simply the result of 'spatial' (or functional) differences, rather than the result of some more widespread temporal change that affected all industries over a wider area. Certainly the fact that comparisons can be made between some of the Epirus industries and the industrial sequence at Franchthi Cave some 500 km to the south, suggests that there are general underlying trends in the industrial sucession that transcend local factors and functional variations.

For an assessment of functional differences, the contemporaneous deposits at Klithi and Kastritsa (Strata 3–1) offer the best insights, and it is clear that they reflect very different sorts of activities. Klithi, as already noted, was highly specialized on ibex and chamois hunting and that specialization is reflected in an artefact inventory dominated by microlithic projectile barbs, and the manufacture of lithics (endscrapers and piercers) and bone tools (needles and spatulae) dedicated to hide-working. Kastritsa, in contrast, has different types of lithic and bone tools. Amongst the former are the distinctive shouldered points, which may represent an alternative projectile tip more suited to the different prey species at Kastritsa — cattle, equid and red deer, as opposed to chamois and ibex. Among the bone inventory, points, presumably used as projectile heads, predominate (a type virtually absent at Klithi), and are common at Kastritsa not least because supplies of antler, which is stronger than bone and the preferred material for point manufacture, were more easily available (Adam & Kotjabopoulou, Chapter 13). The decorative materials also show some important contrasts as well as similarities. Pierced deer canine teeth are present in small numbers at both sites, but there is nothing at Kastritsa comparable to the large numbers of pierced marine shells at Klithi, a difference that hints at differences of social composition between the two sites (Adam & Kotjabopoulou, Chapter 13).

It is probable too that the sites were used by different-sized communities and for different durations, and represent different types of settlement as well as different types of activities. Klithi, as has been repeatedly emphasized, was a specialized site used by a relatively small group of people. Asprochaliko, rather like Boïla, was used for a greater diversity of activities, but neither seems to have supported substantial communities for long periods at a time. Kastritsa is the exceptional site, with its diversity of artefacts and faunal prey, the variety of raw materials, some evidence of greater investment in site facilities, and the much higher economic potential of its local exploitation territory, capable of supporting a human population an order of magnitude bigger than at Klithi (Sturdy *et al.*, Chapter 30). It seems to have been the central node of activities in the Epirus hinterland and represents perhaps the best case for being considered as a summer aggregation site.

Mobility and transhumance

The nature of the links between sites and seasonally complementary areas brings us to the question of transhumance. Here it is helpful to break the problem down into at least three separate issues: the degree of seasonal mobility between complementary resource areas; the nature of the relationships between people and animals; and the degree of continuity between Palaeolithic and present-day patterns of land use.

The weight of our evidence demonstrates that the hinterland of eastern Epirus and the high Pindus was a seasonally available territory that could not have been used except by seasonally mobile parties moving inland in spring from bases at lower altitude and nearer the coast in western and southern Epirus (see Fig. 27.1 for geographical subdivisions). Moreover, our data show that this seasonal hinterland was visited and made use of throughout the Palaeolithic sequence, even in the Middle Palaeolithic period, although the intensity with which it was used varied considerably. During Last Glacial climatic and environmental conditions, most populations of the larger herd animals would have vacated the hinterland in winter, the only possible exceptions being some scattered groups of chamois and ibex, which might have found shelter and some winter browse in the most sheltered low-lying areas of the Doliana basin. Thus the hinterland made available a seasonal abundance of resources that could not have been exploited except by seasonal movement. It does not follow, however, that the reverse applies, namely that all the animal and human populations overwintering in the coastal lowlands moved into the hinterland of eastern Epirus in summer. On the contrary, the palaeogeographic analysis shows that the lower altitude areas of western Epirus supported the great majority of animal resources, and consequently the greater part of the regional human population (Sturdy *et al.*, Chapter 30). We do not have to suppose that these populations were sedentary: at least local and short-distance movements of animals to higher terrain are likely, and there is certainly some summer terrain available in close proximity; but it seems certain that viable subsistence economies could have been pursued without requiring use of the eastern Epirus hinterland.

As for the 'man–animal' relationship, there is no evidence to suppose that people maintained close year-round relationships with individual animal herds in quite the manner originally envisaged by the original Higgsian hypothesis, nor indeed that they would have been forced to do so to avoid over-predation in the longer term — an important corollary of the original hypothesis. The complex, tectonically created topography of Epirus, with its enclosed basins and natural barriers, seems to have benefited both prey and predator, removing incentives for either to establish closer relationships. From the point of view of the human predator, the possibilities of monitoring and controlling the movement of prey animals by use of topographic barriers and constraints were well taken advantage of by Upper Palaeolithic times (King *et al.*, Chapter 28). Indeed the perception and manipulation of the landscape in this way encourages us to think of the use of the landscape as in some ways an extension of the human technological capacity. At any rate it would have obviated the need for closer control, and was perhaps one disincentive to the sort of close relationships that are commonly implied by the term 'domestication'. From the prey point of view, the topography creates many possibilities of escape and seclusion especially at low densities, and even from technologically sophisticated predators. As Winder's simulations (Chapter 31) demonstrate, patchiness of prey distributions provides an important restraint on over-predation, and encourages the long-term viability and stability of both prey and predator populations.

Both Gamble (Chapter 12) and Winder (Chapter 31) raise the question of why the ibex hunters of Klithi, who after all are broadly contemporary with the goat and gazelle herders of the Near East, did not, unlike their more eastern neighbours, go down the pathway towards animal domestication. One answer to this must be that the loose but stable relationship encouraged by the Epirus topography, with its low risk of over-exploitation in a patchy environment, removed the need for such closer measures of control. Another reason suggested by our analyses is that the expansion of woodland vegetation in the Late Glacial greatly restricted the ibex habitat and caused the breakdown of the highly successful late Upper Palaeolithic system of exploitation focused on Klithi. An additional factor may have been that the long-distance seasonal round of the human groups that moved into the Voïdomatis basin in spring and summer was quite different from the seasonal round of the ibex and chamois herds, which were able to subsist in winter in nearby inland valleys that offered inadequate alternative winter food supplies for the human population. This mismatch between the annual territories of humans and ibex would also surely have militated against the establishment of a close year-round relationship.

Finally, we should consider the relationship between Palaeolithic mobility and the historically known transhumance patterns for which the region is famous. One question that our data do throw some light on is the question of how far back in time transhumance in association with domestic animals can be traced. The conventional argument against using modern transhumance, particularly the large-scale, long-distance transfer of herds, as an analogy for the Palaeolithic is that it is very much the product of historical circumstances and the establishment of market economies of quite recent origin, and that in any case upland areas in prehistory were cloaked with extensive woodlands offering inadequate summer grazing for large herds of animals, until large-scale forest clearance got under way (Bailey, Chapter 1). Although our archaeological focus has not extended in detail to the more recent periods of prehistory, the pollen data, particularly from the high altitude Rezina Marsh (Willis, Chapter 20), appear to show clear indications of vegetational disturbance by human activity in the prehistoric period, from as early as about 6000 years ago. If livestock were being grazed at this altitude, they must have been taken elsewhere in winter, and while those wintering areas may not have been very far away, the evidence suggests that a system of seasonal movement of livestock may already have been present with the earliest Neolithic occupants of Epirus, whose arrival is dated in the Ioannina basin from the evidence of the Asfaka site to about 7000 years ago (Bailey, Chapter 1), only shortly before we see signs of vegetational disturbance in the Rezina, Gramousti and Tseravinas pollen diagrams further to the north in the Doliana basin.

On the other hand, seasonal use of the hinterland was certainly not continuous throughout prehistory. For at least 3000 years and possibly longer, the Epirus hinterland seems to have been a virtually unused and closed woodland environment, following the breakdown of the Upper Palaeolithic system of exploitation focused on Klithi and Katritsa. There is little evidence that Mesolithic populations were present, or it they were, as is suggested for example by the Megalakkos date of 8800 BP, that this was anything more than an occasional visit. Whether Mesolithic populations were truly absent from the hinterland, and, if so, why they should have ignored it, is an unresolved question, considered in the final section below. At any rate it is difficult, on the basis of the available archaeological or palynological evidence, to argue for continued large-scale seasonal movements of herd animals into the eastern Epirus hinterland between the termination of Upper Palaeolithic occupation at Kastritsa and Klithi and the beginning of the local Neolithic, and this gap may have lasted for as much as 6000 years.

The implication of these remarks is that the historically known pattern of transhumance may indeed have its roots in the Neolithic period, but it is certainly not possible on the available evidence to trace a direct historical link further back in time to the Palaeolithic era. This leaves open the question of whether there are functional similarities between Palaeolithic patterns of seasonal movement and historical transhumance. Let us accept that the seasonal use of the hinterland in different periods may have been motivated by altogether different social, economic and political circumstances. Let us even accept that there were some periods when the hinterland was not used at all, or at any rate much less intensively than at other periods. What is left of the original notion that Palaeolithic and historical patterns of seasonal movement are simply variations on a long-term theme of seasonal mobility determined by the environment? As Green emphasizes in Chapter 32, the physical landscape does play an important role in the embodied experience of the people who live there, however much the environmental determinism implied by long-term continuities in economic strategies may be anathema to the social anthropologist. If there is continuity, it is a continuity of resilience to an unstable landscape, a resilience made possible by the active and indeed skilled and varied responses of successive human populations, and selected for by the physical characteristics of the landscape, including the varied dynamics of environmental change that have affected those characteristics.

During the Palaeolithic, people used the complex topography as a means of predicting and controlling animal movements; they selected those focal points in the landscape which, with their complex topography and combination of sediment traps and natural barriers, offered the best chances of sustained and predictable access to large numbers of herd animals; and they combined different locations and different areas of the landscape in various ways as a flexible response to shorter-term climatic and vegetational changes. Moreover, that flexibility of response seems to have included periods when the hinterland zone was virtually abandoned or visited only fleetingly. During the historical period, the use of different resources and seasonal grazing territories was achieved through a complex layering of social linkages, which facilitated complementarity of activities, and avoidance of disturbances on a variety of scales from local landslips to larger-scale intrusions of marauding bandits, Ottoman tax-collectors or foreign armies.

If environmental determinism is discernible, it is certainly not a passive environmental determinism in which people played no active part. Indeed the language of determinism seems as inadequate to describe the long-term interactions between people and environment as does the language of choice and individual agency. We are not dealing with people as passive automata any more than we are dealing with people as disembodied actors engaged in purely cerebral or symbolic exercises. If there is an underlying theme that links together the different periods in the history of the Epirus landscape, it is the theme of resilience to a changeable environment liable to adventitious physical and social changes, in which mobility — of individuals and small groups as well as whole communities — and economies based on mobile animal herds, played a unifying role.

Inter-regional comparisons and long-term perspectives

Discussion of transhumance and the time depth through which it can be traced brings us to some final questions about long-term changes on the largest geographical scale. If there are functional continuities in the ways in which people have responded to the Epirus landscape at different periods, are there nevertheless cumulative changes or directional trends, or evidence of external influences and contacts, and can these be corroborated by the evidence from adjacent regions (Fig. 33.1)?

Here it has to be admitted that the problems of patchiness in the data, particularly the differential survival or discovery of sites, and the potential confounding problems of poor spatial and temporal control, become formidable. These uncertainties are compounded by major climatically-induced environmental changes which are likely to have compelled large-scale reorganization of human activities and their locations in the landscape. In Epirus, for example, our most detailed evidence is limited to sites in the hinterland of eastern Epirus, which were clearly vulnerable to the climatic extremes of the Last

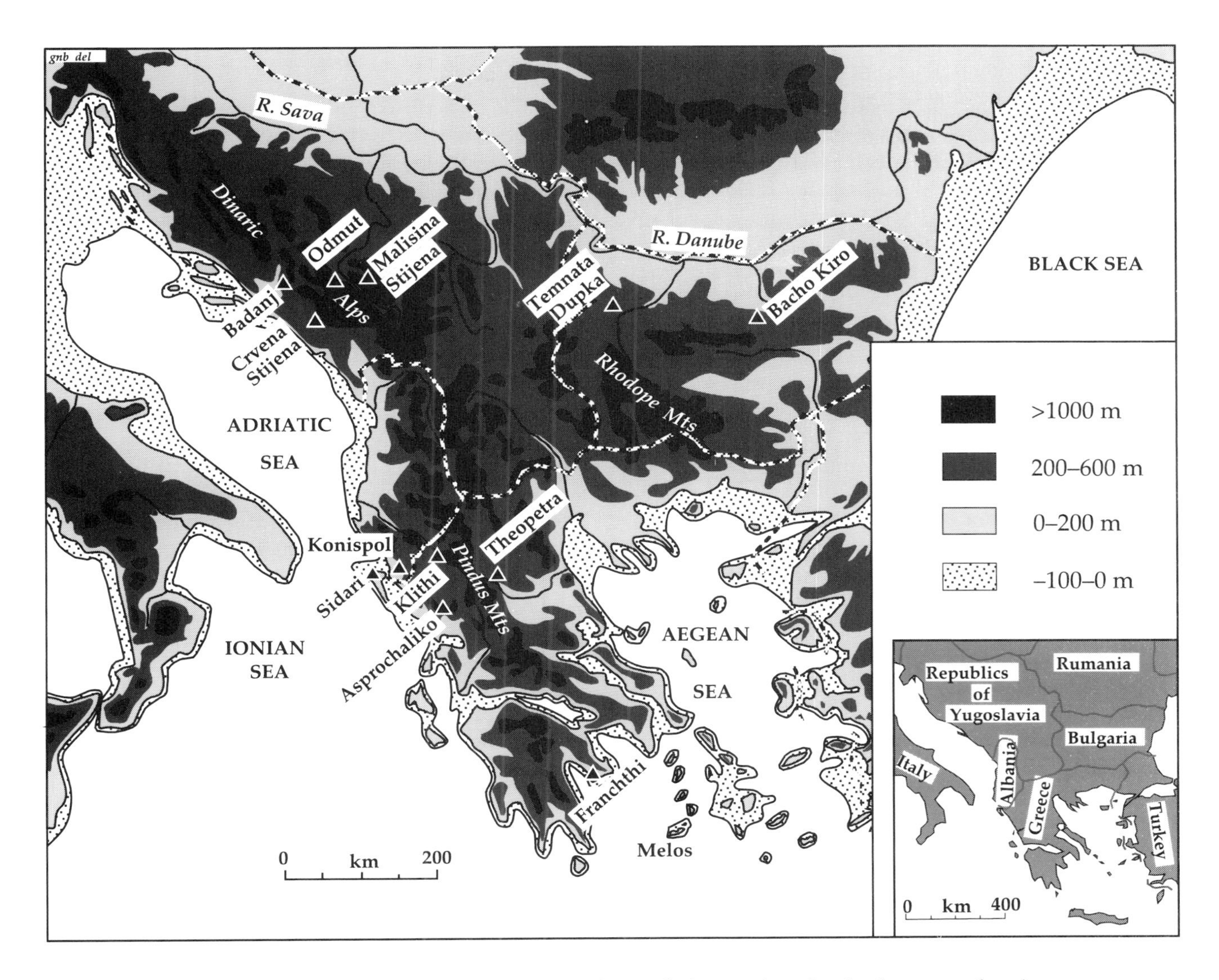

Figure 33.1. *General map of the Balkan region showing sites and places referred to in the text and major palaeogeographical features.*

Glacial, but we have no comparable windows into the sequence of activities nearer the coast, where the impact of increased cold and aridity is likely to have been more subdued. Conversely in the Argolid, the most detailed evidence comes from Franchthi Cave, which would have been vulnerable to changes in use with changes in sea level, but which lacks comparable detail of evidence about the use of a complementary hinterland.

Moreover, as our Epirus data base clearly demonstrates, environmental changes are likely to have had different effects in different areas, and even at different locations within the same valley. In the Voïdomatis basin, discontinuities at one site are not necessarily matched at nearby sites, and reliance on the sequence of activities represented at a single site could clearly be misleading when making comparisons with other areas. Even within the Epirus region, this is a serious difficulty: the Ioannina basin is represented by just one site, Kastritsa, which may not be representative of the full range of activities carried out in the wider basin, and the Louros Valley is represented by just two sites, Asprochaliko and Kokkinopilos, the latter of which has poor chronological control and no organic remains. As for the extensive areas of western Epirus and Kerkyra, we have only one excavation with Upper Palaeolithic remains, namely Grava, and this site probably has a longer sequence than that identified in the limited excavations so far undertaken there (Sordinas, pers. comm.).

With all these difficulties in mind, we must

recognize that such patterns as do emerge point to tentative hypotheses and questions in need of further investigation as much as to final conclusions.

One of the clearest and most striking temporal patterns in the Epirus sequence is the reduction of activity in the hinterland during the extreme conditions of the Last Glacial Maximum, and the subsequent re-expansion of settlement with the Late Glacial amelioration of climate. A similar sequence is apparent elsewhere. In the western Balkans, there is a marked increase in Palaeolithic sites with occupation dated to the Late Glacial period (Bailey & Gamble 1990), and those sites that have long sequences extending into earlier periods appear to indicate a hiatus of activity at about the Last Glacial Maximum, particularly in the mountainous hinterland, notably at Malisina Stijena (Radovanovic 1986). On the karst plateaux of Bulgaria, Temnata Cave shows repeated occupation from Mousterian times through to the Late Glacial but detailed analysis of the data suggests that during the Last Glacial Maximum the site was used much less intensively than in earlier and later periods (Kozlowski *et al.* 1992). Theopetra Cave, on the east side of the Pindus Mountains on the edge of the plain of Thessaly (Fig. 33.1) also appears to have a hiatus between about 25 ka and 14 ka (Kyparissi 1994).

More intriguingly, sites in lowland positions in the southern Balkans, where one might expect the effects of climatic extremes to be less severe, also appear to show a hiatus at this period, for example at Badanj in Bosnia, which lacks evidence of occupation before about 13 ka (Whallon 1989; pers. comm.), arguably at Asprochaliko (with a probable hiatus from 20 ka or earlier to the Postglacial), and most clearly at Franchthi Cave (with a hiatus from about 23 ka to 14 ka). Climatic factors may conceivably play some role in the first two cases, which are situated well inland, but removal of terrestrial resources from the vicinity of Franchthi Cave by extreme climatic conditions seems unlikely, and some other factor must be sought to explain the abandonment of this site during the Last Glacial Maximum. Assuming that the excavations are representative of the original deposit and that there is not some purely local explanation for site abandonment (such as rockfalls that blocked occupation), the most plausible factor is the extreme reduction of sea level at this period, and the consequent exposure of a more extensive coastal lowland with different opportunities for the organization of regional patterns of settlement and land use which rendered the Franchthi location less attractive as a base of activities until rising sea levels once again restored it to an advantageous position.

The difficulty in judging these sequences is that the associated environmental changes are of a cyclical nature: the periodic rise and fall of sea level, for example, and the contraction and expansion of regional tree cover. Hence too narrow a temporal or geographical perspective may persuade us that we are seeing a cumulative change in human responses, involving intensification and population growth, when in fact all we are seeing is a re-adaptation to changed environmental conditions, involving such responses as re-occupation of abandoned areas or dietary broadening no different from that practised at an equivalent stage in an earlier cycle.

Indeed this is the key question at Klithi itself, which offers an instructive example of a rockshelter site that was clearly available for use before 16,500 BP, as demonstrated by the thick buildup of archaeological sterile deposit below the cultural layers, but which was not so used. Is this relatively late appearance of occupation at Klithi linked to a unique window of environmental opportunity of limited duration, to the development of Upper Palaeolithic technologies and techniques of exploiting elusive prey in remote and inaccessible hinterlands and integrating their exploitation into a wider regional network of activities, or to a process of intensification driven perhaps by growing population pressure on existing and more easily available lowland resources?

Gamble (1993) has suggested that the mountain zones of Europe were largely ignored in earlier periods of the Palaeolithic sequence because they represented marginal areas with elusive, unpredictable or low-yielding resources, and that it was only during the Upper Palaeolithic period that effective exploitation of these resources became possible through the development of patterns of social organization that allowed rapid monitoring of and movement between far-flung resource zones, logistic modes of exploitation involving specialist hunting parties, and a host of other social and technical skills that encouraged the development of 'uncertainty specialists' (see also Chapter 12). There is certainly much in the Epirus evidence that would support this general view. One difficulty, however, is why these developments should have been so long delayed in Epirus, if they depended only on an Upper Palaeolithic package of skills that were supposedly available in Europe from at least as early as 40,000 years ago.

One delaying factor could, of course, have been lack of environmental opportunity. A long-standing difficulty with purely environmental explanations for the delayed onset of occupation at Klithi is that similar windows of opportunity should have existed at earlier periods of the Last Glacial sequence, for example during the complex of interstadial conditions that are widely recorded in Europe between about 40,000 and 30,000 years ago. The sedimentary record at Klithi, however, suggests uniform local conditions of aridity and intensive catchment-wide erosion throughout the sequence of archaeologically sterile deposits, in contrast to the upper levels which contain the archaeological material (Woodward, Chapter 18). While we have no dates for the base of this sequence, and no local pollen records extending beyond about 17 ka, it seems possible that the particular combination of ameliorating effects apparent after 17 ka that so favoured the intensification of ibex and chamois hunting — local glacial retreat, reduced erosion of limestone slopes, increased precipitation, river incision and moderate re-afforestation — may be unique to late-glacial conditions, and that we have to go back to the end of the penultimate glacial, some 130,000 years ago, to find an exact environmental analogue.

Another possibility is that the arrival of the Upper Palaeolithic 'package', assuming that it was introduced by the intrusion of anatomically modern populations from the Near East, was delayed by the relative geographical isolation of the Epirus region, and did not reach there until the environmental window of opportunity at Klithi had been closed by climatic deterioration leading up to the Last Glacial Maximum. Certainly the most obvious pathways of population dispersal into southeast Europe from the Near East are along the Danube valley and down the east coast of the Greek peninsula (Fig. 33.1), and both regions have early-dated industries of Aurignacian or similar type at the base of the Upper Palaeolithic sequence, notably at Bacho Kiro in Bulgaria (Kozlowski 1992), and probably at Theopetra Cave in Thessaly (Kyparissi 1994), Franchthi Cave (Perlès 1987), and Kephalari (Felsch 1973; Reisch 1976). Conversely the more broken topography and relatively more favourable climatic conditions of the western Balkans, particularly in Epirus, and the protection afforded by the barriers of the Pindus Mountains and the Dinaric Alps, may have slowed down or filtered the introduction of new influences, resulting in a mosaic of populations including the persistence of local pockets of Mousterian activity. It is certainly intriguing that the earliest Upper Palaeolithic industry at Asprochaliko is relatively late in date and of Gravettian type, and that the final Mousterian at this site is the highly distinctive and localized Asprochaliko industry, which has no analogue elsewhere in Greece or indeed further afield, and marks a sharp technological break with the preceding and more widely distributed Middle Palaeolithic industries (Papaconstantinou 1988; Gowlett & Carter, Chapter 23; Papaconstantinou & Vassilopoulou, Chapter 24). Dating of this industry should have a high priority in any future dating programme. Similarly, the earliest Upper Palaeolithic at Crvena Stijena, though assigned by the original excavators to the Aurignacian (Basler 1975; Benac & Brodar 1958), has not been dated and shows stronger similarities with later Epigravettian industries (Mihailovich 1994). On the other hand Runnels *et al.* (1994) have reported Aurignacian-type material in as yet undated surface collections in western Epirus. In this regard we should note that the coastline may have represented another potential route of dispersal around the south and west of the Greek peninsula, especially at periods of lowered sea level (Fig. 33.1).

Another delaying factor, even for Upper Palaeolithic groups of people, could of course be lack of incentive or pressure, rather than lack of ability. A general difficulty with 'pressure' explanations of this sort, such as population pressure, is that they beg the further question of what caused the pressure. In the Epirus case, there are some intriguing potential answers to this question. For, as the hinterland became more accessible with Late-Glacial climatic amelioration, the coastal zone was beginning to contract with rising sea level. At present we know very little about the resources or archaeology of this now submerged landscape — though the potential for exploration of submerged Palaeolithic finds clearly exists (Flemming 1983) — except that at the maximum lowering of sea level it must have added a sizeable increment to the Epirus landscape. Our current understanding of sea-level change suggests that the maximum regression, and hence the maximum area of coastal lowlands, persisted for some 4000 years, with rapid inundation after about 16 ka (Fig. 28.9). If this lowland environment was rich in exploitable resources, as seems likely, and encouraged the expansion of regional population size, then progressive loss by inundation could well have dislocated pre-existing patterns of subsistence and forced a search for alternative resources or an intensified exploitation of existing ones, including the chamois and ibex populations of the hinterland.

The culmination of marine inundation and the establishment of an essentially modern coastline was completed during the Mesolithic period, perhaps the most enigmatic part of the Epirus sequence. Our evidence for this period is confined to the coast or near-coast regions. The best documented Mesolithic site is the shell midden of Sidari, dated to the eighth millennium BP (Sordinas 1969; 1970; Bailey, Chapter 1). The radiocarbon dates from the Grava rockshelter in the ninth millennium BP (Bailey, Chapter 1; Gowlett *et al.*, Chapter 2) are more problematic, because they are associated with an industry more typical of the Late Glacial and quite unlike the Mesolithic industries recorded at Franchthi Cave from the same time period (Perlès 1990). These surprisingly late dates may perhaps represent a case of isolation at a time when the Kerkyra peninsula was becoming cut off from the mainland by the final rise in sea level, or there may be uncertainties about their stratigraphic associations. However that may be, other Mesolithic material identified by the presence of geometric microliths has been reported from surface sites in coastal locations on mainland Epirus by Runnels *et al.* (1994). At Franchthi Cave, both the artefactual and subsistence data suggest that in the Mesolithic period the site was used as a year-round base with subsistence focused on plant and marine resources (Deith & Shackleton 1988; Hansen 1991; Perlès 1990). This does not mean that there was no exploitation of the hinterland, though none has yet been found, but elsewhere in Europe Mesolithic occupation of wooded hinterlands is notoriously elusive, notably in northern Spain, where human settlement seems to have been confined to the coast edge in the form of shell middens (Bailey 1983; Clark 1983; Straus 1979). On the other hand Mesolithic material has been recovered from inland locations in other parts of western Europe. Mesolithic deposits of demonstrably Postglacial date in inland locations have also been recorded at Medena Stijena (located very close to Malisina Stijena) and the Odmut Cave in Montenegro (Srejovic 1989), and at Theopetra Cave in Thessaly (Kyparissi 1994), none of which can be described as coastal (Fig. 33.1), and even the trace of Mesolithic activity at Asprochaliko is rather a long way inland to be described as a coastal location. It is of course conceivable that the evidence of the Mesolithic in Epirus is more elusive and located in less well-preserved open-air locations, or that we have not yet looked in the right places. Winder (Chapter 31), on the other hand, provides some compelling arguments based on modelling of the long-term interactions between human and animal populations and environmental change, to suggest that human populations at, or shortly before, this time may indeed have been exposed to increased risks of overexploiting their traditional prey by the joint encroachment of rising sea level on one side and expanding forests on the other, forcing exploitation of alternative resources.

One pattern stands out throughout the Epirus sequence, and that is the dominance of the lowland and coastal regions of western Epirus as the primary core of human settlement at all periods, with the longest sequences of occcupation, the earliest dates, the greatest continuity of settlement, and the highest population densities. All signs point to the hinterland of eastern Epirus as a rather specialized and marginal zone of seasonal activity, used intermittently in a cyclical pattern determined in part by fluctuating environmental conditions. This leads to the paradoxical conclusion that the rockshelter sites in eastern Epirus that have been our major focus of attention, which have the best conditions of preservation, and which have produced most of our well-dated evidence and by far our biggest collections of lithic and faunal assemblages, represent quite a small fragment of the regional settlement pattern, and that the lowland sites of western Epirus, in spite of the poor preservation and dating of most of them, represent the main regional focus of settlement. The lowlands of western Epirus would always have been the most favourable environmental zone, with more equable climates, greater faunal and floristic diversity, and the widest range and greatest abundance of resources, particularly at periods of lowered sea level, and perhaps also the possibility of more far-reaching contacts along coastlines and through sea-borne connections. The nature and history of the now submerged coastal landscape and the use made of it by prehistoric human populations emerges as one of our greatest areas of ignorance, and one of the greatest challenges to future research.

Conclusion

After more than a decade of sustained investigation and 32 chapters of analysis and interpretation, this discussion would not be complete without some attempt to evaluate whether the effort was worth it, and whether it should be repeated.

Does our approach provide a model for future research, or does it point to a need to rethink the most fundamental terms and categories that underpin the study of a regional prehistory? Some of the questions posed at the beginning of this project have been answered, or answered to an acceptable degree of approximation. In other cases, decisive evidence that would help to resolve the uncertainties raised by the results, or to reduce the extent of our ignorance, is still beyond our grasp, although the nature of the data that needs to be sought out is at least a little clearer, and some at least of that data is technically within our reach. Yet other questions appear to be intrinsically unanswerable, or to require investment of resources on a scale which far exceeds the will or capacity of current institutional arrangements for funding archaeological research.

The combination of different disciplines and different specialists has been a major feature of the project, and has produced benefits often hard won in the face of conflicting ideas and ambiguous field data, generating its own momentum of unresolved tensions and resulting in changed perceptions, new questions, different methods of observation, and unanticipated challenges for future investigation.

Our work has been conducted on a variety of different scales, and questions about the adequacy of the samples and the resolution of the data have cropped up at many different points in the investigation. The smallest scale, that of the individual site and its contents, presents us with some of our most difficult challenges, both of practice and of philosophy. If Klithi represents such a small fragment, temporally and geographically, of Palaeolithic activity in the region at large, should it deserve so much time and effort in its investigation, however much it may have served as a focus for synthesizing the evidence from a wider area? How many more Klithis, and how many more lifetimes of endeavour, are needed to provide a representative coverage of the region? Could we have obtained the same result from Klithi by digging faster, or by digging less? Our experience emphatically rules out the option of digging faster, and it is to be hoped that any future excavation of the site will take note of the lessons to be learned from our results. Digging less may seem to offer a more desirable option, especially in view of the uniformity of the bone and lithic assemblages, but that result was not predictable at the outset and has only emerged as the outcome of the excavation strategy originally adopted.

This brings us to the question of intra-site analysis and the search for spatial patterning and activity areas, which has formed such a prominent objective of the excavation. At one level this must be deemed a failure, at least to the extent that it has yielded the barest glimmer of any patterning that ethnographic studies of camping arrangements, social interactions and fine-grained variability might have led us to expect, and we have to ask whether this is a failure of our techniques, of the data available, or of our expectations.

It cannot, on any view, be said to be a failure of techniques, given the amount of care and time devoted to the collection and analysis of the data. No amount of further stratigraphic refinement or multivariate number-crunching will squeeze more resolution out of Klithi (see Winder, Chapter 14; Galanidou, Chapter 15).

As for the inadequacies of the data, Pompeii-like sites are sometimes claimed in Palaeolithic contexts, and may indeed yield fine-grained interpretations in terms of individual actions and inter-individual social interactions. But these sites are rare and lie at the extreme end of a very wide spectrum, at the other end of which are palimpsests on surface sites that cannot be dated with a resolution much better than tens of millennia. To privilege the high-resolution sites over all the others would be to write off as worthless virtually all of the data available in Epirus, and indeed most of the Palaeolithic record elsewhere.

In truth, to describe the data as inherently inadequate may be simply a way of externalizing the failure to ask appropriate questions, or to recognize the inappropriateness of existing preconceptions. Klithi may not give us a sharply defined moment frozen in time, but it certainly gives evidence of spatial structure, a structure that persisted virtually without change for nearly 4000 years (Galanidou, Chapter 15). It seems more rewarding to ask why that structure should have persisted for that particular span of time and in that particular place in the wider context of a regional prehistory, rather than to bemoan the fact that Klithi cannot give us a more detailed image of everyday life in the Epigravettian, or to attempt to create such an image by speculative means or the application of untestable theories of doubtful relevance to produce a narrative that is little better than fiction.

Similarly at the regional scale we have to accept that the great majority of human activity in the landscape has left its trace on open-air sites with poor and often non-existent stratigraphic control and exceedingly poor temporal resolution. No amount of wishful thinking, typological argument or geological guesswork can infuse such data with chronological control to compare even with a well-excavated rockshelter. We have to accept that such data must be treated in a different way, and used to focus on a different scale of activity. Indeed once we begin to think more carefully about terms such as contemporaneity in such a context, the very concept itself turns out to be an illusion (Papaconstantinou & Vassilopoulou, Chapter 24).

If increased time depth seems necessarily to

reduce temporal resolution and takes us further away from the conventional expectations of a fine-grained anthropological or ecological study, does an expanded temporal perspective offer compensating advantages? One of the dominant strands in current archaeological theory is the emphasis on the individual as the prime unit of study and interpretation, not least because this is also the dominant orthodoxy in those disciplines which archaeologists most often resort to for theoretical inspiration, whether it is biological theory, at least in its neo-Darwinian form, or sociological theory, both of which, as Mithen (1989) aptly points out, share an emphasis on the individual.

It seems unsurprising that theories based on small-scale participant observation of present phenomena should focus on individuals as units of behaviour. But it seems equally remarkable that anyone should expect theories and concepts built around such observations to provide a sufficient key to the interpretation of an archaeological site like Klithi, where the irreducible unit of behavioural observation has a time span of at least 500 years, is one of many other such units which in aggregate span a duration of at least 100,000 years, and is set within a landscape which has undergone a process of continual and sometimes dramatic remoulding, often under the impetus of processes which happen too slowly or with too little impact to be visible in the lifetime of an individual. If there is any sort of theory, whether we call it ecological, social or otherwise, that can be built around such a record, it is not a theory that will be instantly recognizable let alone acceptable to the theorist of modern social or biological phenomena, or that can be acquired by diligent scouring of the textbook literature. It is a theory that we will have to create for ourselves, and one that will only grow from the experience of working with the primary evidence.

The two most overtly theoretical chapters in this volume, by Winder (Chapter 31) and Green (Chapter 32), provide some interesting pointers as to how such a theory or set of theories might develop. Both approach the problem of interpreting the Palaeolithic past from radically different starting points and with radically different methodologies, rooted in conventional biological theory and mathematical modelling on the one hand, and social theory and participant observation on the other. But both find that thinking through their core variables in the context of a 100,000 year old prehistoric landscape moves them far from their starting point. It is of particular interest that from such different origins both have converged on issues of mobility, competition and dispersal in a topographically complex and changing environment.

Winder shows that modelling long-term interactions between humans, plants and animals as a self-organizing system leads inescapably to processes of 'meta-selection', meshed in with specific features of the physical environment, that operate on entities at a much larger scale than the individual. This is a conclusion which demolishes along the way the myth that humans had no impact on their environment before the development of agriculture, and drives a large hole through neo-Darwinian orthodoxy. Green emphasizes the impact of the physical landscape and the theme of mobility as a constant in an unstable physical and political environment, resulting in an 'interweaving' of social, physical and cognitive factors. The common element emphasized in both approaches is the particular physical features of the landscape in which social and ecological relations are played out, and the ways in which this affects mobility, dispersal and escape from or tolerance of competitors and predators. Both chapters bring out the altered theoretical perspective which results from an expanded time perspective, and highlight the entirely arbitrary nature of the conventional separation between 'nature' and 'culture' in the context of present and prehistoric patterns of land use.

It is not that the role of individuals or of historical contingency has ceased to be important. On the contrary these continue to have a place as proximate and sometimes dominant factors in both theoretical approaches. It is rather that they are nested within and to some extent shaped by larger-scale and longer-term processes which cannot be properly evaluated without a long-term perspective. It is difficult to resist the conclusion that the physical features of the landscape, the perceptions of the people who live in it, their social relations of settlement and dispersal, and their ecological relations with plants and animals, form a co-evolutionary whole, with resultant structures of great durability and flexibility which continue to be embodied in the activities of the present-day inhabitants.

Either we accept that the prehistoric record cannot deliver the sorts of answers that existing conventions require, or can do so only by speculative reconstructions that make virtually no contact with the empirical realities supplied by field investigation, or we accept that the sorts of questions we ask and the terms in which we answer them have to be rethought along lines that are intrinsically alien to established orthodoxies of social and biological theory or current intellectual fashions, and which take due account of the changed focus that comes with a longer-term perspective. Either we take seriously the notion that the deeper record of the prehistoric past has the capacity to alter the way we think about ourselves and our past, or we accept that it is doomed to reflect in a merely passive manner pre-existing conceptions, and hence to play an essentially peripheral role in the drama of human existence.

If these volumes help to focus attention on these choices and their further implications, to highlight the value of a long-term perspective, to encourage optimism about the virtues of grappling long and purposefully with the hard realities of human artefacts in unyielding landscapes, to stimulate genuine dialogue across disciplinary boundaries with all the uncomfortable exposure of unrecognized preconceptions that must necessarily follow, and to create a sense of future possibility about the exploration of unknown territory, both physical and intellectual, then they will have served a wider purpose than that of simply filling in a few blanks on another page in a descriptive narrative of a regional prehistory.

Note

1. There are 69 dp4s, one of the best represented anatomical elements, in Gamble's faunal sample. Assume that each comes from a different animal. Double the number to allow for the adult animals whose heads are under-represented (138). Double this number again to allow for the bone data from the 1988 excavations not included in the Gamble sample (276). Assume that the volume of excavated deposit is just 3 per cent of the total (Chapter 3), and multiply the MNI accordingly (9200). Divide by a total span of occupation of 3000 years.

Appendices

Appendix A

Thermoluminescence Dating of Sediment from Epirus

Nick Debenham

Eighteen sediment samples were examined by thermoluminescence (TL), ten from the Doliana basin (DOL), four from the Voidomatis Gorge (VOI), and four from Kokkinopilos (KOK). A list of samples, TL measurements and TL ages is summarized in the accompanying table.

A general description of the method of thermoluminescence dating is given by Aitken (1985). The TL method for dating sediments relies on the removal of TL ('bleaching') when the material was deposited and exposed to light. For this reason, those parts of the samples which may have been exposed to light at the time of collection were first discarded. Fine grains from the rest of the samples were dispersed in dilute hydrochloric acid, and those settling in times between 2 and 20 minutes were selected. They were washed in distilled water, methanol and acetone, and deposited onto aluminium discs. About half of the discs were exposed to daylight for a few days to remove the bleachable TL signal. These discs were then irradiated with various doses of beta or alpha radiation to regenerate their TL. Measurement of these discs yielded the growth curve of regenerated TL against dose. The growth measurements were fitted by a curve of sub-linear form. The doses which induced a TL intensity equal to that of the natural material (natural regeneration doses) were then evaluated from data at 300°C.

The dose rates due to alpha and beta radiations were assessed by alpha counting and potassium analyses of the samples (see listing below for measurements). The environmental dose rates contributed by gamma radiation and cosmic rays were measured *in situ* by means of gamma spectrometry, and by alpha counting and potassium analyses of the sediments. The dose rate assessments for the samples are also summarized below.

TL dates were determined by an iterative calculation, in which alpha induced TL intensity and that generated by beta, gamma and cosmic rays are determined. The method yields the time required to produce intensities of these signals which sum to the natural TL level. The dates have been corrected for fading of the TL signal assuming a saturating exponential dependence of TL date against true age (see Debenham 1985). The quoted errors combine random and systematic uncertainties, and refer to the 68 per cent confidence level. Minimum dates only are given for those samples whose dates are indistinguishable from the practical upper age limit for dating sediments, which is approximately 150 ka.

BM reference	Site reference	Beta dose rate AD (Grays)	Alpha dose rate AD (μm^{-2})	Alpha dose rate (μm^{-2}/ka)	Beta dose rate (Gy/ka)	External dose rate (Gy/ka)	TL age (ka BP)
DOL1	TL-86-1 Avlaki Rema: Unit C Section PA5 Loess	457 ± 142	395 ± 54	0.719	1.552	0.997	>150
DOL2	TL-86-2 Mazaraki SE: Unit A Section PA18 Cherty fan	179 ± 32	179 ± 42	1.242	1.460	1.510	51 ± 14

BM reference	Site reference	Beta dose rate AD (Grays)	Alpha dose rate AD (μm^{-2})	Alpha dose rate (μm^{-2}/ka)	Beta dose rate (Gy/ka)	External dose rate (Gy/ka)	TL age (ka BP)
DOL3	TL-86-3 Mazaraki SE: Unit B Section PA18 Chert/clay-banded fan	504 ± 75	310 ± 52	1.368	1.766	1.440	>105
DOL6	TL-86-6 Roupsia: Unit B Section PA3/1 Loess	276 ± 50	546 ± 110	0.732	1.236	1.157	>140
DOL7	TL-86-7 Roupsia: Unit C Section PA3/1 Red clay	343 ± 53	375 ± 118	0.889	1.746	1.497	126+48–32
DOL8	TL-86-8 Kephalovrisi: Unit F Section PA12	592 ± 50	398 ± 40	1.023	1.365	0.765	>150
DOL9	TL-86-9 Kephalovrisi: Unit C Section PA12 Chert/clay-banded fan	382 ± 92	210 ± 35	0.829	0.956	0.765	>140
DOL18	TL-86-18 Doliana–Tseravinas Rd: Unit C Section PA45 Loess	296 ± 65	245 ± 54	0.859	1.583	1.133	119+47–32
DOL26	TL-87-6 Katarraktes: Unit B Section PA30 30 m terrace of Kalamas River	12.7 ± 2.3	9.7 ± 1.8	0.559	1.051	0.802	4.2 ± 0.6
DOL31	Sitaria Loess	179 ± 26	126 ± 20	2.848	2.784	2.747	19.7 ± 3.8
VOI23	VOI-87-3 Klithonia Old Bridge: 50 m upstream Red soil over Aristi Unit gravels	77 ± 16	97 ± 18	0.728	1.358	1.066	28.2 ± 7.1
VOI24	VOI-87-4 Bar A: 1 km upstream of Aristi Road Bridge Soil on surface of Vikos Unit	65 ± 7	67 ± 5	0.755	1.434	1.208	19.6 ± 3.0
VOI25	VOI-87-5 Bar C: Aristi Road Bridge Red soil over Aristi Unit	7.1 ± 1.8	6.7 ± 1.0	1.078	1.769	1.158	1.2 ± 0.4
VOI26	VOI-87-6 Kipi Unit	517 ± 80	446 ± 37	0.471	1.435	0.673	>150
KOK10	TL-86-10 SW side of 'bow': Layer D Red/gray gravel	403 ± 80	–	1.046	1.452	1.427	>150
KOK11	TL-86-11 NE side of 'bow': Layer D Red/gray clay	438 ± 37	–	1.141	1.375	1.427	>150
KOK13	TL-86-13 Site beta: Layer D/C Yellow bed	538 ± 70	–	1.259	1.458	1.576	>150
KOK14	TL-86-14 Site beta: Layer D Red bed	560 ± 80	–	0.913	1.311	1.398	>150

Notes

1. These analyses were undertaken at the British Museum.
2. Uncertainties in alpha dose rates are approximately ± 12 per cent, in beta dose rates approximately ± 11 per cent. The external dose rate uncertainties vary between ± 9 per cent and ± 21 per cent.
3. For samples from Kokkinopilos (KOK), dates were calculated assuming a β-value of 1.1 ± 0.3 Gy.μm^2

Appendix B

Participants in the Klithi Field Seasons

Names are listed with their institutional affiliation or home base at the time in question.

1983

E. Adam (London University), G.N. Bailey (Cambridge University), S. Bailey (Cambridge), P.L. Carter (Cambridge University), S. Coleman (Cambridge University), V. Fotou (Ioannina University), C.S. Gamble (Southampton University), A. Gibbs (Cambridge University), J.A.J. Gowlett (Oxford University), H. Higgs (Cambridge University), B. Higgs (Cambridge), M. Higgs (Cambridge), P. Higgs (Cambridge), H. Jones (Cambridge University), S. King (London University), E. Morris (Southampton University), V. Papaconstantinou (Université Paris X), C. Roubet (Institut de Paléontologie Humaine, Paris), C.A. Shell (Cambridge University), D. Sturdy (Bermuda Maritime Museum), C. Sturdy (Bermuda Maritime Museum), N. Tiley (Cambridge), E. Utsi (Cambridge University), V. Utsi (Cambridge), D. Webley (Cardiff University), J. Webley (Cardiff), D. Vassilopoulou (Université Paris X), T. Wasilewski (Cambridge), P. Wilby (Devon).

1984

E. Adam (London University), S. Allen (Southampton University), G.N. Bailey (Cambridge University), V. Fotou (Ioannina University), C.S. Gamble (Southampton University), S. Goodale (Cambridge University), S.F. Green (Cambridge University), J.A.J. Gowlett (Oxford University), H. Higgs (Cambridge University), M-J. Holmes (Cambridge University), H. Kellett (Barrow-in-Furness), B. Ibbs (Cambridge University), M. Johnson (Cambridge University), S. Joyce (Southampton University), D. Kamarinou (Ioannina University), G.C.P. King (Cambridge University), H. Kloosterman (Cambridge), E. Kotjabopoulou (Ioannina University), N. Kyriazis (Ioannina University), L. Martin (London University), C. Merchant (Southampton University), R. Montague (Cambridge University), E. Moss (London University), R. Mühlen-Schulte (ANU, Canberra), M. Newbury (Southampton University), M. Newcomer (London University), M. Nicola (Cambridge University), V. Papaconstantinou (Université Paris X), R. Perry (Southampton University), M. Rawling (Southampton University), C. Roubet (Institut de Paléontologie Humaine, Paris), A. Sampson (Chalkis Ephoreia), J. Sherman (Cambridge University), A. Sinclair (Cambridge University), F. Suffield (Southampton University), C. Turner (Open University, Milton Keynes), D. Vassilopoulou (Université Paris X), S. Wilford (Southampton University), K. Zachos (Speleology Ephoreia Athens).

1985

E. Adam (London University & Speleology Ephoreia Athens), V. Adamandidou (Ioannina University), F. Allard (Cambridge University), S. Allen (Southampton University), G.N. Bailey (Cambridge University), C. Batho (London University), T. Cadbury (Cambridge), D. Cleasby (Cambridge University), C. Councell (Southampton University), K. Dalton (Southampton University), S. Duffin (Cambridge University), R. Eames (Cambridge University), P. Edwards (Southampton University), R. Fowler (Cambridge University), C.S. Gamble (Southampton University), N. Garnett (London University), P. Godfrey (Ipswich), J.A.J. Gowlett (Oxford University), R. Grace (London University), S.F. Green (Cambridge University), E. Hall (London University), H. Higgs (Cambridge University), S. Hinds (Southampton University), M. Horton (London University), S. Joyce (Southampton University), E. Kostala (Cambridge University), G.C.P. King (Cambridge University), E. Kotjabopoulou (Ioannina University), N. Kyriazis (Ioannina University), M. Macklin (Newcastle University), T. Marchant (Southampton University), C. Merchant (Southampton University), R. Montague (Cambridge University), E. Moss (London University), P. Nash (London University), M. Newcomer (London University), P. Newcomer (London), M. Nicola (Cambridge University), J. Ogden (Berkeley,

California), S. Olsen (London University), E. Osborn (London), C. Roubet (Institut de Paléontologie Humaine, Paris), A. Sinclair (Cambridge University), M. Sioboti (Ioannina University), S. Smith (Cambridge University), J. Steele (Southampton University), K. Storey (Cambridge University), K. Struthers (Southampton University), D. Sturdy (Bermuda Maritime Museum), C. Sturdy (Bermuda Maritime Museum), C. Turner (Open University, Milton Keynes), S. Voutsaki (Cambridge University), D. Webley (Cardiff University), J. Webley (Cardiff), S. Wilford (Southampton University), K. Willis (Cambridge University), G. Wilson (Southampton University), M. Ydo (Amsterdam University), A. Zaouri (Ioannina University).

1986

G.N. Bailey (Cambridge University), C. Batho (London University), T. Cadbury (Southampton University), C.S. Gamble (Southampton University), B. Ibbs (Cambridge University), E. Kotjabopoulou (Ioannina University), M. Koumouzeli (Speleology Ephoreia Athens), J. Kozlowski (Jagellionian University Krakow), J. Lewin (University College Wales Aberystwyth), J. Lewin (Aberystwyth), M. Macklin (Newcastle University), R. Mason (Dunedin), C. Roubet (Institut de Paléontologie Humaine, Paris), A. Sinclair (Cambridge University), S. Smith (Cambridge University), M. Sioboti (Ioannina University), D. Sturdy (Bermuda Maritime Museum), C. Sturdy (Bermuda Maritime Museum), G. Thomas (Kidwelly), C. Turner (Open University, Milton Keynes), D. Webley (Cardiff University), J. Webley (Cardiff), K. Willis (Cambridge University), J. Woodward (Cambridge University), M. Ydo (Amsterdam University), A. Zaouri (Ioannina University).

1987

L. Adams (Southampton University), G.N. Bailey (Cambridge University), N. Debenham (British Museum), C.S. Gamble (Southampton University), S. Goodale (Cambridge University), S.F. Green (Cambridge University), H. Higgs (Cambridge University), G.C.P. King (US Geological Survey Denver), B. Knight (London University), E. Kotzambopoulou (Ioannina University), Z. Kuzundjic (Sarajevo Museum), J. Lewin (University College Wales Aberystwyth), J. Lewin (Aberystwyth), M. Macklin (Newcastle University), R. Mason (Dunedin), P. Miracle (Ann Arbor University Michigan), M. Newcomer (London University), S. Olsen (London University), C. Roubet (Institut de Paléontologie Humaine, Paris), S. Scaife (London University), W. Shawcross (ANU, Canberra), S. Smith (Cambridge University), S. Stiros (IGME Athens), T. Stone (ANU Canberra), D. Sturdy (Bermuda Maritime Museum), C. Sturdy (Bermuda Maritime Museum), F. Wenban-Smith (London), J. Whitney (US Geological Survey Denver), S. Wilford (Cambridge University), N. Winder (Cambridge University), J. Woodward (Cambridge University).

1988

G.N. Bailey (Cambridge University), N. Galanidou (Athens), W. Giles (Sheffield), S. Kemp (London University), M. Lewin (Aberystwyth), K. Marabeli (Speleology Ephoreia Athens), Ph. Papaiannou-Stathaki (Athens), C. Roubet (Institut de Paléontologie Humaine, Paris), D. Sturdy (Liverpool University), C. Sturdy (Liverpool), G. Thomas (Kidwelly), C. Turner (Open University, Milton Keynes), T. Way (London University), D. Webley (Cardiff University), J. Webley (Cardiff), F. Wenban-Smith (London), J. Woodward (Cambridge University).

1989

E. Adam (Athens), G.N. Bailey (Cambridge University), T. Cadbury (Southampton University), C. Clements (Cambridge University), S. Crowe (Liverpool University), J.A.J. Gowlett (Liverpool University), K. Gowlett (Liverpool), R. Jameson (Liverpool University), E. Kotjabopoulou (Speleology Ephoreia Athens), S. Milliken (Oxford University), D. Papagianni (Athens University), C. Roubet (Institut de Paléontologie Humaine, Paris), K. Skourtopoulou (Thessaloniki University), T. Wilson (Cambridge University), N. Winder (Cambridge University).

1992

E. Adam (Ioannina), G.N. Bailey (Cambridge University), T. Cadbury (Cambridge University), R. Cosgrove (La Trobe University Melbourne), F. Cosgrove (Melbourne), N. Galanidou (Cambridge University), S.F. Green (Cambridge University), C. Ioakim (IGME Athens), E. Kotjabopoulou (Speleology Ephoreia Athens), T. Murray (La Trobe University Melbourne), D. Papagianni (Athens University), C. Turner (Open University, Milton Keynes), S. Van der Leeuw (Cambridge University).

White. Philadelphia (PA): University of Philadelphia Press, 181–97.

Dibble, H.L., 1989. The implications of stone tool types for the presence of language during the Lower and Middle Palaeolithic, in Mellars & Stringer (eds.), 415–32.

Dibble, H.L. & O. Bar-Yosef, 1995. *The Definition and Interpretation of Levallois Technology*. (Monographs in World Archaeology 23.) Madison (WI): Prehistory Press.

Drobniewicz, B., B. Ginter, S. Ivanova & N. Sirakov, 1982. Middle Palaeolithic finds, in Kozlowski (ed.), 81–116.

Drobniewicz, B., B. Ginter & J.K. Kozlowski, 1992. The Gravettian sequence, in Kozlowski *et al.* (eds.), 95–501.

Escalon de Fonton, M. & G. Onoratini, 1982. Éléments de structures d'habitat des gisements de Provence et du Languedoc, in *Les Habitats du Paléolithique Superieur. Actes du Colloque International en Hommage au Professeur A. Leroi-Gourhan*. Roanne-Villerest: C.N.R.S., 72–6.

Everett, J.R., M. Morisawa & M.N. Short, 1986. Tectonic landforms, in *Geomorphology from Space: a Global Overview of Regional Landforms*, eds. N.M. Short & R.W. Blair. Washington (DC): NASA, 27–185.

Fairbanks, R.G., 1989. A 17,000-year-old glacioeustatic sea level record: influence of glaial melting rates on the Younger Dryas event and deep ocean circulation. *Nature* 342, 637–42.

Farrand, W.R., 1975. Sediment analysis of a prehistoric rockshelter: the Abri Pataud. *Quaternary Research* 5, 1–26.

Farrand, W.R., 1979. Chronology and palaeoenvironment of Levantine prehistoric sites as seen from sediment studies. *Journal of Archaeological Science* 6, 369–92.

Farrand, W.R., 1985. Rockshelter and cave sediments, in Stein & Farrand (eds.), 21–40.

Felsch, R.C.S., 1973. Die Höhle von Kephalari. Eine jungpaläolithishce Siedlung in der Argolis. *Αρχαιολογικαϖ Αναλεκτα εξ Αθηνων* 6, 13–27.

Flannery, K., J. Marcus & J. Reynolds, 1989. *Flocks of the Wamani*. New York (NY): Academic Press.

Flemming, N.C., 1983. Survival of submerged lithic and bronze age artifact sites: a review of case histories, in Masters & Flemming (eds.), 135–73.

Follieri, M., D. Magri & L. Sadori, 1988. 250,000-year pollen record from Valle di Castiglione (Roma). *Pollen et Spores* 30, 329–56.

Ford, D.C. & P.W. Williams, 1989. *Karst Geomorphology and Hydrology*. London: Unwin-Hyman.

Foss, A., 1978. *Epirus*. London: Faber.

Friedman, E., N. Goren-Inbar, A. Rosenfeld, O. Marder & F. Burian, 1995. Hafting during Mousterian times: further indication. *Journal of the Israel Prehistoric Society* 26, 8–31.

Friedman, G.M. & J.E. Sanders, 1978. *Principles of Sedimentology*. New York (NY): Wiley.

Fuller, I.C., M.G. Macklin, D.G. Passmore, P.A. Brewer, J. Lewin & A.G. Wintle, 1996. Geochronologies and environmental records of Quaternary fluvial sequences in the Guadalope basin, northeast Spain, based on luminescence dating, in *Global Continental Changes: the Context of Palaeohydrology*, eds. J. Branson, A.G. Brown & K.J. Gregory. (Special Publication 115.) London: Geological Society, 99–120.

Furlan, D., 1977. The climate of southeast Europe, in *Climates of Central and Southern Europe*, ed. C.C. Wallen. Amsterdam: Elsevier Scientific Publishing Company, 185–223.

Gabori-Csank, V., 1968. *La Station du Paléolithique moyen d'Erd–Hongrie*. Budapest: Academie des Sciences de Hongrie.

Gabori-Csank, V., 1983. La Grotte Remete 'Felso' (Supérieure) et le 'Szeletien de Transdanubie'. *Acta Archaeologica Academiae Scientarum Hungaricae* 35, 249–85.

Gaki-Papanastassiou, K. & H. Maroukian, 1995. Late Quaternary controls on river behaviour in the eastern part of the Argive plain, eastern Peloponnese, Greece, in Lewin *et al.* (eds.), 89–95.

Gamble, C.S., 1986. *The Palaeolithic Settlement of Europe*. Cambridge: Cambridge University Press.

Gamble, C.S., 1993. *Timewalkers: the Prehistory of Global Colonization*. Stroud: Sutton.

Gaudreau, D.C., S.T. Jackson & T. Webb III, 1989. Spatial scale and sampling strategy in palaeoecological studies of vegetation patterns in mountain terrain. *Acta Botanica Neerlandica* 38(4), 369–90.

Gause, G., 1934. *The Struggle for Existence*. Baltimore (MD): Williams & Wilkins.

Gilbertson, D.D., D.A. Holyoak, C.O. Hunt & F.N. Paget, 1983. Palaeoecology of Late Quaternary floodplain deposits in Tuscany: the Feccia valley at Frosini. *Archeologia Medievale* 10, 340–50.

Gillespie, R., J.A.J. Gowlett, E.T. Hall, R.E.M. Hedges & C. Perry, 1985. Radiocarbon dates from the Oxford AMS system: Archaeometry datelist 2. *Archaeometry* 27(2), 237–46.

Gillieson, D., 1986. Cave sedimentation in the New Guinea Highlands. *Earth Surface Processes and Landforms* 11, 533–43.

Gillieson, D., F. Oldfield & A. Krawiecki, 1986. Records of prehistoric soil erosion from rockshelter sites in Papua New Guinea. *Mountain Research and Development* 6, 315–24.

Goldberg, P., 1972. Analyses of sediments of Jerf Ajla and Yabrud rockshelters, Syria. *Proceedings of the VIII INQUA Congress, Paris*, 747–54.

Gomez, B., 1987. The alluvial terraces and fills of the Lower Vasilikos Valley, in the vicinity of Kalavasos, Cyprus. *Transactions of the Institute of British Geographers* (New Series) 12, 345–59.

Gordon, A.D. & H.J.B. Birks, 1972. Numerical methods in Quaternary palaeoecology. *New Phytologist* 71, 961–7.

Gould, R.A., 1977. *Puntutjarpa Rockshelter and the Australian Desert Culture*. (Anthropological Papers 54.) New York (NY): American Museum of Natural History.

Gowlett, J.A.J., R.E.M. Hedges, I.A. Law & C. Perry, 1987. Radiocarbon dates from the Oxford AMS system: Archaeometry datelist 5. *Archaeometry* 29, 125–55.

Green, S., 1994. Contemporary change in use and perception of the landscape in Epirus: an ethnographic study, in *Understanding the Natural and Anthropogenic Causes of Land Degradation in the Mediterranean Basin*, vol. I, ed. S.E. van der Leeuw. Land Degradation in Epirus; Report for Directorate General XII of the Commission of the European Union, 171–324.

Green, S. & M. Lemon, 1996. Perceptual landscapes in agrarian systems: degradation processes in northwestern Epirus and the Argolid Valley, Greece. *Ecumene* 3(2), 183–201.

Greig, J.R.A. & J. Turner, 1974. Some pollen diagrams from Greece and their archaeological significance. *Journal of Archaeological Science* 1, 177–94.

Griffin, G.M., 1971. Interpretation of X-ray diffraction data, in Carver (ed.), 541–69.

Gross, M.G., 1971. Carbon determination, in Carver (ed.), 573–96.

Grün, R., H.P. Schwarcz & S. Zymela, 1987. ESR dating of tooth enamel. *Canadian Journal of Earth Science* 24, 1022–37.

Hack, J., 1942. The changing physical environment of the Hopi Indians of Arizona. *Harvard University Peabody Museum of Archaeology and Ethnology Papers* 35, 1–85.

Halácsy, E. von, 1894. Beiträg zur Flora von Epirus. *Denkschriften der mathematisch-naturwissenschaftlichen Classe der Kaiserlichen Akademie der Wissenschaften* 61, 1–52.

Halstead, P., 1987. Traditional and ancient rural economy in Mediterranean Europe: plus ça change. *Hesperia: Journal of Hellenic Studies* 107, 77–87.

Hammond, N.G.L., 1967. *Epirus: the Geography, the Ancient Remains, the History and the Topography of Epirus and Adjacent Areas*. Oxford: Clarendon Press.

Hansen, J.M., 1991. *The Palaeoethnobotany of Franchthi Cave*. (Excavations at Franchthi Cave, Greece 7.) Bloomington (IN): Indiana University Press.

Hardy, D.A. & A.C. Renfrew (eds.), 1991. *Thera and the Aegean World III, Proceedings of the Third International Congress, Santorini, Greece, 3–9 September 1989*, vol. 3: *Chronology*. London: Thera Foundation.

Hardy, D.A., C.G. Doumas, J.A. Sakellarakis & P.M. Warren (eds.), 1991a. *Thera and the Aegean World III, Proceedings of the Third International Congress, Santorini, Greece, 3–9 September 1989*, vol. 1: *Archaeology*. London: Thera Foundation.

Hardy, D.A., J. Keller, V.P. Galanopoulos, N.C. Flemming & T.H. Druitt (eds.), 1991b. *Thera and the Aegean World III, Proceedings of the Third International Congress, Santorini, Greece, 3–9 September 1989*, vol. 2: *Earth Sciences*. London: Thera Foundation.

Harris, D.R. & C. Vita-Finzi, 1968. Kokkinopilos — a Greek badland. *Geographical Journal* 134, 527–46.

Harrison, S.P. & G. Digerfeldt, 1993. European lakes as palaeohydrological and palaeoclimatic indicators. *Quaternary Science Reviews* 12, 233–48.

Harvey, A.M. & S.G. Wells, 1987. Response of Quaternary fluvial systems to differential epeirogenic uplift: Aguas and Feos river systems, southeast Spain. *Geology* 15, 689–93.

Hassan, F.A., 1978. Sediments in archaeology: methods and implications for palaeoenvironmental and cultural analysis. *Journal of Field Archaeology* 5, 197–213.

Hastings, A., 1976. Spatial heterogeneity and the stability of predator–prey systems. *Theoretical Population Biology* 12, 37–48.

Hayden, B., 1993. The cultural capacities of Neandertals: a review and re-evaluation. *Journal of Human Evolution* 24, 113–46.

Hedberg, H.D., 1976. *International Stratigraphic Guide*. New York (NY): J. Wiley & Sons.

Hedges, R.E.M., R.A. Housley, C.R. Bronk & G.J. Van Klinken, 1990. Radiocarbon dates from the Oxford AMS System: Archaeometry datelist 11. *Archaeometry* 32, 211–37.

Herzfeld, M., 1985. *The Poetics of Manhood: Contest and Identity in a Cretan Mountain Village*. Princeton (NJ): Princeton University Press.

Higgs, E.S., 1963a. Epirus: Palaeolithic survey. *Archaiologikon Deltion, Chronika* 18, 157–8.

Higgs, E.S., 1963b. A Middle Palaeolithic industry in Greece: preliminary report. *Man* 63, 2–3.

Higgs, E.S., 1965a. Some recent Old Stone Age discoveries in Epirus. *Archaiologikon Deltion, Chronika* 20, 361–74.

Higgs, E.S., 1965b. Search for Greece of the Stone Age. *Natural History* 74, 18–25.

Higgs, E.S., 1966. Excavations at the rock shelter of Asprochaliko. *Archaiologikon Deltion, Chronika* 21, 292–4.

Higgs, E.S., 1967. Asprochaliko, Kastritsa. *Archaiologikon Deltion, Chronika* 22, 350.

Higgs, E.S., 1968a. Asprochaliko and Kastritsa. *Antiquity* 42, 235.

Higgs, E.S., 1968b. Epirus: Palaeolithic sites. *Archaeologikon Deltion (Chronika)* 23, 296–8.

Higgs, E.S., 1968c. The stone industries of Greece, in *La Préhistoire: Problèmes et Tendances*. Paris: C.N.R.S., 223–35.

Higgs, E.S., 1978. Environmental changes in Northern Greece, in Brice (ed.), 41–9.

Higgs, E.S. & C. Vita-Finzi, 1966. The climate, environment and industries of Stone Age Greece, part II. *Proceedings of the Prehistoric Society* 32, 1–29.

Higgs, E.S. & D. Webley, 1971. Further information concerning the environment of Palaeolithic man in Epirus. *Proceedings of the Prehistoric Society* 27(2), 367–80.

Higgs, E.S., C. Vita-Finzi, D.R. Harris & A.E. Fagg, 1967. The climate, environment and industries of Stone Age Greece, part III. *Proceedings of the Prehistoric Society* 33, 1–29.

Hilborn, R., 1975. The effect of spatial heterogeneity on the persistence of predator-prey interactions. *Theoretical Population Biology* 8, 346–55.

Hilton, J. & J.P. Lishman, 1985. The effect of redox changes on the magnetic susceptibility of sediments from a seasonal anoxic lake. *Limnology and Ocenography* 30(4), 907–9.

Hobhouse, J.C. (Lord Broughton), 1813. *A Journey Through Albania, and Other Provinces of Turkey in Europe and Asia, to Constantinople: During the Years 1809 and 1810*. London. (2nd edition published by John Murray in 1855 as *Travels in Albania and Other Provinces of Turkey in 1809 and 1810*.)

Hobsbawm, E., 1985. *Bandits*. 2nd edition. Harmondsworth: Penguin.

Hofman, J.L., 1981. The refitting of chipped-stone artefacts as an analytical and interpretive tool. *Current Anthropology* 22, 691–3.

Hofman, R.R., 1973. *The Ruminant Stomach*. Nairobi: East African Literature Bureau.

Hofman, R.R., 1985. Digestive physiology of the deer — their morphophysiological specialisation and adaptation, in *Biology of Deer Production*, eds. P.F. Fennessy & R.R. Drew. Wellington: Royal Society of New Zealand, 393–407.

Holling, C.S., 1973. Resilience and stability of ecological systems. *Annual Review of Ecology and Systematics* 4, 1–24.

Holt, M.E., 1976. An investigation of the internal parasite burden of the deer and associated animals at Knebworth Park, Herts. *Deer* 4, 40–41.

Horigan, S., 1988. *Nature and Culture in Western Discourse*. London: Routledge.

Huffaker, C., 1958. Experimental studies on predation: dispersion factors and predator–prey oscillations. *Hilgardia* 27, 343–83.

Huntington, E., 1910. The burial of Olympia. *Geographical Journal* 36, 657–86.

Huntley, B. & H.J.B. Birks, 1983. *An Atlas of Past and Present Pollen Maps for Europe 0–13,000 Years Ago*. Cambridge: Cambridge University Press.

Huxtable, J., J.A.J. Gowlett, G.N. Bailey, P.L. Carter & V. Papaconstantinou, 1992. Thermoluminescence dates and a new analysis of the Early Mousterian from Asprochaliko. *Current Anthropology* 33, 109–14.

IGME, 1987. *1:50,000 Geological Map of Greece, Konitsa Sheet*. Athens: IGME (Institute of Geological and Mineralogical Research).

IGRS, 1968. *1:50,000 Geological Map of Greece, Doliana*. L'Institut de Géologie et Recherches du Sous-Sol. Athens: IGME (Institute of Geological and Mineralogical Research).

IGRS, 1969. *1:50,000 Geological Map of Greece, Arta*. L'Institut de Géologie et Recherches du Sous-Sol. Athens: IGME (Institute of Geological and Mineralogical Research).

IGRS, 1970. *1:50,000 Geological Map of Greece, Tsepelovon*. L'Institut de Géologie et Recherches du Sous-Sol. Athens: IGME (Institute of Geological and Mineralogical Research).

IGRS/IFP, 1966. *Etude Géologique de l'Epire (Grèce Nord-occidental)*. L'Institut de Géologie et Recherches du Sous-Sol, Athènes, et L'Institut Francais du Pétrole, Mission Grèce. Paris: Editions Technip.

Ingold, T., 1986. *The Appropriation of Nature: Essays on Human Ecology and Social Relations*. Manchester: Manchester University Press.

Ingold, T., 1992a. Culture and the perception of the environment, in *Bush Base: Culture, Environment and Development*, eds. E. Croll & D. Parkin. London: Routledge, 39–56.

Ingold, T., 1992b. Foraging for data, camping with theories: hunter-gatherers and nomadic pastoralists in archaeology and anthropology. *Antiquity* 66, 790–803.

Isaac, G.Ll., 1977. *Olorgesailie: Archaeological Studies of a Middle Pleistocene Lake Basin*. Chicago (IL): University of Chicago Press.

Iwanowa, S., 1979. Differentiation of Middle Palaeolithic cultures in the Balkan Peninsula. *Arkheologiya* 21(2), 1–12.

Jackson, R.G., 1978. Preliminary evaluation of lithofacies models for meandering alluvial streams, in *Fluvial Sedimentology*, ed. A.D. Miall. (Memoir 5.) Calgary: Canadian Society of Petroleum Geologists, 543–77.

Jackson, S.T., 1990. Pollen source areas and representation in small lakes of the northeastern United States. *Review of Palaeobotany and Palynology* 63, 53–76.

Jacobson, G.L., 1979. The palaeoecology of the white pine (*Pinus strobus*) in Minnesota. *Journal of Ecology* 67, 697–726.

Jacobson, G.L. & R.H.W. Bradshaw, 1981. The selection of sites for paleovegetational studies. *Quaternary Research* 16, 80–96.

Jahns, S., 1993. On the Holocene vegetation history of the Argive Plain (Peloponnese, southern Greece). *Vegetation History and Archaebotany* 2, 187–203.

Jalut, G., V.Andrieu, G. Delibrias, M. Fontugné & P. Pagès, 1990. Palaeoenvironnment of the valley of Ossau (western French Pyrénées) during the last 27,000 years. *Pollen et Spores* 30(3/4), 357–94.

Jameson, M.H., C.N. Runnels & T.H. van Andel, 1994. *A Greek Countryside: the Southern Argolid from Prehistory to the Present Day*. Stanford (CA): Stanford University Press, 228–46.

Jancin, M. & D.D. Clark, 1993. Subsidence-sinkhole development in light of mud infiltrate structures within interstratal karst of the Coastal Plain, southeast of United States. *Environmental Geology* 22, 330–36.

Janssen, C.R., 1966. Recent pollen spectra from the deciduous and coniferous-deciduous forests of northeastern Minnesota: a study in pollen dispersal. *Ecology* 47, 804–25.

Jarman, P.J., 1974. The social organisation of antelope in relation to their ecology. *Behaviour* 58, 215–67.

Jelinek, A.J., 1990. The Amudian in the context of the Mugharan Tradition at the Tabun Cave (Mount Carmel), Israel, in Mellars (ed.), 81–90.

Jennings, J.N., 1985. *Karst Geomorphology*. Oxford: Blackwell.

Johnsen, S.J., H.B. Clausen, W. Dansgaard, K. Fuhrer, N. Gundestrup, C.U. Hammer, P. Iversen, J. Jouzel, B. Stauffer & J.P. Steffensen, 1992. Irregular glacial interstadials recorded in a new Greenland ice core. *Nature* 359, 311–13.

Jones, G., 1984. Interpretation of archaeological plant remains: ethnographic models from Greece, in *Plants and Ancient Man*, eds. W. van Zeist & W.A. Casparie. Rotterdam: Balkema, 43–61.

Jones, G. & A.H.F. Robertson, 1991. Tectono-stratigraphy and evolution of the Mesozoic Pindos ophiolite and related units, northwestern Greece. *Journal of the Geological Society, London* 148, 267–88.

Jones, K.P.N., I.N. McCave & P.D. Patel, 1988. A computer-interfaced sedigraph for modal size analysis of fine-grained sediment. *Sedimentology* 35, 163–72.

Kavvadias, G.B., 1984. *Palaeolithic Kephalonia*. Athens: Phutraki. (In Greek.)

Kelley, H., 1957. A propos des pseudo-pointes levalloisiennes. *Bulletin de la Société Préhistorique Française* 54, 9–12.

Khazanov, A.M., 1984. *Nomads and the Outside World*. Cambridge: Cambridge University Press.

King, G.C.P. & G.N. Bailey, 1985. The palaeoenvironment of some archaeological sites in Greece: the influence of accumulated uplift in a seismically active region. *Proceedings of the Prehistoric Society* 51, 273–82.

King, G.C.P., A. Tselenis, J. Gomberg, P. Molnar, S.W. Roecke, H. Sinvhal, C. Soufleris & J.M. Stock, 1983. Micro-earthquake seismicity and active tectonics of northwestern Greece. *Earth and Planetary Science Letters* 66, 279–88.

King, G.C.P., D.A. Sturdy & J. Whitney, 1993. Landscape geometry and active tectonics of Northwest Greece. *Geological Society of America Bulletin* 105, 137–61.

King, G.C.P., G.N. Bailey & D.A. Sturdy, 1994. Active tectonics and human survival strategies. *Journal of Geophysical Research—Solid Earth* 99(B10), 20,063–78.

Kislev, M.E., D. Nadel & I. Carmi, 1992. Epipalaeolithic (19,000 bp) cereal and fruit diet at Ohalo II, Sea of Galilee, Israel. *Review of Palaeobotany and Palynology* 73, 161–6.

Knox, J.C., 1977. Human impacts on Wisconsin stream channels. *Annals of the Association of American Geographers* 76, 323–42.

Koestler, A., 1967. *The Ghost in the Machine*. New York (NY): Macmillan.

Kourtessi-Philippakis, G., 1986. *Le Paléolithique de la Grèce Continentale*. Paris: Publications de la Sorbonne.

Kozlowski, J.K. (ed.), 1982. *Excavation in the Bacho Kiro Cave, Bulgaria (Final Report)*. Warsaw: Paristwowe Wydarunictwo. Naukowe.

Kozlowski, J.K., 1992. The Balkans in the Middle and Upper Palaeolithic: the gate to Europe or a cul-de-sac? *Proceedings of the Prehistoric Society* 58, 1–20.

Kozlowski, J.K., 1994. Gravettian/Epigravettian sequence in the Balkans: environment, technologies, hunting strategies and raw materials procurement. Paper presented to the First International Conference on the Palaeolithic Archaeology of Greece and Adjacent Areas. Ioannina, September 1994.

Kozlowski, J.K., H. Laville & B. Ginter (eds.), 1992. *Temnata Cave. Excavations in Karlukovo Karst Area, Bulgaria*, vol. 1, part 1. Krakow: Jagellonian University Press.

Kremmidas, V., 1990. *Recent History: Greece and Europe*. Athens: Gnosis Publishers. (In Greek.)

Kruuk, H., 1972. *The Spotted Hyaena: a Study of Predation and Social Behaviour*. Chicago (IL): University of Chicago Press.

Kuhn, S.L., 1995. *Mousterian Lithic Technology: an Ecological Perspective*. Princeton (NJ): Princeton Univesity Press.

Kutzbach, J.E. & P.J. Guetter, 1986. The influence of changing orbital parameters and surface boundary conditions on climate simulations for the past 18 000 years. *Journal of Atmospheric Sciences* 43, 1726–59.

Kyparissi-Apostolika, N., 1994. The Palaeolithic deposits of Theopetra Cave. Paper presented to the First International Conference on the Palaeolithic Archaeology of Greece and Adjacent Areas. Ioannina, September 1994.

Lang, G., 1970. Florengeschichte und mediterran-mitteleuropäische Florenbeziehungen. *Feddes Repertorium* 81, 315–35.

Larrick, R.R., 1983. The Circulation of Solutrean Foliate Point Cherts in the Perigord. Unpublished Ph.D. thesis, S.U.N.Y., Binghampton.

Latour, B., 1993. *We Have Never Been Modern*. London: Harvester Wheatsheaf.

Latour, B., 1994. Pragmatogonies. *American Behavioural Scientist* 37(4), 791–808.

Lautridou, J.P., 1988. Recent advances in cryogenic weathering, in Clark (ed.), 33–47.

Laville, H., 1976. Deposits in calcareous rock shelters: analytical methods and climatic interpretation, in *Geoarchaeology*, eds. D.A. Davidson & M.L. Shackley. London: Duckworth, 137–55.

Laville, H., J.P. Rigaud & J. Sackett, 1980. *Rockshelters of the Perigord*. New York (NY): Academic Press.

Le Borgne, E., 1955. Abnormal magnetic susceptibility of the top soil. *Annals of Geophysics* 11, 399–419.

Lear, E., 1851. *Journal of a Landscape Painter in Greece and Albania*. London. (Edited reprints in 1965 and 1988.)

Legge, A.J., 1972. Cave climates, in *Papers in Economic Prehistory*, ed. E.S. Higgs. London: Cambridge University Press, 97–103.

Leroi-Gourhan, A., 1964. Découvertes Paléolithiques en Elide. *Bulletin de Correspondance Hellénique* 88, 1–8.

Leroi-Gourhan, A., 1976. Les structures d'habitat au Paléolithique supérieur, in *La Préhistoire Française*, tome 1, ed. H. de Lumley. Paris: C.N.R.S., 656–63.

Leroi-Gourhan, A., N. Chavaillon & J. Chavaillon, 1963a. Premières résultats d'une prospection de divers sites préhistoriques en Elide occidentale. *Annales Géologiques des Pays Helléniques* 14, 324–9.

Leroi-Gourhan, A., N. Chavaillon & J. Chavaillon, 1963b. Paléolithique du Péloponnèse. *Bulletin de la Société Préhistorique Française* 60, 249–65.

Lewin, J., M.G. Macklin & J.C. Woodward, 1991. Late Quaternary fluvial sedimentation in the Voïdomatis basin, Epirus, northwest Greece. *Quaternary Research* 35, 103–15.

Lewin, J., M.G. Macklin & J.C. Woodward (eds.), 1995. *Mediterranean Quaternary River Environments*. Rotterdam: Balkema.

Lieberman, D.E., T.W. Deacon & R.H. Meadow, 1990. Computer image enhancement and analysis of cementum increments as applied to teeth of *Gazella gazella*. *Journal of Archaeological Science* 17, 519–33.

Lorsong, J.A., 1979. Sedimentation and Deformation of the Pindos and Ionian Flysches, Northwestern Greece. Unpublished Ph.D. Thesis, University of Cambridge, Cambridge.

Lovari, S. (ed.), 1985. *The Biology and Management of Mountain Ungulates*. London: Croom Helm.

Lowe, J., 1992. Lateglacial and early Holocene lake sediments from the northern Appenines, Italy: pollen stratigraphy and radiocarbon dating. *Boreas* 21, 194–208.

Lumley, H. de & A. Darlas, 1994. La grotte de Kalamakia (Aréopolis, Péloponnèse, Grèce). *Bulletin de Correspondance Hellénique* 118, 535–59.

McBrearty, S., 1988. The Sangoan-Lupemban and Middle Stone Age sequence at the Muguruk site, western Kenya. *World Archaeology* 19(3), 388–420.

McBurney, C.B.M., 1967. *The Haua Fteah (Cyrenaica) and the Stone Age of the South-East Mediterranean*. Cambridge: Cambridge University Press.

MacCormack, C. & M. Strathern (eds.), 1980. *Nature, Culture and Gender*. Cambridge: Cambridge University Press.

McGlade, J., 1995. Archaeology and the ecodynamics of human-modified landscapes. *Antiquity* 69, 113–32.

Macklin, M.G. & J. Lewin, 1986. Terraced fills of Pleistocene and Holocene age in the Rheidol valley, Wales. *Journal of Quaternary Science* 1, 21–34.

Macklin, M.G., J. Lewin & J.C. Woodward, 1995. Quaternary fluvial systems in the Mediterranean basin, in Lewin *et al.* (eds.), 1–25.

Macleod, D.A., 1980. The origin of the red Mediterranean soils in Epirus, Greece. *Journal of Soil Science* 31, 125–36.

Macleod, D.A. & C. Vita-Finzi, 1982. Environment and provenance in the development of recent alluvial deposits in Epirus, northwest Greece. *Earth Surface Processes and Landforms* 7, 29–43.

McManus, J., 1988. Grain size determination and interpretation, in *Techniques in Sedimentology*, ed. M. Tucker. Oxford: Blackwell, 63–85.

McNeill, J.R., 1992. *The Mountains of the Mediterranean World: an Environmental History*. Cambridge: Cambridge University Press.

Magri, D., 1994. Late Quaternary changes of plant biomass as recorded by pollen stratigraphical data: a discussion of the problem at Valle di Castiglione, Italy. *Review of Palaeobotany and Palynology* 81, 313–25.

Magri, D. & M. Follieri, 1992. Caratteri della biostratigrafia pollinica dell'olocene in Italia Centrale. *Memoria Societa Geologica Italiana* 42, 147–53.

Maher, B.A., 1986. Characterisation of soils by mineral magnetic measurements. *Physics of the Earth and Planetary Interiors* 42, 76–92.

Makris, E.P., 1990. *Ζωη και Παραδοση των Σαρακατσαναιων*. *[The Life and Traditions of the Sarakatsani.]* Ioannina: E.P. Makris.

Mania, D., 1995. Umwelt und Mensch im Pleistozän Mitteleuropas am Beispiel von Bilzingsleben, in *Man and Environment in the Palaeolithic*, ed. H. Ullrich. (Etudes et Recherches Archéologiques de l'Université de Liège.) Liège: University of Liège, 49–65.

Maniatis, Y., E. Aloupi & A. Hourmouziadi, 1989. An attempt to identify flint origin and heat treatment by ESR spectroscopy, in *Archaeometry: Proceedings of the 25th International Symposium*, ed. Y. Maniatis. Amsterdam: Elsevier, 645–59.

Markgraf, V., 1980. Pollen dispersal in a mountain area. *Grana* 19, 127–46.

Mason, S.L.R., J.G. Hather & G.C. Hillman, 1994. Preliminary investigations of the plant macro-remains from Dolní Vestoniče II, and its implications for the role of plant foods in Palaeolithic and Mesolithic Europe. *Antiquity* 68, 48–57.

Masters, P.M. & N.C. Flemming (eds.), 1983. *Quaternary Coastlines and Marine Archaeology*. London: Academic Press.

Mather, A.E. & A.M. Harvey, 1995. Controls on drainage evolution in the Sorbas basin, southeast Spain, in Lewin *et al.* (eds.), 65–76.

May, R.M., 1981. *Theoretical Ecology: Principles and Applications*. Oxford: Blackwell.

Maynard-Smith, J., 1974. *Models in Ecology*. Cambridge: Cambridge University Press.

Mayr, E., 1964. *Systematics and the Origin of Species*. New York (NY): Dover.

Mellars, P., 1964. The Middle Palaeolithic surface artifacts at Kokkinopilos, in Dakaris *et al.*, 229–35.

Mellars, P. (ed.), 1990. *The Emergence of Modern Humans: an Archaeological Perspective*. Edinburgh: Edinburgh University Press.

Mellars, P. & C. Stringer (eds.), 1989. *The Human Revolution: Behavioural and Biological Perspectives on the Origins of Modern Humans*. Edinburgh: Edinburgh University Press.

Mercier, N., H. Valladas, G. Valladas, J.L. Reyss, A. Jelinek, L. Meignen & J.-L. Joron, 1995. TL dates of burnt flints from Jelinek's excavations at Tabun and their implications. *Journal of Archaeological Science* 22, 495–509.

Messerli, B., 1967. Die Eiszeitliche und die gegenwartige Vergletscherung im Mittelmeeraum. *Geographica Helvetica* 22, 105–228.

Meulenkamp, J.E., 1985. Aspects of the Late Cenozoic evolution of the Aegean region, in *Geological Evolution of the Mediterranean Basin*, eds. D.J. Stanley & F. Wezel. New York (NY): Springer-Verlag, 307–21.

Mihailovich, D., 1994. The stone industries of the Upper Palaeolithic and Mesolithic of Montenegro. Paper presented to the First International Conference on the Palaeolithic Archaeology of Greece and Adjacent Areas. Ioannina, September 1994.

Milojčić, V., J. Boessneck, D. Jung & H. Schneider, 1965. *Paläolithikum um Larissa in Thessalien*. Bonn: Habelt.

Miracle, P.T. & D.A. Sturdy, 1991. Chamois and the karst of Herzegovina. *Journal of Archaeological Science* 18, 89–108.

Mithen, S., 1989. Evolutionary theory and post-processual archaeology. *Antiquity* 63, 483–94.

Mithen, S., 1993. Simulating mammoth hunting and extinction: implications for the Late Pleistocene of the Central Russian plain, in *Hunting and Animal Exploitation in the Later Palaeolithic and Mesolithic of Eurasia*, eds. G.L. Peterkin, H.M. Bricker & P. Mellars. (Archeological Papers of the American Anthropological Association 4.) Washington (DC): American Anthropological Association, 163–78.

Monopolis, D. & A. Bruneton, 1982. Ionian Sea (western Greece): its structural outline deduced from drilling and geophysical data. *Tectonophysics* 83(3–4), 227–42.

Moseley, M.E., 1983. The good old days *were* better: agrarian collapse and tectonics. *American Anthropologist* 85, 773–99.

Moseley, M.E. & R.A. Feldman, 1988. Fishing, farming and the foundations of Andean civilization, in *The Archaeology of Prehistoric Coastlines*, eds. G.N. Bailey & J.E. Parkington. Cambridge: Cambridge University Press, 125–34.

Mueller, J.W. (ed.), 1975. *Sampling in Archaeology*. Tucson (AZ): University of Arizona Press.

Mueller-Dombois, D. & H. Ellenberg, 1974. *Aims and Methods of Vegetation Ecology*. New York (NY): Wiley.

Mullins, C.E., 1977. Magnetic susceptibility of the soil and its significance in soil science — a review. *Journal of Soil Science* 28, 223–46.

Murray, P. & N. Kardulias, 1986. A modern-site survey in the Southern Argolid, Greece. *Journal of Field Archaeology* 17, 21–41.

Nadel, D. & I. Hershkovitz, 1991. New subsistence data and human remains from the earliest Levantine Epipalaeolithic. *Current Anthropology* 32, 631–5.

Nandris, J.G., 1985. The stina and the Katun: foundations of a research design in European highland zone ethnoarchaeology. *World Archaeology* 17(1), 256–68.

Nitsiakos, V., 1985. A Vlach Pastoral Community in Greece: the Effects of its Incorporation into the National Economy and Society. Unpublished Ph.D. Dissertation, University of Cambridge, Cambridge.

Nitsiakos, V., 1986. The development of semi-nomadic pastoral communities in the context of national peasant relations. *Ipeirotika Chronika (Ioannina, Greece)*, 261–84. (Title translated from Greek.)

O'Neill, R.V., 1989. Perspectives in hierarchy and scale, in *Perspectives in Ecological Theory*, eds. J. Roughgarden, R. May & S. Levin. Princeton (NJ): Princeton University Press, 140–56.

O'Neill, R.V., D.L. de Angelis, J.B. Waide & T.F.H. Allen, 1986. *A Hierarchical Concept of Ecosystems*. Princeton (NJ): Princeton University Press.

Oldfield, F., 1991. Environmental magnetism — a personal perspective. *Quaternary Science Reviews* 10, 73–87.

Ollier, C.D., 1975. *Weathering*. London: Longman.

Osborne, R., 1987. *Classical Landscape with Figures: the Ancient Greek City and its Countryside*. London: George Philip.

Otte, M., I. Yalcinkaya, J. Kozlowski, O. Bar-Yosef, H. Taskiran & P. Noiret, 1995. Evolution technique au Paléolithique ancien de Karaïn (Turquie). *L'Anthropologie* 99(4), 529–61.

Palmentola, G., P. Acquafredda & S. Fiore, 1990. A new correlation of the glacial moraines in the Southern Appennines, Italy. *Geomorphology* 3, 1–8.

Papaconstantinou, E., 1986. Le concept de contemporanéité en archéologie préhistorique. *L'Ethnographie* 82, 11–25.

Papaconstantinou, E., 1991. Indications of Palaeolithic settlement in Aetolia and Acharnania. *Proceedings of the First Archaeological and Historical Colloquium of Aetolia and Acharnania*. Agrinio, 23–6.

Papaconstantinou, V., 1988. Micromoustérien, Les Idées et Les Pierres: Le Micromoustérien d'Asprochaliko (Grèce) et le Problème des Industries Microlithique du Moustérien. Thèse de Doctorat, Paris X, Nanterre.

Pawlikowski, M., 1992. The origin of lithic raw materials, in Kozlowski *et al.* (eds.), 241–87.

Payne, S. & P.J. Munson, 1985. Ruby and how many squirrels? The destruction of bones by dogs, in *Palaeobiological Investigations: Research Design, Methods and Data Analysis*, eds. N.R.J. Fieller, D.D. Gilbertson & N.G.A. Ralph. (British Archaeological Reports International Series 266.) Oxford: BAR, 31–48.

Pechoux, P., 1970. Traces d'activité glaciaire dans les montagnes de Grèce centrale. *Rev. Géographie Alpine* 58, 211–24.

Peñalba, C., 1989. Dynamique de végétation Tardiglaciaire et Holocène du Centre–Nord de l'Espagne d'après l'analyse pollinique. Unpublished Ph.D. thesis, Université d'Aix-Marseille.

Pérez Obiol, R. & R. Julià, 1994. Climatic change on the Iberian Peninsula recorded in a 30,000-yr pollen record from Lake Banyoles. *Quaternary Research* 41, 91–8.

Perlès, C., 1986. New ways with an old problem: chipped stone-assemblages as an index of cultural discontinuity in early Greek prehistory, in *Problems in Greek Prehistory*, eds. E.B. French & K.A. Wardle. Bristol: Bristol Classical Press, 477–88.

Perlès, C., 1987. *Les Industries Lithiques Taillées de Franchthi (Argolide, Grèce)*, tome I: *Présentation Général et Industries Paléolithiques*. (Excavations at Franchthi Cave, Greece 3.) Bloomington (IN): Indiana University Press.

Perlès, C., 1990. *Les Industries Lithiques Taillées de Franchthi (Argolide, Grèce)*, tome II: *Les Industries du Mésolithique et du Néolithique Initial*. (Excavations at Franchthi Cave, Greece 5.) Bloomington (IN): Indiana University Press.

Petsas, F.M. & G.A. Saralis, 1982. *Aristi and West Zagori, Enosis Aristis-Vikou Zagoriou*. Athens: K. Politi. (In Greek.)

Peyrony, D. & E. Peyrony, 1932. *Les gisements préhistoriques de Bourdeilles*. (Archives de l'Institut de Paléontologie

Humaine, Mémoire 10.) Paris: Masson et Cie.

Pickett, S.T. & P.S. White, 1985. *The Ecology of Natural Disturbance and Patch Dynamics*. Orlando (FA): Academic Press.

Pimm, S.L., 1982. *Food Webs*. London: Chapman & Hall.

Polunin, O., 1980. *Flowers of Greece and the Balkans: a Field Guide*. Oxford: Oxford University Press.

Pope, K.O. & T.H. Van Andel, 1984. Late Quaternary alluviation and soil formation in the southern Argolid: its history, causes and archaeological implications. *Journal of Archaeological Science* 11, 281–306.

Pope, K.O., C.N. Runnels & K. Teh-Lung, 1984. Dating Middle Palaeolithic red beds in southern Greece. *Nature* 312, 264–6.

Porter, S.C., 1989. Some geological implications of average Quaternary glacial conditions. *Quaternary Research* 32, 245–61.

Prentice, I.C., J. Guiot & S.P. Harrsion, 1992. Mediterranean vegetation, lake levels and palaeoclimate at the last glacial maximum. *Nature* 360, 658–60.

Putnam, R., 1988. *The Natural History of Deer*. New York (NY): Cornell University Press.

Pye, K., 1984. Loess. *Progress in Physical Geography* 8, 176–217.

Pye, K., 1987. *Aeolian Dust and Dust Deposits*. London: Academic Press.

Pye, K., 1992. Aeolian dust transport and deposition over Crete and adjacent parts of the Mediterranean Sea. *Earth Surface Processes and Landforms* 17, 271–88.

Rackham, O., 1983. Observations on the historical ecology of Boeotia. *Annual of the British School of Archaeology at Athens* 78, 291–351.

Radovanovich, I., 1986. Recent research on the Palaeolithic and Mesolithic of Montenegro. *Glasnik Srpskog Arheoloskog Drustva* 3, 63–77.

Rapp, G. & J.A. Gifford, 1982. Archaeological geology. *American Scientist* 70, 45–53.

Raunkiaer, C., 1937. *Plant Life Forms*. Oxford: Clarendon.

Reille, M., 1990. *Leçons de Palynologie et d'Analyse Pollinique*. Paris: C.N.R.S.

Reisch, L., 1976. Beobachtungen an Vogelknochen aus dem Spätpleistozän der Höhle von Kephalari (Argolis) Griechenland. *Archäologisches Korrespondenzblatt* 6(4), 26–5.

Reisch, L., 1982. The transition from Lower to Middle Palaeolithic in Greece and the southern Balkans, in *The Transition from Lower to Middle Palaeolithic and the Origin of Modern Man*, ed. A. Ronen. (British Archaeological Reports International Series 151.) Oxford: BAR, 223–32.

Richter, D., I. Mariolakos & H. Risch, 1978. The main flysch stages of the Hellenides, in *Alps, Appennines, Hellenides*, ed. H. Closs. Vertagsbuch, Stuttgart: Schweizerbart, 434–38.

Ritchie, J.C. & S. Litchi-Federovich, 1967. Pollen dispersal phenomena in arctic-subarctic Canada. *Review of Palynology and Palaeobotany* 3, 255–66.

Rolland, N., 1986. Recent findings from La Micoque and other sites in south-western and Mediterranean France: their bearing on the 'Tayacian' problem and Middle Palaeolithic emergence, in *Stone Age Prehistory: Studies in Memory of Charles McBurney*, eds. G.N. Bailey & P. Callow. Cambridge: Cambridge University Press, 121–51.

Rolland, N., 1990. Middle Palaeolithic socio-economic formations in western Eurasia: an exploratory survey, in Mellars (ed.), 347–88.

Runnels, C., 1988a. A prehistoric survey of Thessaly: new light on the Greek Middle Paleolithic. *Journal of Field Archaeology* 15, 277–90.

Runnels, C., 1988b. The early prehistory of Greece: new Palaeolithic finds from Thessaly. *Boston University: Center for Archaeological Studies* 6, 1–7.

Runnels, C., 1995. Review of Aegean prehistory IV: the Stone Age of Greece from the Palaeolithic to the Advent of the Neolithic. *American Journal of Archaeology* 99, 699–728.

Runnels, C. & T.H. Van Andel, 1993a. A handaxe from Kokkinopilos, Epirus, and its implications for the Paleolithic of Greece. *Journal of Field Archaeology* 20, 191–203.

Runnels, C. & T.H. Van Andel, 1993b. The Lower and Middle Paleolithic of Thessaly, Greece. *Journal of Field Archaeology* 20, 299–317.

Runnels, C., T.H. Van Andel, C. Zachos & P. Paschos, 1994. Human Settlement and Landscape in the Preveza Region (Epirus) in the Pleistocene and Early Holocene. Paper presented to the First International Conference on the Palaeolithic Archaeology of Greece and Adjacent Areas. Ioannina, September 1994.

Sanchez-Goñi, M.-F., 1991. On the Last Glacial Maximum and Interstadials during the Solutrean: a contradiction? *Current Anthropology* 32, 573–5.

Schein, M.D., 1975. When is an ethnic group? Ecology and class structure in northern Greece. *Ethnology* 14, 83–97.

Schick, K.D., 1991. On making behavioral inferences for early sites, in *Approaches to Understanding Early Hominid Life-ways in the African Savanna. Romisch-Germanisches Zentralmuseum Forschungsinstitut für Vor- und Fruhgeschichte in Verbindung mit der UISSP, 11 Kongress, Mainz, 31 August–5 September 1987*, ed. J.D. Clark. (Monographien Band 19.) Bonn: Dr Rudolf Habelt GMBH, 79–107.

Schmid, E., 1969. Cave sediments and prehistory, in *Science in Archaeology*, eds. D.R. Brothwell & E.S. Higgs. 2nd edition. London: Thames & Hudson, 151–66.

Schröder, W. & H. Kofler, 1985. Do parasites play an important role in competition between ibex and chamois?, in Lovari (ed.), 265–8.

Schumm, S.A. & R.W. Lichty, 1965. Time, space and causality in geomorphology. *American Journal of Science* 263, 110–19.

Selby, M.J., 1993. *Hillslope Materials and Processes*. 2nd edition. Oxford: Oxford University Press. (First printed in 1982.)

Sestini, A., 1933. Tracce glaciali nel Pindo epirota. *Bollettino della Societa Geografica Italiana* 10, 136–56.

Sfikas, G., 1979. *The Mountains of Greece*. Athens: Efstathiadis.

Shackleton, J.C., 1988. *Marine Molluscan Remains from Franchthi Cave*. (Excavations at Franchthi Cave, Greece 4.) Bloomington (IN): Indiana University Press.

Shackleton, J.C. & T.H. Van Andel, 1986. Prehistoric shore environments, shellfish availability, and shellfish gathering at Franchthi, Greece. *Geoarchaeology* 1, 127–43.

Shawcross, W. & N. Winder, 1987. A pilot investigation of the Klithi flint technology. Manuscript in possession of the authors.

Shea, J., 1989a. A functional study of the lithic industries associated with hominid fossils in the Kebara and Qafzeh Caves, Israel, in Mellars & Stringer (eds.), 611–25.

Shea, J. 1989b. Spear points from the Middle Palaeolithic of the Levant. *Journal of Field Archaeology* 15(4), 441–50.

Shorrocks, B., 1978. *The Genesis of Diversity*. London: Hodder & Stoughton.

Shott, M., 1986. Technological organisation and settlement mobility: an ethnographic examination. *Journal of Anthropological Research* 42, 15–51.

Sibrava, V., D.Q. Bowen & G.M. Richmond, 1986. Quaternary glaciations in the northern hemisphere. *Quaternary Science Reviews* 5, 1–511.

Sinclair, A., 1990. Technology as phenotype: an extended examination of Torrence's 'Time, energy and stone tools'. *Archaeological Review from Cambridge* 9(1), 71–81.

Sinclair, A., 1991. Technology, Design and the Division of Labour in Solutrean Europe. Unpublished Ph.D. thesis, University of Cambridge, Cambridge.

Sirakov, N., 1983. Reconstruction of the Middle Palaeolithic flint assemblages from the cave Samuilitsa II (northern Bulgaria) and their taxonomical position seen against the Palaeolithic of southeastern Europe. *Folia Quaternaria* 55, 1–100.

Slobodkin, L.B., 1961. *Growth and Regulation of Animal Populations*. New York (NY): Holt, Reinhart & Winston.

Smart, P.L., P.A. Bull, J. Rose, M. Laverty, H. Friedrich & M. Noel, 1985. Surface and underground fluvial activity in the Gunung Mulu National Park, Sarawak, in *Environmental Change and Tropical Geomorphology*, eds. I. Douglas & T. Spencer. London: Allen & Unwin, 123–48.

Smith, A.G. & E.M. Moores, 1974. Hellenides, in *Mesozoic and Cenozoic Orogenic Belts*, ed. R.A. Spencer. (Special Publication 4.) London: Geological Society of London, 159–85.

Smith, A.G., N.H. Woodcock & M.A. Naylor, 1979. The structural evolution of a Mesozoic continental margin, Othris Mountains, Greece. *Journal of the Geological Society of London* 136, 589–603.

Solomon, A.M. & A.B. Silkworth, 1986. Spatial patterns of atmospheric pollen transport in a montane region. *Quaternary Research* 25, 150–62.

Sonneville-Bordes, D. de & J. Perrot, 1954. Lexique typologique du paléolithique supérieur, outillage lithique, I grattoirs, II outils solutréens. *Bulletin de la Société Préhistorique Française* 51, 327–35.

Sonneville-Bordes, D. de & J. Perrot, 1955. Lexique typologique du paléolithique supérieur, outillage lithique, III outils composites-perçoirs. *Bulletin de la Société Préhistorique Française* 52, 76–9.

Sonneville-Bordes, D. de & J. Perrot, 1956a. Lexique typologique du paléolithique supérieur, outillage lithique, IV burins. *Bulletin de la Société Préhistorique Française* 53, 408–12.

Sonneville-Bordes, D. de & J. Perrot, 1956b. Lexique typologique du paléolithique supérieur, outillage lithique (suite et fin), V outillage à bord abattu, VI pièces tronquées, VII lames retouchées, VIII pièces variées, IX outillage lamellaire, pointe azilienne. *Bulletin de la Société Préhistorique Française* 53, 547–59.

Sordinas, A., 1965. Investigations of the prehistory of Corfu during 1965. *Kerkyraïka Chronica* 11, 141. (In Greek.)

Sordinas, A., 1969. Investigations of the prehistory of Corfu during 1964–1966. *Balkan Studies* 10, 393–424.

Sordinas, A., 1970a. *Stone Implements from Northwestern Corfu, Greece*. Memphis (TN): Anthropological Research Center, Memphis State University.

Sordinas, A., 1970b. Stone tools from prehistoric Zakynthos. *Kerkyraïka Chronica* 7, 122–30. (In Greek.)

Sordinas, A., 1983. Quaternary shorelines in the region of Corfu and adjacent islets, western Greece, in Masters & Flemming (eds.), 335–44.

Srejovic, D., 1989. The Mesolithic of Serbia and Montenegro, in *The Mesolithic in Europe*, ed. C. Bonsall. Edinburgh: Edinburgh University Press, 481–515.

Starkel, L., 1985. Late glacial and Postglacial history of river valleys in Europe as reflection of climatic changes. *Zeitschrift fur Gletscherkunde und Glazialgeologie* 21, 159–64.

Steele, J.H., 1978. *Spatial Pattern in Plankton Communities*. New York (NY): Plenum Press.

Stein, J.K. & W.R. Farrand (eds.), 1985. *Archaeological Sediments in Context*. Orono (MN): University of Maine Centre for the Study of Early Man, Institute of Quaternary Studies.

Steinhauser, H., 1970. *Climatic Atlas of Europe*, vol. 1. Geneva: World Meteorological Organization; Paris: Unesco.

Stiner, M.C., 1991. *Honor Among Thieves: a Zooarchaeological Study of Neandertal Ecology*. Princeton (NJ): Princeton University Press.

Stockton, E.D., 1973. Shaw's Creek shelter: human displacement of artefacts and its significance. *Mankind* 9, 112–17.

Stoller, P., 1995. *Embodying Colonial Memories: Spirit Possession, Power and the Hauka in West Africa*. London & New York (NY): Routledge.

Straus, L.G., 1979. Mesolithic adaptations along the northern coast of Spain. *Quaternaria* 21, 305–27.

Straus, L.G., 1980. The role of raw materials in lithic assemblage variability. *Lithic Technology* 3, 68–72.

Strid, A. (ed.), 1986 & 1991. *Mountain Flora of Greece*, vols.

1 & 2. Cambridge: Cambridge University Press.

Stringer, C.B. & C.S. Gamble, 1993. *In Search of the Neanderthals: Solving the Puzzle of Human Origins*. London: Thames & Hudson.

Stringer, C.B., R. Grün, H.P. Schwarcz & P. Goldberg, 1989. ESR dates for the hominid burial site of Es Skhul in Israel. *Nature* 338, 756–8.

Sturdy, D.A., 1969. Untitled ms. Cambridge: Unpublished ms.

Sturdy D.A. & D.P. Webley, 1988. Palaeolithic geography: or where are the deer? *World Archaeology* 19, 262–80.

Sugden, D.E. & B.S. John, 1976. *Glaciers and Landscape*. London: Arnold.

Tallon, P.W.J., 1978. Geological setting of the hominid fossils and Acheulian artifacts from the Kapthurin Formation, Baringo District, Kenya, in *Geological Background to Fossil Man*, ed. W.W. Bishop. Edinburgh: Scottish Academic Press, 361–74.

Tauber, H., 1965. Differential pollen dispersion and the interpretation of pollen diagrams. *Danmarks Geologiske Undersøgelse Raekke* II, 89.

Tauber, H., 1977. Investigations of aerial pollen transport in a forested area. *Dansk Botanisk Arkiv* 32.

Taussig, M., 1993. *Mimesis and Alterity: a Particular History of the Senses*. London: Routledge.

Taylor, K.C., C.U. Hammer, R.B. Alley, H.B. Clausen, D. Dahl-Jensen, A.J. Gow, N.S. Gundestrup, J. Kipfstuhl, J.C. Moore & E.D. Waddington, 1993. Electric conductivity measurements from the GISP2 and GRIP Greenland ice cores. *Nature* 366, 549–52.

Theocharis, D., 1967. *The Dawn of Thessalian Prehistory*. Volos: Thessalika Meletimata. (In Greek.)

Thomas, K.D., 1987. Prehistoric coastal ecologies: a view from outside Franchthi Cave, Greece. *Geoarchaeology* 2, 231–40.

Thompson, R. & F. Oldfield, 1986. *Environmental Magnetism*. London: Allen & Unwin.

Tixier, J., 1963. *Typologie de l'Epipaleolithique du Maghreb*. (Mémoires de Centre de Recherches Anthropologiques, Préhistoriques et Ethnologiques 2.) Paris: R. Alger, Arts et Métiers Graphiques.

Tixier, J., M.-L. Inizan & H. Roche, 1980. *Préhistoire de la Pierre Taillée*, I: *Terminologie et Technologie*. Paris: C.R.E.P.

Torrence, R., 1983. Time-budgetting and hunter-gatherer technology, in *Hunter-Gatherer Economy in Prehistory*, ed. G.N. Bailey. Cambridge: Cambridge University Press, 11–22.

Torrence, R., 1989. Re-tooling: towards a behavioural theory of stone tools, in *Time, Energy and Stone Tools*, ed. R. Torrence. Cambridge: Cambridge University Press, 57–66.

Toth, N., 1987. Behavioral inferences from Early Stone artifact assemblages: an experimental model. *Journal of Human Evolution* 16, 763–87.

Turner, C., 1985. Problems and pitfalls in the application of palynology to Pleistocene archaeological sites in Western Europe, in *Palynologie Archéologie*, ed. J. Renault-Miskovsky, Bui-Thi-Mai & M. Girard. (Notes et monographies techniques 17.) Paris: C.N.R.S.

Turner, C. & G.E. Hannon, 1988. Vegetational evidence for late Quaternary climatic changes in southwest Europe in relation to the influence of the North Atlantic Ocean. *Philosophical Transactions of the Royal Society* B 3318, 451–85.

Turner, C. & R.G. West, 1968. The subdivision and zonation of interglacial periods. *Eiszeitalter und Gegenwart* 19, 93–101.

Turner, J. & J.R.A. Greig, 1975. Some Holocene pollen diagrams from Greece. *Review of Palaeobotany and Palynology* 20 171–204.

Turrill, W.B., 1929. *The Plant-life of the Balkan Peninsula: a Phytogeographical Study*. Oxford: Clarendon Press.

Tzedakis, C., 1993. Long-term tree populations in northwest Greece in response to Quaternary climatic cycles. *Nature* 364, 437–40.

Tzedakis, P.C., 1991. Vegetation Dynamics in Northwest Greece in Response to Quaternary Climatic Cycles. Unpublished Ph.D. thesis, University of Cambridge, Cambridge.

Tzedakis, P.C., 1994. Vegetation change through glacial-interglacial cycles: a long term pollen sequence perspective. *Philosphical Transactions of the Royal Society of London* B 345, 403–32.

Valladas, H., J.L. Reyss, J.L. Joron, G. Valladas, O. Bar-Yosef & B. Vandermeersch, 1988. Thermoluminescence dating of Mousterian 'Proto-Cro-Magnon' remains from Israel and the origin of modern man. *Nature* 331, 624–6.

Van Andel, T.H., 1989. Late Quaternary sea level changes and archaeology. *Antiquity* 63, 733–45.

Van Andel. T.H., 1990. Addendum to 'Late Quaternary sea-level changes and archaeology'. *Antiquity* 64, 151–2.

Van Andel, T.H. & J.C. Shackleton, 1982. Late Paleolithic and Neolithic coastlines of Greece and the Aegean. *Journal of Field Archaeology* 9, 445–54.

Van Andel, T.H. & E. Zangger, 1990. Landscape stability and destabilization in the prehistory of Greece, in Bottema *et al.* (eds.), 139–57.

Van Campo, M., 1984. Relations entre la végétation de l'Europe et les températures de surface océanique après le dernier maximum glaciaire. *Pollen Spores* 26, 497–518.

Van der Hammen, T., T.A. Wijmstra & W.H. Zagwijn, 1971. The floral record of the late Cenozoic of Europe, in *The Late Cenozoic Glacial Ages*, ed. K.K. Turekian. Newhaven (CT): Yale University Press, 391–424.

Van Geel, B., G.R. Coope & T. Van der Hammen, 1989. Palaeocology and stratigraphy of the Lateglacial type section at Usselo (The Netherlands). *Review of Palaeobotany and Palynology* 60, 25–129.

Vereshchagin, N.K., 1967. Primitive hunters and Pleistocene extinctions in the Soviet Union, in *Pleistocene Extinctions: the Search for a Cause*, eds. P.S. Martin & H.E. Wright Jr. New Haven (CT) & London: Yale University Press, 365–98.

Villa, P., 1982. Conjoinable pieces and site formation processes. *American Antiquity* 47, 276–90.

Villa, P. & J. Courtin, 1983. The interpretation of stratified sites: a view from underground. *Journal of Archaeological Science* 10, 267–81.

Vita-Finzi, C., 1969. *The Mediterranean Valleys: Geological Changes in Historical Times.* Cambridge: Cambridge University Press.

Vita-Finzi, C., 1975. Chronology and implications of Holocene alluvial history of the Mediterranean basin. *Biuletyn Geologiczny* 19, 137–47.

Vita-Finzi, C., 1978. *Archaeological Sites in their Setting.* London: Thames & Hudson.

Vita-Finzi, C., 1986. *Recent Earth Movements.* London: Academic Press.

Vita-Finzi, C. & G.C.P. King, 1985. The seismicity, geomorphology and structural evolution of the Corinth area of Greece. *Philosophical Transactions of the Royal Society of London* 314 A, 379–407.

Wagstaff, J.M., 1981. Buried assumptions: some problems in the interpretation of the 'Younger Fill' raised by recent data from Greece. *Journal of Archaeological Science* 8, 247–64.

Walker, M.J.C. & J.J. Lowe, 1990. Reconstructing the environmental history of the lateglacial-interglacial transition: evidence from the Isle of Skye, Inner Hebrides, Scotland. *Quaternary Science Reviews* 9, 15–49.

Walter, H. & H. Leith, 1960. *Klimadiagramm-Weltatlas.* Jena.

Waters, D.W., 1994. The Tectonic Evolution of Epirus Northwest Greece. Unpublished Ph.D. Thesis, University of Cambridge, Cambridge.

Waters, M.R., 1988. Holocene alluvial geology and geoarchaeology of the San Xavier reach of the Santa Cruz River, Arizona. *Geological Society of America Bulletin* 100, 479–91.

Watt, A., 1947. Pattern and process in the plant community. *Journal of Ecology* 35, 1–22.

Watts, W.A., 1980. Regional variation in response of vegetation to Late Glacial climatic events in Europe, in *Studies in the Late Glacial of Northwest Europe*, eds. J.J. Lowe, J.M. Gray & J.E. Robinson. Oxford: Pergamon, 1–21.

Wendorf, F. & R. Schild, 1974. *A Middle Stone Age Sequence from the Central Rift Valley, Ethiopia.* Warsaw: Institute for History and Material Culture, Polish National Academy.

Weniger, G., 1989. The Magdalenian in western central Europe: settlement pattern and regionality. *Journal of World Prehistory* 3, 323–72.

West, R.G., 1980. Pleistocene forest history in East Anglia. *New Phytologist* 85, 571–622.

Whallon, R., 1984. Unconstrained clustering for the analysis of spatial distributions in archaeology, in *Intrasite Spatial Analysis in Archaeology*, ed. H. Hietala. Cambridge: Cambridge University Press, 242–77.

Whallon, R., 1989. The Palaeolithic site of Badanj: recent excavations and results of analysis. *Glasnik Zemaljskog muzeja Bosne i Hercegovine, Arheolgija, Nova serija* 44, 7–20.

White, C., 1968. *Report on Field Survey, June–August 1968.* Canberra: Australian Institute of Aboriginal Studies, Document 68/738 (mimeographed).

White, W.B., 1988. *Geomorphology and Hydrology of Karst Terrains.* Oxford: Oxford University Press.

Whitelaw, T.M., 1991. The ethnoarchaeology of recent rural settlement and land use in northwest Keos, in *Landscape Archaeology as Long-Term History: Northern Keos in the Cycladic Islands*, eds. J.F. Cherry, J.L. Davis & E. Mantzourani. Los Angeles (CA): Institute of Archaeology, University of California, 403–54.

Whittle, A., 1985. *Neolithic Europe: a Survey.* Cambridge: Cambridge University Press.

Wijmstra, T.A., 1969. Palynology of the first 30 m of 120 m deep section in Northern Greece. *Acta Botanica Neerlandica* 18(4), 511–27.

Willis, K.J., 1989. The Late Quaternary Vegetational History of Epirus, Northwest Greece. Unpublished Ph.D. Thesis, University of Cambridge, Cambridge.

Willis, K.J., 1992a. The late Quaternary vegetational history of northwest Greece, I: Lake Gramousti. *New Phytologist* 121, 101–17.

Willis, K.J., 1992b. The late Quaternary vegetational history of northwest Greece, II: Rezina Marsh. *New Phytologist* 121, 119–38.

Willis, K.J., 1992c. The late Quaternary vegetational history of northwest Greece, III: A comparative study of two contrasting sites. *New Phytologist* 121, 139–56.

Willis, K.J., 1994a. Altitudinal variation in the late Quaternary vegetational history of northwest Greece. *Historical Biology* 9, 100–116.

Willis, K.J., 1994b. A review of the vegetational history of the Balkans. *Review of Palaeobotany and Palynology* 13, 769–88.

Willis, K.J. & K.D. Bennett, 1994. The Neolithic transition, fact or fiction? Paleoecological evidence from the Balkans. *The Holocene* 4, 326–30.

Wilson, L., 1988. Petrography of the Lower Palaeolithic tool assemblage of the Caune de l'Arago (France). *World Archaeology* 19(3), 376–87.

Winder, N., 1995. Herbivores in an extinct landscape: Palaeolithic Epirus and the Overkill Hypothesis, in *L'homme et la degradation de l'environment. XVe Rencontres Internationales d'Archéologie et d'Histoire d'Antibes*, ed. S.E. van der Leeuw. Juan Les Pins: Editions APDCA.

Winder, N., 1996. Perception, prediction and policy: the Master Equation as a tool for theory building, in *Environmental Perception and Policy Making: Cultural and Natural Heritage and the Preservation of Degradation-Sensitive Environments in Southern Europe*, ed. S.E. van der Leeuw. Report on Contract EV5V-CT94-0486 submitted to Directorate General XII of the European Commission.

Winnifrith, T.J., 1987. *The Vlachs: the History of a Balkan People.* London: Duckworth.

Wintle, A.G., N.J. Shackleton & J.P. Lautridou, 1984. Thermoluminescence dating of periods of loess deposition and soil formation in Normandy. *Nature* 310,

491–3.
Wobst, M., 1974. Boundary conditions for Paleolithic social systems: a simulation approach. *American Antiquity* 39, 147–78.
Wood, P.A., 1978. Fine sediment mineralogy of source rocks and suspended sediment, Rother catchment, West Sussex. *Earth Surface Processes and Landforms* 3, 255–63.
Woodward, J.C., 1990. Late Quaternary Sedimentary Environments in the Voidomatis basin, northwest Greece. Unpublished Ph.D. Thesis, University of Cambridge, Cambridge.
Woodward, J.C., 1995. Patterns of erosion and suspended sediment yield in Mediterranean river basins, in *Sediment and Water Quality in River Catchments*, eds. I.D.L. Foster, A.M. Gurnell & B.W. Webb. Chichester: John Wiley, 365–89.
Woodward, J.C., 1996. Rockshelter sediment records in the Pindus Mountains, Greece. Paper presented at the First International Conference on Geoarchaeology in Tropical and Mediterranean Environments. Brussels, April 1996.
Woodward, J.C., J. Lewin & M.G. Macklin, 1992. Alluvial sediment sources in a glaciated catchment: the Voïdomatis basin, northwest Greece. *Earth Surface Processes and Landforms* 17, 205–16.
Woodward, J.C., M.G. Macklin & J. Lewin, 1994. Pedogenic weathering and relative-age dating of Quaternary alluvial sediments in the Pindus Mountains of northwest Greece, in *Rock Weathering and Landform Evolution*, eds. D.A. Robinson & R.B.G. Williams. Chichester: John Wiley, 259–83.
Woodward, J.C., J. Lewin & M.G. Macklin, 1995. Glaciation, river behaviour and Palaeolithic settlement in upland northwest Greece, in Lewin *et al.* (eds.), 115–29.
Woodward, J.C., M.G. Macklin & J. Lewin, 1997. *Fine-grained Infiltrates in the Pindus Karst of Northwest Greece: Sedimentology, Provenance and Depositional Environment*. (School of Geography Working Paper.) Leeds: University of Leeds.
Wright, H.E., 1967. A square-rod piston sampler for lake sediments. *Journal of Sedimentary Petrology* 37, 975–6.
Wright, H.E., Jr, J.H. McAndrews & W. Van Zeist, 1967. Modern pollen rain in Western Iran and its relation to the plant geography and Quaternary vegetational history. *Journal of Ecology* 55, 415–43.
Zeuner, F.E., 1946. *Dating the Past*. London: Methuen.